Robert M. Bohm

Professor
Department of Criminal Justice
And Legal Studies
University of Central Florida
Orlando, Florida

Keith N. Haley

Dean/Professor
School of Criminal Justice
Tiffin University
Tiffin, Ohio

 **Glencoe McGraw-Hill**

New York, New York   Columbus, Ohio   Woodland Hills, California   Peoria, Illinois

Glencoe/McGraw-Hill

A Division of The **McGraw·Hill** *Companies*

Introduction to Criminal Justice, Third Edition

Printed in United States of America.

Send all inquiries to:
Glencoe/McGraw-Hill
21600 Oxnard Street, Suite 500
Woodland Hills, California 91367

ISBN 0-07-824928-7 (Student Edition–hard cover)
1 2 3 4 5 6 7 8 9   027   05 04 03 02 01

ISBN 0-07-825368-3 (Student Edition–soft cover)
1 2 3 4 5 6 7 8 9   027   05 04 03 02 01

Brief Contents

Expanded Contents

Introduction to Criminal Justice
Third Edition
By Robert M. Bohm and Keith N. Haley

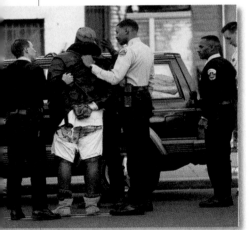

Chapter 3 Explaining Crime

68

Chapter 4 The Rule of Law

112

Chapter 5 History and Structure of American Law Enforcement   156

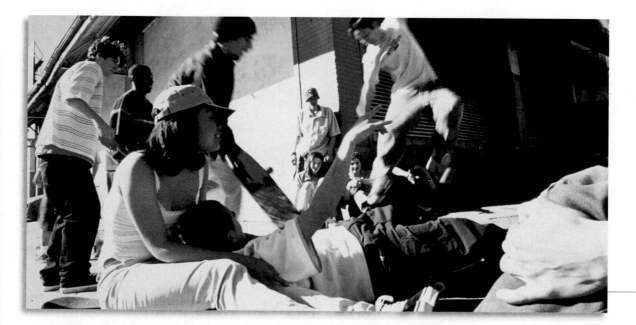

Introduction to Criminal Justice
Third Edition

Learning System

This book is designed to help students learn. It contains 14 chapters, divided into six parts. You will learn more if you use a learning system. *Introduction to Criminal Justice, Third Edition* uses the following integrated learning system:

1. **Concept Preview** — The chapter opener introduces the key concepts to be learned.

2. **Concept Development** — The chapter text explains concepts in structured, visual format.

3. **Concept Reinforcement** — In-text examples, graphics, and special features enhance and strengthen your learning.

4. **Concept Review and Application** — End-of-chapter exercises and activities encourage you to apply what you learned.

1. Concept Preview

Chapter objectives alert you to the major concepts to learn. Turn the objectives into questions, and, as you read the chapter, look for the answers to the questions.

The **opening photograph** sets the stage for the chapter content and provides a visual connection to the chapter.

A **chapter outline** introduces the topics that will be discussed. Scan the outline to familiarize yourself with the subject matter.

2. Concept Development

The **heading structure** shows the relationship among the topics in a section and breaks the material into easily digestible segments of information. Scan the headings to locate the information that will help you answer the questions you formed from the chapter objectives.

Key terms are defined when introduced and are printed in boldface to make them easy to find.

Key terms are also defined in the margin to make it easy for you to learn them.

5.5 American Private Security

Private security is a huge enterprise that complements public law enforcement in the United States. The Department of Labor's Bureau of Labor Statistics projects the continued growth of private security employment well into the 21st century. There may be as many as 1.8 million people now working in private security. Conservative estimates suggest that twice as many people work in private security as in public law enforcement. According to the National Association of Security Companies, the nation spends 73 percent more each year on private security than it does on public policing.[27]

A common way to categorize private security employment is to classify the agencies and personnel as either contract or proprietary. **Contract security** companies offer protective services for a fee to people, agencies, and companies that do not employ their own security personnel or that need extra protection. A state university, for example, may employ private security officers to work at a football game. Contract security employees are not peace officers. **Proprietary security** agents and personnel provide protective services for the entity that employs them. They are also not classified as sworn peace officers. For example, the Ford Motor Company employs its own security forces at its large manufacturing plants.

In 2000, the services provided by the private security agencies of this nation were expected to cost $104 billion, substantially more than the $40 billion projected for public law enforcement.[28]

Reasons for Growth

A number of factors have stimulated the phenomenal growth of private security since the 1970s.

Declining Revenues for Public Policing In virtually all major cities and in state governments in the United States, the competition for limited funds to operate public services is fierce. Public police agencies have experienced their share of across-the-board government belt-tightening, and that has caused limitations and even freezes on the hiring of additional police officers. As a result, police departments have curtailed services no longer deemed critical. Often, businesses have filled the service gap by employing private security personnel.

The Private Nature of Crimes in the Workplace A business depends on a positive reputation to remain competitive. Widespread employee theft, embezzlement scandals, and substance abuse harm an organization's public image and may cause potential customers to question the quality of a company's products and services. By employing private security personnel to prevent and repress crime in their facilities, businesses can either hide the crimes that occur or minimize the negative publicity.

contract security Protective services that a private security firm provides to people, agencies, and companies that do not employ their own security personnel or that need extra protection. Contract security employees are not peace officers.

proprietary security In-house protective services that a security staff, which is not classified as sworn peace officers, provide for the entity that employs them.

188 · PART 2 · Law Enforcement

3. Concept Reinforcement

Careers in Criminal Justice features alert you to the issues facing criminal justice professionals.

Special features reinforce and enhance your understanding of the topics presented.

Examples help you understand the concepts presented.

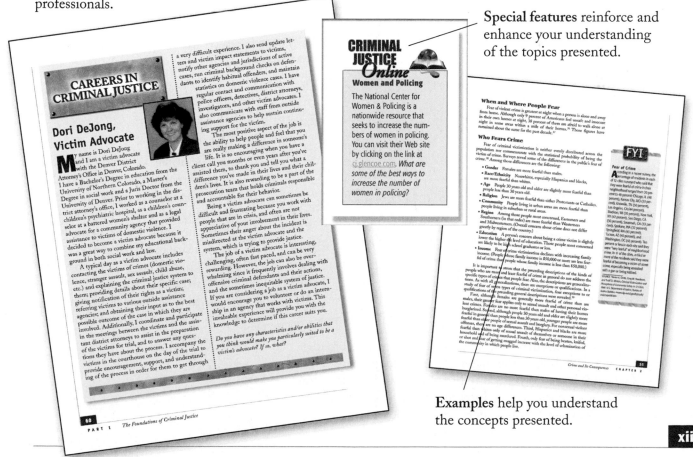

4. Concept Review and Application

Summary by Chapter Objectives sums up the chapter's major themes. The summary is organized by chapter objectives and provides you with general answers to the questions you posed when you began the chapter.

Key Terms consolidates the juvenile justice vocabulary presented in the chapter. If you can't remember what term means, the page reference alerts you to the location of its definition in the chapter.

Questions for Review re-examine key points presented in the chapter. These questions test your knowledge of the chapter concepts and can help you review for exams.

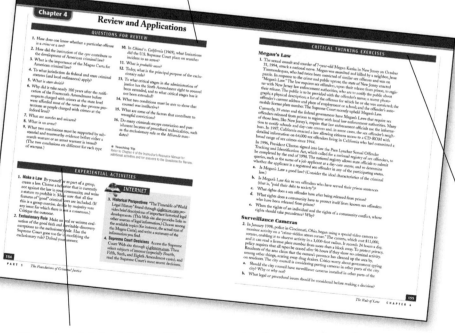

Critical Thinking Exercises encourage you to apply the concepts you have learned. Each scenario provides you the opportunity to analyze a situation, using the knowledge you have gained from the chapter, and to then propose a solution, evaluate a proposal, or make a decision.

Experiential Activities offer opportunity for you to broaden your understanding of the material presented, prepare yourself to participate in classroom discussions, and enhance your performance on exams. An Internet project encourages you to take advantage of this important technology.

Additional Study and Tutorial Resources

Tutorial With Simulation Applications CD-ROM

This *Tutorial With Simulation Applications CD-ROM* is a comprehensive interactive study tool designed to assist you in learning and applying concepts. It contains a visual tutorial of major concepts with reinforcement exercises, followed by simulation applications:

■ **Interactive Content Tutorial**

This visually oriented tutorial covers all concepts in the textbook. Chapter content is divided into sections followed by reinforcement and interactive assessment.

■ **Application Simulations**

Chapter concepts and issues are explored and applied through application simulations (two simulations per Chapter), which pose real-world situations to which you are asked to respond. You receive immediate feedback regarding the appropriateness of your choices.

■ **Knowledge Checkpoint**

Test your grasp of concepts through a variety of interactive reinforcement tools:
- Self-check exercises
- Practice tests
- Career planning
- Interactive exercises
- Study tips

Criminal Justice Web Site

- **cj.glencoe.com**
  This site provides information on currents trends, links to relevant sites, bulletin board, plus multiple reinforcement, assessment, and research tools.

- Links to Glencoe's Criminal Justice Web page for a complete list of texts and resources.

State Supplements

- California
- Florida
- Texas

Student Success in Criminal Justice

You have purchased *Introduction to Criminal Justice, Third Edition*, Glencoe/McGraw-Hill's new criminal justice textbook. You have taken a major step toward your career. However, it is not enough to own this book, you must read it, study it and take advantage of the many learning aids that are provided. If you follow the strategies outlined, you will be successful in this course. Also you will gain a broad and comprehensive understanding of juvenile justice and the juvenile justice system. That knowledge will serve you well as a strong foundation for other more specialized courses in juvenile justice and the social sciences.

How This Volume is Organized

This book is divided into 14 chapters that are organized in six parts and is organized to provide a logical approach to understanding the operation of criminal justice in the United States. The first chapter presents a brief overview of the entire criminal justice response to crime; that is, the stages of the process from the commission of a crime through the law enforcement response and the administration of justice (courts and prosecutions) to corrections. We recommend that you familiarize yourself with the basic elements of this process as soon as possible. This knowledge will help you understand how the different parts of the process fit together. This chapter also provides a detailed description of the costs of criminal justice in the United States — a subject that concerns nearly everyone — and introduces the aforementioned principal theme of the book: myths about crime and criminal justice.

Chapter 2, 3, and 4 furnish the context for understanding criminal justice in the United States. A critical understanding of criminal justice requires a critical understanding of the context in which it operates. The second chapter examines the nature of crime and its consequences, focusing on definitions, measurements, costs, fear, and victims. Chapter 3 surveys theories or explanations of crime and delinquency, their policy implications, and their problems. We believe that criminal justice policies should be based on well-supported and compelling theories of crime. All too often they are not. Finally, Chapter 4 addresses criminal law and its application. The purpose of criminal justice is to enforce criminal law. Much of Chapter 4 is devoted to procedural law, which deals with the rights afforded people accused of crimes.

The next seven chapters examine in detail what was briefly described in Chapter 1: the components and the operation of criminal justice in the United States. Chapters 5 and 6 cover law enforcement; Chapter 7 and 8, the administration of justice (courts and prosecution); and Chapter 9, 10, and 11, corrections. Chapter 12 is devoted to juvenile justice, and Chapter 13 explores the future of criminal justice.

Why Study Criminal Justice?

No one has to tell you how important criminal justice is in the United States today. Most people are in agreement that crime is one of the most pressing issues in the United States. The ways individuals and society respond to crime are commonplace in our daily lives. We cannot escape them. We fear crime. We distrust strangers. We avoid going to certain places, especially at night. We carry mace and whistles. We lock our car doors, as well as the doors and windows of our homes. We install burglar alarms. We buy theft insurance. We own guns for protection. We keep ferocious dogs. We hire people to protect us. We participate in neighborhood watches. We travel in groups.

We also find crime and reactions to it fascinating. We read about them in newspapers, magazines, and books and on the Internet. We are enthralled by portrayals of them on television and in the movies. Unfortunately, crime victimizes too many of us, including the perpetrators themselves, whose young lives, like those of their victims, are likely to be forever diminished because of their crimes.

Criminal justice is a response to crime, but unlike the personal responses listed above, juvenile justice is a formal response by agents of local, state, and federal governments.

Many of you are probably interested in joining the numerous individuals with careers in criminal justice. An important purpose of this book is to enable you to make an informed decision about pursuing a career in juvenile justice. For example it is important to know that juvenile justice officials in the United States have tried to significantly reduce juvenile crime. By nearly all available measures, they have not succeeded. There are many reasons for this failure and plenty of blame to go around. We believe that a major reason for the sad state of modern juvenile justice is that many juvenile justice personnel, particularly law enforcement and correctional offices, lack postsecondary education. We are convinced that a good postsecondary education in criminal justice, and in the liberal arts generally, can significantly improve the performance of most criminal justice officials.

The need for postsecondary criminal justice education becomes more evident everyday as the law changes. What was a crime years ago, may no longer be a crime today. New forms of crime emerge to befuddle the best efforts of those who deal with crime. Police officers, for example, have to contend with sophisticated computer crimes and criminals' advanced communication techniques. We are certain that juvenile justice personnel who have juvenile justice degrees and have used this book as directed, and then go to work in the field, will be better at their jobs for using it.

Introduction to Criminal Justice, Third Edition is not just for students interested in careers in criminal justice. It is also for students who want to learn more about this important social institution. Knowledge of criminal justice is vital to a free and democratic people. All individuals need to know their legal rights and responsibilities. The better informed individuals are, the better able they are to protect themselves. A major theme of this book is that much of what the public "knows" about criminal justice in the United States is myth – that is, simply wrong or significantly misunderstood. *Introduction to Criminal Justice, Third Edition* presents current and accurate information about juvenile justice in the United States and standard and generally accepted interpretations of historical and modern developments. With an education in juvenile justice, you will feel more comfortable and better equipped to participate in juvenile justice policy formulation. You will also be more effective in solving problems in your community. More generally, a good criminal justice education will help you develop the critical thinking skills you need to be a constructive participant in a democratic nation and to have greater control over your own destiny.

How to Study Criminal Justice

As stated, here is a detailed and, we believe, foolproof strategy for succeeding in your criminal justice course. (The strategy can also be applied successfully in other courses.) Before beginning, however, it is important to emphasize three qualities that are important in the learning process and that we cannot teach you: *desire, commitment, and perseverance.*

Criminal justice, like any other course, builds in stages. Information presented in later chapters often assumes knowledge of information introduced in earlier chapters. You cannot afford to fall behind and then expect to catch up in one massive cramming session.

To get off to a good start, prepare yourself before the course begins by setting learning goals, organizing your time, studying your syllabus, and examining your own learning style.

Set Learning Goals for Yourself

The purpose of setting goals is to understand exactly what you plan to accomplish. Ask yourself what you want out of this course. Is it a specific grade? Perhaps you need an A or a B to keep up your grade average. Perhaps you need a certain body of knowledge from this course to get into a higher level course. Perhaps you need a specific set of skills. You may be taking this course to meet a requirement for your job, to attain a personal career goal, or simply to satisfy your curiosity about the subject. Be forewarned, however, if you sent your goals too low, you are likely to achieve only those low goals. For example, if you are not interested in the course but are taking it only because it is required of all majors, you should not be disappointed if you earn less than an A or a B.

Organize Your Time

Now that you have set your goals, you need to organize your time to accomplish them. Time management allows you to meet your goals and still have time for activities. It helps you work smarter, not just harder. As a rule of thumb, for every class hour, allow two study hours. If an exam is coming up, allow more study time. Plan to study when you are most alert. You will retain information longer if you study on a regular basis, rather than during one or two cramming sessions. Either before or after a study session, have some fun! Timely breaks from studying enhance the learning process.

Study Your Syllabus

Usually the course syllabus is available on the first day of class, but sometimes it is available sooner. If you can get a copy early, you will be that much ahead. The syllabus is your map for navigating the course. It should define the goals or objectives of the course, specify the textbook and supporting materials to be used, and explain course requirements, including the method or formula for determining final grades. The syllabus will also include a course schedule indicating when particular topics will be covered, what material needs to be read for each class, and when tests will be given. Other useful information on a course syllabus may include the instructor's name, office location, phone number, and office hours, and perhaps, the types of extra credit or special projects you may complete. Keep the syllabus in your notebook or organizer at all times. Review it at the beginning of each class and study session so you will know what course material will be covered and what you will be expected to know. Write down important due dates and test dates on your calendar.

Eight-Step Study Plan to Maximize Your Learning

This plan is based on research that shows that people learn — and remember — best when they have repeated exposure to the same material. This technique not only helps you learn better but can also reduce anxiety by allowing you to become familiar with material step by step. You will go over material at least six times before you take an exam.

Step 1: Use a Reading Strategy

In most cases, you will be asked to read material before each class. The SQ3R (Survey, Question, Read, Recite, and Review) method can help you get the most out of the material in every chapter of your book. Reading the material before class will acquaint you with the subject matter, arouse your interest in the subject, and help you know what questions to ask in class.

Survey By surveying an assignment, you are preparing yourself for a more thorough reading of the material.

Read the Chapter Title, the Chapter Objectives, and the Chapter Outline What topics does the chapter cover? What are the learning objectives? Do you already know something about the subject?

Read the Summary by Chapter Objectives This will give you an overview of what is covered in the chapter.

Look for Key Terms Key terms are the names for or words associated with the important concepts covered in the chapter. Key terms are printed in boldface type in the text. Definitions of the key terms appear in the margins near the text in which they are introduced.

Question Turn the chapter objectives into questions. For example, if the objective is, "Identify the deciding factors in waiving a juvenile to court," turn it into a question by asking yourself, "What are the deciding factors in waiving a juvenile to court?" Look for the answers to your questions as you read the chapter. By beginning the study of a chapter with questions, you will be more motivated to read the chapter to find the answers. To make sure your answers are correct, consult the summary at the end of the chapter.

You can also write a question mark in pencil in the margin next to any material you don't understand as you read the chapter. Your goal is to answer all your questions and erase the question marks before you take an exam.

Read Before you begin a thorough reading of the material, make sure that you are rested and alert and that your reading area is well-lighted and ventilated. This will not only make your reading time more efficient but help you understand what you read.

Skim the Material Generally, you will need to read material more than once before you really understand it. Start by skimming or reading straight through the material. Do not expect to understand everything at once. You are getting the big picture and becoming familiar with the material.

Read, Highlight, Outline The second time, read more slowly. Take time to study explanations and examples. Highlight key terms, important concepts, numbered lists or other items that will help you understand the material. Most students use colored highlighting markets for this step. Put question marks in pencil in the margin beside any points or concepts you don't understand.

Outline the chapter in your notebook. By writing the concepts and definitions into your notebook, you are using your tactile sense to reinforce your learning and to remember better what you read. Be sure you state concepts and definitions accurately. You can use brief phrases to take more extensive notes for your outline, depending on the material.

Apply What You Read In juvenile justice, as in other course, you must be able to apply what you read. The experiential activities and critical thinking exercises at the end of each chapter allow you to do this. Complete those activities and exercises when you have finished studying the chapter.

Recite In this step, you do a self-check of what you have learned in reading the chapter. Go back to the questions you formed from the chapter objectives and see if you can answer them. Also, see if you can answer the Questions for Review at the end of each chapter. Try explaining the material to a friend so that he or she understands it. These exercises will reveal your strengths and weaknesses.

Review Now go back and review the entire chapter. Erase any question marks that you have answered. If you still don't understand something, put a Post-it by it or mark it in your text. These items are the questions you can ask in class.

Study Plan

1) Use a Reading Strategy
2) Combine Learning Styles in Class
3) Review Class Notes
4) Reread the Text
5) Get Help if Necessary
6) Study Creatively for Test

Step 2: Combine Learning Styles in Class

Think of the time you spend in class as your opportunity to learn by listening and participating. You are combing visual, aural, and tactile learning styles in one experience.

Attendance: More Than Just Showing Up Your attitude is a critical element. Attend class *ready to learn*. That means being prepared by having read and reread the assignment, having your questions ready, and having your note-taking materials organized.

Because juvenile justice, like other courses, builds in stages, it is important for you to attend every class. You cannot ask questions if you are not there. And you may miss handouts, explanations, or key points that often are included on a test.

One final note. If you cannot attend a class, call the instructor or a classmate to find out what you have missed. You do not want to show up the next day and find out the instructor is giving a test!

Attention: Active Listening and Learning During most classes, you spend more time listening than you do reading, writing, or speaking. Learning by listening, however, calls for you to become an *active listener* and to participate in the class. This means you come to class prepared, you focus on the subject, you concentrate on what the instructor or other students are saying, and you ask questions. Block out distractions such as street noises or people walking by the classroom.

Participation In reading the material before class, you will have made a list of questions. If those questions are not answered in class, then ask your instructor to answer

them. If the instructor makes a point you do not understand, jot it down and ask him or her to explain it as soon as you can.

Note Taking Why take notes? We forget nearly 60 percent of what we hear within one hour after we hear it. Memory is highly unreliable. This is why taking notes during class is so important.

Note taking involves both listening and writing at the same time. You must learn not to concentrate too much on one and forget the other. Follow these tips for taking good notes:

Listen for and Record Main Ideas You do not need to write down everything your instructor or other students say. By reading your assignment before class, you will know what the main topics are. Listen for those topics when your instructor goes over the material in class, then take notes on what he or she says about them. If the instructor emphasizes the importance of a topic for a test, be sure to make a note of this information as well (for example, "This section really important for exam"). If you think you have missed a point, either ask your instructor to repeat or rephrase it right away, or mark the point with a question mark and ask your instructor about it later.

Use Outline Style and Abbreviations Set up your notes in outline style, and use phrases instead of complete sentences. Use abbreviations of symbols whenever possible (& for and, w for with, and so on). This technique will help you write faster to keep up with the instructor.

Step 3: Review Class Notes

Listening and taking notes are critical steps in Learning, but reviewing your notes is equally important. Remember — Repetition reinforces learning. The more times you go over material, the better you learn it.

Fill in the Blanks As soon as possible after a class, review your notes to fill in any missing information. Make sure you do it the same day. Sometimes you may be able to recall the missing information. If you can't, check your textbook or ask to see another student's notes to obtain what you need. Spell out important abbreviations that you may not recognize later.

Highlight Important Information Marking different types of information helps organize your notes. You want to find what you need when you need it. Try these suggestions for highlighting your notes:

1. Use different colored highlighting pens to mark key terms, important Supreme Court decisions, and other

kinds of information. Then, you will know that green, for example, always indicates key terms; blue indicates Supreme Court decisions; and so on. This method will help you find specific information quickly and easily.

2. Write a heading such as "Deciding Factors in Waiving a Juvenile to Court" at the beginning of each key topic. These headings can either correspond to those in the chapter, or you may make up your own headings to help you remember key information.

Step 4: Reread the Text

After reviewing your notes, you are ready to reread the chapter to fix the concepts in your mind.

Read for Details

■ Go over the key points and main ideas carefully. Make sure you understand them thoroughly and can explain them to someone in your own works.

■ Review the Chapter Objectives (that you have turned into questions) and the Questions for Review. Make sure you can answer all the questions and that you understand your answers.

Mark Your Text

■ Highlight any important terms or concepts you may have missed in your previous reading

■ Highlight any Myth/Fact boxes, FYIs, or figures you feel are important to remember.

■ Erase any question marks in the margin that represent questions you have answered.

■ Use Post-It notes to mark anything of which you are still unsure. Ask questions about those points in the next class, talk them over with other students, or make an appointment to meet with your instructor to discuss your questions.

Step 5: Get Help if Necessary

What if you have read the material, taken notes, and asked questions, and you still do not understand the material? You can get further help. As soon as it becomes apparent that you need some help, ask for it. If you wait until the semester is nearly over, it may be too late. Here are several sources of help.

Your Instructors Most instructors are willing to spend extra time with students who need help. Find out what your instructor's office hours are and schedule an appointment to go over the material in more detail. You may need several sessions. Remember to take notes during those sessions.

Study Groups Join a study group in your class, or start your own. What one person does not learn, another does. Study groups take advantage of each member's expertise. You can often learn best by listening and talking to others in such groups. Chances are that, together, you will be able to master the material better than any one of you could alone. This is an example of power in numbers.

Learning Labs Many schools have learning labs that offer individual instruction or tutoring for students who are having trouble with course material. Ask your instructor or classmates for information about the learning labs in your college or university.

Private Tutors You might consider getting help from a private tutor if you can afford the fee. Although this route will cost you more, it may take only a few sessions to help you understand the material and keep up with the class. Check with your instructor about the availability of private tutors.

Step 6: Study Creatively for Tests

If you have read your assignments, attended class, taken notes and reviewed them, answered the Questions for Review, and completed the Experiential Activities and Critical Thinking Exercises, then you have been studying for tests all along. This kind of preparation means less stress when test time comes around.

Review: Bring It All Together You should enter all exam dates on your calendar so that you know well in advance when to prepare for a test. If you plan extra time for study during the week, you will not have to cram the night before the test.

During that week, bring together all your textbook notes, all your handouts, and other study materials. Reread them, paying particular attention to anything you marked that the instructor emphasized or that you had trouble understanding.

In addition to studying the Summary by Chapter Objectives, Key Terms, and Questions for Review at the end of each chapter, it is a good idea to make a summary sheet of your own that lists all the major points and other information that will be covered on the test. If you have quizzes or tests you have already taken, review them as well. Focus on the material you either missed or did not do well on before.

Do not hesitate to ask the instructor for information about the test, in particular:

- The types of test items he or she will use (multiple-choice, true-false, matching, fill-in-the-blanks, short answer, essay)
- What material, if any, will be emphasized, and what material, if any, will not be included
- How much time you will have to take the test

Step 7: Test-taking Strategies

No matter how well you prepare for a test, you will feel some anxiety just before and even during the exam. This is natural — *everybody* feels this way. The guidelines in this section will help you manage your anxiety so that you can do your best.

Before the Test: Get Ready Use this checklist to help you prepare the night before or a few hours before an exam.

- Gather supplies: unless instructed otherwise, at least 2 sharpened pencils with good erasers, a watch for timing yourself, and other items if you need them (such as a blue book for essay exams).
- If the test is in your first class, get up at least an hour before the exam to make sure you will be fully awake.
- Eat well before the test, but avoid having a heavy meal, which can make you sleepy.
- Arrive early to review your notes and study materials. Remember: Luck favors the prepared!

During the Test: Go for It! Memorize these strategies to help you during the exam.

- Follow the directions. Listen carefully to the instructor's directions and read the printed directions carefully. Ask questions if the directions are unclear.
- Preview the test. Take a few minutes to look over the entire test. This will give you an idea of how much time to allot to each of the components.
- Do the easier sections first. If you get stumped on a question, skip it for now. You can come back to it later. Finish with the harder sections.
- Go back over the test. If you finish ahead of time, double-check your work and look for careless errors. Make sure your writing is legible if you are taking an essay exam or an exam that requires short answers. Make sure that your name and other information the instructor requires are on the test papers.

Step 8: Reviewing Your Results

Never throw away any of your quizzes or tests. Tests give you direct feedback on your progress in the courses. Whether the test is a weekly quiz or a mid-term, do not just look at the grade and put the paper in your file or notebook. Use the results of each quiz or test to help you achieve your goals.

Learn From Your Successes First review the test for those questions you answered correctly. Ask yourself the following questions:

- What are my strongest areas? You will know which topics to spend less time studying for the next exam.
- What types of items did I find easiest to answer (multiple-choice, true-false, etc.)? You might want to start with these types of items on the next exam, giving you more time to work on the harder items.

Learn From Your Mistakes Look over your errors, and ask yourself these questions:

- What types of items did I miss? Is there a pattern (for instance, true-false items, Supreme Court decisions)?
- Did I misunderstand any items? Was it clear to me what each item was asking for?
- Were my mistakes the result of carelessness? Did I read the items incorrectly or miss details? Did I lose track of time? Was I so engrossed in a test section that I forgot to allow myself enough time to get through the entire test at least once?

Look back through the textbook, your notes, class handouts, and other study materials to help you understand how and why you made the mistakes you did. Ask your instructor or classmates to go over your test with you until you know exactly why you missed the items. Evaluating your errors can show you where you need help and what to watch out for in the next test.

Refine Your Action Plan: The Learning Spiral You can think of the eight-step action plan as an upward spiral. Each time you travel a full cycle of the plan, you accumulate more knowledge and experience. You go one turn higher on the spiral.

Use your test feedback and classroom work to help you refine your plan. Perhaps you need to spend more time reading the textbook or reviewing key terms. Perhaps you did not allow enough time for study during the week. Or you might need extra help from your instructor, your classmates, or tutors. Make adjustments in your plan as you tackle the next part of the course.

Acknowledgements

This book, like any book, is the product of a collaborative effort. We would like to acknowledge and thank the many people who helped to make both the first and this second edition possible. First, our thanks go to Kevin I. Minor and H. Preston Elrod, both at Eastern Kentucky University, for their significant contributions to the chapters on corrections and the juvenile justice system, respectively. We would also like to thank the following colleagues for their substantial help with revisions: James R. Acker, State University of New York at Albany (Chapter 4: The Rule of Law), John O. Smykla, University of Alabama (Chapter 12: Community Corrections), and Donna M. Bishop, University of Central Florida (Chapter 13: Juvenile Justice). In addition, for their insightful reviews, criticism, helpful suggestions, and information, we would like to thank:

Brandon Applegate
University of Central Florida

Richard L. Ashbaugh
Clackamas Community College

Gregg Barak
Eastern Michigan University

Michael Barrett
Ashland University

Denny Bebout
Central Ohio Technical College

Anita Blowers
University of North Carolina at Charlotte

Jack Bohm
Leawood, Kansas

Lorie Bohm
Denver, Colorado

Richard Bohm
New York, New York

Robert J. Boyer
Luzerne Country Community College

William D. Burrell
Probation Services Division, State of New Jersey

Michael Cain
Coastal Bend Community College

Vincent J.Capozzella
Jefferson Community College

Jonathan Cella
Central Texas Community College

Charles Chastain
University of Arkansas at Little Rock

Daryl Cullison
Columbus State Community College

Vicky Dorworth
Montgomery College

Joyce K. Dozier
Wilmington College

Mary Ann Eastep
University of Central Florida

Randy Eastep
Brevard Community College

John W. Flickinger
Tiffin University

Kenneth A. Frayer
Schoolcraft College-Radcliff

David O. Friedrichs
University of Scranton

Rodney Friery
Jacksonville State University

Gary Green
Minot State University

Alex Greenberg
Niagara County Community College

Bob Hale
Southeastern Louisiana University

David O. Harding
Ohio University at Chillicothe

Stuart Henry
Eastern Michigan University

Joseph Hogan
Central Texas College

Thomas E. Holdren
Muskingum Technical College

Michael Hooper
Pennsylvania State University at Harrisburg

James L. Hudson
Clark State Community College

W. Richard Janikowski
University of Memphis

Lamar Jordan
Southern Utah University

Don Knueve
Defiance College

Peter C. Kratcoski
Kent Sate University

Gregory C. Leavitt
Green River Community College

Vivian Lord
University of North Carolina at Charlotte

Karol Lucken
University of Central Florida

Richard Lumb
State University of New York at Brockport

Kathleen Maguire
Hindelang Criminal Justice Research Center

Bradley Martin
University of Findlay

Richard M. Martin
Elgin Community College

Alida Merlo
Indiana University of Pennsylvania

Dale Mooso
San Antonio College

James Newman
Rio Hondo College

Sarah Nordin
Solano Community College

Les Obert
Casper College

Mary Carolyn Purtill
San Joaquin Delta College

Joseph B. Sanborn, Jr.
University of Central Florida

Martin D. Schwartz
Ohio University

Lance Selva
Middle Tennessee State University

James E. Smith
West Valley College

Jeffrey B. Spelman
North Central Technical College

Gene Stephens
University of South Carolina

James Stinchcomb
Miami-Dade Community College

David Streater
Catawba Valley Community College

William L. Tafoya
University of Illinois at Chicago

Roger D. Turner
Shelby State Community College

Ronald E. Vogel
California State University at Long Beach

Robert R. Eiggins
Cedarville College

Harold Williamson
Northeastern Louisiana University

Peter Wood
Mississippi State University

Finally, we would like to express our appreciation to our families and friends for their understanding and patience over the several years we have worked on this project.

About the Authors

Robert M. Bohm is Professor of Criminal Justice and Legal Studies at the University of Central Florida in Orlando. He has also been a faculty member in the Departments of Criminal Justice at the University of North Carolina at Charlotte (1989-1995) and at Jacksonville State University in Alabama (1979-1989). From 1973 to 1974, he worked for the Jackson County Department of Corrections in Kansas City, Missouri, first as a corrections officer and later as an instructor/counselor in the Model Inmate Employment Program, a Law Enforcement Assistance Administration sponsored work-release project. He received his Ph.D. in Criminology from Florida State University in 1980. He has published numerous journal articles and book chapters in the areas of criminal justice and criminology. Besides being the co-author of *Introduction to Criminal Justice, 3rd ed.* (Glencoe/McGraw-Hill, 2002), he is the editor of *The Death Penalty in America: Current Research*, the author of *A Primer on Crime and Delinquency Theory, 2nd ed.*, and *Deathquest: An Inquiry into the Theory and Practice of Capital Punishment in the United States*, and an editor (with James R. Acker and Charles S. Lanier) of *America's Experiment with Capital Punishment: Reflections on the Past, Present, and Future of the Ultimate Sanction*. He has been active in the American Society of Criminology, the Southern Criminal Justice Association, and especially the Academy of Criminal Justice Sciences, having served as Trustee-at-Large (1987-90), Second Vice-President (1990-91), First Vice-President (1991-92), and President (1992-93). In 1989, he was selected as the *Outstanding Educator of the Year* by the Southern Criminal Justice Association. In 1999, he was elected a Fellow of the Academy of Criminal Justice Sciences and, in 2001, he was presented with the Founder's Award of the Academy of Criminal Justice Sciences.

Keith N. Haley is the Dean of the School of Criminal Justice at Tiffin University in Tiffin, Ohio. He has also served in the following positions: Coordinator of the Criminal Justice Program at Collin County Community College in Texas; Executive Director of the Ohio Peace Office Training Council, the state's law enforcement standards and training commissions; Chairman of the Criminal Justice Department at the University of Cincinnati, which offers B.S., M.S., and Ph. D. degrees in criminal justice; police officer in Dayton, Ohio; Community School Director in Springfield, Ohio; Director of the Criminal Justice Program at Redlands Community College in Oklahoma; and electronics repairman and NCO in the U.S. Marines. Haley holds a B.S. in Education for Wright State University and an M.S. in Criminal Justice from Michigan State University. Haley has written or co-authored several books, including *How to Take a Test and Score With Memory Power* (Imprint Publications, 1977) and *Crime and Punishment in the Lone Star State* (McGraw-Hill Custom, 1997), as well as many articles and papers. He has also served as a consultant to many public service, business, and industrial organizations. Mr. Haley is also active in the affairs of the Academy of Criminal Justice Sciences and is the 1998-99 chair of the Academy's Membership Committee.

Dedication

To Linda Taconis, with love.

Robert M. Bohm

To my wife, Shelby, and daughter, Jill, with love.

Keith N. Haley

PART 1

The Foundations of Criminal Justice

CHAPTER OUTLINE

Chapter 1

Crime and Justice in the United States

CHAPTER OBJECTIVES

After completing this chapter, you should be able to:

1. Describe how the type of crime routinely presented by the media compares with crime routinely committed.

2. Identify institutions of social control and explain what makes criminal justice an institution of social control.

3. Summarize how the criminal justice system responds to crime.

4. Explain why criminal justice in the United States is sometimes considered a nonsystem.

5. Describe the costs of criminal justice in the United States and compare those costs among federal, state, and local governments.

6. Explain how myths about crime and criminal justice affect the criminal justice system.

1.1 Crime in the United States

Crime and the Media

A study conducted jointly by researchers at eight universities (Miami, Columbia, Northwestern, Syracuse, Southern California, Texas, Oregon, and Ball State) found that crime stories dominate local television news shows, confirming the adage, "If it bleeds, it leads." The researchers reported that stories about crime and criminal justice, particularly those involving blood and mayhem, accounted for nearly 30 percent of the broadcasts. Stories about government and politics, once the mainstay of local news, were given the second largest amount of time (about 15 percent). Natural disaster stories were third, with about 10 percent of the time. One of the researchers speculated that excessive crime news "has a numbing effect on the public." He added that "people withdraw from activities because of fear."

SOURCE: "Crime Is Tops on TV News, Study Says," *The Orlando Sentinel*, May 7, 1997, p. A-10.

Every day we read about crime in newspapers, magazines, and news programs. We also see crime on TV docudramas and on such popular shows as the fictional *NYPD Blue*, *Law & Order*, and *Homicide* and the reality-based *America's Most Wanted*, *Cops*, and *Unsolved Mysteries*. There is also Court TV, an entire network devoted to crime and justice issues. Crime is also a favorite subject of movies and novels. Unfortunately, some of us encounter crime more directly, as victims. We cannot escape the subject of crime in our everyday lives. No wonder crime is a top concern of the American public.

However, the crimes presented by the media are usually more sensational than the crimes routinely committed. Some of the top crime news stories in the United States for 2000 (through mid-July) were as follows:[1]

- On January 19, Michael Skakel, a nephew of Ethel Kennedy, widow of the late Senator Robert F. Kennedy, was charged with the 1975 murder of Martha Moxley, a 15-year-old neighbor. Skakel was 15 years old at the time of the murder.

- Early February 14, two sophomores at Columbine High School in Littleton, Colorado, were shot to death at a sandwich shop near the school. In April 1999, the high school had been the scene of the worst school-shooting spree in U.S. history.

- A jury in Albany, New York, on February 25, acquitted four New York City police officers of second-degree murder and lesser charges in the February 1999 shooting death of Amadou Diallo, 22, an unarmed black immigrant from the West African country of Guinea. The white, plain-clothes officers had fired 41 shots at Diallo, hitting him 19 times, while he was standing in the entrance hallway of his apartment building in the New York City borough of the Bronx. The officers, members of the NYPD's Street Crimes Unit, claimed to have opened fire after Diallo acted suspiciously and pulled out of his pocket a black object that they thought was a gun. The object was later determined to be a wallet.

- A six-year-old boy shot and killed classmate Kayla Rolland at Theo J. Buell Elementary School in Mount Morris Township, Michigan, on February 29. The shooting came a day after the two first-grade students had fought on the school playground. The boy was believed to be the youngest student ever arrested in a school-shooting death. The county prosecutor said that he would not bring charges against the boy because of his age.

- On March 1, the Los Angeles Police Department released the findings of its investigation into a widening corruption scandal that was described as the worst in the department's history. The scandal had originated with the discovery of extreme misconduct, including the beating, shooting, and framing of scores of innocent people, by members of a special antigang unit based at the LAPD's Rampart Division, which is located in a neighborhood west of downtown Los Angeles. As of March 9, the revelations of corruption at the Rampart unit had led to the overturning of some 40 criminal convictions and the dismissal, suspension, or resignation of 20 officers.

- Once-prominent civil rights activist Jamil Abdullah Al-Amin, formerly known as H. Rap Brown, was arrested on March 20 in a rural area of Alabama three days after he was accused of shooting to death a sheriff's deputy in Atlanta.

- U.S. Army colonel James Hiett, 48, former head of U.S. antinarcotics efforts in Colombia, pleaded guilty on April 17 to charges that he had known his wife, Laurie Hiett, was laundering profits from drug smuggling but failed to report her crimes. Laurie Hiett was charged with sending $700,000 worth of heroin to New York City addresses through the diplomatic mail service of the U.S. embassy in Bogotá, Colombia. She pleaded guilty on January 27 to charges that she had traveled to the United States to collect proceeds from accomplices who had sold the smuggled drugs. She said that her husband did not know of her illegal activities. James Hiett, who was scheduled to retire from the Army in June, faced a 12- to 18-month prison sentence. Laurie Hiett could be sentenced to prison for as long as nine years.

- Richard Baumhammers, 34, a white immigration lawyer, was arrested on April 28 for killing five people and critically wounding a sixth in suburban Pittsburgh. Police described the attacks as racially driven. Those killed in the rampage included three Asian men, one African-American man, and a Jewish woman. The attacks were the second series of racially motivated murders to occur in the Pittsburgh area in two months. On March 1, Ronald Taylor, a 39-year-old African-American man, was arrested for a shooting spree in two fast-food restaurants where he shot five white men, killing three of them. Authorities found writings in Taylor's apartment describing "racist, biased doctors and nurses" who had treated him "like dirt."

- On May 15, the Jefferson County Sheriff's Department released its final report about the 1999 Columbine High School shootings in Littleton, Colorado. The report concluded that it took two students 16 minutes to fire the shots that killed 13 people and wounded 21 others.

- On May 16, an Alabama grand jury indicted two former Ku Klux Klan members, Thomas Blanton Jr., 61, and Bobby Frank Cherry, 69, for their roles in the 1963 bombing of an Alabama church, in which four black girls were killed. They were charged with eight counts each of first-degree murder—four counts of intentional murder and four

CRIMINAL JUSTICE Online
Crime in the News

You can read more about past and present crime news stories by visiting the APB News Web site through the link at cj.glencoe.com. *Does this Web site provide a balanced picture of crime in the United States or does it primarily provide sensational news coverage?*

Criminal cases involving Michael Skakel, Amadou Diallo, and Kayla Rolland were among the top crime news stories of 2000. *What factors make these crimes so sensational?* ▼

Crime and Justice in the United States CHAPTER 1

counts of murder with universal malice. Both men were held without bond. The 1963 bombing was a turning point in the civil rights movement. It caused many politically apathetic whites to support the crusade led by Rev. Martin Luther King, Jr.

Some of these crime stories are likely to remain top news stories for 2001 and beyond. However, taken together, those sensational crime news stories do not provide a very accurate image of the types of crime by which the average citizen is victimized. Nor do such stories accurately depict the kinds of crime to which the police respond on a daily basis.

To provide a more accurate idea of the kinds of crimes more typically committed, we reviewed a list of calls for police service in Chicago, Illinois, for the month of June 2000.[2] There were 181,748 calls for police service in Chicago during the period selected.

A close examination of the list of police calls (see Figure 1–1) reveals that the most frequent type of call for service in Chicago involves disturbances (for example, domestic quarrels, neighbor or landlord-tenant squabbles, gang altercations, bar or street fights, or even loud music or a dog barking). This type of call accounted for 30.2 percent of the total. (In the list, three separate types of disturbances are cataloged—general disturbances (20.9 percent),

FIGURE 1–1
Distribution of Calls for Police Service

Police Calls	Percentage
Disturbance	20.9
Alarm	9.4
Domestic Disturbance	7.6
Parking Violation	6.5
Selling Narcotics	4.5
Auto Accident	3.9
Domestic Battery	2.4
Vice Complaint	2.2
Suspicious Person	1.9
Gang Disturbance	1.7
Shots Fired	1.7
Battery (just occurred)	1.6
Person with Gun	1.4
Suspicious Auto (no occupant)	1.2
Fire	1.2
Missing Person	1.1
Assault (in progress)	1.0
Theft (just occurred)	1.0
Fireworks	1.0

Calls for police service to the Chicago, Illinois, Police Department during June, 2000. There were a total of 181,748 police calls.

domestic disturbances (7.6 percent), and gang disturbances (1.7 percent).) Other calls for service ranged from burglar alarms (9.4 percent) to parking violations (6.5 percent); from selling narcotics (4.5 percent) to auto accidents (3.9 percent); and from domestic battery (2.4 percent) to vice complaints (2.2 percent). The calls for police service listed in Figure 1–1 represent only those calls that accounted for at least one percent of the total calls. In all, there were 122 categories of calls for police service. There were also serious crimes or potential crimes not included in the list (because they accounted for less than one percent of the total calls): 1,241 robbery calls, 111 death investigation calls, 78 kidnapping calls, and 69 arson calls. Police are also called to assist motorists and to provide escorts for funeral processions—to name just two additional police services. Police services and responsibilities will be discussed further in Chapter 5.

Here it is important to observe that the calls to which the police routinely respond rarely involve the sensational crimes reported by the media. In many cases, they do not involve crimes at all. Critics argue that the news media have a dual obligation to (1) present news that reflects a more balanced picture of the overall crime problem and (2) reduce their presentation of sensational crimes, especially when such crimes are shown not so much to inform as to pander to the public's curiosity and its simultaneous attraction *and* repulsion to heinous crimes. The more fundamental problem, however, is that the public's conception of crime is to a large extent shaped by the media, and what the media present, for the most part, misleads the public about the nature of crime.

1.1 CRITICAL THINKING

1. Do you think the news media is obligated to present a balanced picture of the overall crime problem and reduce their presentation of sensational crimes? Why or why not?

2. How much do you think the public conception of crime is influenced by the media? How do you think the media select crime stories on which to focus?

1.2 Criminal Justice: An Institution of Social Control

In the United States, there is a variety of responses to crime. When a child commits a criminal act, even if that act does not come to the attention of the police, parents or school authorities nevertheless may punish the child for the offense (if they find out about it). Attempts to prevent crime by installing burglar alarms in automobiles and homes are other ways of responding to crime. Throughout this book, we focus on the criminal justice response to crime.

Like the family, schools, organized religion, the media, and the law, criminal justice is an **institution of social control** in the United States. A primary role of such institutions is to persuade people, through subtle and not-so-subtle means, to abide by the dominant values of society. Subtle means of

institution of social control
An organization that persuades people, through subtle and not-so-subtle means, to abide by the dominant values of society.

7

persuasion include gossip and peer pressure, whereas expulsion and incarceration are examples of not-so-subtle means.

As an institution of social control, criminal justice differs from the others in two important ways. First, the role of criminal justice is restricted officially to persuading people to abide by a limited range of social values: those whose violation constitutes crime. Thus, although courteous behavior is desired of all citizens, rude behavior is of no official concern to criminal justice, unless it violates the criminal law. Dealing with noncriminal rude behavior is primarily the responsibility of the family. Second, criminal justice is generally society's "last line of defense" against people who refuse to abide by dominant social values and commit crimes. Usually, society turns to criminal justice only after other institutions of social control have failed.

1.2 CRITICAL THINKING

1. Given what you know about crime in the United States, do you think that the criminal justice system is a strong institution of social control? Why?

2. Do you think that other institutions such as the family, schools, and organized religion are better institutions of social control than the criminal justice system? If so, which ones? Why?

1.3 Criminal Justice: The System

Criminal justice in the United States is administered by a loose confederation of more than 50,000 agencies of federal, state, and local governments. Those agencies consist of the police, the courts, and corrections. Together they are commonly referred to as the *criminal justice system.* Although there are differences in the ways the criminal justice system operates in different jurisdictions, there are also similarities. The term **jurisdiction,** as used here, means a politically defined geographical area (for example, a city, a county, a state, or a nation).

The following paragraphs will provide a brief overview of a typical criminal justice response to criminal behavior. Figure 1–2 on pages 12–13 is a graphic representation of the process. It includes the variations for petty offenses, misdemeanors, felonies, and juvenile offenses. A more detailed examination of the criminal justice response to crime and delinquency will be provided in later chapters of this book.

Police

The criminal justice response to crime begins when a crime is reported to the police or, far less often, when the police themselves discover that a crime has been committed. Sometimes solving the crime is easy—the victim or a witness knows the perpetrator, or where to find him or her. Often, an arrest supported by witness statements and crime scene evidence is sufficient to close a case, especially with a less serious crime. More often, though, the police must conduct an in-depth investigation to determine what happened

jurisdiction
A politically defined geographical area.

CAREERS IN CRIMINAL JUSTICE

Law Enforcement/ Security

BATF Agent
Border Patrol Agent
Campus Police Officer
Crime Prevention Specialist
Criminal Investigator
Criminal Profiler
Customs Officer
Deputy Sheriff
Deputy U.S. Marshal
Drug Enforcement Officer
Environmental Protection Agent
FBI Special Agent
Federal Agency Investigator
Fingerprint Technician
Forensic Scientist
Highway Patrol Officer
INS Officer
Insurance Fraud Investigator
Laboratory Technician
Loss Prevention Officer
Military Police Officer
Park Ranger
Police Administrator
Police Dispatcher
Police Officer
Polygraph Examiner
Postal Inspector
Private Investigator
Secret Service Agent
State Trooper

Courts/Legal

Arbitrator
Attorney General
Bailiff
Clerk of Court
Court Reporter
District Attorney
Judge
Jury Assignment Commissioner
Jury Coordinator
Juvenile Magistrate
Law Clerk
Law Librarian
Legal Researcher
Mediator
Paralegal
Public Defender
Public Information Officer
Trial Court Administrator
Victim Advocate

Teaching/ Research

Agency Researcher
Community College, College, or University Lecturer or Professor

Corrections/ Rehabilitation

Activity Therapy Administrator
Business Manager

Case Manager
Chaplain
Chemical Dependency Manager
Child Care Worker
Children's Services Counselor
Classification Officer
Client Service Coordinator
Clinical Social Worker
Community Liaison Officer
Correctional Officer
Dietary Officer
Drug Court Coordinator
Field Administrator
Fugitive Apprehension Officer
Home Detention Supervisor
Human Services Counselor
Job Placement Officer
Juvenile Detention Officer
Juvenile Probation Officer
Mental Health Clinician
Parole/Probation Officer
Presentence Investigator
Prison Industries
    Superintendent
Program Officer/Specialist
Programmer/Analyst
Psychologist
Recreation Coordinator
Rehabilitation Counselor
Researcher
Residence Supervisor
Sex Offender Therapist
Social Worker
Statistician
Substance Abuse Counselor
Teacher
Vocational Instructor
Warden or Superintendent
Youth Service
    Worker/Coordinator
Youth Supervisor

arrest
The seizing and detaining of a person by lawful authority.

booking
The administrative recording of an arrest. Typically, the suspect's name, the charge, and perhaps the suspect's fingerprints or photograph are entered in the police blotter.

misdemeanor
A less serious crime generally punishable by a fine or by incarceration in jail for not more than one year.

ordinance violation
Usually the violation of a law of a city or town.

complaint
A charging document specifying that an offense has been committed by a person or persons named or described.

felony
A serious offense punishable by confinement in prison for more than one year or by death.

information
A document that outlines the formal charge(s) against a suspect, the law(s) that have been violated, and the evidence to support the charge(s).

grand jury indictment
A written accusation by a grand jury that one or more persons have committed a crime.

arrest warrant
A written order directing law enforcement officers to arrest a person.

---

in a particular crime. Even when the police start with a known crime or a cooperative victim or witness, the investigation can be lengthy and difficult.

If police investigation of the crime is successful, a suspect is arrested. An **arrest** is the seizing and detaining of a person by lawful authority. After an arrest has been made, the suspect is brought to the police station to be booked. **Booking** is the administrative recording of the arrest. It typically involves entering the suspect's name, the charge, and perhaps the suspect's fingerprints or photograph in the police blotter.

Courts

Soon after a suspect has been arrested and booked, a prosecutor reviews the facts of the case and the available evidence. Sometimes a prosecutor reviews the case before arrest. The prosecutor decides whether to charge the suspect with a crime or crimes. If no charges are filed, the suspect must be released.

Charging Documents   There are three principal kinds of charging documents:

1. A complaint
2. An information
3. A grand jury indictment

If the offense is a **misdemeanor** (a less serious crime) or an **ordinance violation** (usually the violation of a law of a city or town), then in many jurisdictions the prosecutor prepares a complaint. A **complaint** is a charging document specifying that an offense has been committed by a person or persons named or described. If the offense is a **felony** (a serious offense punishable by confinement in a prison for more than one year or by death), an information is used in about half the states. A grand jury indictment is used in the other half. An **information** outlines the formal charge or charges, the law or laws that have been violated, and the evidence to support the charge or charges. A **grand jury indictment** is a written accusation by a grand jury that one or more persons have committed a crime. (Grand juries will be described later in this discussion.) On rare occasions, police may obtain an arrest warrant from a lower-court judge before making an arrest. An **arrest warrant** is a written order directing law enforcement officers to arrest a person. The charge or charges against a suspect are specified on the warrant. Thus, an arrest warrant may also be considered a type of charging document.

▲ Suspects who remain in custody must be brought before a judge for an initial appearance without unnecessary delay. *Why is this policy important?*

Pretrial Stages   After the charge or charges have been filed, the suspect, who is now the **defendant,** is brought before a lower-court judge for an initial appearance. At the **initial appearance** the defendant is given formal notice of the charge or charges against him or her and advised of his or her constitutional rights (for example, the right to counsel). In the case of a misdemeanor or an ordinance violation, a **summary trial** (an immediate trial without a jury) may be held. In the case of a felony, a hearing is held to determine whether the defendant should be released or whether there is probable cause to hold the defendant for a preliminary hearing. **Probable cause** is a standard of proof that requires trustworthy evidence sufficient to make a reasonable person believe that, more likely than not, the proposed action is justified. If the suspect is to be held for a preliminary hearing, bail is set if the judge believes release on bail is appropriate. **Bail,** usually a monetary guarantee deposited with the court, is meant to ensure that the defendant will appear at a later stage in the criminal justice process.

In about half of all states, the initial appearance is followed by a preliminary hearing. Preliminary hearings are used only in felony cases. The purpose of the **preliminary hearing** is for a judge to determine whether there is probable cause to believe that the defendant committed the crime or crimes with which he or she is charged. If the judge finds probable cause, the defendant is bound over for possible indictment in a state with grand juries or for arraignment on an information in a state without grand juries.

Grand juries are involved in felony prosecutions in about half the states. A **grand jury** is a group of citizens who meet in closed sessions for a specified period to investigate charges coming from preliminary hearings and to fulfill other responsibilities. Thus, a primary purpose of the grand jury is to determine whether there is probable cause to believe that the accused committed the crime or crimes with which the prosecutor has charged her or him. The grand jury can either indict or fail to indict a suspect. If the grand jury fails to indict, the prosecution must be dropped.

Once an indictment or information is filed with the trial court, the defendant is scheduled for arraignment. The primary purpose of **arraignment** is to hear the formal information or indictment and to allow the defendant to enter a plea. About 90 percent of criminal defendants plead guilty to the charges against them, in an arrangement called *plea bargaining.* **Plea bargaining** is the practice whereby the prosecutor, the defense attorney, the defendant, and, in many jurisdictions, the judge agree on a specific sentence to be imposed if the accused pleads guilty to an agreed-upon charge or charges instead of going to trial.

Trial   If a defendant pleads not guilty or not guilty by reason of insanity, a trial date is set. Although all criminal defendants have a constitutional right to a trial (when imprisonment for six months or more is a possible outcome), only about ten percent of all criminal cases are disposed of by trial. Approximately five percent of criminal cases involve jury trials. The remaining cases that are not resolved through plea bargaining are decided by a judge in a **bench trial** (without a jury). Thus, approximately 90 percent of all criminal cases are resolved through plea bargaining, about 5 percent through jury trials, and about 5 percent through bench trials. (See Figure 1–3.) In most jurisdictions the choice between a jury trial and a bench trial is the defendant's to make.

defendant
A person against whom a legal action is brought, a warrant is issued, or an indictment is found.

initial appearance
A pretrial stage in which a defendant is brought before a lower court to be given notice of the charge(s) and advised of her or his constitutional rights.

summary trial
An immediate trial without a jury.

probable cause
A standard of proof that requires evidence sufficient to make a reasonable person believe that, more likely than not, the proposed action is justified.

bail
Usually a monetary guarantee deposited with the court to ensure that suspects or defendants will appear at a later stage in the criminal justice process.

preliminary hearing
In a felony case, a pretrial stage at which a judge determines whether there is probable cause.

grand jury
A group of citizens who meet to investigate charges coming from preliminary hearings.

arraignment
A pretrial stage to hear the information or indictment and to allow a plea.

plea bargaining
The practice whereby a specific sentence is imposed if the accused pleads guilty to an agreed-upon charge or charges instead of going to trial.

bench trial
A trial before a judge without a jury.

Crime and Justice in the United States   **CHAPTER 1**

FIGURE 1-2

Overview of the Criminal Justice System

The Criminal Justice System

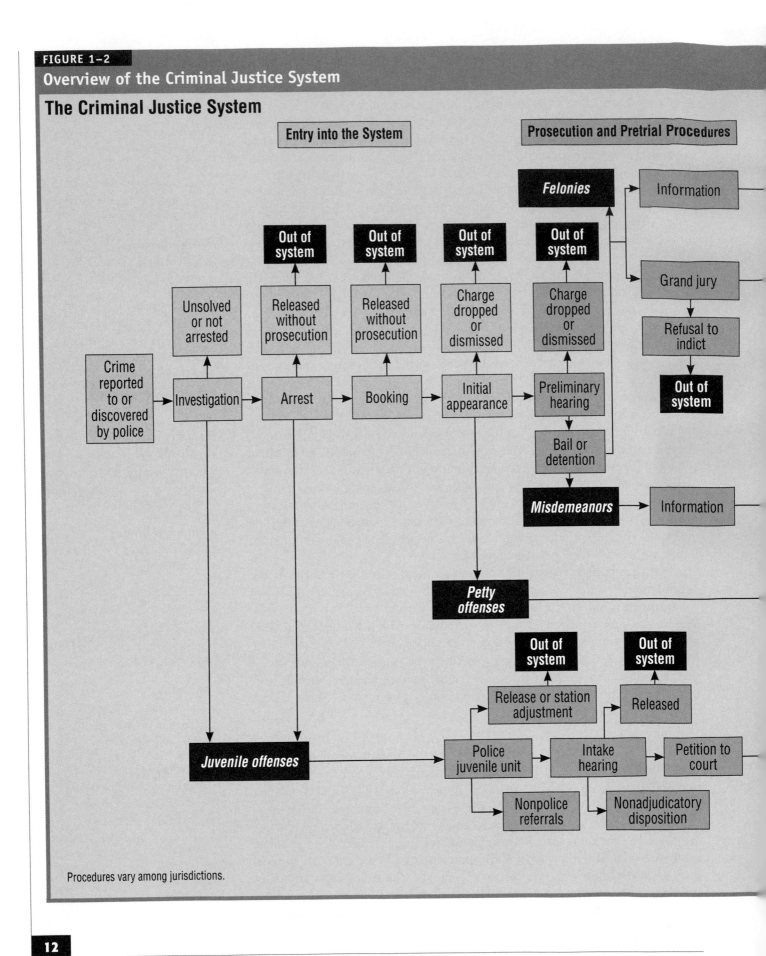

Entry into the System

Prosecution and Pretrial Procedures

Felonies — Information

Out of system — Unsolved or not arrested

Out of system — Released without prosecution

Out of system — Released without prosecution

Out of system — Charge dropped or dismissed

Out of system — Charge dropped or dismissed

Grand jury — Refusal to indict — Out of system

Crime reported to or discovered by police → Investigation → Arrest → Booking → Initial appearance → Preliminary hearing

Bail or detention

Misdemeanors → Information

Petty offenses

Out of system — Release or station adjustment

Out of system — Released

Juvenile offenses → Police juvenile unit → Intake hearing → Petition to court

Nonpolice referrals → Nonadjudicatory disposition

Procedures vary among jurisdictions.

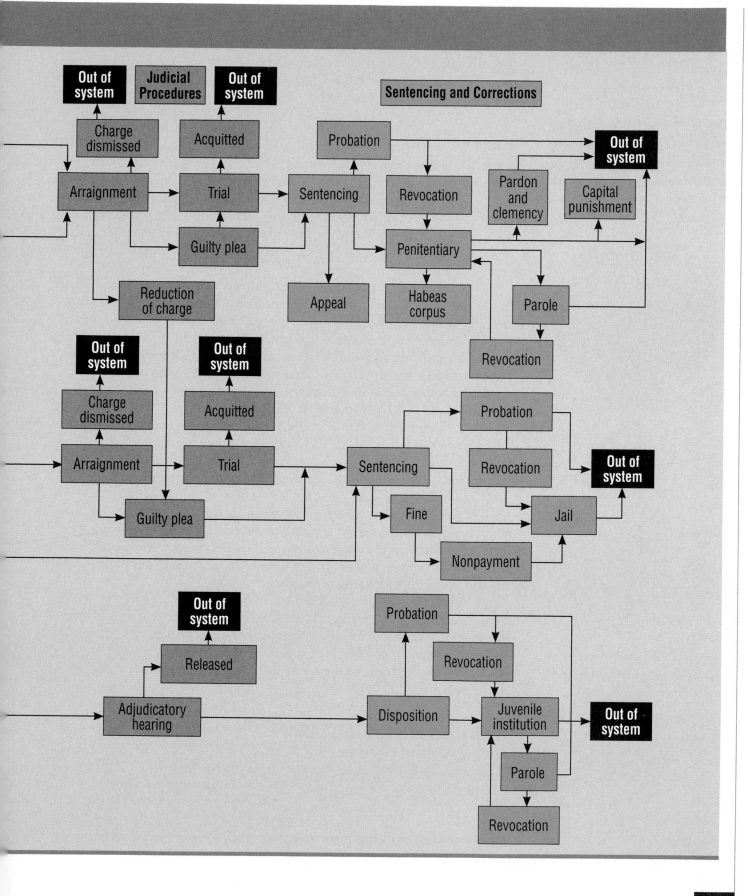

Out of system

Charge dismissed

Acquitted

Probation

Out of system

Arraignment

Trial

Sentencing

Revocation

Pardon and clemency

Capital punishment

Guilty plea

Penitentiary

Reduction of charge

Appeal

Habeas corpus

Parole

Revocation

Out of system

Charge dismissed

Out of system

Acquitted

Probation

Arraignment

Trial

Sentencing

Revocation

Out of system

Guilty plea

Fine

Jail

Nonpayment

Out of system

Released

Probation

Adjudicatory hearing

Disposition

Revocation

Juvenile institution

Out of system

Parole

Revocation

If the judge or the jury finds the defendant guilty as charged, the judge begins to consider a sentence. In some jurisdictions the jury participates to varying degrees in the sentencing process. The degree of jury participation depends on the jurisdiction and the crime. If the judge or jury finds the defendant not guilty, the defendant is released from the jurisdiction of the court and becomes a free person.

Corrections

Judges cannot impose just any sentence. There are many factors which restrict sentencing decisions. They are limited by statutory provisions. They are guided by prevailing philosophical rationales, by organizational considerations, and by presentence investigation reports. They are also influenced by their own personal characteristics. Presentence investigation reports are used in the federal system and in the majority of states to help judges determine appropriate sentences.

Currently, five general types of punishment are in use in the United States: fines, probation, intermediate punishments (various punishments that are more restrictive than probation but less restrictive and less costly than imprisonment), imprisonment, and death. As long as a judge imposes one or a combination of the five punishments and the sentence length and type are within statutory limits, the judge is free to set any sentence he or she wants.

Defendants who are found guilty can appeal their convictions either on legal grounds or on constitutional grounds. Examples of legal grounds include defects in jury selection, improper admission of evidence at trial, and mistaken interpretations of law. Constitutional grounds include illegal search and seizure, improper questioning of the defendant by the police, identification of the defendant through a defective police lineup, and incompetent assistance of counsel.

The appellate court can either *affirm* the verdict of the lower court and let it stand; modify the verdict of the lower court, without totally reversing it; reverse the verdict of the lower court, which requires no further court action; or reverse the decision and *remand*, or return, the case to the court of original jurisdiction for either a retrial or resentencing.

A defendant sentenced to prison may be eligible for parole (in those jurisdictions that grant parole) after serving a portion of his or her sentence. **Parole** is the conditional release of prisoners before they have served their full sentences. Generally, the decision to grant parole is made by a parole board. Once offenders have served their sentences, they are released from criminal justice authority.

FIGURE 1–3
Criminal Case Dispositions

Bench Trial 5%

Jury Trial 5%

Plea Bargain 90%

parole
The conditional release of prisoners before they have served their full sentences.

1.3 CRITICAL THINKING

1. Do you think the criminal justice system "works" in the United States? Why or why not?

2. What improvements do you think should be made to the criminal justice system?

3. Do you think judges should be limited in the sentences they are allowed to impose? Why or why not?

1.4 Criminal Justice: The Nonsystem

As noted earlier, the many police, court, and corrections agencies of the federal, state, and local governments, taken together, are commonly referred to as the criminal justice system. However, the depiction of criminal justice—or, more specifically, of the interrelationships and inner workings of its various components—as a "system" may be inappropriate and misleading for at least two reasons.

First, there is no single "criminal justice system" in the United States. Rather, as noted earlier, there is a loose confederation of many independent criminal justice agencies at all levels of government. This loose confederation is spread throughout the country with different, sometimes overlapping, jurisdictions. Although there are some similarities among many of those agencies, there are also significant differences. The only requirement they all share, a requirement that is the basis for their similarities, is that they follow procedures permitted by the U.S. Constitution.

Second, if a **system** is thought of as a smoothly operating set of arrangements and institutions directed toward the achievement of common goals, one is hard pressed to call the operation of criminal justice in the United States a system. Instead, because there is considerable conflict and confusion between different agencies of criminal justice, a more accurate representation may be that of a criminal justice *nonsystem*.

For example, police commonly complain that criminal offenders who have been arrested after weeks or months of time-consuming and costly investigation are not prosecuted or are not prosecuted vigorously enough. Police often maintain that prosecutors are not working with them or are making their jobs more difficult than necessary. Prosecutors, on the other hand, often gripe about shoddy police work. Sometimes, they say, they are unable to prosecute a crime because of procedural errors committed by the police during the investigation or the arrest.

Even when a criminal offender is prosecuted, convicted, and sentenced to prison, police often argue that the sentence is not severe enough to fit the seriousness of the crime, or they complain when the offender is released from prison after serving only a portion of his or her sentence. In such situations, police frequently argue that the courts or the correctional agencies are undermining their efforts by putting criminals back on the streets too soon.

system
A smoothly operating set of arrangements and institutions directed toward the achievement of common goals.

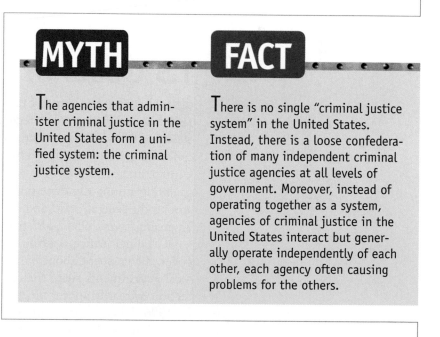

MYTH

The agencies that administer criminal justice in the United States form a unified system: the criminal justice system.

FACT

There is no single "criminal justice system" in the United States. Instead, there is a loose confederation of many independent criminal justice agencies at all levels of government. Moreover, instead of operating together as a system, agencies of criminal justice in the United States interact but generally operate independently of each other, each agency often causing problems for the others.

Conflicts between the courts and corrections sometimes occur when judges continue to impose prison sentences on criminal offenders, especially so-called petty offenders, even though the judges know that the prisons are under court orders to reduce overcrowding.

Additionally, there is a mostly separate process for juvenile offenders. Criminal justice officials frequently complain that their jobs are made more difficult because of the practice, common in many states, of sealing juvenile court records. That practice withholds juvenile court records from the police, prosecutors, and judges even though the records may be relevant and helpful in making arrests, prosecuting criminal cases, and determining appropriate sentences. A rationale for concealing juvenile court records is to prevent, as much as possible, the labeling of juvenile offenders as delinquents, which could make them delinquents. (Labeling theory will be discussed in Chapter 3.)

In short, rather than operating together as a system, agencies of criminal justice in the United States generally operate independently of each other, each agency often causing problems for the others. Such conflicts may not be entirely undesirable, however, since they occur in a context of checks and balances by which the courts ensure that the law is enforced according to constitutional principles.

1.4 CRITICAL THINKING

1. What do you think are some of the positive aspects of having a criminal justice "nonsystem"?

2. What do you think are some of the disadvantages of having a criminal justice "nonsystem"?

1.5 Costs of Criminal Justice

Each year in the United States, an enormous amount of money is spent on criminal justice at the federal, state, and local levels. In 1996 (the latest year for which figures are available), a total of $120 billion was spent on civil and criminal justice. That represents $454 for every resident of the United States. Figure 1–4 on pages 18 and 19 shows the breakdown of spending among the three main segments of the criminal justice system and among the federal, state, and local levels. The $120 billion was an increase of 7 percent from 1995 and 85 percent from 1985.[3]

Criminal justice is primarily a state and local function; state and local governments spent about 85 percent of the 1996 total. Note that state and local governments share the costs of criminal justice by making police protection primarily a local function and corrections primarily a state function. In 1996, local governments spent 72 percent of the total spent on police protection, while state governments spent nearly 62 percent of the total spent on corrections. The expense of judicial and legal services was more evenly divided between state and local governments; still, local governments (primarily counties) spent more than state governments on those services (47 percent versus 31 percent).

It is important to note that although the bulk of government spending on criminal justice is at the state and local levels, the federal government uses its expenditures strategically to influence criminal justice policy at the other levels of government. For example, the federal government develops and tests new approaches to criminal justice and crime control. It then encourages state and local criminal justice agencies to duplicate effective programs and practices by awarding monetary grants to interested and willing agencies. Grants are also awarded to state and local criminal justice agencies to implement programs that address the federal government's crime control priorities, such as its current emphasis on violent and drug-related crimes. In 1996, the federal government spent 14.5 percent of the total expenditures on criminal and civil justice.

It is also noteworthy that despite the billions of dollars spent on criminal and civil justice at the federal, state, and local levels, as a percentage of all government expenditures, the amount spent on criminal justice represents only a tiny fraction—about 4.4 percent (1.8 percent for police protection, 1.7 percent for corrections, and 0.9 percent for judicial and legal services). In other words, only about four cents of every federal, state, and local tax dollar is spent on criminal justice—an amount that has stayed about the same for the past 15 years. Thus, compared with expenditures on other government services, such as social insurance, national defense, international relations, interest on debt at the federal level, and public welfare and education at the state and local levels, spending on criminal justice remains a relatively low priority —a point apparently not missed by the American public.[4]

For the past 25 years, public opinion polls have shown that about two-thirds of all Americans believe that too little money is spent on crime control. Very few people think that too much is being spent.[5] In a 1998 public opinion poll, for example, 61 percent of people surveyed believed that too little was being spent to halt the rising crime rate (down from 75 percent in 1994). Only 28 percent believed that the amount being spent was about right (up from 16 percent in 1994).[6] What is not clear, however, because no data are available, is whether those people who believe more money should be spent to fight crime are willing to pay higher taxes to provide that money.

The data presented so far in this section provide a general overview of the aggregate costs of criminal justice in the United States. They do not, however, reveal the expenses of individual-level justice, which vary greatly. On one hand, administering justice to people who commit capital or death-eligible crimes costs, on average, between $2 and $3 million per case (the cost of the entire process); extraordinary cases can cost much more. For example, the state of Florida reportedly spent $10 million to administer justice to serial murderer Ted Bundy.

On the other hand, the routine crimes processed daily cost much less. A better idea of the costs of justice in more typical cases comes from an examination of the costs of each stage of the local criminal justice process. The results

CRIMINAL JUSTICE Online

Crime Statistics

You can learn more about crime statistics in your area by visiting the Crime.com Web site by clicking the link at cj.glencoe.com. Once at the site, enter your zip code and get a breakdown of crime statistics in your area. *Given the crime statistics you have reviewed, do you think that sufficient money is being spent on criminal justice in your area?*

Money and Crime

Americans have definite opinions about crime and the money spent to fight it. To lower the crime rate, most Americans (54 percent) think that the money available should be spent on social and economic problems; 31 percent think it should be spent on criminal justice (police, prisons, and judges); 13 percent think money should be spent on both social and economic problems and criminal justice; and, finally, 2 percent think money should not be spent on either one.

SOURCE: Jurg Gerber and Simone Engelhardt Greer, "Just and Painful: Attitudes Toward Sentencing Criminals," pp. 62–74 in T. J. Flanagan and D. R. Longmire, (eds.) *Americans View Crime and Justice: A National Public Opinion Survey* (Thousand Oaks, CA, Sage, 1996), p. 71, Table 5.3

of such a study are presented below.[7] A 39-year-old male burglar was arrested in Orange County, Florida, in 1995. The state of Florida and Orange County spent $46,106 to administer justice to that offender, who had stolen approximately $5,100 of merchandise and caused about $1,000 in damages to the store. Of course, the costs of the crime include more than just the stolen merchandise and damaged property. They also include the psychological costs of

FIGURE 1-4

Costs of Criminal Justice

In 1996, federal, state, and local governments spent $120 billion in direct expenditures for the criminal and civil justice systems.

Judicial/Legal Services

Police Protection

$53 BILLION

+ $26 BILLION

Police Protection		$ Billions
52%	Municipalities	$27.801
20%	Counties	10.425
12%	States	6.499
16%	Federal	8.281
100%		53.007

Judicial/ Legal Services		
11%	Municipalities	$2.997
36%	Counties	9.358
31%	States	8.110
22%	Federal	5.693
100%		26.158

Corrections		
6%	Municipalities	$2.402
24%	Counties	9.827
62%	States	25.294
9%	Federal	3.506
100%		41.029

Detail may not add to 100% because of rounding.

victimization (for example, the loss of a sense of security, a greater fear of crime), which are difficult to place a dollar figure on. Figure 1–5 on page 20 displays the total cost of the case and the costs for each of the specific criminal justice functions. As shown, corrections costs accounted for the bulk of expenditures (98 percent). Law enforcement, prosecution, and court costs were minimal in comparison. An interesting postscript is that two years after his

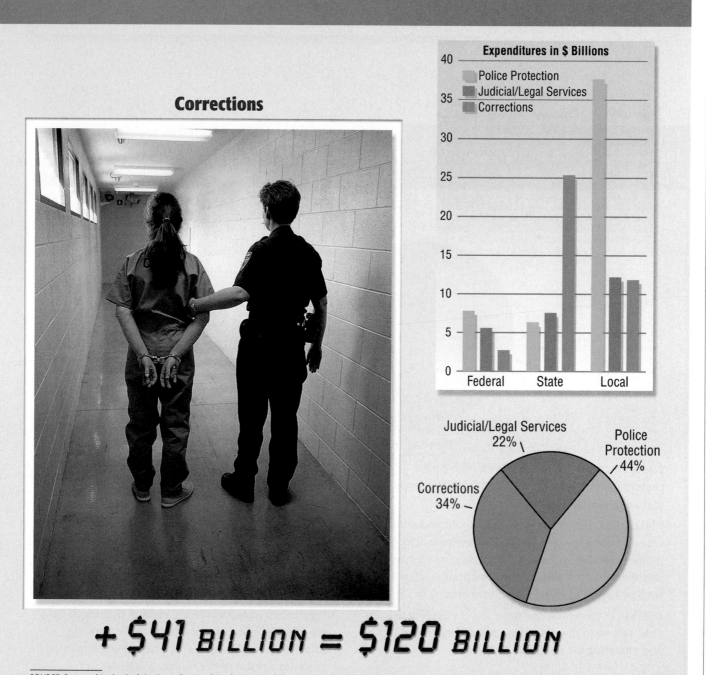

Corrections

Expenditures in $ Billions

- Police Protection
- Judicial/Legal Services
- Corrections

Federal State Local

Judicial/Legal Services 22%

Police Protection 44%

Corrections 34%

+ $41 BILLION = $120 BILLION

SOURCE: Bureau of Justice Statistics Expenditure and Employment Statistics, Summary Findings 1996, <www.ojp.usdoj.gov/bjs/eande.htm#top> (July 2000); Table in individual spreadsheets from the 1996 Justice Expenditure and Employment Extracts (provided by the Bureau of Justice Statistics.)

Crime and Justice in the United States **CHAPTER 1**

release from prison, the offender in the case was arrested again for burglary of a structure and resisting arrest with violence. At this writing, he was awaiting trial and, if found guilty, could once again cost the taxpayers of Florida thousands of dollars.

1.5 CRITICAL THINKING

Do you think more money needs to be spent on criminal justice? Why or why not?

FIGURE 1–5
Total Costs of the Orange County, Florida, Burglary Case by Specific Criminal Justice Functions

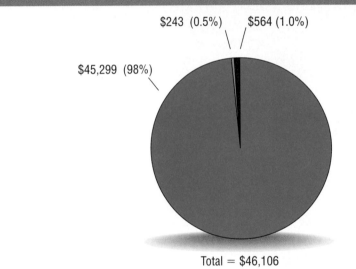

$243 (0.5%) $564 (1.0%)

$45,299 (98%)

■ Law Enforcement Costs
☐ Prosecution and Court Costs
▨ Corrections Costs

*percentages do not total 100% because of rounding errors.

Total = $46,106

- Law enforcement costs include the time spent capturing and arresting the offender, writing reports, and conducting the investigation.

- Prosecution costs include the time spent reviewing the case and filing charges, negotiating a plea with the public defender, and attending the sentencing hearing and the support staff who performed various tasks such as filing and forwarding documents.

- Defense costs include the time spent reviewing the case, talking to the defendant, negotiating a plea, and attending the sentencing hearing.

- Judicial costs include time spent at the initial appearance and arraignment and completing required paperwork.

- Court support staff costs include time spent filing the charges, entering the file into the computer, assigning the case number, scheduling the arraignment, preparing subpoenas, and recording minutes of the formal proceedings.

- Corrections costs include the costs of booking the offender, detaining him in jail while awaiting adjudication of the case, and incarcerating him in prison as a result of the sentence imposed.

P A R T   1   *The Foundations of Criminal Justice*

1.6 Myths About Crime and Criminal Justice

A major theme of this book is to expose and correct misconceptions the American public has about crime and criminal justice. Much of the public's understanding of crime and criminal justice is wrong; it is based on myths. **Myths** are "simplistic and distorted beliefs based upon emotion rather than rigorous analysis" or "at worst . . . dangerous falsifications."[8] More specifically, myths are "credible, dramatic, socially constructed representation[s] of perceived realities that people accept as permanent, fixed knowledge of reality while forgetting (if they were ever aware of it) [their] tentative, imaginative, created, and perhaps fictional qualities."[9] For example, during the Middle Ages in Europe, people commonly believed that guilt or innocence could be determined through *trial by ordeal*. The accused might be required to walk barefoot over hot coals, hold a piece of red-hot iron, or walk through fire. The absence of any injury was believed to be a sign from God that the person was innocent. Although we may now wonder how such a distorted and simplistic belief could have been taken as fact and used to determine a person's guilt or innocence, people did not consider the belief a myth during the time that it was official practice. The lesson to be learned from this example is that a belief that is taken as fact at one time may in retrospect be viewed as a myth. In this book, we attempt to place such myths about crime and criminal justice in perspective.[10] In each chapter, we present at least one generally accepted belief about crime or the justice system that can be considered a myth because it can be contradicted with fact.

myths
Beliefs based on emotion rather than analysis.

- -

1.6 CRITICAL THINKING

What do you think are some of the most common myths about the criminal justice system?

Review and Applications

1. Describe How the Type of Crime Routinely Presented by the Media Compares with Crime Routinely Committed

Crime presented by the media is usually more sensational than crime routinely committed.

2. Identify Institutions of Social Control and Explain What Makes Criminal Justice an Institution of Social Control

Institutions of social control include the family, schools, organized religion, the media, the law, and criminal justice. Such institutions attempt to persuade people to abide by the dominant values of society. Criminal justice is restricted to persuading people to abide by a limited range of social values, the violation of which constitutes crime.

3. Summarize How the Criminal Justice System Responds to Crime

The typical criminal justice response to the commission of a crime involves the following: investigation; arrest (if the investigation is successful); booking; the formal charging of the suspect; an initial appearance; a preliminary hearing (for a felony); either indictment by a grand jury followed by arraignment, or arraignment on an information; either a plea bargain or a trial; sentencing; possible appeal; and punishment (if the defendant is found guilty).

4. Explain Why Criminal Justice in the United States is Sometimes Considered a Nonsystem

Criminal justice in the United States is sometimes considered a nonsystem for two major reasons. First, there is no single system, but instead a loose confederation of more than 50,000 agencies on federal, state, and local levels. Second, rather than being a smoothly operating set of arrangements and institutions, the agencies of the criminal justice system interact with one another, but generally operate independently, often causing problems for one another.

5. Describe the Costs of Criminal Justice in the United States and Compare Those Costs Among Federal, State, and Local Governments

An enormous amount of money is spent each year on criminal justice in the United States. In 1996, federal, state, and local governments spent a total of $120 billion on police protection ($53 billion), judicial/legal services ($26 billion), and corrections ($41 billion). The bulk of government spending on criminal justice is at the state and local levels, but the federal government spends money strategically to influence criminal justice policy at the other levels of government.

6. Explain How Myths About Crime and Criminal Justice Affect the Criminal Justice System

The acceptance and perpetuation of myths, or simplistic beliefs based on emotion rather than rigorous analysis, can harm the criminal justice system by contributing to the failure to reduce crime and to the waste of money in the battle against crime.

institution of social control, p. 7
jurisdiction, p. 8
arrest, p. 10
booking, p. 10
misdemeanor, p. 10
ordinance violation, p. 10
complaint, p. 10
felony, p. 10

information, p. 10
grand jury indictment, p. 10
arrest warrant, p. 10
defendant, p. 11
initial appearance, p. 11
summary trial, p. 11
probable cause, p. 11
bail, p. 11

preliminary hearing, p. 11
grand jury, p. 11
arraignment, p. 11
plea bargaining, p. 11
bench trial, p. 11
parole, p. 14
system, p. 15
myths, p. 21

QUESTIONS FOR REVIEW

1. What is the fundamental problem with the types of crime routinely presented by the media?

2. What was the most frequent type of call for police service in Chicago during the period examined in the text (see Figure 1–1)?

3. What is an *institution of social control*?

4. Why is criminal justice sometimes considered society's "last line of defense"?

5. What three agencies make up the criminal justice system?

6. What is a *jurisdiction*?

7. What is the difference between an *arrest* and a *booking*?

8. Who decides whether or not to charge a suspect with a crime?

9. What are three principal kinds of charging documents?

10. What is the difference between a *misdemeanor* and a *felony*?

11. What is a *defendant*, and when does a suspect become a defendant?

12. What is the difference between an *initial appearance* and a *preliminary hearing*?

13. Define *bench trial, summary trial, bail, grand jury, arraignment, plea bargaining,* and *parole.*

14. What is meant by *probable cause*?

15. Why are the conflicts between the different agencies of criminal justice not entirely undesirable?

16. Which levels of government—federal, state, or local—bear most of the costs of criminal justice in the United States?

17. What is a lesson to be learned from myths about crime and criminal justice?

EXPERIENTIAL ACTIVITIES

1. **Crime and the Media** Watch a local television station's broadcast of the evening news for one or more days and record the crimes reported. Then obtain from your local police department a copy of the log of calls for police service for one of those days. Compare the crimes reported on the nightly news with the calls for police service. Describe similarities and differences between the two different sources of crime information. What have you learned?

2. **Costs of Crime** Follow a criminal case in your community and determine the costs of processing the case. You will have to contact the police, the prosecutor, the defense attorney, the judge, and other relevant participants. Remember to consider both monetary and psychological costs. After you have determined the costs, decide whether you think they were justified. Defend your answer.

3. Costs of Justice In 1995, 7.4 percent of state spending and 7.9 percent of local spending were for criminal justice. By contrast, 31.6 percent of state spending was for public welfare, 20 percent for education and libraries, and 18.4 percent for social insurance payments. The biggest expense for local governments, nearly 38 percent of all spending, was for education and libraries. Divide into groups. Using the preceding data, debate within your group whether or not states and localities spend enough of their budgets on criminal justice. Share group results with the class.

INTERNET

4. Criminal Justice in Other Countries Learn about the criminal justice systems of other countries by visiting the Web site of the U.S. Justice Department's *The World Factbook of Criminal Justice Systems* through the link at cj.glencoe.com.

5. FBI's Most Wanted Access the FBI's "Top Ten Most Wanted Fugitives" Web site by clicking the link at cj.glencoe.com. Read the descriptions of the fugitives. Write a report describing the characteristics they share. Also, try to determine what unique features qualify these fugitives, and not others, for the list.

CRITICAL THINKING EXERCISES

Plea Bargaining

1. Shirley Smith pleaded guilty to third-degree murder after admitting she had put rat poison in drinks her husband ingested at least 12 times during the course of their 13-month marriage. Sentenced to a maximum of 20 years in prison, she would have to serve at least 10 years before she could be considered for parole. The prosecutor defended the plea bargain against much public criticism. The prosecutor claimed that the costs of a murder trial and subsequent appeals were not paramount. However, the prosecutor did acknowledge that the case could have been the most expensive in county history, exhausted his entire $2 million budget for the fiscal year, and required a tax increase to cover the costs. As an elected official, the prosecutor attempted to seek justice while exercising a sense of fiscal responsibility.

   a. Do you think the prosecutor made the correct decision to plea bargain? Defend your answer.

   b. In potentially expensive cases, should the prosecutor seek a referendum on the matter (to determine whether residents are willing to pay additional taxes to try a defendant rather than accept a plea bargain)?

Prison versus Rehabilitation

2. The city council of a midsize East Coast city is locked in a debate concerning how to address the rising incidence of violent crime. John Fogarty, one of the most influential people in the city, is pushing for more police and stiffer penalties as the solution. He is the leader of a group that is proposing the construction of a new prison. Another group thinks putting more people in prison is not the answer. They

believe that early intervention, education, and prevention programs will be most effective. There is not enough money to fund both sides' proposals.

a. Which side would you support? Why?

b. What do you think is the number one crime problem in your community? List ways of dealing with that problem. What would be the most cost-effective way to lower the rate of that crime?

ADDITIONAL READING

Kappeler, Victor E., Mark Blumberg, and Gary W. Potter. *The Mythology of Crime and Criminal Justice*, 3d ed. Prospect Heights, IL: Waveland, 2000.

Pepinsky, Harold E., and Paul Jesilow. *Myths That Cause Crime*, 2d ed. Cabin John, MD: Seven Locks, 1985.

Reiman, Jeffrey H. *The Rich Get Richer and the Poor Get Prison: Ideology, Class, and Criminal Justice*, 6th ed. Boston: Allyn & Bacon, 2001.

Walker, Samuel. *Sense and Nonsense About Crime, and Drugs: A Policy Guide*, 4th ed. Belmont, CA: Wadsworth, 1998.

Wright, Kevin N. *The Great American Crime Myth*. Westport, CT: Greenwood, 1987

ENDNOTES

1. The top crime news stories for 2000 are taken from *Facts on File: World News Digest with Index*, No. 3085, January 20, 2000, p. 31; No. 3094, March 23, 2000, p. 196; No. 3091, March 2, 2000, p. 126; No. 3092, March 9, 2000, p. 151; No. 3092, March 9, 2000, p. 152; No. 3094, March 23, 2000, p. 195; No. 3094, March 23, 2000, p. 196; No. 3098, April 20, 2000, p. 266; No. 3100, May 4, 2000, p. 301; No. 3105, May 18, 2000, p. 336; No. 3103, May 25, 2000, p. 357.

2. Our thanks to Chicago Police Officer Monica Chester of the Research and Development Division and Tom Dugan of the Office of Emergency Communications, for their help in securing and explaining these data.

3. Unless otherwise indicated, the data in this section are from *Bureau of Justice Statistics Expenditure and Employment Statistics, Summary Findings 1996*, <www.ojp.usdoj.gov/bjs/eande.htm#top> (July 2000); tables in individual spreadsheets from the 1996 *Justice Expenditure and Employment Extracts* (provided by the Bureau of Justice Statistics); Lea S. Gifford with assistance from Sue A. Lindgren, "Justice Expenditures and Employment in the United States, 1995," *Bureau of Justice Statistics Bulletin*, U.S. Department of Justice (Washington, DC: GPO, 1999).

4. Lea S. Gifford with assistance from Sue A. Lindgren, "Justice Expenditures and Employment in the United States, 1995," *Bureau of Justice Statistics Bulletin*, U.S. Department of Justice (Washington, DC: GPO, 1999.)

5. Timothy J. Flanagan, "Public Opinion on Crime and Justice: History, Development, and Trends," pp. 1–15 in Timothy J. Flanagan and Dennis R. Longmire (eds.), *Americans View Crime and Justice: A National Public Opinion Survey* (Thousand Oaks, CA: Sage, 1996).

6. Kathleen Maguire and Ann L. Pastore (eds.), *Sourcebook of Criminal Justice Statistics 1998*, U.S. Department of Justice, Bureau of Justice Statistics (Washington, DC: GPO, 1999), pp. 124–25, Table 2.48.

7. Laurie A. Gould, "A Case Study of the Monetary Costs of Criminal Justice in a Local Jurisdiction" (unpublished manuscript, 2000).

8. D. Nimmo and J. E. Combs, *Subliminal Politics: Myths and Mythmakers in America* (Englewood Cliffs, NJ: Prentice-Hall, 1980), p. 6.

9. Ibid., p. 16.

10. Many of the myths presented in this book were taken from the following sources: Jeffrey H. Reiman, *The Rich Get Richer and the Poor Get Prison: Ideology, Class, and Criminal Justice*, 6th ed. (Boston: Allyn & Bacon, 2001); Harold E. Pepinsky and Paul Jesilow, *Myths That Cause Crime*, 2d ed. (Cabin John, MD: Seven Locks, 1985); Kevin N. Wright, *The Great American Crime Myth* (Westport, CT: Greenwood, 1987); also see Robert M. Bohm, "Myths About Criminology and Criminal Justice: A Review Essay," *Justice Quarterly*, Vol. 4, 1987, pp. 631–42.; William Wilbanks, *The Myth of a Racist Criminal Justice System* (Belmont, CA: Wadsworth, 1987); Victor E. Kappeler, Mark Blumberg, and Gary W. Potter, *The Mythology of Crime and Criminal Justice*, 3d ed. (Prospect Heights, IL: Waveland, 2000); Samuel Walker, *Sense and Nonsense About Crime, and Drugs: A Policy Guide*, 4d ed. (Belmont, CA: Wadsworth, 1998). For a discussion of why these myths exist, see Robert M. Bohm, "Crime, Criminal and Crime Control Policy Myths," *Justice Quarterly*, Vol. 3, 1986, pp. 193–214.

CHAPTER OUTLINE

CHAPTER OBJECTIVES

After completing this chapter, you should be able to:

1. Distinguish between a social definition and a legal definition of crime and summarize the problems with each.

2. List the technical and ideal elements of a crime.

3. Identify some of the legal defenses or legal excuses for criminal responsibility.

4. Explain why crime and delinquency statistics are unreliable.

5. Identify the two major sources of crime statistics in the U.S.

6. Describe the principal finding of the national crime victimization surveys.

7. Summarize the general finding of self-report crime surveys.

8. Identify the costs of crime.

9. Describe the extent of fear of crime in the United States and the characteristics of people most likely to fear crime.

10. List the characteristics of people who are the most likely and the least likely to be victims of crime.

2.1 Definitions of Crime

The object of criminal justice in the United States is to prevent and control crime. Thus, to understand criminal justice, it is necessary to understand crime. An appropriate definition of crime, however, remains one of the most critical unresolved issues in criminal justice today. One problem is that many dangerous and harmful behaviors are not defined as crimes, while many less dangerous and less harmful behaviors are. We begin, then, by examining how crime is defined and the problems with defining what is a crime.

Social Definitions

The broadest definitions of crime are social definitions. A typical social definition of crime is behavior that violates the norms of society—or, more simply, antisocial behavior. A **norm** is any standard or rule regarding what human beings should or should not think, say, or do under given circumstances. Because social definitions of crime are broad, they are less likely than narrower definitions to exclude behaviors that ought to be included. Nevertheless, there are several problems with social definitions of crime.

First, norms vary from group to group within a single society. There is no uniform definition of antisocial behavior. Take, for example, the acts involved in gambling, prostitution, abortion, and homosexual behavior. As current public debates indicate, there is much controversy in the United States over whether those acts should be crimes. Even with acts about which there seems to be a consensus, like murder and rape, there is no agreement on what constitutes such acts. For example, if a patient dies from a disease contracted from a doctor who did not wash his or her hands before examining the patient, has the doctor committed murder? Or, if a man has forcible sexual intercourse with a woman against her will but, before the act, at the woman's request, puts on a condom so that the woman will not get a sexually transmitted disease, has the man committed rape? Those examples illustrate the difficulty of determining what, in fact, constitutes antisocial behavior, let alone crime.

Second, norms are always subject to interpretation. Each norm's meaning has a history. Consider abortion, for example. For some people, abortion is the killing of a fetus or a human being. For other people, abortion is not killing because, for them, human life begins at birth and not at conception. For the latter group, the abortion issue concerns women's freedom to control their own bodies. For the former group, abortion constitutes an injustice to the helpless.

Third, norms change from time to time and from place to place. For example, the consumption of alcohol was prohibited in the United States during the 1920s and early 1930s but is only regulated today. Until the passage of the Harrison Act, in 1914, it was legal in the United States to use opiates such as opium, heroin, and morphine without a doctor's prescription. Such use is prohibited today. Casino gambling is allowed in some states but forbidden in other states. Prostitution is legal in a few counties in Nevada, but illegal in the rest of the United States. Prior to the mid-1970s, a husband could rape his wife with impunity in all but a handful of states. Today, laws in every state prohibit a husband from raping or assaulting his wife.

norm
Any standard or rule regarding what human beings should or should not think, say, or do under given circumstances.

Crime
Crime is from the Latin *crimen*, meaning "accusation" or "fault."

SOURCE: *Webster's New Twentieth Century Dictionary of the English Language Unabridged* (Williams Collins, 1980.)

▲ More and more states are legalizing casino gambling as a means of generating income. *Is this a desirable trend? Why or why not?*

A Legal Definition

In an attempt to avoid the problems with social definitions of crime, a legal definition of crime is used in criminal justice in the United States. A typical **legal definition of crime** is an intentional violation of the criminal law or penal code, committed without defense or excuse and penalized by the state. The major advantage of a legal definition of crime, at least on the surface, is that it is narrower and less ambiguous than a social definition of crime. If a behavior violates the criminal law, then by definition it is a crime. However, although a legal definition eliminates some of the problems with social definitions of crime, a legal definition of crime has problems of its own.

First, some behaviors prohibited by the criminal law arguably should not be. This problem of **overcriminalization** arises primarily in the area of so-called victimless crimes. Lists of victimless crimes typically include gambling, prostitution involving consenting adults, homosexual acts between consenting adults, and the use of some illegal drugs, such as marijuana. Ultimately, whether those acts should or should not be prohibited by criminal law depends on whether they are truly victimless—an issue we will not debate here.

A second problem with a legal definition of crime is that for some behaviors prohibited by the criminal law, the law is not routinely enforced. **Nonenforcement** is common for many white-collar and government crimes. It is also common for blue laws, which require stores and other commercial establishments to be closed on Sundays. Many jurisdictions in the United States have blue laws, or they did until recently. The principal problem with the nonenforcement of prohibitions is that it causes disrespect for the law. People come to believe that because criminal laws are not routinely enforced, there is no need to routinely obey them.

legal definition of crime
An intentional violation of the criminal law or penal code, committed without defense or excuse and penalized by the state.

overcriminalization
The prohibition by the criminal law of some behaviors that arguably should not be prohibited.

nonenforcement
The failure to routinely enforce prohibitions against certain behaviors.

29

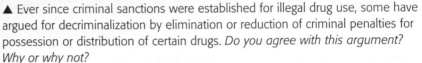

▲ Ever since criminal sanctions were established for illegal drug use, some have argued for decriminalization by elimination or reduction of criminal penalties for possession or distribution of certain drugs. *Do you agree with this argument? Why or why not?*

undercriminalization
The failure to prohibit some behaviors that arguably should be prohibited.

A third problem with a legal definition of crime is the problem of **undercriminalization.** That is, some behaviors that arguably should be prohibited by the criminal law are not. Have you ever said to yourself that there ought to be a law against whatever it is you are upset about? Of course, most of the daily frustrations that people claim ought to be crimes probably should not be. Some people argue, however, that some very harmful and destructive actions or inactions that are not criminal should be. Examples include the government allowing employers (generally through the nonenforcement of laws) to maintain unsafe working conditions that cause employee deaths and injuries, and corporations' intentional production of potentially hazardous products to maximize profits.[1]

Elements of Crime

A legal definition of crime is the basis of criminal justice in the United States. The legal definition of crime provided earlier in this chapter, however, is only a general definition. It does not specify all the elements necessary to make a behavior a crime. Technically and ideally, a crime has not been committed unless all seven of the following elements are present:[2]

1. Harm
2. Legality
3. *Actus reus*
4. *Mens rea*

5. Causation
6. Concurrence
7. Punishment

It is only in a technical and ideal sense that all seven elements must be present. In actual practice, a behavior is often considered a crime when one or more of the elements is absent. We will examine each of the seven elements in turn, indicating exceptions to the technical and ideal where relevant.

Harm   For crime to occur, there must be an external consequence, or **harm.** A mental or emotional state is not enough. Thus, thinking about committing a crime or being angry enough to commit a crime, without acting on the thought or the anger, is not a crime.

The harm may be physical or verbal. Physically striking another person without legal justification is an example of an act that does physical harm. An example of an act that does verbal harm is a threat to strike another person, whether or not the threat is carried out. Writing something false about another person that dishonors or injures that person is a physical harm called *libel.* The spoken equivalent of libel is called *slander.*

Whether the legal element of harm is present in all crimes is sometimes questioned. Some crimes, such as gambling, prostitution, marijuana consumption, and certain consensually committed sexual acts such as sodomy, have come to be called "victimless crimes" by those who argue that only those people involved in these behaviors are harmed, if at all. Other people maintain that the participants, their families, and the moral fabric of society are jeopardized by such behavior. In short, there is considerable debate as to whether so-called victimless crimes really are harmless.

Legality   The element of **legality** has two aspects. First, the harm must be legally forbidden for a behavior to be a crime. Thus, violations of union rules, school rules, religious rules, or any rules other than those of a political jurisdiction may be "wrong," but they are not crimes unless they are also prohibited by criminal law. Furthermore, rude behavior may be frowned upon, but it is not criminal.

Second, a criminal law must not be retroactive, or *ex post facto.* An *ex post facto* **law** (1) declares criminal an act that was not illegal when it was committed, (2) increases the punishment for a crime after it is committed, or (3) alters the rules of evidence in a particular case after the crime is committed. The first meaning is the most common. The United States Constitution (Article I, Section 10.1) forbids *ex post facto* laws.

Actus reus   The Latin term *actus reus* refers to criminal conduct—specifically, intentional or criminally negligent (reckless) action or inaction that causes harm. Crime involves not only things people do but also things they do not do. If people do not act in situations where the law requires them to act, they are committing crimes. For example, parents are legally required to provide their children with adequate food, clothing, and shelter. If parents fail to provide those necessities—that is, if they fail to act when the law requires them to—they are committing a crime.

harm
The external consequence required to make an action a crime.

legality
The requirement (1) that a harm must be legally forbidden for the behavior to be a crime and (2) that the law must not be retroactive.

ex post facto law
A law that (1) declares criminal an act that was not illegal when it was committed, (2) increases the punishment for a crime after it is committed, or (3) alters the rules of evidence in a particular case after the crime is committed.

actus reus
Criminal conduct—specifically, intentional or criminally negligent (reckless) action or inaction that causes harm.

mens rea
Criminal intent; a guilty state of mind.

negligence
The failure to take reasonable precautions to prevent harm.

duress
Force or coercion as an excuse for committing a crime.

Actus Reus

A confusing example of the legal element *actus reus* involves the crime of conspiracy. Conspiracy is the plotting by two or more persons to commit a crime. What is sometimes confusing is that the plot does not have to be carried out for a person to be convicted of conspiracy. If the plan is not executed, however, what is the *actus reus*? It is the act of plotting the crime.

juvenile delinquency
A special category of offense created for young offenders, usually those between 7 and 18 years of age.

Mens rea   The Latin term **mens rea** refers to criminal intent or a guilty state of mind. It is the mental aspect of a crime. Ideally, criminal conduct is limited to intentional or purposeful action or inaction and not to accidents. In practice, however, reckless actions or *negligence* may be criminal. **Negligence** is the failure to take reasonable precautions to prevent harm.

In some cases, offenders lack the capacity (sometimes called competence) to form *mens rea*. If they do not have that capacity, they are not to be held responsible for their criminal conduct. If they have a diminished capacity to form *mens rea*, they are to be held less than fully responsible. In other cases, offenders who have the capacity to form *mens rea* are not held responsible for their crimes, or are held less responsible for them, either because they did not have *mens rea* when they acted or because there were extenuating circumstances when they did act with *mens rea*.

Legal Defenses for Criminal Responsibility. In the United States, an offender is not considered responsible or is considered less responsible for an offense if he or she, for example, (1) acted under duress, (2) was underage, (3) was insane, (4) acted in self-defense or in defense of a third party, (5) was entrapped, or (6) acted out of necessity. Those conditions are legal defenses or legal excuses for criminal responsibility.

If a person did not want to commit a crime but was forced or coerced to do so against his or her will, he or she committed the crime under **duress** and is generally excluded from criminal liability. Suppose that an intruder held a gun to the head of a loved one and threatened to kill that person if you did not rob a local convenience store and return immediately to give the intruder the money. If you committed the robbery to save the life of your loved one, you would probably not be held legally responsible for the crime, because you committed it under duress. There were extenuating circumstances when you acted with *mens rea*. To prevent all offenders from claiming duress, the burden of proof is placed on the defendant.

Another legal excuse or legal defense against criminal responsibility is being underage. Although the age at which a person is considered legally responsible for his or her actions varies by jurisdiction, in most American jurisdictions a child under the age of seven is not held responsible for a crime. It is assumed that a child under seven years of age does not have the capacity to form *mens rea*. A child under seven years of age is considered a *legal infant* or of *legal nonage*. Such a child is protected by the criminal law but not subject to it. Thus, if a six-year-old child picks up a shotgun and shoots his or her parent, the child is unlikely to be charged with a crime. On the other hand, if a parent abuses a child, the criminal law protects the child by holding the abusive parent responsible for his or her actions.

In most developed countries children under 18 years of age are not considered entirely responsible for their criminal acts. It is assumed that their capacity to form *mens rea* is not fully developed. A special category of offense called **juvenile delinquency** has been created for those children. In most American jurisdictions, the upper age limit for juvenile delinquency is 18. The lower limit is usually seven. The criminal law generally treats anyone who is 18 or older as an adult. However, the upper age limit of juvenile delinquency is lower in some jurisdictions and sometimes varies with the sex of the offender. In some jurisdictions there is a legal borderland between the ages of 16 and 18. An offender in that age range may be treated as a juvenile or as an adult, depending on the severity of the offense. In some cases, an offense is considered heinous enough for a court to certify a juvenile, regardless of age, as an adult and to treat him or her accordingly. The subject of juvenile delinquency will be discussed more fully in Chapter 13.

A third legal defense or legal excuse from criminal responsibility is insanity. **Insanity** is a legal term, not a medical one. It refers to mental or psychological impairment or retardation. Like many of the other legal defenses or excuses, an insanity defense rests on the assumption that someone who is insane at the time of a crime lacks the capacity, or has diminished capacity, to form *mens rea*. Thus, that person either should not be held responsible or should be held less responsible for crime.

In most western European nations, legal insanity is determined solely by the judgment and testimony of medical experts. British and American law, by contrast, provide guidelines for judges, juries, and medical experts to follow in determining whether or not a defendant is legally insane. The oldest—and, until recently, the most popular—of those guidelines is the M'Naghten rule, which was first used in an English trial in 1843.

Under the M'Naghten rule:

> [E]very man is to be presumed to be sane, and . . . to establish a defense on the ground of insanity, it must be clearly proved that, at the time of the committing of the act, the party accused was laboring under such a defect of reason, from disease of the mind, as not to know the nature and quality of the act he was doing; or if he did know it, that he did not know he was doing what was wrong.[3]

In short, according to the M'Naghten rule, a person is legally insane if, at the time of the commission of the act, he or she (1) did not know the nature and quality of the act or (2) did not know that the act was wrong. The burden of proof is on the defendant.

One problem with the M'Naghten rule is the difficulty of determining what a person's state of mind was at the time of the commission of the criminal act. The rule has also been criticized for its ambiguity. What is a "defect of reason," and by whose standards is the act a product of defective reason? Does "disease of the mind" refer to organic diseases, nonorganic diseases, or both? What does it mean to "know" the nature and quality of the act? Does it mean an intellectual awareness, an emotional appreciation, or both? Does "wrong" mean legally wrong, morally wrong, or both?

Perhaps the most serious problem with the M'Naghten rule is that it does not address the situation of a defendant who knew the difference between right and wrong but was unable to control his or her actions. To remedy that problem, some states have adopted the *irresistible-impulse* or *control test* and use it in conjunction with the M'Naghten rule. In those states a defense against conviction on grounds of insanity is first made by using the M'Naghten rule. If the conditions of M'Naghten are met, the irresistible-impulse or control test is applied. If it is determined that the defendant knew that he or she was doing wrong at the time of the commission of the criminal act but nevertheless could not control his or her behavior, the defendant is entitled to an acquittal on the grounds of insanity. The major problem with the irresistible-impulse or control test is distinguishing between behavior that is uncontrollable and behavior that is simply uncontrolled.

insanity
Mental or psychological impairment or retardation as a defense against a criminal charge.

Daniel M'Naghten

Daniel M'Naghten was acquitted of the murder of a person he had mistaken for his real target, Sir Robert Peel, then the Prime Minister of Great Britain. M'Naghten claimed that he was delusional at the time of the killing. Go to cj.glencoe.com and research the M'Naghten case. *Explain the insanity defense in that case and give your opinion about the court's ruling.*

▲ In a 1994 trial in Virginia, attorneys for Lorena Bobbitt, who had sliced off her husband's penis with a kitchen knife while he was sleeping, successfully used the *irresistible-impulse* defense against charges of malicious wounding. She was acquitted of the crime. *Was Bobbitt's act of slicing off her husband's penis uncontrollable or uncontrolled? Defend your answer.*

entrapment
A legal defense against criminal responsibility when a person, who was not already predisposed to it, is induced into committing a crime by a law enforcement officer or by his or her agent.

Since 1980, the test for insanity used by most states has been the *substantial-capacity test* of the American Law Institute's Model Penal Code. Under that test, a defendant is not to be found guilty of a crime "if at the time of such conduct as a result of mental disease or defect he lacks substantial capacity either to appreciate the criminality of his conduct or to conform his conduct to the requirements of law." By using the term *substantial capacity*, the test does not require that a defendant be completely unable to distinguish right from wrong. The test has been criticized for its use of the ambiguous terms *substantial capacity* and *appreciate*. It also does not resolve the problem of determining whether behavior is uncontrollable or uncontrolled.

Following the public uproar over the 1982 acquittal of John Hinckley, the would-be assassin of President Ronald Reagan, on the grounds that he was legally insane, several states enacted "guilty but insane" or "guilty but mentally ill" laws. Defendants who are found guilty but insane generally receive sentences that include psychiatric treatment until they are cured. Then they are placed in the general prison population to serve the remainder of their sentences.

A fourth legal defense or legal excuse from criminal responsibility is self-defense or the defense of a third party. Generally, people are relieved of criminal responsibility if they use only the amount of force reasonably necessary to defend themselves or others against an apparent threat of unlawful and immediate violence. When it comes to the protection of property, however, the use of force is much more limited. Deadly force is not allowed, but non-deadly force may be used to protect one's property. The reason people are not held legally responsible for acting in self-defense or in defense of a third party is that due to extenuating circumstances, they do not act with *mens rea*.

Entrapment is a fifth legal defense or legal excuse from criminal responsibility. People are generally considered either not responsible or less responsible for their crimes if they were entrapped, or induced into committing them, by a law enforcement officer or by someone acting as an agent for a law enforcement officer, such as an informer or an undercover agent. A successful entrapment defense, however, requires proof that the law enforcement officer or his or her agent instigated the crime or created the intent to commit the crime in the mind of a person who was not already predisposed to committing it. Thus, it is not entrapment if a law enforcement officer merely affords someone an opportunity to commit a crime, as, for example, when an undercover agent poses as a drug addict and purchases drugs from a drug dealer.

The final legal defense or legal excuse from criminal responsibility to be discussed here is necessity. A **necessity defense** can be used when a crime has been committed to prevent a greater or more serious crime. In such a situation, there are extenuating circumstances, even though the act was committed with *mens rea*. Although it is rarely used, the necessity defense has been invoked occasionally, especially in cases of "political" crimes. The necessity defense was used successfully by Amy Carter (daughter of former President Jimmy Carter), Jerry Rubin, and other activists who were charged with trespassing for protesting apartheid on the property of the South African embassy in Washington, D.C. The court agreed with the protesters that apartheid was a greater crime than trespassing. Interestingly, the law does not recognize economic necessity as a defense against or an excuse from criminal responsibility. Therefore, the unemployed and hungry thief who steals groceries cannot successfully employ the necessity defense.

The availability of an insanity defense allows dangerous offenders to escape conviction and go free.

Defendants found not guilty by reason of insanity rarely go free. Generally, they are confined to a mental institution until they are deemed by the committing court or some other judicial body to be sane or no longer dangerous. Also, there are only about 300 insanity pleas per year in the entire United States, approximately 0.1 percent of all felony complaints in a year.[4]

Causation A fifth ideal legal element of crime is causation, or a causal relationship between the legally forbidden harm and the *actus reus*. In other words, the criminal act must lead directly to the harm without a long delay. In a recent case in Georgia, for example, a father was accused of murdering his baby daughter. The murder charges were dropped, however, because too much time had passed between the night the three-and-a-half-month-old girl was shaken into a coma and her death 18 months later. Because of Georgia's year-and-a-day rule, the father was not charged with murder, but he still faced a charge of cruelty to children, which in Georgia carries a maximum sentence of 20 years. The purpose of the requirement of causation is to prevent people from facing the threat of criminal charges the rest of their lives.

Concurrence Ideally, for any behavior to be considered a crime, there must be concurrence between the *actus reus* and the *mens rea*. In other words, the criminal conduct and the criminal intent must occur together. For example, suppose you call someone to repair your broken washing machine, and that person comes to your home, fixes your washing machine, and on the way out takes your television set. The repair person cannot be found guilty of entering your home illegally (trespass) because that was not his or her initial intent. However, the repair person can be found guilty of stealing your television set.

The Year-And-A-Day Rule
The rule that a person cannot be prosecuted for murder if the victim dies more than a year and a day after the injury is based on thirteenth century English common law.

SOURCE: *Tennessee v. Rogers*, 992 S.W.2d 393 (1999); *United States v. Jackson*, 528A.2d 1211, 1214 (D.C.1987).

Punishment The last of the ideal legal elements of a crime is punishment. For a behavior to be considered a crime, there must be a statutory provision for punishment or at least the threat of punishment. Without the threat of punishment, a law is unenforceable and is therefore not a criminal law.

Degrees or Categories of Crime

Crimes can be classified according to the degree or severity of the offense, according to the nature of the acts prohibited, or on some other basis, such as a statistical reporting scheme. One way crimes are distinguished by degree or severity of the offense is by dividing them into *felonies* and *misdemeanors*. The only way to determine whether a crime is a felony or misdemeanor is by knowing the legislated punishment. Consequently, a felony in one jurisdiction might be a misdemeanor in another jurisdiction, and vice versa. Generally, a felony, as noted in Chapter 1, is a relatively serious offense punishable by death, a fine, or confinement in a state or federal prison for more than one year. A misdemeanor, on the other hand, is any lesser crime that is not a felony. Misdemeanors are usually punishable by no more than a $1,000 fine and one year of incarceration, generally in a county or city jail.

Another way of categorizing crimes is to distinguish between offenses that are *mala in se* and offenses that are *mala prohibita*. Crimes **mala in se** are "wrong in themselves." They are characterized by universality and timelessness. That is, they are crimes everywhere and have been crimes at all times. Examples are murder and rape. Crimes **mala prohibita** are offenses that are illegal because laws define them as such. They lack universality and timelessness. Examples are trespassing, gambling, and prostitution.

For statistical reporting purposes, crimes are frequently classified as *crimes against the person* or *violent crimes* (for example, murder, rape, assault), *crimes against property* or *property crime* (for instance, burglary, larceny, auto theft), and *crimes against public decency, public order, and public justice* or *public order crimes* (for example, drunkenness, disorderly conduct, vagrancy).

Figure 2–1 is a list of selected crimes and their definitions, grouped by type. The selection, placement, and definition of the crimes are somewhat arbitrary. There are many different types of crime, and some crimes can be placed in more than one category. Legal definitions of crime vary among jurisdictions and frequently list numerous degrees, conditions, and qualifications. A good source of legal crime definitions is *Black's Law Dictionary*.

mala in se
Wrong in themselves. A description applied to crimes that are characterized by universality and timelessness.

mala prohibita
Offenses that are illegal because laws define them as such. They lack universality and timelessness.

2.1 CRITICAL THINKING

1. Are there any acts that are currently legal that you think should be illegal? If so, what?

2. Do you think there should be other elements of crime besides the seven listed in this section? If so, what other elements should there be?

FIGURE 2–1

Types and Definitions of Selected Crimes

Violent Crimes	Crimes that involve force or threat of force.
Murder	The unlawful killing of another human being with malice aforethought.
Manslaughter	The unlawful killing of another human being without malice aforethought.
Aggravated assault	An assault committed (1) with the intention of committing some additional crime, (2) with peculiar outrage or atrocity, or (3) with a dangerous or deadly weapon.
Forcible rape	The act of having sexual intercourse with a woman, by force and against her will.
Robbery	Theft from a person, accompanied by violence, threat of violence, or putting the person in fear.
Kidnapping	The unlawful taking and carrying away of a human being by force and against his or her will.
Property Crimes	Crimes that involve taking money or property, but usually without force or threat of force.
Larceny	The unlawful taking and carrying away of another person's property with the intent of depriving the owner of that property.
Burglary	Entering a building or occupied structure to commit a crime therein.
Embezzlement	The willful taking or converting to one's own use another person's money or property, which was lawfully acquired by the wrongdoer by reason of some office, employment, or position of trust.
Arson	Purposely setting fire to a house or other building.
Extortion/blackmail	The obtaining of property from another by wrongful use of actual or threatened force, violence, or fear, or under color of official right.
Receiving stolen property	Knowingly accepting, buying, or concealing goods which were illegally obtained by another person.
Fraud	The false representation of a matter of fact, whether by words or by conduct, by false or misleading allegations, or by concealment of that which should have been disclosed, which deceives and is intended to deceive, and causes legal harm.
Forgery	The fraudulent making of a false writing having apparent legal significance.
Counterfeiting	Under federal law, falsely making, forging, or altering any obligation or other security of the United States, with intent to defraud.
"Morals" Offenses	Violations of virtue in sexual conduct (for example, fornication, seduction, prostitution, adultery, illicit cohabitation, sodomy, bigamy, and incest).
Public Order Offenses	Violations that constitute a threat to public safety or peace (for example, disorderly conduct, loitering, unlawful assembly, drug offenses, driving while intoxicated).
Offenses Against the Government	Crimes motivated by the desire to effect social change or to rebel against perceived unfair laws and governments (for example, treason, sedition, hindering apprehension or prosecution of a felon, perjury, and bribery).
Offenses by Government	Harms inflicted upon people by their own governments or the governments of others (for example, genocide and torture, police brutality, civil rights violations, and political bribe taking).
Hate Crimes	Criminal offenses committed against a person, property, or society which are motivated, in whole or in part, by the offender's bias against a race, a religion, an ethnic/national origin group, or a sexual-orientation group.
Organized Crimes	Unlawful acts of members of highly organized and disciplined associations engaged in supplying illegal goods and services, such as gambling, prostitution, loansharking, narcotics, and labor racketeering.
White-Collar and Corporate Crimes	Generally nonviolent offenses committed for financial gain by means of deception by entrepreneurs and other professionals who utilize their special occupational skills and opportunities (for example, environmental pollution, manufacture and sale of unsafe products, price fixing, price gouging, and deceptive advertising).
Occupational Crimes	Offenses committed through opportunities created in the course of a legal business or profession and crimes committed by professionals, such as lawyers and doctors, acting in their professional capacities.
"Victimless" Crimes	Offenses involving a willing and private exchange of goods or services that are in strong demand but are illegal (for example, gambling, prostitution, drug law violations, and homosexual acts between consenting adults).

dark figure of crime
The number of crimes not officially recorded by the police.

crime index
An estimate of crimes committed.

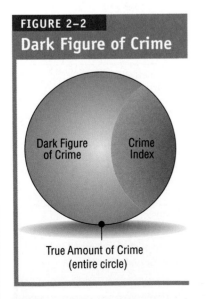

FIGURE 2–2
Dark Figure of Crime

Dark Figure of Crime

Crime Index

True Amount of Crime
(entire circle)

2.2 Measurement of Crime

Many people who read the daily newspaper or watch the nightly news on television believe that crime is the most pressing problem in the United States. But is it? How do you know how much crime is committed? How do you know if crime is, in fact, increasing or decreasing? Besides what you learn from the media, perhaps you have been the victim of crime or know someone who has been. Although that information is important, it does not indicate whether your experience with crime or the experience of someone you know is typical. The fact is that what we and the media know about crime, by and large, is based on statistics supplied by government agencies.

Crime Statistics

The difficulty in relying on crime statistics to measure the prevalence of crime is that "statistics about crime and delinquency are probably the most unreliable and most difficult of all social statistics."[5] In other words, "it is impossible to determine with accuracy the amount of crime [or delinquency] in any given jurisdiction at any particular time."[6] Why? There are several reasons. First, "some behavior is labeled . . . 'crime' by one observer but not by another."[7] If a behavior is not labeled a crime, it is not counted. On the other hand, if a behavior is wrongly labeled a crime, then it may be wrongly counted as a crime. Both situations contribute to the inaccuracy of crime statistics. Second, a large proportion of crimes are undetected. Crimes that are not detected obviously cannot be counted. Third, some crimes may not be reported to the police. If they are not reported to the police, they are unlikely to be counted. Fourth, crimes that are reported to the police may not be officially recorded by them, for various reasons (to be discussed later), or may be inaccurately recorded. Crimes that are not officially recorded by the police are called the **dark figure of crime** (see Figure 2–2).

For all of the foregoing reasons, any record of crimes—such as "offenses known to the police," arrests, convictions, or commitments to prison—can be considered at most a **crime index,** or an estimate of crimes committed. Unfortunately, no index or estimate of crimes is a reliable indicator of the actual amount of crime. The indexes or estimates vary independently of the true amount of crime, whatever that may be. Figure 2–2 portrays one possible relationship of a crime index to the dark figure of crime and the true amount of crime. It shows how great a discrepancy there can be between the index and the actual amount of crime.

Adding to the confusion is the reality that any index of crime varies with changes in police practices, court policies, and public opinion—to name just three factors. Suppose, for example, that a large city is hosting a major convention and city leaders want to make a good impression on visitors. The mayor asks the police chief to order officers to "sweep" the streets of prostitutes. As a result of that police policy, there is a dramatic increase in arrests for prostitution and in the index measuring prostitution. Does the increase in the index mean that the true amount of prostitution increased in the city? The answer is that we do not know and, for that matter, can never know. All we do know is that the index measuring prostitution increased as a result of police practices.

Thus, despite what some government agencies or the media may suggest, we do not know, nor can we ever know, the true amount of crime. For the same reasons, we can never know for sure whether crime is increasing, decreasing, or remaining at the same level. The sophisticated student of crime knows only that indexes of crime are imperfect estimates that vary widely. Those variations, which are independent of variations in the true amount of crime, depend on such things as police practices, court policies, and public opinion. Therefore, comparisons of crime measures are an especially dubious exercise. Criminal justice officials and professors routinely compare crime measures in different jurisdictions and at different times. What they are doing, though they rarely acknowledge it, even when they are aware of it, is comparing indexes or estimates of crime. Although such comparisons tell us nothing about differences in true amounts of crime, they do provide insights into police practices, court policies, and public opinion.

Probably the best index of crime—that is, the least inaccurate!—is **offenses known to the police.** That index, which is reported in the FBI's uniform crime reports (to be discussed later), is composed of crimes that are both reported to and recorded by the police. The reason it is an inaccurate measure of the true amount of crime is that the number of offenses known to the police is always much smaller than the number of crimes actually committed. One reason is that victims do not report all crimes to the police. There are many reasons for the nonreporting of crimes:[8]

1. Victims may consider the crime insignificant and not worth reporting.
2. They may hope to avoid embarrassing the offender, who may be a relative, school friend, or fellow employee.
3. They may wish to avoid the publicity which might result if the crime were reported.
4. They might have agreed to the crime, as in gambling offenses and some sexual offenses.
5. They may wish to avoid the inconvenience of calling the police, [filling out a report, appearing in court, and so on].
6. They may be intimidated by [or afraid of] the offender.
7. They may [dislike] the police or [be] opposed to the punitive policies of the legal system.
8. They may feel that the police are so inefficient that they will be unable to catch the offender even if the offense is reported.

Another reason the number of offenses known to the police is necessarily much smaller than the number of crimes actually committed is that the police do not always officially record the crimes that are reported to them. In practice, police officers often use their discretion to handle informally an incident reported to them; that is, they do not make an official report of the incident. Or they may exercise discretion in enforcing the law (for instance, by not arresting the customer in a case of prostitution). The law is often vague, and officers may not know the law or how to enforce it. Still another reason is that some police officers feel they are too busy to fill out and file police reports. Also, some officers, feeling an obligation to protect the reputations of their cities or being pressured by politicians to "get the crime rate down," may manipulate statistics to show a decrease in crime.[9]

CRIMINAL JUSTICE *Online*

Crime on Campus

Go to cj.glencoe.com for a link to the U.S. Department of Education's Office of Post Secondary Education Campus Security Statistics Web site for information and statistics on reported criminal offenses at colleges and universities across the United States. *What do the statistics say about crime at schools in your area?*

offenses known to the police
A crime index, reported in the FBI's uniform crime reports, composed of crimes that are both reported to and recorded by the police.

Crimes Reported to Police

According to the national crime victimization surveys for 1973 through 1999, only about 35 percent of crimes, on average, are reported to the police. In 1999, approximately 36 percent of all crime victimizations were reported to the police: 44 percent of violent crime victimizations and 34 percent of property crime victimizations.

SOURCE: Callie Marie Rennison, "Criminal Victimization 1999: Changes 1998–99 with Trends 1993–99," U.S. Department of Justice, Bureau of Justice Statistics, *National Crime Victimization Survey* (Washington, DC: GPO, August 2000), p. 11; Kathleen Maguire and Ann L. Pastore (eds.), *Sourcebook of Criminal Justice Statistics 1993*, U.S. Department of Justice, Bureau of Justice Statistics (Washington, DC: GPO, 1994), p. 255, Table 3.9.

Underreporting Crime

In 1998, Philadelphia police failed to report 13,000 to 37,000 major crimes including robberies, aggravated assaults, and thefts. The review of city crime statistics by the city controller's office also revealed that other crimes were wrongly classified as less serious crimes.

SOURCE: "Philly underreports crime," *The Orlando Sentinel* (September 15, 2000), p. A-11.

crime rate

A measure of the incidence of crime expressed as the number of crimes per unit of population or some other base.

Additionally, the number of offenses included in the index is much smaller than the actual number of crimes because of the way crimes are counted. For the FBI's uniform crime reports, when more than one crime is committed during a crime event, only the most serious is counted for statistical purposes. The seriousness of the crime is determined by the maximum legal penalty associated with it. Thus, for example, if a robber holds up ten people in a tavern, takes their money, shoots and kills the bartender, and makes a getaway in a stolen car, only one crime, the murder, is counted for statistical purposes. However, the offender could legally be charged with several different crimes. (The practice of counting only the most serious offense in a multiple-crime event is being changed with the implementation of the National Incident-Based Reporting System, which will be discussed later in this chapter.)

Despite the problems in recording crime events, *offenses known to the police* is a more accurate index of crime than arrest statistics, charging statistics, trial statistics, conviction statistics, sentencing statistics, or imprisonment statistics. As shown in Figure 2–3, the further a crime index is from the initial commission of crime, the more inaccurate it is as a measure of the true amount of crime.

Crime Rates

When crime indexes are compared, rarely are total numbers of crimes used. Instead, crime is typically reported as rates. A **crime rate** is expressed as the number of crimes per unit of population or some other base. Crime rates are used instead of total numbers because they are more comparable. For example, suppose you wanted to compare the crime of murder in the United States for the years 1960 and 1999. There were 9,110 murders and nonnegligent manslaughters reported to and recorded by the police in 1960; there were 15,533 murders and nonnegligent manslaughters reported to and recorded by the police in 1999. According to those data, the total number of murders and nonnegligent manslaughters reported to and recorded by the police in 1999 increased about 70 percent from the number reported and recorded by the police in 1960. Although this information may be helpful, it ignores the substantial increase in the population of the United States—and thus in the number of potential murderers and potential murder victims—between 1960 and 1999.

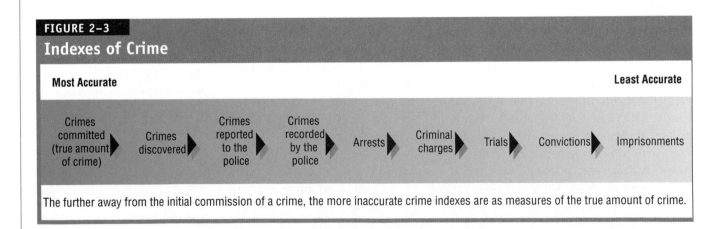

FIGURE 2–3
Indexes of Crime

Most Accurate   **Least Accurate**

Crimes committed (true amount of crime) → Crimes discovered → Crimes reported to the police → Crimes recorded by the police → Arrests → Criminal charges → Trials → Convictions → Imprisonments

The further away from the initial commission of a crime, the more inaccurate crime indexes are as measures of the true amount of crime.

FIGURE 2-4
Calculating Crime Rates

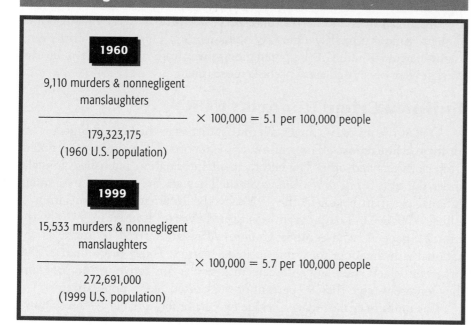

1960

$$\frac{9{,}110 \text{ murders \& nonnegligent manslaughters}}{179{,}323{,}175 \text{ (1960 U.S. population)}} \times 100{,}000 = 5.1 \text{ per } 100{,}000 \text{ people}$$

1999

$$\frac{15{,}533 \text{ murders \& nonnegligent manslaughters}}{272{,}691{,}000 \text{ (1999 U.S. population)}} \times 100{,}000 = 5.7 \text{ per } 100{,}000 \text{ people}$$

A better comparison—though, of course, not an accurate one—would be a comparison that takes into account the different population sizes. To enable such a comparison, a population base, such as "per 100,000 people" is arbitrarily chosen. Then the total number of murders and nonnegligent manslaughters for a particular year is divided by the total population of the United States for the same year. The result is multiplied by 100,000. When those calculations are made for the years 1960 and 1999, the rate of murders and nonnegligent manslaughters is 5.1 per 100,000 people for 1960 and 5.7 per 100,000 people for 1999 (see Figure 2–4). According to those figures, the rate of murder and nonnegligent manslaughter in 1999 was about 12 percent higher than it was in 1960. Thus, although both sets of data show that murders and nonnegligent manslaughters reported to and recorded by the police increased between 1960 and 1999, the increase is not nearly as great when the increase in the size of the population is taken into account. Crime rates provide a more accurate indication of increases or decreases in crime indexes than do total numbers of crimes. Remember, however, that what are being compared are indexes and not true amounts.

A variety of factors indirectly related to crime can affect crime rates. For example, burglary rates might increase, not because there are more burglaries, but because more things are insured, and insurance companies require police reports before they will reimburse their policyholders. Changing demographic characteristics of the population can also have an effect. For example, because of the post–World War II baby boom (1945–1964), between 1963 and 1988 there were more people in the age group most prone to committing recorded crime (18- to 24-year-olds). All other things being equal, higher crime rates would be expected between 1963 and 1988 simply because there were more people in the age group that commits the most recorded crime. By the same token, a decrease in crime rates might be expected after 1988, all

uniform crime reports
A collection of crime statistics and other law enforcement information gathered under a voluntary national program administered by the FBI.

eight index crimes
The Part I offenses in the FBI's uniform crime reports. They are (1) murder and nonnegligent manslaughter, (2) forcible rape, (3) robbery, (4) aggravated assault, (5) burglary, (6) larceny-theft, (7) motor vehicle theft, and (8) arson, which was added in 1979.

other things being equal, because the baby boom generation is no longer at those crime-prone ages. However, an increase in crime might be expected when their children reach the age range 18 to 24.

Urbanization is another factor, especially with regard to violent crime. Violent crime is primarily a big-city phenomenon. Thus, violent crime rates might increase as more of the population moves from rural to urban areas or as what were once rural areas become more urban.

Uniform Crime Reports (UCR)

One of the primary sources of crime statistics in the United States is the **uniform crime reports.** The uniform crime reports (UCR) are a collection of crime statistics and other law enforcement information published annually under the title *Crime in the United States.* They are the result of a voluntary national program begun in the 1920s by the International Association of Chiefs of Police.[10] The program was turned over to the FBI in 1930 by the attorney general, whose office Congress had authorized to serve as the national clearinghouse for crime-related statistics. Today more than 17,000 city, county, and state law enforcement agencies are active in the program; they represent more than 95 percent of the United States population.[11]

The uniform crime reports include two major indexes: (1) offenses known to the police, discussed earlier, and (2) statistics about persons arrested. The section on offenses known to the police, or offenses reported to the police, provides information about the **eight index crimes,** or Part I offenses:

1. Murder and nonnegligent manslaughter
2. Forcible rape
3. Robbery
4. Aggravated assault
5. Burglary
6. Larceny-theft
7. Motor vehicle theft
8. Arson (added in 1979)

The first four offenses are considered violent offenses; the last four are considered property offenses. According to the UCR, in 1999 more than 11.6 million index offenses, excluding arson, were reported to the police, down 6.8 percent from the previous year.

The 1996 edition of the uniform crime reports included for the first time data reported on crimes motivated by bias against individuals on account of race, religion, disability, sexual orientation, or ethnicity/national origin. The UCR designated these as hate crimes or bias crimes. In 1999, crimes against persons made up 67 percent of the 9,031 hate crime offenses reported; crimes against property accounted for 33 percent, and less than 1 percent to crimes against society.[12] Intimidation was the single most frequently reported offense, accounting for 35 percent of the total, followed by damage, destruction, or vandalism of property, 29 percent; simple assault, 19 percent; and aggravated assault, 12 percent.[13] Of all the hate crimes reported, 56 percent were motivated by racial bias, 16.5 percent by religious bias, 16 percent by sexual-orientation bias, 11 percent by ethnic bias, and 0.2 percent by disability bias.[14]

The other major crime index in the uniform crime reports is based on arrest statistics. Arrest data are provided for the eight index crimes, as well as

FIGURE 2–5

Part I and Part II Offenses of the FBI's Uniform Crime Reports

Part I Offenses—Index Crimes	Part II Offenses
Violent Crime	1. Other assaults (simple)
1. Murder and nonnegligent manslaughter	2. Forgery and counterfeiting
2. Forcible rape	3. Fraud
3. Robbery	4. Embezzlement
4. Aggravated assault	5. Stolen property: buying, receiving, possessing
	6. Vandalism
Property Crime	7. Weapons: carrying, possessing, etc.
5. Burglary–breaking or entering	8. Prostitution and commercialized vice
6. Larceny-theft	9. Sex offenses
7. Motor vehicle theft	10. Drug abuse violations
8. Arson	11. Gambling
	12. Offenses against the family and children
	13. Driving under the influence
	14. Liquor laws
	15. Drunkenness
	16. Disorderly conduct
	17. Vagrancy
	18. All other offenses
	19. Suspicion
	20. Curfew and loitering laws
	21. Runaway

status offense
An act that is illegal for a juvenile but would not be a crime if committed by an adult.

Decline in Violent Crime Rates

According to the FBI's 1999 uniform crime report, the rate of violent crimes reported to the police declined for a record eighth consecutive year. Among the factors that police chiefs and academics cite for the decline are (1) aging-out of the crime-prone years by the post-war baby boom generation; (2) fewer turf battles over crack cocaine distribution because of market maturation and consolidation; (3) police efforts to disarm criminals and juveniles; (4) more police officers on the beat; (5) smarter policing; (6) tougher criminal justice legislation, such as the federal law that ties financial aid for prison building to a requirement that states keep violent offenders incarcerated for at least 85 percent of their sentences; (7) increased interest in "grass-roots" crime prevention; and (8) a better economy that has provided jobs and given cities more to invest in crime control.

SOURCE: "Serious Crimes Decline for 8th Consecutive Year," *The Orlando Sentinel,* (May 8, 2000), p. A–7; "Violent Crimes Plummet 7%–Drop Biggest in 35 Years," *The Orlando Sentinel,* (June 2, 1997), p. A–4; "FBI Report: Crime Rate Still Falling," *The Orlando Sentinel,* (October 5, 1997), p. A–3.

21 other crimes and status offenses. The 21 other crimes and status offenses are referred to as Part II offenses. A **status offense** is an act that is illegal for a juvenile but would not be a crime if committed by an adult (such as truancy or running away from home). Figure 2–5 lists the Part I and Part II offenses in the FBI's uniform crime reports.

According to the UCR, law enforcement agencies made about 14 million arrests for violations of Part I and Part II offenses nationwide in 1999, down five percent from the previous year.[15] The offenses for which the most arrests were made in 1999 (approximately 1.5 million arrests each) were drug abuse violations and driving under the influence.[16] The second largest number of arrests (about 1.3 million) was for simple assault.[17] Arrestees generally were young (45 percent were under 25 years of age), male (78 percent), and white (69 percent).[18] The index crime for which women were most frequently arrested was larceny-theft, which accounted for 71 percent of all female arrests for index offenses and 14 percent of all female arrests. More than half the female larceny-theft arrestees were under 25.[19]

crime index offenses cleared
The number of offenses for which at least one person has been arrested, charged with the commission of the offense, and turned over to the court for prosecution.

In addition to statistics on offenses known to the police and persons arrested, the uniform crime reports include statistics on crime index offenses cleared by the police. **Crime index offenses cleared** (also called *clearance rates* or *percent cleared by arrest*) is a rough index of police performance in solving crimes. According to the UCR, an offense that is cleared is one for which "at least one person is arrested, charged with the commission of the offense, and turned over to the court for prosecution."[20] The arrest of one person may clear several crimes, or one offense may be cleared by the arrest of several people. Clearances recorded in one year may be for offenses committed in previous years. Clearance rates remain remarkably stable from year to year. Generally, the police are able to clear about 70 percent of murders and nonnegligent manslaughters, 50 percent of forcible rapes, 25 percent of robberies, 60 percent of aggravated assaults, 15 percent of burglaries, 20 percent of larceny-thefts, 15 percent of motor vehicle thefts, and 15 percent of acts of arson.[21] Annually, the police are able to clear about 20 percent of all index offenses (21 percent in 1999).[22]

MYTH

When the media report that crime has increased or decreased from one year to the next, they are generally referring to increases or decreases in the true amount of crime.

FACT

What the media are usually referring to when they report that "crime" has increased or decreased from one year to the next is an increase or decrease in the aggregate rate of the eight index crimes (that is, the "crime index total"), not the rates of other crimes or the true amount of crime.

The uniform crime reports also provide statistics about law enforcement personnel, such as the number of full-time sworn officers in a particular jurisdiction and the number of law enforcement officers killed in the line of duty.

Finally, in recent editions of the uniform crime reports, special sections have been devoted to topical studies. For example, the 1996 special section, entitled "Drugs in America: 1980–1995," presented a relatively detailed examination of the national drug arrest trends during that period. In the 1999 edition of the uniform crime reports the special section is entitled "The Chances of Lifetime Murder Victimization, 1997." Among data presented are comparisons of age-specific murder rates, by race and sex, for the years 1978 and 1997. Among the findings are that in 1997, black males were the most likely murder victims (victimization ratio = 1 out of 40), followed by black females (1 out of 199), white males (1 out of 280), and white females (1 out of 794).[23]

National Incident-Based Reporting System (NIBRS)

In 1982, a joint task force of the Bureau of Justice Statistics (BJS) and the Federal Bureau of Investigation (FBI) was created to study and recommend ways to improve the quality of information contained in the uniform crime reports.[24] The result is the National Incident-Based Reporting System (NIBRS), which collected its first data in 1991. Under NIBRS, participating law enforcement authorities provide offense and arrest data on 22 broad categories of crime, covering 46 offenses (as compared to the 8 UCR index offenses), and provide only arrest information on 11 other offenses (as compared to the 21 Part II UCR offenses) (see Figure 2–6 on page 45).

FIGURE 2–6

The National Incident-Based Reporting System

Group A Offenses	Group B Offenses
Arson	Bad checks
Assault offenses	Curfew/loitering/vagrancy
Bribery	Disorderly conduct
Burglary/breaking and entering	Driving under the influence
Counterfeiting/forgery	Drunkenness
Destruction/damage/vandalism	Liquor law violations
Drug/narcotic offenses	Nonviolent family offenses
Embezzlement	Peeping Tom
Extortion/blackmail	Runaways
Fraud offenses	Trespassing
Gambling offenses	All other offenses
Homicide offenses	
Kidnapping/abduction	
Larceny/theft offenses	
Motor vehicle theft	
Pornography/obscene material	
Prostitution offenses	
Robbery	
Sex offenses, forcible	
Sex offenses, nonforcible	
Stolen property offenses	
Weapons law violations	

Perhaps the greatest and most important difference between the NIBRS and the UCR is that the NIBRS contains more data on each crime, making it possible to examine crimes in much more detail. The NIBRS contains more than 50 different pieces of information about a crime, divided into six segments, or categories. It is hoped that the increased amount of information in the NIBRS will provide the basis for a much greater understanding of crime and its causes (or at least of crime reporting and recording behavior) than is possible with the data from the UCR. Figure 2–7 on page 46 lists the NIBRS data elements.

The BJS and the FBI hope that eventually the NIBRS will replace the UCR as the source of official FBI crime counts. As of July 1999, 18 states have been NIBRS certified, that is, have shown that they are capable of meeting NIBRS' data submission requirements, 18 states are in the process of testing NIBRS, and an additional 6 states are developing NIBRS with plans to test in the future.[25] So far, the biggest impediment to implementation of the NIBRS is that it is a "paperless" reporting system and, thus, requires the use of a computerized records management system. Many larger law enforcement agencies have older computer systems that require extensive and costly modifications. Many smaller agencies do not have computer systems.

Switching Reporting Systems

In 1997, the state of Florida decided to abandon incident-based reporting after using it for nearly eight years. The Florida Department of Law Enforcement expects to save $1 million a year by switching to summary-based reporting, which requires less information.

SOURCE: "Crime Drop: More Fiction Than Fact?" *The Orlando Sentinel,* (May 11, 1997), p. B–1.

FIGURE 2-7

NIBRS Data Reporting Elements

Administrative Segment
1. ORI (originating agency identifier) number
2. Incident number
3. Incident date/hour
4. Exceptional clearance indicator
5. Exceptional clearance date

Offense Segment
6. UCR offense code
7. Attempted/completed code
8. Alcohol/drug use by offender
9. Type of location
10. Number of premises entered
11. Method of entry
12. Type of criminal activity
13. Type of weapon/force used
14. Bias crime code

Property Segment
15. Type of property loss
16. Property description
17. Property value
18. Recovery date
19. Number of stolen motor vehicles
20. Number of recovered motor vehicles
21. Suspected drug type
22. Estimated drug quantity
23. Drug measurement unit

Victim Segment
24. Victim number (ID)
25. Victim UCR offense code
26. Type of victim
27. Age of victim
28. Sex of victim
29. Race of victim
30. Ethnicity of victim
31. Resident status of victim
32. Homicide/assault circumstances
33. Justifiable homicide circumstances
34. Type of injury
35. Related offender murder
36. Relationship of victim to offender

Offender Segment
37. Offender number (ID)
38. Age of offender
39. Sex of offender
40. Race of offender

Arrestee Segment
41. Arrestee number (ID)
42. Transaction number
43. Arrest date
44. Type of arrest
45. Multiple clearance indicator
46. UCR arrest offense code
47. Arrestee armed indicator
48. Age of arrestee
49. Sex of arrestee
50. Race of arrestee
51. Ethnicity of arrestee
52. Resident status of arrestee
53. Disposition of arrestee under 18

Although some agencies have received federal and state grants to upgrade or buy computer systems for the NIBRS, the amounts allocated have covered only a small part of the need.

Adding to the implementation problem are benefit and policy concerns.[26] Some law enforcement agencies question who, other than researchers, will benefit from their reporting NIBRS data. Others fear that, because NIBRS reports multiple offenses within an incident, crime will appear to increase, causing a public relations nightmare for law enforcement officials. Some law enforcement administrators are concerned that the detailed incident reporting required for NIBRS will tie up patrol officers, keeping them from responding to the needs of the community.

National Crime Victimization Surveys (NCVS)

The other major source of crime statistics in the United States is the **national crime victimization surveys (NCVS)**. The surveys provide a detailed picture of crime incidents, victims, and trends from the victim's perspective. Formerly called the national crime surveys (NCS), they have been conducted annually since 1972 by the Bureau of the Census for the U.S. Department of Justice's Bureau of Justice Statistics.[27] The NCVS, published under the title Criminal Victimization in the United States, were created not only as a basis for learning more about crime and its victims, but also as a means of complementing and assessing what is known about crime from the FBI's uniform crime reports. (From 1996 on, the NCVS are available only in electronic formats, see www.ojp.usdoj.gov.)

From a nationally representative sample of about 50,000 households, respondents aged 12 or older are asked in interviews whether they have been victims of any of the FBI's index offenses (except murder, nonnegligent manslaughter, and arson) or any other crimes during the past six months. If they have, they are asked to provide information about the experience. Because major changes were made in the format and methodology of the NCVS in 1992, adjustments have been made to the data before 1993 to make them comparable with data collected since the changes. Like the UCR, the NCVS is merely an index of crime and not an accurate measure of the true amount of crime that is committed.

Generally, the national crime victimization surveys produce different results from the FBI's uniform crime reports. For nearly all offenses, the NCVS shows more crimes being committed than the UCR. This underestimation by the UCR may result from victims' failure to report crimes to the police or from failure by the police to report to the FBI all the crimes they know about. The UCR counts more of some kinds of offenses (such as assault) and counts them differently. For example, the UCR counts each report of a domestic assault at the same address separately; the NCVS counts the repeated assaults as one victimization. The UCR counts crimes reported by people and businesses that the NCVS doesn't reach. Unlike the UCR, the NCVS relies on random samplings of victims and their memories of things that may have happened months ago, both of which are subject to some degree of error. Other problems with the NCVS are interviewers who may be biased or who may cheat, and respondents who may lie or exaggerate, or may respond without understanding the questions.

Differences in the data sources help explain the differences in the trends indicated by the NCVS and the UCR. For example, in one year (1990), NCVS respondents indicated that they had experienced about 50 percent more crimes, on average, than were recorded by the FBI. However, the differences varied by offense. The smallest difference between the two indexes for that year was for motor vehicle theft (20 percent). The largest difference was for burglary (67 percent). The smaller difference for motor vehicle theft was probably due to insurance companies requiring a police report before reimbursing policyholders for their losses.

national crime victimization surveys

A source of crime statistics based on interviews in which respondents are asked whether they have been victims of any of the FBI's index offenses (except murder, nonnegligent manslaughter, and arson) or other crimes during the past six months. If they have, they are asked to provide information about the experience.

Gallup Crime Polls

The Gallup Organization conducts public opinion polls on a variety of topics that affect Americans. You can learn more about the public's view of crime issues by visiting the Gallup Web site from links available at cj.glencoe.com. *What connection, if any, is there between public opinion toward crime and crime statistics?*

Sometimes overall changes in the two indexes differ. For example, between 1984 and 1985, the total number of crimes in the UCR increased 4.6 percent, while the total number of crimes in the NCVS decreased 1.9 percent. The difference probably stems from the difference in what the two indexes measure. Thus, between 1984 and 1985, there was an apparent increase in the number of crimes reported to and recorded by the police, but an apparent decrease in the number of crimes to which people said they had been subjected. Figure 2–8 on page 49 displays the trends in four measures or indexes of serious violent crime. Remember that serious violent crimes include murder, rape, robbery, and aggravated assault.

self-report crime surveys
Surveys in which subjects are asked whether they have committed crimes.

Self-Report Crime Surveys

Whereas other tallies of crime rely on summary police reports, incident-based reports, or victim interviews, **self-report crime surveys** ask selected subjects whether they have committed crimes. Self-report crime surveys, like all crime measures, are indexes of crime; they are not accurate measures of the true amount of crime. To date, most self-report crime surveys conducted in the United States have been administered to school-children, especially high school students. Some examples of such nationwide self-report crime survey efforts are the National Youth Survey, begun in 1975, and the effort to ascertain and to gauge fluctuations in the levels of smoking, drinking, and illicit drug use among secondary school students, begun by the National Institute on Drug Abuse in 1975 (see Figure 2–9 on pages 50 and 51).

MYTH
Criminal activity is concentrated among certain groups of people.

FACT
Early self-report crime surveys of adults found an enormous amount of hidden crime in the United States. They found that more than 90 percent of all Americans had committed crimes for which they could have been imprisoned.

Earlier self-report crime surveys of adults interestingly enough found an enormous amount of hidden crime in the United States. Those self-report crime surveys indicated that more than 90 percent of all Americans had committed crimes for which they could have been found guilty and imprisoned.[28] This is not to say that all Americans are murderers, thieves, or rapists, for they are not, but only that crime serious enough to warrant an individual's imprisonment is more widespread among the U.S. population than many people might think or imagine. Moreover, it is unlikely that the pervasiveness of crime in the population has lessened significantly since the earlier self-report crime surveys were conducted.

One lesson that can be learned from the aforementioned survey findings is that most people are better described as representing a continuum, that is, as having committed more crime or less crime, rather than simply being described as criminal or noncriminal. In society, there are probably few "angels," that is, people who have never committed a crime. Likewise, there are probably few criminals whose whole lives are totally oriented toward the commission of crimes. Most people have committed one crime at some point in their lives and some have committed crimes repeatedly. It probably makes more sense for us, then, to talk about relative degrees of criminality, rather than to talk about all-encompassing criminality or its absence.

Common Offenses
The most commonly reported offenses in self-report crime surveys are larceny, indecency, and tax evasion.

SOURCE: Thomas Gabor, *Everybody Does It! Crimes by the Public.* (Toronto: University of Toronto Press, 1994).

FIGURE 2-8

Four Measures of Serious Violent Crime

Offenses in millions

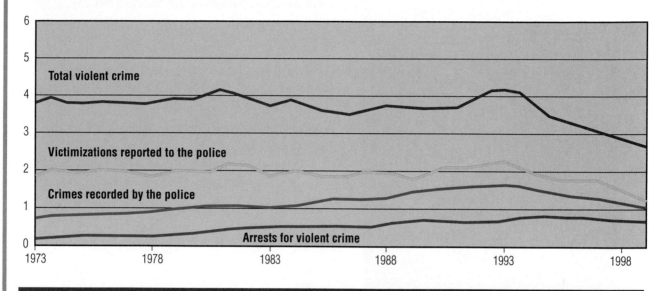

Total violent crime

Victimizations reported to the police

Crimes recorded by the police

Arrests for violent crime

1973   1978   1983   1988   1993   1998

Note:

The serious violent crimes included are rape, robbery, aggravated assault, and homicide. Because of changes made to the victimization survey, data prior to 1993 are adjusted to make them comparable to data collected under the redesigned methodology. Estimates for 1993 and beyond are based on collection year while earlier estimates are based on data year.

The measures of violent crime came from two sources of data:

1. The National Crime Victimization Survey (NCVS), a household survey ongoing since 1972, that interviews about 80,000 persons age 12 and older in 43,000 households twice each year about their victimizations from crime.

2. The Uniform Crime Reports (UCR) that collects information on crimes and arrests reported by law enforcement authorities to the FBI.

Definitions:

- *Total violent crime:*
  The number of homicides recorded by police plus the number of rapes, robberies, and aggravated assaults from the victimization survey whether or not they were reported to the police. From the NCVS + homicide from the UCR.

- *Victimizations reported to the police:*
  The number of homicides recorded by police plus the number of rapes, robberies, and aggravated assaults from the victimization survey that victims said were reported to the police. From the NCVS + homicide from the UCR.

- *Crimes recorded by the police:*
  The number of homicides, forcible rapes, robberies, and aggravated assaults included in the Uniform Crime Reports of the FBI excluding commercial robbery and those that involved victims under age 12. From the the UCR.

- *Arrests for violent crimes:*
  The number of person arrested for homicide, forcible rape, robbery, or aggravated assault as reported by law enforcement agencies to the FBI. From the UCR.

SOURCE: Bureau of Justice Statistics, <www.ojp.usdoj.gov/bjs/>.

FIGURE 2-9

How Crime is Counted

National Crime Victimization Surveys (NCVS)

- Begun in 1972

- Compile data from interviews with victims of crime

- Collect data from nationally representative sample of approximately 50,000 households and all household members at least 12 years of age

- Provide information about victims, offenders, and crimes

- Estimate the proportion of each crime type reported to law enforcement and summarize the victims' reasons for reporting or not reporting crimes to the police

- Provide yearly reports under the title Criminal Victimization in the United States

- Administered by Bureau of Justice Statistics (BJS)

Self-Report Crime Surveys

- Government surveys begun in 1970s

- Ask subjects if they have committed crimes

- Administered generally to students to ascertain levels of smoking, drinking, and illicit drug use

One of the criticisms of the National Youth Survey, and a problem with many self-report crime surveys, is that it asks about less serious offenses, such as cutting classes, disobeying parents, and stealing items worth less than $5, while omitting questions about serious crimes, such as robbery, burglary, and sexual assault. Self-report crime surveys also suffer from all the problems of other surveys, problems that were described in the last subsection—they produce different results from other surveys, and they are not an accurate measure of crime.

Uniform Crime Reports (UCR)

- Begun in 1920s

- Administered by Federal Bureau of Investigation (FBI)

- Compile aggregate reports from state and local law enforcement agencies

- Collect data on 8 index crimes and 21 other offenses

- Provide crime counts for the nation as a whole, as well as for regions, states, counties, cities, and towns

- Represent 95 percent of the U.S. population

- Report two major indexes: offenses known to the police and statistics about persons arrested

- Publish yearly reports under the title Crime in the United States

National Incident-Based Reporting System (NIBRS)

- Begun in 1991 as a redesign of UCR to provide more comprehensive and detailed crime statistics

- Collects information on each criminal incident in 22 broad categories of crime, covering 46 offenses

- Collects data through computerized records-management systems

- Reports data on victim-offender relationship, type and location of the incident, type of weapon used, type of injury sustained by the victim, and sex, age, and race of offender and victim

- Administered by BJS and FBI

2.2 CRITICAL THINKING

1. Of the various methods of measuring crime presented in this section, which one do you think is the most accurate? Why? Which one do you think is the least accurate? Why?

2. Do you think there are ways to get more victims of crime to report criminal incidents? If so, what would you suggest?

2.3 Costs of Crime

According to data from the national crime victimization survey, in 1998 the total economic loss to victims of crime in the United States was $17 billion.[29] Figure 2–10 shows the breakdown of this amount among categories of personal and property crimes. The total includes losses from property theft or damage, cash losses, medical expenses, and income lost from work because of injuries, police and court-related activities, or time spent repairing or replacing property.[30] It does not include the cost of the criminal justice process (described in Chapter 1), increased insurance premiums, security devices bought for protection, losses to businesses (which are substantial), or corporate crime.[31]

Until recently, the national crime victimization surveys provided the best estimates of the costs of crime. Those cost estimates, however, are deficient in two ways. First, they include only a limited number of personal and property crimes. And, as noted previously, they do not include the cost of the criminal justice process, increased insurance premiums, security devices bought for protection, losses to businesses, or corporate crime. Second, they report estimates only of relatively short-term and tangible costs. They do not include long-term and intangible costs associated with pain, suffering, and reduced quality of life.

Costs of Corporate Crime

The $17 billion cost to victims of crimes reported in the 1998 national crime victimization survey is less than one-tenth as great as the annual losses of victims of corporate crimes, estimated at $200 billion. The crime of price-fixing, in which competing companies explicitly agree to keep prices artificially high to maximize profits, is estimated by itself to cost consumers about $60 billion a year.

SOURCE: David R. Simon, *Elite Deviance*, 6th ed. (Boston: Allyn and Bacon, 1999) p. 93, p. 104.

FIGURE 2–10

Total Economic Loss to Victims of Personal and Property Crimes, 1998

Type of Crime	Gross Loss (in millions of dollars)
All crimes	17,056
Personal crimes	**1,454**
Crimes of violence	1,415
Rape/sexual assault	23
Robbery	657
Assault	735
Purse snatching	8
Pocket picking	31
Property crimes	**15,601**
Household burglary	3,680
Motor vehicle theft	6,143
Thefts	5,778

Note: Detail may not add to total shown because of rounding.

SOURCE: *Criminal Victimization in the United States 1998 Statistical Tables,* Table 82, <www.ojp.usdoj.gov/bjs/pub/pdf/cvus98pdf>.

To compensate for the deficiencies of the NCVS, a recent study was sponsored by the National Institute of Justice.[32] In addition to the more standard cost estimates in the NCVS, the new study estimated long-term costs as well as the intangible costs of pain, suffering, and reduced quality of life. Intangible costs were calculated in a number of ways. For example, the costs of pain, suffering, and reduced quality of life for nonfatal injuries were estimated by analyzing jury awards to crime and burn victims. Only the portion of the jury award intended to compensate the victim for pain, suffering, and reduced quality of life was used; punitive damages were excluded from the estimates.

Furthermore, although the new study includes only "street crimes" and "domestic crime," it expands on the crime categories and information included in the NCVS by (1) including crimes committed against people under the age of 12, (2) using better information on domestic violence and sexual assault, (3) more fully accounting for repeat victimizations, and (4) including child abuse and drunk driving. Excluded from the new study are crimes committed against business and government, personal fraud, white-collar crime, child neglect, and most "victimless" crimes, including drug offenses.

The study estimates that the annual tangible cost of personal and property crime—including medical costs, lost earnings, and public program costs related to victim assistance—is $105 billion, or more than $400 per U.S. resident. When the intangible costs of pain, suffering, and reduced quality of life are added, the annual cost increases to an estimated $450 billion, or about $1,800 per U.S. resident. Figure 2–11 shows how the $450 billion is divided into specific costs of crime.

Violent crime (including drunk driving and arson) accounts for $426 billion of the total, while property crime accounts for the remaining $24 billion. The study found that violence against children accounts for more than 20 percent of all tangible costs and more than 35 percent of all costs (including pain, suffering, and reduced quality of life).

War on Drugs

Between 1980 and 1997, the United States spent about $290 billion on federal, state, and local antidrug efforts. That is more than the federal government spent on medical research into cancer, heart disease, or AIDS. In 1999, the federal government alone spent an estimated $17.7 billion to combat illegal drugs. The 2000 expenditure is estimated to be $18.5 billion. About one-third of the 2000 federal expenditures is designated for demand reduction (programs and research related to drug abuse treatment and prevention) and about two-thirds is designated for supply reduction (a wide scope of law enforcement-related activities). Of the two-thirds devoted to supply reduction, about half is for domestic law enforcement, about eight percent for international law enforcement, and about ten percent for interdiction.

SOURCE: Michael Griffin, "Drug War Strategies Are Not Poles Apart," *The Orlando Sentinel,* October 29, 1996, p. A-1; Ann L. Pastore and Kathleen Maguire (eds.), *Sourcebook of Criminal Justice Statistics 1999,* U.S. Department of Justice, Bureau of Justice Statistics (Washington, DC: GPO, 2000), p. 15, Table 1.12.

FIGURE 2–11

Annual Cost of Crime in the United States

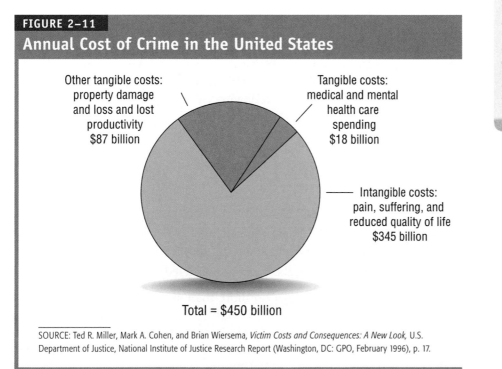

Other tangible costs: property damage and loss and lost productivity $87 billion

Tangible costs: medical and mental health care spending $18 billion

Intangible costs: pain, suffering, and reduced quality of life $345 billion

Total = $450 billion

SOURCE: Ted R. Miller, Mark A. Cohen, and Brian Wiersema, *Victim Costs and Consequences: A New Look,* U.S. Department of Justice, National Institute of Justice Research Report (Washington, DC: GPO, February 1996), p. 17.

Of the crimes included in the study, rape has the highest annual victim costs, at $127 billion a year (excluding child sexual abuse). Second is assault, with victim costs of $93 billion a year, followed by murder (excluding arson and drunk driving deaths), at $71 billion annually. Drunk driving (including fatalities) is next at $61 billion a year, and child abuse is estimated to cost $56 billion annually.

Among the tangible costs of crime excluded from the study are the costs of the criminal justice process and private security expenditures. Omitted also are the intangible costs of fear of crime, a fear that makes people prisoners in their own homes, divides people, and destroys communities.

2.3 CRITICAL THINKING

1. What would you estimate is the cost of crimes that go unreported?

2. Why are the highest costs of crimes the intangible costs?

2.4 Fear of Crime

A by-product of crime, beyond actual physical or material loss, is fear. For many crime victims, it is the most burdensome and lasting consequence of their victimizations. However, fear of crime is also contagious. One does not have to be a victim of violent crime to be fearful of violent crime. In fact, research shows that people who have heard about other people's victimizations are nearly as fearful as the people who have been victimized themselves.[33]

What People Fear

Fear of crime, especially violent crime, is widespread. For example, a public opinion poll found that 80 percent of Americans are "concerned . . . about becoming a victim of crime"; 29.4 percent are "somewhat concerned" and 50.6 percent are "very concerned."[34] When Americans are asked specifically what they fear, surveys show the following categories:[35]

- Forty percent worry about sexual assault, either against themselves or against a family member.
- Forty percent are concerned about burglaries when they are not home.
- Thirty percent worry about being attacked while driving their cars.
- Thirty percent worry about being mugged.
- Twenty-five percent worry about being beaten up, knifed, or shot.
- Twenty-five percent worry about burglaries when they are home.
- Twenty percent worry about being murdered.

It is interesting to note that no more than 40 percent of Americans are fearful of any specific type of crime, though 80 percent of Americans are fearful of crime in general. Those survey results suggest that there is a greater fear of being a crime victim in general—that is, a greater abstract fear of crime—than there is of being the victim of a specific crime.

Youth Fear Crime

According to a 1998 survey (completed before the Columbine High School shootings), half of 9- to 17-year olds in the United States are worried that they will die young, and 36 percent fear they will be attacked in school.

SOURCE: Erik Sherman, "New Study: America's Children Live in Fear" <www.apbnews.com/newscenter/breakingnews/1999/04/24/kidfear0424_01.html>

When and Where People Fear

Fear of violent crime is greatest at night when a person is alone and away from home. Although only 9 percent of Americans feel unsafe and insecure in their own homes at night, 38 percent of them are afraid to walk alone at night in some areas within a mile of their homes.[36] Those figures have remained about the same for the past decade.[37]

Who Fears Crime

Fear of criminal victimization is neither evenly distributed across the population nor commensurate with the statistical probability of being the victim of crime. Surveys reveal some of the differences in the public's fear of crime.[38] Among those differences are the following:

- **Gender** Females are more fearful than males.
- **Race/Ethnicity** Nonwhites, especially Hispanics and blacks, are more fearful than whites.
- **Age** People 30 years old and older are slightly more fearful than people less than 30 years old.
- **Religion** Jews are more fearful than either Protestants or Catholics.
- **Community** People living in urban areas are more fearful than people living in suburban or rural areas.
- **Region** Among those people most concerned, Easterners and Southerners (in that order) are more fearful than Westerners and Midwesterners. (Overall concern about crime does not differ greatly by region of the country.)
- **Education** A person's concern about being a crime victim is slightly lower the higher the level of education. Those people most concerned are likely to be high school graduates or less.
- **Income** Fear of crime victimization declines with increasing family income. (People whose family income is $50,000 or more are less fearful of crime than people whose family income is less than $50,000.)

It is important to stress that the preceding descriptions of the kinds of people who are most and least fearful of crime in general do not address the specific types of crimes that people fear. Also, the descriptions are generalizations. As with all generalizations, there are exceptions or qualifications. In a study of fear of seven types of criminal victimization, four exceptions to or qualifications of the preceding general descriptions were revealed.[39]

First, although females are generally more fearful of crime than are males, their greater fear applies only to sexual assault and other personal violent crimes. Females are no more fearful than males of having their homes burglarized. Second, although people 30 years old and older are slightly more fearful in general than people less than 30 years old, younger people are more fearful than older people of sexual assault and burglary. For nonsexual violent offenses, there are no age differences. Third, Hispanics and blacks are more fearful than whites only of sexual assault of themselves or someone in their household and of being murdered. Fourth, only fear of being beaten, knifed, or shot and fear of getting mugged increase with the level of urbanization of the community in which people live.

FYI

Fear of Crime

According to a recent survey, the percentage of residents in each of 12 cities surveyed who said that they were fearful of crime in their neighborhood ranged from 20 percent to 48 percent: Chicago, IL (48 percent), Kansas City, MO (33 percent), Knoxville, TN (30 percent), Los Angeles, CA (44 percent), Madison, WI (20 percent), New York, NY (42 percent), San Diego, CA (30 percent), Savannah, GA (33 percent), Spokane, WA (32 percent), Springfield, MA (45 percent), Tucson, AZ (40 percent), and Washington, DC (48 percent). Ten percent or less in each city said they were "very fearful" of neighborhood crime. In 11 of the cities, a third or more of the residents said they were fearful of becoming a victim of street crime, especially being assaulted with a gun or being robbed.

SOURCE: Steven K. Smith, Greg W. Steadman, and Todd D. Minton, *Criminal Victimization and Perceptions of Community Safety in 12 Cities, 1998.* U.S. Department of Justice, Bureau of Justice Statistics <www.ojp.usdoj.gov/bjs/pub/ascii/cvpcs98.txt>

MYTH

The people most fearful of crime are the people most vulnerable to crime.

FACT

The people most fearful of crime are not necessarily members of groups with the highest rates of victimization. For example, the demographic group most afraid of crime, elderly women, is the least likely to be victimized.

As noted previously, the groups that are the most fearful of crime are not necessarily those with the highest rates of victimization. For example, elderly women, the demographic group most afraid of crime, are the least likely to be victimized.[40] More generally, women and older people are more fearful of crime than are men and younger people, even though women and older persons are less likely to be victims of crime.[41]

Fear of crime has many detrimental consequences. It makes people feel vulnerable and isolated, it reduces a person's general sense of well-being, it motivates people to buy safety devices with money that otherwise could be used to improve their quality of life, and it also contributes to neighborhood decline and the crime problem. As Wesley Skogan explains:

> Fear . . . can work in conjunction with other factors to stimulate more rapid neighborhood decline. Together, the spread of fear and other local problems provide a form of positive feedback that can further increase levels of crime. These feedback processes include (1) physical and psychological withdrawal from community life; (2) a weakening of the informal social control processes that inhibit crime and disorder; (3) a decline in the organizational life and mobilization capacity of the neighborhood; (4) deteriorating business conditions; (5) the importation and domestic production of delinquency and deviance; and (6) further dramatic changes in the composition of the population. At the end lies a stage characterized by demographic collapse.[42]

2.4 CRITICAL THINKING

1. What steps could be taken, if any, to reduce people's overall fear of crime?

2. Why do you think there is no correlation between those who fear crime the most and the most likely victims of crime?

3. What factors contribute to people's fear of crime?

4. What are the costs, if any, of a fear of crime?

2.5 Victims of Crime

Findings from the 1999 NCVS reveal that in 1999 a total of 28.8 million crimes were attempted or completed against U.S. residents aged 12 or older—approximately 7.5 million personal crimes (rape and sexual assault, robbery, aggravated and simple assault, pocket picking, purse snatching, and attempted purse snatching) and about 21 million property crimes (household burglary, motor vehicle theft, and other thefts).[43] Of the approximately 7.5 million personal crimes, 7.35 million were violent.[44] However, in 69 percent of all violent crimes, the crime was attempted or threatened but not completed.[45] Still, in about 25 percent of the violent crimes, a victim was injured.[46]

Victimization Trends

According to 1999 NCVS data, the violent and property crime victimization rates were 33 and 198 per 1,000 persons age 12 or older, respectively. The violent crime rate was ten percent lower than the 1998 rate, a decline that continued a trend that began in 1994 (see Figure 2–12, top graph).[47] The 1999 property crime rate decreased nine percent from the 1998 rate, a decline that continued a trend that began in 1974 (see Figure 2–12, bottom graph).[48] Combined, the 1999 violent and property crimes rates were the lowest recorded since the survey was first administered in 1973.[49] Figure 2–12 shows that the decline in the violent crime rate is primarily a result of a decline in simple assaults, while the decrease in the property crime rate is almost entirely attributable to a decrease in thefts.

Who the Victims Are

Although each year millions of people are victimized by crime, victimization—like the fear of crime—is not spread evenly throughout the population. Certain types of people are much more likely to be crime victims. The types of people that were most vulnerable to victimization in the past continue to be the most vulnerable.

Based on 1999 NCVS data the demographic groups with the highest rates of violent crime victimization per 1,000 persons age 12 or older (from highest to lowest overall rate) were:[50]

- **Younger persons**   Persons 12–24 had about double the violent crime victimization rates of persons 25 or older and about 20 times the rate of persons 65 or older. Persons 16–19 had the highest rate, 77.4, and persons 65 and older had the lowest rate, 3.8.

- **Never married, divorced, or separated persons**   Never married, divorced, or separated persons were nearly four times more likely than married persons and nearly nine times more likely than widowed persons to be violent crime victims. The rates for never married and separated persons were 60.6 and 53.6, respectively, compared to the rate of 14.4 for married persons and 6 for widowers.

- **Poorer persons**   Persons with annual household incomes of less than $7,500 had violent victimization rates 2.5 times higher than victims with annual household incomes of $75,000 or more. The rate for the lower income category was 57.5; the rate for the highest income category was 22.9.

National Crime Victims' Fund

In 1984, during the Reagan administration, a national crime victims' fund was created to help crime victims and the nonprofit organizations that serve them, such as shelters for battered women, rape crisis centers, and children's advocacy centers. Money for the fund comes from federal fines, penalties, and forfeitures collected from convicted criminals. Between 1985 and 1999, nearly $3 billion was deposited in the fund. In 1996 alone, the fund was increased $440 million by fines paid by just two federal defendants. With money from the fund, states can aid crime victims with unpaid medical bills, lost wages, health counseling, emergency transportation to court, and funeral costs.

SOURCE: Office for Victims of Crime, OVC Fact Sheet, U.S. Department of Justice <www.ojp.usdoj.gov/ovc/factshts/cvfvca.htm>; Bruce M. Taylor, "Changes in Criminal Victimization, 1994-95," U.S. Department of Justice, Bureau of Justice Statistics (Washington, DC: GPO, April 1997), p. 2, Table 1; Michael R. Rand, James P. Lynch, and David Cantor, "Criminal Victimization, 1973-95," U.S. Department of Justice, Office of Justice Programs, Bureau of Justice Statistics (Washington, DC: GPO, April 1997), p. 1.

Violence on Television

The relationship between the viewing of violence on television and the violence in society is a hotly debated topic. However, television violence may have more to do with fear of crime than it does with actual violent behavior. George Gerbner, a professor and dean emeritus at the Annenberg School for Communication at the University of Pennsylvania, has studied the subject for more than 20 years. He says, "The contribution of television to the committing of violence is relatively minor, maybe five percent. Whereas the contribution of television to the perception of violence is much higher. People are almost paralyzed by fear." From his research, Gerbner has concluded that heavy television viewers tend to suffer from what he calls the "mean world syndrome." Heavy viewers are more likely than light viewers to overestimate their chances of encountering violence, to believe that their neighborhoods are unsafe, and to assume that crime is rising, whether or not it actually is. They are also more likely to buy guns for protection.

SOURCE: Elizabeth Kolbert, "Aggression in Kids Linked to TV Violence: Experts Say Connection Isn't Cause," *The Charlotte (NC) Observer* (December 18, 1994), p. 18A.

FIGURE 2–12

Trends in Violent and Property Crime Rates

Violent victimization rate per 1,000 persons age 12 and older, 1973–99

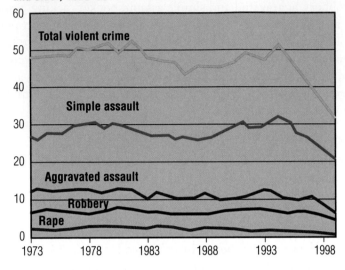

Property crime rate per 1,000 households, 1973–99

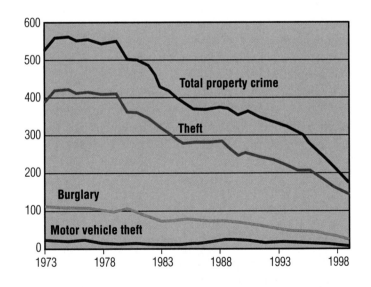

Note: From 1973 through June 1992 data were collected under the National Crime Survey (NCS) and made comparable to data collected under the redesigned methods of the NCVS that began in July 1992.

SOURCE: Callie Marie Rennison, *Criminal Victimization 1999: Changes 1998–99, Trends 1993–99,* U.S. Department of Justice, Bureau of Justice Statistics, National Crime Victimization Survey (Washington, DC: GPO, August 2000), p. 2.

▲ Young, economically disadvantaged black males are the most likely victims of personal violent crime. *Why and what can be done about it?*

- **Blacks** The rate of violent crime victimization for blacks was 41.6; for whites, 31.9; and for others, 24.5. The rate for Hispanics was 33.8.

- **Urban residents** The violent crime victimization rates for urban, suburban, and rural residents were 39.8, 32.8, and 24.9, respectively.

- **Men** The violent crime victimization rate for men was 37; the rate for women was 28.8.

- **Persons living in the West or Midwest** Persons living in the West and Midwest had violent crime victimization rates of 36.9 and 35.5, respectively, while persons living in the South and Northeast had rates of 30.2 and 29.6, respectively.

Whereas violent crime victimization rates are measures of the characteristics of victims age 12 and older, property crime victimization rates are measures of the characteristics of victimized households or heads of households. Consequently, there are no property crime victimization rates by gender, age,

Dori DeJong, Victim Advocate

My name is Dori DeJong and I am a victim advocate with the Denver District Attorney's Office in Denver, Colorado. I have a Bachelor's Degree in education from the University of Northern Colorado, a Master's Degree in social work and a Juris Doctor from the University of Denver. Prior to working in the district attorney's office, I worked as a counselor at a children's psychiatric hospital, as a children's counselor at a battered women's shelter and as a legal advocate for a community agency that provided assistance to victims of domestic violence. I decided to become a victim advocate because it was a great way to combine my educational background in both social work and law.

A typical day as a victim advocate includes contacting the victims of crimes (domestic violence, stranger assault, sex assault, child abuse, etc.) and explaining the criminal justice system to them; providing details about their specific case; giving notification of their rights as a victim; referring victims to various outside assistance agencies; and obtaining their input as to the best possible outcome of the case in which they are involved. Additionally, I coordinate and participate in the meetings between the victims and the assistant district attorneys to assist in the preparation of the victims for trial, and to answer any questions they have about the process. I accompany the victims in the courthouse on the day of the trial to provide encouragement, support, and understanding of the process in order for them to get through a very difficult experience. I also send update letters and victim impact statements to victims, notify other agencies and jurisdictions of active cases, run criminal background checks on defendants to identify habitual offenders, and maintain statistics on domestic violence cases. I have regular contact and communication with police officers, detectives, district attorneys, investigators, and other victim advocates. I also communicate with staff from outside assistance agencies to help sustain continuing support for the victim.

The most positive aspect of the job is the ability to help people and feel that you are really making a difference in someone's life. It is so encouraging when you have a client call you months or even years after you've assisted them, to thank you and tell you what a difference you've made in their lives and their children's lives. It is also rewarding to be a part of the prosecution team that holds criminals responsible and accountable for their behavior.

Being a victim advocate can sometimes be difficult and frustrating because you work with people that are in crisis, and often are not appreciative of your involvement in their lives. Sometimes their anger about the incident is misdirected at the victim advocate and the system, which is trying to provide justice.

The job of a victim advocate is interesting, challenging, often fast paced, and can be very rewarding. However, the job can also be overwhelming since it frequently involves dealing with offensive criminal defendants and their actions, and the sometimes inequitable system of justice. If you are considering a job as a victim advocate, I would encourage you to volunteer or do an internship in an agency that works with victims. This invaluable experience will provide you with the knowledge to determine if this career suits you.

Do you have any characteristics and/or abilities that you think would make you particularly suited to be a victim's advocate? If so, what?

or marital status, but there is the new category of home ownership. The characteristics of households or heads of households with the highest 1999 rates of property crime victimization per 1,000 households (from highest to lowest overall rate) were:[52]

- **Urban residences** The property crime victimization rates for urban, suburban, and rural residences were 256.3, 181.4, and 159.8, respectively.

- **Renters** The rate of property crime victimization of renters was 251.9; the rate for homeowners was 170.4.

- **Black households** The property crime victimization rate of black households was 249.9; for white households, 190, and for the households of other races, 206.3. The rate for Hispanics was 232.5.

- **Western households** The rate of property crime victimization for households in the West was 243.1; in the Midwest, 199.9, in the South, 191.4, and in the Northeast, 159.5.

MYTH · · · · · FACT · · · · ·

Adults are more likely to be forcibly raped than are children.

Girls younger than 18 are the victims of nearly half the forcible rapes reported to police, even though the younger the rape victim, the less likely the crime is to be reported to the police. Girls younger than 18 make up about 25 percent of the U.S. female population. Girls younger than 12 are the victims in about 12 percent of forcible rapes reported to the police; girls 12–17 years of age are the victims of about one-third of forcible rapes reported to the police. The younger the victim, the more likely that the attacker is a relative and not a stranger. More than 80 percent of forcible rapists are 18 years of age or older.[51]

There was not much difference in the property crime victimization rates for households of different incomes. For example, the rate for households with incomes of less than $7,500 was 220.8, while the rate for households with incomes of $75,000 or more was 220.4.

There were two other interesting findings in the 1999 NCVS. The first deals with the victim-offender relationship. While strangers victimized a majority of men (55 percent), a majority of women (68 percent) were victimized by someone they knew.[53] The second finding was that in two-thirds of violent victimizations no weapon was used. A weapon was known to be used in 47 percent of robberies, 23 percent of assaults, and only 5 percent of rapes or sexual assaults.[54]

2.5 CRITICAL THINKING

Why do you think that certain types of people are more likely to become crime victims than others?

Review and Applications

SUMMARY BY CHAPTER OBJECTIVES

1. Distinguish Between a Social Definition and a Legal Definition of Crime and Summarize the Problems with Each

A typical social definition of crime is behavior that violates the norms of society or, more simply, anti-social behavior. A typical legal definition of crime is an intentional violation of the criminal law or penal code, committed without defense or excuse and penalized by the state. There are problems with both definitions. Problems with the social definition are that (1) there are no uniform norms of behavior accepted by all of society, (2) norms of behavior are subject to interpretation, and (3) norms change from time to time and from place to place. Problems with the legal definition of crime are (1) overcriminalization, (2) nonenforcement, and (3) undercriminalization.

2. List the Technical and Ideal Elements of a Crime

The technical and ideal elements of a crime are (1) harm, (2) legality, (3) *actus reus*, (4) *mens rea*, (5) causation, (6) concurrence, and (7) punishment.

3. Identify Some of the Legal Defenses or Legal Excuses for Criminal Responsibility

Among the legal defenses or legal excuses for criminal responsibility in the United States are that the defendant (1) acted under duress, (2) was underage, (3) was insane, (4) acted in self-defense or in defense of a third party, (5) was entrapped, or (6) acted out of necessity.

4. Explain Why Crime and Delinquency Statistics are Unreliable

Among the reasons why crime and delinquency statistics are unreliable are the following: First, some behavior is labeled crime by one observer but not by another. Second, a large proportion of crimes are undetected. Third, not all crimes are reported to the police. Fourth, not all crimes that are reported are officially recorded by the police.

5. Identify the Two Major Sources of Crime Statistics in the United States

The two major sources of crime statistics in the United States are the uniform crime reports (UCR) compiled by the FBI and the national crime victimization surveys (NCVS) compiled by the Bureau of Justice Statistics.

6. Describe the Principal Finding of the National Crime Victimization Surveys

The national crime victimization surveys (NCVS) produce different results from the FBI's uniform crime reports (UCR). The NCVS generally show more crimes being committed than the UCR. The NCVS count more of some kinds of crimes and count them differently.

7. Summarize the General Finding of Self-Report Crime Surveys

Self-report crime surveys show that the amount of hidden crime in the United States is enormous; more than 90 percent of all Americans have committed crimes for which they could have been imprisoned.

8. Identify the Costs of Crime

According to data from the NCVS, in 1998 the total economic loss to victims of crime in the United States was $17 billion. This figure does not include the tangible costs of the criminal justice process, security devices bought for protection, losses to businesses, losses from corporate crimes, or the intangible costs of pain, suffering, and reduced quality of life. When all costs are totaled, it is estimated that crime costs about $450 billion annually.

9. Describe the Extent of Fear of Crime in the United States and the Characteristics of People Most Likely to Fear Crime

Fear of crime, especially violent crime, is widespread. However, it is neither evenly distributed across the population nor commensurate with the statistical probability of being a victim. In general, those more likely to fear crime are females, nonwhites, people 30 years old and older, Jews, people living in urban areas, Easterners and Southerners, high school graduates or people with less education, and people whose family income is less than $50,000.

10. List the Characteristics of People Who are the Most Likely and the Least Likely to be Victims of Crime

According to data from the 1999 NCVS, the most likely victims of personal violent crimes are young (12–24 years old), never married, divorced, or separated, poor, black, urban men living in the West or Midwest. The group least likely to experience violent crime victimization is persons aged 65 or older. The most likely victims of household property crimes are households in urban areas headed by renters and blacks in the West.

KEY TERMS

norm, p. 28
legal definition of crime, p. 29
overcriminalization, p. 29
nonenforcement, p. 29
undercriminalization, p. 30
harm, p. 31
legality, p. 31
ex post facto law, p. 31
actus reus, p. 31
mens rea, p. 32
negligence, p. 32
duress, p. 32
juvenile delinquency, p. 32
insanity, p. 33
entrapment, p. 34
necessity defense, p. 35
mala in se, p. 36
mala prohibita, p. 36
dark figure of crime, p. 38
crime index, p. 38
offenses known to the police, p. 39
crime rate, p. 40
uniform crime reports, p. 42
eight index crimes, p. 42
status offense, p. 43
crime index offenses cleared, p. 44
national crime victimization surveys, p. 47
self-report crime surveys, p. 48

Review and Applications

1. What is a *norm*?
2. What is the *harm* of crime?
3. What is the *mens rea* of crime?
4. What is *legal infancy* or *legal nonage*?
5. What is *juvenile delinquency*?
6. What is *insanity*?
7. Does the availability of the insanity defense allow a large number of dangerous criminals to go free?
8. What is the difference between a *felony* and a *misdemeanor*?
9. What percentages of all crime are violent crime, property crime, and public order crime?
10. Why aren't any records or indexes of crime very reliable measures of the true amount of crime?
11. What is *offenses known to the police*, and what are an advantage and disadvantage of using it?

12. What is a *crime rate*, and why are crime rates used?
13. What is a *status offense*?
14. When the media report that crime has increased or decreased from one year to the next, to what are they referring?
15. What is the NIBRS?
16. What are some of the detrimental consequences of a fear of crime?
17. What long-term trends in violent and property crime victimization rates are revealed by the national crime victimization surveys?

EXPERIENTIAL ACTIVITIES

1. **Crime Victimization Survey** As an individual project or a group project, construct and conduct a crime victimization survey. (Use the national crime victimization survey as a model.) Either orally or in writing, present and discuss the results. Be sure to discuss problems encountered in constructing the survey and problems with the accuracy and trustworthiness of responses.

2. **Self-Report Crime Survey** As an individual project or a group project, construct and conduct a self-report crime survey. (Make sure you tell respondents not to put their names or any other identifying information on the survey. Also, be sure to include both serious and less serious crimes.) Either orally or in writing, present and discuss the results. Be sure to discuss problems encountered in constructing the survey and problems with the accuracy and trustworthiness of responses.

INTERNET

3. **Crime Statistics** Examine the latest edition of the FBI's uniform crime reports by clicking the link at cj.glencoe.com. Then choose one of the eight index crimes listed in Figure 2–5, and search the site for statistics about that crime. Write a brief report summarizing the results of your research. As an alternative, examine the printed version, *Crime in the United States,* at an area library.

4. **Victimization Data** Examine the latest edition of the NCVS at the Bureau of Justice Statistics site through the cj.glencoe.com site. Click on "criminal victimization, general" and scroll to the newest edition (hardcopies of the NCVS are no longer available). Compare the latest victimization data with the data presented in your textbook. Write a brief report summarizing any changes.

The Twinkie Defense

1. Dan White had been elected as city supervisor of San Francisco. White resigned on November 10, 1978. Four days later, he changed his mind and asked Mayor George Moscone to reappoint him to his former position. The mayor refused and appointed Harvey Milk, a leader in San Francisco's gay community. On the morning of November 27, White confronted the mayor and demanded to be reappointed. When the mayor refused, White shot the mayor five times. White reloaded the gun, walked across the hall to Milk's office, and shot him four times. White fled, but shortly thereafter went to the police and confessed. He was charged with first-degree murder. During his trial, several psychologists called by the defense testified that White's behavior was the result of long-term depression exacerbated by a craving for junk food. They testified that White's judgment and ability to control his behavior were altered by the huge amount of sugar he had consumed the night before the killings. The so-called "Twinkie defense" worked. White was convicted of voluntary manslaughter instead of first-degree murder, and on May 21, 1979, he was sentenced to a prison term of five years to seven years eight months.

    a. What is the legal rationale for accepted legal defenses against or excuses from criminal responsibility? Do you agree with the rationale?

    b. Should all legal defenses or excuses be abolished? Why or why not?

Fighting Illegal Drugs

2. Activists are advocating a different strategy in the fight against illegal drugs. In agreement with the American Medical Association, they maintain that drug addiction is a disease. They believe it should be treated as a public health problem, not as a law enforcement problem. They propose a change in strategy from prohibition to decriminalization or legalization. According to these activists, decriminalization or legalization would do the following:

    - Reduce profits from drug trafficking, crime caused by the need to support drug habits, and the prison population.
    - Allow money used for incarceration to fund new models of drug control.
    - Allow drugs such as marijuana to be regulated and taxed.
    - Reduce the negative health consequences from using drugs of unknown potency and purity.
    - Improve pain control options for certain medical conditions.
    - Free physicians from fear of entrapment for prescribing certain drugs.
    - Shift the focus of criminal justice to more serious crime problems.

    a. One of the seven elements of a crime is harm. Do you think that illegal drug use is harmful? Explain.

    b. If the use of addictive drugs is illegal, should addictive substances such as nicotine (in cigarettes) or caffeine (in coffee) also be made illegal? Explain.

ADDITIONAL READING

Barak, Gregg (ed.). *Crimes by the Capitalist State: An Introduction to State Criminality.* New York: State University of New York Press, 1991.

Coleman, James W. *The Criminal Elite: Understanding White Collar Crime,* 4th ed. New York: St. Martin's, 1998.

Friedrichs, David O. *Trusted Criminals: White Collar Crime in Contemporary Society.* Belmont, CA: Wadsworth, 1995.

Green, Gary S. *Occupational Crime,* 2d ed. Chicago: Nelson-Hall, 1995.

Reiman, Jeffrey J. *The Rich Get Richer and the Poor Get Prison: Ideology, Class, and Criminal Justice,* 6th ed. Boston: Allyn & Bacon, 2001.

Simon, David R. *Elite Deviance,* 6th ed. Boston: Allyn & Bacon, 1999.

ENDNOTES

1. For additional examples and further discussion of this issue, see Robert M. Bohm, "Some Relationships That Arguably Should Be Criminal Although They Are Not: On the Political Economy of Crime," pp. 3–29 in K. D. Tunnell (ed.), *Political Crime in Contemporary America: A Critical Approach* (New York: Garland, 1993); Gregg Barak (ed.), *Crimes by the Capitalist State: An Introduction to State Criminality* (New York: State University of New York Press, 1991); Gregg Barak and Robert M. Bohm, "The Crimes of the Homeless or the Crime of Homelessness? On the Dialectics of Criminalization, Decriminalization, and Victimization," Contemporary Crises, Vol. 13, 1989, pp. 275–88; James W. Coleman, *The Criminal Elite: Understanding White Collar Crime,* 4th ed. (New York: St. Martin's, 1998); David O.Friedrichs, *Trusted Criminals: White Collar Crime in Contemporary Society.* (Belmont, CA: Wadsworth, 1995); Gary S. Green, Occupational Crime, 2d ed. (Chicago: Nelson-Hall, 1996); David R. Simon, *Elite Deviance,* 6th ed. (Boston: Allyn and Bacon, 1999).

2. These elements and the discussion that follows are based on material from Edwin H. Sutherland and Donald R. Cressey, *Criminology,* 9th ed. (Philadelphia: J. B. Lippincott, 1974), pp. 13–15.

3. *M'Naghten's Case,* 8 Eng. Rep. 718 (1843).

4. Herbert Modlin, "Crime and Insanity," Firing Line, May 25, 1984; Samuel Walker, *Sense and Nonsense about Crime and Drugs: A Policy Guide,* 3rd ed. (Belmont, CA: Wadsworth, 1994), p. 151.

5. Sutherland and Cressey, op. cit., p. 25.

6. Ibid. The remainder of the discussion in this section is based on material from the aforementioned source, pp. 25–30.

7. Ibid.

8. Ibid., pp. 27–28.

9. D. Seidman and M. Couzens, "Getting the Crime Rate Down: Political Pressure and Crime Reporting," Law and Human Behavior, Vol. 8, 1974, pp. 327–42. See also

L. DeFleur, "Biasing Influences on Drug Arrest Records: Implications for Deviance Research," American Sociological Review, Vol. 40, 1975, pp. 88–103; W. L. Selke and H. E. Pepinsky, "The Politics of Police Reporting in Indianapolis, 1948-1978," Law and Human Behavior, Vol. 6, 1982, pp. 327–42.

10. Federal Bureau of Investigation, *Crime in the United States 1999,* U.S. Department of Justice (Washington, DC: GPO, 2000).

11. Ibid.

12. Ibid., pp. 58–61.

13. Ibid., p. 60.

14. Ibid., p. 61.

15. Ibid., p. 211

16. Ibid.

17. Ibid.

18. Ibid., p. 212.

19. Ibid.

20. Ibid., p. 201.

21. Ibid., p. 202.

22. Ibid., p. 201.

23. Ibid., pp. 279–289.

24. Unless indicated otherwise, all information in this section is from Brian A. Reaves, "Using NIBRS Data to Analyze Violent Crime," U.S. Department of Justice, Bureau of Justice Statistics Technical Report (Washington, DC: GPO, October 1993).

25. The Federal Bureau of Investigation <www.fbi.gov/ucr/nibrs/faqs.htm>

26. U.S. Department of Justice, "Implementing the National Incident-Based Reporting System: A Project Status Report," (Washington, DC: GPO, July 1997).

27. U.S. Department of Justice, Office of Justice Programs, Bureau of Justice Statistics, *Criminal Victimization in the United States, 1994* (Annapolis, MD: Bureau of Justice Statistics Clearinghouse, 1997).

28. See, for example, J. S. Wallerstein and C. J. Wylie, "Our Law-Abiding Lawbreakers," Probation, Vol. 25, 1947, pp. 107–12; I. Silver, Introduction to *The Challenge of Crime in a Free Society* (New York: Avon, 1968). See also C. Tittle, W. Villemez, and D. Smith, "The Myth of Social Class and Criminality," American Sociological Review, Vol. 43, 1978, pp. 643–56. Juvenile delinquency is also widespread. See, for example, Jerald Bachman, Lloyd Johnston, and Patrick O'Malley, *Monitoring the Future* (Ann Arbor: University of Michigan, Institute for Social Research, 1992); Martin Gold, "Undetected Delinquent Behavior," Journal of Research in Crime and Delinquency, Vol. 3, 1966, pp. 27–46; Martin Gold, Delinquent Behavior in an American City (Belmont, CA: Brooks/Cole, 1970); Maynard Erickson and LaMar Empey, "Court Records, Undetected Delinquency, and Decision-Making," Journal of Criminal Law, Criminology, and Police Science, Vol. 54, 1963, pp. 446–69; James Short and F. Ivan Nye, "Extent of Unrecorded Delinquency," Journal of Criminal Law, Criminology, and Police Science, Vol. 49, 1958, pp. 296–302.

29. *Criminal Victimization in the United States 1998* Statistical Tables, Table 82, <www.ojp.usdoj.gov/bjs/pub/pdf/cvus98pdf>.

30. U.S. Department of Justice, Office of Justice Programs, Bureau of Justice Statistics, *Criminal Victimization in the United States, 1992* (Annapolis, MD: Bureau of Justice Statistics Clearinghouse, 1994), p. 148.

31. Simon, op. cit., p. 93

32. Ted R. Miller, Mark A. Cohen, and Brian Wiersema, "Victim Costs and Consequences: A New Look," U.S. Department of Justice, National Institute of Justice Report (Washington, DC: GPO, February 1996).

33. Wesley Skogan, "Fear of Crime and Neighborhood Change," in Albert J. Reiss, Jr., and Michael Tonry (eds.), Communities and Crime, Vol. 8 of Crime and Justice: A Review of Research (Chicago: The University of Chicago Press, 1986).

34. Sourcebook of Criminal Justice Statistics Online, June 1997, p. 156, Table 2.37 (1995 data).

35. Kathleen Maguire and Ann L. Pastore (eds.), *Sourcebook of Criminal Justice Statistics 1993*, U.S. Department of Justice, Bureau of Justice Statistics (Washington, DC: GPO, 1994), p. 182, Table 2.30; Bahram Haghighi and Jon Sorensen, "America's Fear of Crime," in Timothy J. Flanagan and Dennis R. Longmire (eds.), Americans View Crime and Justice: A National Public Opinion Survey (Thousand Oaks, CA: Sage, 1996), p. 22, Table 2.1.

36. Ann L. Pastore and Kathleen Maguire (eds.), *Sourcebook of Criminal Justice Statistics 1999*, U.S. Department of Justice, Bureau of Justice Statistics (Washington, DC: GPO, 2000), p. 119, Table 2.43.

37. Ibid.

38. Kathleen Maguire and Ann L. Pastore (eds.), *Sourcebook of Criminal Justice Statistics 1996*, U.S. Department of Justice, Bureau of Justice Statistics (Washington, DC: GPO, 1997), p. 134, Tables 2.30, 2.31, and 2.32; Kathleen Maguire and Ann L. Pastore (eds.), *Sourcebook of Criminal Justice Statistics 1994*, U.S. Department of Justice, Bureau of Justice Statistics (Washington, DC: GPO, 1995) (from draft data); Haghighi and Sorensen, op. cit., p. 19.

39. Haghighi and Sorensen, op. cit., pp. 26–27.

40. Wesley Skogan and Michael G. Maxwell, *Coping With Crime: Individual and Neighborhood Reactions* (Beverly Hills, CA: Sage, 1981).

41. Haghighi and Sorensen, op. cit., p. 19.

42. Skogan, "Fear of Crime and Neighborhood Change," op. cit., p. 215.

43. Callie Marie Rennison, "Criminal Victimization 1999: Changes 1998–99 with Trends 1993–99," U.S. Department of Justice, Bureau of Justice Statistics, National Crime Victimization Survey (Washington, DC: GPO, August 2000), p. 3, Table 1.

44. Ibid.

45. Ibid.

46. Ibid.

47. Ibid., p. 1

48. Ibid

49. Ibid.

50. Howard N. Snyder, *Sexual Assault of Young Children as Reported to Law Enforcement: Victim, Incident, and Offender Characteristics*, U.S. Department of Justice, Bureau of Justice Statistics (Washington, DC: GPO, July 2000).

51. Ibid.

52. Ibid., p. 9, Table 6.

53. Ibid., p. 8, Table 4.

54. Ibid., p. 9, Table 5.

Chapter 3

Explaining Crime

CHAPTER OBJECTIVES

After completing this chapter, you should be able to:

1. Define criminological theory.

2. State the causes of crime according to classical and neoclassical criminologists.

3. Describe the biological theories of crime causation and their policy implications.

4. Describe the different psychological theories of crime causation.

5. Explain sociological theories of crime causation.

6. Distinguish major differences among classical, positivist, and critical theories of crime causation.

7. Describe how critical theorists would explain the causes of crime.

3.1 Introduction to Criminological Theory

theory
An assumption (or set of assumptions) that attempts to explain why or how things are related to each other.

A theory is an assumption (or set of assumptions) that attempts to explain why or how things are related to each other. A theory of crime attempts to explain why or how a certain thing or certain things are related to criminal behavior. For example, some theories assume that crime is part of human nature, that some human beings are born evil. In those theories, human nature is examined in relation to crime. Other theories assume that crime is caused by biological things (for example, chromosome abnormalities, hormone imbalances), psychological things (for example, below-normal intelligence, satisfaction of basic needs), sociological things (for example, social disorganization, inadequate socialization), economic things (for example, unemployment, economic inequality); or some combination of all four kinds of things. In this chapter, we will examine a variety of crime theories and discuss the policy implications of each. (Unless indicated otherwise, the term crime includes delinquency.)

criminological theory
The explanation of criminal behavior, as well as the behavior of police, attorneys, prosecutors, judges, correctional personnel, victims, and other actors in the criminal justice process.

Criminological theory is important because most of what is done in criminal justice is based on criminological theory, whether we or the people who propose and implement policies based on the theory know it or not. The failure to understand the theoretical basis of criminal justice policies leads to at least two undesirable consequences. First, if criminal justice policy makers do not know the theory or theories on which their proposed policies are based, then they will be unaware of the problems that are likely to undermine the success of the policies. Much time and money could be saved if criminal justice policies were based on a thorough theoretical understanding. Second, criminal justice policies invariably intrude on people's lives (for example, people are arrested and imprisoned). If people's lives are going to be disrupted by criminal justice policies, it seems only fair that there be very good reasons for the disruption.

Technically, criminological theory refers not only to explanations of criminal behavior but also to explanations of police behavior and the behavior of attorneys, prosecutors, judges, correctional personnel, victims, and other actors in the criminal justice system. However, in this chapter, our focus is on theories of crime causation. Figure 3–1 outlines the crime causation theories presented in this chapter.

- -

3.1 CRITICAL THINKING

What is a theory? Why is it important to understand the various theories of criminal behavior?

FIGURE 3–1

Theories of Crime Causation

Classical and Neoclassical

Theories	Theorists	Causes	Policy Implications
	Beccaria	Free-willed individuals commit crime because they rationally calculate that crime will give them more pleasure than pain.	Deterrence: Establish social contract. Enact laws that are clear, simple, unbiased, and reflect the consensus of the population. Impose punishments that are proportionate to the crime, prompt, certain, public, necessary, the least possible in the given circumstances, and dictated by law, not judges' discretion. Educate the public. Eliminate corruption from the administration of justice. Reward virtue.

Positivist

Theories	Theorists	Causes	Policy Implications
Biological			
	Lombroso, Sheldon	Biological inferiority or biochemical processes cause people to commit crimes.	Isolate, sterilize, or execute offenders. For specific problems, brain surgery, chemical treatment, improved diets, and better mother and child health care.
Psychological			
Intelligence	Goddard	Mental inferiority (low IQ) causes people to commit crimes.	Isolate, sterilize, or execute offenders.
Psychoanalytic	Freud	Crime is a symptom of more deep-seated problems.	Provide psychotherapy or psychoanalysis.
Humanistic	Maslow Halleck	Crime is a means by which individuals can satisfy their basic human needs (Maslow). Crime is an adaptation to helplessness caused by oppression (Halleck).	Help people satisfy their basic needs legally (Maslow). Eliminate sources of oppression. Provide legal ways of coping with feelings of helplessness caused by oppression; psychotherapy (Halleck).
Sociological			
Durkheim	Durkheim	Crime is a social fact. It is a "normal" aspect of society, although different types of societies should have greater or lesser degrees of it. Crime is also functional for society.	Contain crime within reasonable boundaries.
Chicago School	Park, Burgess, Shaw, McKay	Delinquency is caused by detachment from conventional groups, which is caused by social disorganization.	Organize and empower neighborhood residents.

Continued on page 72

FIGURE 3-1

Theories of Crime Causation (continued)

Theories	Theorists	Causes	Policy Implications
Anomie or strain	Merton, Cohen	For Merton, it is the contradiction between cultural goals and the social structure's capacity to provide the institutionalized means to achieve those goals. For Cohen and gang delinquency, it is caused by an inability to conform to middle-class values and to achieve status among peers legally.	Reduce aspirations. Increase legitimate opportunities. Do both.
Learning	Tarde, Sutherland, Burgess, Akers, Jeffery	Crime is committed because it is positively reinforced, negatively reinforced, or imitated.	Provide law-abiding models. Regulate association. Eliminate crime's rewards. Reward law-abiding behavior. Punish criminal behavior effectively.
Control	Reiss, Toby, Nye, Reckless, Hirschi	Crime is a result of improper socialization.	Properly socialize children so that they develop self-control and a strong moral bond to society.

Critical

Theories	Theorists	Causes	Policy Implications
Labeling	Lemert	Does not explain the initial cause of crime and delinquency (primary deviance); explains only secondary deviance with the acceptance of a criminal label.	Do not label. Employ radical nonintervention. Employ reintegrative shaming.
Conflict	Vold, Turk	Crime is caused by relative powerlessness.	Dominant groups give up power to subordinate groups. Dominant groups become more effective rulers and subordinate groups better subjects.
Radical	Quinney, Chambliss, Platt	Competition among wealthy people and among poor people as well as between rich and poor (the class struggle) and the practice of taking advantage of other people cause crime.	Define crime as a violation of basic human rights. Replace the criminal justice system with "popular" or "socialist" justice. Create a socialist society appreciative of human diversity.
British or Left Realism	Young	Directs attention to the fear and victimization experienced by working-class individuals.	Employ police power to protect people living in working-class communities.
Peacemaking	Quinney, Pepinsky	Same as radical (different prescription for change).	Transform human beings so that they are able to experience empathy with those less fortunate and respond to other people's needs. Reduce hierarchical structures. Create communities of caring people. Champion universal social justice.
Feminist theory	Daly, Chesney-Lind, Simpson	Patriarchy (men's control over women's labor and sexuality) is the cause of crime.	Abolish patriarchal structures and relationships. Champion greater equality for women in all areas.
Postmodernism	Henry, Milovanovic	The denial of responsibility for other people and to other people.	Similar to peacemaking criminal theory.

3.2 Classical and Neoclassical Approaches to Explaining Crime

The causes of crime have long been the subject of much speculation, theorizing, research, and debate among scholars and the public. Each theory of crime has been influenced by the religious, philosophical, political, economic, social, and scientific trends of the time. One of the earliest secular approaches to explaining the causes of crime was the classical theory, developed in Europe at the time of profound social and intellectual change. Before classical theory, crime was generally equated with sin and was considered the work of demons or the devil.

Classical Theory

Classical theory is a product of the Enlightenment period, or the Age of Reason, a period of history that began in the late 1500s and lasted until the late 1700s. The Enlightenment thinkers, including members of the classical school of criminology, promoted a new, scientific view of the world. In so doing, they rejected the then-dominant religious view of the world, which was based on revelation and the authority of the Church. The Enlightenment thinkers assumed that human beings could understand the world through science—the human capacity to observe and to reason. Moreover, they believed that if people could understand the world and its functioning, they could change it. The Enlightenment thinkers rejected the belief that either the nature of the world or the behavior of the people in it was divinely ordained or predetermined.

Instead, the Enlightenment thinkers believed that people exercise *free will*, or the ability to choose any course of action, for which they are completely responsible. Human behavior was considered motivated by a *hedonistic rationality*, in which a person weighs the potential pleasure of an action against the possible pain associated with it. In that view, human beings commit crime because they rationally calculate that the crime will give them more pleasure than pain.

Classical criminologists, as Enlightenment thinkers, were concerned with protecting the rights of humankind from the corruption and excesses of the existing legal institutions. Horrible and severe punishments were common both before and during the Enlightenment. For example, in England during the eighteenth century, almost 150 offenses carried the death penalty including stealing turnips, associating with gypsies, cutting down a tree, and picking pockets. Barbarous punishments were not the only problem. At the time, crime was rampant, yet types of crime were poorly defined. What we today call *due process of law* was either absent or ignored. Torture was employed routinely to extract confessions. Judgeships were typically sold to wealthy persons by the sovereign, and judges had almost total discretion. Consequently, there was little consistency in the application of the law or in the punishments imposed.

It was within that historical context that Cesare Beccaria, perhaps the best known of the classical criminologists, wrote and published anonymously in 1764 his truly revolutionary work, *An Essay on Crimes and Punishments*

classical theory
A product of the Enlightenment, based on the assumption that people exercise free will and are thus completely responsible for their actions. In classical theory, human behavior, including criminal behavior, is motivated by a hedonistic rationality, in which actors weigh the potential pleasure of an action against the possible pain associated with it.

Cesare Beccaria

Cesare Beccaria, the best known of the classical criminologists, opposed the death penalty. In *An Essay on Crimes and Punishments*, he wrote: The death penalty cannot be useful, because of the example of barbarity it gives . . . It seems to me absurd that the laws, which are an expression of the public will, which detest and punish homicide, should themselves commit it, and that to deter citizens from murder, they order a public one.

(*Dei Delitti e delle Pene*). His book is generally acknowledged to have had an enormous practical influence on the establishment of a more humane system of criminal law and procedure.[1] In the book, Beccaria sets forth most of what we now call classical criminological theory.

According to Beccaria, the only justified rationale for laws and punishments is the principle of **utility**, that is, "the greatest happiness shared by the greatest number."[2] The basis of society, as well as the origin of punishments and the right to punish, is the **social contract**. The social contract is an imaginary agreement entered into by persons who sacrifice the minimum amount of their liberty necessary to prevent anarchy and chaos.

Beccaria believed that the only legitimate purpose of punishment is deterrence, both special and general.[3] **Special** or **specific deterrence** is the prevention of the punished persons from committing crime again. **General deterrence** is the use of the punishment of specific individuals to prevent people in general or society at large from engaging in crime. To be both effective and just, Beccaria argued, punishments must be "public, prompt, necessary, the least possible in the given circumstances, proportionate to the crime, dictated by the laws."[4] It is important to emphasize, however, that Beccaria promoted crime prevention over punishment.

In addition to the establishment of a social contract and the punishment of people who violate it, Beccaria recommended four other ways to prevent or to deter crime.[5] The first was to enact laws that are clear, simple, and unbiased and that reflect the consensus of the population. The second was to educate the public. Beccaria assumed that the more educated people are, the less likely they are to commit crimes. The third was to eliminate corruption from the administration of justice. Beccaria believed that if the people who dispense justice are themselves corrupt, people lose respect for the justice system and become more likely to commit crimes. The fourth was to reward virtue. Beccaria asserted that punishing crime is not enough; it is also important to reward law-abiding behavior. Such rewards might include public recognition of especially meritorious behavior or, perhaps, an annual tax deduction for people who have not been convicted of a crime.

The application of classical theory was supposed to make criminal law fairer and easier to administer. To those ends, judges would not select sentences. They could only impose the sentences dictated by legislatures for specific crimes. All offenders would be treated alike, and similar crimes would be treated similarly. Individual differences among offenders and unique or mitigating circumstances about the crime would be ignored. A problem is that all offenders are not alike and similar crimes are not always as similar as they might appear on the surface. Should first offenders be treated the same as those who commit crime repeatedly? Should juveniles be treated the same as adults? Should the insane be treated the same as the sane? Should a crime of passion be treated the same as the intentional commission of a crime? The classical school's answer to all of those difficult questions would be a simple "yes."

Despite those problems, Beccaria's ideas, as previously noted, were very influential. France, for example, adopted many of Beccaria's principles in its Code of 1791—in particular, the principle of equal punishments for the same crimes. However, because classical theory ignored both individual differences among offenders and mitigating circumstances, it was difficult to apply the law in practice. Because of that difficulty, as well as new developments in the emerging behavioral sciences, modifications of classical theory and its application were introduced in the early 1800s.

Neoclassical Theory

Several modifications of classical theory are collectively referred to as **neoclassical theory**. The principal difference between the two theories has to do with classical theory's assumption about free will. In the neoclassical revision, it was conceded that certain factors, such as insanity, might inhibit the exercise of free will. Thus, the idea of premeditation was introduced as a measure of the degree of free will exercised. Also, mitigating circumstances were considered legitimate grounds for an argument of diminished responsibility.

Those modifications of classical theory had two practical effects on criminal justice policy. First, they provided a reason for nonlegal experts such as medical doctors to testify in court as to the degree of diminished responsibility of an offender. Second, offenders began to be sentenced to punishments that were considered rehabilitative. The idea was that certain environments, for example, environments free of vice and crime, were more conducive than others to the exercise of rational choice.

The reason we have placed so much emphasis on the classical school of criminology and its neoclassical revisions is that, together, they are essentially the model on which criminal justice in the United States is based today. During the past 25 years or so, at least in part because the public frequently perceived as too lenient the sentences imposed by judges for certain crimes, such measures as legislatively imposed sentencing guidelines have limited the sentencing authority of judges in many jurisdictions. Public outrage over the decisions of other criminal justice officials has led to similar measures. For example, parole has been abolished in the federal jurisdiction and in some states because many people believe that parole boards release dangerous criminals from prison too soon.

The revival of classical and neoclassical theories during the past two decades, and the introduction of a more modern version called *rational choice theory*, are also probably a reaction to the allegation of some criminologists and public officials that criminologists have failed to discover the causes of crime. As a result of that belief, there has been a renewed effort to deter crimes by sentencing more offenders to prison for longer periods of time and, in many jurisdictions, by imposing capital punishment for heinous crimes. Ironically, one reason the theory of the classical school lost favor in the nineteenth century was the belief that punishment was not a particularly effective method of preventing or controlling crime.

neoclassical theory
A modification of classical theory in which it was conceded that certain factors, such as insanity, might inhibit the exercise of free will.

Americans Behind Bars

At midyear 2000, there were nearly 2 million people incarcerated in the United States. More than 1.2 million were in state prisons, nearly 131,000 were in federal prisons, and more than 600,000 were in local jails. Between 1990 and midyear 2000, the state prison population increased 72 percent, the federal prison population 123 percent, and jail populations 53 percent. Between 1990 and midyear 2000, the population grew on average 5.6% annually. On June 30, 2000, one in every 142 U.S. residents was incarcerated.

SOURCE: Allen J. Beck and Jennifer C. Karbeg, "Prison and Jail Inmates at Midyear 2000," U.S. Department of Justice, Bureau of Justice Statistics Bulletin (Washington, DC: GPO, March 2001).

3.2 CRITICAL THINKING

1. Name four of the ways that classical criminologist Cesare Beccaria thought were best to prevent or deter crime.

Do you agree with Beccaria? Why or why not?

2. What are the main differences between classical and neoclassical theories?

3.3 Positivist Approaches to Explaining Crime

The theory of the positivist school of criminology grew out of positive philosophy and the logic and basic methodology of empirical or experimental science. Positive philosophy was an explicit rejection of the critical and "negative" philosophy of the Enlightenment thinkers. Among the founders of positivism was Auguste Comte, who also has been credited with founding sociology. Comte acknowledged that the Enlightenment thinkers had contributed to progress by helping to break up the old system and by paving the way for a new one.[6] However, Comte argued that the ideas of the Enlightenment period had outlived their usefulness and had become obstructive.

At about the same time that positivist philosophy was developing, experimentation with animals was becoming an increasingly accepted way of learning about human beings in physiology, medicine, psychology, and psychiatry. Human beings were beginning to appear to science as one of many creatures, with no special connection to God. Human beings were beginning to be understood, not as free-willed, self-determining creatures who could do anything that they wanted to do, but rather as beings whose action was determined by biological and cultural factors.

Positivism was a major break with the classical and neoclassical theories that had preceded it. The following are key assumptions of the positivist school of thought.

1. Human behavior is determined and not a matter of free will. Consequently, positivists focus on cause-and-effect relationships.

2. Criminals are fundamentally different from noncriminals. Positivists search for such differences by scientific methods.

3. Social scientists (including criminologists) can be objective, or value-neutral, in their work.

4. Crime is frequently caused by multiple factors.

5. Society is based on consensus but not on a social contract.

As the social sciences developed and social scientists directed their attention to the problem of crime, they adopted, for the most part, positivist assumptions. For example, theories of crime were (and continue to be) based on biological positivism, psychological positivism, sociological positivism, and so on. However, as theories based on positivist assumptions were developed, it became apparent to close observers that there were problems, not only with the theories, but with the positivist assumptions as well. We will briefly discuss five of those problems.[7] In subsequent subsections, we will also describe problems peculiar to specific positivist theories of crime causation.

The first problem with positivism is overprediction: positivist theories generally account for too much crime. They also do not explain exceptions very well. For example, a positivist theory that suggests crime is caused by poverty overpredicts because not all poor people commit crime.

Second, positivist theories generally ignore the criminalization process, the process by which certain behaviors are made illegal. They separate the

CAREERS IN CRIMINAL JUSTICE

Criminologist

My name is Alida Merlo, and I am a professor of criminology at Indiana University of Pennsylvania. I have taught criminal justice and criminology for 25 years. I have a Ph.D. in sociology from Fordham University, a master's degree in criminal justice from Northeastern University, and a bachelor's degree from Youngstown State University. As an undergraduate, I majored in sociology and corrections.

I became interested in criminology while taking an undergraduate course in juvenile delinquency. That course inspired me to pursue a career in criminal justice as a probation officer and then as an intake supervisor for the Mahoning County Juvenile Court in Youngstown, Ohio. These experiences led me to enroll in graduate school to learn more about crime causation and the criminal justice process.

During graduate school, I realized I would like to teach criminology and criminal justice. I was attracted to the profession for a variety of reasons: It would enable me to do research, teach, develop programs, and pursue professional activities and community service. Teaching and studying criminal justice and criminology seemed a wonderful opportunity.

Being a criminologist involves developing and teaching courses, reading and contributing to the literature in the field, serving on departmental and university committees, advising students about courses, research, career options, and graduate education, meeting prospective students and their families, applying for funding research, conducting research, sharing research findings with colleagues at state, regional, national, and international meetings, being involved in professional organizations, and serving on community boards or assisting in community programs.

One great joy of teaching criminology and criminal justice is assisting students as they develop and blossom in the discipline. Many of my students work in the field. Former students have been awarded doctoral degrees, and teach criminal justice. It is exciting to have played a part in their professional development.

One disadvantage of being a criminologist is the inability to communicate to the public and to policy makers the realities of criminal justice and the implications of one's research. Confronting the fact that policies are often developed and enforced with little enlightenment is frustrating, but I am confident that criminologists will play a greater role in the future.

Do you think effective public speaking skills are important in this position? Why?

---

study of crime from a theory of the law and the state and take the legal definition of crime for granted. Ignored is the question of why certain behaviors are defined as criminal while other, similar behaviors are not.

A third problem with positivism is its consensual worldview, the belief that most people agree about most things most of the time. Such a view ignores a multitude of fundamental conflicts of value and interest in society. It also tends to lead to a blind acceptance of the status quo.

A fourth problem is positivism's belief in determinism, the idea that choice of action is not free, but is determined by causes independent of a person's will. Positivists generally assume that humans only adapt or react, but humans also create. How else could we explain new social arrangements or ways of thinking? A belief in determinism allows positivists to present an absolute situation uncomplicated by the ability to choose.

Finally, a fifth problem with positivist theories is the belief in the ability of social scientists (criminologists) to be objective, or value-neutral, in their work. Positivists fail to recognize that to describe and evaluate such human actions as criminal behavior is fundamentally a moral endeavor and, therefore, subject to bias.

Biological Theories

Biological theories of crime causation (biological positivism) are based on the belief that criminals are physiologically different from noncriminals. Early biological theories assumed that structure determined function. In other words, criminals behave differently because, structurally, they are different. Today's biocriminologists are more likely to assume that biochemistry determines function or, more precisely, the difference between criminals and noncriminals is the result of a complex interaction between biochemical and environmental factors. To test biological theories, efforts are made to demonstrate, through measurement and statistical analysis, that there are or are not significant structural or biochemical differences between criminals and noncriminals.

Historically, the cause of crime, from this perspective, was **biological inferiority**. Biological inferiority in criminals was assumed to produce certain physical or genetic characteristics that distinguished criminals from noncriminals. It is important to emphasize that in these theories, the physical or genetic characteristics themselves did not cause crime, they were only the symptoms, or *stigmata*, of the more fundamental inferiority. The concept of biological inferiority has lost favor among today's biocriminologists who generally prefer to emphasize the biological differences between criminals and noncriminals without adding the value judgment. In any event, several different methodologies have been employed to detect physical differences between criminals and noncriminals. They are criminal anthropology; study of body types; heredity studies, including family trees, statistical comparisons, twin studies, and adoption studies; and, in the last 10 to 15 years or so, studies based on new scientific technologies that allow, for example, the examination of brain chemistry processes.

biological inferiority
According to biological theories, a criminal's innate physiological makeup produces certain physical or genetic characteristics that distinguish criminals from noncriminals.

criminal anthropology
The study of "criminal" human beings.

Criminal Anthropology
Criminal anthropology is the study of "criminal" human beings. It is associated with the work of an Italian army doctor and later, university professor, Cesare Lombroso. Lombroso first published his theory of a physical criminal type in 1876.

Lombroso's theory consisted of the following propositions:[8]

1. Criminals are, by birth, a distinct type.
2. That type can be recognized by physical characteristics, or *stigmata*, such as enormous jaws, high cheekbones, and insensitivity to pain.
3. The criminal type is clearly distinguished in a person with more than five stigmata, perhaps exists in a person with three to five stigmata, and does not necessarily exist in a person with fewer than three stigmata.
4. Physical stigmata do not cause crime; they only indicate an individual who is predisposed to crime. Such a person is either an **atavist**—that is, a reversion to a savage type—or a result of degeneration.
5. Because of their personal natures, such persons cannot desist from crime unless they experience very favorable lives.

atavist
A person who reverts to a savage type.

Lombroso's theory was popular in the United States until about 1915, although variations of his theory are still being taught today. The major problem with Lombroso's criminal anthropology is the assumption that certain physical characteristics are indicative of biological inferiority. Unless there is independent evidence to support that assumption, other than the association of the physical characteristics with criminality, then the result is circular reasoning. In other words, crime is caused by biological inferiority, which is itself indicated by the physical characteristics associated with criminality.

Body-Type Theory   Body-type theory is an extension of Lombroso's criminal anthropology. William Sheldon, whose work in the 1940s was based on earlier work by Ernst Kretchmer in the 1920s, is perhaps the best known of the body-type theorists. According to Sheldon, human beings can be divided into three basic body types, or *somatotypes*, which correspond to three basic temperaments.[9] The three body types are the endomorphic (soft, fat), the mesomorphic (athletically built), and the ectomorphic (tall, skinny).

Sheldon argued that everyone has elements of all three types, but that one type usually predominates. In a study of 200 Boston delinquents between 1939 and 1949, Sheldon found that delinquents were more mesomorphic than nondelinquents, and that serious delinquents were more mesomorphic than less severe delinquents. Subsequent studies by the Gluecks in the 1950s and by Cortes in the 1970s also found an association between mesomorphy and delinquency.

The major criticism of the body-type theory is that differences in behavior are indicative of the social selection process and not biological inferiority. In other words, delinquents are more likely to be mesomorphic than nondelinquents because, for example, mesomorphs are more likely to be selected for gang membership. Also, the finding that delinquents are more likely than nondelinquents to be mesomorphic contradicts, at least with regard to physique, the theory's general assumption that criminals (or delinquents) are biologically inferior.

In any event, if one believes that crime is the product of biological inferiority, then the policy implications are limited. Either criminals are isolated from the rest of the population by imprisoning them, for example, or they are executed. If they are isolated, they may also need to be sterilized to ensure that they do not reproduce.

CRIMINAL JUSTICE *Online*

Biological Causes of Crime

Learn more about the biological causes of criminal, violent, and psychopathic behavior. Go to cj.glencoe.com for a link to the Crime Times Web site. Review the issue and/or subject index and read a few articles related to biology and criminal behavior. *Do you think that biological theories of crime causation adequately explain criminal behavior?*

▲ William Sheldon, a well-known body-type theorist, divided humans into three basic body types. Left: endomorphic (soft fat); center: mesomorphic (athletically built); right: ectomorphic (tall, skinny). *Why would delinquents more likely have a mesomorphic body type rather than an endomorphic or ectomorphic body type?*

The Family Tree Method

The family tree method was used by Dugdale (1877) and Estabrook (1916), who both compared the Jukes family with the Jonathan Edwards family. The Jukes family presumably had 7 murderers, 60 thieves, 50 prostitutes, and assorted other criminals. The Edwards family, on the other hand, presumably had no criminals but, instead, had Presidents of the United States, governors, Supreme Court justices, federal court justices, and assorted writers, preachers, and teachers. As it turns out, the Edwards family was not as crime-free as originally believed. Apparently, Jonathan Edwards's maternal grandmother had been divorced on grounds of adultery, a grandaunt had murdered her son, and a granduncle had murdered his sister.

SOURCE: Richard L. Dugdale, *The Jukes: A Study in Crime, Pauperism, Disease and Heredity* (New York: Putnam, 1877); Arthur H. Estabrook, *The Jukes in 1915* (Washington, DC: Carnegie Institute of Washington, 1916).

Heredity Studies   A variety of methods has been employed to test the proposition that criminals are genetically different from noncriminals.

Family Tree Studies   Perhaps the earliest method was the use of family trees, in which a family known to have many "criminals" was compared with a family tree of "criminals." (See FYI.) However, a finding that criminality appears in successive generations does not prove that criminality is inherited or is the product of a hereditary defect. For example, the use of a fork in eating has been a trait of many families for generations, but that does not prove that the use of a fork is inherited. In short, the family tree method cannot adequately separate hereditary influences from environmental influences.

Statistical Comparisons   A second method used to test the proposition that crime is inherited or is the product of a hereditary defect is statistical comparison. The rationale is that if criminality exhibits the same degree of family resemblance as other physical traits, such as eye or hair color, then criminality, like those other traits, must be inherited. Although there is some evidence to support the notion, statistical comparisons also fail to separate adequately hereditary influences from environmental influences.

Twin Studies   A third, more sophisticated method of testing the proposition that crime is inherited or is the result of a hereditary defect is the use of twin studies. Heredity is assumed to·be the same in identical twins because they are the product of a single egg. Heredity is assumed to be different in fraternal twins because they are the product of two eggs fertilized by two sperm. The logic of the method is that if there is greater similarity in behavior between identical twins than between fraternal twins, the behavior must be due to heredity, since environments are much the same. More than a half century of this methodology has revealed that identical twins are more likely to demonstrate concordance (both twins having criminal records) than are fraternal twins, thus supporting the hereditary link. A problem with the twin studies, however, is the potential confounding of genetic and environmental influences. Identical twins tend to be treated more alike by others, spend much more time together, and have a greater sense of shared identity than do fraternal twins.

Adoption Studies   A fourth method, the most recent and most sophisticated method of examining the inheritability of criminality, is the adoption study. The first such study was conducted in the 1970s. In this method, the criminal records of adopted children (almost always boys) who were adopted at a relatively early age are compared with the criminal records of both their biological parents and their adoptive parents (almost always fathers). The rationale is that if the criminal records of adopted boys are more like those of their biological fathers than like those of their adoptive fathers, the criminality of the adopted boys can be assumed to be the result of heredity.

The findings of the adoption studies reveal that the percentage of adoptees who are criminal is greater when the biological father has a criminal record than when the adoptive father has one. However, there also is an interactive effect. A greater percentage of adoptees have criminal records when both fathers have criminal records than when only one of them does. Like the twin studies, the adoption studies presumably demonstrate the influence of heredity but cannot adequately separate it from the influence of the environment. A problem with the adoption studies is the difficulty of interpreting the relative influences of heredity and environment, especially when the adoption does not take place shortly after birth or when, as is commonly the case, the adoption agency attempts to find an adoptive home that matches the biological home in family income and socio-economic status.

If criminals are genetically different from noncriminals or the product of genetic defect, then the policy implications are the same as for other theories that propose that criminals are biologically inferior: isolate, sterilize, or execute. However, in the future, new technologies may make possible genetic engineering—that is, the removal or alteration of defective genes.

Modern Biocriminology   Ongoing research has revealed numerous biological factors associated either directly or indirectly with criminal or delinquent behavior. Among such factors are certain chemical, mineral, and vitamin deficiencies in the diet, diets high in sugar and carbohydrates, hypoglycemia (low blood sugar level), certain allergies, ingestion of food dyes and lead, exposure to radiation from fluorescent tubes and television sets, and all sorts of brain dysfunctions such as attention deficit/hyperactivity disorder.[10] This section focuses on a few more of the biological factors linked to criminality and delinquency: disorders of the limbic system and other parts of the brain, brain chemical dysfunctions, minimal brain damage, and endocrine abnormalities.

Limbic System Disorders   At least some unprovoked violent criminal behavior is believed to be caused by tumors and other destructive or inflammatory processes of the limbic system.[11]

The **limbic system** (see Figure 3–2) is a structure surrounding the brain stem that, in part, controls the life functions of heartbeat, breathing, and sleep. It also is believed to moderate expressions of violence; such emotions as anger, rage, and fear; and sexual response. Violent criminal behavior has also been

Genetic Unity (DNA)

Based on the analysis of thousands of DNA samples, preliminary findings of the Human Genome Diversity Project—the first worldwide survey of humankind—demonstrate the "genetic unity that binds our diverse, polyglot species." The data show that "any two people, regardless of geography or ethnicity, share at least 99.99 percent of their genetic makeups." As for the 0.01 percent of the genome that makes people different, "it doesn't shake out along racial lines. . . . Instead, some 85 percent of human genetic diversity occurs within ethnic groups, not between them."

Source: Paul Salopek, "What's Next for Mankind?" *The Orlando Sentinel* (from the *Chicago Tribune*), June 1, 1997, p. G-1.

limbic system
A structure surrounding the brain stem that, in part, controls the life functions of heartbeat, breathing, and sleep. It also is believed to moderate expressions of violence; such emotions as anger, rage, and fear; and sexual response.

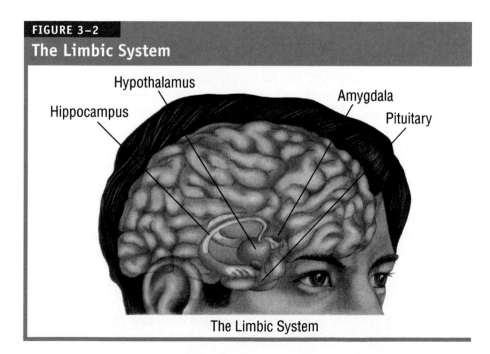

FIGURE 3–2
The Limbic System

Hypothalamus
Hippocampus
Amygdala
Pituitary

The Limbic System

linked to disorders in other parts of the brain. Recent evidence suggests that chronic violent offenders have much higher levels of brain disorder when compared to the general population. Surgical removal of the affected area sometimes eliminates expressions of violence. A problem with that type of intervention, however, is that it can cause unpredictable and undesirable behavior changes and, of course, is irreversible. Irreversibility is less a problem with newer chemical interventions, but the problem of unpredictable and undesirable behavior changes remains.

Chemical Dysfunctions   Some criminal behaviors are believed to be influenced by low levels of brain neurotransmitters (substances brain cells use to communicate).[12] For example, low levels of the brain neurotransmitter *serotonin* have been found in impulsive murderers and arsonists. Research is currently being conducted to determine whether low levels of another neurotransmitter, *norepinephrine*, are associated with compulsive gambling. Another interesting discovery in this area may help explain cocaine use. Apparently cocaine increases the level of the neurotransmitter *dopamine*, which activates the limbic system to produce pleasure. If such chemical deficiencies are linked to those behaviors, chemical treatment or improved diets might help. Neurotransmitters are products of the foods people eat.

Research on minimal brain damage has found that it increases an individual's chances of being identified as delinquent.[13] Minimal brain damage is believed to be most commonly caused by nutritional or oxygen deficiencies during pregnancy, or during or shortly after birth, or by insufficient protein and sensory stimulation during a child's formative years. Because minimal brain damage is also strongly associated with lower socioeconomic status, social deprivation must be considered a crucial element in its occurrence.

To reduce minimal brain damage in the population, adequate prenatal medical care and nutrition must be provided to all expectant mothers. To minimize complications during birth, adequate medical assistance must be provided. Further reductions in minimal brain damage would require providing adequate protein and social and intellectual stimulation to developing infants and young children.

Endocrine Abnormalities
Criminal behaviors have also been associated with endocrine, or hormone, abnormalities, especially those involving *testosterone* (a male sex hormone) and *progesterone* and *estrogen* (the female sex hormones).[14] For example, administering estrogen to male sex offenders has been found to reduce their sexual drives. A similar effect has been achieved by administering the drug Depo-Provera®, which reduces testosterone levels. However, a problem with Depo-Provera is that it is successful only for male sex offenders who cannot control their sexual urges. The drug does not seem to work on offenders whose sex crimes are premeditated. Studies have also found a large number of crimes committed by females during the menstrual or premenstrual periods of the female hormonal cycle. Those periods are characterized by a change in the estrogen-progesterone ratio.

In sum, there are probably no positivist criminologists today who would argue that biology or genetics makes people criminals. Nor, for that matter, are there many criminologists today who would deny that biology has some influence on criminal behavior. The position held by most criminologists

Chemical Castration

In 1996, California became the first state to require chemical castration of repeat child molesters. Under the law, molesters who commit a second crime against a child under 13 must receive weekly injections of Depo-Provera. In 1997, Florida and Georgia passed similar legislation requiring repeat offenders to be chemically castrated, and Texas approved voluntary castration for repeat molesters. In all four states, offenders may choose surgical castration instead.

today is that criminal behavior is the product of a complex interaction between biology and environmental or social conditions. What is inherited is not criminal behavior, but rather the way in which the person responds to his or her environment. In short, biology or genetics gives an individual a predisposition, or a tendency, to behave in a certain way. Whether a person actually behaves in that way and whether that behavior is defined as a crime depend primarily on environmental or social conditions.

Psychological Theories

This section examines psychological theories of crime causation, namely, the relationship between intelligence, criminality, and delinquency and discusses psychoanalytic and humanistic psychological theories. Learning or behavioral theories will be discussed along with sociological theories.

Intelligence and Crime   The idea that crime is the product primarily of people of low intelligence was popular in the United States from about 1914 until around 1930. It received some attention again during the mid-1970s and in the mid-1990s. The belief requires only a slight shift in thinking from the idea that criminals are biologically inferior to the idea that they are mentally inferior.

In 1931, Edwin Sutherland reviewed approximately 350 studies on the relationship between intelligence and delinquency and criminality.[15] The studies reported the results of intelligence tests of about 175,000 criminals and delinquents. Sutherland concluded from the review that although intelligence may play a role in individual cases, given the selection that takes place in arrest, conviction, and imprisonment, the distribution of the intelligence scores of criminals and delinquents is very similar to the distribution of the intelligence scores of the general population.

For the next 40 years or so, the issue of the relationship between intelligence and crime and delinquency appeared resolved. However, in the mid-1970s, two studies were published that resurrected the debate.[16] Those studies found that IQ was an important predictor of both official and self-reported juvenile delinquency, as important as social class or race. Both studies acknowledged the findings of Sutherland's earlier review. Both also noted that a decreasing number of delinquents had been reported as being of below-normal intelligence over the years. However, in both studies, it was maintained that the difference in intelligence between delinquents and nondelinquents had never disappeared and had stabilized at about eight IQ points. The studies failed to note, however, that the eight-point IQ difference found between delinquents and nondelinquents was generally within the normal range. The authors of the studies surmised that IQ influenced delinquency through its effect on school performance.

We cannot conclude with any degree of confidence that delinquents, as a group, are less intelligent than nondelinquents. We do know that most adult criminals are not of below-normal intelligence. Obviously, low-level intelligence cannot account for the dramatic increase in the crime rate over the last couple of decades, until recently, unless one is prepared to conclude that the population of offenders is getting less intelligent. Low-level intelligence certainly cannot account for complex white-collar and political crimes.

IQ and Crime

One of the earliest promoters in the United States of the relationship between low IQ and crime was H.H. Goddard. In 1914, he published *Feeblemindedness: Its Causes and Consequences*. In the book, Goddard argued that criminals are feebleminded, an old-fashioned term that means below-normal intelligence.

SOURCE: George B. Vold and Thomas J. Bernard, *Theoretical Criminology*, 3rd ed. (New York: Oxford, 1986) p. 72.

Nevertheless, to the degree, if any, that crime is caused by low-level intelligence, the policy implications are the same as for theories of biological inferiority: isolate, sterilize, or execute. Intelligence is believed to have a large genetic component.

Psychoanalytic Theories   Psychoanalytic theories of crime causation are associated with the work of Sigmund Freud and his followers.[17] Freud did not theorize much about criminal behavior itself, but a theory of crime causation can be deduced from his more general theory of human behavior and its disorders. Had he contemplated the issue, Freud probably would have argued that crime, like other disorders, was a symptom of more deep-seated problems and that if the deep-seated problems could be resolved, the symptom of crime would go away.

Freud believed that some people who had unresolved deep-seated problems were psychopaths (sociologists call them *sociopaths*). **Psychopaths, sociopaths**, or **antisocial personalities** are characterized by no sense of guilt, no subjective conscience, and no sense of right and wrong. They have difficulty in forming relationships with other people; they cannot empathize with other people. Figure 3–3 provides an extended list of the characteristics of psychopaths.

psychopaths, sociopaths, or **antisocial personalities**
Persons characterized by no sense of guilt, no subjective conscience, and no sense of right and wrong. They have difficulty in forming relationships with other people; they cannot empathize with other people.

FIGURE 3–3
Characteristics of the Psychopath

1. Superficial charm and good "intelligence."
2. Absence of delusions and other signs of irrational "thinking."
3. Absence of "nervousness" or psychoneurotic manifestations.
4. Unreliability.
5. Untruthfulness and insincerity.
6. Lack of remorse or shame.
7. Inadequately motivated antisocial behavior.
8. Poor judgment and failure to learn by experience.
9. Pathologic egocentricity and incapacity for love.
10. General poverty in major affective reactions.
11. Specific loss of insight.
12. Unresponsiveness in general interpersonal relations.
13. Fantastic and uninviting behavior, with drink and sometimes without.
14. Suicide rarely carried out.
15. Sex life impersonal, trivial, and poorly integrated.
16. Failure to follow any life plan.

SOURCE: From Hervey Cleckley's "The Mask of Sanity," *Institutions, Etc.: A Journal of Progressive Human Services,* Vol. 8, No. 9 (September 1985), p. 21. Reprinted by permission.

The principal policy implication of considering crime symptomatic of deep-seated problems is to provide psychotherapy or psychoanalysis. *Psychoanalysis* is a procedure first developed by Freud that, among other things, attempts to make patients conscious or aware of unconscious and deep-seated problems in order to resolve the symptoms associated with them. Methods used include a variety of projective tests (such as the interpretation of Rorschach inkblots), dream interpretation, and free association. Another policy implication that derives logically from Freudian theory is to provide people with legal outlets to sublimate or redirect their sexual and aggressive drives. (Freud believed that all human beings are born with those two drives and that those are the primary sources of human motivation.)

Psychoanalysis, and the psychoanalytic theory on which it is based, are components of a medical model of crime causation that has, to varying degrees, informed criminal justice policy in the United States for a century. The general conception of this medical model is that criminals are biologically or, especially, psychologically "sick" and in need of treatment.

Despite the enduring popularity of this theory, a number of problems have been identified with it. First, the bulk of the research on the issue suggests that most criminals are not psychologically disturbed or, at least, are no more disturbed than the rest of the population.[18]

Second, if a person who commits a crime has a psychological disturbance, that does not mean that the psychological disturbance causes the crime. Many people with psychological disturbances do not commit crimes, and many people without psychological disturbances do commit crimes.

Third, psychoanalytic theory generally ignores the environmental circumstances in which the problematic behavior occurs. The problem is considered a personal problem and not a social one.

Fourth, there are problems with psychoanalysis and other forms of psychotherapy. Psychotherapy rests on faith. Much of its theoretical structure is scientifically untestable. The emphasis of psychotherapy as an approach to rehabilitation is on the individual offender and not on the offender in interaction with the environment in which the criminal behavior occurs. The behaviors that are treated in psychotherapy are not criminal; they are the deep-seated problems. It is assumed that criminal behavior is symptomatic of those problems. That assumption may not be true. Many people who do not engage in crime have deep-seated problems, and many people who do not have those problems do engage in crime.

Humanistic Psychological Theory   Humanistic psychological theory, as described here, refers primarily to the work of Abraham Maslow and Seymour Halleck. The theories of Maslow and Halleck are fundamentally psychoanalytic, but they are called humanistic because they assume that human beings are basically good even though they are sometimes influenced by society to act badly. By contrast, Freudian theory assumes that human beings are inherently bad, motivated by sexual and aggressive drives.

Maslow did not apply his theory to crime itself, so we must infer from Maslow's work what we think he would have said about the causes of crime had he addressed the subject. Abraham Maslow believed human beings are motivated by a hierarchy of basic needs. (See Figure 3–4 on page 86.)

CRIMINAL JUSTICE Online

Serial Killers

Serial killers are characterized as psychopaths or sociopaths. Go to cj.glencoe.com for a link to read more about serial killers that are under investigation and some of the most well-known cases involving serial killers in the U.S. *Were you able to note any of the characteristics of a psychopath listed in Figure 3–3 in these articles?*

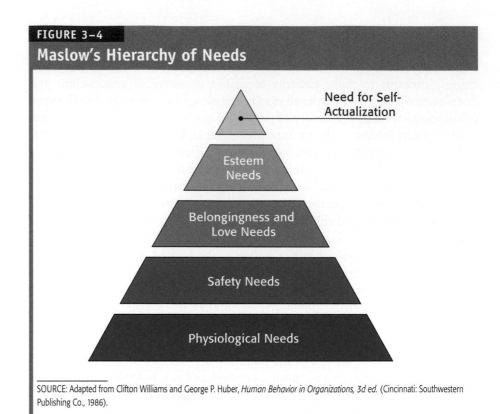

FIGURE 3-4

Maslow's Hierarchy of Needs

Need for Self-
Actualization

Esteem
Needs

Belongingness and
Love Needs

Safety Needs

Physiological Needs

SOURCE: Adapted from Clifton Williams and George P. Huber, *Human Behavior in Organizations, 3d ed.* (Cincinnati: Southwestern Publishing Co., 1986).

1. Physiological (food, water, and procreational sex)
2. Safety (security; stability; freedom from fear, anxiety, chaos, etc.)
3. Belongingness and love (friendship, love, affection, acceptance)
4. Esteem (self-esteem and the esteem of others)
5. Self-actualization (being true to one's nature, becoming everything that one is capable of becoming)[19]

According to Maslow, during a given period, a person's life is dominated by a particular need. It remains dominated by that need until the need has been relatively satisfied, at which time a new need emerges to dominate that person's life. From this view, crime may be understood as a means by which individuals satisfy their basic human needs. They choose crime because they cannot satisfy their needs legally or, for whatever reason, choose not to satisfy their needs legally. An obvious policy implication of the theory is to help people satisfy their basic human needs in legitimate ways. That may require governments to ensure adequate food, shelter, and medical care for those in need or to provide educational or vocational opportunities for those who are unable to obtain them. Those strategies are implied by several sociological theories as well. On a basic, interpersonal level, Maslow's theory might imply the need to make sympathetic listeners available to people who would benefit from sharing their problems.

Seymour L. Halleck views crime as one of several adaptations to the helplessness caused by oppression.[20] For Halleck, there are two general types of oppression, *objective* and *subjective*. Each has two subtypes. The subtypes of objective oppression are (a) social oppression (for example, oppression resulting from racial discrimination) and (b) the oppression that occurs in two-person interactions (for example, a parent's unfair restriction of the activities of a child). The subtypes of subjective oppression are (a) oppression from within (guilt) and (b) projected or misunderstood oppression (a person's feeling of being oppressed when, in fact, he or she is not).

For Halleck, the emotional experience of either type of oppression is helplessness, to which the person sometimes adapts by resorting to criminal behavior. Halleck suggests that the criminal adaptation is more likely when alternative adaptations, such as conformity, activism, or mental illness, are not possible or are blocked by other people. He also maintains that criminal behavior is sometimes chosen as an adaptation over other possible alternatives because it offers gratifications or psychological advantages that could not be achieved otherwise. Halleck's psychological advantages of crime are listed in Figure 3–5.

FIGURE 3–5
Halleck's 14 Psychological Advantages of Crime

1. The adaptational advantages of crime in changing one's environment are more desirable than illness or conformity.

2. Crime involves activity, and when man is engaged in motoric behavior, he feels less helpless.

3. However petty a criminal act may be, it carries with it a promise of change in a favorable direction.

4. During the planning and execution of a criminal act, the offender is a free man. (He is immune from the oppressive dictates of others.)

5. Crime offers the possibility of excitement.

6. Crime calls for the individual to maximize his faculties and talents which might otherwise lie dormant.

7. Crime can relieve feelings of inner oppression and stress.

8. Crime increases external stresses, which allows the individual to concentrate upon these threats to his equilibrium and temporarily allows him to abandon his chronic intrapsychic problems.

9. Once a person has convinced himself that the major pressures in his life come from without, there is less tendency to blame himself for this failure.

10. Adopting the criminal role provides an excellent rationalization for inadequacy.

11. Crime has a more esteemed social status than mental illness.

12. America has an ambivalent attitude toward crime. Although crime is regularly condemned, it is also glamorized.

13. Deviant behavior sometimes helps the criminal to form close and relatively nonoppressive relations with other criminals.

14. Crime can provide pleasure or gratify needs.

SOURCE: Seymour L. Halleck, *Psychiatry and the Dilemmas of Crime* (New York: Harper and Row, 1967) pp. 76–80.

There are at least three crime policy implications of Halleck's theory. First, sources of social oppression should be eliminated wherever possible. Affirmative action programs, which attempt to rectify historic patterns of discrimination in such areas as employment, are an example of such efforts. Second, alternative, legal ways of coping with oppression must be provided. An example is the opportunity to file claims with the Equal Employment Opportunity Commission (EEOC) in individual cases of employment discrimination. Third, psychotherapy should be provided for subjective oppressions. Psychotherapy could make the individual aware of oppressive sources of guilt or sources of misunderstood oppression so that the individual could better cope with them.

A major problem with the theories of Maslow and Halleck is that they do not go far enough. Neither Maslow nor Halleck asks the basic questions: Why can't people satisfy their basic needs legally, or why do they choose not to? Why don't societies ensure that basic needs can be satisfied legally so that the choice to satisfy them illegally makes no sense? Similarly, why does society so oppress many people, and why aren't more effective measures taken to greatly reduce that oppression?

Sociological Theories

Sociologists emphasize that human beings live in social groups and that those groups and the social structure they create (for example, political and economic systems) influence behavior. Most sociological theories of crime causation assume that a criminal's behavior is determined by his or her social environment, which includes families, friends, neighborhoods, and so on. Most sociological theories of crime explicitly reject the notion of the born criminal.

The Contributions of Durkheim

Many of the sociological theories of crime (actually delinquency) causation have their roots in the work of the French sociologist Emile Durkheim. Durkheim rejected the idea that the world is simply the product of individual actions. His basic premise is that society is more than a simple aggregate of individuals; it is a reality *sui generis* (unique).[21] Rejecting the idea that social phenomena, such as crime, can be explained solely by the biology or psychology of individuals, Durkheim argued that society is not the direct reflection of the characteristics of its individual members, because individuals cannot always choose. For Durkheim, social laws and institutions are "social facts" that dominate individuals, and all people can do is submit to them. The coercion may be formal (by means of law) or informal (by means of peer pressure). Durkheim maintained that with the aid of positive science, all people can expect is to discover the direction or course of social laws so that they can adapt to them with the least amount of pain.

For Durkheim, crime, too, is a social fact. It is a normal aspect of society, although different types of societies should have greater or lesser degrees of it. The cause of crime for Durkheim is **anomie**, that is, the dissociation of the individual from the **collective conscience**, or the general sense of morality of the times. He also believed that crime is functional for society by marking the boundaries of morality. In other words, people would not know what acceptable behavior is if crime did not exist. Crime is also functional because it provides a means of achieving necessary social change through, for example, civil

anomie
For Durkheim, the dissociation of the individual from the collective conscience.

collective conscience
The general sense of morality of the times.

disobedience and, under certain circumstances, directly contributes to social change, as in the repeal of prohibition. Durkheim advocated containing crime within reasonable boundaries. He warned, however, that too much crime could destroy society.

The Theory of the Chicago School   In the 1920s, members of the Department of Sociology at the University of Chicago tried to identify environmental factors associated with crime. Specifically, they attempted to uncover the relationship between a neighborhood's crime rate and the characteristics of the neighborhood. It was the first large-scale study of crime in the United States and was to serve as the basis for many future investigations into the causes of crime and delinquency.

The research of the **Chicago School** was based on a model taken from ecology, and as a result, that school is sometimes called the Chicago School of Human Ecology.[22] Ecology is a branch of biology in which the interrelationship of plants and animals is studied in their natural environment. Robert Park was the first of the Chicago theorists to propose this organic or biological analogy—that is, the similarity between the organization of plant and animal life in nature and the organization of human beings in societies.

Park and his colleagues described the growth of American cities like Chicago in ecological terms, saying growth occurs through a process of invasion, dominance, and succession.[23] That is, a cultural or ethnic group *invades* a territory occupied by another group and *dominates* that new territory until it is displaced, or *succeeded*, by another group and the cycle repeats itself.

This model of human ecology was used by other Chicago theorists, most notably Clifford R. Shaw and Henry D. McKay in their studies of juvenile delinquency in Chicago.[24] From the life histories of delinquents, Shaw and McKay confirmed that most of the delinquents were not much different from nondelinquents in their personality traits, physical condition, and intelligence.[25] However, Shaw and McKay did find that the areas of high delinquency were "socially disorganized." For the Chicago theorists, **social disorganization** is the condition in which the usual controls over delinquents are largely absent, delinquent behavior is often approved of by parents and neighbors, there are many opportunities for delinquent behavior, and there is little encouragement, training, or opportunity for legitimate employment.

In 1932, Shaw and his colleagues established the Chicago Area Project (CAP), which was designed to prevent delinquency through the organization and empowerment of neighborhood residents. Neighborhood centers, staffed and controlled by local residents, were established in six areas of Chicago. The centers had two primary functions. One was to coordinate community resources, such as schools, churches, labor unions, and industries, to solve community problems. The other function was to sponsor activity programs, such as scouting, summer camps, and sports leagues, to develop a positive interest by individuals in their own welfare and to unite citizens to solve their own problems. CAP operated continuously for 25 years, until Shaw's death in

▲ Emile Durkheim said in his volume, *Moral Education,* that, "The more detached from any collectivity man is, the more vulnerable to self-destruction he becomes." *Do you agree? Why? Why not?*

Chicago School
A group of sociologists at the University of Chicago who assumed in their research that delinquent behavior was a product of social disorganization.

social disorganization
The condition in which the usual controls over delinquents are largely absent, delinquent behavior is often approved of by parents and neighbors, there are many opportunities for delinquent behavior, and there is little encouragement, training, or opportunity for legitimate employment.

▲ From his analysis of the life histories of individual delinquents, Chicago sociologist Clifford Shaw discovered that many delinquent activities began as play activities at an early age. *What kind of play activities do you think could later contribute to delinquent activities?*

1957. Evaluations of the project suggest that it had a negligible effect on delinquency.

One of the problems with the theory of the Chicago School is the presumption that social disorganization is a cause of delinquency. Both social disorganization and delinquency may be the product of other, more basic factors. For example, one factor that contributes to the decline of city neighborhoods is the decades-old practice of *redlining*, in which banks refuse to lend money in an area because of the race or ethnicity of the inhabitants. Though illegal today, the practice continues. What usually happens in redlined areas is that neighborhood property values decline dramatically. Then land speculators and developers, typically in conjunction with political leaders, buy the land for urban renewal or gentrification and make fortunes in the process. In other words, political and economic elites may cause both social disorganization and delinquency—perhaps not intentionally, but by the conscious decisions they make about how a city will grow—making social disorganization appear to be the basic cause of delinquency.

anomie

For Merton, the contradiction between the cultural goal of achieving wealth and the social structure's inability to provide legitimate institutional means for achieving the goal. For Cohen, it is caused by the inability of juveniles to achieve status among peers by socially acceptable means.

Anomie or Strain Theory In an article published in 1938, Robert K. Merton observed that a major contradiction existed in the United States between cultural goals and the social structure.[26] He called the contradiction **anomie**, a concept first introduced by Durkheim. Specifically, Merton argued that in the United States the cultural goal of achieving wealth is deemed possible for all citizens, even though the social structure limits the legitimate "institutionalized means" available for obtaining the goal. For Merton, legitimate institutionalized means are the Protestant work ethic (hard work, education, and deferred gratification); illegitimate means are force and fraud. Because the social structure effectively limits the availability of legitimate institutionalized means, a *strain* is placed on people (hence the other name of the theory). Merton believed that strain could affect people in all social classes, but he acknowledged that it would most likely affect members of the lower class.

Merton proposed that individuals adapt to the problem of anomie or strain in one of several different ways: (1) conformity, (2) innovation, (3) ritualism, (4) retreatism, and (5) rebellion. Figure 3–6 displays these different adaptations. According to Merton, most people adapt by conforming; they "play the game." Conformers pursue the cultural goal of wealth only through legitimate institutional means. Innovation is the adaptation at the root of most crime. After rejecting legitimate institutional means, innovators pursue the cultural goal of wealth through illegitimate means. Ritualism is the adaptation of the individual who "takes no chances," usually a member of the lower middle class. Ritualists do not actively pursue the cultural goal of wealth (they are willing to settle for less) but follow the legitimate institutional means anyway. Retreatists include alcoholics, drug addicts, psychotics, and other outcasts of society. Retreatists "drop out"; they do not pursue the cultural goal of wealth, so they do not employ legitimate institutional means. Last is the adaptation of rebellion. Rebels reject both the cultural goal of wealth and the legitimate institutional means of achieving it. They substitute both different goals and different means. Rebellion can also be a source of crime.

In summary, Merton believed that a source of some, but not all, crime and delinquency was anomie or strain, a disjunction or contradiction between the cultural goal of achieving wealth and the social structure's ability to provide legitimate institutional means of achieving the goal.

Beginning in the mid-1950s, concern developed over the problem of juvenile gangs. Albert K. Cohen adapted Merton's anomie or strain theory to his attempt to explain gang delinquency.[27] In attempting to explain such behavior, Cohen surmised that it was to gain status among peers. Thus, Cohen substituted the goal of status among peers for Merton's goal of achieving wealth.

For Cohen, anomie or strain is experienced by juveniles who are unable to achieve status among peers by socially acceptable means, such as family name and position in the community or academic or athletic achievement. In response to the strain, either they can conform to middle-class values (generated primarily through the public school) and resign themselves to

Juvenile Delinquency Prevention and Control

When Robert Kennedy was Attorney General of the United States under his brother, President John F. Kennedy, he read Cloward and Ohlin's book *Delinquency and Opportunity: A Theory of Delinquent Gangs* (1960). Kennedy asked Lloyd Ohlin to help shape a new federal policy on juvenile delinquency. That effort, based on anomie theory, produced the Juvenile Delinquency Prevention and Control Act of 1961. The act included a comprehensive action program to provide employment opportunities and work training, in combination with community organization and improved social services, to disadvantaged youths and their families.

SOURCE: George B. Vold and Thomas J. Bernard, *Theoretical Criminology*, 3rd ed. (New York: Oxford, 1986), p. 201.

FIGURE 3-6
Merton's Typology of Modes of Individual Adaptation

Modes of Adaptation	Culture Goals	Institutional Means
I. Conformity	+	+
II. Innovation	+	−
III. Ritualism	−	+
IV. Retreatism	−	−
V. Rebellion	±	±

Key: + signifies "acceptance," − signifies "rejection," and ± signifies "rejection of prevailing values and substitution of new values."

SOURCE: Reprinted by permission of Macmillan Publishing Co, Inc., from *Social Theory and Social Structure*, by Robert K. Merton, Copyright © 1968, 1967 by Robert K. Merton.

▲ According to Albert K. Cohen's version of anomie theory, juveniles who are unable to achieve status among their peers by socially acceptable means sometimes turn to gangs for social recognition. *What are some other reasons why juveniles join gangs?*

imitation or **modeling**

A means by which a person can learn new responses by observing others without performing any overt act or receiving direct reinforcement or reward.

their inferior status among their peers, or they can rebel and establish their own value structures by turning middle-class values on their head. Juveniles who rebel in this way tend to find each other and to form groups or gangs to validate and reinforce their new values. Like Merton, Cohen believed that anomie can affect juveniles of any social class but that it disproportionately affects juveniles from the lower class.

Richard Cloward and Lloyd Ohlin extended Merton's and Cohen's formulations of anomie theory by suggesting that not all gang delinquents adapt to anomie in the same way. Cloward and Ohlin argue that the type of adaptation made by juvenile gang members depends on the *illegitimate opportunity structure* available to them.[28] They identified three delinquent subcultures: the criminal, the violent, and the retreatist. According to Cloward and Ohlin, if illegitimate opportunity is available to them, most delinquents will form *criminal* gangs to make money. However, if neither illegitimate nor legitimate opportunities to make money are available, delinquents often become frustrated and dissatisfied and form *violent* gangs to vent their anger. Finally, there are delinquents who, for whatever reason, are unable to adapt by joining either criminal or violent gangs. They *retreat* from society, as in Merton's retreatist adaptation, and become alcoholics and drug addicts.

The policy implications of anomie or strain theory are straightforward: reduce aspirations or increase legitimate opportunities or do both. Increasing legitimate opportunities, already a cornerstone of the black civil rights movement, struck a responsive chord as the 1960s began. Examples of this strategy are affirmative action employment programs, expansion of vocational education programs, and government grants that enable low-income students to attend college. Reducing aspirations (that is, desires to be wealthy), received little attention, however, because to attempt it would be to reject the "American dream," a principal source of motivation in a capitalist society.

Among the problems with the anomie theories of Merton, Cohen, and Cloward and Ohlin is their reliance on official statistics (police and court records) as measures of crime. Because these theorists relied on official statistics, their theories focus on lower-class crime and delinquency and ignore white-collar and government crimes.

Learning Theories Gabriel Tarde was one of the first theorists to believe that crime was something learned by normal people as they adapted to other people and the conditions of their environment. His theory was a product of his experience as a French lawyer and magistrate and was described in his book *Penal Philosophy*, published in 1890. Reflecting the state of knowledge about the learning process in his day, Tarde viewed all social phenomena as the product of imitation. Through **imitation** or **modeling**, a person can learn new responses, such as criminal behavior, by observing others, without performing any overt act or receiving direct reinforcement or reward.[29]

The first twentieth century criminologist to forcefully argue that criminal behavior was learned was Edwin H. Sutherland. His theory of **differential association**, developed between 1934 and 1947, was that persons who become criminal do so because of contacts with criminal patterns and isolation from noncriminal patterns. Together with its more recent modifications, his theory remains one of the most influential theories of crime causation.[30] The nine propositions of Sutherland's theory are presented in Figure 3–7.

Borrowing a premise from the theory of the Chicago School, Sutherland maintained that differential associations would not produce criminality if it were not for *differential social organization*. In other words, the degree to which communities promote or inhibit criminal associations varies with the way or the degree to which they are organized (that is, the extent of *cultural conflict*).

Since its final formulation in 1947, modifications and additions have been made to Sutherland's theory as new developments in learning theory have emerged. For example, Daniel Glaser modified Sutherland's theory by introducing *role theory* and by arguing that criminal behavior could be learned by identifying with criminal roles and not just by associating with criminals.[31] Thus, a person could imitate the behavior of a drug dealer without actually

differential association
Sutherland's theory that persons who become criminal do so because of contacts with criminal patterns and isolation from anticriminal patterns.

FIGURE 3–7

Sutherland's Propositions of Differential Association

1. Criminal behavior is learned.

2. Criminal behavior is learned in interaction with other persons in a process of communication.

3. The principal part of the learning of criminal behavior occurs within intimate personal groups.

4. When criminal behavior is learned, the learning includes (a) techniques of committing the crime, which are sometimes very complicated, sometimes very simple; (b) the specific direction of motives, drives, rationalizations, and attitudes.

5. The specific direction of motives and drives is learned from definitions of the legal codes as favorable and unfavorable.

6. A person becomes delinquent because of an excess of definitions favorable to violation of law over definitions unfavorable to violation of law. This is the principle of differential association.

7. Differential associations may vary in frequency, duration, priority, and intensity.

8. The process of learning criminal behavior by association with criminal and anti-criminal patterns involves all of the mechanisms that are involved in any other learning.

9. While criminal behavior is an expression of general needs and values, it is not explained by those general needs and values, since noncriminal behavior is an expression of the same needs and values.

SOURCE: Edwin H. Sutherland and Donald R. Cressey, *Criminology,* 9th ed. (Philadelphia: J. B. Lippincott, 1974), pp. 75–77. Reprinted by permission.

having met one. Glaser obviously believed that the media had a greater influence on the learning of criminal behavior than Sutherland believed they had.

Robert L. Burgess and Ronald L. Akers, as well as C. Ray Jeffery, adapted the principles of *operant conditioning* and *behavior modification*, developed by the psychologist B. F. Skinner, and the principles of *modeling*, as developed by Albert Bandura, to the explanation of criminal behavior. Burgess, Akers, and Jeffery integrated psychological concepts with sociological ones. Although they referred to their theories by different names, we will use the more general term *learning theory*.

Learning theory explains criminal behavior and its prevention with the concepts of *positive reinforcement, negative reinforcement, extinction, punishment,* and *modeling* or *imitation*. In this view, crime is committed because it is positively reinforced, negatively reinforced, or imitated. We described the imitation or modeling of criminal behavior in our earlier discussion of Tarde. Here we will focus on the other concepts.[32]

Positive reinforcement is the presentation of a stimulus that increases or maintains a response. The stimulus, or *reward*, can be either material, like money, or psychological, like pleasure. People steal (a response) because of the rewards—for example, the objects or money—that they receive. They use drugs (at least at first) because of the rewards, the pleasure, that the drugs give them.

Negative reinforcement is the removal or reduction of a stimulus whose removal or reduction increases or maintains a response. The stimulus in negative reinforcement is referred to as an *aversive stimulus*. Aversive stimuli, for most people, include pain and fear. Stealing may be negatively reinforced by removing or reducing the aversive stimuli of the fear and pain of poverty. For drug addicts, the use of addictive drugs is negatively reinforced because the drugs remove or reduce the aversive stimulus of the pain of drug withdrawal. In short, both positive and negative reinforcement explain why a behavior, such as crime, is maintained or increases. Both types of reinforcement can simultaneously affect the same behavior. In other words, people may commit crime, in this view, both because the crime is rewarded and because it removes an aversive stimulus.

According to learning theory, criminal behavior is reduced, but not necessarily eliminated, through *extinction* or *punishment*. **Extinction** is a process in which behavior that previously was positively reinforced is no longer reinforced. In other words, the rewards have been removed. Thus, if burglars were to continually come up empty-handed in their quests—not to receive rewards for their efforts—they would no longer continue to commit burglary. **Punishment** is the presentation of an aversive stimulus to reduce a response. It is the principle method used in the United States, and in other countries, to prevent crime or, at least, reduce it. For example, one of the reasons offenders are imprisoned is to punish them for their crimes.

Among the policy implications of learning theory is to punish criminal behavior effectively, that is, according to learning theory principles. For a variety of reasons, punishment is not used effectively in criminal justice in the United States. For example, to employ punishment effectively, one must prevent escape. Escape is a natural reaction to the presentation of an aversive stimulus like imprisonment. In the United States, the chances of an offender's escaping punishment are great. Probation probably does not function as an aversive stimulus, and most offenders, especially first-time offenders, are not incarcerated.

learning theory
A theory that explains criminal behavior and its prevention with the concepts of positive reinforcement, negative reinforcement, extinction, punishment, and modeling or imitation.

positive reinforcement
The presentation of a stimulus that increases or maintains a response.

negative reinforcement
The removal or reduction of a stimulus whose removal or reduction increases or maintains a response.

extinction
A process in which behavior that previously was positively reinforced is no longer reinforced.

punishment
The presentation of an aversive stimulus to reduce a response.

To be effective, punishment must be applied consistently and immediately. As for immediacy, the process of criminal justice in the United States generally precludes punishment immediately after a criminal act is committed. The process is a slow and methodical one. Consistent application of punishment is rare because most criminal offenders are not caught.

In addition, extended periods of punishment should be avoided, or the effectiveness of the punishment will be reduced. The United States currently imprisons more of its offenders for longer periods than any other country in the world, except perhaps Russia, though in many cases inmates actually serve only a fraction of their original sentences. A related issue is that punishment is far less effective when the intensity with which the aversive stimulus is presented is increased gradually than when the stimulus is introduced at full intensity. Prolonged imprisonment is a gradual process of punishment that lacks the full intensity and immediacy of corporal punishment, for example.

To be effective, punishment must also be combined with extinction. That is, the rewards that maintain the behavior must be removed. In the United States, after imprisonment, offenders are generally returned to the environments in which their crimes originally were committed and rewarded.

Finally, for punishment to be effective, it must be combined with the positive reinforcement of alternative, prosocial behaviors.

We must emphasize that for learning theorists, positive reinforcement is a much more effective and preferred method of manipulating behavior than is punishment, because positive reinforcement does not suffer the disadvantages associated with punishment. That point is often overlooked by criminal justice decision makers. Among the disadvantages of punishment are the effort to escape punishment by means other than law-abiding behavior; the development of negative self-concepts by offenders, who come to view themselves (instead of their criminal behaviors) as bad, making rehabilitation difficult and causing aggression.

Among the problems with a learning theory of crime causation is that it ignores the criminalization process. It fails to consider why the normal learned behaviors of some groups are criminalized while the normal learned behaviors of other groups are not. For example, why is marijuana consumption illegal, while cigarette or alcohol consumption is not? Learning theory ignores the effect that political and economic power has on the definition of criminal behavior.

Social Control Theories   The key question for social control theorists is not why people commit crime and delinquency, but rather why do they not. Why do people conform? From the perspective of **social control theory**, people are expected to commit crime and delinquency unless they are prevented from doing so. They will commit crime, that is, unless they are properly socialized.

Like many of the other sociological theories of crime causation, social control theories have their origins in the work of Durkheim. It was not until the 1950s, however, that social control theories began to emerge to challenge other, more dominant theories, such as strain and differential association. Among the early control theorists were Albert J. Reiss, Jackson Toby, F. Ivan Nye, and Walter C. Reckless. Despite the important contributions of those early theorists, modern social control theory in its most detailed elaboration

social control theory
A view in which people are expected to commit crime and delinquency unless they are prevented from doing so.

is attributed to the work of Travis Hirschi. Hirschi's 1969 book, *Causes of Delinquency*, has had a great influence on current criminological thinking.

As did proponents of earlier social control theories, Hirschi argued that delinquency (his was not a theory of adult criminality) should be expected if a juvenile is not properly socialized. For Hirschi, proper socialization involves the establishment of a strong moral bond between the juvenile and society. This *bond to society* consists of (1) *attachment* to others, (2) *commitment* to conventional lines of action, (3) *involvement* in conventional activities, and (4) *belief* in the moral order and law. Thus, delinquent behavior is likely to occur if there is (1) inadequate attachment, particularly to parents and school, (2) inadequate commitment, particularly to educational and occupational success, (3) inadequate involvement in such conventional activities as scouting and sports, and (4) inadequate belief, particularly in the legitimacy and morality of the law. For Hirschi, the units of social control most important in the establishment of the bond are the family, the school, and the law.

In a more recent book, Michael Gottfredson and Travis Hirschi argue that the principal cause of many deviant behaviors, including crime and delinquency, is ineffective child rearing, which produces people with low self-control.[33] Low self-control impairs a person's ability to accurately calculate the consequences of his or her actions and is characterized by impulsivity, insensitivity, physical risk taking, shortsightedness, and lack of verbal skills. This theory posits that everyone has a predisposition toward criminality, therefore low self-control makes it difficult to resist.

One of the appealing aspects of Hirschi's social control theory—and Gottfredson and Hirschi's theory, too—is their seemingly commonsense policy implications. To prevent delinquency, juveniles must be properly socialized; they must develop a strong moral bond to society. As part of that strategy, children must be reared properly so that they develop a high level of self-control.

Although social control theory is currently very influential in the thinking of many criminologists, it has not escaped extensive criticism. Perhaps the major problem, at least for some criminologists, is the theory's assumption that delinquency will occur if not prevented. Some criminologists find it troublesome that the theory rejects altogether the idea of delinquent motivation. Another problem with social control theory is that it does not explain how juveniles are socialized. For example, how are attachments to others produced and changed? Finally, Hirschi's argument, as stated, does not allow for delinquency by juveniles who are properly socialized, nor does it allow for conformity by juveniles who are not properly socialized.

3.3 CRITICAL THINKING

1. What are the five key assumptions of the positivist school of thought?

2. How would you describe body-type theory? What is the major criticism of this theory?

3. Explain psychoanalytic theory and some of the problems associated with it.

4. Explain learning theory. Do you think this theory has merit?

3.4 Critical Approaches to Explaining Crime

Critical theories are, in part, a product of a different conception of American society that began to emerge toward the end of the 1950s. Concepts like racism, sexism, capitalism, imperialism, monopoly, exploitation, and oppression were beginning to be employed with greater frequency to describe the social landscape. In the 1960s, the period of naive acceptance of the status quo and the belief in the purely benevolent actions of government ended for many social scientists, and the seeds of critical theory began to sprout.

Not surprisingly, the basic assumptions of critical theories differ both from those of classical and neoclassical theories and from those of positivist theories. First, unlike classical and neoclassical theories, which assume that human beings have free will, and positivist theories, which assume that human beings are determined, critical theories assume that human beings are both determined *and* determining. In other words, critical theories assume that human beings are the creators of the institutions and structures that ultimately dominate and constrain them. Second, in contrast to both classical and neoclassical theories and positivist theories, critical theories assume that conflict is the norm, that society is characterized primarily by conflict over moral values. Finally, unlike positivist theorists, many critical theorists assume that everything they do is value-laden by virtue of their being human; that is, they believe it is impossible to be objective or value-neutral in anything a person does.

Labeling Theory

The focus of **labeling theory** is the **criminalization process**—the way people and actions are defined as criminal—rather than the positivist concern with the peculiarities of the criminal actor. From this perspective, the distinguishing feature of all "criminals" is that they have been the object of a *negative social reaction*. In other words, they have been designated by the state and its agents as different and "bad."

It is important to note that labeling theorists attempt to explain only what Edwin Lemert called *secondary deviance*.[34] For our purposes, *secondary deviance* is the commission of crime subsequent to the first criminal act and the acceptance of a criminal label. Secondary deviance begins with an initial criminal act, or what Lemert called *primary deviance*. The causes of initial criminal acts are unspecified. Nevertheless, if society reacts negatively to an initial criminal act, especially through official agents of the state, the offender is likely to be *stigmatized*, or negatively labeled. It is possible, even likely, that there will be no reaction at all to an initial criminal act or that the offender will not accept or internalize the negative label. However, if the negative label is successfully applied to the offender, the label may become a *self-fulfilling prophecy*, in which the offender's self-image is defined by the label. Secondary deviance is the prophecy fulfilled.

As is well known, once a person is labeled and stereotyped as a "criminal," he or she probably will be shunned by law-abiding society, have difficulty finding a good job, lose some civil rights (if convicted of a felony), and suffer

labeling theory
A theory that emphasizes the criminalization process as the cause of some crime.

criminalization process
The way people and actions are defined as criminal.

a variety of other disabilities. The "criminal" (or "delinquent") label is conferred by all of the agencies of criminal justice—the police, the courts, and the correctional apparatus—as well as by the media, the schools, churches, and other social institutions. The irony is that in its attempt to reduce crime and delinquency, society may inadvertently be increasing it by labeling people and producing secondary deviance.

A policy implication of labeling theory is simply not to label or to employ *radical nonintervention*.[35] This might be accomplished through decriminalization (the elimination of many behaviors from the scope of the criminal law), diversion (removing offenders from involvement in the criminal justice process), greater due-process protections (replacing discretion with the rule of law), and deinstitutionalization (a policy of reducing jail and prison populations and construction).[36]

An alternative to the nonintervention strategy is John Braithwaite's *reintegrative shaming*.[37] In this strategy, disappointment is expressed for the offender's actions, and the offender is shamed and punished. What is more important, however, is that following the expression of disappointment and shame is a concerted effort on the part of the community to forgive the offender and reintegrate him or her back into society. Braithwaite contends that the practice of reintegrative shaming is one of the principal reasons for Japan's relatively low crime rate.

A problem with labeling theory is that it tends to overemphasize the importance of the official labeling process.[38] On one hand, the impression is given that innocent people are arbitrarily stigmatized by an oppressive society and that as a result, they begin a life of crime. That probably does not happen very much. On the other hand, the impression is given that offenders resist the criminal label and accept it only when they are no longer capable of fighting it. However, in some communities, the criminal label, or some variation of it, is actively sought. Perhaps the most telling problem with labeling theory is the question whether stigmatizing someone as criminal or delinquent causes more crime and delinquency than it prevents. To date, the answer is unknown.

MYTH

Most offenders resist being labeled criminal and accept the label only when they are no longer capable of fighting it.

FACT

In some communities the label *criminal*, or some variation of it, is actively sought.

Conflict Theory

Unlike classical and neoclassical and positivist theories, which assume that society is characterized primarily by consensus, **conflict theory** assumes that society is based primarily on conflict between competing interest groups—for instance, the rich against the poor, management against labor, whites against minorities, men against women, adults against children. In many cases, competing interest groups are not equal in power and resources. Consequently, one group is dominant and the other is subordinate.

One of the earliest theorists in the United States to apply conflict theory to the study of crime was George B. Vold. For Vold and other conflict theorists, such as Austin T. Turk, many behaviors are defined as crimes because it is in the interest of dominant groups to do so.[39]

conflict theory
A theory that assumes that society is based primarily on conflict between competing interest groups and that criminal law and the criminal justice system are used to control subordinate groups. Crime is caused by relative powerlessness.

98

▲ For conflict theorists, conflict between competing interest groups can sometimes lead to crime. *What kinds of group conflicts are more likely to lead to crime?*

According to conflict theorists, criminal law and the criminal justice system are used by dominant groups to control subordinate ones. However, the public image is quite different. The public image of the criminal law and the criminal justice system is that they are value-neutral institutions—that is, that neither institution has a vested interest in who "wins" a dispute. The public image is that the only concern of the criminal law and the criminal justice system is resolving disputes between competing interest groups justly and—more importantly—peacefully. According to conflict theorists, this public image legitimizes the authority and practices of dominant groups and allows them to achieve their own interests at the expense of less powerful groups. In this view, crime also serves the interest of dominant groups. It deflects the attention of subordinate group members from the many problems that dominant groups create for them and turns that attention to subordinate group members who are defined as criminal.

All behavior, including criminal behavior, in this view, occurs because people act in ways consistent with their social positions. Whether white-collar crime or ordinary street crime, crime is a response to a person's social situation. The reason members of subordinate groups appear in official criminal statistics more frequently than members of dominant groups is that the dominant groups have more control over the definition of criminality. Thus they are better able to ensure that the responses of subordinate group members to their social situations will be defined and reacted to as criminal. For

Explaining Crime CHAPTER 3

power differentials
The ability of some groups to dominate other groups in a society.

relative powerlessness
In conflict theory, the inability to dominate other groups in society.

Karz Marx

In an article entitled "Population, Crime and Pauperism," which appeared in the *New York Daily News* on September 16, 1859, Karl Marx observed that "there must be something rotten in the very core of a social system which increases its wealth without decreasing its misery; and increases in crimes even more than in numbers."

radical theories
Theories of crime causation that are generally based on a Marxist theory of class struggle.

conflict theorists, the amount of crime in a society is a function of the extent of conflict generated by **power differentials**, or the ability of some groups to dominate other groups in that society. Crime, in short, is caused by **relative powerlessness**, the inability to dominate other groups.

There are two principal policy implications of conflict theory. One is for dominant groups to give up some of their power to subordinate groups, making the weaker more powerful and reducing conflict. Increasing equality in that way might be accomplished by redistributing wealth through a more progressive tax system, for example. Another way to increase equality, at least in the political arena, would be to strictly limit or eliminate altogether the contributions of wealthy people and corporations to political candidates. The other policy implication is for dominant group members to become more effective rulers and subordinate group members better subjects. To do so, dominant group members would have to do a better job of convincing subordinate group members that the current unfair distribution of power in society is in their mutual interests.

A problem with conflict theory is that it generally fails to specify the sources of power in society. When those sources are identified, they are usually attributed to the personal characteristics of elites; that is, people with power are said to be smarter, better educated, luckier, and better able to defer gratification. Conflict theorists seem to ignore that power in society comes primarily from the ownership of private property.

Another criticism of conflict theory is that it is basically reformist in its policy implications. Conflict theorists generally assume that crime, as well as other social problems, can be corrected by existing social institutions. For example, if only the agencies of criminal justice were more effective, a conflict theorist might argue, crime would be reduced greatly. Historical evidence suggests that this assumption may not be true.

Radical Theory

The social and political turmoil in the United States during the 1960s and 1970s created a renewed interest in Marxist theory. Although Karl Marx wrote very little about crime and criminal justice, **radical theories** of crime causation are generally based on Marx's ideas. Among the first criminologists in the United States to employ Marxist theory to explain crime and justice were Richard Quinney, William J. Chambliss, and Anthony M. Platt.

Radical criminologists argue that *capitalism* is an economic system that requires people to compete against each other in the individualistic pursuit of material wealth. A defining characteristic of a capitalist society is that a very small percentage of people are the big winners in the competitive struggle for material wealth. Figure 3–8 shows the distribution of income (a proxy for wealth) in the United States in 1998.

The winners do everything in their considerable power to keep from becoming losers, including taking advantage of other people, preying on them. Their power is considerable, by virtue of their ownership of material wealth. (The really big winners are members of the *ruling class*.) Losers, relatively speaking, members of the *working class* and the *nonworking class*—in an effort to become winners, usually do what the winners do: prey on weaker people. Radical

FIGURE 3–8

Distribution of 1998 Income in the United States Received by Each Fifth of Families (Households)

Families (Households) by Fifths	Percentage of Total Income	Average Household Income[a]
Poorest fifth	3.6%	$9,223
Second fifth	3.0%	$23,288
Third fifth	15.0%	$38,967
Fourth fifth	23.2%	$60,266
Richest fifth[b]	49.2%	$127,529

a. Average income of all families (households) in 1999 = $37,000.

b. The table fails to accurately convey the inequitable distribution of income/wealth in the highest category. In 1999, there were 267 billionaires in the United States (compared to 71 billionaires in 1991). The richest individual (not household) in 1999 was William Henry Gates, III (Microsoft), whose net worth was conservatively estimated to be $85 billion ($36.4 billion in 1997). The second and third richest individuals were Paul Gardner Allen (Microsoft) worth approximately $40 billion, and Warren Edward Buffett (Berkshire Hathaway) worth about $31 billion. In the past decade, 5 million American families have achieved a net worth of at least $1 million.

SOURCE: U.S. Census Bureau, Income 1998, Table C
<www.census.gov/hhes/income/income98/in98dis.html>,
Forbes.com (July 13, 2000)
<www.forbes.com/tool/toobox/rich400/>

criminologists believe that the more unevenly wealth is distributed in a society, the more likely people are to be able to find persons weaker than themselves.

It is important to understand that for radical criminologists, the destructive effects of capitalism, such as crime, are not caused by income or property inequality or by poverty. Rather, the competition among wealthy people and among poor people and between rich and poor people—the **class struggle** — and the practice of taking advantage of other people cause crime. They also cause income or property inequality, poverty, many of the other problems that are characteristic of a capitalist society. Crime in capitalist societies is a rational response to the circumstances in which people find themselves in the competitive class struggle to acquire material wealth. "Senseless" violent crime, which is most often committed by poor people against each other, is frequently a product of the demoralizing and brutalizing conditions under which many people are forced to live.

Radical criminologists argue that noncapitalist societies should have different types of crime and much lower rates of crime, as traditionally defined, "because the less intense class struggle should reduce the forces leading to and the functions of crime."[40]

class struggle
For radical criminologists, the competition among wealthy people and among poor people and between rich people and poor people, which causes crime.

Radical criminologists also define crime as a violation of human rights. As Tony Platt explains:

> A radical perspective defines crime as a violation of politically defined human rights: the truly egalitarian rights to decent food and shelter, to human dignity and self-determination, rather than the so-called right to compete for an unequal share of wealth and power.[41]

A radical definition of crime includes "imperialism, racism, capitalism, sexism and other systems of exploitation which contribute to human misery and deprive people of their human potentiality."[42] Although many behaviors currently proscribed by criminal law would be included in this radical definition, other behaviors now considered crimes would be excluded, such as prostitution, gambling, and drug use, and some behaviors not now considered crimes would be added, such as racism, sexism, and imperialism.

Consequently, the policy implications of radical theory include demonstrating that the current legal definition of crime supports the ruling class in a capitalist system and redefining crime as the violation of human rights. For nearly all radical criminologists—anarchists are exceptions—the solution to the crime problem is a benevolent socialist society governed by democratically elected representatives of the population. Arguably the biggest difference between the envisioned socialist society and the current capitalist society in the United States is that governments in the socialist society would regulate the economy to promote public welfare. Governments in capitalist America regulate the economy to promote the accumulation of material wealth by individuals. Radical criminologists stress that the difference is primarily a matter of priorities. Some accumulation of private material wealth would probably exist in the socialist society, and even capitalist America provides for the public welfare through such socialistic programs as Social Security, Medicare, and Medicaid. Another important difference between the two societies is that in the socialist society, human diversity in all areas of life would be not only tolerated but also appreciated by government agents (and, one would hope, by the rest of society). In the socialist society, the criminal law would be based on a slightly modified version of the positive sanction of the classical school: that every member of society has a right to do anything that is not prohibited by law without fearing anything but natural consequences. Acts prohibited by law would be those that violate basic human rights or the public welfare, interpreted as liberally as possible. The recognition of "hate crimes" by federal legislation in the United States is an example of an attempt to protect human diversity.

Radical criminologists maintain that creating such a socialist society would first require the development of political awareness among all people disadvantaged by the capitalist system. Such people must be made aware that they are in a class struggle. Once enough people are aware, according to radical criminologists, then only through *praxis* (human action based on theoretical understanding) will the new socialist society be achieved.

One objection to radical theory is that the radical definition of crime as the violation of human rights is itself too broad and vague. Although radical criminologists concede that it may be difficult to determine what a human right is, they generally assume that most people know when a human right has been violated.

Other criticisms of radical theory are that its adherents are pursuing a political agenda and thus are not objective in their work; that its causal

Utopians

Early socialists criticized the rise of industry as the cause of great hardship among working people. During the early 1800s, socialists, who were sometimes called *utopians*, tried to foster communities with ideal social and economic conditions. Their name came from Sir Thomas More's *Utopia*, published in England in 1516. More's book describes an ideal society, with justice and equality for all citizens.

model is wrong, that is, that social arrangements do not cause people to commit crime, as radical theorists argue, but rather that crime is committed by people who are born evil and remain evil; that it has not been tested satisfactorily; that it cannot be tested satisfactorily; and that it is utopian in its policy implications.

Other Critical Theories

The law-and-order climate of the 1980s and 1990s was not a period in which critical theories of crime causation received much attention from government bureaucrats and criminal justice practitioners. Nevertheless, critical scholars continued to produce and to refine critical analyses of government efforts to understand and to address the crime problem. In this subsection we will briefly describe some of the new directions taken by critical theorists. These descriptions will show the diversity of current critical thought.

British or Left Realism   The focus of many critical criminologists has been on crimes committed by the powerful. While pursuing that area of study, however, they have tended either to ignore or to romanticize working-class crime and criminals. By the mid-1980s, a group of social scientists in Great Britain had begun to criticize that tendency and to argue that critical criminologists needed to redirect their attention to the fear and the very real victimization experienced by working-class people.[43] These **left realists** correctly observed that crimes against the working class were being perpetrated not only by the powerful but also by members of their own class. They admonished their critical colleagues to take crime seriously, especially "street crime" and domestic violence. They have argued that police power must be employed to protect people living in working-class communities. Certain versions of community policing are examples of such policy.

Left realism has been criticized for holding a contradictory position regarding the police (and other agencies of criminal justice).[44] On one hand, left realists want to give the police more power to combat crime, especially crime committed against the working class. On the other hand, they want to reduce the power of the police to intervene in people's lives and want to make the police more accountable for their actions. Another criticism of left realism is that its emphasis on the reform of criminal justice practice, rather than on radical change, makes it little different in that regard from conflict theory, classical and neoclassical theories, and many positivist theories.[45]

left realists
A group of social scientists who argue that critical criminologists need to redirect their attention to the fear and the very real victimization experienced by working-class people.

Peacemaking Criminology   This perspective rejects the idea that predatory criminal violence can be reduced by repressive state violence. In this view, "wars" on crime only make matters worse. Consisting of a mixture of anarchism, humanism, socialism, and Native American and Eastern philosophies, **peacemaking criminology** suggests that the solutions to all social problems, including crime, are the transformation of human beings, mutual dependence, reduction of class structures, the creation of communities of caring people, and universal social justice. For peacemaking criminologists, crime is suffering, and, therefore, to reduce crime, suffering must be reduced.[46] Policy emphasis is placed on the transformation of human beings through an inner rebirth or spiritual rejuvenation (inner peace) that enables individuals to experience empathy with those less fortunate and a desire to respond to the needs of other people.

peacemaking criminology
An approach that suggests that the solutions to all social problems, including crime, are the transformation of human beings, mutual dependence, reduction of class structures, the creation of communities of caring people, and universal social justice.

▲ Peacemaking criminology advocates restorative justice, compassion, and community action. *Do you think this theory could have a positive impact on juvenile justice? Explain.*

Peacemaking criminology has been criticized for its extreme idealism and its emphasis on the transformation of individuals as a way of transforming society rather than on the transformation of society as a way of transforming individuals.

Feminist Theory   Although feminism is not new, the application of feminist theory to the study of crime is.[47] Recognizing that the study of crime has always been male-centered, feminist criminologists seek a feminine perspective. Specifically, the focus of **feminist theory** is on women's experiences and ways of knowing because, in the past, men's experiences have been taken as the norm and generalized to the population. As a result, women and girls have been omitted almost entirely from theories of crime and delinquency.

Three areas of crime and justice have commanded most of the attention of feminist theorists: (1) the victimization of women, (2) gender differences in crime, and (3) *gendered justice*, that is, differing treatment of female and male offenders and victims by the agencies and agents of criminal justice. Regarding gender differences in crime, two questions seem to dominate: (1) Do explanations of male criminality apply to women? (2) Why are women less likely than men to engage in crime?

Not all feminists share the same perspective on the issues noted. At least four different types of feminist thought have been identified: liberal, radical, Marxist, and socialist. (Conspicuously omitted from this typology are women of color, whose gender and race place them in a uniquely disadvantaged position.) Radical, Marxist, and socialist feminist thought share, to varying degrees, a belief that the problems of women, including female victimization, lie in the institution of **patriarchy**, men's control over women's labor and sexuality. The principal goal of most feminist theory is to abolish patriarchal relationships by, among other things, ensuring women equal opportunity and equal rights.

One of the principal criticisms of feminist criminology is the focus on gender as a central organizing theme. Such a focus fails to appreciate differences among women—for example, as noted previously, differences between the experiences of black women and white women.[48] Another problem similar to

feminist theory

A perspective on criminality that focuses on women's experiences and seeks to abolish men's control over women's labor and sexuality.

patriarchy

Men's control over women's labor and sexuality.

the one associated with left realism, is many feminists' contradictory position regarding the police (and the criminal justice system in general). On one hand, several feminists call for greater use of the police to better protect women from abuse; on the other hand, some feminists concede that giving more power to the police, under present circumstances, will only lead to further discrimination and harassment of minority males and females.[49] A similar contradictory position is held by many feminists toward using the law to improve gender relations. The law, after all, is almost entirely the product of white males.

Postmodernism   Postmodernism originated in the late 1960s as a rejection of the "modern" or Enlightenment belief in scientific rationality as the route to knowledge and progress. Among the goals of this area of critical thought are to understand the creation of knowledge, and how knowledge and language create hierarchy and domination. Postmodernist ideas began to be introduced in law and criminology during the late 1980s.[50] As applied to the area of crime and criminal justice, the major foci have been critical analyses of the privileged position of "the Law" and the construction of crime theories.

With regard to "the Law," postmodernist criminologists reject the idea "that there is only one true interpretation of a law or for that matter the U.S. Constitution."[51] They argue, instead, that there is a plurality of interpretations that are dependent, in part, on the particular social context in which they arise. As in other critical criminologies, the law, from a postmodernist view, always has a human author and a political agenda.[52] As for crime theories, postmodernist criminologists typically abandon the usual notion of causation. From the postmodernist perspective:

> Crime is seen to be the culmination of certain processes that allow persons to believe that they are somehow not connected to other humans and society. These processes place others into categories or stereotypes and make them different or alien, denying them their humanity. These processes result in the denial of responsibility for other people and to other people.[53]

Postmodernist criminologists would, among other things, replace the prevailing description of the world with new conceptions, words, and phrases, which convey alternative meanings, as Sutherland did when he introduced the concept of "white-collar crime." These new descriptions would tell different stories about the world as experienced by historically subjugated people.[54] Postmodernist criminologists would also replace the formal criminal justice apparatus with informal social controls so that the current functions of criminal justice are handled by local groups and local communities.[55] This strategy is consistent with the one advocated by peacemaking criminologists. Postmodernist criminology has been criticized for its relativism and subjectivism or for being an "anarchy of knowledge": "If truth is not possible, how can we decide anything?"[56]

NVAW Rape Survey

In a victimization survey informed by feminist ideas–The National Violence Against Women survey (NVAW)–researchers found, among other things, that in 1995 and 1996, there were more rapes committed in the United States than were reported by the Bureau of Justice Statistics in the National Crime Victimization Survey (NCVS). Among the findings of the NVAW was that 1 of every 6 U.S. women and 1 of every 33 U.S. men has experienced an attempted or completed rape as a child and/or an adult. Put differently, 18 percent of surveyed women and 3 percent of surveyed men said they experienced a completed or attempted rape at some time in their life. Rape was defined as forced vaginal, oral, and anal sex.

SOURCE: Patricia Tjaden and Nancy Thoennes, "Prevalence, Incidence, and Consequences of Violence Against Women: Findings From the National Violence Against Women Survey," *National Institute of Justice, Centers for Disease Control and Prevention, Research in Brief* (Washington, DC: GPO, November 1998).

postmodernism
An area of critical thought which, among other things, attempts to understand the creation of knowledge, and how knowledge and language create hierarchy and domination.

3.4 CRITICAL THINKING

1. How would you explain labeling theory?

2. What is peacemaking criminology? Is this theory realistic?

3. Explain feminist theory and its key criticisms.

Review and Applications

SUMMARY BY CHAPTER OBJECTIVES

1. Define Criminological Theory

Criminological theory is the explanation of the behavior of criminal offenders, as well as the behavior of police, attorneys, prosecutors, judges, correctional personnel, victims, and other actors in the criminal justice process. It helps us understand criminal behavior and the basis of policies proposed and implemented to prevent and control crime.

2. State the Causes of Crime According to Classical and Neoclassical Criminologists

Classical and neoclassical criminologists theorize that human beings are free-willed individuals who commit crime when they rationally calculate that the crime will give them more pleasure than pain. In an effort to deter crime, classical criminologists advocate the following policies: (1) establish a social contract, (2) enact laws that are clear, simple, unbiased, and reflect the consensus of the population, (3) impose punishments that are proportionate to the crime, prompt, certain, public, necessary, the least possible in the given circumstances, and dictated by law rather than by judges' discretion, (4) educate the public, (5) eliminate corruption from the administration of justice, and (6) reward virtue. Neoclassical criminologists introduced the concepts that mitigating circumstances might inhibit the exercises of free will and that punishment should be rehabilitative.

3. Describe the Biological Theories of Crime Causation and Their Policy Implications

The basic cause of crime for biological positivists has been biological inferiority, which is indicated by physical or genetic characteristics that distinguish criminals from noncriminals. The policy implications of biological theories of crime causation include a choice of isolation, sterilization, or execution. Biological theorists also advocate brain surgery, chemical treatment, improved diets, and better mother and child care.

4. Describe the Different Psychological Theories of Crime Causation

According to psychological theories, crime results from individuals' mental or emotional disturbances, inability to empathize with others, inability to legally satisfy their basic needs, or oppressive circumstances of life. To combat crime, psychological positivists would isolate, sterilize, or execute offenders not amenable to treatment. For treatable offenders, psychotherapy or psychoanalysis may prove effective. Other policy implications are to help people satisfy their basic needs legally, to eliminate sources of oppression, and to provide legal ways of coping with oppression.

5. Explain Sociological Theories of Crime Causation

Sociological theories propose that crime is caused by *anomie*, or the dissociation of the individual from the *collective conscience*; by *social disorganization*; by *anomie* resulting from a lack of opportunity to achieve aspirations; by the learning of criminal values and behaviors; and by the failure to properly socialize individuals. Among the policy implications of sociological theories of crime causation are containing crime within reasonable boundaries; organizing and empowering neighborhood residents; reducing aspirations, increasing legitimate opportunities; providing law-abiding models, regulating associations, eliminating crime's rewards, rewarding law-abiding behavior, punishing criminal behavior effectively; and properly socializing children so that they develop self-control and a strong moral bond to society.

6. Distinguish Major Differences Among Classical, Positivist, and Critical Theories of Crime Causation

Unlike classical theories, which assume that human beings have free will, and positivist theories, which assume that human beings are determined, critical theories assume that human beings are both determined and determining. In contrast to both classical and positivist theories, which assume that society is characterized primarily by consensus over moral values, critical theories assume that society is characterized primarily by conflict over moral values. Finally, unlike positivist theorists, who assume that social scientists can be objective or value-neutral in their work, many critical theorists assume that everything they do is value-laden by virtue of their being human, that it is impossible to be objective.

7. Describe How Critical Theorists Would Explain the Causes of Crime

Depending on their perspective, critical theorists explain crime as the result of labeling and stigmatization; of relative powerlessness, the class struggle, and the practice of taking advantage of other people; or of patriarchy. Those who support labeling theory would address crime by avoiding labeling people as criminals or by employing radical nonintervention or reintegrative shaming. Conflict theorists would address crime by having dominant groups give up some of their power to subordinate groups or having dominant group members become more effective rulers

and subordinate group members better subjects. Radical theorists would define crime as a violation of basic human rights, replace the criminal justice system with popular or socialist justice, and (except for anarchists) would create a socialist society appreciative of human diversity. Left realists would use police power to protect people living in working-class communities. Peacemaking criminologists would transform human beings so that they were able to empathize with those less fortunate and respond to other people's needs, would reduce hierarchical structures, would create communities of caring people, and would champion universal social justice. Feminist theorists would address crime by eliminating patriarchal structures and relationships and promoting greater equality for women. Postmodernist criminologists would replace the prevailing description of the world with new conceptions, words, and phrases, which convey alternative meanings, as experienced by historically subjugated people. They would also replace the formal criminal justice system with informal social controls handled by local groups and local communities.

KEY TERMS

theory, p. 70
criminological theory, p. 70
classical theory, p. 73
utility, p. 74
social contract, p. 74
special or specific deterrence, p. 74
general deterrence, p. 74
neoclassical theory, p. 75
biological inferiority, p. 78
criminal anthropology, p. 78
atavist, p. 78
limbic system, p. 81
psychopaths, p. 84

sociopaths, p. 84
antisocial personalities, p. 84
anomie (Durkheim), p. 88
collective conscience, p. 88
Chicago School, p. 89
social disorganization, p. 89
anomie (Merton), p. 90
imitation or modeling, p. 92
differential association, p. 93
learning theory, p. 94
positive reinforcement, p. 94
negative reinforcement, p. 94
extinction, p. 94
punishment, p. 94

social control theory, p. 95
labeling theory, p. 97
criminalization process, p. 97
conflict theory, p. 98
power differentials, p. 100
relative powerlessness, p. 100
radical theories, p. 100
class struggle, p. 101
left realists, p. 103
peacemaking criminology, p. 103
feminist theory, p. 104
patriarchy, p. 104
postmodernism, p. 105

QUESTIONS FOR REVIEW

1. What are two undesirable consequences of the failure to understand the theoretical basis of criminal justice policies?
2. Before the Enlightenment and classical theory, what was generally believed to be the cause of crime?
3. Who was arguably the best known and most influential of the classical criminologists, and how did his ideas become known?
4. What is the difference between special or specific deterrence and general deterrence?
5. What are five problems with positivist theories?
6. What is the position held by most criminologists today regarding the relationship between biology and crime?
7. What does research indicate about the relationship between intelligence and both juvenile delinquency and adult criminality?
8. What are problems with psychological or psychoanalytic theories of crime and their policy implications?
9. In what ways did Durkheim believe that crime was functional for society?
10. What is a potential problem with the theory of the Chicago School?
11. What is a criticism of most anomie theories?
12. Who was the first twentieth-century criminologist to argue forcefully that crime was learned, and what is his theory called?
13. What is arguably the major problem with control theory?
14. What is *secondary deviance*, and how does it occur, according to labeling theorists?
15. What are major criticisms of conflict theory? The radical theory?
16. What contributions to criminological theory have been made by British or left realism, peacemaking criminology, feminist theory, and postmodernism?

EXPERIENTIAL ACTIVITIES

1. **Professional Perspectives on Crime** Interview representatives of the criminal justice process—a police officer, a prosecutor, a defense attorney, a judge, a correctional officer, and a probation or parole officer. Ask each to explain why crimes are committed. Ask them how they would prevent or reduce crime. After completing the interviews, identify the theories and policy implications described in the textbook that best correspond to their responses. Explain any differences in responses that emerged. Present your findings in a brief written report.
2. **Literary Perspectives on Crime** Read a nonfiction book about crime. Explain the criminal behavior, orally or in writing, using the theories in this chapter. Some good books are Truman Capote's *In Cold Blood*, Vincent Bugliosi's *Helter Skelter*, and Norman Mailer's *The Executioner's Song*.
3. **Explaining Crimes** Select several crimes from Figure 2–1 on page 37 and explain them by using the theories in Chapter 3.

INTERNET

4. **Comparing Crime Rates** Use the Internet to research crime rates of several capitalist and noncapitalist countries. (Remember that crime rates, as discussed in Chapter 2, are not accurate measures of the true amount of crime.) Then write a paragraph in which you support or oppose the proposition that capitalist countries have higher crime rates than noncapitalist countries.
5. **Criminologists** Use the links at cj.glencoe.com to learn more about professional, mostly academic criminologists. Read about the history of the American Society of Criminology. Examine the annual meeting information to see the topics on which criminologists are currently working. Explore specialty areas in criminology. Scan employment information to discover the types of jobs available.

1. **The Dahmer Case** Jeffrey Dahmer, a white male, was sentenced to 936 years in prison (Wisconsin had no death penalty) for the murder and dismemberment of 15 young males—mostly black and homosexual—in Milwaukee, Wisconsin.

   Dahmer was arrested without a struggle at his apartment on Milwaukee's crime-infested west side in August, 1991, after one of his victims had escaped and notified the police. Dahmer was 31 years old and had recently been fired from his job at a chocolate factory. He immediately confessed to 11 murders. He told the police that he lured men from bars and shopping malls by promising them money to pose for pictures. He would then take them to his apartment, drug them, strangle them, and dismember their bodies. He boiled the heads of some of his victims to remove the flesh and had sex with the cadaver of at least one of them. Police found rotting body parts lying around his apartment, along with bottles of acid and chemical preservatives. Photographs of mutilated men were on a freezer that contained two severed heads. Another severed head was in the refrigerator. Dahmer told the police that he had saved a heart to eat later.

   Dahmer's stepmother told the press that as a child, he liked to use acid to scrape the meat of dead animals. When he was 18, his parents divorced. He lived with his mother until, one day, she took his little brother and disappeared, leaving him alone. He went to live with his grandmother, where he started to abuse alcohol. During the six years he lived with his grandmother, mysterious things were occurring in the basement and garage. Dahmer's father, a chemist, discovered bones and other body parts in containers. Dahmer told his father that he had been stripping the flesh from animals he found.

   In 1988, Dahmer spent ten months in prison for fondling a 13-year-old Laotian boy. On his release from prison, he was placed on probation, but his probation officer never visited him.

   Dahmer's defense attorney claimed that his client was insane at the time of the murders. The jury rejected the insanity defense.

   a. Which theory or theories of crime causation described in this chapter best explain Jeffrey Dahmer's criminal behavior?

   b. What crime prevention and correctional policies described in this chapter should be employed with criminal offenders like Jeffrey Dahmer?

2. **Breaking the Law** Stacey Raines drives from Indianapolis to Fort Wayne, Indiana, twice a month as part of her job as a sales representative for a pharmaceutical company. Although the posted speed limit is 65 miles per hour, Stacey generally cruises at 80 to 85, intentionally exceeding the speed limit.

   a. Which theory or theories of crime causation described in this chapter best explain the behavior of intentional speeders?

   b. What crime prevention and correctional policies described in this chapter should be used with intentional speeders?

ADDITIONAL READING

Beccaria, Cesare. *On Crimes and Punishments*. Translated, with an introduction by Harry Paolucci. Indianapolis: Bobbs-Merrill, 1975.

Bohm, Robert M. "Radical Criminology: An Explication." *Criminology*, Vol. 19 (1982), pp. 565–89.

Bohm, Robert M. *A Primer on Crime and Delinquency Theory*. 2d ed. Belmont, CA: Wadsworth, 2001.

Cullen, Francis T. and Robert Agnew. *Criminological Theory: Past to Present*. Los Angeles, CA: Roxbury, 1999.

Currie, Elliott. *Confronting Crime: An American Challenge*. New York: Pantheon, 1985.

Daly, Kathleen and Meda Chesney-Lind. "Feminism and Criminology." *Justice Quarterly*, Vol. 5 (1988), pp. 497–538.

Davis, Nanette J. *Sociological Constructions of Deviance: Perspectives and Issues in the Field*, 2d ed. Dubuque, IA: Wm. C. Brown, 1980.

DeKeseredy, Walter S. and Martin D. Schwartz. *Contemporary Criminology*. Belmont, CA: Wadsworth, 1996.

Fishbein, Diana H. "Biological Perspectives in Criminology." *Criminology*, Vol. 28 (1990), pp. 27–72.

Gould, Stephen Jay. *The Mismeasure of Man*. New York: Norton, 1981.

Jones, David A. *History of Criminology*. Westport, CT: Greenwood, 1987.

Lynch, Michael J. and W. Byron Groves. *A Primer in Radical Criminology*, 2d ed. New York: Harrow and Heston, 1989.

Michalowski, Raymond J. *Order, Law, and Crime: An Introduction to Criminology*. New York: Random House, 1985.

Simpson, Sally S. "Feminist Theory, Crime, and Justice." *Criminology*, Vol. 27 (1989), pp. 605–31.

Sutherland, Edwin H. and Donald R. Cressey. *Criminology*, 9th ed. Philadelphia: J. B. Lippincort, 1974.

Taylor, Ian, Paul Walton, and Jock Young. *The New Criminology: For a Social Theory of Deviance*. New York: Harper and Row, 1974.

Vold, George B., Thomas J. Bernard, and Jeffrey B. Snipes. *Theoretical Criminology*, 4th ed. New York: Oxford, 1997.

Williams, Frank P. III and Marilyn D. McShane. *Criminological Theory: Selected Classic Readings*, 2d ed. Cincinnati: Anderson, 1998.

ENDNOTES

1. Cesare Beccaria, *An Essay on Crimes and Punishments*, trans., with introduction, by Harry Paolucci. (Indianapolis: Bobbs-Merrill, 1975), p. ix.
2. Ibid., p. 8.
3. Ibid., p. 42.
4. Ibid., p. 99.
5. Beccaria, op. cit.
6. See Irving M. Zeitlin, *Ideology and the Development of Sociological Theory*, 3d ed. (Englewood Cliffs, NJ: Prentice Hall, 1987).
7. See Ian Taylor, Paul Walton, and Jock Young, *The New Criminology: For a Social Theory of Deviance*. (New York: Harper and Row, 1974), pp. 24–32.
8. George B. Vold and Thomas J. Bernard, *Theoretical Criminology*, 3d ed. (New York: Oxford, 1986), p. 48.
9. See William H. Sheldon, *Varieties of Delinquent Youth*. (New York: Harper, 1949).
10. Diana H. Fishbein, *The Science, Treatment, and Prevention of Antisocial Behaviors: Application to the Criminal Justice System*. (Kingston, NJ: Civic Research Institute, 2000).
11. See Diana H. Fishbein "Biological Perspectives in Criminology." *Criminology*, Vol. 28 (1990), pp. 27–72. Vold and Bernard, op. cit., pp. 87–92; Daniel J. Curran and Claire

M. Renzetti, *Theories of Crime*. (Boston: Ally and Bacon, 1994), pp. 54–63; James Q. Wilson and Richard J. Herrnstein, *Crime and Human Nature*. (New York: Simon & Schuster, 1985), pp. 75–81, 90–100.
12. See Curran and Renzetti, op. cit., p. 78; Fishbein, op. cit., pp. 38, 47.
13. See National Institute, *ibid.*, pp. 120–122,; Vold and Bernard, op. cit., pp. 101–103.
14. See Fishbein, *ibid.*, pp. 48, 53; National Institute, op. cit.; Curran and Renzetti, *ibid.*, pp. 73–77, 80–81.
15. Edwin H. Sutherland and Donald R. Cressey, *Criminology*, 9th ed. (Philadelphia: J. B. Lippincott, 1974), p. 152.
16. Robert Gordon, "Prevalence: The Rare Datum in Delinquency Measurement and Its Implications for the Theory of Delinquency," in Malcolm W. Klein (ed.), *The Juvenile Justice System*. (Beverly Hills, CA: Sage, 1976), pp. 201–84; Travis Hirschi and Michael J. Hindelang, "Intelligence and Delinquency: A Revisionist Review," *American Sociological Review*, Vol. 42 (1977), pp. 572–87.
17. See Robert S. Woodworth and Mary R. Sheehan, *Contemporary Schools of Psychology*, 3d ed. (New York: The Ronald Press Co., 1964).

18. Walter Bromberg and Charles B. Thompson, "The Relation of Psychosis, Mental Defect, and Personality Types to Crime," *Journal of Criminal Law and Criminology,* Vol. 28 (1937), pp. 70–89; Karl F. Schuessler and Donald R. Cressey, "Personality Characteristics of Criminals," *American Journal of Sociology,* Vol. 55 (1950), pp. 476–84; Gordon P. Waldo and Simon Dinitz, "Personality Attributes of the Criminal: An Analysis of Research Studies, 1950–1965," *Journal of Research in Crime and Delinquency,* Vol. 4 (1967), pp. 185–202; John Monahan and Henry J. Steadman, "Crime and Mental Disorder: An Epidemiological Approach," in Michael Tonry and Norval Morris (eds.), *Crime and Justice,* Vol. 4 (Chicago: University of Chicago Press, 1983).

19. Abraham H. Maslow, *Motivation and Personality,* 2d ed. (New York: Harper and Row, 1970).

20. Seymore L. Halleck, *Psychiatry and the Dilemmas of Crime.* (New York: Harper and Row, 1967).

21. Emile Durkheim, *Rules of Sociological Method.* (New York: Free Press, 1964).

22. Vold and Bernard, op. cit., p. 160.

23. Robert E. Park, Ernest Burgess, and Roderick D. McKenzie, *The City.* (Chicago: University of Chicago Press, 1928).

24. Clifford R. Shaw, *Delinquency Areas.* (Chicago: University of Chicago Press, 1929); Clifford R. Shaw and Henry D. McKay, *Social Factors in Juvenile Delinquency.* (Chicago: University of Chicago Press, 1931); Clifford R. Shaw and Henry D. McKay, *Juvenile Delinquency and Urban Areas.* (Chicago: University of Chicago Press, 1942).

25. Clifford R. Shaw, *The Jackroller.* (Chicago: University of Chicago Press, 1930); Clifford R. Shaw, *The National History of Delinquent Career.* (Chicago: University of Chicago Press, 1931); Clifford R. Shaw, *Brothers in Crime.* (Chicago: University of Chicago Press, 1938).

26. Robert K. Merton, "Social Structure and Anomie," *American Sociological Review,* Vol. 3 (1938), pp. 672–82.

27. Albert K. Cohen, *Delinquent Boys: The Culture of the Gang.* (New York: Free Press, 1960).

28. Richard A Cloward and Lloyd E Ohlin, *Delinquency and Opportunity: A Theory of Delinquent Gangs.* (New York: Free Press, 1960).

29. See, for example, Albert Bandura, *Social Learning Theory.* (Englewood Cliffs, NJ: Prentice Hall, 1977).

30. See, for example, Edwin H. Sutherland and Donald R. Cressey, *Criminology,* 9th ed. (Philadelphia: J. B. Lippincott, 1974).

31. Daniel Glaser, "Criminality Theories and Behavioral Images," *American Journal of Sociology,* Vol. 61 (1956). pp. 433–44.

32. Definitions of learning theory concepts are from Howard Rachlin, *Introduction to Modern Behaviorism,* 2d ed. (San Francisco: W. H. Freeman, 1976).

33. Michael R. Gottfredson and Travis Hirschi, *A General Theory of Crime.* (Stanford, CA: Stanford University Press, 1990).

34. Edwin Lemert, *Social Pathology: A Systematic Approach to the Theory of Sociopathic Behavior.* (New York: McGraw-Hill, 1951).

35. See Edwin M. Schur, *Radical Nonintervention.* (Englewood Cliffs, NT: Prentice Hall, 1973).

36. Robert J. Lilly, Francis T. Cullen, and Richard A. Ball, *Criminological Theory: Context and Consequences.* (Newbury Park, CA: Sage, 1989), pp. 131–135.

37. John Braithwaite, *Crime, Shame and Reintegration.* (Cambridge: Cambridge University Press, 1989).

38. Vold and Bernard, op. cit., p. 256.

39. George B. Vold, *Theoretical Criminology.* (New York: Oxford, 1958).

40. William J. Chambliss, "Functional and Conflict Theories of Crime: The Heritage of Emile Durkheim and Karl Marx," in W. J. Chambliss and M. Mankoff (eds.), *Whose Law, What Order?* (New York: Wiley, 1976), p. 9.

41. Tony Platt, "Prospects for a Radical Criminology in the USA," in I. Taylor et al. (eds.), *Critical Criminology* (Boston: Routledge & Kegan Paul, 1975), p. 103.

42. *Ibid.;* for a similar definition, see also Herman Schwendinger and Julia Schwendinger, "Defenders of Order or Guardians of Human Rights?" in I. Taylor et al. (eds.), *Critical Criminology,* pp. 113–46.

43. See, for example, Richard Kinsey, John Lea, and Jock Young, *Losing the Fight Against Crime.* (London: Basil Blackwell, 1976); Roger Matthews and Jock Young (eds.), *Confronting Crime.* (London: Sage, 1986).

44. Werner Einstadter and Stuart Henry, *Criminological Theory: An Analysis of Its Underlying Assumptions.* (Fort Worth, TX: Harcourt Brace, 1995), p. 256.

45. Ibid., p. 257.

46. See Harold E. Pepinsky and Richard Quinney (eds.), *Criminology as Peacemaking.* (Bloomington: Indiana University Press, 1991).

47. For two excellent reviews, see Kathleen Daly and Meda Chesney–Lind, "Feminism and Criminology," *Justice Quarterly,* Vol. 5 (1988), pp. 497–538; Sally S. Simpson, "Feminist Theory, Crime, and Justice," *Criminology,* Vol. 27 (1989), pp. 605–31.

48. See Einstadter and Henry, op. cit., p. 275.

49. Ibid.

50. Einstadter and Henry, op. cit., p. 278.

51. Einstadter and Henry, op. cit., p. 287.

52. Bruce Arrigo and T.R. Young,"Chaos, Complexity, and Crime: Working Tools for a Postmodern Criminology," in B.D. MacLean and D. Milovanovic (eds.), *Thinking Critically About Crime.* (Vancouver, BC: Collective Press, 1997), p. 77.

53. Einstadter and Henry, op. cit., p. 291.

54. Arrigo and Young, op. cit., pp. 81–2; Stuart Henry and Dragan Milovanovic, *Constitutive Criminology: Beyond Postmodernism.* (London: Sage, 1996).

55. Einstadter and Henry, op. cit., p. 294.

56. Einstadter and Henry, op. cit., p. 280.

Chapter 4

The Rule of Law

CHAPTER OBJECTIVES

After completing this chapter, you should be able to:

1. Distinguish between criminal law and civil law.

2. Distinguish between substantive law and procedural law.

3. List five features of "good" criminal laws.

4. Explain why criminal law is a political phenomenon.

5. Summarize the origins of American criminal law.

6. Relate the role of the courts in defining procedural rights.

7. Describe the procedural rights in the Fourth Amendment.

8. Describe the procedural rights in the Fifth Amendment.

9. Describe the procedural rights in the Sixth Amendment.

10. Describe the procedural rights in the Eighth Amendment.

11. Explain why procedural rights are important to those accused of crimes.

criminal law
One of two general types of law practiced in the United States (the other is civil law); "a formal means of social control [that uses] rules . . . interpreted [and enforced] by the courts . . . to set limits to the conduct of the citizens, to guide the officials, and to define . . . unacceptable behavior."

penal code
The criminal law of a political jurisdiction.

tort
A violation of the civil law.

civil law
One of two general types of law practiced in the United States (the other is criminal law); a means of resolving conflicts between individuals. It includes personal injury claims (torts), the law of contracts and property, and subjects such as administrative law and the regulation of public utilities.

substantive law
The body of law that defines criminal offenses and their penalties.

procedural law
The body of law that governs the ways substantive laws are administered; sometimes called *adjective* or *remedial* law.

4.1 Two Types of Law: Criminal Law and Civil Law

As discussed in Chapter 2, the conventional, though not necessarily the best, definition of *crime* is "a violation of the criminal law." **Criminal law** is one of two general types of law practiced in the United States; the other is civil law. Criminal law is:

> a formal means of social control [that] involves the use of rules that are interpreted, and are enforceable, by the courts of a political community. . . . The function of the rules is to set limits to the conduct of the citizens, to guide the officials (police and other administrators), and to define conditions of deviance or unacceptable behavior.[1]

The purpose of criminal justice is to enforce the criminal law.

A crime, as noted, is a violation of the criminal law, or of the **penal code** of a political jurisdiction. Although crime is committed against individuals, it is considered an offense against the state, that is, the political jurisdiction that enacted the law.[2] A **tort,** on the other hand, is a violation of the **civil law** and is considered a private matter between individuals. Civil law includes the law of contracts and property as well as subjects such as administrative law and the regulation of public utilities.

For legal purposes, a particular act may be considered an offense against an individual or the state or both. It is either a tort or a crime or both, depending on how it is handled. For example, a person who has committed an act of assault may be charged with a crime. If that person is convicted of the crime, the criminal court may order the offender to be imprisoned in the county jail for six months and to pay a fine of $500. Both the jail sentence and the fine are punishments, with the fine going to the state treasury (in federal court to the national treasury). The criminal court could also order the offender to pay restitution to the victim. In that case, the offender would pay the victim a sum of money either directly or indirectly, through an intermediary. In addition, the victim may sue the offender in civil court for damages, such as medical expenses or wages lost because of injury. If the offender is found liable (responsible) for the damages because he or she has committed a tort (civil courts do not "convict"), the civil court may also order the offender to compensate the victim in the amount of $500 for damage to the victim's interests. The payment of compensation in the civil case is not punishment; it is for the purpose of "making the victim whole again."

Substantive versus Procedural Law

There are two types of criminal law: substantive and procedural. **Substantive law** is the body of law that defines criminal offenses and their penalties. Substantive laws, which are found in the various penal codes, govern what people legally may and may not do. Examples of substantive laws are those that prohibit and penalize murder, rape, robbery, and other crimes. **Procedural law,** sometimes called *adjective* or *remedial* law, governs the ways in which the substantive laws are to be administered. It covers such subjects as the way suspects can legally be arrested, searched, interrogated, tried, and punished. In other words, procedural law is concerned with **due process of law,** or the rights of people suspected of or charged with crimes. The last part of this chapter is devoted to a detailed description of procedural law.

Ideal Characteristics of the Criminal Law

Legal scholars identify five features that all "good" criminal laws ideally ought to possess. To the extent that those features are absent in criminal laws, the laws can be considered "bad" laws, and bad laws do exist. The five ideal features of good criminal laws are (1) politicality, (2) specificity, (3) regularity, (4) uniformity, and (5) penal sanction (see Figure 4–1).

Politicality   **Politicality** refers to the legitimate source of criminal law. Only violations of rules made by the state (that is, the political jurisdiction that enacted the laws) are crimes. Violations of rules made by other institutions, such as families, churches, schools, and employers, may be "bad," "sinful," or "socially unacceptable," but they are not crimes because they are not prohibited by the state.

Specificity   **Specificity** refers to the scope of criminal law. Although civil law may be general in scope, criminal law should provide strict definitions of specific acts. The point is illustrated by an old case in which a person stole an airplane but was found not guilty of violating a criminal law that prohibited the taking of "self-propelled vehicles." The judge ruled that at the time the law was enacted, *vehicles* did not include airplanes. Ideally, as the Supreme Court ruled in *Papachristou v. City of Jacksonville* (1972), a statute or ordinance "is void for vagueness . . . [if] it fails to give a person of ordinary intelligence fair notice that his contemplated conduct is forbidden."

Regularity   **Regularity** is the applicability of the criminal law to all persons. Ideally, anyone who commits a crime is answerable for it, regardless of the person's social status. Thus, ideally, when criminal laws are created, they should apply not only to the women who violate them, but also to the men; not only to the poor, but also to the rich. In practice, however, this ideal feature of law has been violated. Georgia's pre-Civil War criminal laws, for example, provided for a dual system of crime and punishment, with one set of laws for "slaves and free persons of color" and another for all other persons.

due process of law
The rights of people suspected of or charged with crimes.

politicality
An ideal characteristic of criminal law, referring to its legitimate source. Only violations of rules made by the state, the political jurisdiction that enacted the laws, are crimes.

specificity
An ideal characteristic of criminal law, referring to its scope. Although civil law may be general in scope, criminal law should provide strict definitions of specific acts.

regularity
An ideal characteristic of criminal law: the applicability of the law to all persons, regardless of social status.

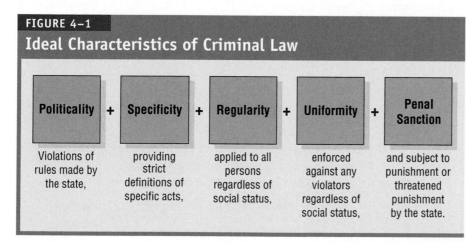

FIGURE 4–1
Ideal Characteristics of Criminal Law

Politicality	+	**Specificity**	+	**Regularity**	+	**Uniformity**	+	**Penal Sanction**
Violations of rules made by the state,		providing strict definitions of specific acts,		applied to all persons regardless of social status,		enforced against any violators regardless of social status,		and subject to punishment or threatened punishment by the state.

uniformity
An ideal characteristic of criminal law: the enforcement of the laws against anyone who violates them, regardless of social status.

penal sanction
An ideal characteristic of criminal law: the principle that violators will be punished or at least threatened with punishment by the state.

Uniformity   **Uniformity** refers to the way in which the criminal law should be enforced. Ideally, the law should be administered without regard for the social status of the persons who have committed crimes or are accused of committing crimes. Thus, when violated, criminal laws should be enforced against both young and old, both rich and poor, and so on. However, as is the case with regularity, the principle of uniformity is often violated because some people consider the strict enforcement of the law unjust in some cases. For example, juveniles who are caught misbehaving in violation of the criminal law are sometimes ignored or treated leniently through the exercise of police or judicial discretion.

Penal Sanction   The last ideal feature of criminal law is **penal sanction,** the principle that violators will be punished, or at least threatened with punishment, by the state. Conventional wisdom suggests that there would be no point in enacting criminal laws if their violation were not responded to with punishment or threat of punishment. Most people assume that sanctionless criminal laws would be ignored. Because all criminal laws carry sanctions, the power of sanctionless laws can be left to philosophers to debate. Figure 4–2 shows the five general types of penal sanctions currently used in the United States, as well as the purpose and focus of each sanction. Combining different penal sanctions in the administration of justice is not uncommon.

Criminal Law as a Political Phenomenon

People sometimes forget that criminal law is a political phenomenon, that it is created by human beings to regulate the behavior of other human beings. Some people, for example, view the criminal law as divinely inspired, something that should not be questioned or challenged. That viewpoint probably comes from a belief in the biblical story of Moses receiving the Ten

FIGURE 4–2
Five General Types of Penal Sanctions

Type	Purpose	Focus
Punishment	Prevent undesired conduct. Provide retribution ("an eye for an eye").	Offending conduct
Restitution	Make the victim "whole again" by having the offender directly or indirectly pay the victim.	Crime victim
Compensation	Make the victim "whole again" by having the state pay for damages to the victim.	Crime victim
Regulation	Control future conduct toward the best interests of the community (e.g., making it a crime or traffic violation to operate a motor vehicle with a blood alcohol content higher than a specified level).	The entire community
Treatment or rehabilitation	Change the offender's behavior and, perhaps, personality.	Criminal offender

Commandments from God on Mount Sinai. However, as critical theorists are quick to point out, criminal law frequently promotes the interests of some groups over the interests of other groups. Thus, regardless of the law's source of inspiration, it is important to understand that what gets defined as criminal or delinquent behavior is the result of a political process in which rules are created to prohibit or to require certain behaviors. Nothing is criminal or delinquent in and of itself; only the response of the state makes it so.

Origins of Laws   Formal, written laws are a relatively recent phenomenon in human existence. The first were created about 5,000 years ago. They emerged with the institutions of property, marriage, and government. "Stateless" societies apparently managed without them for two primary reasons.[3] First, most stateless societies were governed by rigid customs to which citizens strictly adhered. Second, crimes of violence were considered private matters and were usually resolved through bloody personal revenge. Formal, written laws partially replaced customs when nation-states appeared, although customs often remained the force behind the laws. Formal laws also replaced customs with the advent of writing, which allowed recorded legislation to replace the recollections of elders and priests.

The first known written laws (approximately 3000 B.C.) have been found on clay tablets among the ruins of Ur, one of the city-states of Sumeria. Attributed to King Urukagina of Lagash, the laws were truly enlightened for their time and attempted to free poor people from abuse by the rich and everybody from abuse by the priests. For example, one law forbade the high priest from coming into the garden of a poor mother and taking wood or fruit from her to pay taxes. Laws also cut burial fees to one-fifth of what they had been and forbade the clergy and high officials from sharing among themselves the cattle that were sacrificed to the gods. By 2800 B.C., the growth of trade had forced the city-states of Sumeria to merge into an empire governed by a single, all-powerful king.

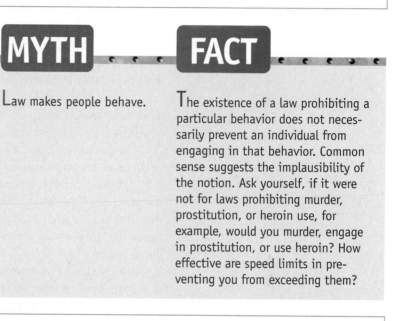

MYTH

Law makes people behave.

FACT

The existence of a law prohibiting a particular behavior does not necessarily prevent an individual from engaging in that behavior. Common sense suggests the implausibility of the notion. Ask yourself, if it were not for laws prohibiting murder, prostitution, or heroin use, for example, would you murder, engage in prostitution, or use heroin? How effective are speed limits in preventing you from exceeding them?

Around 2200 B.C., a war settlement between the Sumerians and the Akkadians produced the Babylonian civilization. Babylonia's best-known king was Hammurabi (2123–2081 B.C.), who ruled for 43 years. Hammurabi is famous for the first great code of laws. The Code of Hammurabi, like the laws of Moses later, presumably was a gift from God. Hammurabi was said to have received it from the sun god, Shamash, about 2100 B.C. There was a total of 285 laws in the code, arranged under the headings of personal property, real estate, trade and business, the family, injuries, and labor. The Code of Hammurabi combined very enlightened aims, such as "to prevent the strong from oppressing the weak, . . . to enlighten the land and to further the welfare of the people," although with very barbaric punishments.

The Rule of Law   **CHAPTER 4**

All the ancient nation-states or civilizations had formal legal codes. In addition to the laws of King Urukagina of Lagash (Sumeria) and the Code of Hammurabi (Babylonia), legal codes were established by the Egyptians, the Assyrians, the Hebrews, the Persians, the Indians, the Chinese, the Greeks (especially the codes of Lycurgus, Draco, Solon, and Plato), and the Romans (for example, the Twelve Tables, the Justinian Code, and the Law of the Nations). The development and the content of those legal codes are of mostly historical interest. The criminal law of the United States, for the most part, is derived from the laws of England.

England's Contribution to American Criminal Law

Before the Norman Conquest in 1066, England was populated by Anglo-Saxon tribes that regulated themselves through custom.[4] Wars between those tribes resulted in the taking of the tribal lands of the losers by the leader of the victorious tribe, who, by force, made the newly acquired land his own private property and himself the feudal lord. By the time of the Norman Conquest, there were about eight large and relatively independent feudal landholdings. In an effort to increase their power, the feudal lords took it on themselves to dispense justice among their subjects and began to require that disputes between subjects be settled in local courts rather than by relatives, as had previously been the custom.

When William I of Normandy conquered England in 1066 and proclaimed himself king, he declared that all land, and all land-based rights, including the administration of justice, were now vested in the king. King William also rewarded the Norman noblemen who had fought with him with large grants of formerly Anglo-Saxon land.

To make the dispensing of justice a profitable enterprise for the king and to make sure the local courts remained under his control, the institution of the *eyre* was created early in the twelfth century. The eyre was composed of traveling judges who represented the king and examined the activities of the local courts.

Of particular interest to the eyre was the resolution of cases of sufficient seriousness as to warrant the forfeiture of the offender's property as punishment. The notion of forfeiture was based on the feudal doctrine that the right to own private property rested on a relationship of good faith between the landowner and his lord. The Norman kings expanded the notion of forfeiture to include any violation of the "king's peace," which enabled the king to claim forfeited property for a variety of offenses, including such minor ones as trespassing. It was the responsibility of the judges in eyre to make sure the king received his portion of forfeited property.

A secondary responsibility of the eyre was to hear common pleas, which consisted primarily of disputes between ordinary citizens. Although common pleas could be handled in the local courts, which in many instances were still influenced by Anglo-Saxon customs, the Norman settlers frequently felt more comfortable having their cases heard in the king's courts, of which the eyre was one. It was the common-plea decisions made by judges in eyre that formed the body of legal precedent that became known as the *common law*, that is, the rules used to settle disputes throughout England. Thus, as the judges of eyre resolved common-plea disputes, they created precedents to be

Felony

The term *felony* originally meant an offense serious enough "to break the relationship between [the landowner and his lord] and to cause the [land] holding to be forfeited to the lord."

SOURCE: S. Francis Milson, *The Historical Foundations of the Common Law* (London: Butterworths, 1969), p. 355.

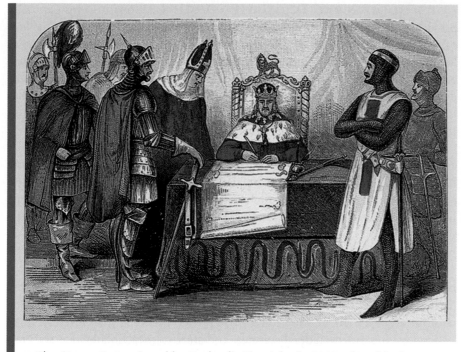

▲ The Magna Carta, signed by England's King John in 1215, placed limits on royal power and established the principle of the rule of law. *Which is preferable: royal power or the rule of law? Why?*

followed in similar cases. Because the common law was built case by case, it is sometimes also called *case law*. Many of the precedents that were created in medieval England became the basis of statutory law in modern England, as well as in the United States. In both countries, some of the early precedents are still used as the basis for settling disputes not covered by statutes.

The efforts of the Norman kings to centralize their power over all of England were only partially successful. In 1215, powerful landholding nobles rebelled against the heavy taxation and autocratic rule of King John and forced him to sign the Magna Carta (the Great Charter). The primary purpose of the Magna Carta was to settle the dispute between the king and his nobles by placing checks on royal power. (It did little for the common person.) From that time forward, kings and queens of England were supposed to be governed by laws and customs rather than by their own wills, and the laws were supposed to be applied in a regular and fair way by the king or queen and his or her judges. Thus, the Magna Carta not only created the idea of the rule of law, but also formed the basis of what would later be called *due process of law*.

Creating Criminal Laws in the United States

In the United States, criminal laws (or criminal statutes) are almost entirely a product of constitutional authority and the legislative bodies that enact them. They are also effected by common law or case law interpretation and by administrative or regulatory agency decisions.

Constitutions and Legislative Bodies   Constitutions generally provide for the creation of legislative bodies empowered to enact criminal and other laws. The U.S. Constitution, for example, created Congress and gave it lawmaking power. The Bill of Rights of the Constitution (the first ten amendments), as well as similar amendments to state constitutions, also describe procedural laws that dictate how substantive laws are to be administered. Constitutions are important to the substantive criminal law because they set limits on what can be defined as a crime.

As noted, criminal laws are products of the lawmaking bodies created by constitutional authority. Thus, federal statutes are enacted by Congress, and state statutes are enacted by state legislatures. Laws created by municipalities, such as by city councils, are generally called *ordinances*. Both the federal criminal statutes and the criminal statutes of particular states, including the definitions of crimes and the penalties associated with them, can be found in penal codes, one for each jurisdiction.

Generally, statutes and ordinances apply only in the particular jurisdiction in which they were enacted. A crime must be prosecuted in the jurisdiction in which it was committed, and it is generally held to have been committed in the jurisdiction in which it was completed or achieved its goal. Federal crimes violate federal statutes, and state crimes violate state statutes. A crime in one state may not be a crime in another state, but a violation of a federal statute is a crime if committed anywhere in the United States. When a certain behavior violates both federal and state statutes, and possibly local ordinances, as is the case with many drug law violations, there is overlapping jurisdiction. In such cases, there is frequently confusion over which jurisdiction has authority for the enforcement of the law and the prosecution of the crime.

Common Law   Common law, also called *case law*, is a by-product of decisions made by trial and appellate court judges, who produce case law whenever they render a decision in a particular case. The decision becomes a potential basis, or **precedent,** for deciding the outcomes of similar cases in the future. Although it is possible for the decision of any trial court judge to become a precedent, it is primarily the written decisions of appellate court judges that do. The reasons on which the decisions of appellate court judges are based are the only ones required to be in writing. This body of recorded decisions has become known as *common law.* Generally, whether a precedent is binding is determined by the court's location. (The different levels of courts in the United States will be described in detail in Chapter 8.)

The principle of using precedents to guide future decisions in court cases is called *stare decisis* (Latin for "to stand by decided cases"). Much of the time spent by criminal lawyers in preparing for a case is devoted to finding legal precedents that support their arguments. The successful outcome of a case depends largely on the success of lawyers in that endeavor.

Although common law was an important source of criminal law in colonial America, it is no longer the case. Currently, what were originally common law crimes, as well as many new crimes, have been defined by statutes created by legislatures in nearly all states. There is no federal criminal common law. Nevertheless, as noted previously, common law or case law remains important for purposes of statutory interpretation.

precedent
A decision that forms a potential basis for deciding the outcomes of similar cases in the future; a by-product of decisions made by trial and appellate court judges, who produce case law whenever they render a decision in a particular case.

stare decisis
The principle of using precedents to guide future decisions in court cases; Latin for "to stand by decided cases."

Administrative or Regulatory Agency Decisions   Administrative or regulatory agencies are the products of statutes enacted by the lawmaking bodies of different jurisdictions. Those agencies create rules, regulate and supervise activities in their areas of responsibility, and render decisions that have the force of law. Examples of federal administrative or regulatory agencies are the Federal Trade Commission (FTC), the Federal Communications Commission (FCC), the Nuclear Regulatory Commission (NRC), the Drug Enforcement Administration (DEA), and the Occupational Safety and Health Administration (OSHA). There are administrative or regulatory agencies at the state and local levels as well. Although violations of many of the rules and regulations of such agencies are handled through civil law proceedings, some violations—especially habitual violations—may be addressed through criminal proceedings. Additionally, legislatures often enact criminal statutes based on the recommendations of regulatory agencies.

The Interdependency Among Sources of Legal Authority

Although federal and state criminal statutes are essentially independent of one another, and although almost all of the action in the enforcement of criminal laws is at the state level, there is an important interdependency among sources of legal authority. For example, suppose a state passed a law requiring teachers in public schools to begin each class by reciting a mandatory prayer. The law would probably be challenged as a violation of the *establishment clause* of the First Amendment to the Constitution, which states that "Congress shall make no law respecting an establishment of religion." The law would certainly be declared unconstitutional because it violated the Constitution. Provisions of the Constitution always take precedence over state statutes. However, if the state statute were not challenged, it would remain in effect in the particular state that enacted it. Figure 4–3 on pages 122–123 summarizes the relationships among the sources of legal authority in the United States.

DEA

You can learn more about the programs, major operations, statistics, etc. of the Drug Enforcement Administration by visiting their Web site through the link at cj.glencoe.com. *How much power should the recommendations of regulatory agencies like the DEA have in shaping criminal justice statutes?*

4.1 CRITICAL THINKING

1. Which of the five features of "good" criminal laws do you think are most important? Why?

2. Are there any other features that could/should be added to "good" criminal laws?

FIGURE 4–3

Sources of Legal Authority in the United States

Constitutions

Constitutions (federal, then state) are the highest forms of legal authority. State constitutions cannot take away rights granted by the federal Constitution, but they can confer greater rights.

Statutes

All statutes must comply with federal constitutional requirements, and the statutes of a particular state must comply with that state's own constitution.

Ordinances

Local ordinances must be consistent with higher forms of law (constitutions, statutes). They can also result in criminal punishment (usually minor) if violated.

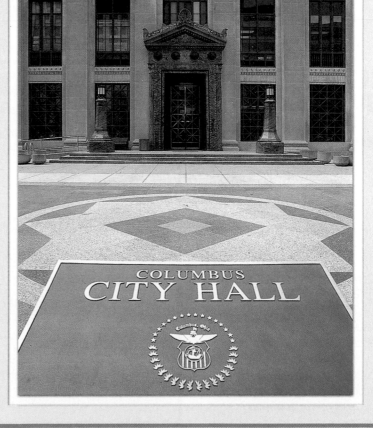

Judicial Decisions

Judicial decisions (common law or case law) interpret and apply both constitutional and statutory provisions and are indispensable to federal and state criminal law.

Sanctions

Violations of administrative or regulatory agency regulations and decisions can result in both civil and criminal sanctions.

4.2 Procedural Law: Rights of the Accused

Most of the procedural, or due-process rights, given to criminal suspects or defendants in the United States are found in the Bill of Rights. The Bill of Rights went into effect on December 15, 1791. Other procedural rights are found in state constitutions and federal and state statutes. Probably the best systematic collection of due-process rights is the *Federal Rules of Criminal Procedure.* Those rules apply only to federal crimes prosecuted in federal courts. Most states also have collections of rules regarding criminal procedures in state courts. Ohio, for example, has 60 such rules in its *Ohio Rules of Criminal Procedure.*

The Bill of Rights

The ink was barely dry on the new Constitution before critics attacked it for not protecting the rights of the people. The First Congress quickly proposed a set of 12 amendments and sent them to the states for ratification. By 1791, the states had ratified ten of the amendments, which became known as the Bill of Rights (the first ten amendments of the Constitution). Although the Bill of Rights originally applied only to the national government, almost all of its provisions have also been applied to the states through a series of U.S. Supreme Court decisions. Figure 4–4 lists the 12 provisions in the Bill of Rights that are applicable to the criminal justice process. Note that only

CRIMINAL JUSTICE Online

ACLU

The American Civil Liberties Union is a nonprofit, nonpartisan, advocacy group devoted to the protection of civil liberties for all Americans. You can learn more about the organization and its defense of the Constitution—especially the Bill of Rights—by clicking the link at cj.glencoe.com. Review "The Issues" section, and look at issues such as criminal justice, cyber-liberties, and drug policy. *Do you think that organizations like the ACLU are necessary? Why or why not?*

FIGURE 4–4

The 12 Provisions in the Bill of Rights Applicable to the Criminal Justice Process

Procedural Right	Amendment
1. Freedom from unreasonable searches and seizures	Fourth
2. Grand jury indictment in felony cases*	Fifth
3. No double jeopardy	Fifth
4. No compelled self-incrimination	Fifth
5. Speedy and public trial	Sixth
6. Impartial jury of the state and district where crime occurred	Sixth
7. Notice of nature and cause of accusation	Sixth
8. Confront opposing witnesses	Sixth
9. Compulsory process for obtaining favorable witnesses	Sixth
10. Counsel	Sixth
11. No excessive bail and fines*	Eighth
12. No cruel and unusual punishment	Eighth

*This right has not been incorporated and is not adhered to by the states.

two of the provisions—the prohibition against excessive bail and fines and the right to a grand jury indictment—are not yet applicable to the states.

The Fourteenth Amendment and the Selective Incorporation of the Bill of Rights

The Fourteenth Amendment was finally ratified by the required three-fourths of all states in 1868, shortly after the conclusion of the Civil War. In part, the amendment reads as follows:

> No State shall make or enforce any law which shall abridge the privileges or immunities of citizens of the United States, nor shall any State deprive any person of life, liberty, or property, without due process of law; nor deny to any person within its jurisdiction the equal protection of the laws.

One of the interesting and long-debated questions about the Fourteenth Amendment was whether its original purpose was to extend the procedural safeguards described in the Bill of Rights to people charged with crimes at the state level. Before the passage of the Fourteenth Amendment, the Bill of Rights applied only to people charged with federal crimes; individual states were not bound by its requirements. Some justices of the Supreme Court—for example, William Douglas (justice from 1939 to 1975), Hugo Black (justice from 1937 to 1971), and Frank Murphy (justice from 1940 to 1949)—believed that the Fourteenth Amendment was supposed to *incorporate* the Bill of Rights and make it applicable to the states. However, other justices, perhaps even a majority of them, did not. Thus, until the 1960s, the Supreme Court did not interpret the Fourteenth Amendment as incorporating the Bill of Rights.

There are at least three different explanations for the actions or, in this case, inactions of the Supreme Court.[5] First, there is little evidence that supporters of the Fourteenth Amendment intended it to incorporate the Bill of Rights. Second, by 1937 a series of court decisions had established the precedent that the due-process clause of the Fourteenth Amendment did not require states to follow trial procedures mandated at the federal level by provisions in the Bill of Rights. The Supreme Court had held that due process was not violated if procedures followed in state courts were otherwise fair. Third, there was the states' rights issue. Because the administration of justice is primarily a state and local responsibility, many people resented what appeared to be unwarranted interference by the federal government in state and local matters. Indeed, the Constitution, for the most part, leaves questions about policing and administering justice to the states, unless a state's procedure violates a fundamental principle of justice.

Regardless of the reason, it was not until the early 1960s that the Supreme Court, then headed by Chief Justice Earl Warren, began to selectively incorporate most of the procedural safeguards contained in the Bill of Rights, making them applicable to the states.

Thus, it took nearly 100 years after the ratification of the Fourteenth Amendment for suspects charged with crimes at the state level to be afforded most of the same due-process protections as people charged with crimes at the federal level. During the past 30 years, however, the composition of the Supreme Court has changed dramatically, and with the change in personnel,

"Evolving Standards of Decency"

In *Trop v. Dulles* (1958) Chief Justice Warren wrote that the protections of the Bill of Rights "must draw [their] meaning from evolving standards of decency that mark the progress of a maturing society."

▲ From left to right: Chief Justices William Rehnquist, Warren Burger, and Earl Warren. Whereas the politically liberal Warren Court of the 1960s championed the rights of criminal suspects by extending procedural safeguards, the politically conservative Burger and Rehnquist Courts of the 1970s, 1980s, and 1990s have actively reversed or altered in other ways the work of the Warren Court. *How can the different direction in criminal procedure taken by the Burger and Rehnquist Courts be explained?*

the Court's views of due-process rights have changed as well. Whereas the politically liberal Warren Court of the 1960s championed the rights of criminal suspects by extending procedural safeguards, the politically conservative Burger and Rehnquist Courts of the 1970s, 1980s, and 1990s have actively reversed or altered in other ways the work of the Warren Court.[6]

In the rest of this section, we will consider the procedural rights in the Bill of Rights, which are found in the Fourth, Fifth, Sixth, and Eighth Amendments to the Constitution.[7] Before we do, however, it is important to emphasize that the specific interpretation of each of the procedural, or due-process, rights has evolved over time through dozens of Supreme Court and lower-court decisions, or precedents. In this introductory examination, we will limit our consideration of the legal development of those rights to what we believe are the most consequential cases, the landmark cases.

The Fourth Amendment

The Fourth Amendment reads as follows:

> The right of the people to be secure in their persons, houses, papers, and effects, against unreasonable searches and seizures, shall not be violated, and no warrants shall issue, but upon probable cause, supported by oath or affirmation, and particularly describing the place to be searched, and the person or things to be seized.

The Fourth Amendment (as well as other provisions of the Constitution) protects individual privacy against certain types of governmental interference. However, it does not provide a general constitutional "right to privacy," as many people wrongly believe. Nearly every governmental action interferes with personal privacy to some extent. Thus, the question in Fourth Amendment cases is limited to whether a governmental intrusion violates the Constitution.[8]

The procedural rights in the Fourth Amendment influence the operation of criminal justice in the United States nearly every day. They concern the legality of searches and seizures and the question of what to do with evidence that is illegally obtained. **Searches** are explorations or inspections, by law enforcement officers, of homes, premises, vehicles, or persons, for the purpose of discovering evidence of crimes or persons who are accused of crimes. **Seizures** are the taking of persons or property into custody in response to violations of the criminal law.

According to the Supreme Court, the Fourth Amendment allows two kinds of searches and seizures: those made with a warrant and those made without a warrant. A **warrant** is a written order from a court directing law enforcement officers to conduct a search or to arrest a person. An **arrest** is the seizure of a person or the taking of a person into custody. An arrest can be either taking actual physical custody, as when a suspect is handcuffed by a police officer, or constructive custody, as when a person peacefully submits to a police officer's control. An arrest can occur without an officer's physically touching a suspect.

The Fourth Amendment requires only that searches and seizures not be "unreasonable." Searches and seizures conducted with a legal warrant are generally considered reasonable. However, what is "reasonable" in warrantless searches remained vague for more than 100 years after the ratification of the amendment. It was not until a series of cases beginning in the 1960s that the Supreme Court began to provide a more precise definition of the term. Because the law concerning warrantless searches and seizures is complex, only a relatively brief and simplified overview will be provided in that section.

Searches and Seizures With a Warrant

First, law enforcement officers must have *probable cause* before a judicial officer can legally issue a search or arrest warrant. Probable cause for a search warrant requires substantial and trustworthy evidence to support two conclusions: (1) that the specific objects to be searched for are connected with criminal activity and (2) that the objects will be found in the place to be searched. In nearly all jurisdictions, law enforcement officers seeking a search warrant must specify in a signed *affidavit,* a written and sworn declaration, the facts that establish probable cause. The facts in the affidavit are the basis for determining later whether there was probable cause to issue the warrant in the first place. Some jurisdictions allow sworn oral testimony to establish probable cause.

The Fourth Amendment requires that a search warrant contain a particular description of the place to be searched and the person or things to be seized. Thus, the warrant must be specific enough that a law enforcement officer executing it would know where to search and what objects to seize, even if the officer was not originally involved in the case. However, absolute technical accuracy in the description of the place to be searched is not necessary. It is required only that an officer executing a warrant can find, perhaps by asking questions of neighborhood residents, the place to be searched.

searches
Explorations or inspections, by law enforcement officers, of homes, premises, vehicles, or persons, for the purpose of discovering evidence of crimes or persons who are accused of crimes.

seizures
The taking of persons or property into custody in response to violations of the criminal law.

warrant
A written order from a court directing law enforcement officers to conduct a search or to arrest a person.

arrest
The seizure of a person or the taking of a person into custody, either actual physical custody, as when a suspect is handcuffed by a police officer, or constructive custody, as when a person peacefully submits to a police officer's control.

The Rule of Law CHAPTER 4

A warrant may also be issued for the search of a person or an automobile, rather than a place. A warrant to search a person should provide the person's name or at least a detailed description. A warrant to search an automobile should include either the car's license number or its make and the name of its owner.

Search warrants are required to be executed in a reasonable amount of time. For example, federal law requires that a search be conducted within ten days after the warrant is issued. The federal government and nearly half of the states also have laws limiting the time of day during which search warrants may be executed. In those jurisdictions, searches may be conducted only during daytime hours unless there are special circumstances.

Generally, before law enforcement officers may enter a place to conduct a search, they must first announce that they are law enforcement officers, that they possess a warrant, and that they are there to execute it. The major exceptions to this requirement are situations in which it is likely that the evidence would be destroyed immediately on notification or in which notification would pose a threat to officers. However, if officers are refused entry after identifying themselves, they may then use force to gain entry, but only after they have given the occupant time to respond. In short, they cannot legally yell "police officers," and immediately kick down the door. Finally, if in the course of conducting a legal search, law enforcement officers discover **contraband** (an illegal substance or object) or evidence of a crime not covered by the warrant, they may seize that contraband or evidence without getting a new warrant specifically covering it. Figure 4–5 on page 129 shows a sample search and arrest warrant and the supporting affidavit.

Arrests With a Warrant   Most arrests are made without a warrant. Generally, an arrest warrant is legally required when law enforcement officers want to enter private premises to make an arrest. An arrest warrant is issued only if substantial and trustworthy evidence supports these two conclusions: (1) a violation of the law has been committed and (2) the person to be arrested committed the violation.

Searches and Seizures Without a Warrant   In guaranteeing freedom from illegal searches and seizures, the Fourth Amendment, as noted previously, protects a person's privacy. Under most circumstances, the amendment requires a warrant signed by a judge to authorize a search for and seizure of evidence of criminal activity. However, Supreme Court interpretations of the Fourth Amendment have permitted warrantless searches and seizures in some circumstances. A person is generally protected from searches and seizures without a warrant in places, such as home or office, where he or she has a legitimate right to privacy. That same protection, however, does not extend to all places where a person has a legitimate right to be. For example, the Supreme Court has permitted the stopping and searching of automobiles under certain circumstances and with probable cause. Several doctrines concerning search and seizure without a warrant have developed over time.

Before 1969, when law enforcement officers arrested a suspect, they could legally search, without a warrant, the entire premises surrounding the arrest. That kind of search is called a *search incident to arrest,* and like a search

contraband
An illegal substance or object.

United States v. Mendenhall

In *United States v. Mendenhall* (1980), the Supreme Court created the following test for determining whether an encounter constitutes a Fourth Amendment seizure: "A person has been 'seized' within the meaning of the Fourth Amendment only if, in view of all the circumstances surrounding the incident, a reasonable person would have believed that he was not free to leave." The Court provided these examples of situations that might be construed as seizures, even if the person did not attempt to leave: (1) the threatening presence of several officers, (2) the display of a weapon by an officer, (3) some physical touching of the person, or (4) the use of language or a tone of voice that indicated that compliance with the officer's request might be compelled.

FIGURE 4-5

Sample Search and Arrest Warrant

SEARCH AND ARREST WARRANT

THE STATE OF TEXAS § 155 E. Main Street
§ Dallas, Dallas County, Texas
COUNTY OF DALLAS §

THE STATE OF TEXAS to the Sheriff or any Peace Officer of Dallas County, Texas, or any Peace Officer of the State of Texas,

GREETINGS:

WHEREAS, the Affiant whose signature is affixed to the Affidavit appearing on the reverse hereof is a Peace Officer under the laws of Texas and did heretofore this day subscribed and swear to said Affidavit before me (which said affidavit is by this reference incorporated herein for all purposes), and whereas I find that the verified facts by Affiant in said Affidavit show that Affiant has probable cause for the belief he expresses therein and establishes the existence of proper grounds for the issuance of this Warrant:

NOW, THEREFORE, you are commanded to enter the s[ ]
described in said Affidavit and to there search for t[ ]
described in said Affidavit and to seize the same an[ ]
And, you are commanded to arrest and bring before[ ]
and accused in said Affidavit. Herein fail not, but h[ ]
this Warrant executed within three days, exclusive [ ]
issuance and exclusive of the day of its execution w[ ]
thereon, showing how you have executed the same.

ISSUED AT ___11:35___ o'clock ___A___ M., on this th[ ]
of ___March___, 19 99 to certify which v[ ]
day.

Sarah H. Solano
MAGISTRATE, DALLAS COUN[ ]

RETURN AND INVENTORY

THE STATE OF TEXAS §
§
COUNTY OF DALLAS §

The undersigned Affiant, being a Peace Officer und[ ]
and being duly sworn, on oath certifies that the forego[ ]
hand on the day it was issued and that it was execute[ ]
of _____, 19_____, by making the se[ ]
therein and seizing during such search the following d[ ]
property:

_____
AFFIANT

SUBSCRIBED AND SWORN to before me, the unders[ ]
the_____day of_____, 19_

_____
Notary Public in and for Dallas Cou[ ]

AFFIDAVIT FOR SEARCH WARRANT AND ARREST WARRANT

THE STATE OF TEXAS § 155 E. Main Street
§ City of Dallas, Dallas County, Texas
COUNTY OF DALLAS §

The undersigned Affiant, being a Peace Officer under the laws of Texas and being duly sworn, on oath makes the following statements and accusations:

1. There is in Dallas County, Texas, a suspected place and premises described and located as follows: A one story family dwelling, which is white in color, with a grey composition roof. The location of this residence is 155 E. Main Street, located in the City of Dallas, Dallas County, Texas.

2. There is at said suspected place and premises personal property concealed and kept in violation of the laws of Texas and described as follows: A CONTROLLED SUBSTANCE: TO WIT: Cocaine

3. Said suspected place and premises are in charge of and controlled by each of the following persons: A white male approximately 25 years of age, 5'10 in height, 160 pounds, with a mustache, black hair and brown eyes and other person or persons whose names, ages, and descriptions are unknown to the affiant.

4. It is the belief of Affiant, and he hereby charges and accuses, that: The above listed white male described in paragraph number 3 was in possession of an amount of cocaine located in the residence at 155 E. Main Street, located in the City of Dallas, Dallas County, Texas.

5. Affiant has probable cause for said belief by reason of the following facts: Affiant, Officer Smith, is employed by the City of Dallas Police Department and is currently assigned to the Narcotics Bureau.

I, the affiant, personally purchased an amount of cocaine from the suspect described in paragraph number 3 out of the aforementioned address at 155 E. Main Street, and that the affiant has been inside the above described residence within the last 24 hours, and personally observed the above described white male and other person, persons, whose names, ages, and identities, and descriptions are unknown to the affiant, in possession of and selling cocaine. Detective Jones purchased 0.3g of cocaine from the above described suspect for twenty dollars U.S. Currency. The cocaine was field tested by the affiant who knows due to his experience as a narcotics officer, what cocaine looks like and how it is packaged for resale.

I, the affiant, observed this on March 22, 1999.

Wherefore, Affiant asks for issuance of a warrant that will authorize him to search said suspected place and premises for said personal property and seize the same and to arrest each said described and accused person.

James C. Smith
AFFIANT

Subscribed and sworn to before me by said Affiant on this the _23rd_ day of ___March___, 19 99 .

Sarah H. Solano
MAGISTRATE, DALLAS COUNTY, TEXAS

with a warrant, it required probable cause. Evidence obtained through a *search incident to arrest* was admissible as long as the arrest was legal.

In 1969, in the case of *Chimel v. California*, the Supreme Court limited the scope of *searches incident to an arrest*. The Court restricted the physical area in which officers could conduct a search to the area within the suspect's immediate control. The Court interpreted the area within the suspect's immediate control as an area near enough to the suspect to enable him or her to obtain a weapon or destroy evidence. The Court also ruled that it is permissible for officers, incident to an arrest, to protect themselves, to prevent a suspect's escape by searching the suspect for weapons, and to preserve evidence within the suspect's grabbing area.

The Supreme Court has continued to refine the scope of warrantless searches and seizures incident to an arrest. For example, in 1981, in *New York v. Belton*, the Court ruled that after police have made a lawful arrest of the occupant of an automobile, they may, incident to that arrest, search the automobile's entire passenger compartment and the contents of any containers found in that compartment. One year later, in *United States v. Ross*, the Court clarified the *Belton* rule, saying that the scope of an automobile search incident to a lawful arrest under *Belton* does not include the car's trunk. Then, in 1991, in the case of *California v. Acevedo*, the Court ruled that police may search the trunk of a car in a warrantless search, even if not incident to an arrest, if they have probable cause to believe that contraband or another seizable object is in the trunk.

Other Supreme Court decisions have established principles governing when private areas may be searched incident to an arrest. In 1968, for instance, in the case of *Harris v. United States*, the Court established the *plain-view doctrine*. Under this doctrine, the police may seize an item—evidence or contraband—without a warrant if they are lawfully in a position to view the item and if it is immediately apparent that the item is evidence or contraband. In 1990, in the case of *Maryland v. Buie*, the Court addressed the issue of *protective sweeps*. The Court held that when a warrantless arrest takes place in a suspect's home, officers may make only a "cursory visual inspection" of areas that could harbor an accomplice or a person posing danger to them.

Even a warrantless search not incident to an arrest may be justified under the Supreme Court's *exigent circumstances* doctrine. It permits police to make warrantless searches in exigent, or emergency, situations. Such situations could include a need to prevent the imminent destruction of evidence, a need to prevent harm to individuals, or the hot pursuit of suspects.

Frequently, law enforcement officers are not hampered by the warrant requirement, because suspects often consent to a search. In other words, law enforcement officers who do not have enough evidence to obtain a search warrant, or who either cannot or do not want to take the time and trouble to obtain one, may simply ask a suspect whether they may conduct a search. If the suspect consents voluntarily, the search can be made legally. Law enforcement officers call this strategy "knock and talk." In 1973, in the case of *Schenckloth v. Bustamonte*, the Supreme Court upheld the legality of *consent searches*. The Court also ruled that officers do not have to tell suspects that they have a right to withhold consent.

It is not surprising that consent searches have become the most common type of searches performed by law enforcement officers. They are used frequently in traffic stops and drug interdiction efforts at airports and bus terminals. In the 1980s, as a new tool in the war on drugs, several police departments adopted programs in which officers boarded buses and asked passengers to consent to searches. The practice was challenged in a 1985 Florida case in which a bus passenger had consented to having his luggage searched. When the police found cocaine, the passenger was arrested and subsequently convicted. The Florida Supreme Court ruled that the search was unconstitutional. In 1991, the U.S. Supreme Court reversed the Florida Supreme Court (in *Florida v. Bostick*) and held that the search was not unconstitutional and that law enforcement officers may make such a search without a warrant or suspicion of a crime—as long as the passenger feels free to refuse the search.

Critics argue that, in most cases, consent searches cannot be truly voluntary, even when permission is granted, because most people are intimidated by the police and would have a hard time telling them no. Moreover, most people probably do not know that they may refuse a warrantless search except under the conditions described earlier.

Arrests Without a Warrant   Officers may not enter a private home to make a warrantless arrest unless the offense is a serious one and there are exigent circumstances, such as the likely destruction of evidence or the hot pursuit of a felony suspect. This is the same *exigent circumstances* doctrine that applies to warrantless searches and seizures.

A suspect who is arrested without a warrant and remains confined is entitled to have a judge determine whether there was probable cause for the arrest. Ordinarily, judges must make such a determination within 48 hours of arrest. The purpose of this proceeding is to ensure that the suspect's continuing custody is based on a judicial determination of probable cause and not merely on the police officer's judgment that probable cause supported an arrest.

Standards of Proof   As mentioned previously and as specified in the Fourth Amendment, neither search nor arrest warrants can be issued legally unless law enforcement officers convince a judge that there is probable cause to believe that the specific items to be searched for are related to criminal activity and the items will be found in the place to be searched or that a violation of the law has been committed and the person to be arrested committed the violation. Probable cause is one among a number of standards of proof for various criminal justice activities. The amount of proof necessary depends on the activity in question. Figure 4–6 on page 132 shows various standards of proof, along a continuum of certainty, and the criminal justice activities that correspond to them.

Toward one end of the continuum is the standard of proof with the least certainty: *mere suspicion*. **Mere suspicion** is equivalent to a "gut feeling." In other words, a law enforcement officer may have a feeling that something is amiss—an uncanny knack that some experienced law enforcement officers possess—but be unable to state exactly what it is. With only mere suspicion, law enforcement officers cannot legally even stop a suspect.

mere suspicion
The standard of proof with the least certainty; a "gut feeling." With mere suspicion, a law enforcement officer cannot legally even stop a suspect.

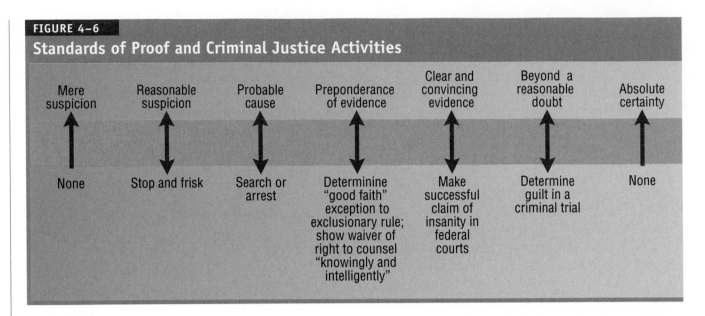

FIGURE 4–6

Standards of Proof and Criminal Justice Activities

Mere suspicion	Reasonable suspicion	Probable cause	Preponderance of evidence	Clear and convincing evidence	Beyond a reasonable doubt	Absolute certainty
None	Stop and frisk	Search or arrest	Determinine "good faith" exception to exclusionary rule; show waiver of right to counsel "knowingly and intelligently"	Make successful claim of insanity in federal courts	Determine guilt in a criminal trial	None

reasonable suspicion

A standard of proof that is more than a gut feeling. It includes the ability to articulate reasons for the suspicion. With reasonable suspicion, a law enforcement officer is legally permitted to stop and frisk a suspect.

frisking

Conducting a search for weapons by lightly patting the outside of a suspect's clothing, feeling for hard objects that might be weapons.

probable cause

The amount of proof necessary for a reasonably intelligent person to suspect that a crime has been committed or that items connected with criminal activity can be found in a particular place. It is the standard of proof needed to conduct a search or to make an arrest.

A standard of proof with greater certainty is *reasonable suspicion.* **Reasonable suspicion** is more than a gut feeling. It includes the ability to articulate reasons for the suspicion. For example, if a law enforcement officer observes a person in front of a bank wearing a heavy trench coat on a hot summer day, the officer might have a reasonable suspicion that something is amiss. The officer could state that idling in front of a bank while wearing a heavy trench coat on a hot summer day is suspect behavior. Until recently, an anonymous tip could be the basis for reasonable suspicion. However, in *Florida v. J.L.* (2000), the Supreme Court ruled that the practice was unconstitutional, despite having allowed the practice for more than three decades.[9] On the other hand, the Court, in *Illinois v. Wardlow* (2000), recently confirmed that running from the police when they enter a high-crime area is reasonably suspicious behavior.[10] With reasonable suspicion, a law enforcement officer is legally permitted to stop and frisk a suspect (*Terry v. Ohio,* 1968). **Frisking** a suspect means conducting a search for weapons by lightly patting the outside of a suspect's clothing, feeling for hard objects that might be weapons. Only if an officer feels something that may be a weapon may he or she search inside a pocket or an article of clothing. If evidence of a crime is discovered, the officer is permitted to make an arrest.

The standard of proof needed to conduct a search or to make an arrest is *probable cause.* The conventional definition of **probable cause** is the amount of proof necessary for a reasonably intelligent person to suspect that a crime has been committed or that items connected with criminal activity can be found in a particular place. Although its meaning is not entirely clear—what is "reasonably intelligent"?—probable cause has a greater degree of certainty than reasonable suspicion. For probable cause, law enforcement officers must have some tangible evidence that a crime has been committed, but that evidence does not have to be admissible at trial. Such evidence might include a tip from a reliable informant or the pungent aroma of marijuana in the air.

The line between probable cause and reasonable suspicion, or even mere suspicion, is a fine one and a matter of interpretation. In practice, there are many gray areas. Consequently, criminal courts and the judicial officers who are authorized to approve search warrants have been given the responsibility of determining whether a standard of proof has been met in a particular situation. As noted, search warrants, for example, must generally be approved by a judicial officer before they can be executed. The way courts and judicial officers determine whether a standard of proof has been met will be discussed in detail in Chapter 8. Here we simply observe that, for much of the public, one of the frustrating aspects of criminal justice is that offenders who are factually guilty of their crimes sometimes escape punishment because a judicial officer did not have probable cause to issue a warrant, or a police officer did not have probable cause to make an arrest or have reasonable suspicion to stop and frisk the suspect.

The next standard of proof along the continuum of legal certainty is *preponderance of evidence*. **Preponderance of evidence** is evidence that outweighs the opposing evidence, or sufficient evidence to overcome doubt or speculation. It is the standard of proof necessary to find a defendant liable in a civil lawsuit. This standard is also used in determining whether the *inevitable-discovery rule* applies. That is, the prosecution must prove by a preponderance of the evidence that evidence actually uncovered as a result of a constitutional violation would inevitably have been discovered through lawful means, independent of the action constituting the violation. Finally, preponderance of evidence is the standard of proof in criminal proceedings by which the state must show that the right to counsel has been waived "knowingly and intelligently."

Next along the continuum of certainty is **clear and convincing evidence.** It is the standard of proof required in some civil cases and, in federal courts, the standard of proof necessary for a defendant to make a successful claim of insanity.

Of greater certainty still is proof **beyond a reasonable doubt,** the standard of proof necessary to find a defendant guilty in a criminal trial. Reasonable doubt is the amount of doubt about a defendant's guilt that a reasonable person might have after carefully examining all the evidence. In the case of *Sandoval v. California* (1994), the Court upheld the following definition of *reasonable doubt*:

> It is *not a mere possible doubt*; because everything relating to human affairs, and *depending on moral evidence*, is open to some possible or imaginary doubt. It is that state of the case which, after the entire comparison and consideration of all the evidence, leaves the minds of the jurors in that they cannot say they feel an abiding conviction, *to a moral certainty*, of the truth of the charge. [Emphasis in original.]

Thus, to convict a criminal defendant in a jury trial, a juror must be convinced of guilt by this standard. However, what is considered reasonable varies, and reasonableness is thus a matter of interpretation. Therefore, the procedural laws in most jurisdictions require that 12 citizens all agree that a defendant is guilty beyond a reasonable doubt before that defendant can be convicted. No criminal justice activity requires absolute certainty as a standard of proof.

preponderance of evidence
Evidence that outweighs the opposing evidence, or sufficient evidence to overcome doubt or speculation.

clear and convincing evidence
The standard of proof required in some civil cases and, in federal courts, the standard of proof necessary for a defendant to make a successful claim of insanity.

beyond a reasonable doubt
The standard of proof necessary to find a defendant guilty in a criminal trial.

exclusionary rule
The rule that illegally seized evidence must be excluded from trials in federal courts.

The Exclusionary Rule   The **exclusionary rule** was created by the Supreme Court in 1914 in the case of *Weeks v. United States*. In *Weeks*, the Supreme Court held that illegally seized evidence must be excluded from trials in federal courts. In 1961, the Warren Court extended the exclusionary rule to state courts in the case of *Mapp v. Ohio*. The exclusionary rule originally had three primary purposes: (1) to protect individual rights from police misconduct, (2) to prevent police misconduct, and (3) to maintain judicial integrity (for citizens to have faith in the administration of justice, courts should not admit evidence that is tainted by the illegal activities of other criminal justice officials). Today, however, the principal purpose of the exclusionary rule is to deter the police from violating people's Fourth Amendment rights.

In practice, when suspects want to claim that incriminating evidence was obtained through an illegal search and seizure, that a confession was obtained without the required warnings or was involuntary, that an identification was made as a result of an invalid police lineup, or that evidence was in some other way illegally obtained, they attempt, through their attorneys, to show at a suppression hearing that the search and seizure, for example, violated the Fourth Amendment. If they are successful in their claims, the evidence that was obtained as a result of the illegal search and seizure will not be admitted at trial.

By the late 1970s, public opinion polls showed that Americans were becoming increasingly alarmed about the problem of crime and especially about what they perceived as the practice of allowing a substantial number of criminals to escape punishment because of legal technicalities. One legal technicality that received much of the public's scorn was the exclusionary rule. In 1984, responding at least in part to public opinion, the Supreme Court, under Chief Justice Warren Burger, decided three cases that had the practical effect of weakening the exclusionary rule.

Many criminals escape punishment because of the exclusionary rule.

Very few criminals escape punishment because of the exclusionary rule.

In two of the three cases, *United States v. Leon* and *Massachusetts v. Sheppard*, a *good faith exception* to the *exclusionary* rule was recognized. The Court ruled that as long as the police act in good faith when they request a warrant, the evidence they collect may be used in court, even if the warrant is illegal or defective. In the *Leon* case, the judge's determination of probable cause turned out to be wrong. Prior to *Leon*, such an error by a judge would have been recognized as a violation of the Fourth Amendment, and the evidence seized with the warrant would have been excluded at trial. The Court reasoned that it was unfair to penalize law enforcement officers who conduct searches in which incriminating evidence is found, when those officers conduct the search in good faith that they have a legal warrant. In the *Sheppard* case, the judge had used the wrong form for the warrant. As in *Leon*, the Court reasoned that it was unfair to penalize law enforcement officers, and the public, just because there was a flaw in the warrant, when the officers had conducted a search in good faith and found incriminating evidence.

The third case, *Nix v. Williams,* established an *inevitable-discovery exception* to the *exclusionary rule.* The *Nix* case involved a murderer whom police had tricked into leading them to the hidden body of his victim. Before *Nix,* illegally seized evidence (in the *Nix* case, the body) had to be excluded from trial. In *Nix,* the Court held that evidence obtained in violation of a defendant's rights can be used at trial if the prosecution can show, by a preponderance of the evidence, that the information ultimately or inevitably would have been discovered by lawful means.

Of all the due-process guarantees in the Bill of Rights, those in the Fourth Amendment are the ones likely to require the most interpretation by the Supreme Court in the future. With advances in the technology of surveillance, the Court will have to determine the legality of increasingly more intrusive ways of gathering evidence. The star of a 1983 science fiction movie was a police helicopter named *Blue Thunder.* The helicopter was able to hover silently outside apartment buildings, record what was being said inside the apartments, and take pictures of what was being done. Although the movie was fictional, it will probably not be long before law enforcement has such equipment—if it does not have at least some of that equipment already. Will evidence obtained by means of the futuristic surveillance technology of *Blue Thunder* violate the Fourth Amendment prohibition against unreasonable searches and seizures? That decision will ultimately be made by the Supreme Court.

The Fifth Amendment

The Fifth Amendment reads as follows:

No person shall be held to answer for a capital, or otherwise infamous crime, unless on a presentment or indictment of a grand jury, except in cases arising in the land or naval forces, or in the militia, when in actual service in time of war or public danger; nor shall any person be subject for the same offense to be twice put in jeopardy of life or limb; nor shall be compelled in any criminal case to be a witness against himself, nor be deprived of life, liberty, or property, without due process of law; nor shall private property be taken for public use without just compensation.

Right to Grand Jury Indictment and Protection Against Double Jeopardy The Fifth Amendment right to a grand jury indictment in felony cases, to be described in detail in Chapter 8, is one of the two Bill of Rights guarantees that has not yet been extended to the states (see *Hurtado v. California,* 1884). But the Fifth Amendment protection against **double jeopardy** has been (see *Benton v. Maryland,* 1969). The protection provides that no person shall "be subject for the same offense to be twice put in jeopardy of life or limb."

When most people think of double jeopardy, they probably think of the classic case in which a defendant cannot be retried for the same crime or a related crime after he or she has been acquitted by a jury. However, the protection against double jeopardy can apply even without an acquittal. Technically, it does not apply until jeopardy has attached. If a trial ends before jeopardy has attached, the prosecution has the right to retry the defendant for the same charge in a new trial. But, when does jeopardy attach? In jury trials, jeopardy attaches when the entire jury has been selected and sworn in. In a

Arizona v. Evans

On March 1, 1995, in the case of *Arizona v. Evans,* the Supreme Court ruled that unlawful arrests based on computer errors do not always require the exclusion of evidence seized by police. In the Arizona case, the Court held that a good faith exception to the exclusionary rule could be made as long as the illegal seizure of evidence was caused by the errors of court employees and not the police. In that case, a Phoenix man who had been stopped for a traffic violation was arrested because a computer record showed an outstanding arrest warrant for some traffic violations. In fact, the warrant had been dropped 17 days earlier, but the action had not been entered into the computer. After the arrest, marijuana was seized from the man's car, and he was arrested for illegal possession.

double jeopardy
The trying of a defendant a second time for the same offense when jeopardy attached in the first trial and a mistrial was not declared.

bench trial (a trial before a judge without a jury), jeopardy attaches when the first witness has been sworn in. In cases that are resolved through a guilty plea, jeopardy attaches when the court unconditionally accepts the defendant's plea. Even after jeopardy has attached, however, the prosecution is generally not barred from retrying a defendant when a mistrial has been declared.

The theoretical rationale behind the protection against double jeopardy is that the state should have one and only one chance to convict a defendant charged with a crime. Otherwise, the state could endlessly harass its citizens, as sometimes happens in countries without this protection.

Protection Against Compelled Self-Incrimination

Arguably, the most important procedural safeguard in the Fifth Amendment is the protection against compelled **self-incrimination.** The protection guarantees that in criminal cases, suspects or defendants cannot be forced to be witnesses against themselves. The protection is based on the belief that confessions may not be truthful if they are not made voluntarily. It also expresses an intolerance for certain methods used to extract confessions, even if the confessions ultimately prove to be reliable. A **confession** is an admission by a person accused of a crime that he or she committed the offense as charged. According to the Supreme Court's **doctrine of fundamental fairness,** confessions are inadmissible in criminal trials if they were obtained by means of either psychological manipulation or "third-degree" methods—for example, beatings, subjection to unreasonably long periods of questioning, or other physical tactics.

Although the Fifth Amendment protection against compelled self-incrimination has long been observed in federal trials, it was not until the 1960s, in the case of *Malloy v. Hogan* (1964), that the Fifth Amendment protection against compelled self-incrimination was extended to trials in state courts. In *Miranda v. Arizona* (1966), the Court broadened the protection against compelled self-incrimination to cover nearly all custodial police interrogations. (Custodial police interrogations essentially mean questionings that take place after an arrest or the functional equivalent of an arrest; they may or may not take place at the police station.) In *Miranda,* the Court added that confessions obtained without suspects' being notified of their specific rights could not be admitted as evidence. Perhaps even more important, it established specific procedural safeguards that had to be followed to avoid violation of the protection against compelled self-incrimination. The court said:

> [P]rocedural safeguards must be employed to protect the privilege [against self-incrimination], and unless other fully effective means are adopted to notify the person of his right of silence and to assure that the exercise of the right will be scrupulously honored, the following measures are required. [The suspect] must be warned prior to any questioning (1) that he has the right to remain silent, (2) that anything he says can be used against him in a court of law, (3) that he has the right to the presence of an attorney, and (4) that if he cannot afford an attorney one will be appointed for him prior to any questioning if he so desires.

---

self-incrimination
Being a witness against oneself. If forced, it is a violation of the Fifth Amendment.

confession
An admission by a person accused of a crime that he or she committed the offense charged.

doctrine of fundamental fairness
The rule that makes confessions inadmissible in criminal trials if they were obtained by means of either psychological manipulation or "third-degree" methods.

Brown v. Mississippi

The first time the Supreme Court held that a coerced confession, brutally beaten out of the suspect, was inadmissible in a state trial was in 1936, in the case of *Brown v. Mississippi.* However, in the *Brown* case, the Court did not find that the coerced confession violated the Fifth Amendment protection against self-incrimination. Rather, the Court found that it violated the Fourteenth Amendment right to due process.

However, if an individual being questioned is not yet in custody, the *Miranda* warnings do not have to be given. Also, volunteered confessions do not violate *Miranda* or the Fifth Amendment.

The Fifth Amendment protection against compelled self-incrimination has been weakened recently by the Supreme Court. For example, in *New York v. Quarles* (1984), the Supreme Court created a public-safety exception to the Fifth Amendment protection. Also, in *Arizona v. Fulminante* (1991), the Court ruled that improper use of a coerced confession is a harmless trial error if other evidence is strong enough to convict the defendant. The burden of proof is on the state to show that a coerced confession is harmless error. The case involved a defendant who had been sentenced to death for killing his 11-year-old stepdaughter. While in prison, the defendant confessed to an FBI informant after the informant promised to protect the defendant from other inmates. Prior to *Fulminante,* such a conviction would most likely have been reversed on appeal because of the use of the coerced confession.

However, in *Dickerson v. United States* (2000), the Court reaffirmed the importance of *Miranda,* even when it inconveniences law enforcement officers. In *Dickerson,* a bank robbery suspect asked the Court to throw out incriminating statements he made to FBI agents because he was not given Miranda warnings prior to questioning. Prosecutors argued that the suspect made voluntary statements, which were admissible under a law approved by Congress in 1968. The law gives federal judges authority to admit statements from suspects if the judges believe that the statements are voluntary. The Court disagreed and held that Congress did not have the authority to supersede the Supreme Court's interpretation of the Constitution. Therefore, the

Rhode Island v. Innis

In the case of *Rhode Island v. Innis* (1980), the Supreme Court stated:

[T]he term "interrogation" under *Miranda* refers not only to express questioning, but also to any words or actions on the part of the police (other than those normally attendant to arrest and custody) that the police should know are reasonably likely to elicit an incriminating response from the suspect.

▲ The Fifth Amendment protection against compelled self-incrimination applies to trial procedures as well as police interrogations. *Why do you think protection against self-incrimination is important?*

incriminating statements made by the bank robbery suspect were inadmissible.[11]

The Fifth Amendment protection against compelled self-incrimination also applies to trial procedures. Not only do defendants have a right to refuse to answer any questions put to them by the prosecution during a trial (by "pleading the fifth"), but they also have the right not to take the witness stand in the first place. Moreover, the prosecution is forbidden to comment on the defendant's silence or refusal to take the witness stand. This protection rests on a basic legal principle: the government bears the burden of proof. Defendants are not obligated to help the government prove they committed a crime. In 1964 and 1965, those Fifth Amendment rights were extended to defendants being tried in state courts in the cases of *Malloy v. Hogan* and *Griffin v. California*, respectively.

The Sixth Amendment

The Sixth Amendment reads as follows:

> In all criminal prosecutions, the accused shall enjoy the right to a speedy and public trial, by an impartial jury of the State and district wherein the crime shall have been committed, which district shall have been previously ascertained by law, and to be informed of the nature and cause of the accusation; to be confronted with the witnesses against him; to have compulsory process for obtaining witnesses in his favor, and to have the assistance of counsel for his defense.

Right to a Speedy and Public Trial   The Sixth Amendment right to a speedy and public trial applies directly to trials in federal courts. It was extended to trials in state courts in 1967, in the case of *Klopfer v. North Carolina* (right to a speedy trial), and in 1942, in the case of *In re Oliver* (right to a public trial). Delays in a trial can severely hamper a defendant's case if favorable witnesses have died, have moved and cannot be found, or have forgotten what they saw. Delays can also adversely affect defendants by forcing them to remain in jail for long periods of time while awaiting trial. A long wait in jail can be a very stressful and sometimes dangerous experience.

In determining what constitutes a speedy trial, the Supreme Court has created a balancing test that weighs both the defendant's and the prosecution's behavior (see *Barker v. Wingo*, 1972). Thus, the reason for the delay in a trial is critical. For example, a search for a missing witness would probably be considered an acceptable reason for delay. Court congestion, on the other hand, typically would not.

The acceptable length of delay in a trial also depends partly on the nature of the charge. In *Barker*, the Court held that "the delay that can be tolerated for an ordinary street crime is considerably less than for a serious, complex conspiracy charge." There has been great variation in the length of delay tolerated by specific courts. However, delays of less than five months have generally been considered acceptable, but delays of eight months or longer have not.

The Sixth Amendment right to a public trial means that a trial must be open to the public, but it need not be open to all who want to attend.

Jury Trials

The fundamental right to a jury trial, itself, is provided in Article 3, Section 2.3, of the U.S. Constitution: The trial of all crimes, except in cases of impeachment, shall be by jury, and such trial shall be held in the State where the said crimes shall have been committed; but when not committed within any State the trial shall be at such place or places as the Congress may have by law directed.

Obviously, the number of people who can attend a trial depends on the size of the courtroom. The right would be violated only if the trial were held, for example, in a prison or in a closed judge's chambers against a defendant's wishes. Defendants have no right to a private trial.

A trial may be closed to the public if the defendant's right to a public trial is outweighed by "a compelling state interest." However, before a trial is closed, "the party seeking to close the hearing must advance an overriding interest that is likely to be prejudiced, the closure must be no broader than necessary to protect that interest, the trial court must consider reasonable alternatives to closing the proceeding, and it must make findings adequate to support the closure" (*Waller v. Georgia*, 1984). In some cases, parts of a trial may be closed—for example, to protect the identity of an undercover informant during his or her testimony.

Right to Impartial Jury of the State and District Wherein the Crime Shall Have Been Committed

The right to an impartial jury promises not only that a jury will be unbiased, but also that there will be a jury trial. As interpreted by the Supreme Court, this right means that defendants charged with felonies or with misdemeanors punishable by more than six months' imprisonment are entitled to be tried before a jury. The right was extended to the states in 1968, in the case of *Duncan v. Louisiana*. Most states also allow defendants to be tried by a jury for less serious misdemeanors, but states are not constitutionally required to do so.

For practical purposes, the right to an impartial jury is achieved by providing a representative jury, that is, a jury randomly selected from a fair cross section of the community. However, whether members of such a jury will be impartial in a particular case is a question that defies an easy answer. Juries will be discussed more extensively in Chapter 8.

Finally, the Sixth Amendment guarantees the specific **venue,** or the place of trial. (Venue is also mentioned in the Constitution in Article III, Section 2: "Trial shall be held in the State where the said crimes shall have been committed. . . . ") The venue of a trial must be geographically appropriate. Generally, a crime must be tried in the jurisdiction—the politically defined geographical area—in which it was committed. However, if a defense attorney believes that a client cannot get a fair trial in the appropriate venue because of adverse publicity or for some other reason, the attorney can ask the court for a change of venue. If the change of venue is granted, the trial will be moved to another location (within the state in cases of state law violations), where, presumably, the adverse publicity or other factors are not as great.

Right to Be Informed of the Nature and Cause of the Accusation

The right to notice and a hearing is the very core of what is meant by due process. In *Twining v. New Jersey* (1908), for example, the Supreme Court held that "due process requires . . . that there shall be notice and opportunity for hearing given the parties. . . . [T]hese two fundamental conditions . . . seem to be universally prescribed in all systems of law established by civilized countries." The reason for the right is to prevent the practice, common in some countries, of holding suspects indefinitely without telling them why they are being held.

venue
The place of the trial. It must be geographically appropriate.

Right to Confront Opposing Witnesses The Sixth Amendment right to confront opposing witnesses was extended to trials in state courts in 1965, in the case of *Pointer v. Texas*. In essence, it means that defendants have a right to be present during their trials (otherwise, they could not confront opposing witnesses) and to cross-examine witnesses against them. However, the right to be present during the trial may be forfeited by a defendant's disruptive behavior. Thus, if a defendant continues to scream, use profanity, or refuse to sit quietly after being warned by the judge, the judge may have the defendant removed from the trial (see *Illinois v. Allen*, 1970).

Right to Compulsory Process for Obtaining Favorable Witnesses This right ensures a defendant the use of the subpoena power of the court to compel the testimony of any witnesses who may have information useful to the defense. A **subpoena** is a written order issued by a court that requires a person to appear at a certain time and place to give testimony. It can also require that documents and objects be made available for examination by the court. Even though the right to compulsory process for obtaining favorable witnesses was already applicable in many states because of its inclusion in state constitutions and laws, the Supreme Court officially extended it to state trials in 1967, in the case of *Washington v. Texas*.

Right to Counsel The Sixth Amendment right to privately retained and paid-for counsel has existed in federal courts since the ratification of the Bill of Rights. Criminal defendants in state courts did not gain the right until 1954. In the case of *Chandler v. Fretag*, the Supreme Court held that the right to a privately retained lawyer is "unqualified," that is, as long as a criminal defendant (or suspect) can afford to hire an attorney, he or she has the right to be represented by that attorney, not only at trial, but at any stage of the criminal justice process. But what if a criminal defendant were indigent, lacking the funds to hire an attorney? It was not until 1938, in the case of *Johnson v. Zerbst*, that the Supreme Court first extended the Sixth Amendment right to counsel to indigent defendants facing felony charges in federal trials. Another 25 years passed before the right to counsel was extended to indigent defendants facing felony charges in state courts, for which imprisonment could be the result of conviction. That right was granted in the famous case of *Gideon v. Wainwright* (1963). Finally, in 1972, in the case of *Argersinger v. Hamlin*, the Court extended the Sixth Amendment right to counsel to defendants in misdemeanor trials in which a sentence to jail might result. Thus, as a result of those decisions, no person may be imprisoned for any offense, whether classified as petty, misdemeanor, or felony, unless he or she is represented by counsel. If the person cannot afford to hire an attorney, then the court is required to appoint one.

In other Supreme Court decisions, the Sixth Amendment right to counsel has been extended to indigents at additional *critical stages* (described in Chapter 8 and elsewhere in this book); and other circumstances in the administration of justice. Those include (by date of Supreme Court decision):

---

subpoena
A written order issued by a court that requires a person to appear at a certain time and place to give testimony. It can also require that documents and objects be made available for examination by the court.

Jury Flexibility
In 1994, the state of Florida passed a law allowing a jury selected in one county to hear a trial in another county. Before the law, trials—not juries—were moved, often causing hardship to victims' families.

1. Arraignment, under most circumstances (*Hamilton v. Alabama,* 1961).
2. The plea bargaining process (*Carnley v. Cochran,* 1962).
3. Initial appearances where defendants may be compelled to make decisions that may later be formally used against them (*White v. Maryland,* 1963).
4. A first appeal that is a matter of right, that is, an appeal made available to all convicted defendants (*Douglas v. California,* 1963).
5. Questioning by law enforcement officers of suspects in police custody (*Escobedo v. Illinois,* 1964).
6. Proceedings after a grand jury indictment (*Massiah v. United States,* 1964).
7. Postindictment police lineups (*Gilbert v. California,* 1967).
8. Sentencing (*Mempa v. Rhay,* 1967).
9. Juvenile court proceedings in which children face possible institutional commitment (*In re Gault,* 1967).
10. Preliminary hearings (*Coleman v. Alabama,* 1970).
11. A psychiatric examination used by the prosecution to show that a murder defendant remains dangerous and should receive the death penalty (*Estelle v. Smith,* 1981).

To date, the Court has not extended the right to counsel to preindictment lineups, booking, grand jury investigations, or appeals after the first one.

The Sixth Amendment not only guarantees the right to counsel in the areas to which it has been extended, it also guarantees the right to the "effective assistance of counsel." However, it was not until 1984, in the case of *Strickland v. Washington,* that the Supreme Court first established standards to define "ineffective assistance of counsel." The Court ruled that two facts must be proved to show that counsel was ineffective: (1) that counsel's performance was "deficient," meaning that counsel was not a "reasonably competent attorney" or that his or her performance was below the standard commonly expected, and (2) that the deficiencies in the attorney's performance were prejudicial to the defense, meaning that there is a "reasonable probability that, but for the counsel's unprofessional errors, the result of the proceeding would have been different." In other words, not only must it be shown that an attorney was incompetent, it must also be shown that the incompetence led to the final result. Thus, if the defendant were clearly guilty of the crime with which he or she was charged, it would most likely be impossible to win a claim of "ineffective assistance of counsel."

Finally, the right to counsel may be waived, but only if the waiver is made "knowingly and intelligently." The burden of proof is on the state to show, by a preponderance of the evidence, that the waiver was made according to the aforementioned standards (see *Colorado v. Connelly,* 1986). Thus, the Sixth Amendment has also been interpreted to mean that defendants have the right to represent themselves, that is, to conduct the defense *pro se* (see *Faretta v. California,* 1975). However, if defendants choose to represent themselves, they cannot claim later, on appeal, that their defense suffered from ineffective assistance of counsel.

Right to Counsel

The Supreme Court extended the right to court-appointed counsel to indigents in death penalty cases in *Powell v. Alabama* (1932). The right, however, was extended only to indigents who were "incapable adequately of making [their] own defense because of ignorance, feeble-mindedness, illiteracy or the like." Moreover, the Court's decision in *Powell* was based on the Fourteenth Amendment right to due process and not on the Sixth Amendment right to counsel.

CAREERS IN CRIMINAL JUSTICE

Public Defender

My name is Junior A. Barrett and I am an assistant public defender in the Major Crimes Unit of the Public Defender Office in the Ninth Judicial Circuit (Orange and Osceola Counties in Florida). I have a Bachelor of Science degree in Criminal Justice Administration and Planning from John Jay College of Criminal Justice, City University of New York. I also have a Juris Doctor from Union University, Albany Law School, Albany, New York.

My decision to represent indigent clients was made before I even started college. I wanted to do something that was not only challenging, but where I felt I could help the poor. Growing up on the island of Jamaica and in Brooklyn, New York, I saw what can happen to people who don't receive proper legal representation. I knew people who were railroaded by the criminal justice system and by lawyers who did not really care, but instead saw what they did as just a job.

I started working for the Public Defender's Office in July of 1991 doing misdemeanor and traffic-related offenses. About six years ago, I was promoted to the Major Crimes Unit where I represent clients charged with capital sexual battery and first degree murder.

My days are never typical. Sometimes they start with a trip to the Orange County Jail to talk to a client about his case and what we will need to do to prepare for court. Another day might begin with me sitting down with an investigator to talk about locating witnesses.

A large portion of my day is spent trying to reconstruct my client's life and reviewing evidence.

Reconstructing my client's life involves contacting family and friends of my client. It also involves my spending a lot of time contacting different agencies in order to get copies of my client's school records, medical records, mental health records, military records, job records, and even records of time the client spent in jail or prison. This information is then used to try and convince a jury that my client should not be executed.

Ultimately, every thing I do is in preparation for trying the case. A first degree murder trial usually takes about a week to try. If the death penalty is involved, it can take two weeks. Often, the case does not end at a trial. There are appeals, rehearings, and sometimes even retrials.

It is hard to say what I like best and least about my job. Sometimes it is seeing the tears of joy running down the cheeks of my client as a jury says not guilty. Sometimes it is knowing that the State of Florida will not be able to execute my client. Other times it is the camaraderie that I find in the Public Defender's Office. On the flip side, one of the things I enjoy least about my job is a verdict of guilty in spite of the evidence. I also dislike the fact that even after a verdict of not guilty, my client's life is ruined forever. I have had clients who have lost many months of their lives because they were in jail awaiting a final disposition of their case. There is no way to give back to an innocent client the months he sat in jail waiting to be tried by a jury.

The job of an Assistant Public Defender is a morally rewarding one. You deal with real life situations that are often interesting, challenging and fast-paced. You put in long hours for little pay. You have to deal with Assistant State Attorneys who think your clients are scum, judges who care little for your clients' rights, and clients who sometimes verbally abuse you. If you can handle all that, at the end of the day you will feel that you have truly helped another human being. You have to be prepared to fight the good fight.

Would you choose to defend indigent clients? Why or why not?

The Eighth Amendment

The Eighth Amendment reads as follows:

> Excessive bail shall not be required, nor excessive fines imposed, nor cruel and unusual punishments inflicted.

Protection Against Excessive Bail and Fines   The Eighth Amendment protection against excessive bail and fines is the second Bill of Rights guarantee dealing directly with criminal justice that has not been extended to the states. (The first is the right to a grand jury indictment in felony cases.) However, there is a good possibility that the protection against excessive bail will be incorporated and made applicable to state-level criminal cases when the issue is finally brought before the Supreme Court.

In any event, it is important to note that the Eighth Amendment to the Constitution does not require that bail be granted to all suspects or defendants, only that the amount of bail not be excessive. What constitutes excessive bail is determined by several factors, including the nature and circumstances of the offense, the weight of evidence against the suspect or defendant, the character of the suspect or defendant, and the ability of the suspect or defendant to pay bail. The subject of bail will be discussed more fully in Chapter 8.

The Eighth Amendment also prohibits excessive fines. What is excessive depends on the seriousness of the crime. For example, in a conviction for illegal possession of a small amount of marijuana, a defendant's having to forfeit his or her home might be considered an excessive fine.

Protection Against Cruel and Unusual Punishment   The final prohibition of the Eighth Amendment is against "cruel and unusual punishment." That prohibition was extended to trials in state courts in 1962, in *Robinson v. California*. Generally, discussions of this issue involve the practice of capital punishment, or the death penalty, which will be discussed in detail in Chapter 9. Here we will provide only a brief history of the definition of cruel and unusual punishment.

For approximately 120 years after the adoption of the Bill of Rights, the Supreme Court employed a fixed, historical meaning for "cruel and unusual punishment." In other words, the Court interpreted the concept's meaning in light of the practices that were authorized and were in use at the time the Eighth Amendment was adopted (1791). Thus, only the most barbarous punishments and tortures were prohibited. Capital punishment itself was not prohibited, because there was explicit reference to it in the Fifth Amendment and it was in use when the Eighth Amendment was adopted.

The Court, in *Wilkerson v. Utah* (1878), provided examples of punishments that were prohibited by the Eighth Amendment because they involved "torture" or "unnecessary cruelty." They included punishments in which the criminal "was emboweled alive, beheaded, and quartered." In another case, *In re Kemmler* (1890), the Court expanded the meaning of cruel and unusual punishment to include punishments that "involve torture or lingering death . . . something more than the mere extinguishment of life." The Court also provided some examples of punishments that would be prohibited under that standard: "burning at the stake, crucifixion, breaking on the wheel, or the like."

In 1910, in the noncapital case of *Weems v. United States,* the Supreme Court abandoned its fixed, historical definition of cruel and unusual punishment and created a new one. Weems was a U.S. government official in the Philippines who was convicted of making two false accounting entries, amounting to 616 pesos.[12] He was sentenced to 15 years of hard labor and was forced to wear chains on his ankles and wrists. After completing his sentence, he was to be under surveillance for life, and he was to lose his voting rights as well. Weems argued that his punishment was disproportionate to his crime, and, therefore, cruel and unusual.

The Court agreed with Weems and, breaking with tradition, held "(1) that the meaning of the Eighth Amendment is not restricted to the intent of the Framers, (2) that the Eighth Amendment bars punishments that are excessive, and (3) that what is excessive is not fixed in time but changes with evolving social conditions." Thus, the Court no longer interpreted the concept of cruel and unusual punishment in the context of punishments in use when the Eighth Amendment was adopted. Instead, it chose to interpret the concept in the context of "evolving social conditions."

The Court further clarified its position nearly 50 years later, in another noncapital case, *Trop v. Dulles* (1958). As punishment for desertion during World War II, Trop was stripped of his U.S. citizenship. In reviewing the case on appeal, the Court ruled that the punishment was cruel and unusual because it was an affront to basic human dignity. Noting that the "dignity of man" was "the basic concept underlying the Eighth Amendment," the Court held that Trop's punishment exceeded "the limits of civilized standards." Referring to the earlier *Weems* case, the Court emphasized that "the limits of civilized standards . . . draws its meaning from the evolving standards of decency that mark the progress of a maturing society." Those "evolving standards of decency" are, in turn, determined by "objective indicators, such as the enactments of legislatures as expressions of 'the will of the people,' the decisions of juries, and the subjective moral judgments of members of the Supreme Court itself." In short, it appears that a punishment enacted by a legislature and imposed by a judge or jury will *not* be considered cruel and unusual, as long as the U.S. Supreme Court determines that (1) it is not grossly disproportionate to the magnitude of the crime, (2) it has been imposed for the same offense in other jurisdictions, and (3) it has been imposed for other offenses in the same jurisdiction (see *Solem v. Helm,* 1983; *Harmelin v. Michigan,* 1991).

4.2 CRITICAL THINKING

1. Which of the amendments within the Bill of Rights do you think are the most protective of the rights of the accused? Why?

2. Why is the Bill of Rights subject to interpretation by the Supreme Court?

CAREERS IN CRIMINAL JUSTICE

Paralegal

My name is Renée Daniel and I have an Associate of Applied Science Degree in Paralegal Studies from State Technical Institute at Memphis now called Southwest Tennessee Community College. Currently I am a senior pursuing a Bachelor of Arts Degree in Criminology and Criminal Justice from the University of Memphis. After graduating from State Tech, I was chosen by the Chairperson and Associate Professors of the Paralegal Studies Department to be the recipient of a scholarship to pursue my Bachelors Degree and also work as a paralegal in the Shelby County Jail Law Library.

Prior to graduating from State Tech, I interned as a paralegal for the Shelby County Division of Corrections. As a paralegal intern I had the opportunity to learn the various duties and responsibilities a paralegal encounters. During my internship I was able to review and answer inmate disciplinary appeals, draft documents, review discovery for litigation, and research case law and brief cases.

As a paralegal in the County Jail I assist inmates/pre-trial detainees with legal research. Inmates are scheduled to report to the law library through program services in groups. My job involves assisting them in locating case law, statutes, sentencing guidelines, information pertaining to criminal procedure, pre-trial motions and petitions. I act as a liaison between the inmates and the courts by verifying all outgoing legal calls. I have contacted attorneys, probation officers, parole officers, court clerks, and on some occasions, Immigration and Naturalization Services. My duties as a paralegal not only involve assisting inmates with preparation for trial/appeal but also managing and organizing the law library. I log and inventory all legal material that comes to the library and supervise the placement and rotation of books and supplements. In order to adequately assist the inmates with significant research, the legal material must be monitored at all times. I consult frequently with practicing attorneys regarding relevant substantive and procedural legal material that would help those who are preparing for trial or filing motions. If we do not already have the material, I submit a request to the Director of Programs to order necessary items.

The aspect I like most about my job is the opportunity I have to utilize the skills I have learned in the Paralegal Studies and Criminology and Criminal Justice programs. I enjoy legal research and applying legal principles to substantive criminal law. My job allows me to see first-hand how the criminal justice system works from arrest to sentencing and appeal. What I like least about my job are the imperfections that exist in the criminal justice system. I often see several inmates who have been detained in the jail for a year or more before they are indicted. There have been cases where inmates have served their entire sentences in the jail by the time they go to trial. Another aspect about my job that I like least is the destructive behavior that some inmates display by destroying legal books. Once these books are destroyed it is difficult to have them replaced.

Paralegals work in several areas of the legal system with knowledge of substantive and procedural law. A paralegal has the opportunity to work in numerous areas of the law. I would advise paralegal students to intern first to gain insight and experience in the area of law in which they wish to work.

What type of growth opportunities would you expect as a paralegal?

4.3 Protecting the Accused From Miscarriages of Justice

The legal system of the United States is unique in the world in the number of procedural rights that it provides people suspected or accused of crimes. The primary reason for procedural rights is to protect innocent people, as much as possible, from being arrested, charged, convicted, or punished for crimes they did not commit. One of the basic tenets of our legal system is that a person is considered innocent until proven guilty. However, even with arguably the most highly developed system of due-process rights in the world, people continue to be victims of miscarriages of justice.

Unfortunately, there is no official record of miscarriages of justice, so it is impossible to determine precisely how many actually occur each year. Nevertheless, in an effort to provide some idea of the extent of the problem, a study was conducted of wrongful convictions—miscarriages of justice at just one of the stages in the administration of justice.[13] In the study, *wrongful convictions* were defined as

> cases in which a person [is] convicted of a felony but later . . . found innocent beyond a reasonable doubt, generally due to a confession by the actual offender, evidence that had been available but was not sufficiently used at the time of conviction, new evidence that was not previously available, and other factors.

The conclusions of the study were based on the findings of a survey. All attorneys general in the United States and its territories were surveyed, and in Ohio, all presiding judges of common pleas courts, all county prosecutors, all county public defenders, all county sheriffs, and the chiefs of police of seven major cities were also surveyed. The authors of the study conservatively estimated that approximately 0.5 percent of all felony convictions are in error. In other words, of every 1,000 persons convicted of felonies in the United States, about 5 are probably innocent. The authors believe that the frequency of error is probably higher in less serious felony and misdemeanor cases.

Although an error rate of 0.5 percent may not seem high, consider that in 1998, a typical year, approximately 14.5 million people were arrested in the United States.[14] Assuming conservatively that 50 percent of all people arrested are convicted[15]—about 7.25 million convictions in 1998—then approximately 36,250 people were probably wrongfully convicted!

Eyewitness misidentification is the most important factor contributing to wrongful convictions. The second and third most important contributing factors are police and prosecutorial errors, respectively. Overzealous police officers and prosecutors, convinced that a suspect or defendant is guilty, may prompt witnesses, suggest to witnesses what may have occurred at the time of the crime, conceal or fabricate evidence, or even commit perjury. Another factor contributing to wrongful convictions is guilty pleas made "voluntarily" by innocent defendants. Innocent defendants are more likely to plead guilty to crimes they did not commit when they are faced with multiple charges and when the probability of severe punishment is great. They are also more likely to plead guilty to crimes they did not commit when they are mentally incompetent.

Death Row Reversals

From 1976, when the Supreme Court reinstated the death penalty, through June, 2000, 87 inmates have been freed from death row because of problems or errors in the legal process. Common reasons for reversals include (1) key witnesses lied or recanted their testimony, (2) police overlooked or withheld important evidence, (3) DNA testing showed someone else committed the crime, (4) the defense lawyer was incompetent or negligent, and (5) prosecutors withheld exculpatory evidence from the defense.

SOURCE: Jonathan Alter, "The Death Penalty on Trial" (*Newsweek*, June 12, 2000).

When the charge is a less serious one, innocent people who are unable to post bail sometimes admit guilt to be released from jail immediately. For many people, release from jail is more important than a minor criminal record. Besides, it is often difficult to prove one's innocence (Remember that in the United States the prosecution is required to prove, beyond a reasonable doubt, that defendants are guilty. Defendants are not required to prove their innocence.) Problems faced by innocent people wrongly accused of crimes include inability to establish an alibi; misidentification by witnesses who swear they saw the defendant commit the crime; a lawyer who lacks the skill, time, or resources to mount a good defense; and a lawyer who is unconvinced of the defendant's innocence. Inadequate legal representation is one of the most important factors in wrongful convictions in death penalty cases.[16]

Other factors contributing to wrongful convictions are community pressures, especially in interracial and rape cases; false accusations; knowledge of a defendant's prior criminal record; judicial errors, bias, or neglect of duty; errors made by medical examiners and forensic experts; and errors in criminal record keeping and computerized information systems.[17] In short, numerous factors can cause wrongful convictions. And remember, the foregoing discussion addresses only wrongful convictions; it does not consider wrongful arrests or other miscarriages of justice.

Despite such miscarriages of justice, many people still resent the provision of procedural safeguards to criminal suspects. The accusation is frequently made that procedural rights protect criminals and penalize victims—that many criminals escape conviction and punishment because of procedural technicalities. For example, a driving force behind the good faith and inevitable-discovery exceptions was the belief that a substantial number of criminal offenders escaped punishment because of the exclusionary rule. The available evidence, however, does not support the belief. One of the most thorough studies of the effect of the exclusionary rule was conducted by the National Institute of Justice (NIJ).[18] The NIJ study examined felony cases in California between 1976 and 1979—a period during which the American public was becoming increasingly alarmed about the problem of crime and especially about what was perceived as the practice of allowing a substantial number of criminals to escape punishment because of legal technicalities. The study found that only a tiny fraction (fewer than 0.5 percent) of the felony cases reaching the courts were dismissed because of the exclusionary rule. It is important to emphasize that the study examined only the cases that reached the courts. It excluded cases that prosecutors elected not to pursue to trial because they assumed that the exclusionary rule would make the cases impossible to win. However, other studies show that although there is some variation between jurisdictions, fewer than one percent of cases overall are dropped by prosecutors before trial because of search and seizure problems.[19] Interestingly, 71.5 percent of the California cases affected by the exclusionary rule involved drug charges. The problem in most of the drug cases was that in the absence of complaining witnesses,

MYTH

Many criminals escape punishment because of the Supreme Court's decision in *Miranda v. Arizona.*

FACT

Very few criminals escape punishment because of that decision.

▲ Specific laws govern the police's right to stop and search a vehicle. *Do you think the police should be entitled to search a vehicle they have stopped because, for example, they suspect drug possession?*

overaggressive law enforcement officers had to engage in illegal behavior to obtain evidence.

A study of the effect of the exclusionary rule at the federal level was conducted by the General Accounting Office (GAO).[20] The GAO examined 2,804 cases handled by 38 different U.S. attorneys in July and August of 1978. The GAO found results similar to those found by the NIJ in California. In only 1.3 percent of the nearly 3,000 cases was evidence excluded in the federal courts. Again, it is important to emphasize that the study included only cases that went to trial. However, as noted earlier, evidence shows that, overall, fewer than one percent of cases are dropped by prosecutors before trial because of search and seizure problems. It is important to understand, moreover, that having evidence excluded from trial does not necessarily mean that a case is impossible to win and that the defendant will escape punishment. A defendant may still be convicted on the basis of evidence that was not illegally obtained.

The *Miranda* mandates, like the exclusionary rule, are also viewed by many people as legal technicalities that allow criminals found guilty to escape punishment. That view is fortified by Supreme Court Justice Byron White's dissent in *Miranda:* "In some unknown number of cases the rule will return a killer, a rapist or other criminal to the streets." No doubt, Justice White's warning is true, but the evidence suggests that only a very small percentage of cases are lost as a result of illegal confessions. In one large survey, for example, fewer than one percent of all cases were thrown out because of confessions illegally obtained.[21]

In another study of decisions made by the Indiana Court of Appeals or the Indiana Supreme Court from November 6, 1980, through August 1, 1986, the researchers found that in only 12 of 2,354 cases (0.51 percent) was a conviction overturned because of the failure of the police to correctly implement the *Miranda* safeguards.[22] In only 213 of the 2,354 cases (9 percent) was a claim even made about improper interrogation procedures by the police, and in 201 of those 213 cases, the conviction was affirmed by the appellate court, resulting in a reversal rate of 5.6 percent for the cases raising a *Miranda* question.

The authors of that study speculated on possible reasons for the low rate of successful appeals. One was that the police routinely comply with the *Miranda* decision. In fact, most police support *Miranda* and the other reforms because it makes them appear more professional. The second possible reason was that the police are able to solve most cases without having to question suspects. Studies show that the *Miranda* warnings rarely stop suspects from confessing anyway. Many suspects attempt to clear themselves in the eyes of the police and end up incriminating themselves instead; other suspects simply do not understand that they have a right to remain silent.[23] Third, the police are able to evade *Miranda* by using more sophisticated strategies, such as skillfully suggesting that suspects volunteer confessions or casually talking with suspects in the back of squad cars.[24] And, fourth, prosecutors, knowing that they cannot win cases involving illegal interrogations, screen them out before trial or settle them through alternative means, such as plea bargaining. However, as with the exclusionary rule, fewer than one percent of cases overall are dismissed or handled in other ways by prosecutors because of *Miranda*.[25] In short, the available evidence suggests that the effects of the exclusionary rule in both Fourth and Fifth Amendment contexts have been minor.[26]

4.3 CRITICAL THINKING

1. Do you think miscarriages of justice are on the increase? Decrease? Why or why not?

2. Do you think that anything can be done to combat miscarriages of justice?

Reforming the Criminal Justice System

The authors of *Actual Innocence* suggest the following reforms: *DNA testing:* Allow postconviction DNA testing nationwide. Test DNA on unsolved crimes where evidence exists. *Witness IDs:* Independent, trained examiner who does not know the suspect should conduct lineups and photo IDs to ensure investigators don't influence witnesses. Videotape lineups, photo spreads, and other identification processes to ensure neutrality. *Confessions:* Videotape all interrogations. *Informants:* Committee of prosecutors should screen all informant testimony before permission to use at trial. All deals between prosecutors and informants must be in writing. *Forensics:* Crime labs should function and be funded separately from police, prosecution, or defense. Strengthen accreditation programs for labs, establish postgraduate forensic programs at universities. *Police, prosecutors:* Establish disciplinary committees to deal with legal misconduct by defense and prosecution. *Defense attorneys:* Increase fees to attract competent lawyers. Public defenders' pay should equal prosecutors' pay. *Wrongful convictions:* Establish innocence commissions to investigate wrongful convictions. Create and fund innocence projects at law schools to represent clients. Provide compensation to those who were clearly wrongly convicted. Moratorium on death penalty.

SOURCE: Jim Dwyer, Peter Neufeld, and Barry Scheck, *Actual Innocence: Five Days to Execution and Other Dispatches from the Wrongly Convicted* (New York: Doubleday, 2000).

Review and Applications

1. Distinguish Between Criminal Law and Civil Law

There are two general types of law practiced in the United States—criminal and civil. Criminal law is a formal means of social control that involves the use of rules that are interpreted, and are enforceable, by the courts of a political community. The violation of a criminal law is a crime and is considered an offense against the state. Civil law is a means of resolving conflicts between individuals. The violation of a civil law is a tort—an injury, damage, or wrongful act—and is considered a private matter between individuals.

2. Distinguish Between Substantive Law and Procedural Law

There are two types of criminal law—substantive and procedural. Substantive law defines criminal offenses and their penalties. Procedural law specifies the ways in which substantive laws are administered. Procedural law is concerned with due process of law—the rights of people suspected of or charged with crimes.

3. List Five Features of "Good" Criminal Laws

Ideally, "good" criminal laws should possess five features: (1) politicality, (2) specificity, (3) regularity, (4) uniformity, and (5) penal sanction.

4. Explain Why Criminal Law is a Political Phenomenon

Criminal law is the result of a political process in which rules are created by human beings to prohibit or regulate the behavior of other human beings. Formal, written laws are relatively recent phenomena; the first were created about 5,000 years ago.

5. Summarize the Origins of American Criminal Law

The criminal law of the United States is, for the most part, derived from the laws of England and is the product of constitutions and legislative bodies, common law, and administrative or regulatory agency rules and decisions.

6. Relate the Role of the Courts in Defining Procedural Rights

The courts, especially the U.S. Supreme Court, have selectively defined the procedural rights of persons accused of crimes as guaranteed by the U.S. Constitution. Procedural rights, or due-process rights, are found in the Fourth, Fifth, Sixth, and Eighth Amendments to the Constitution. Through its power of judicial review, the Supreme Court has overturned federal and state actions and has reversed some of its earlier decisions. Some Supreme Court decisions expanded the rights of accused persons; other decisions limited the actions of law enforcement personnel; still other decisions relaxed the limits that had been placed on the police. Interpretations by the Supreme Court are changeable because of changes in the Court's composition. As justices die or retire, new ones are appointed. New justices bring different legal views to the Court, and, over time, help shift its position on some issues.

7. Describe the Procedural Rights in the Fourth Amendment

The Fourth Amendment protects persons from unreasonable searches and seizures (including arrests). Under most circumstances, it requires that a judge issue a search warrant authorizing law officers to search for and seize evidence of criminal activity, but the warrant can be issued only when there is *probable cause*. In 1914, the Supreme Court adopted the *exclusionary rule*, which barred evidence seized illegally from being used in a criminal trial; in 1961, the rule was made applicable to the states. Subsequent Supreme Court decisions have narrowed the application of the exclusionary rule. The Fourth Amendment also protects persons from warrantless searches and seizures in places where they have a legitimate right to expect privacy. The protection, however, does not extend to every place where a person has a legitimate right to be. The Court has permitted stopping and searching an automobile when there is probable cause to believe the car is carrying something illegal.

8. Describe the Procedural Rights in the Fifth Amendment

The Fifth Amendment provides many procedural protections, the most important of which is the protection against compelled self-incrimination. This protection was extended to most police custodial interrogations in the 1966 case of *Miranda v. Arizona.* According to *Miranda*, police custody is threatening and confessions obtained during custody can be admitted into evidence only if suspects have been (1) advised of their constitutional right to remain silent, (2) warned that what they say can be used against them in a trial, (3) informed of the right to have an attorney paid for by the state if they cannot afford one and to have the attorney present during interrogation, and (4) told of the right to terminate the interrogation at any time. Other due-process rights in the Fifth Amendment are the right to a grand jury indictment in felony cases (in federal court) and protection against double jeopardy.

9. Describe the Procedural Rights in the Sixth Amendment

Many due-process rights are provided by the Sixth Amendment: the right to a speedy and public trial, the right to an impartial jury of the state and district where the crime occurred, the right to be informed of the nature and cause of the accusation, the right to confront opposing witnesses, the right to compulsory process for obtaining favorable witnesses, and the right to counsel. In the 1963 case of *Gideon v. Wainwright,* the Supreme Court extended the right to counsel to any poor state defendant charged with a felony.

10. Describe the Procedural Rights in the Eighth Amendment

The Eighth Amendment protects against "cruel and unusual punishment." The Supreme Court has rarely ruled on this provision, generally approving a punishment as long as it has been enacted by a legislature, it has been imposed by a judge or jury, and the Court determines that (1) it is not grossly disproportionate to the magnitude of the crime, (2) it has been imposed for the same offense in other jurisdictions, and (3) it has been imposed for other offenses in the same jurisdiction. The Eighth Amendment also protects against excessive bail and fines, but those protections have not been made binding on state courts.

11. Explain Why Procedural Rights are Important to Those Accused of Crimes

The primary reason for procedural rights is to protect innocent people, as much as possible, from being arrested, charged, convicted, or punished for crimes they did not commit. However, even with the most highly developed system of procedural, or due-process, rights in the world, criminal defendants in the United States still face miscarriages of justice.

KEY TERMS

criminal law, p. 114
penal code, p. 114
tort, p. 114
civil law, p. 114
substantive law, p. 114
procedural law, p. 114
due process of law, p. 115
politicality, p. 115
specificity, p. 115
regularity, p. 115
uniformity, p. 116
penal sanction, p. 116

precedent, p. 120
stare decisis, p. 120
searches, p. 127
seizures, p. 127
warrant, p. 127
arrest, p. 127
contraband, p. 128
mere suspicion, p. 131
reasonable suspicion, p. 132
frisking, p. 132
probable cause, p. 132
preponderance of evidence, p. 133

clear and convincing evidence, p. 133
beyond a reasonable doubt, p. 133
exclusionary rule, p. 134
double jeopardy, p. 135
self-incrimination, p. 136
confession, p. 136
doctrine of fundamental fairness, p. 136
venue, p. 139
subpoena, p. 140

QUESTIONS FOR REVIEW

1. How does one know whether a particular offense is a *crime* or a *tort*?

2. How did the institution of the *eyre* contribute to the development of American criminal law?

3. What is the importance of the Magna Carta for American criminal law?

4. To what jurisdiction do federal and state criminal statutes (and local ordinances) apply?

5. What is *stare decisis*?

6. Why did it take nearly 100 years after the ratification of the Fourteenth Amendment before suspects charged with crimes at the state level were afforded most of the same due-process protections as people charged with crimes at the federal level?

7. What are *searches* and *seizures*?

8. What is an *arrest*?

9. What two conclusions must be supported by substantial and trustworthy evidence before either a search warrant or an arrest warrant is issued? (The two conclusions are different for each type of warrant.)

10. In *Chimel v. California* (1969), what limitations did the U.S. Supreme Court place on searches incident to an arrest?

11. What is *probable cause*?

12. Today, what is the principal purpose of the exclusionary rule?

13. To what critical stages in the administration of justice has the Sixth Amendment right to counsel been extended, and to what critical stages has it not been extended?

14. What two conditions must be met to show that counsel was ineffective?

15. What are some of the factors that contribute to wrongful convictions?

16. Do many criminals escape conviction and punishment because of procedural technicalities, such as the exclusionary rule or the *Miranda* mandates?

EXPERIENTIAL ACTIVITIES

1. **Make a Law** By yourself or as part of a group, create a law. Choose a behavior that is currently not against the law in your community, and write a statute to prohibit it. Make sure that all five features of "good" criminal laws are included. (If this is a group exercise, decide by majority vote any issue for which there is not a consensus.) Critique the outcome.

2. **Exclusionary Rule** Make an oral or written evaluation of the good faith and inevitable-discovery exceptions to the exclusionary rule. Has the Supreme Court gone too far in modifying the exclusionary rule? Defend your answer.

INTERNET

3. **Historical Perspectives** "The Timetable of World Legal History" found through cj.glencoe.com provides brief descriptions of important historical legal developments. (This Web site also provides links to other sources of legal information.) Choose among the available topics (for instance, the actual text of the Magna Carta), and write a summary of the information you find.

4. **Supreme Court Decisions** Access the Supreme Court Web site through cj.glencoe.com. Then select subjects of interest (especially Fourth, Fifth, Sixth, and Eighth Amendment cases), and read the Supreme Court's most recent decisions.

Megan's Law

1. The sexual assault and murder of 7-year-old Megan Kanka in New Jersey on October 31, 1994, struck a national nerve. Megan was assaulted and killed by a neighbor, Jesse Timmendequas, who had twice been convicted of similar sex offenses and was on parole. In response to the crime and public uproar, the state of New Jersey enacted "Megan's Law." The law requires sex offenders, upon their release from prison, to register with New Jersey law enforcement authorities, who are to notify the public about their release. The public is to be provided with the offender's name; a recent photograph; a physical description; a list of the offenses for which he or she was convicted; the offender's current address and place of employment or school; and the offender's automobile license plate number. The Supreme Court recently upheld Megan's Law.

   Currently, 39 states and the federal government have Megan's Laws that require sex offenders released from prison to register with local law enforcement authorities. Many of those laws, like New Jersey's, require that law enforcement officials use the information to notify schools and day-care centers and, in some cases, the sex offender's neighbors. In 1997, California enacted a law allowing citizens access to a CD-ROM with detailed information on 64,000 sex offenders living in California who had committed a broad range of sex crimes since 1944.

   In 1996, President Clinton signed into law the Pam Lyncher Sexual Offender Tracking and Identification Act, which called for a national registry of sex offenders, to be completed by the end of 1998. The national registry allows state officials to submit queries, such as the name of a job applicant at a day-care center, and to determine whether the applicant is a registered sex offender in any of the participating states.

   a. Is Megan's Law a good law? (Consider the ideal characteristics of the criminal law.)

   b. Is Megan's Law fair to sex offenders who have served their prison sentences (that is, "paid their debt to society")?

   c. What rights does a sex offender have after being released from prison?

   d. What rights does a community have to protect itself from known sex offenders who have been released from prison?

   e. When the rights of an individual and the rights of a community conflict, whose rights should take precedence? Why?

Surveillance Cameras

2. In January 1998, police in Cincinnati, Ohio, began using a special video camera to monitor activity on a "crime-ridden street corner." The camera, which cost $11,000, rotates, enabling it to observe activity in a 1,000-foot radius. It records 24 hours a day, and it can read a license plate number from more than a block away. To protect privacy, policy requires that all tapes be erased after 96 hours if they show no criminal activity. Residents of the area claim that the camera's presence has cleaned up the area by, among other things, scaring away drug dealers. Critics worry about government spying on residents. The city council is considering putting cameras in other parts of the city.

   a. Should the city council have surveillance cameras installed in other parts of the city? Why or why not?

   b. What legal or procedural issues should be considered before making a decision?

Review and Applications

ADDITIONAL READING

Alderman, Ellen and Caroline Kennedy. *In Our Defense: The Bill of Rights in Action.* New York: William Morrow, 1991.

Dwyer, Jim, Peter Neufeld, and Barry Scheck. *Actual Innocence: Five Days to Execution and Other Dispatches from the Wrongly Convicted.* New York: Doubleday, 2000.

ENDNOTES

1. Jay A. Sigler, *Understanding Criminal Law* (Boston: Little, Brown, 1981), p. 3.
2. The discussion in the remainder of this section is based on material from Edwin H. Sutherland and Donald R. Cressey, *Criminology,* 9th ed. (Philadelphia: J. B. Lippincott, 1974), p. 8.
3. Most of the material in this section comes from Will Durant, *Our Oriental Heritage,* Part 1 of *The Story of Civilization* (New York: Simon & Schuster, 1954).
4. Most of the material in this section comes from Raymond J. Michalowski, *Order, Law, and Crime: An Introduction to Criminology* (New York: Random House, 1985).
5. See Archibald Cox, *The Court and the Constitution* (Boston: Houghton Mifflin, 1987), pp. 239–49.
6. For an examination of the influence of the Burger and Rehnquist Courts on criminal procedure, see Mary Margaret Weddington and W. Richard Janikowski, "The Rehnquist Court: The Counter-Revolution That Wasn't: Part II, The Counter-Revolution That Is," *Criminal Justice Review,* Vol. 21 (1997), pp. 231–50.
7. In addition to the Supreme Court cases themselves, much of the information in the remainder of this chapter is from the following sources: John Ferdico, *Criminal Procedure for the Law Enforcement Officer* (St. Paul, MN: West, 1975); Yale Kamisar, Wayne R. LaFave, and Jerold H. Israel, *Modern Criminal Procedure,* 7th ed. (St. Paul, MN: West, 1990); Sanford H. Kadish and Monrad G. Paulsen, *Criminal Law and Its Processes,* 3d ed. (Boston: Little, Brown, 1975); Wayne R. LaFave and Jerold H. Israel, *Criminal Procedure* (St. Paul, MN: West, 1984, Supp. 1991); Jerold H. Israel and Wayne R. LaFave, *Criminal Procedure in a Nutshell* (St. Paul, MN: West, 1975); John M. Scheb and John M. Scheb II, *Criminal Law and Procedure,* 2d ed. (St. Paul, MN: West, 1994).
8. *Katz v. United States,* 389 U.S. 347 (1967).
9. *Florida v. J. L.* (No. 98-1993, decided March 28, 2000).
10. *Illinois v. Wardlow* (No. 98-1036, decided January 12, 2000).
11. *Dickerson v. United States* (No. 99-5525, April 19, 2000).
12. See Raymond Paternoster, *Capital Punishment in America* (New York: Lexington, 1991), p. 51.
13. C. Ronald Huff, Arye Rattner, and Edward Sagarin, "Guilty Until Proven Innocent: Wrongful Conviction and Public Policy," *Crime and Delinquency,* Vol. 32, 1986, pp. 518–44.
14. U.S. Department of Justice, Federal Bureau of Investigation, Crime in the United States, 1998 (Washington: GPO, 1999), p. 210.
15. See Huff et al., op. cit., p. 523.
16. Marcia Coyle, Fred Strasser, and Marianne Lavelle, "Fatal Defense," *The National Law Journal,* Vol. 12 (1990), pp. 30–44.
17. Huff et al., op. cit., pp. 530–33.
18. Samuel Walker, *Sense and Nonsense About Crime: A Policy Guide* (Monterey, CA: Brooks/Cole, 1985), pp. 94–97.
19. F. Feeney, F. Dill, and A. Weir, *Arrests Without Conviction: How Often They Occur and Why* (Washington: U.S. Department of Justice, National Institute of Justice, 1983); P. Nardulli, "The Societal Cost of the Exclusionary Rule: An Empirical Assessment," *American Bar Foundation Research Journal* (1983), pp. 585–609; *Report of the Comptroller General of the United States, Impact of the Exclusionary Rule on Federal Criminal Prosecutions* (Washington: U.S. General Accounting Office, 1979); K. Brosi, *A Cross City Comparison of Felony Case Processing* (Washington: U.S. Department of Justice, Law Enforcement Assistance Administration, 1979); B. Forst, J. Lucianovic, and S. Cox, *What Happens After Arrest: A Court Perspective of Police Operations in the District of Columbia* (Washington: U.S. Department of Justice, Law Enforcement Assistance Administration, 1978).
20. Walker, op. cit.
21. Cited in Tamar Jacoby, "Fighting Crime by the Rules: Why Cops Like Miranda," *Newsweek* (July 18, 1988), p. 53.
22. Karen L. Guy and Robert G. Huckabee, "Going Free on a Technicality: Another Look at the Effect of the Miranda Decision on the Criminal Justice Process," *Criminal Justice Research Bulletin,* Vol. 4 (1988), pp. 1–3.
23. Jacoby, op. cit.
24. Guy and Huckabee, op. cit.
25. Walker, op. cit.
26. For a different view, see Paul G. Cassell and Bret S. Hayman, "Police Interrogation in the 1990s: An Empirical Study of the Effects of Miranda," *UCLA Law Review,* Vol. 43 (1996), pp. 839–931; and George C. Thomas, III, "Is Miranda a Real-World Failure? A Plea for More and Better Empirical Evidence," *UCLA Law Review,* Vol. 43 (1996), pp. 821–37.

PART 2

Law Enforcement

CHAPTER 5

History and Structure of American Law Enforcement

CHAPTER 6

Police Work

CHAPTER 7

Policing America: Issues and Ethics

History and Structure of American Law Enforcement

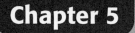

CHAPTER OBJECTIVES

After completing this chapter, you should be able to:

1. Briefly describe the jurisdictional limitations of American law enforcement.

2. Trace the English origins of American law enforcement.

3. Discuss the early development of American law enforcement.

4. Describe the major developments that have occurred in policing in America.

5. Describe the structure of American law enforcement.

6. Discuss the development and growth of private security in the United States.

5.1 The Limited Authority of American Law Enforcement

jurisdiction
The right or authority of a justice agency to act in regard to a particular subject matter, territory, or person.

The United States has almost 19,000 public law enforcement agencies at the federal, state, and local levels of government. The vast majority of those agencies, however, are local, serving municipalities, townships, villages, and counties. The authority of each agency—whether it is the FBI, a state highway patrol, or a city or county sheriff's department—is carefully limited by law. The territory within which an agency may operate is also restricted. The city police, for example, may not patrol or answer calls for service outside the city's boundaries unless cooperative pacts have been developed. **Jurisdiction,** which is defined as a specific geographical area, also means the right or authority of a justice agency to act in regard to a particular subject matter, territory, or person. It includes the laws a particular police agency is permitted to enforce and the duties it is allowed to perform. The Oklahoma Highway Patrol, for example, has investigative and enforcement responsibilities only in traffic matters, while the Kentucky State Police have a broader jurisdiction that includes the authority to conduct criminal investigations throughout the state. Each of the nearly two dozen major federal law enforcement agencies has a specific jurisdiction, although one criminal event may involve crimes that give several federal agencies concurrent jurisdiction. For example, in a bank robbery, if mail of any sort is taken, both the Postal Inspections Service and the FBI are likely to investigate the case.

Beyond the statutes that create and direct law enforcement agencies, the procedural law derived from U.S. Supreme Court decisions also imposes limitations on the authority of those agencies. Giving arrested suspects the familiar *Miranda* warnings before questioning is a good example of the Court's role in limiting the authority of the police. In addition, police civilian review boards, departmental policies and procedures, and civil liability suits against officers who have abused their authority curtail the power of the police in the United States.

Thus, there is a great difference between law enforcement with limited authority, operating under the rule of law in a democratic nation, and law enforcement in countries where the law is by decree and the police are simply a tool of those in power. Even in comparison with other democratic nations of the world, however, the United States has remarkably more police agencies that operate under far more restrictions on their authority. To understand the origin of those unique qualities of law enforcement in the United States, it is necessary to look first at the history of law enforcement in England, the nation that provided the model for most of American criminal justice.

5.1 CRITICAL THINKING

Why do you think it is important that law enforcement agencies have limited authority?

▲ The only police contact most citizens have is in a traffic situation in a local or state jurisdiction. *Should citizens have more contact with the police in non-law enforcement situations? Why or why not?*

5.2 English Roots

If you are the victim of a crime, you might expect that a uniformed patrol officer will respond quickly to your call and that a plainclothes detective will soon follow up on the investigation. Because there are thousands of police departments in local communities across the nation, you might also take for granted that the police handling your case are paid public servants employed by your city or county. Such was not always the case in the United States—nor in England, where the basic concepts of American law enforcement and criminal justice originated. The criminal justice system in England took hundreds of years to develop, but eventually the idea arose of a locally controlled uniformed police force with follow-up plainclothes investigators.

The Tithing System

Before the twelfth century in England, justice was primarily a private matter based on revenge and retribution.[1] Victims of a crime had to pursue perpetrators without assistance from the king or his agents. Disputes were often settled by blood feuds, in which families would wage war on each other.

By the twelfth century, a system of group protection had begun to develop. Often referred to as the **tithing system** or the frankpledge system, it afforded some improvements over past practices. Ten families, or a *tithing*, were required to become a group and agree to follow the law, keep the peace in their areas, and bring law violators to justice. Over even larger areas, ten tithings were grouped together to form a *hundred*, and one or several hundreds constituted a *shire*, which was similar to a modern American county.

tithing system
A private self-help protection system in early medieval England, in which a group of ten families, or a *tithing*, agreed to follow the law, keep the peace in their areas, and bring law violators to justice.

History and Structure of American Law Enforcement **CHAPTER 5**

The shire was under the direction of the **shire reeve** (later called the *sheriff*), the forerunner of the American sheriff. The shire reeve received some assistance from elected constables at the town and village levels, who organized able-bodied citizens into **posses** to chase and apprehend offenders.[2] County law enforcement agencies in the United States still sometimes use posses to apprehend law violators.

The Constable-Watch System

The Statute of Winchester, passed in 1285, formalized the **constable-watch system** of protection. The statute provided for one man from each parish to be selected as **constable,** or chief peacekeeper. The statute further granted constables the power to draft citizens as watchmen and require them to guard the city at night. Watchmen were not paid for their efforts and, as a result, were often found sleeping or sitting in a pub rather than performing their duties. In addition, the statute required all male citizens between the ages of 15 and 60 to maintain weapons and to join in the *hue and cry,* meaning to come to the aid of the constable or the watchman when either called for help. If they did not come when called, the male citizens were subject to criminal penalties for aiding the offender. This system of community law enforcement lasted well into the 1700s.

Two features of this system are worthy of note. First, the people were the police, and second, the organization of the protection system was local. These two ideas were transported to the American colonies centuries later.

The Bow Street Runners

In 1748, Henry Fielding, a London magistrate, founded a group of professional law enforcement agents to apprehend criminals and recover stolen property in the entertainment district of London, known as Bow Street Covent Garden. This publicly funded detective force, named the Bow Street Runners, was by far the most effective official law enforcement organization of its day. Efforts to duplicate it in other parts of London proved unsuccessful, but Fielding's work in organizing the first British detective force, and his writing addressing the shortcomings of the criminal justice system, had a great deal of influence. They helped pave the way for a more professional and better-organized response to the crime problems that were dramatically increasing in London by the end of the eighteenth century.[3]

The London Metropolitan Police

Because of the Industrial Revolution, urban populations in cities like London swelled with an influx of people from the countryside looking for work in factories. A major result of this social transformation was that England began experiencing increasing poverty, public disorder, and crime. There was no clear consensus about what to do. Several efforts to establish a central police force for London had been opposed by people who believed that police of any kind were a throwback to the absolute power formerly wielded by English kings. Parliament eventually responded, in 1829, with the London Metropolitan Police Act. It created a 1,000-officer police force with professional standards to replace the patchwork of community law enforcement systems then in use. Members of the London Police became known as

Henry Fielding
Henry Fielding, founder of the Bow Street Runners, is perhaps better known for his literary accomplishments. His most famous novel is *Tom Jones.*

bobbies or *peelers,* after Robert Peel, the British Home Secretary who had prodded Parliament to create the police force.

To ensure discipline, the London Police were organized according to military rank and structure and were under the command of two magistrates, who were later called commissioners. According to Peel, the main function of the police was to prevent crime, not by force but by preventive patrol of the community. Londoners, who resented such close scrutiny, did not at first welcome this police presence in the community. Eventually, though, the bobbies (the term was originally derogatory) showed that the police could have a positive effect on the quality of life in the community. Peel's military approach to policing, as well as some of his other principles, remain in effect today throughout the world. **Peel's Principles of Policing** are outlined in Figure 5–1.[4]

Peel's Principles of Policing
A dozen standards proposed by Robert Peel, the author of the legislation resulting in the formation of the London Metropolitan Police Department. The standards are still applicable to today's law enforcement.

FIGURE 5–1

Robert Peel's Principles of Policing

1. The police must be stable, efficient, and organized along military lines.

2. The police must be under governmental control.

3. The absence of crime will best prove the efficiency of police.

4. The distribution of crime news is essential.

5. The deployment of police strength both by time and area is essential.

6. No quality is more indispensable to a policeman than a perfect command of temper; a quiet, determined manner has more effect than violent action.

7. Good appearance commands respect.

8. The securing and training of proper persons is at the root of efficiency.

9. Public security demands that every police officer be given a number.

10. Police headquarters should be centrally located and easily accessible to the people.

11. Policemen should be hired on a probationary basis.

12. Police records are necessary to the correct distribution of police strength.

5.2 CRITICAL THINKING

Do you think any of the early English systems of law enforcement (e.g., tithing) could work today? Why or why not?

5.3 The Development of American Law Enforcement

The United States has more police departments than any other nation in the world. The major reason for this is that local control is highly regarded in the United States. Thus, like many other services, even small communities that can barely afford police service provide it locally. This practice is primarily responsible for the disparity in the quality of American police personnel and service. The struggle to improve American law enforcement began even before formal police departments came into existence.

Early American Law Enforcement

The chance for a better life, free of government intervention, was key in the decision of many colonists to cross the Atlantic and settle in the New World. American colonists from England brought with them the constable-watch system with which they were familiar, if not completely satisfied. Boston established a night watch as early as 1634. Except for the military's intervention in major disturbances, the watch system, at least in the cities, was the means of preventing crime and apprehending criminals for the next two centuries. As in England, the people were the police. Citizens could pay for watch replacements, and often the worst of the lot ended up protecting the community. In fact, Boston and other cities frequently deployed the most elderly citizens and occasionally sentenced minor offenders to serve on the watch.[5] Later, in rural and southern areas of the country, the office of sheriff was established and the power of the posse was used to maintain order and apprehend offenders. In essence, two forms of protection began to evolve—the watch in the villages, towns, and cities and the sheriff in the rural areas, unincorporated areas, and counties. Communities in the North often had both systems.

Law Enforcement in the Cities

As had happened in England, the growth of the Industrial Revolution lured people away from the farms to cities. Large groups of newcomers, sometimes immigrants from other countries, settled near factories. Factory workers put in long days, often in unsafe and unhealthy working conditions. Some workers organized strikes, seeking better working conditions, but the strikes were quickly suppressed. As the populations of cities swelled, living conditions in some areas became overcrowded and unhealthy.

Major episodes of urban violence occurred in the first half of the nineteenth century because of the social and economic changes transforming American cities. Racial and ethnic tensions often reached a boiling point, resulting in mob disturbances that lasted for days. A particular source of trouble were the drinking establishments located throughout working-class districts of cities. Regular heavy drinking led to fights, brawls, and even full-scale riots.

Unlike London, which organized its police force in 1829, American citizens resisted the formation of police departments, relying instead on the

The "Leatherheads"

In Dutch-influenced New York in the seventeenth century, the first paid officers on the night watch were known as *leatherheads* because they wore leather helmets similar in appearance to the helmets worn by today's firefighters. The leatherheads were not known for their attention to duty and often spent entirely too much of their watch schedule inside.

SOURCE: Carl Sifakis, "Leatherheads: First New York Police," *The Encyclopedia of American Crimes* (New York: Smithmark Publishers, Inc., 1992).

constable-watch system, whose members lit streetlights, patrolled the streets to maintain order, and arrested some suspicious people. Constables often had daytime duties, which included investigating health hazards, carrying out orders of the court, clearing the streets of debris, and apprehending criminals against whom complaints had been filed. Neither the night watch nor the constables tried to prevent or discover crime, nor did they wear any kind of uniform. This weak protection system was unable to contain the increasing level of lawlessness.

Municipal Police Forces In 1844, New York City combined its day and night watches to form the first paid, unified police force in the United States. Close ties developed between the police and local political leaders. As with the first police in London, citizens were suspicious of the constant presence of police officers in their neighborhoods. Also, citizens had little respect for the New York police because they thought they were political hacks, appointed by local officials who wanted to control the police for their own gain. During the next several years, the struggle to control the police in New York built to a fever pitch.[6]

In 1853, the New York state legislature formed the Municipal Police Department, but within four years that force was so corrupt from taking bribes to overlook crime that the legislature decided to abolish it. It was replaced by the Metropolitan Police, which was administered by five commissioners appointed by the governor. The commissioners then selected one superintendent. Each commissioner was to oversee the others, as well as the superintendent, and keep them all honest. The new structure was an improvement, in the minds of the legislature, that would prevent corruption in the top level of the department. But when the Metropolitan Police Board called on Mayor Fernando Wood to abolish the Municipal Police, he refused. Even after New York's highest court upheld a decision to disband the Municipals, the mayor refused. The Metropolitans even tried to arrest Mayor Wood, but that failed attempt resulted in a pitched battle between the two police forces. When the National Guard was called in, Mayor Wood submitted to arrest but was immediately released on bail.

During the summer of 1857, the two police forces often fought over whether or not to arrest certain criminals. A particularly troubling practice was one police force's releasing from custody the criminals arrested by the other force. Lawbreakers operated freely during the dispute between the two police forces. Criminal gangs had a free hand to commit robberies and burglaries during most of that summer. The public became enraged over this neglect of duty and the increased danger on the streets of New York City. Only when another court order upheld the decision to disband the Municipal Police did Mayor Wood finally comply.

Following the course charted by New York City, other large cities in the United States soon established their own police departments. In 1855, Boston combined its day and night watches to form a city police department. By the end of the decade, police departments had been formed in many major cities east of the Mississippi. The duties of the officers did not vary substantially from the duties of those who had served on the watch. After the Civil War, however, peace officers began to take on the trappings of today's police. They began to wear uniforms, carry nightsticks, and even carry

Devil's Night
The citizens of Detroit, sick and tired of vandals that torched cars and vacant houses during Devil's Night each Halloween, formed street patrols to prevent arson in their neighborhoods. The number of Devil's Night fires that plagued Detroit shrunk in most years between 1984 and 1997. In 1984, firefighters counted 810 fires; in 1997, with 35,000 volunteers patrolling the streets, they recorded only 168.

SOURCE: "Devil's Night Touched By Angels," CBS News.com, October 31, 2000, and Ze've Chafets, *Devil's Night And Other True Stories* (New York: Random House, 1990).

▲ By the early 1900s, most American cities had organized, uniformed police forces similar to the police force of Newport, Rhode Island, pictured circa 1910. *How do current police officers differ from those depicted in the photo?*

firearms, although many citizens resisted giving this much authority to the police.

Tangle of Politics and Policing Until the 1920s in most American cities, party politics prevented the development of professional police departments. Local political leaders understood that controlling the police was a means of maintaining their own political power and of allowing criminal friends and political allies to violate the law with impunity. In fact, in some cities, the police were clearly extensions of the local party machine, which attempted to dominate all activity in a community. If local politicians gave police applicants a job, it became the hired officers' job to get out the vote so that the politicians could keep their positions. The system was so corrupt in some cities that police officers bought their jobs, their promotions, and their special assignments. In collaboration with local politicians, but often on their own, the police were more than willing to ignore violations of the law if the lawbreakers gave them money, valuables, or privileges.

Law Enforcement in the States and on the Frontier

The development of law enforcement on the state level and in the frontier territories was often peculiar to the individual location. Without large population centers that required the control of disorderly crowds, law enforcement was more likely to respond to specific situations—for example, by rounding up cattle rustlers or capturing escaped slaves. Still, out of this kind of limited law enforcement activity, the basic organizational structure of police units with broader responsibilities was born.

Southern Slave Patrols   In the South, the earliest form of policing was the plantation **slave patrols.**[7] Those patrols were created to enforce the infamous slave codes, the first of which was enacted by the South Carolina legislature in 1712. Eventually all the Southern colonies enacted slave codes. The slave codes protected the slaveholders' property rights in human beings, while holding slaves responsible for their crimes and other acts that were not crimes if committed by free persons. Under some slave codes, enslaved people could not hold meetings, leave the plantation without permission from the master, travel without a pass, learn to read and write, carry a firearm, trade, or gamble. Both the slave codes and the slave patrols were created in part because of a fear of bloody slave revolts, such as had already occurred in Virginia and other parts of the South.

Generally consisting of three men on horseback who covered a beat of 15 square miles, a slave patrol was responsible for catching runaway slaves, preventing slave uprisings, and maintaining discipline among the slaves. To maintain discipline, the patrols often whipped and terrorized black slaves who were caught after dark without passes. The slave patrols also helped enforce the laws prohibiting literacy, trade, and gambling among slaves. Although the law required that all white males perform patrol services, the large plantation owners usually hired poor, landless whites to substitute for them. The slave patrols lasted until the end of the Civil War, in 1865. After the Civil War, the Ku Klux Klan served the purpose of controlling blacks just as the slave patrols had before the Civil War.

Frontier Law Enforcement   In the remote and unpopulated areas of the nation, and particularly on the expanding frontier, justice was often in the hands of the people in a more direct way. Vigilantism was often the only way that people could maintain order and defend themselves against renegades and thugs.[8] Even when formal law enforcement procedures were provided by the sheriff or a marshal, courts in many communities were held only once or twice a year, leaving many cases unresolved. This idea of self-protection remains very popular in the South and the West, where firearms laws in many states permit people to carry loaded weapons in a vehicle, or even on their persons if they have completed a qualification and licensing procedure.

State Police Agencies   Self-protection did not prove sufficient as populations and their accompanying problems increased. As early as 1823, mounted militia units in Texas protected American settlers throughout that territory. Called *rangers,* these mounted militia fought Native Americans and Mexican bandits. The Texas Rangers were officially formed in 1835, and the organization remains in existence today as an elite and effective unit of the Texas Department of Public Safety.[9]

The inefficiency and unwillingness of some sheriffs and constables to control crime, along with an emerging crime problem that exceeded the local community's ability to deal with it, prompted other states to form state law enforcement agencies. In 1905, Pennsylvania established the first modern state law enforcement organization with the authority to enforce the law statewide, an authority that made it unpopular in some communities where enforcement of state laws had been decidedly lax.[10] The advent of the

slave patrols
The earliest form of policing in the South. They were a product of the slave codes.

Nat Turner Rebellion
Perhaps the most publicized slave revolt was the Nat Turner Rebellion of 1831 in Virginia. Turner and five other slaves killed Joseph Travis, Turner's owner, and his family. Approximately 70 more rebels joined Turner, whose immediate plan was to capture the county seat, where munitions were stored. Turner was unsuccessful in his plan, but during the siege, he and his rebels killed 57 whites. Turner was tried, convicted, and hanged, along with 16 other rebels. In response to the revolt, white mobs lynched nearly 200 blacks, most of whom were innocent.

SOURCE: John Duff and Peter Mitchell, *The Nat Turner Rebellion: The Historical Event and the Modern Controversy* (New York: Harper & Row, 1971).

▲ The Texas Rangers, organized in the early 1800s to fight Native Americans, patrol the Mexican border, and track down rustlers, were the first form of state police. *Why and how do you think the Rangers have endured for so long?*

Texas Rangers

To learn more about the history of the Texas Rangers, visit cj.glencoe.com and find the Texas Ranger Hall of Fame and Museum Web site. *Why do you think the Texas Rangers have elite status?*

automobile and the addition of miles of state highways extended the authority of state police agencies. Some form of state law enforcement agency existed in every state by the 1930s.

Professionalism and Reform

You will recall that the people themselves were once the police, as they served on the watch. Being an adult citizen was about the only qualification. No training was required, and it was common practice for citizens who did not want to serve to hire replacements, sometimes hiring sentenced offenders. Because of the few services and the little order the watch provided, not much else seems to have been required. Even when organized police forces were developed in the 1840s and 1850s in the United States, qualifications for the job mattered little beyond the right political connections or the ability to purchase one's position outright.

Not until the latter part of the nineteenth century did qualifications for the position of police officer begin to evolve. In the 1880s, Cincinnati posted two qualifications to be a police officer.[11] First, an applicant had to be a person of high moral character—an improvement over earlier times. Three citizens had to vouch for the applicant's character at a city council meeting. If deemed acceptable by the council, the applicant was immediately taken to a gymnasium and tested for the second qualification, foot speed.

Both Cincinnati and New York began police academies in the 1880s, but the curriculum was meager and recruits were not required to pass any examinations to prove their competence. The lack of adequate standards and training for police officers was recognized as a major stumbling block to improved policing. A group of reformers within policing allied themselves with the Progressives, a movement for political, social, and economic change. Among the reformers was August Vollmer, who became chief of police of Berkeley, California, in 1909. During his tenure as chief from 1909 to 1932, Vollmer attempted to create a professional model of policing. With Vollmer and a succession of internal reformers who followed, a new era of professional policing began.

Vollmer and his followers advocated training and education as two of the key ingredients of professionalism in policing. He also believed strongly that the police should stay out of politics and that politics should stay out of policing. Vollmer believed that the major function of the police was fighting crime, and he saw great promise in professionalizing law enforcement by emphasizing that role.[12] He began to hire college graduates for the Berkeley Police Department, and he held college classes on police administration.

Within a few decades, this professional model, sometimes called the reform model, had taken root in police departments across the country. To eliminate political influences, gain control of officers, and establish crime-fighting priorities, departments made major changes in organization and operation. Those changes included the following:

- Narrowing of the police function from social service and the maintenance of order to law enforcement only
- Centralization of authority, with the power of precinct captains and commanders checked
- Creation of specialized, centrally based crime-fighting units, as for burglary
- A shift from neighborhood foot patrol to motorized patrol
- Implementation of patrol allocation systems based on such variables as crime rates, calls for service, and response times
- Reliance on technology, such as police radios, to both control and aid the policing function
- Recruitment of police officers through psychological screening and civil service testing
- Specific training in law enforcement techniques

Conflicting Roles

Throughout American history, Americans have never been sure precisely what role they want their police officers to play. Much of the ambivalence has to do with American heritage, which makes many Americans suspicious of government authority. At one time or another, local police have acted as peace-keepers, social workers, crime fighters, and public servants, completing any task that was requested. Often, the police have been asked to take on all those roles simultaneously.

For most of the nineteenth century, distrust of government was so strong and the need to maintain order in the cities so critical that the police operated almost exclusively as peacekeepers and social service agents, with little or no concern for enforcing the law beyond what was absolutely necessary to maintain tranquility.[13] In this role, the police in many American cities administered the laws that provided for public relief and support of the poor. They fed the hungry and housed the homeless at the request of the politicians who controlled them. Later, other social service agents, such as social workers, began to replace them, and a reform effort developed to remove policing from the direct control of corrupt politicians. As a result, the police began to focus on crime-fighting as early as the 1920s. Having the police enforce the law fairly and objectively was thought to be a major way of professionalizing law enforcement. This approach also fit the professional model of policing advocated by Vollmer and other reformers.

By the end of the 1960s, strong doubts about the role of the police emerged again. The role they had been playing encouraged them to ferret out crime and criminals through such practices as aggressive patrol, undercover operations, and electronic surveillance. In some neighborhoods, the police came to be viewed as armies of occupation. Some confrontations between police and citizens resulted in violence. The civil rights movement produced a series of demonstrations and civil disorders in more than 100 cities across

▲ Brutal tactics by some police officers to suppress civil rights protests during the 1960s led to calls for improved standards of police conduct and training. *Have new standards of conduct and training ended police brutal tactics?*

America, beginning in 1964. As in the labor struggles of the late nineteenth and early twentieth centuries, the police were called in to restore order. Some police officers suppressed the demonstrations with brutal tactics. The anti-Vietnam War movement during the 1960s sparked protests all over the country, especially on college campuses. Again, police officers were called upon to maintain and sometimes to restore order. Thousands of students were sprayed with tear gas, and some were beaten by police.

By the end of the 1960s, it was clear that police standards and training had to be improved. To many observers, fast response and proactive patrols did not seem effective in reducing crime, and officers increasingly were seeing their work world through the windshield of a cruiser. The likelihood of establishing rapport with the people they served was remote as officers dashed from one crime scene to another.

Four blue-ribbon commissions studied the police in the United States. The names of the four commissions and the years in which they released their reports are as follows:

1967   National Advisory Commission on Civil Disorders

1967   President's Commission on Law Enforcement
        and the Administration of Justice

1973   National Advisory Commission on Criminal Justice
        Standards and Goals

1973   American Bar Association's Standards Relating
        to Urban Police Function

All four reports made the same major recommendations: They pointed out the critical role police officers play in American society, called for careful selection of law enforcement officers, and recommended extensive and continuous training. The reports also recommended better police management and supervision, as well as internal and external methods of maintaining integrity in police departments.

In an attempt to follow many of the specific recommendations of the reform commissions' reports, police selection became an expensive and elaborate process. It was designed to identify candidates who had the qualities to be effective law enforcement officers: integrity, intelligence, interpersonal skills, mental stability, adequate physical strength, and agility. Attempts were also made to eliminate discriminatory employment practices that had prevented minorities and women from entering and advancing in law enforcement. Finally, it became more common for police officers to attend college, and some police agencies began to set a minimum number of college credit hours as an employment qualification.

Community Policing

By the 1970s, research began to show that a rapid response to crime does not necessarily lead to more arrests and that having more police officers using methods made popular under the professional or reform model does not significantly reduce crime.[14] What was emerging was the view that unattended disorderly behavior in neighborhoods—such as unruly groups of youths, prostitution, vandalism, drunk and disorderly vagrants, and aggressive street people—is a signal to more serious criminals that residents do not care what goes on in their community and that the criminals can move in and operate with impunity.

The 1970s and 1980s saw some experimentation with community- and neighborhood-based policing projects.[15] Those projects got mixed results, and many were abandoned because of high costs, administrative neglect, and citizen apathy. However, higher crime rates, continued community deterioration, and recognition of the failure to control crime caused law enforcement to again question the role it was playing. The enforcer role still was not working well enough. It appeared senseless simply to respond to calls for service and arrive at scenes of crime and disorder time and time again without resolving the problems or having any lasting effect on the lives of the residents of the community. Out of this failure and frustration came the contemporary concept of **community policing.**

Under a community policing philosophy, the people of a community and the police form a lasting partnership, in which they jointly approach the problems of maintaining order, providing services, and fighting crime.[16] If the police show they care about the minor problems associated with community disorder, two positive changes are likely to occur: citizens will develop better relations with the police as they turn to them for solutions to the disorder, and criminals will see that residents and the police have a commitment to keeping all crime out of the neighborhood. Once again, the emphasis has shifted from fighting crime to keeping peace and delivering social services.

MYTH

Random patrol, as opposed to directed patrol, reduces crime. It is important to have police out in patrol cars, scouting neighborhoods and business districts.

FACT

There is not much value to such random patrols other than perhaps helping people feel safe. They would probably feel even safer if the police were walking a beat. However, little research supports the idea that officers who ride around for three to five hours of their shifts are repressing crime. Even being available to respond to calls from the public is not a strong argument for such patrols. Only a small percentage of reported crimes and other incidents require a rapid response.

community policing
A contemporary approach to policing that actively involves the community in a working partnership to control and reduce crime.

The goal is eradicating the causes of crime in a community, not simply responding to symptoms.

In the early 1990s, many communities across the nation began implementing community policing strategies. Community policing called for a shift from incident-based crime fighting to a problem-oriented approach, in which police would be prepared to handle a broad range of troublesome situations in a city's neighborhoods. There was greater emphasis on foot patrol so that officers could come to know and be known by the residents of a neighborhood. Those citizens would then be more willing to help the police identify and solve problems in the neighborhood. Many other aspects of community policing will be discussed more fully in Chapter 6.

5.3 CRITICAL THINKING

1. Which of the major changes in the organization and operation of police departments listed on page 169 do you think brought about the most significant change? Why?

2. What do you think are the key benefits of community policing? Why?

5.4 The Structure of American Law Enforcement

Describing American law enforcement and its structure is difficult because law enforcement agencies are so diverse. To begin with, you must decide which law enforcement agency you are talking about. For example, Oklahoma Highway Patrol officers cruise the highways and back roads, enforcing traffic laws, investigating accidents, and assisting motorists over seemingly endless miles of paved and unpaved routes. They do not ordinarily investigate criminal violations unless the violations are on state property. In contrast, a sheriff and two deputies in rural Warren County, Georgia conduct criminal investigations, serve subpoenas, and investigate accidents. In the towns of Astoria, Equality, and Newman, Illinois, only one employee, the chief of police, works in each department, and that person is responsible for all law enforcement, public order, and service duties. The 65 sworn law enforcement officers at the University of Texas in Austin are also a part of American law enforcement.[17]

Altogether, tens of thousands of law enforcement officers at the federal, state, county, and municipal levels protect life and property and serve their respective publics. They are employed by government, private enterprise, and quasi-governmental entities. Their responsibilities are specific and sometimes unique to the kind of organization that employs them. Examples of these organizations are airports, transit authorities, hospitals, and parks.

At the state level, there are highway patrols, bureaus of investigation, park rangers, watercraft officers, and other law enforcement agencies and personnel with limited jurisdictions. Colleges and universities employ police officers, and some of those forces are comparable to many medium-sized police departments in the United States.

At the federal level, there are about 50 law enforcement agencies. The Federal Bureau of Investigation (FBI), the U.S. Secret Service, and the Drug Enforcement Administration (DEA) are three of the better-known agencies. The U.S. Marshals Service, the Bureau of Alcohol, Tobacco, and Firearms (ATF), and the Customs Service are other federal law enforcement agencies, as are the Internal Revenue Service's Criminal Investigation Division, the White House Police, the Border Patrol, and nearly three dozen other agencies.

As the aforementioned list of law enforcement agencies suggests, explaining the law enforcement mandate and its execution in the United States is difficult. The structure of American police services is different from those of other countries. Japan and many other nations have only one police department. The United States has almost 19,000 public law enforcement agencies, and probably more when all the special police jurisdictions in the public sector are counted—including game protection agencies, water conservancies, and mental health institutions. Figure 5–2 on pages 172 and 173 summarizes the various law enforcement agencies in the United States.

You have already learned that law enforcement in America is fragmented, locally controlled, and limited in authority; to that, you can also add the terms *structurally* and *functionally different*. Virtually no two police agencies in America are structured alike or function in the same way. Police officers themselves are young and old; well-trained and ill-prepared; educated and uninformed; full-time and part-time; rural, urban, and suburban; generalists and specialists; paid and volunteer; and public and private. These differences lead to the following generalizations about law enforcement in the United States:

1. The quality of police services varies greatly among states and localities across the nation.

2. There is no consensus on professional standards for police personnel, equipment, and practices.

3. Expenditures for police services vary greatly among communities.

4. Obtaining police services from the appropriate agency is often confusing for crime victims and other clients.

Local Policing and Its Functions

If a person knows a law enforcement agent at all, it is probably a local police officer. The officer may have given the person a traffic ticket or investigated an automobile accident. The officer may have conducted a crime prevention survey. Children meet local police officers through Drug Abuse Resistance Education (D.A.R.E.) in public or private schools. Almost everyone has seen the beat cop drive by in a patrol car. Some people have reported thefts or burglaries, but it is doubtful that even they understand what local police officers in America really do, besides what they see on television and in movies.

CRIMINAL JUSTICE *Online*

Secret Service

To learn more about the U.S. Secret Service, visit their Web site by clicking the link at cj.glencoe.com. *Based on what you have learned from the Web site, do you think that you would be interested in a career with the Secret Service? Why or why not?*

171

FIGURE 5–2

Public Law Enforcement Agencies in the United States

The United States has almost 19,000 public law enforcement agencies.

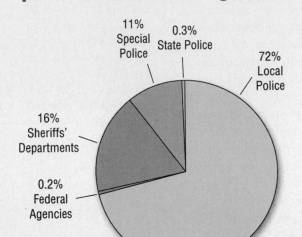

- 11% Special Police
- 0.3% State Police
- 72% Local Police
- 16% Sheriffs' Departments
- 0.2% Federal Agencies

State
State police agencies in every state except Hawaii have statewide jurisdiction and may be set up according to state police or highway patrol models.

Special
Special police agencies operate at local and state levels and have limited jurisdictions.

Local

Local police departments, which make up the bulk of law enforcement agencies in America, are responsible for law enforcement, order maintenance, service, and information gathering.

Federal

Federal agencies investigate violations of federal law and enforce laws that involve interstate crimes.

Almost 780,000 full-time sworn officers are employed by public law enforcement agencies in the United States.

Number of Full-Time Sworn Officers

450,000	
400,000	Local
350,000	
300,000	
250,000	
200,000	
150,000	Sheriff
100,000	
50,000	State / Special / Federal
0	

Local   Sheriff   State   Special   Federal

SOURCE: Data in graphs are calculated from material in Brian A. Reaves and Andrew L. Goldberg, Local Police Departments, 1997, U.S. Department of Justice, Bureau of Justice Statistics (Washington, DC: GPO, February, 2000) and Brian A. Reaves and Timothy C. Hart, Federal Law Enforcement Officers, 1998, U.S. Department of Justice, Bureau of Justice Statistics Bulletin (Washington, DC: GPO, March 2000).

County

County sheriffs' departments enforce the law in most rural and unincorporated areas of the United States.

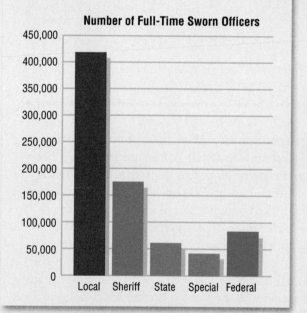

History and Structure of American Law Enforcement   CHAPTER 5

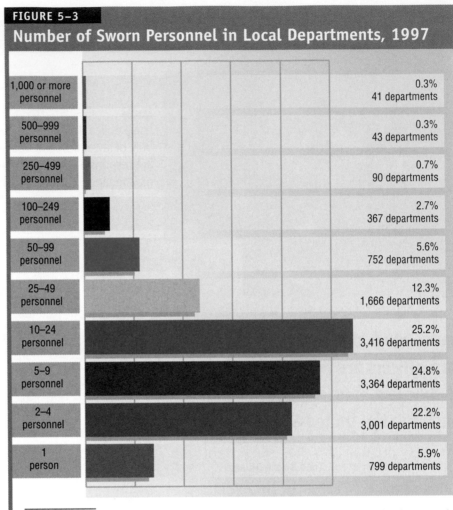

FIGURE 5-3
Number of Sworn Personnel in Local Departments, 1997

Category	Percent	Departments
1,000 or more personnel	0.3%	41 departments
500–999 personnel	0.3%	43 departments
250–499 personnel	0.7%	90 departments
100–249 personnel	2.7%	367 departments
50–99 personnel	5.6%	752 departments
25–49 personnel	12.3%	1,666 departments
10–24 personnel	25.2%	3,416 departments
5–9 personnel	24.8%	3,364 departments
2–4 personnel	22.2%	3,001 departments
1 person	5.9%	799 departments

SOURCE: Brian A. Reaves and Andrew L. Goldberg, *Local Police Departments, 1997,* U.S. Department of Justice, Bureau of Justice Statistics (Washington: GPO, February, 2000).

Lola Baldwin

The first woman to have full police power (1905) was Lola Baldwin of Portland, Oregon. The first uniformed policewoman was Alice Stebbins Wells, who was hired by the Los Angeles Police Department in 1910. By 1916, 16 other police departments had hired policewomen as a result of the success in Los Angeles.

SOURCE: Roy Robert, John Crank, and Jack Kuykendall, *Police and Society* (Los Angeles, CA: Roxbury Publishing Company, 1999) pp. 432–433.

Municipal Police Departments Municipal police departments come in all sizes, but most of them are small in the number of officers employed. The overwhelming majority of police departments in America employ fewer than 50 sworn officers. Figure 5–3 shows the number of sworn officers in local police agencies in the United States. As shown in Figure 5–3, approximately one-half of all local police departments in the United States employ fewer than ten officers, and fewer than one percent employ more than 1,000 sworn personnel.

What are some of the characteristics of the sworn personnel who occupy the ranks of municipal police agencies in the United States? Most police officers are white males. In 1997, 78.4 percent of full-time sworn officers were white men. The larger the police agency, the more likely it is to employ minority officers. Women represented about ten percent of all sworn officers in the nation's local police departments in 1997. Figure 5–4 provides a breakdown of police employment in local agencies by gender, race, and ethnicity.

A high school diploma or higher educational achievement was required by 86 percent of the local police departments of the nation in 1997. Fourteen

FIGURE 5-4

Characteristics of Local Full-Time Police Officers

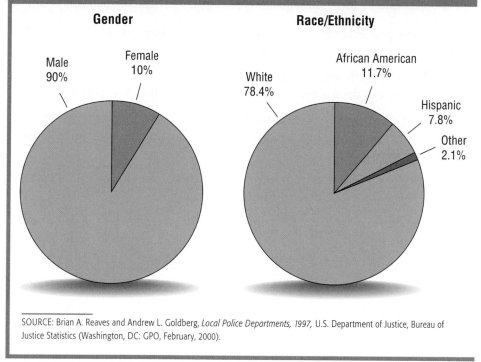

SOURCE: Brian A. Reaves and Andrew L. Goldberg, *Local Police Departments, 1997,* U.S. Department of Justice, Bureau of Justice Statistics (Washington, DC: GPO, February, 2000).

percent of local police departments in 1997 required some college courses (up from 4 percent in 1993), but only 8 percent of the agencies required recruits to have a minimum of two years of college.[18]

Local Police Functions The local police are the workhorses of the law enforcement system in America. They perform many functions and tasks that will never be included in police detective novels or in movies about law enforcement. The functions that local police perform have been categorized in several different ways. One general grouping lists these four categories of local police functions:

1. **Law enforcement**—examples are investigating a burglary, arresting a car thief, serving a warrant, or testifying in court.
2. **Order maintenance or peacekeeping**—examples are breaking up a fight, holding back a crowd at a sporting event, or intervening in a domestic dispute before it gets violent.
3. **Service**—examples are taking people to the hospital, escorting funeral processions, delivering mail for city officials, or chasing bats out of a caller's house.

FYI

Policewomen

It took a long time for police-women to gain the opportunity to perform the same roles and duties as their male counterparts. From the early 1900s until 1972, when the Equal Employment Opportunity Commission began to assist women police officers in obtaining equal employment status with male officers, police-women were responsible for protection and crime prevention work with women and juveniles, particularly with girls. The Los Angeles Police Department created the City Mother's Bureau in 1914 and hired policewomen to work with delinquent and predelinquent children whose mothers did not want formal intervention by a law enforcement agency. Policewomen were also used to monitor, investigate, and punish young girls whose behavior flouted social and sexual conventions of the times.

MYTH   FACT

The police spend most of their time and resources apprehending law violators and combating crime.

Only about ten percent of police time and resources are devoted to apprehending law violators and combating crime. Most of their time and resources are spent "keeping the peace," which means maintaining a police presence in the community, for example, by routine patrolling.

4. **Information gathering**—examples are determining neighborhood reactions to a proposed liquor license in the community, investigating a missing child case, or investigating and reporting on a dangerous road condition.

Some police academies teach recruits the functions of a police officer through the use of the acronym *PEPPAS:*

P—Protect life and property (patrol a business district at night, keep citizens from a fire scene, or recover and return lost property).

E—Enforce the law (ensure traffic laws are obeyed, warn jaywalkers of the inherent danger, make out criminal complaints, or seize illegal weapons).

P—Prevent crime (give home security advice, patrol high crime areas, or work as a D.A.R.E. officer in schools).

P—Preserve the peace (disband disorderly groups, have a visible presence at sporting events, or intervene in neighbor conflicts).

A—Arrest violators (apprehend fleeing suspects, give citations to alcohol permit holders who sell to minors, or conduct drug raids).

S—Serve the public (give directions to travelers, deliver emergency messages, or administer first aid).

There are literally dozens of other functions that the police of a city, town, or village carry out, and much of the work falls into the category of helping out when no one else seems to be available. Because the police are on duty 24 hours a day in nearly every community, they are often called on to perform services that have nothing to do with law enforcement. That round-the-clock availability also significantly affects the structure, work life, and activity of a police agency.

Organizational Structure How a police agency is structured depends on the size of the agency, the degree of specialization, the philosophy the leadership has chosen (such as community policing), the political context of the department (the form of municipal government), and the history and preferences of a particular community. Most medium- to large-staffed police agencies are subdivided into patrol, criminal investigation, traffic, juvenile, and technical and support services. Subspecialties include robbery, gangs, training, bombs, property, victims' services, jail, and mounted patrol.

The Dallas (Texas) Police Department, with 2,873 sworn officers and 724 nonsworn employees, is large, sophisticated, and very specialized. For example, it has a separate detective unit for each major category of crime. Evidence technicians collect and preserve evidence during the preliminary investigation of a crime. An entire contingent of officers is assigned to traffic regulation and enforcement duties. Bicycle patrol officers work the popular West End entertainment and restaurant section downtown. The Dallas police even have sworn officers who serve as crime analysts and collect, analyze, map, and report crime data to enable better prevention and repression of crime by means of scientific deployment of officers and other strategies. Figure 5–5 on page 177 presents the organizational structure of the Dallas Police Department.

FIGURE 5–5
Dallas Police Department Organization Chart

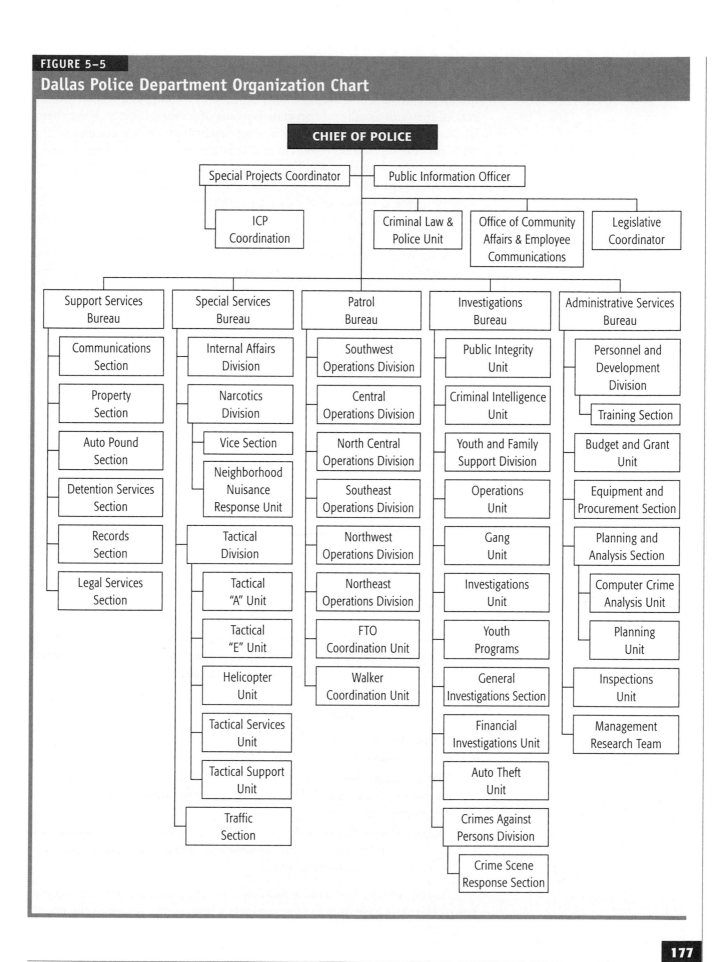

Most police agencies in the United States do not have or need elaborate organizational structures. Police officers on the beat are generalists, and when special circumstances arise, such as a homicide or a complex financial investigation, they can usually rely on state bureaus of investigation to assist them. Moreover, local cooperation pacts among departments in a particular region often provide for sharing resources and specialized assistance when needed.

The infrequent need for homicide investigation skills in communities under 30,000 people, for example, makes it impractical to train one or more officers in the methods of conducting a thorough death investigation. An officer so trained might have to wait an entire career to put into practice the acquired skills, and it is most likely that by the time they were needed, the officer would have forgotten them. The lack of a trained specialist for the infrequent complex investigation, however, is one of the major reasons criminal investigation services in small communities are not equal to those in larger police departments.

The question has been raised whether larger, regional police departments would be more efficient providers of police services, but as you have already discovered, policing in America is a local concern, and that is not likely to change.

The police are organized militarily with regard to accountability, discipline, rank, dress, and decorum. Many people believe that the military structure of a chain of command may be dysfunctional because police work is so varied. Some people believe that a military structure is best suited for situations where the objectives are simple and few, which is not the case in municipal policing. Some commentators think the military structure impedes the flow of communication and the development of good community relations because people are suspicious of the police or even fear them in some neighborhoods. Despite these criticisms, most police departments retain this organizational structure, which originated in the hiring of military leaders as the first police chiefs. Attempts to change the military structure of policing have generally failed. One reason is that police officers have often resisted any type of reorganization.

The Political Context of Policing   A police department of any size is part of a larger government entity. Municipalities generally operate under one of four forms of municipal government:[19]

Strong Mayor-Council—Voters elect the mayor and the city council; the mayor appoints heads of departments.

Weak Mayor-Council—Voters elect the mayor and the city council; the city council appoints heads of departments.

City Manager—Voters elect the city council and, in some cities, a mayor; the city council selects the city manager, who appoints heads of departments.

Commission—Voters elect a board of commissioners, who become the heads of departments; the commission or the voters may choose one commissioner to be mayor.

As you can see, the forms of municipal government vary in the amount of control citizens have over the municipality's leaders, the source of the executive authority of the chief of police, and the degree of insulation a chief of police has from interference by the executive head of the city (mayor or city manager) or the city council. Each form has advantages and disadvantages. At one time it was thought that city manager government was the system under which the police were most likely to develop professionally, be free of political meddling from city lawmakers, and be insulated from local corruption. Although many progressive and effective police departments operate under a city manager form of government, other municipal forms of government have records of both success and failure in local police effectiveness and integrity.

You have probably noticed from reading newspapers and listening to radio and television that chief executives of local police agencies have different titles, depending on the locale. Popular titles are chief of police (Kansas City), director of police (Dayton, Ohio), and commissioner (New York City).

County Law Enforcement

A substantial portion of law enforcement work in the United States is carried out by sheriff's departments. In 1997, the nation had 3,088 sheriffs' departments, employing approximately 263,427 full-time personnel. About 66 percent of the personnel were sworn peace officers. Sheriffs frequently employ part-time personnel who work as special deputies, assisting with county fairs, traffic control, and other duties. Sheriffs' departments represent 16.4 percent of all the law enforcement departments in the United States. In 1997, the cost to provide county law enforcement was $13.1 billion.[20]

Sheriffs' personnel are 81 percent white, 11.8 percent black, 5.9 percent Hispanic, and 1.3 percent other. Women make up 15.6 percent of the sworn personnel working for sheriffs' departments.[21] (See Figure 5–6.)

As are most municipal police departments, most sheriffs' departments in America are small. Figure 5–7 on page 180 shows the number of departments

Female Sheriffs

Before 1992, no woman had ever been elected to the position of sheriff in the United States. The first two were elected in 1992: The first was Jackie Barrett in Fulton County, Georgia, and the second was Judy Pridgen in Saline County, Arkansas.

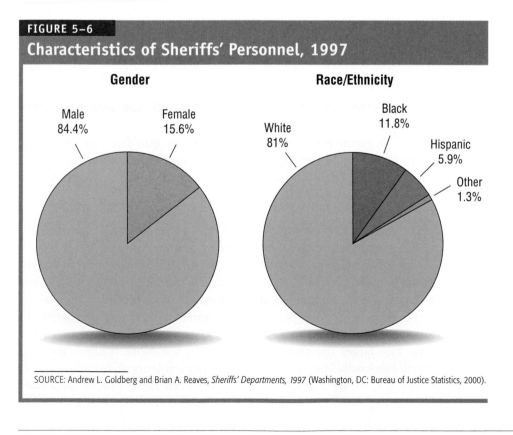

FIGURE 5–6

Characteristics of Sheriffs' Personnel, 1997

Gender

Male 84.4%   Female 15.6%

Race/Ethnicity

White 81%   Black 11.8%   Hispanic 5.9%   Other 1.3%

SOURCE: Andrew L. Goldberg and Brian A. Reaves, *Sheriffs' Departments, 1997* (Washington, DC: Bureau of Justice Statistics, 2000).

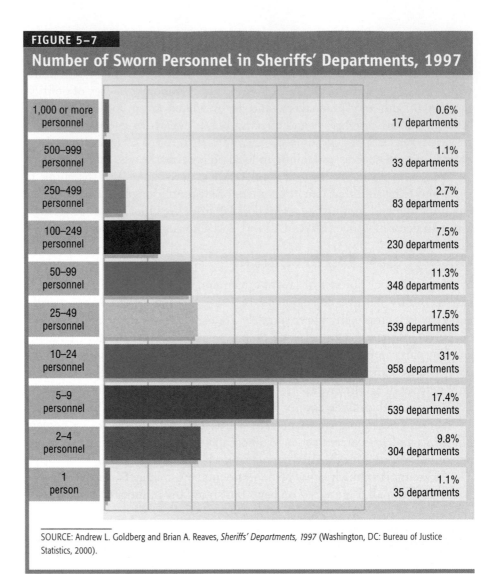

FIGURE 5-7

Number of Sworn Personnel in Sheriffs' Departments, 1997

1,000 or more personnel	0.6% 17 departments
500–999 personnel	1.1% 33 departments
250–499 personnel	2.7% 83 departments
100–249 personnel	7.5% 230 departments
50–99 personnel	11.3% 348 departments
25–49 personnel	17.5% 539 departments
10–24 personnel	31% 958 departments
5–9 personnel	17.4% 539 departments
2–4 personnel	9.8% 304 departments
1 person	1.1% 35 departments

SOURCE: Andrew L. Goldberg and Brian A. Reaves, *Sheriffs' Departments, 1997* (Washington, DC: Bureau of Justice Statistics, 2000).

and their respective sizes. Nearly three dozen sheriffs' departments employ only the sheriff.

Sheriffs' departments often have employment qualifications similar to those of municipal police agencies. Ninety-three percent of sheriffs' departments require new officers to have a high school diploma; 4 percent require some college, usually a two-year degree.

County Law Enforcement Functions The sheriff and department personnel perform functions that range from investigation to supervision of sentenced offenders. Even in the smallest departments, sheriffs are responsible for investigating crimes and enforcing the criminal and traffic laws of the state. They also perform many civil process services for the court, such as serving summonses, warrants, and various writs. In addition, they provide courtroom security and confine and transport prisoners. The larger the sheriff's department, the more confinement and corrections responsibilities it has. Sheriffs' departments frequently operate the county jail, which houses hundreds and even thousands of prisoners, depending on the particular county. In some counties, the sheriff's department shares law enforcement duties with a separate police department.

Politics and County Law Enforcement Most sheriffs are directly elected and depend on an elected board of county commissioners or supervisors for their funding and some oversight of their operations. Sheriffs generally have a freer hand in running their agencies than do police chiefs. In many counties, local politics governs the operation of the sheriff's department, and the sheriff must operate as a partisan politician to remain in office. The authority to appoint special deputies and to award patronage jobs contributes to the sheriff's power and influence in a county.

State Law Enforcement

Filling the complement of law enforcement agencies in a particular state are one or more state law enforcement agencies, which provide criminal and traffic law enforcement, as well as other services peculiar to the needs of that state government. In 1997, the 49 primary state law enforcement agencies (Hawaii has no state police agency) had approximately 83,742 employees, of which 54,587 were sworn officers. Those agencies had budgets that totaled more than $5 billion. Fifteen state agencies employ more than 1,000 personnel. The California Highway Patrol is the largest state law enforcement agency, with more than 9,000 personnel, of which about two-thirds are sworn officers.[22]

For the most part, each state has chosen one of two models for providing law enforcement services at the state level. The first model is the **state police model,** in which the agency and its officers have essentially the same enforcement powers as local police in the state and can work cases and enforce the law anywhere within the state's boundaries. One of the best known state police agencies is the Texas Rangers, part of the Texas Department of Public Safety, which also employs state troopers to enforce criminal and traffic laws. The Rangers usually focus on special and complex investigations, such as the Branch Davidian case in Waco in 1993. A number of states have placed some restrictions on state police activities to avoid clashes with local politicians and local police agencies.

The second model for state law enforcement services is the **highway patrol model,** in which officers focus almost exclusively on highway traffic safety, enforcement of the state's traffic laws, and investigation of accidents on the state's roads and highways. Even highway patrols, however, may retain responsibility for investigating criminal violations on state property and in state institutions or for conducting drug interdictions.

States that employ the highway patrol model often have other state law enforcement agencies with narrow service mandates, such as the following:

- Bureaus of criminal investigation (to investigate white-collar and organized crime, narcotics, etc.)
- State criminal identification services
- Forest, game, and watercraft protection services
- Alcoholic beverage control and enforcement
- Crime laboratory and criminalistics services
- Driver's license examinations

state police model
A model of state law enforcement services in which the agency and its officers have the same law enforcement powers as local police but can exercise them anywhere within the state.

highway patrol model
A model of state law enforcement services in which officers focus on highway traffic safety, enforcement of the state's traffic laws, and the investigation of accidents on the state's roads, highways, and property.

- Drug interdiction activities
- Peace officer training and certification

Both state police and highway patrol agencies help regulate commercial traffic, conduct bomb investigations, protect the governor and the capitol grounds and buildings, and administer computerized information networks for the state, which link up with the National Crime Information Center (NCIC) run by the FBI.

Some tension always seems to exist between state police agencies and local law enforcement over legal jurisdiction and recognition for conducting investigations and making arrests. Recall that policing in America and the political system that governs it are local. Much of the resentment by locals over state interference is similar to the suspicions and doubts concerning federal involvement at the local level.

A significant function performed by a special category of state law enforcement officers is university or campus policing. Some of the large state and private universities and colleges have full-blown police agencies with many special subdivisions. They are very much like municipal police departments—and rightly so, because a community's problems with crime and public order do not end at the university gate.

Federal Law Enforcement

Everyone has heard of a few of the better-known federal law enforcement agencies. The FBI, the U.S. Secret Service, and even the T-men and T-women of the Treasury Department have had their own television shows, creating wider public recognition of those agencies. The unrelenting war on drugs has brought to the attention of the American public the activities of the Drug Enforcement Administration (DEA). There are also other, lesser-known federal police agencies. Their law enforcement jurisdictions are narrowly defined by specific statutes, and their work is unlikely to come to the attention of most American citizens.

Three major differences exist between federal law enforcement and the local and state police agencies with which we are likely to be more familiar. First, federal agencies such as the FBI operate across the entire nation and even have agents serving abroad. Second, federal police agencies do not, as a rule, have the peacekeeping or order maintenance duties typical in local policing. Finally, some federal law enforcement agencies have extremely narrow jurisdictions. (The U.S. Supreme Court Police, for example, provide protective and investigative services for the Supreme Court only.)

As of June 1998, federal agencies employed nationwide about 83,000 full-time personnel authorized to make arrests and carry firearms.[23] Another 1,300 federal officers worked in U.S. territories, and some are employed in foreign countries. One-half of those federal officers were employed by agencies within the Department of Justice, about one-fourth of them worked for agencies within the Treasury Department, and the remainder worked for other agencies.[24] Nearly $11 billion was spent on their law enforcement

FIGURE 5-8

Major Employers of Federal Officers Authorized to Make Arrests and Carry Firearms

Agency	Number of Full-Time Officers
1. Immigration and Naturalization Service	16,552
2. Federal Bureau of Prisons	12,587
3. Federal Bureau of Investigation	11,285
4. U.S. Customs Service	10,539
5. U.S. Secret Service	3,587
6. U.S. Postal Inspection Service	3,490
7. Internal Revenue Service	3,361
8. Drug Enforcement Administration	3,305
9. U.S. Marshals Service	2,705
10. Administrative Office of the U.S. Courts	2,490
11. National Park Service	2,197
12. Bureau of Alcohol, Tobacco, and Firearms	1,723
13. U.S. Capitol Police	1,055
14. GSA–Federal Protective Service	900
15. U.S. Fish and Wildlife Service	831
16. U.S. Forest Service	601

SOURCE: Brian A. Reaves and Timothy C. Hart, *Federal Law Enforcement Officers, 1998* (Washington, DC: U.S. Bureau of Justice Statistics Bulletin, March, 2000) p. 2, Table 1.

activities.[25] The four largest employers of federal officers were the Immigration and Naturalization Service, the Federal Bureau of Prisons, the Federal Bureau of Investigation, and the U.S. Customs Service.[26] Figure 5–8 shows the major employers of federal officers authorized to make arrests and carry firearms.

5.4 CRITICAL THINKING

1. What do you think are the pros and cons of working at the local, state, and federal levels of law enforcement?

2. Do you think that any one of the three major areas of law enforcement (local, state, federal) is more prestigious? Why?

FBI Agent

My name is Michelle L. Rankin and I am an FBI special agent in the field office, Public Corruption Unit. I thoroughly enjoy my career with the FBI. I am a Special Agent in the Public Corruption Unit (PCU) in the Washington, D.C., Field Office, the second largest field office in the FBI.

The PCU investigates allegations of bribery involving public officials, including extortion or using the mail to defraud the public. Examples include the issuance of licenses, permits, contracts, or zoning variances; judicial case fixing; and law enforcement corruption.

The PCU's responsibilities are divided into two squads. My squad focuses on the District of Columbia government. The other squad concentrates on the executive branch of the federal government in the Washington, D.C., area. Twelve agents are assigned to my squad, along with non-agent support specialists.

Prior to transferring to the PCU, I worked on a special inquiry squad, conducting background investigations for White House staff and presidential appointees. It was in this capacity that I had the opportunity to interview Attorney General Janet Reno as well as other prominent politicians.

People often ask about training at the FBI Academy. The program is 16 weeks of rigorous and intellectually challenging work. You have to study 12–15 major subject areas and you often have three hours of homework for the next day's classes and you may also have an exam in another course the next day. Some agents realize that the FBI is not what they thought it was. Others find it difficult to be away from family and friends.

I have a B.A. in Criminal Justice from California State University at San Bernardino. While working on a Certificate in Crime and Intelligence Analysis through the California State University system and the California Department of Justice, I began to volunteer with the Riverside County Sheriff's Department. I eventually obtained a full-time position as an analyst there. Later I went to the Santa Clara Police Department as a Certified Crime and Intelligence Analyst. I designed and directed their crime analysis unit for four years. I left Santa Clara in 1999 to become an FBI agent.

To become an FBI Special Agent, applicants must be between the ages of 23 and 37. The FBI prefers to hire people who are already successful in some other field. Prior work experience need not be in law enforcement. The FBI hires agents from four career categories: law; accounting; foreign languages; and "diversified"—which includes criminal justice. You need to have a minimum of three years of work experience in your chosen field before applying to be an agent. When hired, new FBI Special Agents start at a GS-10, step 1 pay grade, which is now approximately $40,000 per year before overtime.

My advice to someone who wants to become an FBI agent is to maintain the highest standards of conduct in your life. Your first job out of college does not have to be in criminal justice, but be sure to be successful in whatever you do.

After reading this account, what do you think is a key quality of a good FBI agent?

U.S. Customs Special Agent

My name is Jose Pagan and I became a U.S. Customs Special Agent/Criminal Investigator in 1987, and during my career, have served as a Federal Law enforcement Officer in the U.S. Virgin Islands, Puerto Rico, and Orlando, Florida, where I am assigned as of December 2000.

I have had the opportunity to conduct and participate in numerous narcotic interdiction investigations, as well as become a liaison officer between U.S. Customs and other federal and international law enforcement agencies.

As a U.S. Customs Special Agent, I have learned the value of organization, and sound criminal investigation procedures as the primordial law enforcement tools. The investigation of crimes, regardless of type (passion, violence, financial, fraud, narcotic smuggling, counterfeiting, etc.) depend on sound standardized investigatory procedures. I have also mastered many investigative techniques. Among these techniques are: interviewing skills such as detecting and utilizing flaws in elicited responses from a suspect, as well as observing behavior that could assist me in assessing the subject's veracity.

By utilizing proven criminal investigation procedures, in conjunction with the officer's experience, crime investigation becomes a scientific, measurable and reliable method of protecting the public. Even in the investigation of the most heinous crimes, a reliable investigation, based on facts properly discovered and presented in an orderly, organized and logical fashion, will always portray a fair, just and clear case for the jury.

I have participated in operations such as the marine interdiction of narcotics and illegal aliens, as well as serving dozens of search warrants, all of which have demanded a great deal of physical exertion (added to the emotional stress that an assertive law enforcement action creates on the officers). Cases such as joint international investigations of narcotic smuggling, have given me the opportunity to learn other countries law enforcement techniques, customs and points of view. At the same time, counterfeiting cases offer the opportunity to learn about the U.S. and international trade systems, as well as teaching the true impact that unfair trade practices have on the U.S. economy.

There are no typical days at the office in this career. On any given day, I could be on a vessel, sailing to prevent narcotic smuggling into the United States, or interviewing the operation manager of a large company, whose product has been counterfeited.

What parts of the U.S. Customs Special Agent's role do you find most and least appealing? Why?

5.5 American Private Security

Private security is a huge enterprise that complements public law enforcement in the United States. The Department of Labor's Bureau of Labor Statistics projects the continued growth of private security employment well into the 21st century. There may be as many as 1.8 million people now working in private security. Conservative estimates suggest that twice as many people work in private security as in public law enforcement. According to the National Association of Security Companies, the nation spends 73 percent more each year on private security than it does on public policing.[27]

A common way to categorize private security employment is to classify the agencies and personnel as either contract or proprietary. **Contract security** companies offer protective services for a fee to people, agencies, and companies that do not employ their own security personnel or that need extra protection. A state university, for example, may employ private security officers to work at a football game. Contract security employees are not peace officers. **Proprietary security** agents and personnel provide protective services for the entity that employs them. They are also not classified as sworn peace officers. For example, the Ford Motor Company employs its own security forces at its large manufacturing plants.

In 2000, the services provided by the private security agencies of this nation were expected to cost $104 billion, substantially more than the $40 billion projected for public law enforcement.[28]

Reasons for Growth

A number of factors have stimulated the phenomenal growth of private security since the 1970s.

Declining Revenues for Public Policing   In virtually all major cities and in state governments in the United States, the competition for limited funds to operate public services is fierce. Public police agencies have experienced their share of across-the-board government belt-tightening, and that has caused limitations and even freezes on the hiring of additional police officers. As a result, police departments have curtailed services no longer deemed critical. Often, businesses have filled the service gap by employing private security personnel.

The Private Nature of Crimes in the Workplace   A business depends on a positive reputation to remain competitive. Widespread employee theft, embezzlement scandals, and substance abuse harm an organization's public image and may cause potential customers to question the quality of a company's products and services. By employing private security personnel to prevent and repress crime in their facilities, businesses can either hide the crimes that occur or minimize the negative publicity.

---

contract security
Protective services that a private security firm provides to people, agencies, and companies that do not employ their own security personnel or that need extra protection. Contract security employees are not peace officers.

proprietary security
In-house protective services that a security staff, which is not classified as sworn peace officers, provide for the entity that employs them.

▲ Private security is assuming an increasing role in maintaining order, investigating crime, and apprehending criminals. *Is this a positive trend? Why or why not?*

Better Control and Attention to the Problem By employing in-house security personnel or by contracting with an outside firm, the management of a business can direct security personnel to do precisely what is needed to prevent crime, minimize substance abuse, and discipline wayward employees. Public police would have to combine the concerns of a business with the priorities of the citizens of the community.

Fewer Constitutional Limitations Some of the constitutional restrictions that would limit the actions of public police officers working undercover to curtail drug trafficking in an industrial plant, for example, would not restrict private security personnel employed directly by that industry. U.S. Supreme Court prohibitions that restrict a public police officer's right to search and seize property, for instance, would not limit the actions of a private security agent.

Citizen Contact With Private Security

Private officers provide security in many locations where people conduct business. People working in a downtown office, for example, may see security officers patrolling their building during the day or night. The garage where those people park their cars is, more than likely, checked by a security patrol. Visiting a hospital to see a friend often requires passing a security guard, who may be an employee of a contract security agency. Likewise, in many of America's urban centers, participating in a parent-teacher conference or attending school as a student necessitates contact with an officer of a private security force.

Issues Involving Private Security

A number of unresolved problems and issues impinge on the potential for development of the private security industry. Some of them put the industry at odds with public law enforcement.

Legal Status and Authority   Private security officers' legal status and authority derive from the rights of the owner who employs them to protect property on the premises. These rights are essentially the same ones you have to protect your life and property at home.

If this view prevails, private security personnel face few constitutional limitations in investigating crime, obtaining evidence, employing reasonable force, searching personal property stored in corporate spaces, and interrogating suspects. Although this is not a unanimous view among courts, it is the most prevalent one. However, private security officers and their employers face the possibility of being held civilly or criminally liable for violating an individual's civil rights or for false arrest.

Public Policing in a Private Capacity   Although some police departments prohibit moonlighting, thousands of police officers still work in a private capacity during their off-duty hours. Some police agencies even cooperate with private agencies in scheduling their officers for off-duty assignments. With regard to their legal status and authority, are these officers considered public police or private security personnel? The private organization that employs them believes that off-duty police officers are better qualified, have more authority to arrest, and will have a greater deterrent effect on the crimes and disturbances of the peace the employer is trying to prevent.

An equally important question is, "Who is liable should moonlighting officers abuse their authority or make a mistake?" At present, it seems police agencies that take an active role in scheduling off-duty assignments accept greater liability than the police departments that do not. Many agencies limit the assignments officers are allowed to accept and the number of hours they are permitted to work.

Qualifications and Training   Many superbly qualified people work in private security at all levels throughout the United States, but those people are not the norm. Although the minimum qualifications for private security personnel at all levels of employment are increasing, they lag far behind those of the public police. Few states enforce any educational, physical, or background integrity qualifications for private security personnel. In most states, the training required to become a private security officer is less than a week long. In some states, armed security officers must attend a firearms course, including a section on the laws applicable to the use of deadly force, and must successfully complete a practical firearms qualification test. In nearly all states, public police officers who work off duty in a private policing capacity are exempt from any private security training, even if the nature of their private police work is substantially different from their police department functions.

The qualifications of proprietary security officers are generally higher than those of contract security officers, demonstrating corporate demand for high-quality security services even when they cost more.

Diminished Public Responsibility   The current mixture of public and private protection is a matter of concern to many. What does it say about a government's ability to govern and provide for the general welfare—let alone what it says about American society—that ever more frequently it is shifting responsibility for protecting life and property to private security enterprises? To some, it seems to mean that public police officers and the governments that employ them have defaulted on a major portion of the social contract.

5.5 CRITICAL THINKING

1. What do you think are some of the benefits and drawbacks of being a private security officer?

2. Do you think that stricter qualification standards should be established for private security personnel? Why or why not?

History and Structure of American Law Enforcement

Review and Applications

SUMMARY BY CHAPTER OBJECTIVES

1. Briefly Describe the Jurisdictional Limitations of American Law Enforcement

The authority of public law enforcement agencies in the United States, whether they are local, state, or federal agencies, is carefully limited by law. The territory within which each may operate is also restricted.

2. Trace the English Origins of American Law Enforcement

Many institutions of American law enforcement evolved from the English tradition. The medieval tithing system and the constable-watch system were early methods of community protection that led to the development of the positions of sheriff and constable. The Bow Street Runners in the city of London in the 1750s were an early group of crime fighters who patrolled neighborhoods and pursued lawbreakers. The London Metropolitan Police, founded in 1829, became the model for municipal police departments in the United States.

3. Discuss the Early Development of American Law Enforcement

Americans at first adopted the British system of community protection. When the constable-watch system proved inadequate in meeting the peacekeeping needs of the nation's major cities, municipal police forces were established in the mid-1800s. They soon became entangled with local politics. In the states and on the frontier, law enforcement reflected regional differences. In the South, the earliest policing was the plantation slave patrols. On the frontier, vigilantism and later, local sheriffs or U.S. marshals dealt with lawbreakers. In some states, state police agencies, such as the Texas Rangers, were established to enforce laws statewide.

4. Describe the Major Developments that Have Occurred in Policing in America

During the period of professionalism and reform that lasted from about 1920 to 1970, the police became professional crime fighters, relying on the centralization of authority, motorized patrols, specialization, and technological aids. In the 1960s, the crime-fighting role of the police came into conflict with the social and political upheavals of the time, causing critics to call for improved standards and training. By the early 1990s, some police agencies began to turn to community policing, attempting to eliminate crime problems in neighborhoods and return to their role as peacekeepers.

5. Describe the Structure of American Law Enforcement

Law enforcement agencies are found at all levels of government in the United States. Most law enforcement officers work for local governments and are responsible for enforcing laws, maintaining order, providing service, and gathering information. In rural areas, the county sheriff's department is responsible for law enforcement. Every state, except Hawaii, has a state law enforcement agency. The law enforcement agencies of the federal government are concerned primarily with violations of federal laws, especially violations that cross state boundaries.

6. Discuss the Development and Growth of Private Security in the United States

The private security industry has grown rapidly over the past 30 years for a number of reasons: revenues for public policing have declined; crimes in the workplace are often private, costly, and embarrassing; employers have better control of private security officers; and fewer constitutional limits restrict private security officers.

jurisdiction, p. 158
tithing system, p. 159
shire reeve, p. 160
posses, p. 160
constable-watch system, p. 160

constable, p. 160
Peel's Principles of Policing,
p. 161
slave patrols, p. 165
community policing, p. 169

state police model, p. 181
highway patrol model, p. 181
contract security, p. 186
proprietary security, p. 186

QUESTIONS FOR REVIEW

1. What is meant by *jurisdiction*?
2. What was the *tithing system*?
3. Who were the Bow Street Runners?
4. In what year was the London Metropolitan Police founded?
5. Who was Robert Peel? What name is given to his 12 standards for policing?
6. What system of English policing did the colonists bring to America?
7. What were the *slave codes*?
8. What group is considered to be the first state police agency?
9. How did August Vollmer change policing?
10. How did police response to the demonstrations and civil disorders of the 1960s affect policing?
11. What is *community policing*?
12. What are the four main functions of local police?
13. Why do county sheriffs have more political clout than police chiefs?
14. What is the difference between a *state police model* and a *highway patrol model* of state law enforcement?
15. Name some federal law enforcement agencies.
16. Distinguish between *contract* and *proprietary private security services.*
17. How do the employment qualifications for private security personnel in the United States compare and contrast with the qualifications to be a police officer, deputy sheriff, state police, or federal agent?

EXPERIENTIAL ACTIVITIES

1. **Your Local Law Enforcement** Identify all the local law enforcement agencies in your area. Divide up the list among your classmates and arrange to visit your assigned agency. On the day that you visit, find out how many calls the department received and/or how many crimes the agency personnel investigated in the 24-hour period prior to your visit, what types of calls were received or crimes were investigated, and how the agency handled the situation. Categorize the actions of the agency personnel into law enforcement, order maintenance, service, or information gathering. Identify the category with the most action. Share your findings with others in the class. What conclusions can you draw about the operation of the local law enforcement agencies in your area?

2. **Local and Private Police** Describe the possibilities you see for local police departments and private security agencies to work together more closely. To prepare for this activity, interview a local police official and a private security manager, either by telephone or in person, asking them what obstacles prevent closer cooperation between local policing and private security.

INTERNET

3. **Local Police Jobs** Go to cj.glencoe.com for links to sites dedicated to law enforcement careers and select two municipal police departments, one large and one small, and one county sheriff's department that list the agency's employment qualifications on their Web page. Then find the qualifications for a private security officer through other applicable career sites provided at cj.glencoe.com. Make a list of the similarities and differences between police and deputy sheriff qualifications and private security officer qualifications. Given your background and abilities, for which type of work would you be best suited? Why? Compile your findings in a two-page report and present it to the class.

4. **Federal Law Enforcement** To learn about the responsibilities of some of the lesser-known federal law enforcement agencies, access their Web sites through links provided at cj.glencoe.com. Among these agencies are the: (1) *Food and Drug Administration, Office of Criminal Investigations*, (2) *National Park Service, U.S. Park Police*, (3) *U.S. Fish and Wildlife Service, Division of Law Enforcement*, (4) *Amtrak Police*, and (5) *U.S. Capitol Police*. Which agency seems the most interesting? Why?

CRITICAL THINKING EXERCISES

Neighborhood Watch

1. You live in a middle-class community of single-family homes close to the center of a midsize city. Over the past five years, everyone in your neighborhood has noted the rise in burglaries and many people feel that it is not safe to walk around the neighborhood after dark. You think that setting up a neighborhood watch would help lower the burglary rate and make people feel safer. Prepare an oral presentation of your ideas for a community meeting. Use the following questions as a guide.

   a. How would you go about organizing a night watch?

   b. How would you select volunteers?

   c. What training, if any, would volunteers have to have?

   d. How would you maintain interest and participation in the watch?

Public Officer or Private Citizen?

2. An off-duty police officer was seated in a restaurant when two men entered, drew guns, and robbed the cashier. The officer made no attempt to prevent the robbery or apprehend the robbers. Later the officer justified the conduct by stating that an officer, when off duty, is a private citizen with the same duties and rights as all private citizens. Do you agree? Explain.

ADDITIONAL READING

Bouza, Anthony V. *The Police Mystique: An Insider Looks at Cops, Crime, and the Criminal Justice System.* New York: Plenum, 1990.

Goldstein, Herman. *Problem-Oriented Policing.* New York: McGraw-Hill, 1990.

Gordon, Diana R. *The Justice Juggernaut: Fighting Street Crime, Controlling Citizens.* New Brunswick, NJ: Rutgers University Press, 1990.

Klockars, Carl B. *The Idea of Police.* Beverly Hills, CA: Sage, 1985.

Marx, Gary T. *Police Surveillance in America.* Berkeley: University of California Press, 1988.

Sparrow, Malcolm K., Mark H. Moore, and David M. Kennedy. *Beyond 911.* New York: Basic Books, 1990.

ENDNOTES

1. Material in this section was taken from T. A. Critchley, A *History of Police in England and Wales,* 2d ed. rev. (Montclair, NJ: Patterson Smith, 1972).
2. Ibid.
3. Patrick Pringle, *Hue and Cry: The Story of Henry and John Fielding and Their Bow Street Runners* (New York: William Morrow, 1965).
4. Material in this section was taken from A. C. Germann, F. Day, and R. Gallati, *Introduction to Law Enforcement and Criminal Justice* (Springfield, IL: Charles C. Thomas, 1962), pp. 54–55.
5. Edward Savage, *Police Records and Recollections, or Boston by Daylight and Gaslights for Two Hundred and Forty Years* (Boston: John P. Dale, 1873).
6. This material came from Carl Sifakis, *The Encyclopedia of American Crime* (New York: Smithmark, 1992), pp. 579–80.
7. Center for Research on Criminal Justice, *The Iron Fist and the Velvet Glove: An Analysis of the U.S. Police* (Berkeley, CA: Center for Research on Criminal Justice, 1975); Hubert Williams and Patrick V. Murphy, "The Evolving Strategy of Police: A Minority View," *Perspectives on Policing, No. 13* (Washington, DC: U.S. Department of Justice, January 1990).
8. Thad Sitton, *Texas High Sheriffs* (Austin: Texas Monthly Press, 1988).
9. Adrian N. Anderson, Ralph A. Wooster, David G. Armstrong, and Jeanie R. Stanley, *Texas and Texans,* (Glencoe/McGraw-Hill, 1993).
10. Bruce Smith, *Police Systems in the United States* (New York: Harper & Row, 1960), pp. 178–205.
11. *Our Police* (Cincinnati Police Division, 1984).
12. Gene Carte and Elaine Carte, *Police Reform in the United States: The Era of August Vollmer* (Berkeley: University of California Press, 1975).
13. Malcolm K. Sparrow, Mark H. Moore, and David M. Kennedy, *Beyond 911* (New York: Basic Books, 1990).
14. *Response Time Analysis: Executive Summary,* U.S. Department of Justice (Washington, DC: GPO, 1978).
15. Samuel Walker, *The Police in America: An Introduction,* 2d ed. (New York: McGraw-Hill, 1992).

16. Robert C. Trojanowicz and Bonnie Bucqueroux, *Community Policing: A Contemporary Perspective* (Cincinnati: Anderson, 1989); Robert C. Trojanowicz and Bonnie Bucqueroux, *Community Policing: How to Get Started* (Cincinnati: Anderson 1994).
17. Federal Bureau of Investigation, *Crime in the United States, 1999* (Washington, DC: GPO, 2000) <www.fbi.gov>.
18. Brian A. Reaves and Andrew L. Goldberg, *Local Police Departments, 1997* (Washington, DC: Bureau of Justice Statistics, 2000).
19. V. A. Leonard, *Police Organization and Management* (New York: Foundation Press, 1964).
20. Andrew L. Goldberg and Brian A. Reaves, *Sheriff's Departments, 1997* (Washington, DC: Bureau of Justice Statistics, 2000).
21. Ibid.
22. Brian A. Reaves and Andrew L. Goldberg, *Census of State and Local Law Enforcement Agencies, 1996* (Washington, DC: Bureau of Justice Statistics, 1998).
23. Brian A. Reaves and Timothy C. Hart, *Federal Law Enforcement Officers, 1998* (Washington, DC: Bureau of Justice Statistics Bulletin, March 2000).
24. Ibid.
25. Kathleen Maguire and Ann L. Pastore (eds.), *Sourcebook of Criminal Justice Statistics 1998,* U. S. Department of Justice, Bureau of Justice Statistics (Washington, DC: GPO, 1999), p. 13, Table 1.10.
26. Reaves and Hart, 2000, op. cit.
27. William Cunningham, John Strauchs, and Clifford Van Meter, *The Hallcrest Report II: Private Security Trends 1970–2000* (McLean, VA: Hallcrest Systems, 1990).
28. Ibid.

Policing: Roles, Styles, and Functions

CHAPTER OBJECTIVES

After completing this chapter, you should be able to:

1. Identify characteristics of police work.

2. Distinguish among James Q. Wilson's three operational styles in policing.

3. List the three major functions of police departments.

4. Explain the main components of community policing.

5. Identify the four steps in a community policing approach to problem solving.

6.1 Policing in America

The police are at the forefront of the criminal justice process and, for most people, the only personal experience they have with that process is contact with a local police officer. Most people have never been in a courthouse for a criminal matter or in a jail or prison for any reason. This chapter examines what the police do, and the qualities they need to do it.

The Roles of the Police

Our expectations of police behavior depend on where we live and when we consider the question. For example, we saw in the last chapter that Cincinnati wanted its police officers in the 1880s to be fleet-footed and honest. In Dallas, Miami, and New York City, citizens may expect police officers to have a working knowledge of Spanish. In Alaska, we would expect police officers to be self-reliant, enjoy the outdoors, and not mind working by themselves in lonely surroundings. In essence, what we expect from the police depends on how we view their role in society.

A **role** consists of the rights and responsibilities associated with a particular position in society. A related concept is **role expectation,** the behavior and actions that people expect from a person in a particular role. Suppose, for example, that teenagers living in a wealthy neighborhood have been caught drinking alcohol. Their parents probably expect police officers to warn the young people and bring them home. In a less affluent neighborhood, on the other hand, the expectation of community residents might be that the police will arrest the teenagers and bring them into juvenile court. This example illustrates a problem that often arises in our attempt to understand the police role in America. When the public's expectations differ from the official police role, the public may become disenchanted and sometimes hostile toward law enforcement officers. Such negative feelings cause officers personal frustration and role conflict. **Role conflict** is the psychological strain and stress that results from trying to perform two or more incompatible responsibilities. A

role
The rights and responsibilities associated with a particular position in society.

role expectation
The behavior and actions that people expect from a person in a particular role.

role conflict
The psychological stress and frustration that results from trying to perform two or more incompatible responsibilities.

▲ Police officers are expected to respond to traffic accidents. *How might such experiences affect them?*

common source of role conflict for the police is the expectation that they should be social or helping agents at the same time they are expected to be control agents by arresting law violators.

What we expect from police officers, then, depends on how we view the police role—a role that has been described as complex, ambiguous, changing, and repressive. Obviously, not everyone views the role of the police in the same way, but a definition that includes the majority of perspectives is possible. The police:

1. Are community leaders in public safety. (By nature, this makes the work potentially dangerous.)

2. Possess broad discretion.

3. Solve sociological and technological problems for people on a short-term basis.

4. Occasionally serve in a hostile or dangerous environment.[1]

Think about some of the common situations in which police officers find themselves when people call and want something "fixed." One example would be an officer's response to freeway accidents where vehicles are overturned and burning and people are trapped inside. Such situations require leadership, informed and quick decisions, the solving of numerous immediate problems, and the use of extreme caution to prevent further injury to citizens or the police officer. Another example would be intervention in a long-running family dispute that has suddenly turned violent. Such a situation requires caution, quick thinking, and the solving of a number of problems in an effort to ensure the safety of all parties. Still another typical role of a police officer is to provide protection at protests and strikes. Those potentially volatile circumstances clearly illustrate the key elements of the police role. Of course, sometimes an officer's role may be simply to solve problems in the course of providing service, as when retrieving a citizen's dropped keys from below a sewer grate.

Characteristics of Police Work

Police work requires a combination of special characteristics. Personnel with the following qualities are best able to carry out the difficult service role mandated for law enforcement officers.

Quick Decision Making   Sometimes police officers must make on-the-spot decisions about whether to use force, how to maneuver a patrol car, or whether to stop a suspect. Making the wrong decision can be fatal for the officer or the other person. All of the work in a lengthy investigation can be ruined by a single procedural law violation if an officer unintentionally makes a wrong decision.

The Independent Nature of Police Work   The position of peace officer in all states in the United States is a position of honor and trust. After patrol officers attend roll call, stand inspection, check out their equipment, and depart into the streets in their patrol cars, they work virtually unsupervised until the end of their tour of duty.

Figure 6–1 on page 198 shows the Law Enforcement Officer's Code of Ethics, which was written as a guide for working police officers. It offers

FIGURE 6-1

Law Enforcement Officer Code of Ethics

The purpose of the Code of Ethics is to ensure that all peace officers are fully aware of their individual responsibility to maintain their own integrity and that of their agency. Every peace officer, during basic training, or at the time of appointment, shall be administered the [following] Code of Ethics.

As a law enforcement officer, my fundamental duty is to serve mankind; to safeguard lives and property; to protect the innocent against deception, the weak against oppression or intimidation, and the peaceful against violence or disorder; and to respect the constitutional rights of all men to liberty, equality, and justice.

I will keep my private life unsullied as an example to all; maintain courageous calm in the face of danger, scorn, or ridicule; develop self-restraint; and be constantly mindful of the welfare of others. Honest in thought and deed in both my personal and official life, I will be exemplary in obeying the laws of the land and the regulations of my department. Whatever I see or hear of a confidential nature or that is confided to me in my official capacity will be kept ever secret unless revelation is necessary in the performance of my duty. I will never act officiously or permit personal feelings, prejudices, animosities, or friendships to influence my decisions. With no compromise for crime and with relentless prosecution of criminals, I will enforce the law courteously and appropriately without fear or favor, malice or ill will, never employing unnecessary force or violence, and never accepting gratuities.

I recognize the badge of my office as a symbol of public faith, and I accept it as a public trust to be held so long as I am true to the ethics of the police service. I will constantly strive to achieve these objectives and ideals, dedicating myself to my chosen profession—law enforcement.

Canons

1. The primary responsibility of police officers and organizations is the protection of citizens by upholding the law and respecting the legally expressed will of the whole community and not a particular party or clique.

2. Police officers should be aware of the legal limits on their authority and the "genius of the American system," which limits the power of individuals, groups, and institutions.

3. Police officers are responsible for being familiar with the law and not only their responsibilities but also those of other public officials.

4. Police officers should be mindful of the importance of using the proper means to gain proper ends. Officers should not employ illegal means, nor should they disregard public safety or property to accomplish a goal.

5. Police officers will cooperate with other public officials in carrying out their duties. However, the officer shall be careful not to use his or her position in an improper or illegal manner when cooperating with other officials.

6. In their private lives, police officers will behave in such a manner that the public will "regard (the officer) as an example of stability, fidelity, and morality." It is necessary that police officers conduct themselves in a "decent and honorable" manner.

7. In their behavior toward members of the public, officers will provide service when possible, require compliance with the law, respond in a manner that inspires confidence and trust, and will be neither overbearing nor subservient.

8. When dealing with violators or making arrests, officers will follow the law; officers have no right to persecute individuals or punish them. And officers should behave in such a manner so the likelihood of the use of force is minimized.

9. Police officers should refuse to accept any gifts, favors, or gratuities that, from a public perspective, could influence the manner in which the officer discharges his or her duties.

10. Officers will present evidence in criminal cases impartially because the officer should be equally concerned with both the prosecution of criminals and the defense of innocent persons.

SOURCE: Commission on Peace Officer Standards and Training, *Administrative Manual* (State of California: POST, 1990), p. c.-5. Reprinted by permission.

some professional direction in a line of work with many opportunities to go astray. The independent nature of police work increases the chances of malfeasance and corruption—topics to be discussed in the next chapter.

"Dirty Work"   Most people agree that police work needs to be done, but police work is distasteful—for example, dealing with people who have committed horrible acts and viewing mangled, broken, and decomposed bodies. The distasteful part of policing has been referred to as "dirty work."[2]

Danger   Police officers in the United States spend a substantial amount of their time trying to resolve conflicts, frequently in hostile environments.[3] Figure 6–2 identifies dangerous circumstances in which officers find

---

FIGURE 6–2

Law Enforcement Officers Assaulted in the United States, 1998

Circumstances at Scene of Incident	Total
Total	59,545
Percent of Total	100%
Disturbance calls (family quarrel, man with gun, etc.)	17,769
	30%
Burglaries in progress or pursuit of burglary suspects	744
	1.0%
Robberies in progress or pursuit of robbery suspects	642
	1.0%
Other arrest attempts	10,997
	18%
Civil disorders (mass disobedience, riot, etc.)	812
	1.0%
Handling, transporting, custody of prisoners	6,881
	12%
Investigation of suspicious persons and circumstances	6,275
	11%
Ambush (no warning)	236
	0.4%
Mentally deranged	943
	1.6%
Traffic pursuits and stops	6,242
	10%
All other	8,004
	13%

SOURCE: Kathleen Maguire and Ann L. Pastore (eds.), *Sourcebook of Criminal Justice Statistics, 1999,* U.S. Department of Justice, Bureau of Justice Statistics (Washington, DC: GPO, 2000), p. 323, Table 3.178.

operational styles

The different overall approaches to the police job.

themselves. Contrary to the media image, police officers are often afraid on the job, and far too many are injured or killed. The data reveal that disturbance calls (for example, a family quarrel or a man with a gun) and arrests of suspects are the most dangerous circumstances for police officers.

Each year, police officers are also killed while on duty. In 1999, for example, 42 officers were feloniously killed in the line of duty, the lowest recorded figure in more than 35 years and 19 fewer than the year before.[4] Accidents during the performance of official duties claimed the lives of an additional 63 officers, 18 fewer than in 1998. Of the 42 officers feloniously killed in the line of duty in 1999, 12 lost their lives during arrest situations: 6 were serving arrest warrants; 3 were attempting to prevent robberies or apprehend robbery suspects; 2 were investigating drug-related situations; and 1 was attempting to prevent a burglary or apprehend a burglary suspect. Eight officers were murdered while enforcing traffic laws, seven while investigating suspicious persons or circumstances, seven while answering disturbance calls, six while encountering ambush situations, and two while handling prisoners.

From 1972 through 1998, 3,918 law enforcement officers were killed in the line of duty: 2,332 were feloniously killed and 1,586 were accidentally killed. The most officers killed in any one year was 185 in 1975, while the least in any one year was 105 in 1999.[5]

Operational Styles

After police officers are trained and begin to gain experience and wisdom from their encounters with veteran police officers and citizens on the street, it is believed that they develop **operational styles** that characterize their overall approach to the police job. If these styles actually exist, it means that the effort of the police department to systematically train and deploy officers with the same philosophy and practical approach to policing in the community has not been entirely successful. The research on operational styles shows that they vary both between departments and among officers of the same department.

One of the earliest scholars to report on the existence of policing styles was James Q. Wilson, who found the following three styles in a study of eight police departments:

1. Legalistic style. The emphasis is on violations of law and the use of threats or actual arrests to solve disputes in the community. In theory, the more arrests that are made, the safer a community will be. This style is often found in large metropolitan areas.

2. Watchman style. The emphasis is on informal means of resolving disputes and problems in a community. Keeping the peace is the paramount concern, and arrest is used only as a last resort to resolve any kind of disturbance of the peace. This style of policing is most commonly found in economically poorer communities.

3. Service style. The emphasis is on helping in the community, as opposed to enforcing the law. Referrals and diversion to community treatment agencies are more common than arrest and formal court action. The service style is most likely to be found in wealthy communities.[6]

John Broderick, another scholar who studied operational styles among the police, classified police officers by their degree of commitment to maintaining order and their respect for due process:

1. **Enforcers.** The emphasis is on order, with little respect for due process.

2. **Idealists.** The emphasis is on both social order and due process.

3. **Optimists.** The emphasis is on due process, with little priority given to social order.

4. **Realists.** Little emphasis is given to due process or social order.[7]

Another classification is based on the way officers use their authority and power in street police work. The two key ingredients of this scheme are passion and perspective. Passion is the ability to use force or the recognition that force is a legitimate means of resolving conflict; perspective is the ability to understand human suffering and to use force ethically and morally. According to William Muir's styles of policing, police officers may be:

1. **Professionals.** Officers have the necessary passion and perspective to be valuable police officers.

2. **Enforcers.** Officers have passion in responding to human problems but do not recognize limits on their power to resolve them.

3. **Reciprocators.** Officers are too objective in that they have perspective but virtually no passion, resulting in a detachment from the suffering they encounter and often a failure to take action.

4. **Avoiders.** Officers have neither passion nor perspective, resulting in no recognition of people's problems and no action to resolve them.[8]

Are there identifiable styles of policing? What value do these styles hold for us? In any area of human endeavor, classifications have been constructed. We have developed classifications for leaders, prisoners, quarterbacks, and teachers. These classifications give us a framework of analysis, a basis for discussion. But can they be substantiated when we go into a police agency to see if they actually exist?

Ellen Hochstedler examined the issue of policing styles with 1,134 Dallas, Texas, police officers and was not able to confirm the officer styles identified in the literature by Broderick, Muir, and others. Her conclusion was that it is not possible to "pigeonhole" officers into one style or another because the way officers think and react to street situations varies, depending on the particular situation, the time, and the officers themselves.[9]

- -

6.1 CRITICAL THINKING

1. Which characteristics do you think are the most important for police officers to have? Why?

2. Is there an operational style of policing that you think is the most effective? If so, which one?

3. Do you think it is possible to identify styles of policing? If so, how can it be done? If not, what obstacles prevent identification?

6.2 Police Functions

The list of functions that police are expected to carry out is long and varies from place to place. In the following sections, we will look at the major operations of police departments and the services they provide.

Patrol

Police administrators have long referred to patrol as the backbone of the department. It is unquestionably the most time-consuming and resource-intensive task of any police agency. More than half of the sworn personnel in any police department are assigned to patrol. In Houston, Chicago, and New York, for example, patrol officers make up more than 65 percent of the sworn personnel in each department.

Patrol officers respond to burglar alarms, investigate traffic accidents, care for injured people, try to resolve domestic disputes, and engage in a host of other duties that keep them chasing radio calls across their own beats and the entire city and county when no other cars are available to respond. Precisely how to conduct patrol activities, however, is a matter of much debate in the nation today. Indeed, it seems that there are many ways to police a city.

▲ Street patrol is the most resource-intensive task of any police agency. *Are there acceptable alternatives to street patrol? If yes, what are they and why?*

preventive patrol

Patrolling the streets with little direction; between responses to radio calls, officers are "systematically unsystematic" and observant in an attempt to both prevent and ferret out crime. Also known as random patrol.

Preventive Patrol For decades, police officers patrolled the streets with little direction. Between their responses to radio calls, they were told to be "systematically unsystematic" and observant in an attempt to both prevent and ferret out crime on their beats. In many police departments, as much as 50 percent of an officer's time is uncommitted and available for patrolling the beats that make up a political jurisdiction. The simultaneous increases in crime and the size of police forces beginning in the 1960s caused police managers and academics to question the usefulness of what has come to be known as **preventive patrol** or random patrol. To test the usefulness of preventive patrol, the now famous Kansas City (Missouri) Preventive Patrol Experiment was conducted in 1972.

The Kansas City, Missouri, Police Department and the Police Foundation set up an experiment in which 15 patrol districts were divided into three matched groups according to size, record of calls for service, and demographic characteristics. In the first group, the "control beats," the police department operated the same level of patrol used previously in those beats. In the second group of districts, the "proactive beats," the police department doubled or even tripled the number of patrol officers normally deployed in the area. In the third group of districts, the "reactive beats," the police department deployed no officers at all on preventive patrol. Officers only responded to calls for service and did no patrolling on their own. At the end of the one-year study, the results showed no significant differences in crime rates among the three groups of patrol districts. In other words, a group of districts that had no officers on preventive patrol had the same crime rates as groups that had several times the normal level of staffing engaged in patrol activity. The number of officers made no difference in the number of burglaries, robberies, vehicle thefts, and other serious crimes experienced in the three groups of police districts. Perhaps even more important is that the citizens of Kansas City did not even notice that the levels of patrol in two of the three districts had been changed.[10]

The law enforcement community was astounded by the results of the study, which showed that it made no difference whether patrol officers conducted preventive, or random, patrol. The research was immediately attacked on both philosophical and methodological grounds. How could anyone say that having patrol officers on the street made no difference?

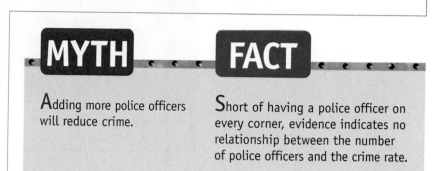

MYTH

Adding more police officers will reduce crime.

FACT

Short of having a police officer on every corner, evidence indicates no relationship between the number of police officers and the crime rate.

One of the criticisms of the study was that no one in the community was told that there were no officers on patrol in reactive districts. What might have happened to the crime rates had the community known no officers were on patrol? Moreover, during the course of the study, marked police cars from other departments and districts crossed the reactive districts to answer calls but then left when the work was completed. Thus, there appeared to be a police presence even in the so-called reactive districts.

This study has forced police executives and academics to reconsider the whole issue of how patrol is conducted, once considered a closed issue. Police administrators have begun to entertain the possibility of reducing the number of officers on patrol. Innovations in patrol methods have also been proposed.

Directed Patrol In **directed patrol,** officers are given guidance or orders on how to use their patrol time. The guidance is often based on the results of crime analyses that identify problem areas. Evidence shows that directed patrol can reduce the incidence of targeted crimes such as thefts from autos and robberies.[11]

directed patrol
Patrolling under guidance or orders on how to use patrol time.

Crime Mapping One technological innovation in crime analysis that has aided directed patrol is Geographic Information Systems (GIS) crime mapping. **GIS crime mapping** is a technique that involves the charting of crime patterns within a geographic area. Crime mapping makes it possible to keep a closer watch on crime and criminals through the generation of crime maps capable of displaying numerous fields of information. If, for example, a series of armed robberies of dry cleaning stores had been committed over a period of several weeks in three adjacent police beats, police crime analysts would be able to record, analyze, determine a definite pattern to these robberies, and make a reasonable prediction as to when and where the next robbery in the series is likely to occur.

GIS crime mapping
A technique that involves the charting of crime patterns within a geographic area.

▲ Field interrogation has been found to reduce crime in targeted areas. *What are some of the problems with field interrogations?*

GIS Crime Mapping

To learn more about GIS crime mapping and how it works, visit the Carolinas Institute for Community Policing through the link at cj.glencoe.com. *Why is crime mapping important?*

aggressive patrol

The practice of having an entire patrol section make numerous traffic stops and field interrogations.

field interrogation

A temporary detention in which officers stop and question pedestrians and motorists they find in suspicious circumstances.

The patrol and investigation forces could be deployed at a prescribed time to conduct surveillance of the prospective target dry cleaning store or stores with a good chance the robber can be arrested. Precisely this kind of use of GIS computer mapping software, coupled with thoughtful crime analysis work, has resulted in the arrest of scores of criminals each month throughout the United States. Dallas, Chicago, New Orleans, and New York are just a few of the cities where the police employ GIS crime mapping and crime analysis. In Dallas, crime analysis has been a part of police operational planning for more than a decade.[12]

Aggressive Patrol   In nearly all police departments, some patrol officers have used aggressive patrol tactics and have been rewarded as high performers because they made many arrests for both minor and serious offenses. When the entire patrol section is instructed to make numerous traffic stops and field interrogations, the practice is referred to as **aggressive patrol**. A **field interrogation** is a temporary detention in which officers stop and question pedestrians and motorists they find in suspicious circumstances. Such procedures have been found to reduce crime in targeted areas.[13]

At least two problems can occur as a result of aggressive patrol. First, random traffic stops and field interrogations inconvenience innocent citizens. To avoid conflict, the police must be certain that those tactics are necessary, and they must explain the necessity to the public. Second, it is often difficult to get all officers on each work shift and in each patrol division motivated to use aggressive patrol tactics. Many officers are reluctant to carry out their duties in an aggressive way. Nevertheless, with crime rates high and research confirming that aggressive patrol can reduce crime, aggressive patrol tactics are likely to continue.

Foot Patrol   During the last few years, there has been renewed interest in having police officers patrol their beats on foot. Is there value in this practice, or is it just nostalgia for a more romantic period in law enforcement? The use of motorized patrols has allowed the police to respond rapidly to citizen calls and to cover large geographical areas. Yet, officers working a busy shift, perhaps responding to more than two dozen calls, come to feel as if they are seeing the world through a windshield. Moreover, it is now generally accepted that rapid response time is useful in only a small portion of the incidents and crimes to which the police are asked to respond.

Challenging conventional wisdom about rapid response, two cities—Flint, Michigan, and Newark, New Jersey—launched substantial programs in foot patrol. In Newark, the results of the foot patrol experiment showed that foot patrol had little or no effect on the level of crime. However, positive effects were identified:

1. Newark residents noticed whether foot patrol officers were present.

2. They were more satisfied with police service when foot patrol officers delivered it.

3. They were less afraid than citizens being served by motorized patrol.[14]

In Flint, Michigan, the extensive neighborhood foot patrol experiment also had positive results:

1. Flint residents had a decreased fear of crime.

2. Their satisfaction with police service increased.

3. There were moderate decreases in crime.

4. There were decreased numbers of calls for police service.

Citizens would wait to talk to their neighborhood foot patrol officer about a problem instead of calling the police department through 911 and speaking with an officer they were not likely to know. One astounding result of the Flint program was that the foot patrol officers became so popular that citizens saw them as real community leaders. They often became more influential than some elected officials. Evidence of the degree of satisfaction with the foot patrol program in Flint was that the community voted three times to continue and expand foot patrol at a time when the city was experiencing one of the nation's highest unemployment rates.[15] Perhaps even more important, the findings of foot patrol research provided the seeds of a much broader concept for law enforcement: community policing, which we will discuss later in this chapter.

Investigation

The role of the detective has generally been glorified by media sources in both fiction and nonfiction accounts. Homicide investigation, in particular, has captured the imagination of fiction readers worldwide. Most police officers aspire to be investigative specialists by attaining the position of detective. But it should be noted that detectives represent only one unit in a police department that conducts investigations. Investigators work in a variety of capacities in a police agency:

1. Traffic homicide and hit-and-run accident investigators in the traffic section.

2. Undercover investigators in narcotics, vice, and violent gang cases.

3. Internal affairs investigators conducting investigations of alleged crimes by police personnel.

4. Investigators conducting background checks of applicants to the police department.

5. Uniformed patrol officers investigating the crimes they have been dispatched to or have encountered on their own while on patrol.

What Is Criminal Investigation? Criminal investigation has been defined as a lawful search for people and things to reconstruct the circumstances of an illegal act, apprehend or determine the guilty party, and aid in the state's prosecution of the offender.[16] The criminal investigation process is generally divided into two parts: the preliminary, or initial, investigation and the continuing, or follow-up, investigation. Most of the time the preliminary investigation in both felony and misdemeanor cases is conducted by patrol officers, although for homicides and other complex, time-consuming investigations, trained investigators are dispatched to the crime scene immediately. The continuing investigation in serious crimes is ordinarily conducted by plainclothes detectives, although small and medium-sized agencies may require patrol officers or a patrol supervisor to follow up on serious criminal offenses.

Investigative Functions In any type of investigation in a police agency, all investigators share responsibility for a number of critical functions. They must:

1. Locate witnesses and suspects.
2. Arrest criminals.
3. Collect, preserve, and analyze evidence.
4. Interview witnesses.
5. Interrogate suspects.
6. Write reports.
7. Recover stolen property.
8. Seize contraband.
9. Prepare cases and testify in court.

The specific application and context of those functions vary considerably, depending on whether the investigation is of the theft of expensive paintings, for example, or the rape of an elderly widow living alone.

The Role of the Detective At first glance, the role of the detective seems highly desirable. To a patrol officer who has been rotating work shifts for several years, seldom getting a weekend off, detectives in the police department seem to have a number of advantages:

1. They do not have to wear uniforms.
2. They have anonymity during work hours if they choose it.
3. They have steady work hours, often daytime hours with weekends off.
4. They have offices and desks.
5. They enjoy the prestige associated with the position.
6. In many agencies, detectives receive higher compensation and hold a higher rank.

▲ Criminal investigation is a time-consuming task that requires much attention to detail. *What aspects of criminal investigations are the most time consuming and why?*

Crime Assessment

For less serious crimes, many police departments use solvability-factor score sheets or software programs to assess information collected at crime scenes. The assessment, which is done by the responding officer, a case-screening officer, or a felony-review unit, determines which cases are likely to be solved, given the initial information obtained. Promising cases are turned over to detectives for follow-up investigation. The rest are often closed on the basis of the preliminary investigation and are reopened only if additional information is uncovered.

SOURCE: Alfred Blumstein and Joan Petersilia, "NIJ and its Research Program," *25 Years of Criminal Justice Research,* (Washington, DC: The National Institute of Justice, 1994) p.13.

7. Perhaps most important, they enjoy more freedom than patrol officers from the police radio, geographical boundaries, and close supervision.

All these advantages add up to a high-status position, both within the police department and in the eyes of the public.

Productivity Despite all the advantages of being a detective, investigators are often faced with insurmountable obstacles and stressful work conditions. Notifying the next of kin in a homicide is one of the worst tasks:

> Of all the dirty tasks that go with the dirty work of chasing a killer, notifying the next of kin is the job that homicide detectives hate most. It's worse than getting up at 3 a.m. on a February night to slog through a field of freezing mud toward a body that needed burying two days ago. Worse than staring into the flat cold eyes of a teenager who bragged about dragging a man through the streets to his death. Worse than visiting every sleazy dive in town until you finally find the one person who can put the murderer away and having that person say as cool as a debutante with a full dance card, "I don't want to get involved."[17]

Detectives have the cards stacked against them most of the time. Unless they discover, during the preliminary investigation, a named suspect or a description or other information that leads to a named suspect, the chances of solving the crime are low. Property crimes with no witnesses are particularly hard to solve. In 1999, for example, the clearance rates for crimes against persons were 69 percent for murder, 59 percent for aggravated assault, 49 percent for forcible rape, and 29 percent for robbery. In crimes against property, the clearance rates were 14 percent for burglary, 19 percent for larceny-theft, and 15 percent for motor vehicle theft. Clearances for crimes against persons are generally higher than for property crimes because crimes against persons receive more intensive investigative effort and because victims and witnesses frequently identify the perpetrators. Overall, the national clearance rate in 1999 was 21 percent.[18] Studies have found that much of what a detective does is not needed and that an investigator's technical knowledge often does little to help solve cases.[19] In one study, for example, fewer than ten percent of all arrests for robbery were the result of investigative work by detectives.[20] Nevertheless, police agencies retain detectives and plainclothes investigators for a number of reasons:

MYTH

Improvements in detective work and criminal investigation will significantly raise clearance rates or lower the crime rate.

FACT

"Cleared" crimes generally solve themselves. The offender either is discovered at the scene or can be identified by the victim or a witness. Investigation rarely solves "cold" or "stranger" crimes.

FYI

DNA

In approximately one-third of DNA examinations, the suspect's DNA cannot be matched with biological evidence from the crime scene. Thus, potential suspects can be eliminated from consideration early in the investigative process, allowing investigators to focus their efforts more effectively on other suspects or cases.

CRIMINAL JUSTICE *Online*

DNA Evidence

The National Commission on the Future of DNA Evidence is a program sponsored by the National Institute of Justice. Visit the program's Web site by clicking on the link at cj.glencoe.com. *How big a role should DNA play in criminal investigations?*

1. Detectives have interrogation and case presentation skills that assist in prosecution.

2. Technical knowledge, such as knowing about burglary tools, does help in some investigations and prosecutions.

3. Law enforcement executives can assign detectives to a major, high-profile case to demonstrate to the public that they are committing resources to the matter.

The major studies of investigative effectiveness emphasize the value of improving the suspect-identification process. Once a suspect is identified by name or some other clearly distinguishing characteristic, the chances of making an arrest are increased substantially.

Recent Identification Developments in Criminal Investigation Two of the most significant advances in criminal investigation have been the development of fingerprinting and DNA profiling. Fingerprinting has resulted in the arrest and conviction of millions of criminal suspects who otherwise might have never been brought to justice. DNA profiling holds even greater promise.

DNA profiling DNA (deoxyribonucleic acid) is a molecule present in all forms of life. A unique genetic profile can be derived from blood, hair, semen, or other bodily substances found at the scene of a crime or on a victim. Not only can bodily substances found at a crime scene be matched with DNA samples from a suspect to give an extremely high probability of identifying the perpetrator, but it is believed that soon DNA from a sample as small as a flake of dandruff will yield a positive, unique identification, with no need to consider mathematical probabilities.

DNA profiling has three distinct functions: linking or eliminating identified suspects to a crime; identifying "cold hits" where a sample from a crime scene is matched against numerous cases in a DNA database and a positive match is made; and clearing convicted rapists and murderers years after they began serving their sentences. DNA profiling would be very useful, for example, in cases where a murderer's blood was found at the scene of a crime after a deadly struggle or in a rape case where seminal fluid could be obtained from the victim.

A serious issue at present is whether DNA databases ought to be assembled and from whom the samples should be taken. Many states permit the taking of DNA samples from arrested and convicted subjects. Some enthusiasts believe that DNA samples should be taken from all suspects in crimes while a smaller number believe the samples should be collected from all people at birth. Undoubtedly the more collected samples in a database, the more likely a match is going to be found. But privacy concerns and the potential for misuse of DNA samples are likely to hinder any more intrusive measures on the part of agents of the justice system.

Automated Fingerprint Identification System An expensive but invaluable tool in criminal investigation is the Automated Fingerprint Identification System (AFIS). This relatively new technology allows investigators to sort through thousands of sets of stored fingerprints for a match with those of a suspect in a crime. In fact, many of the current attempts to match prints would not have been made without AFIS, because the old process would have taken thousands of hours. Large metropolitan police agencies use it to identify 200–500 suspects a year who would have escaped apprehension before the implementation of AFIS. The initial and maintenance costs for an AFIS, however, are expensive.

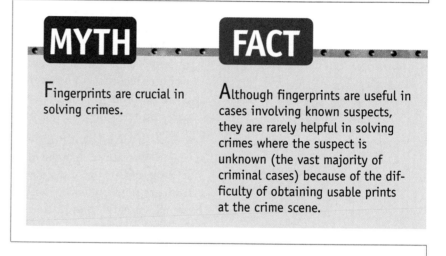

MYTH

Fingerprints are crucial in solving crimes.

FACT

Although fingerprints are useful in cases involving known suspects, they are rarely helpful in solving crimes where the suspect is unknown (the vast majority of criminal cases) because of the difficulty of obtaining usable prints at the crime scene.

cybercrime
The use of computer technology to commit crime.

Cybercrime The use of computer technology to commit crime is of increasing concern to law enforcement officials. The FBI reports that the losses from **cybercrime** each year total $10 billion dollars even though two-thirds of computer crime victims fail to notify the authorities. Some of the reasons for not reporting computer crime are the fear of the loss of public confidence in the organization as a result of being a victim, the attention to their vulnerability that a crime report would attract, and the shame of not providing adequate security to protect trusted assets.

Since so little hardware and expense is involved, any person with a computer and modem connection to the Internet has the potential to attack computer systems and people online. The knowledge to carry out these attacks is often available online at hacker Web sites, message boards, and chat rooms. The cybercriminal can be as unsophisticated as a teenage amateur hacker just out for some fun or a talented computer specialist possessing skills on par with technical experts employed by the nation's top security organizations. Each of these types of computer criminal can wreak destructive havoc on a computer system, invade the privacy of thousands of citizens, and engage in the theft of millions of dollars worth of trade secrets or steal large sums of

CRIMINAL JUSTICE Online
Combatting Cybercrime

To learn more about what the U.S. government is doing to combat cybercrime, visit the U.S. Department of Justice cybercrime Web site through the link at cj.glencoe.com. *Do you think that there is anything more the government can do to prevent cybercrime?*

money. At present, unfortunately, most law enforcement agencies in America are ill prepared to detect, investigate, and prosecute cybercriminals.[21]

A variety of offenses can be committed using computer and Internet technology.

1. Sex Crimes—Predators search the Internet looking for sexually explicit content as well as child pornography. Much of the sexually explicit and pornographic content is in JPEG and MPEG formats which allow it to be downloaded to a person's hard drive easily.[22] Downloading much of this material is illegal in a number of states. The origin of some of this content is often from other nations of the world, thus complicating investigation and prosecution.

2. Illegal Access, Destruction, and Manipulation of Data— Cybercriminals break into computer systems and obtain data that is illegal for them to have, such as credit card numbers, bank records, and software codes. In October of 2000, someone illegally entered Microsoft's computer system and stole software codes for some of its future products. Hackers often illegally enter computer systems and introduce viruses or worms that infect that computer system and any other storage device that interacts with it. Computer data can also be illegally manipulated in a variety of ways. Computer records can be altered at financial, business, and educational institutions. Millions of dollars have been illegally transferred to the accounts of cybercriminals since the inception of electronic data storage.

In a survey involving 114 state and local law enforcement agencies, it was revealed that these agencies lacked the adequate training, equipment, and staff to confront present and future incidents of cybercrime.[23] Cooperative efforts are now underway among law enforcement, business, high tech, and national security organizations to better prepare the nation's police agencies to combat cybercrime.

Traffic

When loss of life, serious injury, suffering, and property damage are all considered, the regulation and control of vehicle and pedestrian traffic are important, if not the most important, police responsibilities. Each year, nearly twice as many people are killed in automobile accidents on the streets and highways of the nation as are murdered.

A large percentage of this highway death and suffering is attributable to alcohol. Enforcement of DUI (driving under the influence) laws is critical to the safety of a community. In addition, automobile insurance rates are based to some degree on a community's level of traffic enforcement. Thus, if the police neglect traffic regulation and enforcement, they are likely to hear about it from both insurance companies and premium payers.

Some of the debate about traffic enforcement concerns whether the major enforcers of traffic regulations should be specialized personnel or uniformed patrol officers. Some traffic responsibilities are already delegated to specialized personnel, such as enforcement of parking regulations and investigations of hit-and-run accidents and traffic fatalities. In some agencies, special **traffic accident investigation crews** are assigned to all traffic accident investigations. Otherwise, patrol officers investigate accidents and attend to other traffic-related duties as a normal part of their everyday workload.

traffic accident investigation crews
In some agencies, the special units assigned to all traffic accident investigations.

Traffic units exist in nearly all medium-to-large police agencies. Some of their more important functions are:

- To educate motorists in a community about traffic safety and proper driving procedures.
- To enforce traffic laws, particularly when violations of those laws cause traffic accidents.
- To recommend traffic engineering changes that will enhance the flow of traffic and promote safety.

Enforcing traffic laws may also reduce criminal activity because stopping vehicles for traffic violations both day and night is likely to put police officers in contact with criminals.

Many veteran officers consider working in the traffic division "clean" police work because it does not normally involve responding to radio calls that take them to the scene of fights, domestic disturbances, or other distasteful incidents, such as those involving drunks. Traffic officers in large police agencies are usually well schooled in scientific accident investigation, a skill that makes them employable in the private sector, usually doing traffic reconstruction for insurance companies. The Traffic Institute at Northwestern University is one of the major schools that prepare officers for sophisticated accident investigation, although many state peace officer and highway patrol academies now have comparable training programs.

6.2 CRITICAL THINKING

1. What do you think are the pros and cons of being an investigator/detective? Does this type of work sound attractive to you?

2. Do you think there are any ways to protect individuals and businesses from becoming victims of cyber-crime? If so, what do you propose?

The Sniffer

Hundreds of police agencies nationwide use the P.A.S. III Sniffer to detect alcohol on motorists' breath. The Sniffer, on the market since 1993, is a tiny, battery-powered device on the end of a flashlight that when placed six inches from a driver's face sucks in breath and analyzes it for traces of alcohol. For daytime use when the flashlight isn't appropriate, a clipboard containing the alcohol sensor can be substituted. The constitutionality of the Sniffer has never been tested in court—it presumably falls under the "plain view doctrine"—and nobody is arrested based solely on a positive reading by the Sniffer. If the device indicates alcohol in the air sample, the driver is held for further tests.

SOURCE: "Tricky flashlight worries ACLU," *The Orlando Sentinel*, August 13, 2000, p. A-4.

6.3 Community Policing

For decades, police followed the professional model, which rested on three foundations: preventive patrol, quick response time, and follow-up investigation. Sensing that the professional model did not always operate as efficiently and effectively as it could, criminal justice researchers set out to review current procedures and evaluate alternative programs. One of the first and best-known of these studies was the Kansas City, Missouri, Preventive Patrol Experiment, discussed earlier in this chapter. That study's conclusion was that preventive patrol did not necessarily prevent crime or reassure citizens. Following the study, some police departments assigned police units to proactive patrol, giving them specific assignments rather than having them randomly cruise the streets.

Another study, again with the Kansas City Police Department, examined the effects of police response time. The study found that police response time was unrelated to the probability of making an arrest. Researchers discovered that the time it takes a citizen to report a crime—not the speed with which police respond—was the major determinant of whether an on-scene arrest took place or witnesses could be located. In 90 percent of crimes, citizens wait five to ten minutes to call the police, precluding catching the criminal at the scene.

As preventive patrol and fast response time were being questioned, so too was follow-up investigation. A study by the Rand Corporation reviewed the criminal investigation process for effectiveness. The researchers concluded that the work of a criminal investigator alone rarely leads to an arrest and that the probability of arrest is determined largely by information that patrol officers obtain at the crime scene in their preliminary investigation.[24]

Criminal justice researchers continued their review of accepted police functions with the aim of making policing more effective by initiating new techniques and procedures. One of the interesting findings of the foot patrol research was that foot patrol officers were better able to deal with minor annoyances—such as rowdy youths, panhandlers, and abandoned cars—that irritate citizens.

In a theory called "broken windows," James Q. Wilson and George Kelling proposed that those minor annoyances are "signs of crime" and that if they are not dealt with early, more serious and more costly problems are likely to occur.[25] Wilson and Kelling concluded that to help solve both minor and major problems in a neighborhood and to reduce crime and fear of crime, police officers must be in close, regular contact with citizens. That is, police and citizens should work cooperatively to build a strong sense of community and should share responsibility in the neighborhood to improve the overall quality of life within the community.

MYTH

Shorter police response time contributes to more arrests.

FACT

For most crimes, police response time is irrelevant. Approximately two-thirds of crimes are "cold"; the offender is gone long before the crime is discovered. In cases where time counts, the critical delay often occurs in the time it takes the victim to call the police.

The Philosophy and Components of Community Policing

With community policing, citizens share responsibility for their community's safety. Citizens and the police work collectively to identify problems, propose solutions, implement action, and evaluate the results in the community. A community policing perspective differs in a number of ways from a traditional policing perspective. For example, in community policing, the police must share power with residents of a community, and critical decisions need to be made at the neighborhood level, not at a downtown police headquarters. Such decentralization of authority means that credit for bringing about a safer and more secure community must be shared with the people of the community, a tall order for any group of professionals to accept. Achieving the goals of community policing requires successful implementation of three essential and complementary components or operational strategies: community partnership, problem solving, and change management.[26] Figure 6–3 on pages 214 and 215 shows some of the varied aspects of community policing.

Community Partnership Establishing and maintaining mutual trust between citizens of a community and the police is the main goal of the first component of community policing. Police have always recognized the need for cooperation with the community and have encouraged members of the community to come forward with crime-fighting information. In addition, police have spoken to neighborhood groups, worked with local organizations, and provided special-unit services. How are those cooperative efforts different from the community partnership of community policing?

In community policing, the police become an integral part of the community culture, and the community, in turn, helps the police define future crime prevention strategies and allocate community protection services. Establishing a community partnership means adopting a policing perspective that exceeds the standard law enforcement emphasis. The police no longer view the community as a passive presence connected to the police by an isolated incident or series of incidents. The community's concerns with crime and disorder become the target of efforts by the police and the community working together.

For patrol officers, building police-community partnerships entails such activities as talking to local business owners to identify their concerns, visiting residents in their homes to offer advice on security, and helping to organize and support neighborhood watch groups and regular community meetings. It also involves ongoing communication with residents. For example, a patrol officer might canvass a neighborhood for information about a string of burglaries and then revisit those residents to inform them when the burglar is caught.

Problem Solving Problem solving requires a lot more thought, energy, and action than traditional incident-based police responses to crime and disorder. In full partnership, the police and a community's residents and business owners identify core problems, propose solutions, and implement a solution. Thus, community members identify the concerns that they feel are most threatening to their safety and well-being. Those areas of concern then become priorities for joint police-community interventions.

For this problem-solving process to operate effectively, the police need to devote time and attention to discovering a community's concerns, and they need to recognize the validity of those concerns. Police and neighborhood groups may not always agree on the specific problems that deserve attention first. For example, the police may regard robberies as the biggest problem in a particular neighborhood, while residents find derelicts who sleep in doorways, break bottles on sidewalks, and pick through garbage cans the number one problem. In community policing, both problems should receive early attention from the police, other government agencies, and the community.

Some community policing advocates recommend a four-step problem-solving process referred to as SARA: *S*canning—identifying problems; *A*nalysis—understanding underlying conditions; *R*esponse—developing and implementing solutions; *A*ssessment—determining the solutions' effect. One useful tool in working toward a solution is known as the *crime triangle*. The crime triangle is a view of crime and disorder as an interaction among three variables: a victim, an offender, and a location. Solutions can be developed that affect one or more of the three elements of the crime triangle. For

FIGURE 6–3
Aspects of Community Policing

Increased Officer Visibility

Neighborhood Substations

Citizen Block Watches

Community Policing Specialists

example, suppose elderly residents are being jeopardized by speeding teenagers in automobiles as they walk across the streets of a suburban residential neighborhood. Using a crime triangle analysis might result in the following police-community solutions: using the juvenile court to alter the probation period of offending drivers (focus on the offender), installing speed bumps in the pavement or changing the cycles of traffic signals on opposite ends of the

Involvement in Neighborhood Functions

Merchant Organizing

House Visits

Interaction with Community Groups

street so that motorists cannot build up speed (focus on the location), holding safety education classes at the senior center to educate elderly residents to use marked crosswalks (focus on the victim). More than likely, in community policing, a combination of those solutions would be used. Such a response to a community problem is much more thorough than merely having a squad car drive by the location when a citizen calls in a complaint.

Change Management Forging community policing partnerships and implementing problem-solving strategies necessitates assigning new responsibilities and adopting a flexible style of management. Traditionally, patrol officers have been accorded lower status in police organizations and have been dominated by the agency's command structure. Community policing, in contrast, emphasizes the value of the patrol function and the patrol officer as an individual. It requires the shifting of initiative, decision making, and responsibility downward within the police organization. The neighborhood police officer or deputy sheriff becomes responsible for managing the delivery of police services to the community or area to which he or she is permanently assigned. Patrol officers are the most familiar with the needs and concerns of their communities and are in the best position to forge the close ties with the community that lead to effective solutions to local problems.

Under community policing, police management must guide, rather than dominate, the actions of the patrol officer and must ensure that patrol officers have the necessary resources to solve the problems in their communities. Management must determine the guiding principles to convert the philosophy of the agency to community policing and then to evaluate the effectiveness of the strategies implemented.

Implementing Community Policing

Implementation plans for community policing vary from agency to agency and from community to community. The appropriate implementation strategy depends on conditions within the law enforcement agency and the community embarking on community policing. Successful implementation requires that the police and the members of the community understand the underlying philosophy of community policing and have a true commitment to the community policing strategy. Communication, cooperation, coordination, collaboration, and change are the keys to putting community policing into action. The community policing philosophy has become so popular and broadly implemented that it exists as the operating method of police departments in colleges and universities, transit systems, and even airports. At the Dallas Love Field, City of Dallas police officers maintain a community police substation in the airport as part of the regular security force and receive specially marked federal funds and airport community police training.

6.3 CRITICAL THINKING

1. Can you think of ways to make community policing even more effective?

2. Do you think there is a certain operational style that is most appropriate for community policing? If so, which one?

CAREERS IN CRIMINAL JUSTICE

Ohio State Highway Patrol Officer

Lieutenant Brenda Sue Collins

I have had an exciting career with the Ohio State Highway Patrol and have worked in a variety of assignments since 1985. Currently I am the post commander for the Fremont post of the State Highway Patrol, responsible for the leadership of all operational and staff personnel serving at the Fremont post. I have also served as a cadet dispatcher (my first job with the patrol) a highway trooper, an academy instructor, an officer in the Traffic and Drug Interdiction Unit, a supervisor in the recruiting section, and a public information officer. I am married to Captain Richard Collins, a district commander of the patrol stationed in Findlay.

An Ohio State Highway Patrol Officer's major responsibility is to patrol the roadways and keep them safe. That responsibility includes investigating vehicle crashes, gaining obedience to the traffic laws by enforcement and other means, giving assistance to motorists 24 hours a day, keeping the roadway free of obstructions, enforcing the extensive commercial vehicle laws, and checking for signs of criminal activity during vehicle stops. One of the toughest parts of the patrol officer's job is to make death notifications to family members of loved ones who have been killed in a fatal crash.

I graduated in the 116th Academy class and was assigned to the Portsmouth post as a trooper where I was somewhat of a novelty with the citizens since there were not that many female highway patrol officers. But when people see that you do your job effectively and professionally just like your male counterparts, the novelty soon wears off. Now we have about 130 female troopers out of a total of approximately 1,400 troopers.

I attended Ohio University where I studied forensic chemistry and law enforcement and Ohio State University in Marion. The OSHP provides tuition assistance that varies depending on the grades you receive in courses.

Being married to another highway patrol officer really has its advantages. First, you can learn from each other because you have worked in different assignments and have experienced common things at different times in your career. Richard and I also know the language and values of the highway patrol, therefore allowing us to communicate a lot more clearly than a married couple working at entirely different jobs. The only disadvantage that I can see is that when both of you are senior officers in the patrol, you have to deal with the issue of promotions. As a married couple we are not allowed to serve in the same posts of the patrol, but can be in adjacent districts if there are openings for our rank. Consequently when promotional opportunities come up for one or the other of us, we have to think of what kind of disruption that will cause in our home life.

The advice I would offer to somebody that wants to be a highway patrol officer is to work in a job you really want until the highway patrol officer's job becomes available. The selection process is long and difficult. I would suggest that you investigate and really find out what a highway patrol officer's job is like. The job entails round-the-clock duty in all sorts of weather, including the worst weather. In fact, you may be the only one out on the highways during bad weather. You are more likely to stick with it when you know these things up front.

What characteristics of your personality do you think would make you best suited to be a highway patrol officer?

Policing: Roles, Styles, and Functions

Review and Applications

SUMMARY BY CHAPTER OBJECTIVES

1. Identify Characteristics of Police Work

The role of the police officer is complex and requires a combination of special characteristics, which involve quick decision making, invisible work, "dirty work," and danger.

2. Distinguish Among James Q. Wilson's Three Operational Styles in Policing

Wilson's three operational styles in policing are legalistic which emphasizes violations of the law and the use of arrests to resolve community disputes; watchman, emphasizing informal means of resolving disputes and using arrest only as a last resort; and service, which emphasizes helping in the community over enforcing the law.

3. List the Three Major Functions of Police Departments

The three major functions of police departments in the United States are patrol, investigation, and traffic.

4. Explain the Main Components of Community Policing

The three main components of community policing are community partnership, problem solving, and change management.

5. Identify Four Steps in a Community Policing Approach to Problem Solving

Community policing relies heavily on problem solving. The four steps in a community policing approach to problem solving are often referred to as SARA: Scanning—identifying problems, Analysis—understanding underlying conditions, Response—developing and implementing solutions, Assessment—determining the solutions' effect.

KEY TERMS

role, p. 196
role expectation, p. 196
role conflict, p. 196
operational styles, p. 200
preventive patrol, p. 202
directed patrol, p. 203
GIS crime mapping, p. 203
aggressive patrol, p. 204
field interrogation, p. 204
cybercrime, p. 209
traffic accident investigation crews, p. 210

1. What is a common source of role conflict for the police?

2. Distinguish among the three sets of operational styles identified by criminal justice scholars.

3. How are preventive patrol, directed patrol, and aggressive patrol different?

4. What are the major uses of GIS crime mapping in law enforcement?

5. What are some of the functions of a criminal investigator?

6. What are three distinct functions of DNA profiling?

7. What are two broad categories of cybercrime?

8. What are some of the more important functions of traffic units?

9. What is the philosophy of community policing?

10. What are the three complementary operational strategies of community policing?

1. **SARA Approach** In groups of three or four, select a local crime or disorder problem. Using the first three components of the SARA approach to problem solving (scanning, analysis, and response) and considering the elements of the crime triangle, formulate some options to deal with the problem. Present your options to the class, and let the whole class vote to determine which option is the best to solve the problem.

   Do you agree with the class vote? Why or why not? What do the results of this vote say about attitudes toward crime-related problem solving?

2. **Law Enforcement Resources** Look through several police periodicals, such as *Law and Order, Police Chief,* or other professional police magazines.

   What do the advertised products tell you about law enforcement? What law enforcement issues are addressed in the articles? Write a brief summary of your findings.

INTERNET

3. **Crime Analysis** Go to the Web page of the International Association of Crime Analysts through the link at cj.glencoe.com. Click on Crime Analysis Units. Examine the crime maps of the police departments listed and write a one-page review of what you found at three of the crime mapping pages.

   How helpful do you think these crime maps are for police patrol and criminal investigation units? Could citizens benefit from these maps? How?

4. **Cybercrime** Ask a local police officer what the needs of the police in combating cybercrime in your area are. Make a list of the types of cyber-crimes that have actually occurred in your area. Compare and contrast that list with what experts on CNET (go to their web page through the link at cj.glencoe.com.) and the material in your text describe as the important concerns in addressing cybercrime.

   Is there cause for concern? Why or why not?

Police Patrol

1. Assume that you are the patrol commander in a southern city that has large numbers of African American and Hispanic residents. All shifts of your patrol division have embraced and supported a "broken windows" and "zero-tolerance" approach to patrol work. Your patrol division's style could clearly be called aggressive, but for the past five years the city's violent, property, and minor offense rates have been dropping steadily. Some citizens have complained each month about the aggressive and sometimes intrusive vehicle stops. Most of the complainants have been African Americans who live in neighborhoods where the recorded crime rate has dropped the most dramatically since the implementation of the aggressive patrol style. They accuse officers of racial profiling. Racial profiling is illegal and occurs when minority citizens are stopped in their cars and on the street for little or nothing more than their race as the cause. (Racial profiling is discussed in greater detail in the next chapter.) When applied to motorists, racial profiling has even acquired a popular name, "Driving While Black" or DWB or DWBB, "Driving While Black or Brown."

   a. What steps would you take as patrol commander to assure the chief of police, the city's leaders, and the public at large that neither racial profiling is occurring in your patrol division nor are infringements on citizens' liberties beyond what are legal and necessary?

   b. What part would validated cases of "Driving While Black or Brown" or (racial profiling) in other cities have on your plan?

Community Policing

2. You are a new community police officer assigned with seven other officers to a low-income, heterogeneous, high-turnover, high-crime neighborhood. How should you and your fellow officers address the following problems?

   a. Neighborhood residents, neighborhood business owners, and community leaders disagree about the most important problems of the neighborhood and what to do about them. What should you and your fellow officers do?

   b. You organize and heavily publicize a meeting to discuss neighborhood problems and their solutions. However, only about ten to twenty percent of neighborhood residents attend and most of them are white and more affluent homeowners who live in the better parts of the neighborhood. Few minorities or renters attend. What should you and your fellow officers do?

   c. Your precinct captain disagrees with neighborhood residents about the most important problems in the neighborhood. Your precinct captain's top priority is abandoned cars used for drug dealing. The top priority of neighborhood residents is the overall appearance of the neighborhood. What should you and your fellow officers do?

ADDITIONAL READING

Ahern, James. *Police in Trouble.* New York: Hawthorn Books, 1972.

Brown, Michael. *Working the Street.* New York: Russell Sage, 1981.

Cordner, Gary and Donna Hale (eds.). *What Works in Policing? Operations and Administration Examined.* Cincinnati: Anderson, 1992.

Skogan, Wesley G. and Susan M. Hartnett. *Community Policing: Chicago Style.* New York: Oxford University Press, 1977.

Sparrow, Malcolm, Mark Moore, and David Kennedy. *Beyond 911, A New Era for Policing.* New York: Basic Books, 1990.

ENDNOTES

1. Keith Haley, "Training," in Gary Cordner and Donna Hale (eds.), *What Works in Policing Operations and Administration Examined* (Cincinnati: Anderson, 1992).

2. Lee Rainwater, "The Revolt of the Dirty Workers," Transaction (November 1967), p. 2.

3. Jerome Skolnick, *Justice Without Trial* (New York: Wiley, 1966).

4. U.S. Department of Justice, Federal Bureau of Investigation, Press Release, May 15, 2000. <www.fbi.gov/pressrm/ pressrel/pressrel00/99leoka.htm>

5. Kathleen Maguire and Ann L. Pastore (eds.), *Sourcebook of Criminal Justice Statistics 1996,* U.S. Department of Justice, Bureau of Justice Statistics (Washington, DC: GPO, 1997), p. 318, Table 3.170; FBI Press Release, May 15, 2000, op. cit.

6. James Q. Wilson, *Varieties of Police Behavior* (Cambridge, MA: Harvard University Press, 1968), pp. 140–227.

7. John Broderick, *Police in a Time of Change* (Morristown, NJ: General Learning Press, 1977), pp. 9–88.

8. William Muir, Jr., *Police: Streetcorner Politicians* (Chicago: University of Chicago Press, 1977).

9. Ellen Hochstedler, "Testing Types: A Review and Test of Police Types," Journal of Criminal Justice, Vol. 9 (1981), pp. 451–66.

10. G. Kelling, T. Pate, D. Dieckman, and C. Brown, *The Kansas City Preventive Patrol Experiment: A Summary Report* (Washington, DC: Police Foundation, 1974).

11. Gary Cordner, "Patrol," in Gary Cordner and Donna Hale (eds.), op. cit.

12. David Michaels, "Obscure Job Is Key in Helping City Track Crime, Police Effectiveness," *Dallas Morning News,* October 28, 2000.

13. James Q. Wilson and Barbara Boland, "The Effect of Police on Crime," *Law and Society Review,* Vol. 12 (1978), pp. 367–84.

14. George Kelling, *The Newark Foot Patrol Experiment* (Washington, DC: Police Foundation, 1981).

15. Robert C. Trojanowicz, *The Neighborhood Foot Patrol Program in Flint, Michigan* (East Lansing, MI: National Neighborhood Foot Patrol Center, n.d.).

16. Bruce L. Berg and John J. Horgan, *Criminal Investigation,* 3d ed. (Westerville: Glencoe/McGraw-Hill, 1998).

17. Christine Wicker, "Death Beat," in Keith N. Haley and Mark A. Stallo, *Texas Crime, Texas Justice* (New York: McGraw-Hill, 1996).

18. U.S. Department of Justice, Federal Bureau of Investigations, *Crime in the United States, 1999* (Washington, DC: GPO, 2000), pp. 201–202.

19. Mark Willman and John Snortum, "Detective Work: The Criminal Investigation Process in a Medium-Size Police Department," *Criminal Justice Review,* Vol. 9 (1984), pp. 33–39; V. Williams and R. Sumrall, "Productivity Measures in the Criminal Investigation Function," *Journal of Criminal Justice,* Vol. 10 (1982), pp. 111–22; I. Greenberg and R. Wasserman, *Managing Criminal Investigations* (Washington, DC: U.S. Department of Justice, 1979); P. Greenwood and J. Petersilia, *The Criminal Investigation Process, Vol. I, Summary and Policy Implications* (Washington, DC: U.S. Department of Justice, 1975); B. Greenberg, C. Elliot, L. Kraft, and H. Procter, *Felony Investigation Decision Model: An Analysis of Investigative Elements of Information* (Washington, DC: GPO, 1975).

20. John Conklin, *Robbery and the Criminal Justice System* (New York: J. B. Lippincott, 1972), p. 149.

21. Hollis Stambaugh, David Beaupre, David Icove, Richard Baker, Waynes Cassady, and Wayne P. Williams, *State and Local Law Enforcement Needs to Combat Local Crime,* National Institute of Justice, August 2000.

22. Ronald T. Holmes, Richard Tewksberry, and Stephen T. Holmes, "Pornography on the Internet" Law and Order, Vol. 45 No. 9 September 1997.

23. Stambaugh, et al., op. cit.

24. Material on research studies based on information in Blumstein and Petersilia, Alfred Blumstein and Joan Petersilia, "NIJ and Its Research Program," *25 Years of Criminal Justice Research,* (Washington, DC: The National Institute of Justice, 1994), pp. 10–14.

25. James Q. Wilson and George L. Kelling, "Broken Windows: The Police and Neighborhood Safety," Atlantic, Vol. 256 (1982), pp. 29–38.

26. Material in this subsection is based on information in the following sources: Community Policing Consortium, Understanding Community Policing: A Framework for Action, monograph. www.communitypolicing.org/ conpubs.html, January 1998; U.S. Department of Justice, National Institute of Corrections, Community Justice: Striving for Safe, Secure, and Just Communities (Louisville, KY: LIS, 1996).

Chapter 7

Policing America: Issues and Ethics

7.1 The Police and the Public

To carry out the functions of law enforcement, order maintenance, service, and information gathering successfully, the police must have the trust and cooperation of the public. The manner in which they carry out those functions, especially law enforcement and order maintenance, determines the community's respect for and trust in the police. Citizens who trust and respect the police are much more likely to help them carry out their functions; citizens who lack that trust and respect may rebel against the police in particular and government in general.

Public Attitudes Toward the Police

What do people think of the police? The answer depends on what and whom you ask. It also depends on people's prior experience with the police. Research shows that citizens who have experienced positive contacts with the police generally have positive attitudes toward the police.[1] Figure 7–1 reveals that, overall, 54 percent of the public has "a great deal" or "quite a lot" of confidence in the police, 33 percent has "some" confidence, and 12 percent has "very little" or "none." However, among nonwhites, only 38 percent have "a great deal" or "quite a lot" of confidence in the police, another 38 percent have "some" confidence, and 21 percent have "very little" or "none." What is it about the police that the public has or does not have confidence? To begin with, a majority of the public has confidence in the ability of the police to protect them from crime in general, to solve crime, and to prevent crime.

Protection From Crime Nearly three-quarters of the public (74 percent) have at least some confidence in the ability of the police to protect them from crime in general. As shown in the first panel of Figure 7–2 on page 225, 30 percent of the public has "a great deal" of confidence, 44 percent has "some" confidence, 16 percent has "little" confidence, and 8 percent has "none at all." Among African Americans, however, confidence in the police's ability to protect them from crime is decidedly lower. Only 18 percent of

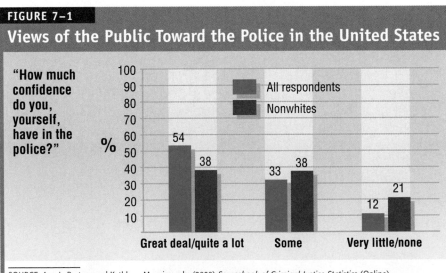

FIGURE 7–1

Views of the Public Toward the Police in the United States

"How much confidence do you, yourself, have in the police?"

SOURCE: Ann L. Pastore and Kathleen Maguire, eds. (2000) *Sourcebook of Criminal Justice Statistics* (Online) <www.albany.edu/sourcebook/> (December 16, 2000), p. 102, Table 2.18.

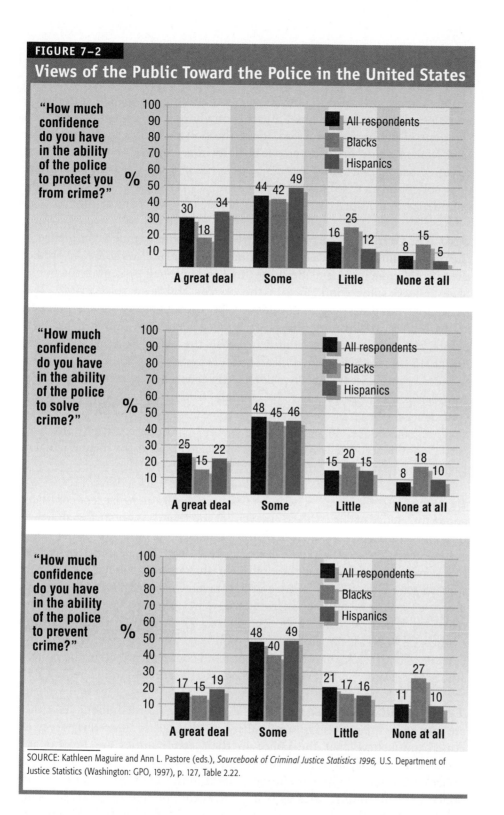

FIGURE 7–2

Views of the Public Toward the Police in the United States

"How much confidence do you have in the ability of the police to protect you from crime?"

%

- All respondents
- Blacks
- Hispanics

A great deal: 30, 18, 34
Some: 44, 42, 49
Little: 16, 25, 12
None at all: 8, 15, 5

"How much confidence do you have in the ability of the police to solve crime?"

%

- All respondents
- Blacks
- Hispanics

A great deal: 25, 15, 22
Some: 48, 45, 46
Little: 15, 20, 15
None at all: 8, 18, 10

"How much confidence do you have in the ability of the police to prevent crime?"

%

- All respondents
- Blacks
- Hispanics

A great deal: 17, 15, 19
Some: 48, 40, 49
Little: 21, 17, 16
None at all: 11, 27, 10

SOURCE: Kathleen Maguire and Ann L. Pastore (eds.), *Sourcebook of Criminal Justice Statistics 1996,* U.S. Department of Justice Statistics (Washington: GPO, 1997), p. 127, Table 2.22.

blacks have "a great deal" of confidence in the police's ability to protect them from crime, 42 percent have "some" confidence, 25 percent have "little" confidence, and 15 percent have "none at all." Among Hispanics, 34 percent have "a great deal" of confidence in the ability of the police to protect them from crime, 49 percent have "some" confidence, 12 percent have "little" confidence, and 5 percent have "none at all."

The public, overall, is less confident in the police's ability to protect them from violent crime. Only one-half the public have either "a great deal" (20 percent) or "quite a lot" (30 percent) of confidence in the police's ability to protect them from violent crime; 39 percent have "not very much" confidence, and 9 percent have "none at all." Again, nonwhites have less confidence than the general public. When asked about the police's ability to protect them from violent crime, only 15 percent of nonwhites (and 16 percent of blacks) have "a great deal" of confidence, 25 percent (22 percent of blacks) have "quite a lot" of confidence, 45 percent (46 percent of blacks) have "not very much" confidence, and 13 percent (14 percent of blacks) have "none at all."[2]

Solving Crime   The public as a whole has about as much confidence in the police's ability to solve crime as it does about the police's ability to protect them from crime in general. Seventy-three and one-half percent of the public have at least some confidence in the police's ability to solve crime; 25.5 percent have "a great deal" of confidence, 48 percent have "some" confidence, 15 percent have "little" confidence, and 8 percent have "none at all." As before, minorities have less confidence than the public as a whole. Among blacks, 15 percent have "a great deal" of confidence in the ability of the police to solve crime, 45 percent have "some" confidence, 20 percent have "little" confidence, and 18 percent have "none at all." Of Hispanics asked to rate their confidence in the ability of the police to solve crime, 22 percent have "a great deal" of confidence, 46 percent have "some" confidence, 15 percent have "little" confidence, and 10 percent have "none at all." (See the second panel of Figure 7–2 on page 225.)

Preventing Crime   The public as a whole is somewhat less confident about the ability of the police to prevent crime than it is about the ability of the police to protect them from crime in general and to solve crime. Only about 65 percent of the public have "a great deal" (17 percent) or "some" (48 percent) confidence in the ability of the police to prevent crime, 21 percent have "little" confidence, and 11 percent have "none at all." On this measure racial and ethnic differences are not as great as on the other measures. The only major exception is that 27 percent of blacks have no confidence at all in the ability of the police to prevent crime, whereas 9.5 percent of both whites and Hispanics have no confidence at all in the police's ability to prevent crime. (See the third panel of Figure 7–2 on page 225.)

Treatment of Citizens   People are also concerned about how they are treated by the police. Opinion polls show that nearly three-quarters of all Americans believe that the police in their communities are helpful and friendly. There are, however, disparities in the way different races rate the police's treatment of citizens. Among blacks, only about 60 percent rate the police in their communities as being "excellent" or "pretty good" at being helpful and friendly; 29 percent rate them as only "fair" and 12 percent rate them as "poor."[3]

When asked whether the police in their communities treat people fairly, 64 percent of the general public say that the police "treat all races fairly"; 26 percent believe that the police "treat one or more groups unfairly"; and 10

Robert Bour, Police Officer

I really enjoy being a police officer in Tiffin, Ohio, a small city of about 20,000 people. My assignment is in the patrol section, but I also work as a bike patrol officer, a field training officer, and a member of the SWAT team. As a SWAT officer, I go out mainly on search warrant and drug raids and in cases where someone has barricaded him or herself in and a life is in danger. In a small police department, you have the opportunity to be involved in a number of specialized assignments.

As a patrol officer, I have the opportunity to interact with the public a great deal. We have always done community policing here in one form or another. Small communities have to. You stop people on the street and say hello, chat with business owners, and meet as many residents as you can. People always have questions for you; often they are about traffic laws and enforcement.

I also have to respond to calls for services and these calls take precedence over everything else. I get one to three calls per hour on the evening and early morning shift, but there are rare times when I don't get any calls during the entire ten hours of work.

My third area of activity involves self-initiated patrol activity. That includes traffic enforcement, of course, but also patrolling the alleys and streets around bars when they are closing in order to protect inebriates who may have passed out outside the establishment. The patrol also includes guarding against people who may be driving under the influence of alcohol. Tiffin has two universities, so sometimes college students may get a little more disorderly than they should and we have to respond.

I graduated in 1992 from a police academy that was hosted by a local community college. Before becoming a police officer in Tiffin, I worked as a sheriff's deputy and a village police officer, both full and part time. The Tiffin police department now requires a two-year college degree as the minimum to become employed. At the time I came on, it was not necessary, but I intend to go back to college and finish my degree anyway.

I can offer a few suggestions for anyone who wants to be a police officer. First, you should have a desire to work with people from diverse backgrounds because that is what police work is. Secondly, you must genuinely want to help people, keeping in mind that you are not always able to help everybody; sometimes that is frustrating. Finally, you must think about your family. They must support you in being a cop because there is some danger involved in the job. Still, police work is one of the best jobs a person can have.

What are the pros and cons of being a police officer?

---

percent don't know how the police treat racial groups. Among blacks, however, only 36 percent respond that the police "treat all races fairly"; 58 percent respond that the police "treat one or more groups unfairly"; and 6 percent don't know.[4]

No treatment is as unfair as is police brutality. Half of all Americans think that police brutality against blacks and Hispanics in their community happens often (8 percent) or occasionally (42 percent). However, among blacks, 76 percent think it occurs often (23 percent) or occasionally (53 percent), while, among Hispanics, 55 percent believe it occurs often (11 percent) or occasionally (44 percent).[5]

Honesty and Ethical Standards   When asked to rate the honesty and ethical standards of the police, 9 percent of the general public rate the police as "very high" on this measure, 43 percent rate them as "high," 38 percent rate them as "average," 8 percent rate them as "low," and 2 percent rate them as "very low." Nonwhites rate the honesty and ethical standards of police lower: Only 7 percent rate the police as "very high," 33 percent rate them as "high," 41 percent rate them as "average," 14 percent rate them as "low," and 5 percent rate them as "very low." (See Figure 7–3.)

In sum, these data clearly show that the public as a whole has more respect for the police and their honesty and ethical standards than it does for a variety of other occupations.[6] Yet, the level of respect is not particularly high, nor is it uniform across races. While most of the public believes that the police do a pretty good job, it also believes there is much room for improvement. One way to improve the police is to employ better police officers.

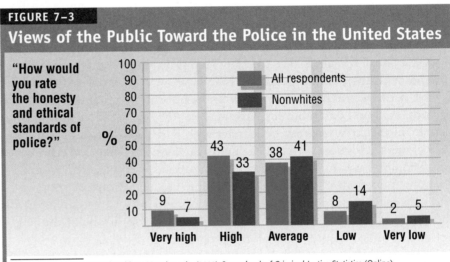

FIGURE 7–3
Views of the Public Toward the Police in the United States

"How would you rate the honesty and ethical standards of police?"

SOURCE: Ann L. Pastore and Kathleen Maguire, eds. (2000) *Sourcebook of Criminal Justice Statistics* (Online) <www.albany.edu/sourcebook/> (December 16, 2000), p. 108, Table 2.26

7.1 CRITICAL THINKING

1. Why do you think that racial groups differ so greatly in their attitudes toward the police?

2. What do you think could be done to improve public attitudes toward the police?

3. How accurate do you think the public's perceptions of the police are?

4. How do the perceptions presented in this section compare with our own?

7.2 Police Recruitment and Selection

Deciding whom to employ should be simple: hire the type of police officer that the citizens of the community want. Of course, that approach assumes that the citizens of a community have some idea of what it takes to be a police officer. Then, there is the matter of which people to consult. Who should decide? The wealthy? The middle class? The politically conservative? The politically liberal? The young? The old? The business community? Some consensus is needed on the type of police officer desired. Seeking that consensus in metropolitan communities is filled with conflict. Police administrators need to be very careful in choosing police officers, who may well be with the agency for 20 years or more. A police department will never reach its full potential without selecting the best available personnel. Selection decisions have momentous long-term implications for a police department.[7]

Entering the World of Policing

Those entering a profession or an occupation will most likely be shaped by it if they spend any length of time on the job. Certainly the socialization process for new police officers has a permanent effect on their attitudes and behaviors. It may also manifest itself in a style of policing.

Entering the world of policing, which may include many experiences with hostility and violence, is not unlike entering the boxing ring. The personnel in policing and boxing are frequently told to "be careful out there" or to "defend yourselves at all times." No boxer would ever enter the ring without having properly trained for the fight. The same is true for police officers. Their training should be realistic, mental, physical, offensive, and defensive, just as it is for boxers. Boxers need to fight according to the rules to avoid being disqualified by the referee. Likewise, police officers must play by the rules of law, or cases will be lost and reputations ruined. At the end of a brutally contested fight, boxers often embrace each other, a rather odd

Police Salaries

In 1999, the average (mean) beginning salary for police officers in cities of 10,000 or more persons was $29,840. The average maximum salary for police officers (who held no promotional rank) was $41,206. On average, it took seven years to reach the maximum salary.

SOURCE: Ann L. Pastore and Kathleen Maguire, eds. (2000) Sourcebook of Criminal Justice Statistics (Online) <www.albany.edu/sourcebook/>, p. 53, Table 1.58.

▲ Police officers must have a variety of qualities in order to be successful on the job. *What qualities would you bring to the position?*

occurrence when you think of what they have been trying to do to each other. The reason is that only a fighter can understand the preparation and pain that goes into being a boxer. Police officers are frequently criticized for socially isolating themselves, but putting their lives on the line every day brings a perspective to living and dying that only other officers can understand. Good police officers, like good boxers, need to keep training, "fight clean," stay close to their fellow officers, and console them when they need it.

Qualities of a Successful Police Officer

Given the complexity of the role of the police officer, it comes as no surprise that deciding what qualities the successful police officer needs is not easy. Indeed, police officers require a combination of qualities and abilities that is rare in any pool of applicants. Robert B. Mills, a pioneer in the psychological testing of police officers, believes that police applicants should possess the following psychological qualities:

- Motivation for a police career.
- Normal self-assertiveness.
- Emotional stability under stress.
- Sensitivity toward minority groups and social deviates.
- Collaborative leadership skills.
- A mature relationship with social authority.
- Flexibility.
- Integrity and honesty.
- An active and outgoing nature.[8]

The Berkeley, California, Police Department lists these qualities:

- Initiative.
- Ability to carry heavy responsibilities and handle emergencies alone.
- Social skills and ability to communicate effectively with persons of various cultural, economic, and ethnic backgrounds.
- Mental capacity to learn a wide variety of subjects quickly and correctly.
- Ability to adapt thinking to technological and social changes.
- Understanding of other human beings and the desire to help those in need.
- Emotional maturity to remain calm and objective and provide leadership in emotionally charged situations.
- Physical strength and endurance to perform these exacting duties.[9]

three I's of police selection
Three qualities of the American police officer that seem to be of paramount importance: intelligence, integrity, and interaction skills.

Three qualities seem to be of paramount importance. One commentator refers to them as the **three I's of police selection:** intelligence, integrity, and interaction skills. In short, police officers need to be bright enough to complete rigorous training. They should be honest enough to resist—and have a lifestyle that allows them to resist—the temptation of corrupting influences in law enforcement. They should also be able to communicate clearly and get along with people of diverse backgrounds.

Nearly as important as the three I's, however, are common sense and compassion. In resolving conflicts and solving problems they encounter, police officers must often choose a course of action without much time to think about it. Common sense is a key quality, for example, in locating a suspect who has just fled a crime scene on foot, or in deciding when to call off a high-speed vehicle pursuit that suddenly endangers innocent citizens and other police officers.

Police agencies also seek to employ officers with the core value of compassion. Without a genuine concern for serving one's fellow human beings, a police officer is not likely to sustain a high level of motivation over a long period of time. Many people the police meet on a daily basis simply need help, sometimes required by law, but more often these officers are spurred by a compassion for helping people no matter what their need.

Other qualities, such as physical strength, endurance, and appearance, seem less important. If you were the one who needed to be dragged from a burning automobile, however, the physical strength of the police officer might be important to you.

The Police Recruitment Process

Few occupations have selection processes as elaborate as the ones used in choosing police officers in most departments of the nation. Before choices are made, a wide net must be cast in the recruiting effort to come up with enough potential applicants to fill the vacancies for an academy class. Police departments, often working with city personnel agencies, are generally guided in their selection decisions by civil service regulations. Those regulations are developed either locally or at the state level. They guarantee a merit employment system with equal opportunity for all.

Because employment qualifications are supposed to be based on perceived needs in policing, law enforcement agencies must be careful not to set unnecessary restrictions that have no bearing on an officer's ability to complete training and perform successfully on the job. The addition of just one seemingly minor qualification, such as requiring four pull-ups instead of three during physical ability testing, or making the eyesight requirement slightly more stringent, may eliminate thousands of men and women from the selection process in a large metropolitan area. It is difficult enough to find capable police candidates without needlessly eliminating them from the selection process.

Recruitment   Most police agencies have finally realized that the kind of officers they desire will not gravitate naturally to the doors of the department. The search for top-notch applicants is very competitive, and many chiefs and sheriffs believe that they have to look at larger pools of applicants than in the past to find the same number of qualified officers. The reasons for the increased difficulty in finding good police candidates involve social maturity and lifestyle issues. Young police applicants today do not seem as mature as those of earlier eras. Problems with drugs and alcohol, sexually transmitted diseases, personal debt, and dependability have also reduced the number of qualified police applicants.

The major goal of the recruiting effort is to cast police work as an attractive and sustaining career, even to those who might initially be turned off by it. Research supports the allure of policing for many people who view a career in law enforcement as financially rewarding and status enhancing. In addition, the work itself is intrinsically satisfying because it is nonroutine, exciting, generally outdoors, and people oriented.[10]

Affirmative Action   Since the passage of the Civil Rights Act of 1964 and the threat of court challenges to the fairness of the police selection process, police agencies have struggled to find the best-qualified applicants and yet achieve satisfactory race and gender representation within the ranks of the department. Failure to seriously pursue equitable representation has led to expensive lawsuits, consent decrees, and court-ordered quotas to achieve the desired diversity. Consequently, affirmative action has become a major concern in police selection and employment. Now affirmative action programs are being questioned on several legal grounds. That questioning may lead to more difficulty in trying to achieve race and gender balance in police departments.

How successful has affirmative action been in accomplishing the desired goal of race and gender balance in police departments? Affirmative action *has* been relatively successful in increasing the percentage of minority members in policing. But it has been less successful in increasing the percentage of women. As noted previously, nearly 80 percent of the sworn officers in the nation's police departments are white males. However, as shown in Figure 7–4 on page 233, the percentage of black and Hispanic officers in local departments is 11.3 and 6.2, respectively. Those figures closely approximate the percentage of blacks and Hispanics in the general population of the United States (11.3 percent for blacks and 9.2 percent for Hispanics). However, women, who compose over 50 percent of the United States population, represent less then 10 percent of the police officers in local police departments.[11]

Education   Given the amount of discretion that law enforcement officers have and the kinds of sociological problems with which they deal, selecting reasonably intelligent, college-educated officers seems a wise

▲ Increasing the number of female officers is a major concern in police selection and employment. *What are some of the advantages of having a greater number of female police officers?*

FIGURE 7-4

Minority Representation in Local Police Departments in the United States, 1997

Race/Ethnicity	Police	Population
Black	11.7%	12.7%
Hispanic	7.8%	10.1%
White	78.4%	82%
Other	2.1%	4.8%

SOURCE: Brian A. Reaves and Andrew Goldberg, *Local Police Departments, 1997* (Washington, DC: Bureau of Justice Statistics and U.S. Cenus Bureau, 2000)

practice. Many police agencies in the country currently require some college background. As a result, the average level of education in policing today is nearly two years of college. Among the advantages of hiring college-educated officers are the following:

1. Better written reports.

2. Enhanced communication with the public.

3. More effective job performance.

4. Fewer citizen complaints.

5. Wiser use of discretion.

6. Heightened sensitivity to racial and ethnic issues.

7. Fewer disciplinary actions.[12]

This list of advantages should impress police administrators and the public. Satisfied citizens, the savings of substantial amounts of money by avoiding lawsuits, and fewer disciplinary actions against officers are good reasons for law enforcement executives to search for police applicants with college backgrounds.

Recognition that college-educated police officers are generally better performers than officers without that level of education is long overdue. And the idea is catching on. Minnesota's Peace Officer Licensing Commission now requires a four-year college degree for licensing. The Peace Officer Council in Ohio now has more than one dozen **college academies,** where students pursue a program that integrates an associate's degree curriculum in law enforcement or criminal justice with the state's required peace officer training. Upon receipt of the associate's degree, students sit for the peace officer certification exam. If they receive a passing score on the exam, they are eligible to be hired by any police agency and to go to work without any additional academy training.

college academies
Schools where students pursue a program that integrates an associate's degree curriculum in law enforcement or criminal justice with the state's required peace officer training.

Successful Recruiting Practices

Where do you find the best-qualified police applicants? Some of the more successful recruiting practices have included going to colleges, neighborhood centers, and schools in minority communities; using television, radio, and newspaper advertisements; and working with local employment offices. Demystifying the nature of police work and the selection process and shortening the time from application to final selection have also helped to attract and retain qualified candidates.

Public Safety Officers   Another promising recruitment strategy has been the employment of 18-year-olds as **public safety officers** (sometimes called community service officers or public service aides), who perform many police service functions but do not have arrest powers. By the time they are 21, the department has had an excellent opportunity to assess their qualifications and potential to be sworn officers.

Police Cadets   **Police cadet programs** have been around since the 1960s (Cincinnati Police), and as recently as the 1990s, the New York City Police launched a cadet program combining a college education with academy training and work experience in the police department. Upon graduation from the university, a cadet is promoted to police officer.

High School Tech Prep Programs   A new idea is beginning to take hold that will attract capable police officers at an even earlier age. The program is known as **tech prep** or **technical preparation** for a criminal justice career. Area community colleges and high schools team up to offer six to nine hours of college law enforcement courses in the 11th and 12th grades, as well as one or two training certifications, such as police dispatcher or local corrections officer. Students who graduate are eligible for employment at age 18. They become interested in law enforcement work early and are ideal police applicants when they become old enough to apply. Accurate law enforcement career information can be passed on to high school students through a tech prep program because the teachers are required to either currently work in law enforcement or have police experience in their backgrounds.

The Police Selection Process

In many communities, selection of police officers takes place through a merit system. A **merit system** of employment is established when an independent civil service commission, in cooperation with the city personnel section and the police department, sets employment qualifications, performance standards, and discipline procedures. Officers employed under such a system are hired and tenured, in theory, only if they meet and maintain the employment qualifications and performance standards set by the civil service commission. Officers in such a system cannot be fired without cause.

To find the best possible recruits to fill department vacancies, police agencies use a selection process that includes some or all of the following steps:

Short Application   This brief form registers the interest of the applicant and allows the agency to screen for such things as minimum age, level of education, residency, and other easily discernible qualifications.

Detailed Application   This document is a major source of information for the department and background investigators. The applicant

---

public safety officers
Police department employees who perform many police services but do not have arrest powers.

police cadet program
A program that combines a college education with agency work experience and academy training. Upon graduation, a cadet is promoted to police officer.

tech prep (technical preparation)
A program in which area community colleges and high schools team up to offer six to nine hours of college law enforcement courses in the 11th and 12th grades, as well as one or two training certifications, such as police dispatcher or local corrections officer. Students who graduate are eligible for police employment at age 18.

merit system
A system of employment whereby an independent civil service commission, in cooperation with the city personnel section and the police department, sets employment qualifications, performance standards, and discipline procedures.

is asked for complete education and work histories, military status, medical profile, references, a record of residence over many years, and other detailed information. Applicants are also asked to submit copies of credentials, military papers, and other certificates.

Medical Examination   This exam determines if applicants are free of disease, abnormalities, and any other medical problems that would disqualify them for police work. This information is critical because retiring a young officer on a medical disability shortly after employment could cost the public hundreds of thousands of dollars.

Physical Ability Test   Physical ability tests are common in police selection despite having been challenged in the courts as having an adverse effect on the hiring of female applicants. Physical ability tests were initially a direct response to the elimination of height and weight standards, which were also discriminatory against female applicants. The first tests required exceptional speed and strength, such as going over walls that were taller than any of the walls in the cities that had such tests. Those tests were struck down by the courts as not being job-related. Today, any physical ability tests must be based on a thorough analysis of the actual work of police officers.

Written Examination   Police agencies once used intelligence tests in their selection process. Most agencies now use some type of aptitude, personality, general knowledge, reading comprehension, writing, or police skill exam. The courts have held that those tests must be true measures of the knowledge and abilities needed to perform police work successfully. Preemployment tests have been the subject of much controversy in the courts.

Background Investigation   Investigators in this process look for any factors in the backgrounds of applicants that would prevent them from performing successfully as police officers. Past drug use or excessive alcohol use, a poor driving record, employer problems, a bad credit history, criminal activity, and social immaturity are areas of concern in the background investigation. The investigator relies heavily on the detailed application, verifies its contents, explores any discrepancies, and develops additional leads to follow.

Psychological Testing   Emotional stability and good mental health are critical to the ability to perform police work, which can be very stressful. Departments have been held liable for not screening their applicants for those psychological traits.[13]

Systematic psychological testing of police officers began in the 1950s. At first, the typical approach was to have the psychological evaluators look for disqualifying factors. The process included a pencil-and-paper test and a one-on-one interview with a psychologist. Today, the testing focus has generally shifted to a search for the positive psychological qualities required in police work. Current tests include multiple versions of both written and clinical evaluations.

The validity of psychological tests has been an issue for decades. Psychologists are often reluctant to rate with any specificity the police

▲ At the end of many police academy training programs, there is a state licensing or certification examination. *Do you believe those examinations are necessary? Why or why not?*

candidates they evaluate. Candidates considered "unacceptable" are sometimes classified as "uncertain" to avoid lawsuits. It is important to remember that understanding and predicting human behavior is an inexact art. So it is easy to appreciate the reluctance of psychologists to be more specific.

Oral Interview/Oral Board This step is frequently the final one in the selection process. Members of the interview team have the results of the previous selection procedures, and they now have an opportunity to clear up inconsistencies and uncertainties that have been identified. The board normally restricts itself to evaluating the following qualities:

1. Appearance, poise, and bearing.
2. Ability to communicate orally and organize thoughts.
3. Attitude toward law enforcement and the job required of police officers.
4. Speech and the ability to articulate.
5. Attitude toward drug, narcotic, and alcohol use.
6. Sensitivity to racial and ethnic issues.[14]

Academy Training The police academy is part of the selection process. Virtually every academy class in any sophisticated police department loses up to ten percent of its students. Thus, to survive academy training, students must be committed to the process. Students undergo from 400 to more than 1,000 hours of academic, skill, and physical training and are tested virtually every week of the process. At the end of many academy training programs, students must take a state licensing or certification examination.

Probation Under local or state civil service requirements, employers may keep a new police officer on probation for six months to a year. The probation period gives the new police officer a chance to learn policing under the guidance of a well-qualified field training officer. Formal field training is a wise investment, and it ensures that new officers get as much knowledge and experience as possible before an agency commits to them for their careers.

A problem is that with police academy training now often extending five or six months, a six-month probation period no longer seems logical. The agency is, in effect, offering the police officer tenure in a matter of weeks after graduation from the academy. This practice defeats the purpose of probation, which was designed to allow the employer to see whether the newly trained officer can successfully perform the job.

Sheriffs

Not all sheriffs have a law enforcement background. In most states, they are not required to be licensed or certified peace officers as their deputies or municipal officers are. As a result, people from various occupations often succeed in being elected sheriff.

The Selection of a Law Enforcement Executive

No less important than the selection of operations-level officers is the choice of the chief executive of a police agency. This executive might be a chief of police, a sheriff, or the head of a state law enforcement organization. A crucial decision in the selection process is whether to allow people from outside the agency to apply. In some police agencies in the United States, civil service regulations prohibit the selection of outside candidates. The rationale for this rule is that there must be qualified internal candidates. In addition, it is discouraging to hard-working and talented police administrators to be denied a chance to lead the agency they have spent many years serving.

Actual hiring decisions are usually shared by members of a selection committee. Frequently, an executive search firm is also employed. The selection committee usually consists of representatives of the local government, the police department, the search firm, and the community. Applicants are put through a rigorous process that includes several visits to the city, written exams, interviews, and assessment center testing, in which candidates try to resolve real-world management problems. Once the interviews and testing have been completed, applicants are normally ranked, and the list is presented to the city manager, the mayor, or others so that a final selection can be made.

The pursuit of a police chief's job is very competitive. Often several hundred candidates contend for a position even in a small suburban community. A typical police chief rarely serves longer than ten years, and life in the chief's seat may not be very comfortable, particularly if a new chief intends to change things. Much of the political controversy and many of the social problems in major cities and counties end up at the door of the police department, so police chiefs must be politically savvy to survive. Many chiefs discover that they cannot please everybody, particularly if they are trying to change the department. Should police chiefs have protection under civil service? Most commentators say no, arguing that mayors and city managers ought to have the authority to pick the management teams that work immediately under their direction. A small number of cities give their police chiefs civil service protection to insulate them from unnecessary political interference.

The selection of a sheriff of one of the nation's counties is just as important as choosing a police chief. The difference in the two processes has to do with who does the selecting. In all but a few of the nation's counties, sheriffs are elected by the county's eligible voters. To be elected, sheriffs must be good politicians. They often have a much better idea of the priorities of a community and wield more influence with prosecutors and in the legislature than chiefs of police. Sheriffs who do not exhibit this political acumen are not likely to be reelected.

7.2 CRITICAL THINKING

1. What do you think are the most important qualities for police officers to have? Why?

2. How much formal education do you think police officers should have? Why?

Executive Salaries

As of July 1, 1999, the average (mean) salary of police chiefs was $58,055. However, salaries varied greatly depending on the city population size. For cities with populations of one million or more, the average salary of police chiefs was $144,788. On the other hand, in cities of fewer than 2,500 the average salary of police chiefs was $39,480. The same is true of county sheriffs. As of July 1, 1999, the average (mean) salary of county sheriffs was $52,067. In counties with a population of one million or more, the average salary was $108,054. In counties with populations of fewer than 2,500 the average salary was $32,490.

SOURCE: Ann L. Pastore and Kathleen Maguire, eds. (2000) Sourcebook of Criminal Justice Statistics (Online)

7.3 Issues in Policing

The discussion of law enforcement thus far has made it clear that not all matters of policing in America are settled. In this final section of the chapter, some of the issues that continue to be major topics of debate in law enforcement and have significant impact on the quality of life in neighborhoods and communities across the nation will be highlighted.

Discretion

discretion

The exercise of individual judgment, instead of formal rules, in making decisions.

Discretion is the exercise of individual judgment, instead of formal rules, in making decisions. No list of policies and procedures could possibly guide police officers in all of the situations in which they find themselves. Even the police officer writing a ticket for a parking meter violation exercises a considerable amount of discretion in deciding precisely what to do.[15] Police even have the discretion to ignore violations of the law when they deem it appropriate in the context of other priorities.

The issue of police discretion is very controversial. Some believe that the discretion of police officers should be reduced. The movement to limit the discretion of police officers is the result of abuses of that discretion, such as physical abuse of citizens or unequal application of the law in making arrests. Other people argue that we should acknowledge that officers operate with great discretion and not attempt to limit it. Advocates of this view believe that better education and training would help officers exercise their judgment more wisely.

Patrol Officer Discretion Patrol officers frequently find it necessary to exercise their discretion. Within the geographical limits of their beats, they have the discretion to decide precisely where they will patrol when they are not answering radio calls. They decide whom to stop and question. For example, they may tell some children playing ball in the street to move, while they ignore others. Patrol officers decide for themselves which traffic violators are worth chasing through busy traffic and which ones are not. They even have the right not to arrest for a minor violation when, for example, they are on the way to investigate a more serious matter.

Some of the more critical situations involve decisions about stopping, searching, and arresting criminal suspects. Many citizens have been inconvenienced and some have been abused because of a police officer's poor use of discretion in those areas.

full enforcement

A practice in which the police make an arrest for every violation of law that comes to their attention.

Police officers cannot make an arrest for every violation of law that comes to their attention—that is, they cannot provide **full enforcement.** The police do not have the resources to enforce the law fully, nor can they be everywhere at once. And even if full enforcement were possible, it may not be desirable. For example, persons intoxicated in front of their own homes may not need to be arrested, but only to be told to go inside. Motorists slightly exceeding the speed limit need not be arrested if they are moving with the flow of traffic. Prostitution may be widely practiced in large metropolitan areas, but police officers have little to gain by searching hotels and motels to stamp it out, particularly when judges will turn the prostitutes right back out on the street. Generally, only when such an activity becomes a clear nuisance, is the subject of a public outcry, or threatens health and safety do the police department and its officers choose to take formal action.

The practice of relying on the judgment of the police leadership and rank-and-file officers to decide which laws to enforce is referred to as **selective enforcement**. The practice allows street police officers to decide important matters about peacekeeping and enforcement of the law. For most violations of the law, but not all felonies, a police officer can usually exercise a number of options:

selective enforcement
The practice of relying on the judgment of the police leadership and rank-and-file officers to decide which laws to enforce.

1. Taking no action at all if the officer deems that appropriate for the situation

2. Giving a verbal warning to stop the illegal action

3. Issuing a written warning for the violation

4. Issuing a citation to the perpetrator to appear in court

5. Making a physical arrest in serious matters or in situations with repeat offenders

Factors Affecting Discretion Dozens of studies have been conducted on the exercise of discretion by police patrol officers. A number of significant factors affect discretion:

- **The Nature of the Crime** The more serious the crime, the more likely it is that police officers will formally report it. In cases involving lesser felonies, misdemeanors, and petty offenses, police officers are more likely to handle the offenses informally. A minor squabble between over-the-fence neighbors is an example of a matter that would probably be handled informally.

- **Departmental Policies** If the leadership of a police department gives an order or issues a policy demanding that particular incidents be handled in a prescribed way, then an officer is not supposed to exercise discretion but is to do as the order or policy directs. Thus, if a city has had many complaints about dangerous jaywalking in a certain downtown area, the chief of police may insist that citations be issued to those found jaywalking, even though, in the past, citations had not been issued.

- **The Relationship Between the Victim and the Offender** Particularly for minor offenses, the closer the relationship between the victim of an alleged offense and the suspected perpetrator, the more discretion the officer is able to exercise. For example, police officers are not likely to deal formally with a petty theft between two lovers if they believe that the victim will not prosecute his or her partner.

- **The Amount of Evidence** If officers do not have enough evidence to substantiate an arrest or to gain a conviction in court, they are likely to handle the case in some way other than making an arrest.

- **The Preference of the Victim** Sometimes the victim of a crime may simply want to talk the matter over with someone, and the police are available on a 24-hour basis. Also, if the officer senses that the victim of a minor assault does not wish to prosecute the perpetrator of the offense, the patrol officer will not make a formal complaint, and the complainant will most likely never know that a report was not made.

- **The Demeanor of the Suspect** Suspects who are disrespectful and uncooperative may very well feel the full brunt of the law. Patrol officers often choose the most severe option possible in dealing with such suspects.

- **The Legitimacy of the Victim** Patrol officers are bound to pass some kind of judgment on the legitimacy of the victim. An assault victim who is belligerent and intoxicated, for instance, will not be viewed favorably by the investigating officer. Criminals victimized by other criminals are also seen as less than fully authentic victims, no matter what the offense.

- **Socioeconomic Status** The more affluent the complainant, the more likely a patrol officer is to use formal procedures to report and investigate a crime. Contrary to popular belief, the personal characteristics of an officer (such as race, gender, and education) do not seem to influence the exercise of discretion.

Discretion and Domestic Violence Police officers have intervened in domestic violence cases and other kinds of family disputes, sometimes off-duty, since the inception of public policing. For the longest period of time, these interventions were looked at as peacekeeping activities when, in fact, they should have been treated as criminal matters. Many women and some men were hurt, and some killed, as a result of the restrictions on the police in making arrests for assault misdemeanors not made in their presence and a view among the police that these calls were the private business of the family and not real police matters. Traditionally, law enforcement has been less interested in arresting perpetrators of crimes when the victim and the perpetrator have a close relationship.

Approximately one million women are victims of domestic violence each year. Even today, with every state requiring the police to have domestic violence intervention training, some commentators believe that the police are not the best qualified of available community helpers to intervene. On the other hand, if crimes are committed in the form of physical abuse, the police are not only the best qualified to intervene, but are required by law to do so. Certainly, the availability of 24-hour service has always made the police the major responder to domestic violence calls.

The police in general do not relish the task of responding to domestic violence calls for several reasons. First, the calls can be dangerous, although generally no more dangerous than other disturbance calls. Nevertheless, officers are hurt each year by responding to domestic violence complaints. Second, police officers know from experience that many of the tense and hostile dynamics that exist between quarreling spouses, couples, and other family members have a way of dissipating over time or at least subsiding for awhile. Third, the police know that they have often conducted investigations, even arrested the suspected batterer, and the victim has later chosen to drop charges. Finally, the police know that responding to the minor assault cases in domestic violence calls is not always the best thing for the family because the arrest creates its own complications that may, in fact, exacerbate the family crisis to a state of irreparable harm.

Police have responded to domestic violence in three distinct ways: mediate the dispute, separate domestic partners in minor disputes, and arrest the perpetrator of the assault. Which of these ways is the most effective? This question was put to the test in a three-year study in the city of Minneapolis. In minor domestic dispute cases, Minneapolis police officers gave up their discretion in handling domestic violence calls. Instead of deciding for themselves the appropriate disposition for each call, they randomly chose either arrest, separation, or mediation. The results of the study showed that the arrested perpetrators were about half as likely to repeat their violence against the original victim.[16] This study may have been the impetus for many states to implement a mandatory arrest domestic violence law. Subsequent studies, however, have not been able to clearly support the mandatory arrest disposition as the most effective way to handle the problem of domestic violence. Yet today nearly half of the states have a mandatory arrest law mandating the arrest of any suspect that has battered a spouse or domestic partner. While victim safety and welfare are indeed the major reasons for police intervention, more research is clearly needed in order to determine the best approaches to handling domestic violence calls.

Discretion and Racial Profiling   Racial profiling is of growing concern to law enforcement officials and the public. Just how frequently this illegal practice occurs is difficult to discern, particularly since the term racial profiling is seldom defined in the discussions found in the national media. Racial profiling is a law enforcement infringement on a citizen's liberty based solely on race. On freeways, highways, and streets throughout the nation blacks and other minorities are stopped for traffic violations and field interrogations in numbers disproportionate to their representation in the population. Many of these stops are pretext stops where the stop is justified by a minor equipment or moving traffic violation that might otherwise be ignored. Where the practice is widely experienced, it has been called "driving while black or brown" (DWBB). At the root of such a practice is racial stereotyping and prejudice.

Racial profiling is a hot topic in the United States Congress, state legislatures, county commissions, and city councils, as well as in the meeting rooms of civil rights and professional police organizations. The American Civil Liberties Union, for example, has started a national project to eliminate racial profiling and even provides citizens with a "Bust Card" that tells them how to respectfully interact with the police (acknowledging the difficulty of their job) even when falling victim to racial profiling.

Racial profiling to any degree is a blight on the record of professional law enforcement and democracy. Some of the methods that have been prescribed to stop racial profiling include racial and cultural diversity training for police personnel, strong discipline for errant officers, videotaping all traffic stops, collecting data on the race of stopped motorists and pedestrians and the disposition of the encounter, and having police officers distribute business cards to all motorists and pedestrians they stop.

The business card may reduce race-based stops because it would allow an officer to be easily identified at a later time. But city leaders throughout the United States are in a quandary as to precisely what to do to stop racial profiling. Thirty-six members of the National League of Cities' public safety

racial profiling
The stopping and/or detaining of individuals by law enforcement officers based solely on race.

CRIMINAL JUSTICE *Online*

ACLU

To learn more about what is being done to combat racial profiling, visit the American Civil Liberties Union (ACLU) Web site on racial profiling by clicking the link at cj.glencoe.com. *What can police departments do to prevent racial profiling?*

job stress
The harmful physical and emotional outcomes that occur when the requirements of a job do not match the capabilities, resources, or needs of the worker.

committees met in Oklahoma City and determined that they oppose police profiling of suspects when it violates a person's civil rights, but they could not agree whether all profiling should be banned.[17]

Factors Limiting Discretion   Several methods are employed to control the amount of discretion exercised by police officers. One method is close supervision by a police agency's management. For example, a department may require that officers consult a sergeant before engaging in a particular kind of action. Department directives or policies also limit the options police officers have in particular situations. Decisions of the United States Supreme Court, such as one restricting the use of deadly force to stop a fleeing felon, limit the options available to officers on the street. Finally, the threat of civil liability suits has reduced the discretion an officer has, for example, in the use of deadly force or in the pursuit of fleeing suspects in an automobile.

The debate over how much control should be placed on the exercise of police discretion is ongoing. Few other professionals have experienced a comparable attack on their authority to make decisions for the good of the clients they serve. The continuing attempt to limit discretion also seems out of place at a time when community policing is being widely advocated. Remember that community policing decentralizes authority and places it in the hands of the local beat officers and their supervisors. Community policing is bound to fail if citizens see that the police they work with every day do not have the authority and discretion to make the decisions that will ultimately improve the quality of life in a community.

Job Stress

Stress in the workplace is common today. A recent survey revealed that 80 percent of responding workers reported at least some degree of stress.[18] Given the nature of police work, no one is surprised to discover that a law enforcement officer's job is stressful. Police officers intervene in life's personal emergencies and great tragedies. Working extended shifts, for example, at the scene of the bombing of the federal building in Oklahoma City would tax the resources of even the most resourceful police officer. Who would deny the stress involved in working deep undercover on a narcotics investigation over a period of several months? Some officers are able to manage stress on the job better than others.

Job stress is defined as the harmful physical and emotional outcomes that occur when the requirements of a job do not match the capabilities, resources, or needs of the worker. Poor health and injury are possible results of prolonged job stress. Police work has long been identified as one of the most stressful of all occupations and many police officers suffer each year from the deleterious effects of a job that tests their physical and emotional limits.

Sources and Effects of Stress   A number of conditions can lead to stress: (1) Design of tasks—heavy lifting, long hours without breaks, and monotonous repetition of dangerous maneuvers; (2) Management style—lack of participation by workers in decision-making, poor communication, lack of family-friendly policies; (3) Interpersonal relationships—poor social environment and lack of support from co-workers and supervisors; (4) Work roles—conflicting or uncertain job expectations, wearing too many hats, too much responsibility.[19] The signs that stress is becoming a problem with an officer are frequent headaches, difficulty in concentrating, short temper, upset stomach, job dissatisfaction, abuse of alcohol and drugs, and low morale. Individually and collectively these symptoms can have other origins, but job stress is often the source.

Stress Management and Reduction

Fortunately, there are ways to manage and reduce stress without leaving police work. The "fixes" for stress come in two general categories. Stress management now encompasses a variety of programs and procedures that include discussing stressful events with colleagues and mental health professionals, regular exercise, relaxation techniques such as structured visualization, a healthy diet that also eliminates caffeine and nicotine, enriched family support, religious support, prayer, mediation, and stress management classes that often involve spouses.

Organizational change can also reduce the potential for stress in the police work environment. Officers, for example, may be given more discretion in determining

▲ Discussing stressful events with colleagues is just one way that police officers can manage stress. *Are there ways that you handle stress that you think would work particularly well in policing?*

their work hours and shifts as long as the police agency is able to respond effectively to the workload requirements of the community. Flattening the organizational structure can help reduce stress by giving officers more discretion in carrying out the responsibilities of their job. Community policing is an effective paradigm for increasing officers' ability to control their work and perhaps minimize stress. Job redesign can assist assigning the right number and type of tasks to a police position when one job requires too much of an officer to maintain emotional stability and good health. Finally, excellent public safety equipment can minimize stress. Proper police weaponry, dependable vehicles, and the best of protective equipment such as high-grade body armor can not only protect officers but can put their minds a little more at ease on those important concerns.[20]

Copicide As if the work of confronting dangerous suspects and preserving the peace were not stressful enough, "copicide" or "death by cop" has entered the worklife of some police officers. **Copicide** is a form of suicide in which a person gets fatally shot after intentionally provoking police officers.[21] A recent study of police shootings resulting in the death of a citizen in Los Angeles found that ten percent could be attributed to copicide.[22] One commentator believes that "dozens of times each year during jittery hostage dramas and routine traffic stops, desperate people lure police officers into shooting them in a phenomenon known in law enforcement circles as 'suicide by cop'."[23] The truth is that no one knows exactly how many times copicide incidents occur each year. Most police officers require a lot of time to emotionally recover from a fatal shooting in circumstances where they were fully authorized to use deadly force. To later discover that they were provoked

copicide
A form of suicide in which a person gets fatally shot after intentionally provoking police officers.

into killing people who simply used police as a tool in a suicide scheme creates an extra emotional burden to bear.

Use of Force

No issue in policing has caused as much controversy in recent decades as the use of force. In New York, Los Angeles, Detroit, Miami, and many other cities, excessive-force charges against police officers have been made and documented and have resulted in the loss of public confidence in the police. Although the vast majority of police officers of this country go to work every day with no intention of using excessive force, far too many instances of brutality still occur.

A precise definition of brutality is not possible. However, the use of excessive physical force is undoubtedly a factor in everyone's definition. For many people, particularly members of racial and ethnic minorities, brutality also includes verbal abuse, profanity, harassment, threats of force, and unnecessary stopping, questioning, and searching of pedestrians or those in vehicles.

Excessive Force   Why do the police have to use force as frequently as they do? A major responsibility of police officers is to arrest suspects so that they can answer criminal charges. No criminal suspect wants his or her liberty taken away, so some of them resist arrest. Invariably, a few suspects are armed with some kind of weapon, and some are prepared to use that weapon against the police to foil the arrest. The police need to establish their authority to control such conflicts. The disrespect and physical resistance that are frequently the result of those encounters have caused the police on occasion to use **excessive force,** which is a measure of coercion beyond that necessary to control participants in a conflict.

Not only is the persistent use of excessive force by the police against citizens unethical, civilly wrong, and criminally illegal, but it also creates a situation where nobody wins. Police may face criminal and civil prosecution in such cases, citizens build up layers of resentment against the police, and law enforcement agencies pay out millions of dollars in damages while losing respect in the eyes of the community. Disturbing events like the brutal beating and sexual assault of Abner Louima in 1997, and the shooting death of Amadou Diallo in 1999 by New York City police officers received nationwide media attention while causing great concern by citizens and law enforcement over the use of excessive force. There were also charges of racism by the police because both incidents involved the use of excessive force by white police officers against black men.

Abner Louima, a 30-year-old Haitian immigrant, was accused of assaulting a police officer outside a nightclub in the city. Louima claimed that following his arrest and arrival at the station house, a white officer, Justin Volpe, savagely beat and sodomized him with a toilet plunger. In 1999, Volpe plead guilty to charges stemming from the beating. Charles Schwarz, another police officer accused of holding Louima down while Volpe attacked him, was convicted separately in a federal trial of violating Louima's rights. Three other NYPD officers said to be involved in the event were acquitted of all charges.

Amadou Diallo, a 22-year-old West African immigrant, was hit by 19 of the 41 bullets shot by police officers from the NYPD street crimes unit.

excessive force

A measure of coercion beyond that necessary to control participants in a conflict.

Diallo died at the scene. The officers claimed that Diallo fit the description of a rape suspect they had been searching for. When the officers tried to stop Diallo, he reached for what police officers thought was a weapon; they then began to shoot. Apparently Diallo, who spoke little English, was reaching for his wallet. The officers involved in the shooting were charged with second-degree murder, however, a state jury found the officers innocent.

Although past and recent incidents of excessive force have been disturbing, research reveals that police brutality does not occur as often as some people might think. For example, in a study conducted in the state of Washington, only four percent of brutality complaints against the police could be substantiated, and most of the charges were of verbal abuse or insults.[24] Widespread media coverage of high-profile cases, such as the Los Angeles police officers' assault on Rodney King, can lead the public to believe that brutality is much more common than it really is. The Los Angeles police, however, had a higher rate of wounding and killing suspects than any other police department in the nation, according to the Christopher Commission, which investigated the assault on Rodney King.

▲ There is much debate on how much control should be placed on the decisions of police officers in arrest situations. *How much control should be placed on them and why?*

Deadly Force The greatest concern over the use of force by the police has to do with the infliction of death or serious injury on citizens and criminal suspects. Since the U.S. Supreme Court's 1985 decision in *Tennessee v. Garner*, the use of deadly force has been severely restricted, and police shootings of suspects and citizens have been reduced. In the *Garner* case, an unarmed teenage boy was shot as he fled a house burglary, failing to heed the warning to stop given by a Memphis police officer. The boy later died of a gunshot wound to the head. He was found with ten dollars in his pocket that he had stolen from the home. The Memphis officer was acting in compliance with his department's policy on the use of deadly force and with the law in Tennessee and in most other states in the nation.

Giving law enforcement officers the authority to use deadly force to stop a fleeing felon, even when they know the suspect is unarmed and not likely to be a danger to another person, derives from the common law in England and the United States, which permitted such a practice. At the time the rule developed, however, unlike today, dozens of crimes were capital offenses, and the fleeing suspect, if apprehended and convicted, would have been executed. The *Garner* decision, no doubt, was long overdue, and it included a rule that many police agencies in the nation had adopted years earlier. The perspective that professional law enforcement agencies had already begun to adopt on deadly force was from the Model Penal Code, Section 307(2)(B).

It reads:

The use of deadly force is not justifiable under this section unless:

1. The arrest is for a felony.
2. The person effecting the arrest is authorized to act as a peace officer or is assisting a person whom he believes to be authorized to act as a peace officer.
3. The actor believes that the force employed creates no substantial risk of injury to innocent persons.
4. The actor believes that: (a.) The crime for which the arrest is made involved conduct including the use or threatened use of deadly force. (b.) There is substantial risk that the person to be arrested will cause death or serious bodily harm if his apprehension is delayed.

Even with explicit guidelines, the decision to use deadly force is seldom clear-cut for police officers, because of the violent and occasionally ambiguous situations in which they find themselves. For example, consider the confrontation a Dallas, Texas, police officer had in the summer of 1993. As a plainclothes officer, he responded at a call to an apartment complex where it was reported that a man had fired shots. It was nighttime, and when he arrived at the parking lot of the complex, he saw a man perhaps 50 feet from him with the butt end of a pistol sticking out of the waistband of his trousers. The police officer told him to stop and put his hands in the air. Instead of doing what he was ordered to do, the man pulled the gun from his waistband and moved it toward the officer. The officer responded by firing his weapon several times at the man and killing him. Later, it was discovered that the man was a Mexican citizen who spoke no English.

Some members of the Hispanic community were enraged that the officer did not offer commands in Spanish, because Dallas officers were required to study 20 hours of the language in the police academy. After several months of investigation and the grand jury's ignoring the case, the officer was exonerated. However, the chief of police assured the community that new police recruits would study three times the previously required amount of Spanish and that annual in-service training would also require the study of Spanish. In addition, the chief stated that in situations such as the one in question, undercover and plainclothes officers would be required, if possible, to put on jackets that would readily identify them as police officers. Some people argue that the man with the gun in this situation not only did not understand English, but also had no idea that the officer with drawn gun was a police officer.

It should not be forgotten that citizens and criminal suspects also attack the police. Mentally ill persons, parties to a family dispute, and suspects trying to avoid arrest feloniously assault between 50 and 100 officers each year. About two-thirds of those assaults are shootings. In response, police officers exercise caution by wearing protective vests, they proactively use what they learn in courses on self-defense (unarmed and armed), and they attempt to defuse hostile situations through peaceful techniques they learn in training.

Unfortunately, research on the police use of force, excessive force, and deadly force has not identified any specific procedures that would significantly reduce the injury or death of police officers and the citizens they confront. Only the number of deaths of citizens is decreasing, and violent regions of the nation with a high density of guns continue to be dangerous areas for police officers.[25]

Police Corruption

Almost from the beginning of formal policing in the United States, corruption of law enforcement officers has been a fact of life. Nothing is more distasteful to the public than a police officer or a whole department gone bad. Throughout history, police officers have bought their positions and promotions, sold protection, and ignored violations of the law for money.

Why is policing so susceptible to bribery and other forms of corruption? Perhaps it has to do with the combination of two critical features of the police role in society. On the one hand, the police have authority to enforce laws and to use power to make sure that those laws are obeyed. On the other hand, they also have the discretion *not* to enforce the law. The combination of those two features makes the police vulnerable to bribes and other forms of corruption. Other features of police work add to the potential for corruption: low pay in relation to important responsibilities, cynicism about the courts' soft handling of criminals that the police spend so much time trying to apprehend, society's ambivalence about vice (most citizens want the laws on the books, but many of them are willing participants), and the practice of recruiting officers from working-class and lower-class backgrounds, where skepticism about obeying the law might be more prevalent.

Types of Corruption   In 1972, the Knapp Commission issued a report on corruption in the New York City Police Department. Two types of corrupt officers were identified: "grass eaters" and "meat eaters." **"Grass eaters"** were officers who occasionally engaged in illegal or unethical activities, such as accepting small favors, gifts, or money for ignoring violations of the law during the course of their duties. **"Meat eaters"** on the other hand, actively sought ways to make money illegally while on duty. For example, they would solicit bribes, commit burglaries, or manufacture false evidence for a prosecution.[26]

More than 30 years ago, Ellwyn Stoddard identified a more complete list of types of police misconduct, with examples, in what he described as the "blue-coat code":

1. Bribery: accepting cash or gifts in exchange for nonenforcement of the law

2. Chiseling: demanding discounts, free admission, and free food

3. Extortion: the threat of enforcement and arrest if a bribe is not given

4. Favoritism: giving breaks on law enforcement, such as for traffic violations committed by families and friends of the police

5. Mooching: accepting free food, drinks, and admission to entertainment

6. Perjury: lying for other officers apprehended in illegal activity

7. Prejudice: unequal enforcement of the law with respect to racial and ethnic minorities

8. Premeditated theft: planned burglaries and thefts

9. Shakedown: taking items from the scene of a theft or a burglary the officer is investigating

10. Shopping: taking small, inexpensive items from a crime scene or an unsecured business or home[27]

"grass eaters"
Officers who occasionally engage in illegal and unethical activities, such as accepting small favors, gifts, or money for ignoring violations of the law during the course of their duties.

"meat eaters"
Officers who actively seek ways to make money illegally while on duty.

internal affairs investigations unit

The police unit that ferrets out illegal and unethical activity engaged in by the police.

Controlling Corruption Corruption in law enforcement strikes at the core of the profession and takes a heavy toll. All peace officer positions are positions of honor and trust, and agencies invest money and time in selecting officers with integrity. To see this investment lost is disheartening. But more than anything else, public confidence and trust plummet after a widely publicized corruption case, such as the police drug-trafficking episode in Miami. In the following list, some ways to control and reduce corruption in policing are described.

- **High Moral Standards** Selecting and maintaining officers with high moral standards is a step in the right direction. Some police agencies in the United States still hire convicted felons to do police work. In-depth academy and in-service training on ethical issues that officers are likely to face would prepare officers for the compromises they may be asked to make later in their careers.

- **Police Policies and Discipline** A police department should develop rigid policies that cover the wide range of activities that corruption comprises. Drug testing of officers, particularly those in narcotics-sensitive positions, may be necessary, although unpopular. Policies mean nothing unless they are enforced. Discipline should be imposed and prosecutions should go forward when officers are found guilty of violating established policies and laws.

- **Proactive Internal Affairs Unit** The **internal affairs investigations unit** of a police department should ferret out illegal and unethical activity. Any internal affairs unit that waits for complaints probably is not going to receive many of them. First-line supervisors should know whether their subordinates are engaging in unethical and illegal violations of department rules and state laws. They should also be held responsible for the actions of their subordinates.

- **Uniform Enforcement of the Law** If a police agency makes it clear that no group of citizens, no matter what their affiliation with the police department is going to receive special treatment from the police department, the incentive for offering bribes and other forms of corruption will be minimized. This process starts with clear policies and procedures and must be backed up with discipline when necessary.

- **Outside Review and Special Prosecutors** Heavily resisted by police leadership and police labor associations is any kind of outside review of their actions. However, both the Christopher Commission and the Knapp Commission are examples of outside reviews that brought about improvements in the agencies they investigated. Special prosecutors are recommended in serious cases to relieve the police and the government of any accusations of a whitewash.

- **Court Review and Oversight** Criminal prosecutions or civil liability suits deriving from police corruption cases can be very costly to a police agency. Such visible forms of oversight often result in adverse media coverage, civil liability awards, and higher insurance rates—all of which should encourage police agencies to control corruption.[28]

Professionalizing Law Enforcement

Many people would argue that policing in America has already reached professional status. Law enforcement is a valued service. Its agents make important decisions daily that substantially affect the lives of people and the quality of life in a community. The police officer's position is one of honor and trust. There are academy programs consisting of hundreds of hours of instruction, as well as law enforcement degree programs. Now there are even signs that law enforcement is attempting to police its own profession. Professional accreditation for police agencies is a rite of passage that is needed if law enforcement is to join the list of the most respected professions. Nevertheless, resistance to it and the other developments is still widespread.

Not everyone has the qualities to be a police officer. To allow into law enforcement those people with no desire to serve, low intelligence, a shady past, poor work habits, and no ability to communicate effectively is to court disaster for every department that does so—and for the entire profession.

Some police officers and their leaders resist 600 hours of initial training and do all they can to avoid continuing education and training. Real professionals seek advanced training.

Professionals in any field make mistakes, and a caring public should forgive most of them. In police work, there are incomplete interviews, evidence left at crime scenes, and bad reports written. In the long run, the consequences of such mistakes are generally insignificant as long as corrections are made. Mistakes can also be technological, such as the failure of a radar gun. No one should blame the police for technological mishaps that are not the result of negligence.

One kind of mistake, however, stands out more than any other: the condoning of racist and brutal tactics like the Los Angeles police officers' beating of Rodney King. The findings of the Christopher Commission confirmed that such tactics were generally condoned and even encouraged. The videotaped replay of that performance will be an embarrassment to professional policing for years to come. Police departments need to remove officers who would participate in or overlook such violence from the profession.

Many police officers go to work each day with a negative attitude, and some may take out their frustrations on the citizens they meet. Police officers need to treat their on-duty time as a professional performance and render the best service possible on any given day. If they treat the citizens they serve with respect and concern, officers will make great progress in improving the public's perception of law enforcement as a profession worthy of trust and admiration.

Accreditation

By the end of 1999, 532 police agencies in the United States were accredited by the Commission on Accreditation for Law Enforcement Agencies (CALEA).

SOURCE: "CALEA, Commission on Accreditation for Law Enforcement Agencies," www.calea.org

---

7.3 CRITICAL THINKING

1. What do you think are the best ways for police officers to handle stress on the job?

2. What do you think are the best ways to recruit new police officers?

Policing in America: Issues and Ethics

Review and Applications

SUMMARY BY CHAPTER OBJECTIVES

1. Describe the General Attitude of the Public Toward the Police

According to surveys, the American public is generally satisfied with the quality of the service the police provide. The level of confidence varies across racial and ethnic groups. As with most services, the public believes there is room for improvement.

2. Summarize the Steps in an Effective Police Officer Selection Process

Police applicants go through several different kinds of testing to become law enforcement officers. Steps in an effective police officer selection process include: recruitment, short application, detailed application, medical examination, physical ability test, written examination, background investigation, psychological testing, oral interview/oral board, academy training, and a probationary employment period.

3. Identify Factors that Affect the Exercise of Police Discretion and Methods of Limiting Discretion

Factors that affect the exercise of police discretion include the nature of the crime, departmental policies, the relationship between the victim and the offender, the amount of evidence, the preference of the victim, the demeanor of the suspect, the legitimacy of the victim, and the suspect's socioeconomic status. Methods of limiting police discretion are close supervision by a police agency's management, department directives and policies, U.S. Supreme Court decisions, and the threat of civil liability suits.

4. Describe Two General Ways that Law Enforcement Agencies Can Reduce Stress on the Job

Two general ways that law enforcement agencies can reduce job stress for police officers are (1) to employ *stress management* strategies, such as discussing stressful events with colleagues and mental health professionals, regular exercise, relaxation techniques, healthy diet,

religious support, enriched family support, prayer, meditation, and stress management classes that often involve spouses, and (2) to implement *organizational change*, such as allowing officers more discretion in determining work hours and shifts, flattening the organizational structure and giving officers more discretion in carrying out their responsibilities, job redesign which assigns unwanted or unnecessary tasks for a police officer to another position, and having excellent public safety equipment such as weaponry, vehicles, and body armor.

5. Explain the Circumstances under which Police Officers May Be Justified in Using Deadly Force

The use of deadly force by a police officer may be justifiable if (1) the arrest is for a felony; (2) the person effecting the arrest is authorized to act as a peace officer or is assisting a person whom he believes to be authorized to act as a peace officer; (3) the officer believes that the force employed creates no substantial risk of injury to innocent persons; (4) the officer believes that the crime for which the arrest is made involved conduct including the use or threatened use of deadly force; and (5) the officer believes there is substantial risk that the person to be arrested will cause death or serious bodily harm if his or her apprehension is delayed.

6. List Some of the Ways to Control and Reduce Police Corruption

Ways to control and reduce police corruption include selecting and maintaining officers with high moral standards, developing rigid departmental policies that cover the wide range of activities that corruption comprises, disciplining and prosecuting officers who are guilty of violating established policies and laws, utilizing a proactive internal affairs investigations unit, holding first-line supervisors responsible for the actions of their subordinates, employing outside review and special prosecutors, and emphasizing to officers the costs to police agencies of criminal prosecutions and civil liability suits.

three I's of police selection, p. 230
college academies, p. 233
public safety officers, p. 234
police cadet program, p. 234
tech prep (technical preparation), p. 234
merit system, p. 234
discretion, p. 238
full enforcement, p. 238
selective enforcement, p. 239
racial profiling, p. 241
job stress, p. 242
copicide, p. 243
excessive force, p. 244
"grass eaters," p. 247
"meat eaters," p. 247
internal affairs investigations unit, p. 248

QUESTIONS FOR REVIEW

1. In general, what is the attitude of the American public toward the police?

2. Explain how the three I's of police selection (intelligence, integrity, and interaction skills) relate to the success of a police officer.

3. What are some advantages of hiring college-educated police officers?

4. What are some arguments in favor of and opposing the reduction of police discretion?

5. Why do police generally not like to respond to domestic violence calls?

6. What is *racial profiling* in law enforcement, and what are some of the methods that have been prescribed to stop it?

7. What are some of the conditions that can lead to police job stress?

8. What is meant by *copicide*?

9. What is meant by *excessive force*?

10. What are some types of police misconduct?

Review and Applications

1. **Neighborhood Survey** Conduct a survey about the police in your neighborhood. Use the same survey questions and categories as in Figures 7–1 on page 224, 7–2 on page 225, and 7–3 on page 228. Try to get respondents from as many races, genders, and age groups as possible. Compare the results of your survey with the results in Figures 7–1, 7–2, and 7–3.
   Note any gender, race, or age differences in responses.

2. **Police Recruiting** Contact your local police department, and find out what it does to recruit police candidates.
   Does it run a police academy? Does it generally recruit officers from other jurisdictions? Compare your findings with those of others in the class and what you have learned from your textbook.

INTERNET

3. **Racial Profiling** Go to the Web site of the American Civil Liberties Union by clicking on the link at cj.glencoe.com and look at its report on "Driving While Black: Racial Profiling on Our Nation's Highways," by Professor David A. Harris from the University of Toledo College of Law. Read Professor Harris' report and his five recommendations for ending racial profiling. Which of the five recommendations do you agree with and why? Which do you disagree with and why? Discuss these findings in class and see if other students share your views.

4. **Job Qualifications** Following the links at cj.glencoe.com, look at five large police department Web sites (for example, New York City, Chicago, etc.) and identify the major qualifications to be a police officer that are listed there. What qualifications are the same or similar among the agencies you examined? What qualifications are unique among those listed by the five agencies? Which employment qualifications are the most difficult to meet? Do you agree that all of the qualifications most difficult to meet are necessary? Would you add any qualifications? If so, what would they be? What would be the impact of your new qualifications on the recruitment and selection of police officers?

Police Academy

1. Recently, "Police Corps," a new military-style police academy, has opened in cities such as Jacksonville and Tampa, Florida. The cadets of the mentally exhausting six-month program eat, sleep, and live together in rooms near the academy with no televisions and with the constant threat of surprise inspections. Their days involve marching in military formation with a platoon leader barking out cadences, weightlifting, and classes on self-defense as well as law and criminal procedure. Afternoons are spent at the firing range, where they train with pistols, MP-5 submachine guns, and AR-15 assault rifles. After ending their days at 10 p.m. with little or no time to themselves to relax or study, they are occasionally awakened at 2 a.m. as instructors push them for practice in high-speed driving and patrolling tactics. At some point in the course, the cadets are put through 24 to 72 hours of sleep deprivation to teach them the effects of stress and lack of sleep on their bodies. The punishment for not following orders correctly is pushups.

    Supporters of the new academy maintain that the Navy SEAL-type training will help officers become more disciplined and community oriented. Critics contend that the program is too extreme and isn't necessary for a community police force, that it "isn't needed in our society unless we're in a warfare environment."

    What are the pros and cons of this new military-style police academy training?

    What effects, if any, are such training methods likely to have on police recruitment?

    Is such training needed in our society?

Stress

2. You are the commander of the operations division of a medium-sized police department, in charge of the patrol, criminal investigation, and traffic sections.

    What would you do if several officers from each of the sections came to you and said that they believed that job stress was hindering officer performance and endangering the health of several officers in each of the units?

    How would you go about validating their claims of job stress in the work environment?

    If it were determined that stressors such as too frequent shift changes, poor communication among the various ranks, and a lack of sufficient safety equipment were present, what would be your plan to improve working conditions and reduce job stress?

    Provide a step-by-step summary of what you would do.

ADDITIONAL READING

Guyot, Dorothy. *Policing as Though People Mattered.* Philadelphia, PA: Temple University Press, 1991.

Kappeler, Victor. *Critical Issues in Police Liability.* Prospect Heights, IL: Waveland Press, 1997 2nd ed.

Kenney, Dennis and Robert McNamara. *Police and Policing: Contemporary Issues.* Westport, CT, Praeger, 1999 2nd.

Moriarity, Laura and David Carter. *Criminal Justice Technology in the 21st Century.* Springfield, IL: Charles C. Thomas Publisher, 1998.

Roberg, Roy, John Crank, and Jack Kuykendall. *Police and Society.* Los Angeles, CA: Roxbury Publishing Company, 2000.

Sanders, William. *Detective Work.* New York: Free Press, 1977.

ENDNOTES

1. W.S. Wilson Huang and Michael S. Vaughn, "Support and Confidence: Public Attitudes Toward the Police," pp. 31–45 in Timothy J. Flanagan and Dennis R. Longmire (eds.), *Americans View Crime and Justice: A National Public Opinion Survey* (Thousand Oaks, CA: Sage, 1996), p. 44.

2. Kathleen Maguire and Ann L. Pastore (eds.), *Sourcebook of Criminal Justice Statistics 1996,* U.S. Department of Justice, Bureau of Justice Statistics (Washington, DC: GPO, 1997), p. 129, Table 2.23.

3. Humphrey Taylor, "In Spite of Amadou Diallo, Public Perceptions of Police Show Marked Improvements." Harris Interactive/The Harris Poll <www.louisharris.com/harris_poll/index.asp?PID=76> (December 16, 2000); Kathleen Maguire, Ann L. Pastore, and Timothy J. Flanagan (eds.), *Sourcebook of Criminal Justice Statistics 1992,* U.S. Department of Justice, Bureau of Justice Statistics (Washington, DC: GPO, 1993), p. 171, Table 2.18.

4. Ann L. Pastore and Kathleen Maguire, eds. (2000) Sourcebook of Criminal Justice Statistics (Online) <www.albany.edu/sourcebook/> (December 16, 2000), p. 110, Table 2.30.

5. Taylor, op. cit.

6. Pastore and Maguire, op. cit., 2000, p. 106, Table 2.22.

7. Larry Gaines and Victor Kappeler, "Police Selection," in Gary Cordner and Donna Hale (eds.), op. cit.

8. Robert B. Mills, "Psychological, Psychiatric, Polygraph, and Stress Evaluation," in Calvin Swank and James Conser (eds.), *The Police Personnel System* (New York: Wiley, 1981).

9. O. W. Wilson and Roy McLaren, *Police Administration* (New York: McGraw-Hill, 1972), p. 261.

10. Albert Reiss, *The Police and the Public* (New Haven, CT: Yale University Press, 1971).

11. Brian A. Reaves and Andrew L. Goldberg, *Local Police Departments, 1997,* U.S. Department of Justice, Bureau of Justice Statistics (Washington, DC: GPO, 2000) and U.S. Census Bureau.

12. David Carter, Allen Sapp, and Darrel Stephens, *The State of Police Education: Policy Direction for the 21st Century* (Washington, DC: Police Executive Research Forum, 1989).

13. Hild v. Bruner, 1980; Bonsignore v. City of New York, 1981.

14. Jack Gregory, "The Background Investigation and Oral Interview," in Calvin Swank and James Conser (eds.), op. cit.

15. Skolnick, op. cit., p. 45.

16. Lawrence W. Sherman and Richard A. Berk, *The Minneapolis Domestic Violence Experiment.* Washington, D.C.: The Police Foundation, 1984.

17. Steve Lackmeyer and Ken Raymond, "City Leaders Balk at Ban on Police Profiling," The Oklahoman, June 3, 2000.

18. Alex Johnson, "Fear and Loathing on the Job," MSNBC, September 4, 2000.

19. NIOSH, "Stress at Work," www.cdc.gov/niosh/stresswk.html

20. NIOSH, "Stress at Work," www.cdc.gov/niosh/stresswk.html

21. Http://www.LOGOPHILIA.com/WordSpy/c.html

22. "10% of Police Shootings Found to Be 'Suicide by Cop,'" Criminal Justice Newsletter, Vol. 29, No. 17, September 1, 1998, pp. 1–2.

23. Alan Feuer, "Drawing a Bead on a Baffling Endgame: Suicide by Cop," *The New York Times,* June 25, 1998.

24. John Dugan and Daniel Breda, "Complaints About Police Officers: A Comparison Among Types and Agencies," Journal of Criminal Justice, Vol. 19 (1991), pp. 165–71.

25. David Lester, "The Murder of Police Officers in American Cities," Criminal Justice and Behavior, Vol. 11 (1984), pp. 101–13.

26. Knapp Commission, *Report on Police Corruption* (New York: George Braziller, 1972).

27. Ellwyn R. Stoddard, "The Informal 'Code' of Police Deviancy: A Group Approach to Blue-Coat Crime," Journal of Criminal Law, Criminology, and Police Science, Vol. 59 (1968), p. 204.

28. Candace McCloy, "Lawsuits Against Police: What Impact Do They Have?" Criminal Law Bulletin, Vol. 20 (1984), pp. 49–56.

The Courts

CHAPTER OUTLINE

The Administration of Justice

8.1 The American Court Structure

dual court system

The court system in the United States, consisting of one system of state and local courts and another system of federal courts.

jurisdiction

The authority of a court to hear and decide cases.

original jurisdiction

The authority of a court to hear a case when it is first brought to court.

appellate jurisdiction

The power of a court to review a case for errors of law.

general jurisdiction

The power of a court to hear any type of case.

special jurisdiction

The power of a court to hear only certain kinds of cases.

subject matter jurisdiction

The power of a court to hear a particular type of case.

personal jurisdiction

A court's authority over the parties to a lawsuit.

The United States has a **dual court system**—a separate judicial system for each of the states and a separate federal system. Figure 8–1 displays this dual court system and routes of appeal from the various courts. The only place where the two systems connect is in the U.S. Supreme Court.

The authority of a court to hear and decide cases is called the court's **jurisdiction.** It is set by law and is limited by territory and type of case. A court of **original jurisdiction** has the authority to hear a case when it is first brought to court. Courts having the power to review a case for errors of law are courts of **appellate jurisdiction.** Courts having the power to hear any type of case are said to exercise **general jurisdiction.** Those with the power to hear only certain types of cases have **special jurisdiction. Subject matter jurisdiction** is the court's power to hear a particular type of case. **Personal jurisdiction** is the court's authority over the parties to a lawsuit.

The Federal Courts

The authority for the federal court system is the U.S. Constitution, Article III, Section 1, which states, "The judicial power of the United States shall be vested in one Supreme Court, and in such inferior courts as Congress may from time to time ordain and establish." The federal court system includes the Supreme Court, the federal courts of appeals, and the federal district courts. The federal court system is shown in Figure 8–2 on page 259.

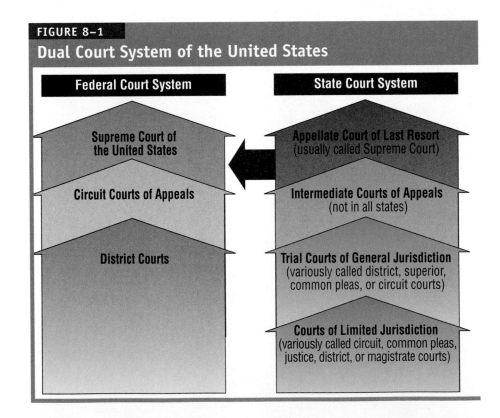

FIGURE 8–1

Dual Court System of the United States

Federal Court System	State Court System
Supreme Court of the United States	Appellate Court of Last Resort (usually called Supreme Court)
Circuit Courts of Appeals	Intermediate Courts of Appeals (not in all states)
District Courts	Trial Courts of General Jurisdiction (variously called district, superior, common pleas, or circuit courts)
	Courts of Limited Jurisdiction (variously called circuit, common pleas, justice, district, or magistrate courts)

FIGURE 8-2
The Federal Court Structure

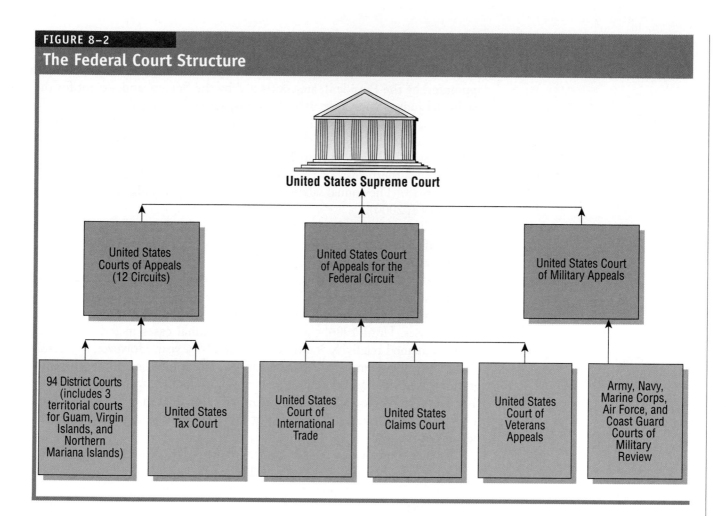

United States Supreme Court

United States Courts of Appeals (12 Circuits)

United States Court of Appeals for the Federal Circuit

United States Court of Military Appeals

94 District Courts (includes 3 territorial courts for Guam, Virgin Islands, and Northern Mariana Islands)

United States Tax Court

United States Court of International Trade

United States Claims Court

United States Court of Veterans Appeals

Army, Navy, Marine Corps, Air Force, and Coast Guard Courts of Military Review

United States District Courts   Forming the base of the federal court structure are the U.S. district courts. These are courts of original jurisdiction, or courts where most violations of federal criminal and civil law are first adjudicated and where decisions of fact are made. Today, there are 94 district courts divided into 13 circuits, with at least one federal district court in each state, one each in the District of Columbia and the commonwealths of Puerto Rico and the Northern Mariana Islands, and one each in the U.S. territories of the Virgin Islands and Guam. In some states, the courts are divided into districts geographically. New York, for example, has northern, eastern, southern, and western district courts.

Two factors determine the jurisdiction of federal district courts: the subject matter of a case and the parties to a case. Federal district courts have subject matter jurisdiction over cases that involve federal laws, treaties with foreign nations, or interpretations of the Constitution. Cases involving admiralty or maritime law—the law of the sea, including ships, their crews, and disputes over actions and rights at sea—also come under federal district court jurisdiction.

Federal district courts have personal jurisdiction in cases if certain parties or persons are involved. These include (1) ambassadors and other representatives of foreign governments, (2) two or more state governments, (3) the U.S. government or one of its offices or agencies, (4) citizens of different states, (5) a state and a citizen of a different state, (6) citizens of the same state claiming lands under grants of different states, and (7) a state or its citizens and a foreign country or its citizens.

U.S. district courts are presided over by district court judges who are appointed by the President, are confirmed by the Senate, and, except for the territorial judges who serve 10-year terms, serve for life (if they choose, do not resign, or are not impeached and convicted by Congress). In 1999, there were 655 authorized federal district judgeships. Several district courts, such as the eastern-district court in Muskogee, Oklahoma, had only one judge, while the southern-district court of New York in New York City had the most with 28.[1] The annual salary of a U.S. district court judge is $141,300 (as of January 1, 2000).

Usually a single federal judge presides over a trial, and trial by jury is allowed if requested by a defendant. Some complex civil cases are heard by a special panel of three judges. The bulk of the workload of the U.S. district courts is devoted to civil cases, the number of which has risen dramatically in recent years, to more than 260,000 in 1999. Federal criminal cases involve such crimes as bank robbery, counterfeiting, mail fraud, kidnapping, and civil rights abuses. Until 1980, the number of criminal cases in federal district courts remained relatively stable at about 30,000 a year. However, as a result of the federal government's War on Drugs and an increase in illegal immigration cases, the number of criminal cases had doubled to nearly 60,000 by the end of 1999. Nearly half of the criminal cases filed in U.S district courts in 1999 were drug cases (29 percent of the total) and immigration cases (18 percent of the total).[2]

To ease the caseload of U.S. district court judges, Congress created the judicial office of federal magistrate in 1968. The title changed to magistrate judge in 1990. As their caseloads require and as funding from Congress permits, district judges may appoint magistrate judges to part-time or full-time positions. Magistrate judges handle civil consent cases, misdemeanor trials, preliminary hearings, pretrial motions and motion hearings, and conferences in felony cases.[3]

Circuit Courts

The circuit courts are so named because early in the nation's history, federal judges traveled by horseback to each of the courts in a specified region, or "circuit," in a particular sequence. In short, they rode the circuit.[6]

SOURCE: Howard Ball, "The Federal Court System," pp. 554–568 in R.J. Janosik (ed.) *Encyclopedia of the American Judicial System: Studies of the Principal Institutions and Processes of Law* (New York: Charles Scribner's Sons, 1987) p. 556.

Circuit Courts of Appeals A person or group that loses a case in district court may appeal to a federal circuit court of appeals or, in some instances, directly to the Supreme Court. Congress created the U.S. circuit courts of appeals in 1891 to reduce the case burden of the Supreme Court. The U.S. circuit courts of appeals have only appellate jurisdiction and review a case for errors of law, not of fact. Most appeals arise from the decisions of district courts, the U.S. Tax Court, and various territorial courts (see Figure 8–2). Federal courts of appeals also hear appeals of the rulings of regulatory agencies, such as the Federal Trade Commission. An appeal to the U.S. circuit court of appeals is a matter of right—the court cannot refuse to hear the case. However, unless appealed to the Supreme Court, decisions of the courts of appeals are final. U.S. courts of appeals hear more than 50,000 cases annually; less than 30 percent of those cases are criminal.[4]

There are currently 13 U.S. circuit courts of appeals (see Figure 8–3 on page 261). Twelve of them have jurisdiction over cases from particular geographic areas. The Court of Appeals for the Federal Circuit, created in 1982, has national jurisdiction over specific types of cases, such as appeals from the U.S. Court of International Trade.[5] Like U.S. district judges, federal appellate judges are nominated by the President, are confirmed by the Senate, and may serve for life. Currently, 179 judges serve on the 13 U.S. circuit courts (167 on the 12 regional courts and 12 on the federal circuit).[6] The yearly salary of a U.S. circuit court of appeals judge is $149,900 (as of January 1, 2000). The number of judges assigned to each court of appeals ranges from six (the First Circuit) to 28 (the Ninth Circuit) and, normally, three judges sit as a panel. Jury trials are not allowed in these courts. In highly controversial cases, all of the judges in a circuit may sit together and hear a case. Those *en banc* hearings are rare; there probably are no more than 100 of them in all of the circuits in one year.

The United States Supreme Court   The U.S. Supreme Court is the court of last resort in all questions of federal law (see Figure 8–2 on page 259). It has the final word in any case involving the Constitution, acts of Congress, and treaties with other nations. Under the Supreme Court's appellate jurisdiction, the Court hears cases appealed from federal courts of appeals, or it may hear appeals from federal district courts in certain circumstances in which an act of Congress has been held unconstitutional.

The Supreme Court may also hear cases that are appealed from the high court of a state, if claims under federal law or the Constitution are involved. In such cases, however, the Court has the authority to rule only on the federal issue involved, not on any issues of state law. For example, suppose a state

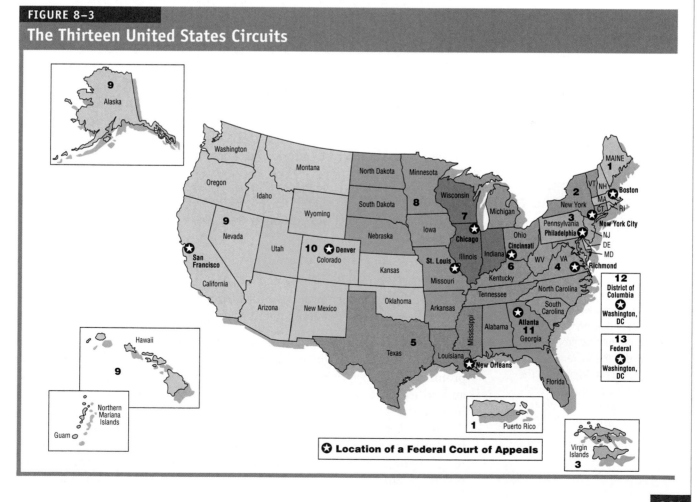

FIGURE 8–3

The Thirteen United States Circuits

☼ **Location of a Federal Court of Appeals**

tries a person charged with violating a state law. During the trial, the accused claims that the police violated Fourth Amendment rights with an illegal search at the time of the arrest. The defendant may appeal to the Supreme Court on the constitutional issue only. The Supreme Court generally has no jurisdiction to rule on the state issue (whether the accused actually violated state law). The Court would decide only whether Fourth Amendment rights were violated. Decisions of the Supreme Court are binding on all lower courts.

The Supreme Court is composed of a chief justice, officially known as the Chief Justice of the United States, and eight associate justices. They are appointed for life by the President with the consent of the Senate and, like other federal judges, can be removed from office against their will only by "impeachment for, and Conviction of, Treason, Bribery, or other high Crimes and Misdemeanors." The Chief Justice, who is specifically nominated by the President for the position, presides over the Court's public sessions and private conferences, assigns justices to write opinions (when the Chief Justice has voted with the majority), and supervises the entire federal judiciary. (When the Chief Justice has voted with the minority, the Associate Justice who has the greatest seniority, that is, has been on the Court the longest, assigns who writes the opinion.) The salary of the Chief Justice is $181,400; the salaries of the Associate Justices are $173,600 (as of January 1, 2000).

For a case to be heard by the Supreme Court, at least four of the nine justices must vote to hear the case (the "rule of four"). When the required number of votes has been achieved, the Court issues a **writ of *certiorari*** to the lower court whose decision is being appealed, ordering it to send the records of the case forward for review. The Court is limited by law and custom in the types of cases for which it issues writs of *certiorari*. The Court will issue a "writ" only if the defendant in the case has exhausted all other avenues of appeal and the case involves a substantial federal question as defined by the appellate court. A substantial federal question, as noted, is one in which there is an alleged violation of either the U.S. Constitution or federal law.

When the Supreme Court decides a case it has accepted on appeal, it can do one of the following:

1. Affirm the verdict or decision of the lower court and "let it stand."
2. Modify the verdict or decision of the lower court, without totally reversing it.
3. Reverse the verdict or decision of the lower court, requiring no further court action.
4. Reverse the verdict or decision of the lower court and remand the case to the court of original jurisdiction, for either retrial or resentencing.

In some cases, the Supreme Court has ordered trial courts to resentence defendants whose original sentences violated the Eighth Amendment prohibition against cruel and unusual punishment. In other cases, prison authorities have been ordered to remedy unconstitutional conditions of imprisonment.

Appeals to the Supreme Court are heard at the discretion of the Court, in contrast to appeals to the U.S. circuit courts, which review cases as a matter of right. Generally, the Supreme Court's refusal to hear a case ends the process of direct appeal. In fiscal year 1998, for example, the Supreme Court

writ of *certiorari*
A written order, from the U.S. Supreme Court to a lower court whose decision is being appealed, to send the records of the case forward for review.

Court Fees

The fee for filing an appeal with the U.S. Supreme Court is $300. Fees are waived for indigent defendants. Approximately 90 percent of the criminal proceedings appealed to the Supreme Court involve indigent defendants. The fees do not include the costs of printing various documents required under other court rules.

SOURCE: Clerk of the Supreme Court; 28 U.S.C. § 1911.

▲ Current U.S. Supreme Court Justices. Top row (L-R): Associate Justices Ruth Bader Ginsburg, David Souter, Clarence Thomas, and Stephen Breyer. Bottom row (L-R): Associate Justices Antonin Scalia and John Paul Stevens, Chief Justice William Rehnquist, Associate Justices Sandra Day O'Connor and Anthony Kennedy. *How well does the Supreme Court reflect the demographic distribution of the U.S. population?*

Justices

The Supreme Court Justices of the United States have varied biographical, legal, and educational backgrounds. Learn more about the current justices by clicking on the link at cj.glencoe.com. *What do the justices have in common? How do their backgrounds differ?*

denied nearly 99 percent of the petitions for review on writ of *certiorari* in criminal proceedings.[7] Writs of *certiorari* in criminal proceedings accounted for 37 percent of such writs filed with the Court; the rest were either civil appeals or administrative appeals.[8] In certain circumstances, an imprisoned defendant whose appeal has been denied may still try to have the Supreme Court review his or her case on constitutional grounds by filing a writ of *habeas corpus.* A **writ of *habeas corpus,*** which is guaranteed by Article I, Section 9, of the Constitution, the Federal Habeas Corpus Act, and state *habeas corpus* laws, is a court order directing a law officer to produce a prisoner in court to determine if the prisoner is being legally detained or imprisoned. The *habeas corpus* proceeding does not test whether the prisoner is guilty or innocent.

The Supreme Court also has original jurisdiction. However, Article III, Section 2.2, of the Constitution limits the Court's original jurisdiction to two types of cases: (1) cases involving representatives of foreign governments; and (2) certain cases in which a state is a party. Many cases have involved two states and the federal government. When Maryland and Virginia argued over oyster fishing rights, and when a dispute broke out between California and Arizona over the control of water from the Colorado River, the Supreme

writ of *habeas corpus*
An order from a court to an officer of the law to produce a prisoner in court to determine if the prisoner is being legally detained or imprisoned.

The Administration of Justice **CHAPTER 8**

The Judicial Conference of the United States

The Judicial Conference of the United States governs the federal court system. The conference is composed of 27 federal judges and is presided over by the Chief Justice of the U.S. Supreme Court. The conference meets twice a year to consider policies affecting the federal courts, to make recommendations to Congress on legislation affecting the judicial system, to propose amendments to the federal rules of practice and procedure, and to address administrative problems of the courts.

SOURCES: Administrative Office of the U.S. Courts, Federal Judiciary Web site, "About the U.S. Courts," <www.uscourts.gov>; "The 1999 Year-End Report on the Federal Judiciary, <www.uscourts.gov/ttb/jan00ttb/jan2000.html>.

summary trials
Trials without a jury.

trial *de novo*
A trial in which an entire case is reheard by a trial court of general jurisdiction because there is an appeal and there is no written transcript of the earlier proceeding.

Court had original jurisdiction in the matters. Original jurisdiction cases are a very small part of the Court's yearly workload. Most of the cases the Court decides fall under its appellate jurisdiction.

The State Courts

The state courts have general power to decide nearly every type of case, subject only to the limitations of the U.S. Constitution, their own state constitutions, and state law. State and local courts are the courts with which citizens most often have contact. These courts handle most criminal matters and the majority of day-to-day legal matters. The laws of each state determine the organization, function, and even the names of its courts. Thus, no two state court systems are exactly alike. For discussion purposes, it is useful to distinguish four levels of state courts: trial courts of limited jurisdiction, trial courts of general jurisdiction, intermediate appellate courts, and state courts of last resort.[9]

Trial Courts of Limited Jurisdiction   At the base of the state court structure (see Figure 8–1 on page 258) are the approximately 13,000 trial courts of limited jurisdiction, sometimes referred to generally as "inferior trial courts" or simply as "lower courts." Depending on the jurisdiction, those courts are called city courts, municipal courts, county courts, circuit courts, courts of common pleas, justice-of-the-peace courts, district courts, or magistrate courts. (Technically, most of the lower courts are not really part of the state judicial structure because they are the creation of, and funded by, either city or county governments.) In several states, judges of the lower courts are not required to have any formal legal training.

The lower courts typically deal with minor cases, such as ordinance and traffic violations, some misdemeanors, and—in many jurisdictions—civil cases involving less than $1,000. For those types of offenses, the lower courts in many states are allowed to conduct **summary trials**, or trials without a jury. Typically, the greatest penalty that can be imposed is a fine of $1,000 and a maximum of 12 months in jail. Unlike trial courts of general jurisdiction, the lower courts are not courts of record, where detailed transcripts of the proceedings are made. Because they are not courts of record, an appeal from such a lower court requires a **trial *de novo***, in which the entire case must be reheard by a trial court of general jurisdiction.

In addition to handling minor cases, the lower courts in most states hear the formal charges against persons accused of felonies, set bail, appoint counsel for indigent defendants, and conduct preliminary hearings for crimes that must be adjudicated at a higher level. The legal proceedings in these courts are typically less formal, and many cases are resolved without defense attorneys. Lower courts process and quickly dispose of large numbers of cases, approximately 70 million a year.

Trial Courts of General Jurisdiction   Variously called district courts, superior courts, and circuit courts, depending on the jurisdiction, the more than 3,000 trial courts of general jurisdiction have the authority to try all civil and criminal cases and to hear appeals from lower courts. They are courts of record (formal transcripts of the proceedings are made), and judges and lawyers in those courts have formal legal training. Trial courts of general jurisdiction are funded by the state.

CAREERS IN CRIMINAL JUSTICE

Trial Court Administrator

My name is Todd Nuccio. I am the trial court administrator for the 26th Judicial District in North Carolina. The district encompasses Charlotte and greater Mecklenburg County. It is the largest jurisdiction in the state serving approximately 700,000 people.

I have a B.A. in political science from Northern Illinois University and an M.S. in judicial administration from the University of Denver, College of Law. I recently received another B.A. in psychology from the University of North Carolina at Charlotte because I have come to learn that 90 percent of successfully managing an organization depends upon one's ability to understand and motivate people.

During my final undergraduate semester, a constitutional law professor told me about a program that combined aspects of public administration and law.

Since graduation, I have held the position of assistant court administrator in the 7th Judicial District of Iowa, the trial court administrator position in the 12th Judicial District in North Carolina, and my current position here in Charlotte.

The responsibilities of a trial court administrator are similar to the more commonly known position of hospital administrator. The only difference is that the hospital administrator manages operations for doctors, whereas the trial court administrator manages operations for lawyers serving in the capacity of judges.

Court administration involves everything that goes into making a court system good or bad. The court manager's mission is to improve the administration of justice by: 1) working with other court officials to facilitate change, 2) initiating and coordinating discussions that form the basis of consensus, and 3) identifying problems and recommending solutions that lead to a more accessible, accountable, effective, and efficient court system.

My primary responsibilities include developing local rules and administrative policies to facilitate calendaring and administrative activities, research, strategic planning, case-flow and jury management, budgeting, personnel oversight, facilities management, grant procurement, program development, project management, coordination of alternative dispute-resolution programs, and oversight of the drug treatment and family court operations and collections department.

What I like best about my job is the variety. There are always new programs to develop and projects to manage.

What do you think are the pros and cons of being a trial court administrator?

Some states have created specialty courts to deal with increases in certain types of crimes or chronic social problems. In 1989, for instance, Dade County, Florida, became the first jurisdiction to establish a drug court. Within a decade, all but ten states had at least one such court. Drug courts have been established to (1) help handle the dramatic increase in drug cases resulting from the War on Drugs that have been overwhelming the trial courts of general jurisdiction, and (2) use the court's authority to reduce crime by changing defendants' drug-using behavior. In exchange for the possibility of dismissed charges or reduced sentences, defendants accept diversion to drug treatment programs during the judicial process. Drug court judges preside over drug court proceedings, monitor the progress of defendants by means of

Drug Courts

As of June 1, 1998, there were 264 drug court programs in operation. Another 151 drug courts were being planned. Drug courts are now operating or being planned in 48 states, the District of Columbia, Puerto Rico, Guam, and two Federal jurisdictions, including more than 15 Native American tribal courts. Since 1989, the programs have admitted more than 65,000 offenders. The average completion rate for the programs is 48 percent (the range is from 8 percent to 95 percent).

SOURCES: U.S. Department of Justice, Drug Courts Program Office, "Looking at a Decade of Drug Courts" (Washington: GPO, 1998), p. 8; "Drug Courts: Overview of Growth, Characteristics, and Results," GAO/GGD-97-106 <www.ncjrs.org/txtfiles/dcourts.txt>, July 31, 1997.

▲ The county courthouse is a familiar sight in many local areas. *Where is the county courthouse in your county?*

frequent status hearings, and prescribe sanctions and rewards as appropriate, in collaboration with prosecutors, defense attorneys, treatment providers, and others.[10]

In 1997, Broward County in south Florida instituted the first mental-health court in the nation. This court is charged with ensuring treatment for mentally ill or developmentally disabled individuals who have been charged with nonviolent misdemeanors and, at the same time, the court is charged with protecting the public. Before the court was created, mentally disabled people often sat in jail for weeks or months for crimes that typically warranted no more than several days of confinement for other offenders. Mentally disabled arrestees often remained in jail for such long periods because they were unable to make a telephone call or post bond. The specialty court speeds up first appearances for those defendants and generally orders them to be hospitalized for evaluation.[11]

The state of New York has recently begun developing "community courts" that aim to restore distressed New York neighborhoods by making low-level, nonviolent offenders clean streets and remove graffiti as punishment for their crimes. Also being developed are "domestic-violence courts" that emphasize victim safety and defendant accountability.[12]

Intermediate Appellate Courts   In some of the geographically smaller and less-populous states, there is only one appellate court, the state court of last resort, usually called the state supreme court. Many states, however, have created intermediate appellate courts to reduce the overwhelming case burden of the state supreme court. As of January 1, 1998, 39 states had intermediate courts of appeal.[13]

The intermediate appellate courts have no trial jurisdiction. They hear only appeals in both civil and criminal cases from the trial courts of general jurisdiction. An appeals court is charged with reviewing a case for errors of law and ensuring that legal procedures were followed. The decision rendered by the appeals court is based on a review of the trial court's official transcript

CAREERS IN CRIMINAL JUSTICE

Assistant State Attorney

My name is Wilson Green and I am an Assistant State Attorney (prosecutor) in Orlando. I received a B.A. from Vanderbilt, an M.Div. From Reformed Theological Seminary and my J.D. from the University of Mississippi, with some Navy time along the way. I interviewed for and began my current job about 20 years ago here at the State Attorney's Office.

I am in the homicide unit. Most of us deal either with misdemeanor or felony cases that are set for trial. Most cases are resolved by defendants pleading guilty (or no contest) and being sentenced by a judge, while others proceed to a jury trial. The prosecutor is assigned cases as they come to our office from law enforcement agencies and after the defendants have been formally charged by other attorneys in our office.

The first step is to "work-up" each case—to review the entire file (police reports, witness statements, photos, tape recordings, lab reports, etc.) and to send out appropriate "discovery" to the defendant's attorney. Witnesses must be listed and subpoenaed for trial. Requests for further investigation may be needed as the prosecutor anticipates what the defense will probably be. Often the defense attorney will take depositions of state witnesses before trial, which we attend. There may also be pretrial hearings on legal issues, as well as plea negotiations.

Jury trials generally may last a day or so or up to a week or more. A prosecutor may have as many as a hundred cases pending at one time (spread over a few month period), with new ones coming in as fast as others are resolved. The stress level can be high at times, due to the caseload, problem cases, witness problems, cases being postponed at the last minute, not knowing which case will actually go to trial until the last minute, and having to make appropriate plea offers. On the plus side, prosecutors (who are to be "ministers of justice," not just "win" cases) have a beneficial role in society, have much discretion in handling their cases, are in the courtroom on a regular basis, and are in touch with the "real world" through their contact with police agencies, witnesses, victims, families of victims, judges and juries. They can use both common sense and legal training. Each case seems to have something new.

Those considering becoming prosecutors might think about sampling criminal justice and pre-law undergraduate courses, taking advantage of internships with law enforcement agencies or prosecutors' offices, or simply observing court proceedings as a citizen. Use any employment opportunities as a way to gain common sense experience that will help in a later career. Take advantage of any group or public speaking opportunities as well.

What do you think is the most challenging part of a prosecutor's job? Explain.

and any other legally relevant information that may be submitted. Brief oral arguments by the attorneys for both sides are also allowed.

Like their federal counterparts, the intermediate appellate courts cannot refuse to hear any legally appealed case. The number of judges assigned to intermediate appellate courts ranges from three in some states to 93 in California.[14] Normally, three judges sit as a panel to decide cases.

State Courts of Last Resort In most states, the state court of last resort is referred to as the state supreme court, although, as noted above, some states use different names. In Massachusetts and Maine, for example, the state court of last resort is called the Supreme Judicial Court; in Maryland and New York, it is called the Court of Appeals. Oklahoma and Texas have two courts of last resort: the Court of Criminal Appeals (for criminal appeals) and the Supreme Court (for civil cases). The Court of Last Resort in 13 states or the Chief Justice of the Court of Last Resort in 36 states is the designated head of a state's judicial branch. In one state, Utah, the Judicial Council is the designated head of the judicial branch.

As previously noted, the primary responsibility of state courts of last resort is to hear appeals from either trial courts of general jurisdiction (in those states without intermediate appellate courts) or intermediate appellate courts. In states with intermediate courts of appeal, the state court of last resort, like the U.S. Supreme Court, has discretion in which cases it will hear. And, like the U.S. Supreme Court, most state courts of last resort have original jurisdiction over a few types of cases.

Depending on the state, the number of judges that serve on the state court of last resort ranges from five to nine, though more than half the states have seven.[15] However, unlike judges of intermediate courts of appeal, judges of the state court of last resort are not divided into panels to hear cases. Instead, all of the judges hear all of the cases; that is, they sit *en banc*. State courts of last resort have the final word on matters involving interpretation of state law. Although defendants dissatisfied with a verdict rendered in a state court of last resort may appeal the decision to the Supreme Court, as noted previously, the Supreme Court will hear the appeal only if it involves an alleged violation of the Constitution or federal law. In deciding cases, most state courts of last resort follow procedures similar to those employed by the Supreme Court.

8.1 CRITICAL THINKING

1. What are some of the benefits of a dual court system?

2. Why is it difficult for a case to make it all the way to the Supreme Court? Should it be that difficult? Why or why not?

8.2 Purposes of Courts

Ted Rubin, former juvenile court judge and noted expert on juvenile justice, court, and rehabilitation issues, outlines ten purposes of courts.[16] The first is to "do justice." However, whether justice is done usually depends on the interests and viewpoints of the parties involved in a dispute. Typically, the "winning" party believes that justice has been done, while the "loser" thinks otherwise.

A second purpose of courts is "to appear to do justice." Even when a decision rendered by a court seems unjust to some people, it is still important that

Public Opinion and the Courts

Although the public is generally satisfied with the courts as a social institution, there is a fair amount of dissatisfaction with certain aspects of the court system, especially among racial and ethnic minorities and people who are fearful of crime. For example, 57 percent of Americans believe that political considerations influencing court decisions and differential treatment of the poor are problems. Sixty-seven percent of Americans oppose plea bargaining, and more than half believe the courts disregard victims' interests. Sixty-five percent of Americans are dissatisfied with courts that permit six months to pass between arrest and trial, and 75 percent of Americans feel that the courts are too expensive.

SOURCE: Laura B. Myers, "Bringing the Offender to Heel: Views of the Criminal Courts," in Timothy J. Flanagan and Dennis R. Longmire (eds.) *Americans View Crime and Justice: A National Public Opinion Survey* (Thousand Oaks, CA: Sage, 1996) pp. 46–61.

the court appear to "do justice." The appearance of justice is accomplished primarily by providing due process of law. **Due process of law,** as noted in Chapter 4, refers to the procedures followed by courts to ensure that a defendant's constitutional rights are not violated.

A third purpose of courts is "to provide a forum where disputes between people can be resolved justly and peacefully." Until the creation of courts of law, disputes were often settled violently, through blood feuds and other acts of revenge. Aggrieved parties would gather their extended families and friends and make war against the families and friends of the person or persons who had presumably violated their rights. Sometimes those feuds would span generations, as did the legendary battles between the Hatfields and the McCoys. Courts were instituted, at least in part, to prevent those calamities. Thus, regardless of which side in a dispute "wins," what is important, from the standpoint of the court, is that the dispute be resolved justly and, perhaps more important, peacefully.

A fourth purpose of courts is "to censure wrongdoing." To *censure* means to condemn or to blame. In this context, it refers to condemning or blaming people who have violated the law.

Purposes five through eight involve specific outcomes that courts hope to achieve by their actions. They are **incapacitation,** or the removal or restriction of the freedom of those found to have violated criminal laws; **punishment,** or the imposition of a penalty for criminal wrongdoing; **rehabilitation,** or the attempt to "correct" the personality and behavior of convicted offenders through educational, vocational, or therapeutic treatment and to return them to society as law-abiding citizens; and **general deterrence,** or the attempt to prevent people in general from engaging in crime by punishing specific individuals and making examples of them. (Omitted from Rubin's list is special or specific deterrence.) These purposes are discussed at greater length in the next chapter under the goals of sentencing.

A ninth purpose of courts is to determine legal status. For example, courts determine marital status by dissolving marriages and granting divorces. Similarly, parental status is determined by approving adoptions.

A tenth and critically important purpose of courts is to protect individual citizens against arbitrary government action. Recourse through the courts is available to citizens who have been abused by government agencies and agents. Examples of such abuses include illegal invasion of a person's privacy; interference with a person's First Amendment rights of religious choice, speech, press, and assembly; and denial of public employment because of race, gender, or age. In summary, by custom and law, courts have become an integral and seemingly indispensable part of modern life.

due process of law
The procedures followed by courts to ensure that a defendant's constitutional rights are not violated.

incapacitation
The removal or restriction of the freedom of those found to have violated criminal laws.

punishment
The imposition of a penalty for criminal wrongdoing.

rehabilitation
The attempt to "correct" the personality and behavior of convicted offenders through educational, vocational, or therapeutic treatment and to return them to society as law-abiding citizens.

general deterrence
The attempt to prevent people in general from engaging in crime by punishing specific individuals and making examples of them.

8.2 CRITICAL THINKING

1. The first purpose of the court is to "do justice." Given what you know about the American court system, do you think that justice is done? Why or why not?

2. Of the remaining nine purposes of the courts, which ones do you think can be most easily achieved? Why?

nolle prosequi (nol. pros.)
The notation placed on the official record of a case when prosecutors elect not to prosecute.

8.3 Key Actors in the Court Process

The three key actors in the court process are the prosecutor, the defense attorney, and the judge. In this section, we will examine the roles those three officers of the court play in the administration of justice.[17]

The Prosecutor

Because most crimes violate state laws, they fall under the authority, or jurisdiction, of the state court system and its prosecutors. The prosecutor is a community's chief law enforcement official and is responsible primarily for the protection of society.[18] Depending on the state, the prosecutor may be referred to as the district attorney, the county attorney, the state's attorney, the commonwealth's attorney, or the solicitor. In large cities, the day-to-day work of the prosecutor's office is performed by assistant district attorneys. Whatever the name, the prosecutor is the most powerful actor in the administration of justice. Not only do prosecutors conduct the final screening of each person arrested for a criminal offense, deciding whether there is enough evidence to support a conviction, but in most jurisdictions they also have unreviewable discretion in deciding whether to charge a person with a crime and whether to prosecute the case. In other words, regardless of the amount (or lack) of incriminating evidence, and without having to provide any reasons to anyone, prosecutors have the authority to charge or not charge a person with a crime and to prosecute or not prosecute the case. If they decide to prosecute, they also determine what the charge or charges will be. (The charge or charges may or may not be the same as the one or ones for which the person was arrested.) Prosecutors are not required to prosecute a person for all the charges that the evidence will support. However, the more charges they bring against a suspect, the more leverage prosecutors have in plea bargaining, which will be discussed later in this section.

Regardless of the reason, when prosecutors elect not to prosecute, they enter a notation of ***nolle prosequi (nol. pros.)*** on the official record of the case and formally announce in court the decision to dismiss the charge or charges.

The Decision to Charge and Prosecute   The exercise of prosecutorial discretion in charging contrasts sharply with the way prosecutors are supposed to behave in their professional capacities. Ideally, prosecutors are supposed to charge an offender with a crime and to prosecute the case if after full investigation three, and only three, conditions are met:

1. They find that a crime has been committed.
2. A perpetrator can be identified.
3. There is sufficient evidence to support a guilty verdict.

On the other hand, prosecutors are not supposed to charge suspects with more criminal charges or for more serious crimes than can be reasonably supported by the evidence. They are not supposed to be deterred from prosecution because juries in their jurisdiction have frequently refused to convict persons of particular kinds of crimes. Conversely, they are not supposed to prosecute simply because an aroused public demands it. Prosecutors are not supposed to be influenced by the personal or political advantages or disadvantages that might be involved in prosecuting or not prosecuting a case. Nor, for that matter, are they supposed to be swayed by their desire to enhance their records of successful convictions. It would be naive, however, to believe that those factors do not have at least some influence on prosecutors' decisions to pursue or to drop criminal cases.

Prosecutors sometimes choose not to charge or prosecute criminal cases for any of the following nine additional reasons. The first is their belief that an offense did not cause sufficient harm. This decision is usually a practical one. Given limited time and resources, overworked and understaffed prosecutors often have to choose which cases go forward and which do not.

A second reason involves the relationship between the statutory punishment and the offender or the offense. In today's legal climate of increasingly harsh sentencing laws, a prosecutor may feel that the statutory punishment for a crime is too severe for a particular offender (for example, a first-time offender) or for a particular offense. In an effort to be fair, at least in their own minds, prosecutors in such cases impose their own sense of justice.

A third reason for not prosecuting, even when the three ideal conditions are met, is an improper motive on the part of a complainant. The prosecutor may feel that a criminal charge has been made for the wrong reasons. For example, if a prosecutor were convinced that a woman who caught her husband cheating had lied when charging her husband with beating her, the prosecutor might elect not to charge the husband with assault or some other crime.

A fourth reason prosecutors sometimes choose not to prosecute a case is that the particular law has been violated with impunity for a long time with few complaints by the public. In the case of "blue laws," for example, which may require stores to be closed on Sundays, prosecutors would occasionally get complaints from outraged churchgoers. In some cases, prosecutors simply ignored the complaints because the law, although on the books for decades, had not been enforced for years and few complaints had been received. In most states, incidentally, blue laws have been declared unconstitutional.

A fifth reason prosecutors often choose not to prosecute a case, even though, ideally, prosecution is required, is that a victim may refuse to testify. In rape cases, for example, prosecutors realize that it is nearly impossible to secure a conviction without the testimony of the victim. Thus, if the victim refuses to testify, the prosecutor may decide to drop the case, knowing that the chances of obtaining a conviction are reduced dramatically without the cooperation of the victim.

A sixth reason for not prosecuting has to do with humanitarian concerns for the welfare of the victim or the offender. In child sexual molestation cases, for example, conviction depends on the victim's testimony. Prosecutors may decline to prosecute because of the possible psychological injury to a child who is forced to testify. When offenders are suffering from mental illness, prosecutors may decide that diverting the offender to a mental health facility rather than prosecuting for a crime is in the best interests of all concerned.

Seventh, prosecutors sometimes do not prosecute a case otherwise worthy of prosecution because the accused person cooperates in the apprehension or conviction of other criminal offenders. In drug cases, for example,

Prosecuting Cases

Insufficient evidence is the most frequent reason given by prosecutors for not prosecuting cases. In most cities, prosecutors refuse to formally charge a person in about one-half of all felony arrests.

Conviction rates

About 90 percent of all convictions in felony cases are the result of guilty pleas. Guilty pleas account for an even higher percentage of convictions in misdemeanor cases.

SOURCE: See, for example, Jodi M. Brown, Patrick A. Langan, and David J. Levin, "Felony Sentences in State Courts, 1996," U.S. Department of Justice, *Bureau of Justice Statistics Bulletin* (Washington, DC: GPO, May 1999) p. 8, Table 10.

plea bargaining or **plea negotiating**
The practice whereby the prosecutor, the defense attorney, the defendant, and—in many jurisdictions—the judge agree on a specific sentence to be imposed if the accused pleads guilty to an agreed-upon charge or charges instead of going to trial.

prosecutors often "cut deals" (make promises not to prosecute) with users or low-level dealers in order to identify "higher-ups" in the drug distribution network. Prosecutors make similar deals with low-level operatives in organized crime.

An eighth reason prosecutors sometimes choose not to prosecute is that the accused is wanted for prosecution of a more serious crime in another jurisdiction. Thus, there is little reason to expend resources prosecuting a case if an offender is likely to receive greater punishment for a crime committed elsewhere. It is easier and cheaper simply to extradite, or to deliver, the offender to the other jurisdiction.

Finally, if an offender is on parole when he or she commits a new crime, prosecutors may not prosecute the new crime because they consider it more cost-effective to simply have the parole revoked and send the offender back to prison.

The Decision to Plea Bargain Unreviewable discretion in deciding whether to charge and prosecute citizens for their crimes is the principal reason the prosecutor is considered the most powerful figure in the administration of justice, but it is by no means the prosecutor's only source of power. Probably the most strategic source of power available to prosecutors is their authority to decide which cases to "plea-bargain." **Plea bargaining** or **plea negotiating** refers to the practice whereby the prosecutor, the defense attorney, the defendant, and—in many jurisdictions—the judge agree to a negotiated plea. For example, they may agree on a specific sentence to be imposed if the accused pleads guilty to an agreed-upon charge or charges instead of going to trial. It is the prosecutor alone, however, who chooses what lesser plea, if any, will be accepted instead of going to trial. Contrary to popular belief, justice in the United States is dispensed mostly through plea bargaining. Criminal trials are relatively rare events; plea bargaining is routine. Plea bargaining and the different types of plea bargains will be discussed in more detail later in this chapter.

▲ Prosecutors strategically decide which cases to plea-bargain. *What factors might influence a prosecutor's plea-bargaining decision? Are all of those factors legitimate?*

Recommending the Amount of Bail In addition to control over charging, prosecuting, and plea bargaining, another source of power for the prosecutor in many jurisdictions is the responsibility of recommending the amount of bail. Although the final decision on the amount or even the opportunity for bail rests with the judge, the prosecutor makes the initial recommendation. By recommending a very high bail amount, an amount that a suspect is unlikely to be able to raise, a prosecutor can pressure a suspect to accept a plea bargain. Bail will be discussed later in this chapter.

Rules of Discovery Perhaps the only weakness in a prosecutor's arsenal of weapons is the legal rules of discovery. The **rules of discovery** mandate that a prosecutor provide defense counsel with any exculpatory evidence in the prosecutor's possession. Exculpatory evidence is evidence favorable to the accused that has an effect on guilt or punishment. Examples of possible exculpatory evidence are physical evidence, evidentiary documents (such as a defendant's recorded statements to police, or reports of medical examinations or scientific tests), and lists of witnesses. A prosecutor's concealment or misrepresentation of evidence is grounds for an appellate court's reversal of a conviction. Defense attorneys, on the other hand, are under no constitutional obligation to provide prosecutors with incriminating evidence. However, most states and the federal system have by statute or by court rules given the prosecution some discovery rights (for example, the right to notice of the defense's intent to use an alibi or an insanity defense). The rationale for the rules of discovery is that, ideally, the prosecutor's job is to see that justice is done and not necessarily to win cases.

rules of discovery
Rules that mandate that a prosecutor provide defense counsel with any exculpatory evidence (evidence favorable to the accused that has an effect on guilt or punishment) in the prosecutor's possession.

Selection and Career Prospects of Prosecutors Given the power of prosecutors in the administration of justice, the public can only hope that prosecutors wield their power wisely and justly. We believe that many of them do. Unfortunately, political considerations and aspirations may be too enticing to some prosecutors, causing them to violate the canons of their position. The partisan political process through which the typical prosecutor is elected increases the chances that political influence will affect the prosecutor's decisions.

The potential for political influence is increased even further by prosecutors' frequent use of the position as a stepping-stone to higher political office (several mayors, governors, and presidents have been former prosecutors). There are very few career prosecutors. Those who are not elected to higher political office and those who choose not to seek it typically go into private law practice.

Assistant District Attorneys The workhorses of the big-city prosecutor's office, as already noted, are the assistant district attorneys (or deputy district attorneys), who are hired by the prosecutor. Generally, assistant district attorneys are hired right out of law school or after a brief and usually unsuccessful stint in private practice. Most of them remain in the prosecutor's office for only two to four years and then go into, or back into, private law practice. Reasons for leaving the prosecutor's office include low pay, little chance for advancement, physical and psychological pressures, boredom, and disillusionment with the criminal adjudication process.

Running for Office
In most jurisdictions, prosecutors run for office on either the Democratic or Republican ticket, although in some jurisdictions, they are elected in nonpartisan races—that is, without party affiliation. Although prosecutors can be removed from office for criminal acts or for incompetence, removal is rare.

Assistant district attorneys provide an important social service, and the job is a good way of gaining legal experience. Lawyers who occupy the position, however, usually do not consider it anything more than temporary employment before they go into private practice.

The Defense Attorney

The Sixth Amendment to the U.S. Constitution and several modern Supreme Court decisions, discussed in Chapter 4, guarantee the right to the "effective assistance" of counsel to people charged with crimes.[19] (The terms *counsel, attorney,* and *lawyer* are interchangeable.)

The right to counsel extends not only to representation at trial but also to other critical stages in the criminal justice process, "where substantial rights of the accused may be affected." Thus, defendants have a right to counsel during custodial interrogations, preliminary hearings, and police lineups. They also have a right to counsel at certain posttrial proceedings, such as their first (and only the first) appeal, and probation and parole revocation hearings. The Supreme Court has also extended the right to counsel to juveniles in juvenile court proceedings.

A defendant may waive the right to counsel and appear on his or her own behalf. However, given the technical nature of criminal cases and the stakes involved (an individual's freedom!), anyone arrested for a crime is well advised to secure the assistance of counsel at the earliest opportunity. The phone call routinely given to arrested suspects at the police station is for the specific purpose of obtaining counsel. If a suspect cannot afford an attorney and is accused of either a felony or a misdemeanor for which imprisonment could be the result of conviction, the state is required to provide an attorney at the state's expense.

Lawyers are sometimes vilified by the media and the public for defending people unquestionably guilty of crimes. That lawyers sometimes succeed in getting guilty persons "off" by the skillful use of "legal technicalities" only makes matters worse. However, what some people fail to understand is that in the American system of justice, it is not the role of defense lawyers to decide their clients' guilt or innocence. Rather, the role of defense lawyers is to provide the best possible legal counsel and advocacy within the legal and ethical limits of the profession. Legal and ethical codes forbid lawyers, for example, to mislead the court by providing false information or by using perjured testimony (false testimony under oath). The American system of justice is based on the premise that a person is innocent until proven guilty. In the attempt to ensure, as far as possible, that innocent people are not found guilty of crimes, all persons charged with crimes are entitled to a rigorous defense. The constitutional right to counsel and our adversarial system of justice would be meaningless if lawyers refused to defend clients that they "knew" were guilty.

Not all lawyers are adequately trained to practice in the specialized field of criminal law. Law schools generally require only a one-semester course in criminal law and a one-semester course in criminal procedure, though additional courses may be taken as electives in a typical six-semester or three-year program. Many lawyers prefer to practice other, often more lucrative areas of law, such as corporate, tax, or tort law. Compared with those other areas of legal practice, the practice of criminal law generally provides its practitioner less income, prestige, and status in the community.

Public Opinion and Lawyers

In 1999, only 13 percent of Americans rated the honesty and ethical standards of lawyers "high" (12 percent) or "very high" (1 percent), 45 percent rated lawyers' honesty and ethical standards "average," 41 percent rated them "low" (28 percent) or "very low" (13 percent).

SOURCE: Sourcebook of Criminal Justice Statistics, Online, Table 2.23.

For those reasons, criminal defendants in search of counsel are limited by practical considerations. They can choose a privately retained lawyer who specializes in criminal law, if they can afford one. Or, if they are indigent and cannot afford one, they will receive a court-appointed attorney (who may or may not be skilled in the practice of criminal law), a public defender, or a "contract" lawyer. In large cities, there is little problem in locating a criminal lawyer. They are listed in the Yellow Pages of the local telephone book. In rural areas, however, finding a lawyer who specializes in criminal law may be more difficult. Because of the lower volume of criminal cases in rural areas, attorneys who practice in those areas generally must practice all kinds of law to make a living; they cannot afford to specialize. Outside of large cities, then, a criminal defendant may have no better option than to rely on the services of a court-appointed attorney, a public defender, or a contract lawyer, whichever is provided in that particular jurisdiction.

During the mid-1990s, about three-fourths of the inmates in state prisons and about half of those in federal prisons received publicly provided legal counsel. Among all prosecutorial districts, 28 percent used a public defender program exclusively, 23 percent employed assigned counsel exclusively, and 8 percent utilized contract attorneys exclusively. Forty-one percent of prosecutors' offices reported that a combination of methods was used in their jurisdictions. The most prevalent, used in 23 percent of jurisdictions, was a combination of an assigned-counsel system and a public defender program.[20] Court-appointed attorneys, public defenders, and contract lawyers will be discussed later in this section.

Criminal Lawyers   In discussing privately retained criminal lawyers, it is useful to think of a continuum. At one end are a very few nationally known, highly paid, and successful criminal lawyers, such as Gerry Spence, Johnnie Cochran Jr., and Alan Dershowitz. Those criminal lawyers generally take only three kinds of cases: (1) those that are sensational or highly publicized, (2) those that promise to make new law, or (3) those that involve large fees. A little further along the continuum is another small group of criminal

Wrongful Convictions

An estimated 36,250 people are convicted wrongfully in American courts every year.

SOURCE: Based on figures provided in C. Ronald Huff, Arye Rattner, and Edward Sagarin, "Guilty Until Proven Innocent: Wrongful Conviction and Public Policy," *Crime and Delinquency*, Vol. 32 (1986), pp. 518–44, and U.S. Department of Justice, Federal Bureau of Investigation, *Crime in the United States*, 1998 (Washington, DC: GPO, 1999) p. 210.

▲ From left to right, Johnnie Cochran Jr., Gerry Spence, and Alan Dershowitz are among the very few nationally known, highly paid, and successful criminal lawyers. *What do you think distinguishes these lawyers from all other lawyers?*

lawyers, those who make a very comfortable living in the large cities of this country by defending professional criminals, such as organized crime members, gamblers, pornographers, and drug dealers. Toward the other end of the continuum are the vast majority of criminal lawyers who practice in the large cities of this country.

Most criminal lawyers must struggle to earn a decent living. They have to handle a large volume of cases to make even a reasonable salary. To attract clients, some criminal lawyers engage in the unethical practice of paying kickbacks to ambulance drivers, police officers, jailers, and bail bonds people for client referrals. Some criminal lawyers also engage in the unethical practice of soliciting new clients in courthouse hallways.

Although a few criminal lawyers are known for their criminal trial expertise, most relatively successful criminal lawyers gain their reputations from their ability to "fix" cases, that is, their ability to produce the best possible outcome for a client, given the circumstances of the case. Fixing cases usually involves plea bargaining but may also include the strategic use of motions for continuances and for changes in the judge assigned to the case. *Who* a lawyer knows is often more important than *what* the lawyer knows. In other words, a close personal relationship with the prosecutor or a hearing before the "right" judge is often far more important to the case's outcome (for example, a favorable plea bargain) than is an attorney's legal ability.

Besides legal expertise and good relationships with other actors in the adjudication process, the only other commodity criminal lawyers have to sell is their time. Thus, for the typical criminal lawyer, time is valuable. As a result, criminal lawyers try to avoid time-consuming court battles and are motivated to get their clients to plead guilty to reduced charges.

Another reason most criminal lawyers prefer plea bargaining to trials is that they are more likely to receive a fee, however small, from their typically poor clients for arranging the plea. When cases go to trial and the legal fee has not been paid in advance, there is the possibility that the lawyer will receive no compensation or inadequate compensation from his or her client, especially if the case is lost.

To prevent nonpayment for services, criminal lawyers sometimes engage in unethical, if not illegal, behavior. Sometimes criminal lawyers plea-bargain cases that they know they can win at trial. They do this because they know that their clients do not have the money to compensate them for the time they would put into a trial. If clients have only a few hundred dollars, some unscrupulous criminal lawyers reason that those clients can afford only "bargain" justice. Another unethical tactic employed by some criminal lawyers to secure a fee from their clients is to seek delays in a case and allow their clients to remain in jail until they have been paid for services yet to be performed. Getting a client to pay a legal fee is not a legitimate basis for seeking a court delay.

Criminal lawyers often spend more time at the county jail and the courthouse, where their clients are, than in their offices, which generally are spartan compared with the plush offices of their corporate counterparts. They are sometimes told by their clients about grisly crimes that have been committed or will be committed in the future. Because of attorney-client privilege, the lawyer in possession of this information cannot reveal it, under penalty of disbarment (the revocation of his or her license to practice law). In short, many criminal lawyers are considered somewhat less than respectable by their professional colleagues and much of the general public because their clients are "criminals," they deal with some of the more unsavory aspects of human existence, and a few may engage in unethical behavior to earn a living.

The Court-Appointed Lawyer   In some jurisdictions, criminal suspects or defendants who cannot afford to hire an attorney are provided with court-appointed lawyers. The court-appointed lawyer is usually selected in one of two ways. In some jurisdictions, lawyers volunteer to represent indigent offenders and are appointed by judges on a rotating basis from a list or from lawyers present in the courtroom. In other jurisdictions, lawyers are appointed by a judge from a list of attorneys who are members of the county bar association.

In the past, appointed lawyers frequently represented indigent clients *pro bono* (without pay). Today, however, the vast majority of appointed lawyers are paid by the jurisdiction. Hourly fees are usually much less than would be charged by privately retained counsel. Seldom is money available to hire investigators or to secure the services of expert witnesses, the lack of which weakens the defense that can be provided a client.

In addition, although appointed attorneys may be experts in some areas of law, they may not be familiar with the intricacies of a criminal defense. They may have never before represented a client charged with a crime. Nevertheless, many lawyers view their appointments as a public service and do their best to represent their clients in a professional manner. Some, however, take cases grudgingly (they can refuse an appointment only for very good reasons) and regard an appointment as a financially unrewarding and unpleasant experience. They perform well enough only to escape charges of malpractice. In many cases, an appointed attorney first meets his or her client in the courtroom, where they have a brief conference before a guilty plea is arranged.

The Public Defender   In many jurisdictions today, people who are charged with crimes and cannot afford an attorney are provided with public

Female Lawyers

In 1971, just 3 percent of all lawyers were female. By 1980, the percentage of women lawyers had increased to 8 percent, and by 1998, 28.5 percent of all (non-government) lawyers were women. Moreover, 43.5 percent of all law degrees conferred in 1996 went to women. Despite those increases and the fact that women hold some of the nation's top legal jobs (including two U.S. Supreme Court Justices), women still face bias in the legal profession. According to a report by the American Bar Association (ABA), only 13 percent of law firm partners in 1994 were women, although women made up 39 percent of associate lawyers. The report also noted that female corporate lawyers generally were paid less than their male counterparts.

SOURCE: "Despite Gains, Women Lawyers Still Face Bias," *The Orlando Sentinel,* August 18, 1996, p. A-20; U.S. Census Bureau, Statistical Abstract of the United States: 1999 (119th edition) (Washington, DC: 1999), p. 424, no. 675.

▲ Defense lawyers spend much of their time at the local jail. *Do you think that the jail setting influences a lawyer's opinion of his or her client?*

277

defenders. Public defenders are paid a fixed salary by a jurisdiction (city, county, state, or federal) to defend indigents charged with crimes. Frequently, public defenders are assigned to courtrooms instead of to specific clients. They defend all of the indigent clients who appear in their courtrooms. As a result, a defendant may have a different public defender at different stages in the process (for example, preliminary hearing, arraignment, and trial). Public defenders commonly spend only five to ten minutes with their clients. In addition, this bureaucratic arrangement makes the public defender a part of a courtroom work group that includes the judge, the prosecutor, and the other courtroom actors with whom the public defender interacts daily. This work group, in turn, may be more interested in processing cases efficiently and maintaining cooperative relationships with each other than in pursuing adversarial justice. Nevertheless, despite the method of assignment, the impersonal nature of the defense, and the potential conflict of interest, most indigent clients in criminal cases prefer public defenders to court-appointed attorneys because public defenders practice criminal law full-time.

Like prosecutors, many public defenders regard their position not as a career, but as a valuable learning experience that will eventually lead to private law practice.

The Contract Lawyer A relatively new and increasingly popular way of providing for indigent defense is the contract system. In this system, private attorneys, law firms, and bar associations bid for the right to represent a jurisdiction's indigent defendants. Terms of contracts differ, but in the typical contract, counsel agrees to represent either all or a specified number of indigent defendants in a jurisdiction during a certain period of time, in exchange for a fixed dollar amount. Contracts are awarded on the basis of costs to the jurisdiction, qualifications of bidders, and other factors.

In certain situations, some jurisdictions employ a combination of indigent defense systems. For example, jurisdictions that regularly use public defenders sometimes contract out the defense of cases where there is a conflict of interest (for example, multiple-defendant cases) or cases that require special expertise (such as some death penalty cases).

The Judge

For most people, black-robed judges are the embodiment of justice, and although they are generally associated with trials, judges actually have a variety of responsibilities in the criminal justice process.[21] Among their nontrial duties are determining probable cause, signing warrants, informing suspects of their rights, setting and revoking bail, arraigning defendants, and accepting guilty pleas. Judges spend much of the workday in their chambers (offices), negotiating procedures and dispositions with prosecutors and defense attorneys. The principal responsibility of judges in all their duties is

MYTH

Crafty defense attorneys help criminals escape conviction.

FACT

Although this may be true in a very small fraction of cases, most felony cases are handled by conscientious but overworked public defenders.

Public Defenders

In many jurisdictions, public defenders represent up to 85 percent of all criminal defendants. Public defenders represent approximately 60 percent of all indigent defendants nationwide. (Another 22 percent of indigent defendants nationwide are represented by assigned counsel.) In some jurisdictions, indigency is determined by the examination of tax returns or the filing of affidavits documenting resources. Generally, defendants are deemed indigent if their resources place them below the government's official poverty level. In other jurisdictions, indigency is determined simply by defendants' response to the judge's question whether they can afford an attorney.

SOURCE: See, for example, Steven K. Smith and Carol J. DeFrances, "Indigent Defense," U.S. Department of Justice, *Bureau of Justice Statistics Selected Findings* (Washington, DC: GPO, February 1996), Table 8.

to ensure that suspects and defendants are treated fairly and in accordance with due process of law.

Furthermore, in jurisdictions without professional court administrators, judges are responsible for the management of their own courtrooms and staff. Judges in some jurisdictions are also responsible for the entire courthouse and its personnel, with the added duties of supervising building maintenance, budgeting, and labor relations.

In jury trials, judges are responsible for allowing the jury a fair chance to reach a verdict on the evidence presented. Judges must ensure that their behavior does not improperly affect the outcome of the case. Before juries retire to deliberate and reach a verdict, judges instruct them on the relevant law. This involves interpreting legal precedents and applying them to the unique circumstances of the case. Those jury instructions are reviewable by an appellate court.

Characteristics of Judges   In the United States, judges are overwhelmingly white and male. They generally come from upper middle-class backgrounds, are Protestant, are better educated than most citizens, and average over 50 years of age. A majority of them were in private legal practice before becoming judges. Most were born in the communities in which they preside and attended college and law school in that state.

Selection of Judges   States vary in the ways they select judges. The two most common selection methods are election and merit selection. Other, less common, ways of selecting judges are gubernatorial appointment and legislative election.

Like prosecutors, many state judges are elected to their positions in either partisan (with political party designation) or nonpartisan elections. This selection process exposes judges, like prosecutors, to potential charges of political influence. It may also discourage some of the best lawyers from becoming judges. Successful lawyers with lucrative practices may not want to interrupt their careers to take the chance of becoming a judge, only to lose the position in the next election. Besides, successful lawyers generally earn much more money than judges.

▲ Judges spend much of their workday in their chambers (offices). *How does this differ from what the public generally believes about judges?*

In an attempt to reduce the appearance of possible political influence, several states have adopted merit selection, sometimes referred to as the "Missouri Plan," as their method of selecting judges. First used in Missouri in 1940, merit selection is a process in which the governor appoints judges from a list of qualified lawyers compiled by a nonpartisan nominating commission composed of both lawyers and other citizens. After serving a short term on the bench, usually one year, the appointed judges face the voters in an uncontested election. Voters are instructed to vote yes or no on whether the judge should be retained in office. If a majority vote yes, the judge remains in office for a full term (usually six years; the range is four years to life). In Illinois, a judge must receive at least 60 percent of the votes. Toward the end of the term, the judge must face the voters again in the same kind of election. The merit plan does not entirely eliminate political influence from the selection process, it seems to have less potential for influence than the direct popular election of judges.

- As of July 1999, states used the following methods for initially selecting their highest *appellate court judges:*
  Merit selection—23 states (and the District of Columbia)
  Nonpartisan election—13 states
  Partisan election—8 states
  Appointment by the governor—4 states
  Election by the legislature—1 state
  Judicial selection committee—1 state

- As of the same date, states used the following methods for initially selecting their *general-jurisdiction court judges:*
  Nonpartisan election—17 states
  Merit selection—17 states (and the District of Columbia)
  Partisan election—12 states
  Appointment by the governor—4 states
  Election by the legislature—1 state
  In California, local voters can choose either nonpartisan elections or gubernatorial appointment of general-jurisdiction court judges.[22]

Qualifications and Training   Although in most jurisdictions lower-court judges are not required to be lawyers or to possess any special educational or professional training, nearly all states require judges who sit on the benches of appellate courts and trial courts of general jurisdiction to be licensed attorneys and members of the state bar association. However, being a lawyer is not the same as being a judge. Many judges come to the bench without any practical experience with criminal law or procedure. Consequently, many states now require new appellate court and trial court judges to attend state-sponsored judicial training seminars. In addition, more than 1,500 judges a year take one- to four-week summer courses offered by the National Judicial College, founded in 1963 and located at the University of Nevada, Reno. Despite those efforts, most judges still learn the intricacies of their profession "on the job."

8.3 CRITICAL THINKING

1. Of the key actors in the administration of justice, which one, in your opinion, wields the most power?

2. Of the different types of attorneys a defendant might have, which one do you think will do the best job of defending the accused? Why?

8.4 Pretrial Stages

As described in Chapter 2, probably fewer than one-half of the crimes committed each year are reported to the police, and of those, only a fraction are officially recorded. Of the crimes that are recorded by the police, only about 20 percent are "cleared by arrest." Still, an arrest by no means guarantees prosecution and conviction. As a result of initial prosecutorial screening, for example, about 25 percent of all arrests are rejected, diverted, or referred to other jurisdictions. Another 20 percent or so of all people arrested are released later for various reasons during one of the pretrial stages. Thus a powerful "funneling" or screening process in the administration of justice eliminates about one-half of all persons arrested. Figures 8–4 and 8–5 illustrate this funneling or screening process.

The pretrial stages do not have the same names or order in every jurisdiction. So what follows should be considered only a general overview. States are required to provide only a prompt, neutral review of the evidence to

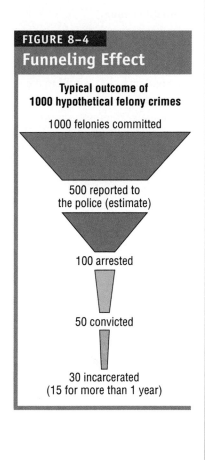

FIGURE 8–4
Funneling Effect

Typical outcome of 1000 hypothetical felony crimes

1000 felonies committed

500 reported to the police (estimate)

100 arrested

50 convicted

30 incarcerated (15 for more than 1 year)

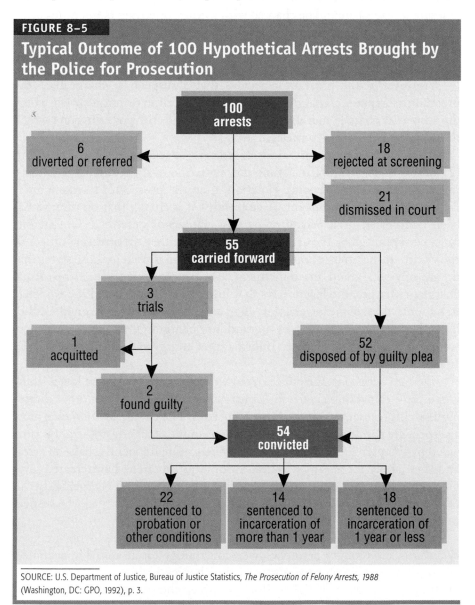

FIGURE 8–5
Typical Outcome of 100 Hypothetical Arrests Brought by the Police for Prosecution

100 arrests

6 diverted or referred

18 rejected at screening

21 dismissed in court

55 carried forward

3 trials

52 disposed of by guilty plea

1 acquitted

2 found guilty

54 convicted

22 sentenced to probation or other conditions

14 sentenced to incarceration of more than 1 year

18 sentenced to incarceration of 1 year or less

SOURCE: U.S. Department of Justice, Bureau of Justice Statistics, *The Prosecution of Felony Arrests, 1988* (Washington, DC: GPO, 1992), p. 3.

determine whether there is probable cause that the suspect/defendant committed the crime or crimes with which he or she is charged. **Probable cause,** which was described in more detail in Chapter 4, is an abstract term that basically means that a law enforcement officer or a judge has trustworthy evidence that would make a reasonable person believe that, more likely than not, the proposed action, such as an arrest, is justified. Figure 1–2 in Chapter 1 provides a simplified view of the case flow through the criminal justice process, highlighting pretrial stages. We will describe the pretrial stages typical of many jurisdictions in the following sections.[23]

From Arrest Through Initial Appearance

Soon after most suspects are arrested, they are taken to the police station to be "booked." **Booking** is the process in which suspects' names, the charges for which they were arrested, and perhaps their fingerprints or photographs are entered on the police blotter. Following booking, a prosecutor is asked to review the facts of the case and, considering the available evidence, to decide whether a suspect should be charged with a crime or crimes (sometimes prosecutors review a case prior to the arrest). As a result of the review, the prosecutor may tell the police that they do not have a case or that the case is weak, requiring further investigation and additional evidence.

However, if the prosecutor decides that a suspect is "chargeable," the prosecutor prepares a charging document. The crime or crimes with which the suspect is charged may or may not be the same crime or crimes for which the suspect was originally arrested.

There are three primary kinds of charging documents: (1) a complaint, (2) an information, and (3) a grand jury indictment. If the offense is either a misdemeanor or an ordinance violation, then the prosecutor in many jurisdictions prepares a complaint. A **complaint** is a charge that an offense has been committed by a person or persons named or described. Complaints must be supported by the oath or affirmation of either the arresting officer or the victim. If the offense is a felony, an information is used in those states that do not rely on a grand jury indictment. An **information** outlines the formal charge or charges, the law or laws that have been violated, and the evidence to support the charge or charges. A **grand jury indictment,** on the other hand, is a written accusation by a grand jury charging that one or more persons have committed a crime. Informations and grand juries are described later in this section.

On rare occasions, the police obtain an arrest warrant from a lower-court judge prior to making an arrest. An **arrest warrant** is a written order directing law enforcement officers to arrest a person. The charge or charges against a suspect are specified on the warrant. An example of an arrest warrant is provided in Chapter 4, Figure 4–5. Police officers more frequently make an arrest and then apply for an arrest warrant. Some jurisdictions have created joint police-prosecution teams so that decisions about arrest and chargeability can be coordinated and can be made early on. If no charges are filed, the suspect must be released.

After the charge or charges have been filed, suspects, who are now *defendants,* are brought before a lower-court judge for an initial appearance, where they are given formal notice of the charges against them and advised of their constitutional rights (for example, the right to counsel). For misdemeanors or ordinance violations, a summary trial may be held. About 75 percent of misdemeanants and ordinance violators plead guilty at the initial appearance and are sentenced on the spot. For felonies, a hearing is held to determine whether the suspect should be released or whether there is probable cause to hold the suspect for a preliminary hearing. If the suspect is to be held for a preliminary hearing, bail may be set if the judge believes release on bail is appropriate.

One of the critical questions about the initial appearance is how long suspects may be held in jail before being brought before a judge. In some countries the answer to the question is "indefinitely," but in the United States there is a limit so that innocent persons are not left in jail too long. If suspects are freed after having posted station-house bail (based on a bail fee schedule for minor offenses posted at the police station), then the initial appearance may be several days after the arrest. However, if suspects remain in custody (the usual scenario), they must be brought for an initial appearance "without unnecessary delay." In 1975, in *Gerstein v. Pugh*, the Supreme Court held that a "prompt" judicial hearing is required in a warrantless arrest to determine if the officer had probable cause to make the arrest. The vast majority of arrests are warrantless. If suspects are not brought before a judge promptly, then they are to be released. The one exception to this requirement is suspects arrested on a Friday night and not brought before a judge until Monday morning.

A problem with the Supreme Court's promptness requirement is that the Court did not define *prompt*. The norm in most jurisdictions was between 24 and 72 hours. Even after the ruling, however, some jurisdictions held suspects much longer than that. For example, in 1975, a district court judge in Birmingham, Alabama, ruled that because of abusive holding practices in that city, suspects arrested on a felony charge could not be held longer than 24 hours. In 1984, the same judge set a new limit of eight hours for holding suspects, because his previous order had been ignored. The judge added, however, that in certain cases a limited time extension could be obtained. In 1991, in *County of Riverside v. McLaughlin*, the Supreme Court finally clarified the situation by ruling that anyone arrested without a warrant may be held no longer than 48 hours before a judge decides whether the arrest was justified.

Bail and Other Methods of Pretrial Release

A **bail bond** or **bail** is usually a monetary guarantee deposited with the court that is supposed to ensure that the suspect or defendant will appear at a later stage in the criminal justice process. In other words, it allows suspects or defendants to remain free while awaiting the next stage in the adjudication process. It is *not* a fine or a penalty; it is only an incentive to appear. Opportunities for bail follow arrest, initial appearance, preliminary hearing, arraignment, and conviction.

Although bail-setting practices vary widely by jurisdiction, the amount of bail, assuming that bail is granted, generally depends on the likelihood that the suspect or defendant will appear in court as required. If the suspect or defendant has strong ties to the community—for example, a house, a family, or a job—then the amount of bail will be relatively low (depending on the seriousness of the offense and other factors). However, if the suspect or defendant has few or no ties to the community, the amount of bail will be relatively high, or the judge may refuse to grant bail.

Bail

The granting of bail and pretrial release to criminal suspects was common practice in England by the twelfth century. It was officially recognized and legally regulated by the Statute of Westminster in 1275.

SOURCE: No author, "Bail: An Ancient Practice Reexamined," *Yale Law Journal*, Vol. 70 (1961), pp. 966-77.

CRIMINAL JUSTICE Online

Bail Agents

You can learn more about how bail agents work by clicking on the link for The Professional Bail Agents of the United States at cj.glencoe.com. Once at the site, review the code of ethics for bail agents. *What does the code of ethics tell you about the different responsibilities of a bail agent?*

bail bond/bail
Usually a monetary guarantee deposited with the court that is supposed to ensure that the suspect or defendant will appear at a later stage in the criminal justice process.

preventive detention

Holding suspects or defendants in jail without giving them an opportunity to post bail, because of the threat they pose to society.

Next to likelihood of appearance, the most important factor in a judge's determination of the amount of bail—and, perhaps, whether bail is granted at all—is the seriousness of the crime. Generally, the more serious the crime, the higher the bail amount. A third influence on the amount of bail is prior criminal record. A prior criminal record usually increases the amount of bail. Jail conditions are a fourth influencing factor—at least on whether bail is set. If the jail is overcrowded, as are many of the jails in the United States, judges are more likely to grant bail, particularly in borderline cases.

In rare cases, when a judge believes that a suspect or defendant would pose a threat to the community if released, the judge can refuse to set bail. Holding suspects or defendants in jail without giving them an opportunity to post bail, because of the threat they pose to society, is called **preventive detention.** Preventive detention is used most often in cases involving violent crimes, drug crimes, and immigration offenses. However, in *U.S. v. Salerno* (1987), the Supreme Court made clear that before a judge can legally deny bail for reasons of preventive detention, a suspect or defendant must have the opportunity for a hearing on the decision. At the hearing, the individual circumstances of the suspect or defendant (such as community ties, convictions, and past dangerous tendencies) must be considered. About 60 percent of all states and the federal jurisdiction have enacted laws that provide for some form of preventive detention, although the laws, at least at the state level, are rarely implemented. The reason is that they are unnecessary. Judges have traditionally imposed high bail amounts on dangerous suspects or defendants. Preventive detention has been employed more frequently at the federal level.

MYTH

Preventive detention will reduce violent crime.

FACT

Preventive detention is not new and has always been used by judges in the United States, even though it was not referred to by that name. Judges simply set bail at a level beyond the financial means of a person suspected of violent crime.

For suspects or defendants who cannot afford to post bail, professional bonds people, who are private entrepreneurs, are available to post it for them for a nonrefundable fee. The fee is typically ten percent of the required amount. Thus, a bonds person would collect $500 for posting a $5,000 bond. If a suspect or a defendant is considered a greater than average risk, then the bonds person can require collateral—something of value like money or property—in addition to the fee.

Bail bonds people are under no obligation to post a surety bond if they believe that a suspect or a defendant is a bad risk. If bonds people believe that a client might flee and not appear as required, they have the right to revoke the bond without refunding the fee. Bail bonds people or their agents (modern-day bounty hunters known as "skip tracers") are also allowed, without a warrant, to track down clients who fail to appear and to return them forcibly, if necessary, to the jurisdiction from which they fled. If the client crosses state lines, the bonds person does not have to seek extradition, as would a law enforcement official, to bring the client back. Clients sign extradition waivers as a condition of receiving bail.

▲ Without the cooperation of the bail bond industry, jail populations would be unmanageable. *Is that reason enough to allow the bail bond industry to exist?*

Release on Bail

About 85 percent of all suspects or defendants are released prior to the final disposition of their cases, but in some jurisdictions, as many as 90 percent of them are held in jail because they are unable to afford bail.

In practice, most bail bonds people assume little risk. Many of them use part of their fee (generally 30 percent) to secure a surety bond from a major insurance company, which then assumes financial liability if the bail is forfeited. However, even this practice is unnecessary in many jurisdictions because the courts do not collect forfeited bonds. Judges are able to use their discretion to simply vacate outstanding bonds and, by doing so, relieve the bail bonds person or the insurance company of any financial obligation. Judges vacate bonds because they realize that without the cooperation of bail bonds people, the courts would be faced with an unmanageably large jail population and prohibitively high pretrial detention costs.

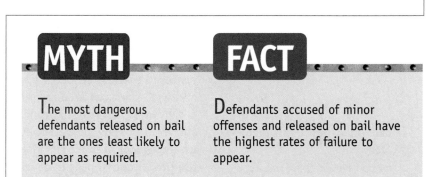

MYTH

The most dangerous defendants released on bail are the ones least likely to appear as required.

FACT

Defendants accused of minor offenses and released on bail have the highest rates of failure to appear.

Suspects or defendants who post their own bail ("full cash bond," 100 percent of the amount required), or have family members or friends do it for them, get it all back after they appear. Sometimes the court will accept property instead of cash. If the suspect or defendant does not appear, the bail is forfeited and the judge issues a **bench warrant** or *capias* authorizing the suspect's or defendant's arrest. Once arrested, the absconder must be brought before the judge who issued the warrant and cannot be released on bail again. Failure to appear also constitutes a new offense, "bond jumping," that carries criminal penalties.

Courts in Illinois, Kentucky, and Pennsylvania, as well as the federal courts, allow defendants to post ten percent of the required bond (*deposit bond*) directly with the court, thereby circumventing the need for bail bonds people. When a defendant makes all required court appearances, 90 percent

bench warrant or *capias*
A document that authorizes a suspect's or defendant's arrest for not appearing in court as required.

of the amount posted is refunded (the remaining 10 percent covers administrative costs). Defendants who fail to appear are still liable for the entire bail amount.

As noted in Chapter 4, the Eighth Amendment to the Constitution does not require that bail be granted to all suspects or defendants. It requires only that the amount of bail, when granted, not be excessive. What constitutes excessive bail is determined by several factors, including the nature and circumstances of the offense, the weight of evidence against the suspect/defendant, the character of the suspect/defendant, and the ability of the suspect/defendant to provide bail.

The bail system has been criticized for unfairly discriminating against the poor, who are the least likely to have the assets for their own bail and are least able to pay the fee to a bail bonds person. In most jurisdictions, defendants held in jail because they are unable to post bail (about one-half of the jail population nationwide) are mixed with the rest of the jail population, that is, convicted offenders. They are also treated in the same way as the rest of the jail population. One of the tragedies of this practice is the occasional brutalization (for example, rape) of the jailed indigent defendant whose case is later dismissed for lack of evidence or who is found not guilty at trial. Although brutalization of any prisoner is horrible and reprehensible, it is particularly so when the prisoner is an innocent person.

Jailed indigent defendants are also likely to lose their jobs and have their personal lives disrupted in other ways as a result of their detention. Studies consistently show that jailed defendants, who are frequently brought into court in jail clothes and handcuffs, are more likely to be indicted and convicted and are sentenced more severely than defendants who have been released pending the next stage in the process. However, it is not clear whether those disparities are the result of pretrial detention or of the selection process in which suspects or defendants charged with more serious crimes and with prior criminal records are more likely to be denied bail.

When the crime is minor and suspects or defendants have ties to the community, they are generally released on their own recognizance. **Release on own recognizance (ROR)** is simply a release secured by a suspect's written promise to appear in court. Another nonfinancial means of release, more restrictive than ROR, is **conditional release.** This form of release (sometimes called *supervised release*) usually requires that a suspect/defendant maintain contact with a pretrial release program or undergo regular drug monitoring or treatment. Some conditional release programs also require a third-party custody agreement (that is, a promise by a reputable person to monitor the person released). Another way that suspects or defendants are released without a financial requirement is by **unsecured bond.** Under this arrangement, bail is set, but no money is paid to the court. Suspects or defendants are liable for the full amount of bail if they do not appear as required.

Information

As noted previously, if the decision is made to prosecute a defendant, in states that do not use grand juries, the prosecutor drafts a document called an *information*. The information outlines the formal charge or charges, the law or laws that have been violated, and the evidence to support the charge or

release on own recognizance (ROR)

A release secured by a suspect's written promise to appear in court.

conditional release

A form of release that requires that a suspect/defendant maintain contact with a pretrial release program or undergo regular drug monitoring or treatment.

unsecured bond

An arrangement in which bail is set but no money is paid to the court.

charges. The information is generally filed with the court at the preliminary hearing or, if the preliminary hearing is waived, at the arraignment.

Preliminary Hearing

The purpose of the **preliminary hearing,** used in about one-half of all states, is for a judge to determine whether there is probable cause to support the charge or charges imposed by the prosecutor. Preliminary hearings are used only in felony cases, and defendants may waive the right to the hearing. A preliminary hearing is similar to a criminal trial in two ways but also differs from a criminal trial in two ways. It is similar in that defendants can be represented by legal counsel and can call witnesses on their behalf. It differs in that the judge must determine only that there is probable cause that the defendant committed the crime or crimes with which he or she is charged. At criminal trials, guilt must be determined "beyond a reasonable doubt." Also, at preliminary hearings, unlike criminal trials, defendants have no right to be heard by a jury.

If the judge determines that there is probable cause that a defendant committed the crime or crimes with which he or she is charged, then the defendant is bound over for possible indictment in states with grand juries or for arraignment on an information in states without grand juries. In grand jury states, even if the judge at the preliminary hearing rules that there is insufficient evidence to proceed, the case is not necessarily dropped. The prosecutor could take the case directly to the grand jury. If the case is not dropped for lack of evidence, then the judge may set bail again or may continue the previous bail to ensure that the defendant appears at the next stage in the process.

Although judges at preliminary hearings are supposed to examine the facts of the case before making a probable cause determination, in practice they seldom do. In big cities, judges do not generally have the time to inquire into the facts of a case. Consequently, at most preliminary hearings, judges simply assume that if a police officer made an arrest and a prosecutor charged the defendant with a crime or crimes, then there must be probable cause that the defendant, in fact, committed the crime or crimes. Few cases are dismissed for lack of probable cause at preliminary hearings.

Grand Jury

A **grand jury** is generally a group of 12 to 23 citizens who, for a specific period of time (generally three months), meet in closed sessions to investigate charges coming from preliminary hearings or to engage in other responsibilities. Thus a primary purpose of the grand jury is to determine whether there is probable cause to believe that the accused is guilty of the charge or charges brought by the prosecutor. Grand juries are involved in felony prosecutions in about half the states and in the federal system. The alternative to the grand jury is the filing of an information.

Before appearing before a grand jury, the prosecutor drafts an **indictment,** a document that outlines the charge or charges against a defendant. Because the grand jury has to determine only whether there is probable cause that a defendant committed the crime or crimes with which he or she is charged, only the prosecution's evidence and witnesses are heard. In most jurisdictions, neither the defendant nor the defendant's counsel has a right to

preliminary hearing
A pretrial stage used in about one-half of all states and only in felony cases. Its purpose is for a judge to determine whether there is probable cause to support the charge or charges imposed by the prosecutor.

Preliminary Hearings
In some jurisdictions, preliminary hearings are frequently waived by defendants. Perhaps the best example is the federal courts, where the majority of criminal cases begin with a grand jury indictment rather than with an arrest.

grand jury
Generally a group of 12 to 23 citizens who meet in closed sessions to investigate charges coming from preliminary hearings or to engage in other responsibilities. A primary purpose of the grand jury is to determine whether there is probable cause to believe that the accused committed the crime or crimes.

indictment
A document that outlines the charge or charges against a defendant.

subpoena
A written order to testify issued by a court officer.

be present during the proceedings. Furthermore, in grand jury proceedings, unlike criminal trials, prosecutors are allowed to present *hearsay* evidence (information learned from someone other than the witness who is testifying). They may also use illegally obtained evidence because the exclusionary rule does not apply to grand jury proceedings. Prosecutors can subpoena witnesses to testify. A **subpoena** is a written order to testify issued by a court officer. A witness who refuses to testify can be held in contempt and can be jailed until he or she provides the requested information. In practice, however, a witness jailed for contempt is generally held only as long as the grand jury is in session and no longer than 18 months in the federal jurisdiction.

After hearing the prosecutor's evidence and witnesses, the grand jury makes its probable cause determination and, usually on a majority vote, either indicts (issues a *true bill*) or fails to indict (issues *no bill*). If the grand jury fails to indict, then in most jurisdictions, the prosecution must be dropped. However, in some jurisdictions, the case can be brought before another grand jury.

In practice, the grand jury system is criticized for merely providing a rubber stamp for whatever the prosecutor wants to do. In other words, in cases where the prosecutor wants an indictment, the grand jury is likely to indict. Likewise, in cases where the prosecutor does not want to indict, the grand jury tends to fail to indict. The reason that prosecutors are so successful with grand juries is that they manage the entire proceedings (remember, only the prosecution's evidence and witnesses are heard). So it should not be surprising that suspects waive the right to a grand jury hearing in about 80 percent of cases. Defendants may also waive the right to a grand jury hearing to speed up their trial date.

You might be wondering why prosecutors would want a grand jury to fail to indict after they have gone to the trouble of bringing a case to the grand jury in the first place. The reason is political. To avoid losing marginal cases or looking cowardly by dropping charges, prosecutors can bring a case to the grand jury, have the grand jury fail to indict, and then blame the grand jury for its failure. The strategy deflects criticism from the prosecutor to the anonymous members of the grand jury. Sometimes prosecutors delay preliminary hearings to await a grand jury action to avoid disclosing evidence in open court that might help defense attorneys at trial. Because of the way the grand jury is used today, some critics of the system suggest that it ought to be abolished.

Arraignment

The primary purpose of an **arraignment** is to hear the formal information or indictment and to allow the defendant to enter a plea. The two most common pleas are "guilty" and "not guilty." "Not guilty" is the most common plea at arraignments. However, some states and the federal courts allow defendants to plead *nolo contendere* to the charges against them. ***Nolo contendere*** is Latin for "no contest." When defendants plead "*nolo*," they do not admit guilt but are willing to accept punishment anyway. The *nolo* plea is used for strategic purposes. If a defendant does not admit guilt in a criminal trial, admission of guilt cannot be the basis for a subsequent civil lawsuit. If there is a subsequent civil lawsuit, the lack of an admission of guilt in a criminal trial may allow the defendant to avoid a penalty of treble, or triple, damages. Furthermore, in some states, defendants can stand mute or can plead

Grand Jury Indictments

Fourteen states require grand jury indictments for all felony prosecutions and an additional four states require them for capital cases or life imprisonment cases. In the federal system, a grand jury indictment is required in all felony prosecutions, unless the defendant waives that right.

SOURCE: U.S. Department of Justice, *Bureau of Justice Statistics*, <www.ojp.usdoj.gov/bjs/courts.htm>.

arraignment
A pretrial stage; its primary purpose is to hear the formal information or indictment and to allow the defendant to enter a plea.

nolo contendere
Latin for "no contest." When defendants plead *nolo,* they do not admit guilt but are willing to accept punishment.

"not guilty by reason of insanity." Standing mute at arraignment is interpreted as pleading "not guilty." In states that do not accept a plea of "not guilty by reason of insanity," defendants plead "not guilty" and assume the burden of proving insanity at trial.

If a defendant pleads guilty, the judge must determine whether the plea was made voluntarily and whether the defendant is fully aware of the consequences of his or her action. If the judge doubts either of those conditions, then the judge can refuse to accept the guilty plea and can enter in the record a plea of "not guilty" for the defendant.

At arraignment, the judge also determines whether a defendant is competent to stand trial. Defendants can seek a delay before trial to consult further with their attorneys. A defendant who does not already have an attorney can ask for one to be appointed. Finally, defendants sometimes attempt to have their cases dismissed at arraignment. For example, they may assert that the state lacks sufficient evidence or that improper arrest procedures were used.

8.4 CRITICAL THINKING

Do you agree with the criticism that the poor are unfairly discriminated against because they are the least able to pay their own bail and the least able to pay the fee to a bail bonds person? Why or why not?

8.5 Plea Bargaining

As noted earlier in this chapter, justice in the United States is dispensed mostly through plea bargaining.[24] About 90 percent of all convictions in felony cases are the result of guilty pleas; criminal trials are relatively rare. We already saw in Figure 8–5 the typical outcome of 100 felony arrests and the prevalence of plea bargaining.

There are three basic types of plea bargains. First, the defendant may be allowed to plead guilty to a lesser offense. For example, a defendant may be allowed to plead guilty to manslaughter rather than to first-degree murder. Second, at the request of the prosecutor, a defendant who pleads guilty may receive a lighter sentence than would typically be given for the crime. Note, however, that the prosecutor can only recommend the sentence; the judge does not have to grant it. Third, a defendant may plead guilty to one charge in return for the prosecutor's promise to drop other charges that could be brought.

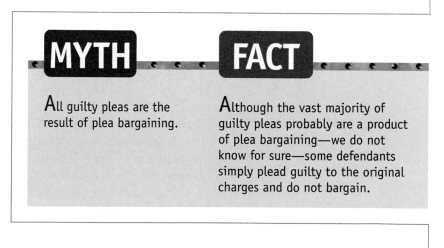

MYTH

All guilty pleas are the result of plea bargaining.

FACT

Although the vast majority of guilty pleas probably are a product of plea bargaining—we do not know for sure—some defendants simply plead guilty to the original charges and do not bargain.

The bargain a prosecutor will strike generally depends on three factors. The most important factor is the seriousness of the offense. Generally, the more serious the crime, the more difficult it is to win concessions from the prosecutor. A second factor is the defendant's criminal record. Defendants with criminal records usually receive fewer concessions from prosecutors. The final factor is the strength of the prosecutor's case. The stronger the case, the stronger is the position of the prosecutor in plea negotiations.

Surprisingly, there is neither a constitutional basis nor a statutory basis for plea bargaining. It is a custom that developed because of the mutual interests it serves. The custom received formal recognition from the Supreme Court in 1970 in the case of *Brady v. United States*. In that case, the Court upheld the use of plea bargaining because of the "mutuality of advantage" it provided the defendant and the state. In two later cases, the Court provided safeguards for the bargaining process. In the 1971 case of *Santobello v. New York*, the Court held that the "deal" offered by a prosecutor in a plea negotiation must be kept. In 1976, in the case of *Henderson v. Morgan*, the Court held that to be valid, a guilty plea must be based on full knowledge of its implications and must be made voluntarily. However, prosecutors are under no obligation to plea-bargain. Once defendants plead guilty and are sentenced, they are almost always stuck with the bargain, even if they have a change of heart. Nevertheless, in most jurisdictions, defendants are allowed to withdraw their guilty pleas before sentencing.

As just noted, the reason justice in the United States is administered primarily through plea bargaining is that the process seemingly serves the interests of all the court participants by, among other things, reducing uncertainty. Uncertainty is a characteristic of all criminal trials because neither the duration of the trial, which may be a matter of minutes or of months, nor the outcome of the trial can ever be predicted with any degree of accuracy. Plea bargaining eliminates those two areas of uncertainty by eliminating the need for a trial.

Plea bargaining also serves the interests of the individual participants in the administration of justice. Prosecutors, for example, are guaranteed high conviction rates. For prosecutors and, apparently, the general public, a conviction is a conviction, whether it is obtained through plea bargaining or as the result of a trial. A prosecutor's conviction rate is one of the principal indicators of job performance, and job performance certainly helps determine whether the prosecutor will fulfill his or her aspirations for higher political office.

Plea bargaining also serves the interests of judges by reducing their court caseloads, allowing more time to be spent on more difficult cases. In addition, if a large proportion of the approximately 90 percent of felony cases that are handled each year by plea bargaining were to go to trial instead, the administration of justice in the United States would be even slower than it already is.

Federal judges and the judges in seven states are legally prohibited from participating in plea negotiations. In other states, their role in the process is limited by law.

Plea bargaining serves the interests of criminal defense attorneys by allowing them to spend less time on each case. It also allows them to avoid trials. Trials are relatively expensive events. Because most criminal defendants are poor, they are usually unable to pay a large legal fee. Thus, when criminal defense attorneys go to trial, they are frequently unable to recoup all of their expenses.

Plea Bargaining
Plea bargaining became a common practice in state courts shortly after the Civil War. The practice was instituted at the federal level during Prohibition, in the 1930s, as a result of the tremendous number of liquor law violations.

SOURCES: Albert W. Alschuler, "Plea Bargaining and Its History," *Law and Society Review,* Vol. 13 (1979), pp. 211–45; John F. Padgett, "Plea Bargaining and Prohibition in the Federal Courts, 1908–1934," *Law and Society Review,* Vol. 24 (1990), pp. 413–50.

Even most criminal defendants are served by plea bargaining. A guilty plea generally results in either no prison sentence or a lesser prison sentence than the defendant might receive if found guilty at trial. Plea bargaining also often allows defendants to escape conviction of socially stigmatizing crimes, such as child abuse. By "copping" a plea to assault rather than to statutory rape, for example, a defendant can avoid the embarrassing publicity of a trial and the wrath of fellow inmates or of society in general.

Two types of criminal defendants are not served by the practice of plea bargaining. The first are innocent, indigent, highly visible defendants who fear being found guilty of crimes they did not commit and receiving harsh sentences. Such defendants are sometimes pressured by unscrupulous defense attorneys into waiving their constitutional right to trial.

The second type is the habitual offender. In this context, a habitual offender is a person who has been convicted under a state's habitual-offender statute (sometimes called a "three strikes and you're out" law). Most such statutes provide that upon conviction of a third felony, a defendant must receive life imprisonment. Although habitual-offender statutes would seem to imprison offenders for life, they actually are used mostly as bargaining chips by prosecutors in plea negotiations and not as they were intended.

A problem with those statutes is illustrated by the Supreme Court case of *Bordenkircher v. Hayes* (1978). The defendant, who had previously been convicted of two minor felonies, was arrested and charged with forging an $88 check. The prosecutor in the case told the defendant that if he did not plead guilty to the charge and accept a five-year prison sentence, which on its face seemed very harsh, then the prosecutor would invoke the state's habitual-offender statute. The statute required the judge to impose a sentence of life imprisonment if the defendant were found guilty at trial. The defendant elected to play "you bet your life" and turned down the prosecutor's plea offer. At trial, the defendant was found guilty of forging the check and was sentenced to life imprisonment. Clearly, the defendant in this case was not served by plea bargaining or, perhaps, was not served by refusing the prosecutor's offer. In either case, with the possible exception of habitual offenders and innocent people, plea bargaining serves the interests of all the actors in the administration of justice. It does so by allowing cases to be disposed of predictably, quickly, and with little of the adversarial conflict associated with criminal trials.

MYTH • • •

Abolishing plea bargaining would reduce the level of serious crime.

FACT • • •

Despite the administrative nightmare it would cause, the abolition of plea bargaining would probably only shift discretion to another area. It would be unlikely to have any effect on crime.

FYI

Three Strikes Law

Although habitual-offender statutes have existed in many jurisdictions for decades, the first state to enact a "three strikes and you're out" law was Washington, in 1993. The Washington law, called the Persistent Offender Accountability Act, allows three-time felons to be imprisoned for life without parole. In August 1996, the Washington Supreme Court upheld the law as constitutional.

SOURCE: "Washington Court Deems '3 Strikes' Constitutional," *The Orlando Sentinel,* August 9, 1996, p. A-12.

8.5 CRITICAL THINKING

1. Do you think that the plea-bargaining process is beneficial? Why or why not?

2. How could the plea-bargaining process be improved?

8.6 The Criminal Trial

One of the distinctive features of criminal justice in the United States is trial by a jury of one's peers.[25] The principal purpose of jury trials—and of criminal trials without juries—is to discover the truth of whether defendants are guilty or innocent of the crimes with which they are charged. The process by which truth is sought is an adversarial one regulated by very specific procedures and rules. The adversaries in a criminal trial are the state (represented by the prosecutor) and the defendant (usually represented by defense counsel). The burden of proof is on the prosecution to show, beyond a reasonable doubt, that the defendant is guilty. The goal of defense counsel is to discredit the prosecution's case and to create reasonable doubt about the defendant's guilt. It is the responsibility of the jury (in jury trials) or the judge (in trials without juries) to determine and assign guilt.

Although all criminal defendants have a constitutional right to a jury trial (when imprisonment for six months or more is a possible outcome), only about five percent of all criminal cases are disposed of in this way. Approximately 90 percent of cases are resolved through a guilty plea, as previously noted, and the remaining cases are decided by a judge in a **bench trial** (without a jury). In most jurisdictions, defendants may choose whether they want to exercise their right to a jury trial or whether they prefer a bench trial. Figure 8–6 on page 293 shows the type of conviction of felony defendants in 1996, by type of offense. The principal reason that so few criminal cases are decided by criminal trials is undoubtedly the advantages associated with plea bargaining.

The Jury

Trial by a jury of one's peers is an exalted American tradition.[26] Its principal purposes are:

1. To protect citizens against arbitrary law enforcement.

2. To prevent government oppression.

3. To protect citizens from overzealous or corrupt prosecutors and from eccentric or biased judges.

But jury trials in the United States are relatively rare. So on those rare occasions when defendants are tried by a jury, seldom is the jury composed of their peers. Until the mid-twentieth century, many states excluded women and people of color from jury service. Even today, class, gender, and racial biases enter into the jury selection process.

In many jurisdictions, jury pools are selected from voter registration lists. About 30 percent of eligible voters do not register; in some jurisdictions, the rate is as high as 60 percent. People not registered to vote are excluded from jury service. Studies show that the poor, the poorly educated, the young, and

---

MYTH

Criminal justice in the United States is dispensed primarily through jury trials.

FACT

Jury trials are relatively rare. Approximately 90 percent of all criminal cases are resolved through guilty pleas. Only about ten percent are decided by bench or jury trials.

---

bench trial

A trial before a judge without a jury.

FIGURE 8-6

Offenses of Felons Convicted in State Courts, by Type of Conviction, 1996

Most Serious Conviction Offense	Percent of Felons Convicted by—		
	Trial		Guilty Plea
	Jury	Bench	
All Offenses[a]	4%	5%	91%
Violent Offenses	11%	7%	83%
Murder[b]	40%	7%	54%
Sexual Assault[c]	11%	7%	81%
Robbery	10%	7%	84%
Aggravated Assault	7%	8%	85%
Other Violent[d]	15%	7%	78%
Property Offenses	2%	5%	94%
Burglary	3%	5%	92%
Larceny[e]	2%	4%	94%
Fraud[f]	1%	5%	94%
Drug Offenses	3%	5%	92%
Possession	2%	7%	91%
Trafficking	3%	4%	92%
Weapons Offenses	4%	5%	91%
Other Offenses[g]	2%	6%	92%

a. Data on conviction type were available for 629,593 cases.

b. Includes nonnegligent manslaughter.

c. Includes rape.

d. Includes offenses such as negligent manslaughter and kidnapping.

e. Includes motor vehicle theft.

f. Includes forgery and embezzlement.

g. Composed of nonviolent offenses such as receiving stolen property and vandalism.

SOURCE: Jodi M. Brown, Patrick A. Langan, David J. Levin, "Felony Sentences in State Courts, 1996" U.S. Department of Justice, *Bureau of Justice Statistics Bulletin,* Washington, DC, May 1999, p. 8, Table 10.

FYI

Trial By Jury

Trial by a jury of one's peers originated in England as a way of limiting the power of the king. When the Magna Carta was signed in 1215, it contained the following provision: No freeman shall be seized or imprisoned, or stripped of his rights or possessions, or outlawed or exiled, or deprived of his standing in any other way, nor will we proceed with force against him, or send others to do so, except by the lawful judgment of his equals or by the law of the land.

SOURCE: <www.wwlia.org/uk-magna.htm>.

---

people of color are least likely to register to vote and, as a result, are least likely to be called for jury service. To remedy this problem, some jurisdictions now use multiple-source lists for obtaining jurors. In addition to voter registration lists, their sources include lists of licensed drivers, lists of utility users, and names listed in the telephone directory. Appellate courts have ruled that master jury lists must reflect an impartial and representative cross-section of the

venire
The pool from which jurors are selected.

voir dire
The process in which potential jurors who might be biased or unable to render a fair verdict are screened out.

Jury Exemptions

In October 1997, the Iowa Supreme Court ruled that farmers can be excused from jury duty during the harvest and planting seasons because of the "unique circumstances" of the profession. In the 1994 case in question, the defendant had argued on appeal that, without farmers, his jury was not a true cross section of the community.

SOURCE: "Court: Farmers Can Miss Jury Duty in Crop Seasons," *The Orlando Sentinel,* October 23, 1997, p. A-18.

population. People of color and women cannot be excluded systematically from juries solely because of race, ethnicity, or gender. But this does not mean that people of color and women must be included on all juries, only that they cannot be denied the opportunity of being chosen for jury service.

From the master list of all eligible jurors (sometimes called the *master wheel* or the *jury wheel*), a sufficient number of people are randomly chosen to make up the jury pool, or **venire.** Those chosen are summoned for service by the sheriff. However, not all those summoned will actually serve on the venire. Potential jurors must generally be U.S. citizens, residents of the locality of the trial, of a certain minimum age, and able to understand English. Convicted felons and insane persons are almost always excluded. Most jurisdictions also require that jurors be of "good character" and be "well-informed," which eliminates other potential jurors.

In addition, members of other groups often escape jury service. Professionals such as doctors, lawyers, and teachers; some elected officials; military personnel on active duty; and law enforcement personnel frequently are not called for jury duty because their professional services are considered indispensable or because they are connected to the criminal justice process. Many jurisdictions allow citizens to be excused from jury service if it would cause them physical or economic difficulties. Compensation for jury service is minimal, currently averaging $15 a day nationwide, and not all employers pay for time lost from work. Consequently, only about 15 percent of adult Americans have ever served on juries. The result is that juries are composed disproportionately of retired persons, the unemployed, and homemakers with grown children—those people least likely to be inconvenienced by the requirement of many states for jurors to serve for 30 days.

From the venire, as many as 30 people (in felony prosecutions that mandate 12 jurors) are randomly selected by the court clerk for the jury panel from which the actual trial jury is selected. To ensure a fair trial, potential trial jurors go through **voir dire,** a process in which persons who might be biased or unable to render a fair verdict are screened out. During *voir dire,* which means "to speak the truth," the defense, the prosecution, and the judge question jurors about their backgrounds and knowledge of the case and the defendant. If it appears that a juror might be biased or unable to render a fair verdict, the juror can be challenged "for cause" by either the defense or the prosecution. If the judge agrees, the juror is dismissed from jury service. In death penalty trials, for example, death penalty opponents can be excluded from juries for cause if they are opposed to the death penalty under any circumstances (*Lockhart v. McCree,* 1986). Generally, there is no limit to the number of jurors that can be eliminated for cause. In practice, however, few potential jurors are eliminated for cause, except in high-profile trials, such as the O.J. Simpson murder trial in 1995.

Another way that either the defense or the prosecution can eliminate potential jurors from jury service is by the use of *peremptory challenges,* which allow either prosecutors or defense attorneys to excuse jurors without having to provide a reason. Peremptory challenges are frequently used to eliminate jurors whose characteristics place them in a group likely to be unfavorable to the case of either the prosecution or the defense. For example, in death penalty cases, prosecutors often use their peremptory challenges to eliminate people of color and women from the juries because, statistically, people of

▲ Attorneys from opposing sides in a trial sometimes confer with the judge. *Why does this happen and what do you think is discussed?*

color and women are less likely to favor capital punishment. However, prosecutors must be careful in their use of peremptory challenges for such purposes because the Supreme Court has forbidden the use of peremptory challenges to exclude potential jurors solely on account of their race (*Batson v. Kentucky,* 1989) or gender (*J.E.B. v. Alabama,* 1994). The number of peremptory challenges is limited by statute. In most jurisdictions, the prosecution is allowed from six to eight peremptory challenges and the defense from eight to ten. *Voir dire* continues until the required number of jurors have been selected. The *voir dire* process may take an hour or two or, in rare cases, months.

Traditionally, a jury in a criminal trial, sometimes called a *petit jury* to distinguish it from a grand jury, consists of 12 citizens plus one or two alternates, who will replace any jurors unable to continue because of illness, accident, or personal emergency. Recently, however, primarily to reduce expenses, some states have gone to six-, seven-, and eight-member juries in noncapital criminal cases. The Supreme Court will not allow criminal trial juries with five or fewer members, and 12-member juries are still required in all states in capital (death penalty) cases.

Recently, attempts have been made to reduce the burden of jury service. In many jurisdictions, jurors can now call a number to find out whether they will be needed on a particular day during their term of service. Some jurisdictions have instituted "one day/one trial" jury systems, which require jurors to serve either for one day or for the duration of one trial. Once they have served, they are exempt from jury service for one or two years. Each year in the United States, approximately two million jurors serve in about 200,000 criminal and civil trials.

The Trial Process

Before a criminal trial formally begins, attorneys in about ten percent of felony cases file pretrial motions. A motion is an application to a court,

The Jury Pool

The jury pool in Timothy McVeigh's trial for the Oklahoma City bombing favored the prosecution. Most members of the jury pool were white and well educated, had close ties to the military, and believed in God, family, and the justice system. All of them had vivid memories of the Oklahoma City bombing, and nearly every one of them said they could look McVeigh in the eye and sentence him to death. According to a former U.S. attorney for Colorado, Bob Miller, "As a prosecutor, I would feel pretty comfortable. And I wouldn't feel so comfortable if I was a defense attorney."

SOURCE: "McVeigh's Jury Pool: Educated, Patriotic," *The Orlando Sentinel,* April 20, 1997, p. A-5.

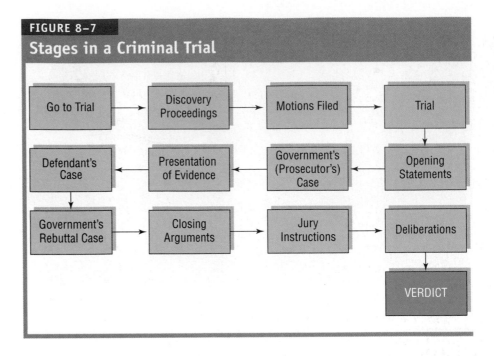

FIGURE 8-7

Stages in a Criminal Trial

Go to Trial → Discovery Proceedings → Motions Filed → Trial

Defendant's Case ← Presentation of Evidence ← Government's (Prosecutor's) Case ← Opening Statements

Government's Rebuttal Case → Closing Arguments → Jury Instructions → Deliberations

VERDICT

requesting a judge to order a particular action. Motions can also be made during and after a trial. Common pretrial motions are to obtain discovery of the prosecution's evidence and to have some of the prosecution's evidence suppressed (for example, to have a confession ruled inadmissible because of *Miranda* violations).

The following is a general description of the stages in a criminal trial.[27] Figure 8–7 shows that process and includes some pretrial stages as well (not all stages occur in every trial). After the jury has been sworn in (if the case is tried before a jury) and the court clerk has read the criminal complaint, the prosecution begins the trial with an opening statement, outlining its case. Next is the opening statement by the defense. However, the defense is not required to make an opening statement. In some jurisdictions, the defense is allowed to defer its opening statement until after the prosecution has presented its case. Opening statements are rarely made in bench trials.

The prosecution then submits its evidence and questions its witnesses. The prosecution must establish beyond a reasonable doubt each element of the crime. If the defense believes that the prosecution has failed to make its case, then the defense may choose to *rest*, that is, not to defend against the charge or charges. At this point, the defense in most states is allowed to request a *directed verdict* or to make a motion for dismissal. If the judge agrees with the defense that the prosecution's evidence is insufficient for conviction, then the judge can either direct the jury to acquit the defendant or "take the case from the jury" and grant the motion for dismissal.

If the defense does not seek a dismissal or a dismissal is not granted, the defense follows the prosecution with its witnesses and any contrary evidence. Then the prosecution and the defense take turns offering rebuttals to the other side's evidence, cross-examining witnesses, and reexamining their own witnesses. Following the rebuttal period, the prosecution summarizes its case. The defense then summarizes its case and makes its closing statement. The closing statement by the prosecution ends the adversarial portion of the trial.

Normally, after the closing statement by the prosecution, the judge instructs, or *charges,* the jury concerning the principles of law the jurors are to utilize in determining guilt or innocence. The judge also explains to the jury the charges, the rules of evidence, and the possible verdicts. In some jurisdictions, the judge summarizes the evidence presented from notes taken during the trial. The jury then retires to deliberate until it reaches a verdict. In a room where it has complete privacy, the jury elects from its members a foreperson to preside over the subsequent deliberations. Jurors are not allowed to discuss the case with anyone other than another juror. In some cases, a jury is sequestered at night in a hotel or motel to prevent any chance of outside influence.

To find a defendant guilty as charged, the jury must be convinced "beyond a reasonable doubt" that the defendant has committed the crime. Some juries reach a verdict in a matter of minutes; some juries have taken weeks or more. If the jury finds the defendant guilty as charged, as it does in two-thirds of criminal cases, the judge begins to consider a sentence. In some jurisdictions, the jury participates to varying degrees in the sentencing process. If the jury finds the defendant not guilty, the defendant is released from the jurisdiction of the court and is a free person. After the verdict has been read in the courtroom, either the defense or the prosecution may ask that the jury be polled individually, with each juror stating publicly how he or she voted.

In the federal courts and in nearly every state, a unanimous verdict is required. If, after serious deliberation, even one juror cannot agree with the others on a verdict, the result is a **hung jury.** In that case, the judge declares a mistrial, and the prosecutor must decide whether to retry the case.

Hung Juries

In 1966, it was estimated that about 5.5 percent of all criminal jury trials ended with a hung jury. Between 1992 and 1994, in contrast, the average hung-jury rate in the nine most ethnically diverse California counties, including Los Angeles, was 13 percent. Also, between 1992 and 1996, the hung-jury rate in all federal criminal trials in Washington, D.C., was 13 percent, compared with only 5 percent in 1991.

SOURCE: Jeffrey Rosen, "One Angry Woman: Why Are Hung Juries on the Rise?" *The New Yorker,* February 24 & March 3, 1997, p. 55.

hung jury
The result when jurors cannot agree on a verdict. The judge declares a mistrial. The prosecutor must decide whether to retry the case.

8.6 CRITICAL THINKING

1. What are some of the benefits of having a trial by jury?

2. How could the jury system be improved so that there is a more diverse mix of people?

Review and Applications

1. Identify the Type of Court Structure in the United States and Describe its Various Components

The United States has a dual court system—a separate judicial system for each of the states and a separate federal system. The only place where the two systems "connect" is in the U.S. Supreme Court. The federal court system is composed of U.S. district courts, U.S. circuit courts of appeals, and the U.S. Supreme Court. The state court system consists of trial courts of limited jurisdiction, trial courts of general jurisdiction, intermediate appellate courts (in most states), and state courts of last resort.

2. Summarize the Purposes of Courts

The purposes of courts are (1) to do justice, (2) to appear to do justice, (3) to provide a forum where disputes between people can be resolved justly and peacefully, (4) to censure wrongdoing, (5) to incapacitate criminal offenders, (6) to punish offenders, (7) to rehabilitate offenders, (8) to deter people from committing crimes, (9) to determine legal status, and (10) to protect individual citizens against arbitrary government action.

3. Identify the Most Powerful Actors in the Administration of Justice and Explain what Makes them so Powerful

Prosecutors are the most powerful actors in the administration of justice because they conduct the final screening of all persons arrested for criminal offenses, deciding whether there is enough evidence to support a conviction, and because, in most jurisdictions, they have unreviewable discretion in deciding whether to charge a person with a crime and prosecute the case.

4. Summarize the Types of Attorneys a Person Charged with a Crime Might Have

People charged with crimes may have privately retained counsel, or if indigent, they may have court-appointed attorneys, public defenders, or "contract" lawyers, depending on which is provided by the jurisdiction.

5. Describe the Responsibilities of a Judge

Judges have a variety of responsibilities in the criminal justice process. Among their nontrial duties are determining probable cause, signing warrants, informing suspects of their rights, setting and revoking bail, arraigning defendants, and accepting guilty pleas. Judges spend much of the workday in their chambers, negotiating procedures and dispositions with prosecutors and defense attorneys. The principal responsibility of judges in all of those duties is to ensure that suspects and defendants are treated fairly and in accordance with due process of law. In jury trials, judges are responsible for allowing the jury a fair chance to reach a verdict on the evidence presented. A judge must ensure that his or her behavior does not improperly affect the outcome of the case. Before juries retire to deliberate and reach a verdict, judges instruct them on the relevant law. Additionally, in jurisdictions without professional court administrators, each judge is responsible for the management of his or her own courthouse and its personnel, with the added duties of supervising building maintenance, budgets, and labor relations.

6. Describe the Purposes of an Initial Appearance

At the initial appearance—the first pretrial stage—defendants are given formal notice of the charges against them and are advised of their constitutional rights. For a misdemeanor or an ordinance violation, a summary trial may be held. For a felony, a hearing is held to determine whether the suspect should be released or whether the suspect should be held for a preliminary hearing.

7. Explain what Bail is and Describe the Different Methods of Pretrial Release

Bail is usually a monetary guarantee deposited with the court that is supposed to ensure that the suspect or defendant will appear at a subsequent stage in the criminal justice process. Different pretrial release options include station-house bail, surety bonds, full cash bonds, deposit bonds, release on own recognizance (ROR), conditional release, and unsecured bonds.

8. Explain What a Grand Jury is and What its Purposes Are

A grand jury is a group of 12 to 23 citizens who, for a specific period of time, meet in closed sessions to investigate charges coming from preliminary hearings or to engage in other responsibilities. A primary purpose of the grand jury is to determine whether there is probable cause to believe that the accused committed the crime or crimes with which he or she is charged by the prosecutor. Other purposes of a grand jury are to protect citizens from unfounded charges and to consider the misconduct of government officials.

9. Describe the Purposes of the Arraignment and the Plea Options of Defendants

The primary purpose of arraignment is to hear the formal information or grand jury indictment and to allow defendants to enter a plea. Plea options include "guilty," "not guilty," and in some states and the federal courts, *"nolo contendere."* In some states, defendants can also stand mute or can plead "not guilty by reason of insanity."

10. Describe the Interests Served and Not Served by Plea Bargaining

Plea bargaining seemingly serves the interests of all the court participants by, among other things, reducing uncertainty about the length or outcome of trials. Plea bargains serve prosecutors by guaranteeing them high conviction rates; judges by reducing court caseloads; defense attorneys by allowing them to avoid trials and spend less time on each case; and even some criminal offenders by enabling them to escape a prison sentence altogether, to receive a lesser sentence than they might have received if convicted at trial, or to escape conviction of socially stigmatizing crimes. Two types of criminal offenders are not served by plea bargaining: (1) innocent, indigent defendants who fear being found guilty of crimes they did not commit and receiving harsh sentences, and (2) habitual offenders.

11. List the Stages in a Criminal Trial

The stages in a criminal trial are as follows: (1) selection and swearing in of the jury, in jury trials; (2) opening statements by the prosecution and the defense; (3) presentation of the prosecution's case; (4) presentation of the defense's case; (5) rebuttals, cross-examination, and reexamination of witnesses; (6) closing arguments by the defense and the prosecution; (7) the judge's instructing, or charging, the jury; and (8) deliberation and verdict.

KEY TERMS

dual court system, p. 258
jurisdiction, p. 258
original jurisdiction, p. 258
appellate jurisdiction, p. 258
general jurisdiction, p. 258
special jurisdiction, p. 258
subject matter jurisdiction, p. 258
personal jurisdiction, p. 258
writ of *certiorari*, p. 262
writ of *habeas corpus*, p. 263
summary trials, p. 264
trial *de novo*, p. 264
due process of law, p. 269
incapacitation, p. 269
punishment, p. 269

rehabilitation, p. 269
general deterrence, p. 269
nolle prosequi (nol. pros.), p. 270
plea bargaining or plea
  negotiating, p. 272
rules of discovery, p. 273
probable cause, p. 282
booking, p. 282
complaint, p. 282
information, p. 282
grand jury indictment, p. 282
arrest warrant, p. 282
bail bond/bail, p. 283
preventive detention, p. 284
bench warrant or *capias*, p. 285

release on own recognizance
  (ROR), p. 286
conditional release, p. 286
unsecured bond, p. 286
preliminary hearing, p. 287
grand jury, p. 287
indictment, p. 287
subpoena, p. 288
arraignment, p. 288
nolo contendere, p. 288
bench trial, p. 292
venire, p. 294
voir dire, p. 294
hung jury, p. 297

QUESTIONS FOR REVIEW

1. What is the difference between *original* and *appellate jurisdiction*? Between *general* and *special jurisdiction*? Between *subject matter* and *personal jurisdiction*?

2. Under what circumstances will the U.S. Supreme Court issue a writ of *certiorari*?

3. Ideally, what are the three conditions that must be met before a prosecutor charges a person with a crime and prosecutes the case?

4. Why do prosecutors sometimes choose not to prosecute criminal cases?

5. In general, when does an individual accused of a crime have the right to counsel?

6. By what methods are judges selected?

7. Describe the "funneling" or screening process in the administration of justice.

8. When do suspects officially become defendants?

9. How long may suspects arrested without a warrant be held in jail before being brought before a judge for an initial appearance?

10. In what two ways are preliminary hearings similar to criminal trials, and in what two ways do preliminary hearings differ from criminal trials?

11. What is the primary purpose of a grand jury?

12. What are three basic types of plea bargains?

13. What are three principal purposes of jury trials?

14. What is *voir dire,* and what is its purpose?

EXPERIENTIAL ACTIVITIES

1. **Bail Bonds** Visit the office of a local bail bonds person. It is generally near the courthouse and well marked. Ask the bonds person to describe the job. Ask about major problems with the business and satisfactions of the job. Specific questions could be: (1) For what type of offender is it most risky to provide bail? (2) How does a bail transaction work? (3) Do bonds people actually have to give money to the court when they put up bail?

2. **Court Proceedings** Visit several different types of courts, such as a lower court, a trial court, an appellate court, state courts, and federal courts. Observe the proceedings and describe how they differ from or are similar to those described in this chapter and to each other.

3. **Report on a Criminal Trial** Scan a local newspaper for a story of a criminal trial. Write a report that includes information about (1) the type of court in which the trial is being held and why it has jurisdiction, (2) the type of case being tried (misdemeanor or felony), (3) the outcome of the case.

INTERNET

4. **District Courts** Go to cj.glencoe.com for links to the Federal Judiciary Web site and find the directory of district courts. Look up the number of districts your state is divided into, where the courts for the districts are located, and how many judgeships are authorized for each district. Report the results to your class or instructor.

5. **State Courts** Go to cj.glencoe.com and click on U.S. Department of Justice, Bureau of Justice Statistics *State Court Organization 1998* document. Examine the material in each table for your state. Write a report about your state court system.

What Would You Do?

1. As a defense attorney, what would you do under the following circumstances?

   a. Your client tells you that he committed the crime or crimes for which he is being prosecuted.

   b. Your client tells you about a serious crime that will be committed sometime next week.

   c. Your client tells you that if you lose the case, his friends will harm your family.

   d. You learn that your client, who has paid you nothing so far for your services, will not be able to pay your fee.

   e. Your client insists on testifying, even though you believe that it is not in his best interests to do so.

Jury Nullification

2. In John Grisham's 1992 novel, *A Time To Kill,* the defendant, a black man whose young daughter was viciously raped by two white men, is on trial for gunning down the two men on the courthouse steps in full view of many bystanders. Even though it was obvious to all that the defendant had killed the two men, the jury in the case returned a not-guilty verdict, and the defendant was allowed to walk free. This is an example of *jury nullification,* the power of a jury in a criminal case to acquit a defendant despite overwhelming evidence. The jury can acquit for any reason or for no reason at all, and the decision of the jury cannot be appealed. Jury nullification is one of the problems cited by critics who call for the abolition of the present American jury system. Another complaint about the jury system is the inability of some jurors in some trials to understand legal arguments, the evidence presented, or the instructions of the judge. Critics of the jury system suggest replacing jury trials with bench trials or with trials before a panel of judges or substituting professionally trained jurors for the current "amateur" jurors.

   a. Should the American jury system be abolished? Why or why not?

   b. Do you believe that any of the alternatives suggested by jury critics would produce a better or more just system? Defend your answer.

ADDITIONAL READING

Eisenstein, James, Roy Flemming, and Peter Nadulli. *The Contours of Justice: Communities and Their Courts.* Boston: Little, Brown, 1988.

Feely, Malcolm. *The Process Is the Punishment: Handling Cases in Lower Criminal Court.* New York: Russell Sage Foundation, 1979.

Hans, Valerie P. and Neil Vidmar. *Judging the Jury.* New York: Plenum, 1986.

Heilbroner, David. *Rough Justice: Days and Nights of a Young D.A.* New York: Pantheon, 1990.

Kalven, Harry, Jr. and Hans Zeisel. *The American Jury.* Boston: Little, Brown, 1966.

Levine, James P. *Juries and Politics.* Pacific Grove, CA: Brooks/Cole, 1992.

Loftus, Elizabeth and E. Ketcham. *For the Defense.* New York: St. Martin's, 1991.

McIntyre, Lisa J. *The Public Defender: The Practice of Law in the Shadows of Repute.* Chicago: Univ. of Chicago Press, 1987.

Neubauer, David W. *America's Courts and the Criminal Justice System,* 4th ed. Pacific Grove, CA: Brooks/Cole, 1992.

Neubauer, David W. *Judicial Process: Law, Courts and Politics in the United States.* Pacific Grove, CA: Brooks/Cole, 1991.

O'Brien, David M. *Storm Center: The Supreme Court in American Politics,* 3d ed. New York: W. W. Norton & Co., 1993.

Satter, Robert. *Doing Justice: A Trial Judge at Work.* New York: Simon & Schuster, 1990.

Smith, Christopher. *Courts, Politics, and the Judicial Process.* Chicago: Nelson-Hall, 1993.

Stumpf, Harry P. and John H. Culver. *The Politics of State Courts.* New York: Longman, 1992.

Wice, Paul. *Judges and Lawyers: The Human Side of Justice.* New York: Harper-Collins, 1991.

Wice, Paul. *Chaos in the Courthouse: The Inner Workings of the Urban Criminal Courts.* New York: Praeger, 1985.

Wishman, Seymour. *Confessions of a Criminal Lawyer.* New York: Penguin, 1982.

ENDNOTES

1. Administrative Office of the U.S. Courts, Federal Judiciary Web site, "About the U.S. Courts," <www.uscourts.gov>; "The 1999 Year-End Report on the Federal Judiciary," <www.uscourts.gov/ttb/jan00ttb/jan2000.html>.

2. Administrative Office of the U.S. Courts, Federal Judiciary Web site, "The 1999 Year-End Report on the Federal Judiciary," <www.uscourts.gov/ttb/jan00ttb/jan2000.html>.

3. Administrative Office of the U.S. Courts, Federal Judiciary Web site, "About the U.S. Courts," <www.uscourts.gov>.

4. Kathleen Maguire and Ann L. Pastore (eds.), *Sourcebook of Criminal Justice Statistics 1998,* U.S. Department of Justice, Bureau of Justice Statistics (Washington, DC: GPO, 1999), p. 443, Table 5.63; also Administrative Office of the U.S. Courts, Federal Judiciary Web site, "The 1999 Year-End Report on the Federal Judiciary," op. cit.

5. Administrative Office of the U.S. Courts, Federal Judiciary Web site, "About the U.S. Courts," op. cit.; also "The 1999 Year-End Report on the Federal Judiciary," op. cit.

6. Ibid.

7. Maguire and Pastore, op. cit., p. 446, Table 5.66 (calculated from data in the tables).

8. Ibid.

9. Material on the state courts is based on information from the following sources: David B. Rottman, Carol R. Flango, Melissa T. Cantrell, Randall Hansen, Neil LaFountain, *State Court Organization 1998,* U.S. Department of Justice, Bureau of Justice Statistics (Washington, DC: GPO, June 2000); David W. Neubauer, *America's Courts and the Criminal Justice System,* 4th ed. (Pacific Grove, CA: Brooks/Cole, 1992); Christopher Smith, *Courts, Politics, and the Judicial Process* (Chicago: Nelson-Hall, 1993); N. Gary Holten and Lawson L. Lamar, *The Criminal Courts: Structures, Personnel, and Processes* (New York: McGraw-Hill, 1991); Lawrence Baum, *American Courts,* 3d ed. (Boston: Houghton Mifflin, 1994). U.S. Department of Justice, Bureau of Justice Statistics, *Report to the Nation on Crime and Justice,* 2d ed. (Washington, DC: GPO, 1988); H. Ted Rubin, *The Courts: Fulcrum of the Justice System* (Santa Monica, CA: Goodyear, 1976); James Eisenstein, Roy Flemming, and Peter Nadulli, *The Contours of Justice: Communities and Their Courts* (Boston: Little, Brown, 1988); Malcolm Feeley, *The Process Is the Punishment: Handling Cases in Lower Criminal Court* (New York: Russell Sage, 1979); Harry P. Stumpf and John H. Culver, *The Politics of State Courts* (New York: Longman, 1992); Paul Wice, *Chaos in the Courthouse: The Inner Workings of the Urban Criminal Courts* (New York: Praeger, 1985).

10. Material in this section about drug courts is from "Drug Courts: Overview of Growth, Characteristics, and Results," GAO/GGD-97-106, <www.ncjrs.org/txtfiles/dcourts.txt>, July 31, 1997; Rottman et al., op. cit., p. 207.

11. Maya Bell, "Mentally Ill Get Court of Their Own—and Help," *The Orlando Sentinel*, July 13, 1997, p. A–1.
12. Judith S. Kaye, "Making the Case for Hands-On Courts," (*Newsweek*, October 11, 1999), p. 13.
13. *Sourcebook of Criminal Justice Statistics*, Online, Table 1.48.
14. Rottman et al., op. cit., p. 7.
15. Ibid.
16. Rubin, op. cit.
17. In addition to the other sources cited, material on the key actors in the court process is from Neubauer, op. cit.; David W. Neubauer, *Judicial Process: Law, Courts and Politics in the United States* (Pacific Grove, CA: Brooks/Cole, 1991); Smith, op. cit.; Holten and Lamar, op. cit.; Baum, op. cit.
18. Material about prosecutors is also taken from David Heilbroner, *Rough Justice: Days and Nights of a Young D.A.* (New York: Pantheon, 1990).
19. In addition to the other sources cited, material on defense attorneys is from Elizabeth Loftus and E. Ketcham, *For the Defense* (New York: St. Martin's, 1991); Paul Wice, *Judges and Lawyers: The Human Side of Justice* (New York: Harper-Collins, 1991); Paul Wice, *Criminal Lawyers: An Endangered Species* (Newbury Park, CA: Sage, 1978); Seymour Wishman, *Confessions of a Criminal Lawyer* (New York: Penguin, 1982); Lisa J. McIntyre, *The Public Defender: The Practice of Law in the Shadows of Repute* (Chicago: Univ. of Chicago Press, 1987).
20. Steven K. Smith and Carol J. DeFrances, "Indigent Defense," U.S. Department of Justice, *Bureau of Justice Statistics Selected Findings*, (Washington, DC), February 1996.
21. In addition to the other sources cited, material on judges is from Paul Ryan, Allan Ashman, Bruce D. Sales, and Sandra Shane-DuBow, *American Trial Judges* (New York: Free Press, 1980); Robert Satter, *Doing Justice: A Trial Judge at Work* (New York: Simon & Schuster, 1990); Wice (1991), op. cit.; Wice (1985), op. cit.
22. *Sourcebook of Criminal Justice Statistics*, Online, Tables 1.51 and 1.53.
23. In addition to the other sources cited, material on pretrial stages is from Neubauer (1992), op. cit.; Holten and Lamar, op. cit.
24. In addition to the other sources cited, material on plea bargaining is from Neubauer (1992), op. cit.; Neubauer (1991), op. cit.; Holten and Lamar, op. cit.; Baum, op. cit.
25. In addition to the other sources cited, material on criminal trials is from Neubauer (1992), op. cit.; Neubauer (1991), op. cit.; Smith, op. cit.; Holten and Lamar, op. cit.
26. In addition to the other sources cited, material on juries is from Rottman et al., op. cit.; Holten and Lamar, op. cit.; Valerie P. Hans and Neil Vidmar, *Judging the Jury* (New York: Plenum, 1986); Harry Kalvan Jr. and Hans Zeisel, *The American Jury* (Boston: Little, Brown, 1996); James P. Levine, *Juries and Politics* (Pacific Grove, CA: Brooks/Cole, 1992).
27. In addition to the other sources cited, material on the trial process is from Satter (1990), op. cit.

Chapter 9

Sentencing, Appeals, and the Death Penalty

After completing this chapter, you should be able to:

1. Identify the general factors that influence a judge's sentencing decisions.

2. Describe how judges tailor sentences to fit the crime and the offender.

3. Distinguish between indeterminate and determinate sentences.

4. Explain the three basic types of determinate sentences.

5. List five rationales or justifications for criminal punishment.

6. Explain the purposes of presentence investigation reports.

7. List the legal bases for appeal.

8. Identify the type of crime for which death may be a punishment.

9. Summarize the three major procedural reforms the U.S. Supreme Court approved for death penalty cases in the *Gregg* decision.

9.1 Sentencing

If a criminal defendant pleads guilty or is found guilty by a judge or jury, then the judge must impose a sentence.[1] In a few jurisdictions, sentencing is the responsibility of the jury for certain types of offenses (for example, capital crimes). Figure 9–1 on page 307 displays, by the most serious offense, the amount of time from conviction to sentencing for defendants in the 75 largest U.S. counties in 1996. As Figure 9–1 shows, for most offenses a majority of defendants are sentenced either on the day of conviction or the next day.

Sentencing is arguably a judge's most difficult responsibility. Judges cannot impose just any sentence. They are limited by statutory provisions and guided by prevailing philosophical rationales, organizational considerations, and presentence investigation reports. They are also influenced by their own personal characteristics.

Statutory Provisions

As described in Chapter 4, state and federal legislative bodies enact penal codes that specify appropriate punishments for each statutory offense or class of offense, such as a class B felony or class C felony. Currently, five general types of punishment are in use in the United States: fines, probation, intermediate punishments (various punishments that are more restrictive than probation but less restrictive and costly than imprisonment), imprisonment, and death. As long as judges impose one or a combination of those five punishments, and the sentence type and length are within statutory limits, judges are free to set any sentence they want.

Thus, within limits, judges are free to tailor the punishment to fit the crime and the offender. As noted, judges can impose a combination sentence of, for example, imprisonment, probation, and a fine. They can suspend the imprisonment portion of a combination sentence, or they can suspend the entire sentence if the offender stays out of trouble, makes **restitution** (pays money or provides services to victims, their survivors, or the community to make up for the injury inflicted), or seeks medical treatment. If the offender has already spent weeks, months, or sometimes even years in jail awaiting trial, judges can give the offender credit for jail time and deduct that time from any prison sentence. When jail time is not deducted from the sentence, it is called "dead time." In some cases, the sentence that a judge intends to impose closely matches the time an offender has already spent in jail awaiting trial. In such cases, the judge may impose a sentence of "time served" and release the offender. When an offender is convicted of two or more crimes, judges can order the prison sentences to run concurrently (together) or consecutively (one after the other). Judges can also delay sentencing and retain the right to impose a sentence at a later date if conditions warrant. Figure 9–2 on page 308 shows, by offense, the types of felony sentences imposed by state courts in 1996. Note that two-thirds of all offenders were incarcerated; only one-third received probation, a fine, or both. Even the majority of misdemeanants were incarcerated, almost all in jail. The largest percentage of offenders incarcerated were violent offenders (80 percent) and drug offenders (72 percent).

The Longest Sentence

The longest prison sentence in the United States is believed to be a 10,000-year sentence imposed on Dudley Wayne Kyzer, 40, on December 4, 1981, in Tuscaloosa, Alabama, for a triple murder committed in 1976.

SOURCE: George E. Rush, *The Dictionary of Criminal Justice,* 5th Ed. (Sluice Dock, Guilford, CT: Dushkin/McGraw-Hill, 2000), p. 295.

restitution
Money paid or services provided by a convicted offender to victims, their survivors, or the community to make up for the injury inflicted.

FIGURE 9–1

Time from Conviction to Sentencing for Convicted Defendants, by Most Serious Offense, 1996

Most serious conviction offense	Number of defendants	Total	Percent of convicted defendants in the 75 largest counties who were sentenced within:			
			0–1 day	2–30 days	31–60 days	61 days or more
All offenses	30,696	100%	66%	16%	12%	7%
All felonies	24,398	100%	60%	19%	14%	8%
Violent offenses	4,102	100%	50%	21%	18%	10%
Murder	70	100	34	34	23	9
Rape	246	100	47	16	23	14
Robbery	1,320	100	56	21	15	9
Assault	1,475	100	56	20	17	8
Other violent	991	100	37	26	22	15
Property offenses	8,018	100%	66%	15%	11%	8%
Burglary	2,097	100	64	18	11	7
Theft	3,157	100	64	15	12	9
Other property	2,764	100	69	13	11	7
Drug offenses	9,813	100%	59%	21%	13%	7%
Trafficking	4,888	100	52	25	14	9
Other drug	4,925	100	66	17	12	5
Public-order offenses	2,342	100%	62%	13%	16%	9%
Weapons	983	100	66	17	11	6
Driving-related	846	100	55	12	22	11
Other public-order	513	100	67	10	14	10
Misdemeanors	6,298	100%	88%	4%	5%	3%

Note: Data on time from conviction to sentencing were available for 96 percent of cases that had reached sentencing. Total for all felonies includes cases that could not be classified into one of the four major offense categories. Detail may not add to total because of rounding.

SOURCE: Timothy C. Hart and Brian A. Reaves, *Felony Defendants in Large Urban Counties, 1996.* U.S. Dept. of Justice, Bureau of Justice Statistics (Washington, DC: GPO, 1999), p. 29, Table 29.

FIGURE 9–2

Types of Felony Sentences Imposed by State Courts and Percentage of All Convictions in 1996, by Offense

Most serious conviction offense	Number of defendants	Total	Percent of convicted defendants in the 75 largest counties who were sentenced to:					
			Incarceration			Nonincarceration		
			Total	Prison	Jail	Total	Probation	Fine
All offenses	28,755	100%	67%	30%	37%	33%	31%	2%
All felonies	24,229	100%	69%	35%	34%	31%	30%	1%
Violent offenses	4,073	100%	80%	51%	29%	20%	20%	—
Murder	66	100	100	100	0	0	0	0
Rape	243	100	77	56	21	23	23	0
Robbery	1,307	100	90	71	19	10	10	—
Assault	1,455	100	73	40	33	27	26	—
Other violent	1,002	100	76	36	40	24	24	0
Property offenses	7,943	100%	62%	30%	32%	38%	38%	—
Burglary	2,093	100	74	43	31	26	25	1
Theft	3,121	100	66	32	34	34	34	—
Other property	2,728	100	48	17	31	52	52	1
Drug offenses	9,761	100%	72%	34%	38%	28%	28%	1%
Trafficking	4,915	100	78	44	34	22	22	—
Other drug	4,846	100	65	23	42	35	34	1
Public-order offenses	2,317	100%	69%	34%	35%	31%	29%	2%
Weapons	962	100	64	37	27	36	34	2
Driving-related	850	100	75	35	40	25	21	3
Other public-order	506	100	66	27	40	34	32	1
Misdemeanors	4,547	100%	57%	3%	54%	43%	36%	7%

Note: Data on type of sentence were available for 90 percent of cases involving defendants who had been convicted. Sixty-seven percent of jail sentences and five percent of prison sentences included a probation term. Twenty-three percent of prison sentences, 31 percent of jail sentences, and 29 percent of probation sentences included a fine. Fines may have included restitution or community service. Total for all felonies includes cases that could not be classified into one of the four major offense categories. Prison category includes seven defendants who received a death sentence. Detail may not add to total because of rounding.

SOURCE: Timothy C. Hart and Brian A. Reaves, *Felony Defendants in Large Urban Counties, 1996.* U.S. Department of Justice, Bureau of Justice Statistics (Washington, DC: GPO, 1999), p. 30, Table 30.

The sentence of death is generally limited to offenders convicted of "aggravated" murder, and because most criminal offenders are poor, fines are seldom imposed for serious crimes. (When they are, it is generally for symbolic reasons.) Thus, in practice, judges have three sentencing options — probation, intermediate punishments, and imprisonment. Later chapters in this text will cover those options. The death penalty will be discussed at the end of this chapter.

The type of sentence imposed on an offender can be a highly volatile issue. Also controversial is the length of the sentence imposed. Judges in states that have indeterminate sentencing statutes generally have more discretion in sentencing than do judges in states with determinate sentencing laws. An **indeterminate sentence** has a fixed minimum and maximum term of incarceration, rather than a set period. Sentences of 10 to 20 years in prison or of not less than 5 years and not more than 25 years in prison are examples of indeterminate sentences. The amount of the term that is actually served is determined by a parole board.

Indeterminate sentences have been a principal tool in the effort to rehabilitate offenders for much of the past 75 years. They are based on the idea that correctional personnel must be given the flexibility necessary to successfully treat offenders and return them to society as law-abiding members. The rationale underlying indeterminate sentencing is that the time needed for "correcting" different offenders varies so greatly that a range in sentence length provides a better opportunity to achieve successful rehabilitation.

Beginning in the early 1970s, social scientists and politicians began to question whether the rehabilitation of most criminal offenders was even possible. Skepticism about rehabilitation of offenders, a public outcry to do something about crime, and a general distrust of decisions made by parole boards, continued to grow. By the mid-1970s, several state legislatures had abandoned or at least deemphasized the goal of rehabilitation and had begun to replace indeterminate sentencing with determinate sentencing.

A **determinate sentence** has a fixed period of incarceration, which eliminates the decision-making responsibility of parole boards. The hope of determinate sentencing is that it will at least get criminals off the street for longer periods of time. Some people also consider a determinate sentence more humane because prisoners know exactly when they will be released, something that they do not know with an indeterminate sentence. Several states and the federal government have developed guidelines for determinate sentencing; other states have established sentencing commissions to do so.

FYI

Sentencing

In 1975, Maine became the first state to replace indeterminate sentencing with determinate sentencing. It abolished parole at the same time.

SOURCE: Robert Carter, "Determinate Sentences," pp. 147–49 in M.D. McShane and F.P. Williams III (eds.) *Encyclopedia of American Prisons* (New York: Garland, 1996), p. 148.

indeterminate sentence
A sentence with a fixed minimum and maximum term of incarceration, rather than a set period.

MYTH ‹ ‹ ‹ ‹ **FACT** ‹ ‹ ‹ ‹ ‹ ‹ ‹ ‹

Determinate sentencing, especially mandatory sentencing, has a signifi-

In practice, this myth has at least two problems. First, "mandatory" aspects of the laws are easy to evade. Second, the basic assumption on which the myth rests is wrong: that "soft" judges release too many dangerous offenders on probation. A recent study shows that two-thirds of all offenders convicted in the 75 largest counties were sentenced to either prison or jail; only one-third received probation. Even 57 percent of misdemeanants were incarcerated, 54 percent in jail. Eighty percent of violent offenders and 72 percent of drug offenders were incarcerated.[2]

determinate sentence
A sentence with a fixed period of incarceration, which eliminates the decision-making responsibility of parole boards.

flat-time sentencing
Sentencing in which judges may choose between probation and imprisonment but have little discretion in setting the length of a prison sentence. Once an offender is imprisoned, there is no possibility of reduction in the length of the sentence.

good time
The number of days deducted from a sentence by prison authorities for good behavior or for other reasons.

mandatory sentencing
Sentencing in which a specified number of years of imprisonment (usually within a range) is provided for particular crimes.

presumptive sentencing
Sentencing that allows a judge to retain some sentencing discretion, subject to appellate review. The legislature determines a sentence range for each crime.

There are three basic types of determinate sentences: flat-time, mandatory, and presumptive. With **flat-time sentencing,** judges may choose between probation and imprisonment but have little discretion in setting the length of a prison sentence. Once an offender is imprisoned, there is no possibility of a reduction in the length of the sentence. Thus, parole and **good time** (the number of days deducted from a sentence by prison authorities for good behavior or for other reasons) are not options under flat-time sentencing. Before New York imposed the first indeterminate sentence in the United States in 1924, nearly all sentences to prison in the United States were flat-time sentences. Flat-time sentences are rarely imposed today.

With **mandatory sentencing,** the second type of determinate sentencing, a specified number of years of imprisonment, usually within a range, is provided for particular crimes. Mandatory sentencing usually allows credit for good time but does not allow release on parole. Beginning in the 1980s, two principal variations of mandatory sentencing emerged. The first was *mandatory minimum* sentences, which require that offenders serve a specified amount of prison time. Mandatory minimum sentences are most frequently imposed on offenders who commit certain types of offenses such as drug offenses, offenses committed with weapons, and offenses committed by repeat or habitual ("three strikes and you're out") offenders. All states and the federal government have one or more mandatory minimum sentencing laws.

Similar to mandatory minimum sentences are sentences based on *truth-in-sentencing* laws. First enacted in the state of Washington in 1984, truth-in-sentencing laws require offenders to serve a substantial portion of their prison sentence, usually 85 percent of it. Most truth-in-sentencing laws target violent offenders and restrict or eliminate parole eligibility and good-time credits. Probably because of incentive grants authorized by Congress in 1994 to build or expand correctional facilities, nearly all states and the District of Columbia have enacted truth-in-sentencing laws modeled after the federal government's, which requires that for certain offenses 85 percent of a prison sentence must be served.

The third type of determinate sentencing is presumptive sentencing. **Presumptive sentencing** allows a judge to retain some sentencing discretion, subject to appellate review. In presumptive sentencing, the legislature determines a sentence range for each crime usually based on the seriousness of the crime and the criminal history of the offender. The judge is expected to impose the typical sentence, specified by statute, unless mitigating or aggravating circumstances justify a sentence below or above the range set by the legislature. Any sentence that deviates from the norm, however, must be explained in writing and is subject to appellate review. Generally, with presumptive sentencing, credit is given for good time, but there is no opportunity for parole. Presumptive sentencing is a compromise between legislatively mandated determinate sentences and their indeterminate counterparts. Figure 9–3 on page 311 displays Minnesota's presumptive sentencing guidelines grid.

Presumptive sentences may also be based on *sentencing guidelines* developed, not by legislatures, but by *sentencing commissions* comprised of both criminal justice professionals and private citizens. Sentencing guidelines are a different way of restricting the sentencing discretion of judges. In 1984, Congress created the nine-member U.S. Sentencing Commission, which is charged with creating and amending federal sentencing guidelines.

FIGURE 9–3

Sample Sentencing Guidelines

MINNESOTA SENTENCING GUIDELINES GRID

Presumptive Prison Sentence Lengths in Months

LESS SERIOUS ⬅————————————➡ MORE SERIOUS

SEVERITY OF OFFENSE (Illustrative Offenses)	CRIMINAL HISTORY SCORE						6 or more
	0	1	2	3	4	5	
Sale of simulated controlled substance	12*	12*	12*	13	15	17	19 _18–20_
Theft Related Crimes ($2500 or less) Check Forgery ($200–$2500)	12*	12*	13	15	17	19	21 _20–22_
Theft Crimes ($2500 or less)	12*	13	15	17	19 _18–20_	22 _21–23_	25 _24–26_
Nonresidential Burglary Theft Crimes (over $2500)	12*	15	18	21	25 _24–26_	32 _30–34_	41 _37–45_
Residential Burglary Simple Robbery	18	23	27	30 _29–31_	38 _36–40_	46 _43–49_	54 _50–58_
Criminal Sexual Conduct 2nd Degree	21	26	30	34 _33–35_	44 _42–46_	54 _50–58_	65 _60–70_
Aggravated Robbery	48 _44–52_	58 _54–62_	68 _64–72_	78 _74–82_	88 _84–92_	98 _94–102_	108 _104–112_
Criminal Sexual Conduct, 1st Degree Assault, 1st Degree	86 _81–91_	98 _93–103_	110 _105–115_	122 _117–127_	134 _129–139_	146 _141–151_	158 _153–163_
Murder, 3rd Degree Murder, 2nd Degree (felony murder)	150 _144–156_	165 _159–171_	180 _174–186_	195 _189–201_	210 _204–216_	225 _219–231_	240 _234–246_
Murder, 2nd Degree (with intent)	306 _299–313_	326 _319–333_	346 _339–353_	366 _359–373_	386 _379–393_	406 _399–413_	426 _419–433_

▨ At the discretion of the judge, up to a year in jail and/or other non-jail sanctions can be imposed instead of prison sentences as conditions of probation for most of these offenses. If prison is imposed, the presumptive sentence is the number of months shown.

☐ Presumptive commitment to state prison for all offenses.

Notes: 1. Criminal history score is based on offender's prior record and seriousness of prior offenses. 2. Numbers in italics represent the range of months within which a judge may sentence without the sentence being deemed a departure from the guidelines. 3. First degree murder is excluded from the guidelines by law and carries a mandatory life sentence.

*One year and one day

SOURCE: Minnesota Sentencing Guidelines Commission. Effective August 1, 1994; reprinted in _Seeking Justice: Crime and Punishment in America,_ New York: The Edna McConnell Clark Foundation, 1995, p. 24.

CRIMINAL JUSTICE Online

U.S. Sentencing Commission

To learn more about the U.S. Sentencing Commission, visit its Web site by clicking the link at cj.glencoe.com. *Why do you think sentencing commissions are necessary?*

FYI

Truth-in-Sentencing

Violent offenders released from prison in 1996 were sentenced to serve an average of 85 months in prison. Prior to release they served about half of their prison sentences or 45 months. Under a truth-in-sentencing law requiring 85 percent of the sentence to be served, violent offenders would be expected to serve an estimated 15 months longer.

SOURCE: Paula M. Ditton and Doris Jane Wilson, "Truth in Sentencing in State Prisons." (U.S. Department of Justice, Bureau of Justice Special Report, 1999).

In today's "law and order" climate, state legislatures, as noted, are increasingly replacing indeterminate sentences with determinate ones. This trend, however, has not escaped criticism. For example, it has been argued that the consequences of determinate sentencing include longer prison sentences and overcrowded prisons. Whether it is the result of a shift in sentencing philosophy or some other factor or factors, there is no question that the United States has been experiencing a dramatic increase in the number of people sentenced to prison and in the length of terms of incarceration. A result has been a crisis of prison overcrowding. In recent years, the United States has had one of the highest imprisonment rates in the world. Furthermore, as of September 30, 1999, the entire adult correctional departments of 14 states (Alabama, Arkansas, Arizona, California, Idaho, Indiana, Kentucky, Mississippi, New Jersey, Ohio, Oklahoma, Texas, Washington, and Wisconsin) were under court orders to reduce overcrowding or improve other conditions of confinement.[3] In another nine states (Connecticut, Florida, Georgia, Illinois, Louisiana, Michigan, Missouri, Montana, and New York) and the Federal Bureau of Prisons, one or more institutions were under court orders to reduce overcrowding or improve other conditions of confinement.

A related criticism of determinate sentencing is that it produces an unusually harsh prison system. For example, because of prison overcrowding, many states have all but abandoned even the pretense of rehabilitating offenders. Prisons are increasingly becoming places where offenders are simply "warehoused." In addition, because of the abolition of good time and parole under some determinate sentencing schemes, prison authorities are having a more difficult time maintaining discipline and control of their institutions. Eliminating good time and parole removed two of the most important incentives that prison authorities use to get inmates to behave and to follow prison rules. Also, because of the perceived harshness of some of the determinate sentencing schemes, some judges simply ignore the guidelines. Other judges have ignored sentencing guidelines because they believe they are too lenient. In short, many judges resent sentencing guidelines and refer to their use as "justice by computer."

A third criticism of determinate sentencing is that it merely shifts sentencing discretion from judges to legislatures and prosecutors (through plea bargaining). Whether or not this shift in sentencing responsibility is desirable is a matter of debate. On one hand, prosecutors generally exercise their discretion in secret, whereas judges exercise discretion in the open. Also, prosecutors and legislators are generally subject to more political influence than are judges.

Yet, on the other hand, one of the major criticisms of indeterminate sentencing and a principal reason for the adoption of determinate sentencing schemes by some states is judicial disparity in sentencing. Judges vary widely in the sentences they impose for similar crimes and offenders. For example, in one study, 41 New York state judges were asked to review files of actual cases and to indicate the sentences they would impose. Sentences for the same crime were quite different. In one case, a heroin addict robbed an elderly man at gunpoint. The assailant was unemployed, lived with his pregnant wife, and had a minor criminal record. He was convicted of first-degree robbery, and under New York's indeterminate sentencing statute, the actual sentence was between 0 and 5 years. When the 41 judges were asked what sentence they

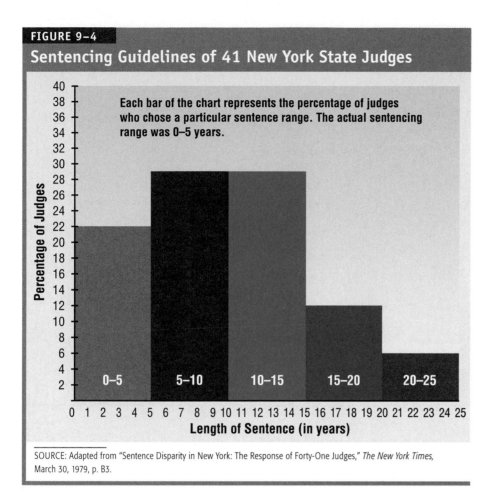

SOURCE: Adapted from "Sentence Disparity in New York: The Response of Forty-One Judges," *The New York Times*, March 30, 1979, p. B3.

would impose in the case, 22 percent of them chose the actual sentence (between 0 and 5 years), 29 percent chose a sentence of 5 to 10 years, another 29 percent selected a sentence of 10 to 15 years, 12 percent opted for a sentence of 15 to 20 years, and 7 percent of them chose a sentence of 20 to 25 years.[4] Figure 9–4 displays the judges' choices. Obviously, different judges view the same circumstances very differently. Critics have charged that disparity in sentencing has resulted in discrimination against people of color and the poor.

A fourth, related criticism of determinate sentencing in those jurisdictions that retain good time is that sentencing discretion, at least to some degree, actually shifts from legislators and prosecutors to correctional personnel. By charging inmates with violations of prison rules, correctional personnel can

MYTH

Judges are "soft" on crime, allowing many dangerous criminals to escape imprisonment.

FACT

Whether or not an offender is imprisoned usually depends on the facts of the case. In cases of robbery and burglary, for example, judges are generally "hard" on robberies involving strangers and relatively "soft" on prior-relationship burglaries. According to a 1996 public opinion poll, 78 percent of Americans think that the courts are not harsh enough with criminals. In general, however, the "softness" or "hardness" of a judge's sentence depends on the seriousness of the offense, and only about 10 percent of all felonies reported to the police are violent.

▲ In response to overcrowding, some states are erecting tents on prison grounds, as in this Huntsville, Texas, facility. *Do you think that the use of tents to deal with prison overcrowding is acceptable? Why or why not?*

reduce (if the charges are upheld) the amount of good time earned by inmates and, by doing so, increase an inmate's time served.

A fifth criticism of determinate sentencing is that it is virtually impossible for legislatures or sentencing commissions to define in advance all of the factors that ought to be considered in determining a criminal sentence. You may recall from the discussion in Chapter 3 that this was a problem with one of the crime prevention implications of the classical school (equal punishment for equal crime) and the major reason for neoclassical reforms.

Philosophical Rationales

At the beginning of Chapter 2, the goals of criminal justice in the United States were identified as the prevention and the control of crime. Those are also the goals of **criminal sanctions** or **criminal punishment**—the penalties that are imposed for violating the criminal law. What has always been at issue, however, is how best to achieve those goals. This decision is the main problem faced by legislators who determine what the criminal sanctions will be in general and by judges who make sentencing decisions in individual cases. Historically, four major rationales or justifications have been given for the punishment imposed by the criminal courts: retribution, incapacitation, deterrence, and rehabilitation. A fifth rationale, restoration, has also been receiving greater attention.

Frequently, judges impose sentences for all five reasons, but at certain times in history, one or more of the reasons have been seen as less important than the others. Today, for example, punishment is imposed less for rehabilitative

criminal sanctions or **criminal punishment**
Penalties that are imposed for violating the criminal law.

purposes than it once was because of the prevalent view that we do not know how to change the behavior of criminal offenders. We will now examine each of the rationales for criminal punishment.

Retribution   From biblical times through the eighteenth century, **retribution** was the dominant justification for punishment. Although it has probably always played some role in sentencing decisions, it is now increasingly popular with the public as a rationale for punishment. However, *retribution* is an imprecise term that has been defined in many ways.[5] Nevertheless, when people say that criminal punishment should be imposed for retribution, what most of them want is probably either *revenge* or *just desserts*. **Revenge** is the justification for punishment expressed by the biblical phrase, "An eye for an eye, and a tooth for a tooth." People who seek revenge want to pay back offenders by making them suffer for what they have done. **Just desserts** is another justification in which punishment is seen as a paying back, but one that is based on something more than vindictive revenge and supposedly does not contain the emotional element of vengeance. *Just desserts* draws part of its meaning from the idea, attributed to the German philosopher Immanuel Kant (1724–1804), that offenders should be punished automatically, simply because they have committed a crime—they "deserve" it. Another aspect of *just desserts* is proportionality of punishment. That is, a punishment should fit the crime and should not be more nor less than the offender deserves.

Based on the assumption that the desire for revenge is a basic human emotion, retributivists generally believe that state-authorized punishment greatly reduces the likelihood that individual citizens will take it upon themselves to pay back offenders for what they have done. Vigilante justice is thereby avoided. Retributivists also believe that if offenders are not punished for their crimes, then other people will lose respect for the criminal law and will not obey it.

Finally, retribution is the only rationale for criminal punishment that specifically addresses what has happened in the past; that is, to pay back offenders for their crimes. All of the other rationales focus on the future and seek to influence it; for example, to restrain or prevent an offender from committing future crimes.

Incapacitation   **Incapacitation** is the removal or restriction of the freedom of those found to have violated criminal laws. Incapacitation makes it virtually impossible for offenders to commit crimes during the period of restraint. Banishment or exile was once used to achieve incapacitation. Even today, foreign nationals are deported after conviction of certain crimes. Currently, incapacitation is achieved primarily through imprisonment, which keeps inmates from committing further crimes (at least outside the prison). Some states, as noted previously, have habitual-offender statutes or "three strikes and you're out" laws that are intended to incapacitate repeat felons for life. Capital punishment is the ultimate means of incapacitation. An executed offender can never commit a crime again.

retribution
A dominant justification for punishment.

revenge
The punishment rationale expressed by the biblical phrase, "An eye for an eye, and a tooth for a tooth." People who seek revenge want to pay back offenders by making them suffer for what they have done.

just desserts
The punishment rationale based on the idea that offenders should be punished automatically, simply because they have committed a crime—they "deserve" it—and the idea that the punishment should fit the crime.

incapacitation
The removal or restriction of the freedom of those found to have violated criminal laws.

special or **specific deterrence**
The prevention of individuals from committing crimes again by punishing them.

general deterrence
The prevention of people in general from engaging in crime by punishing specific individuals and making examples of them.

rehabilitation
The attempt to "correct" the personality and behavior of convicted offenders through educational, vocational, or therapeutic treatment and to return them to society as law-abiding citizens.

Purpose of Sentencing

Most Americans (53 percent) think the most important purpose in sentencing should be retribution, 21 percent think it should be rehabilitation, and 13 percent each choose deterrence or incapacitation. Retribution is chosen more frequently than rehabilitation even though three-fifths (61 percent) of Americans think that most or some offenders could be rehabilitated "given early intervention with the right program." Only 9 percent of Americans think that no offenders can be rehabilitated.

SOURCE: Timothy J. Flanagan, "Reform or Punish: Americans' Views of the Correctional System," pp. 75–92 in Timothy J. Flanagan and Dennis R. Longmire (eds.), *Americans View Crime and Justice: A National Public Opinion Survey* (Thousand Oaks, CA: Sage, 1996), p. 69, Table 5.1 and p. 78.

Deterrence   As described in Chapter 3, in keeping with their goal of achieving the "greatest happiness for the greatest number," Beccaria and other classical theorists believed that the only legitimate purpose for punishment is the prevention or deterrence of crime. They generally viewed punishment for purely retributive reasons as a pointless exercise.

There are two forms of deterrence. **Special** or **specific deterrence** is the prevention of individuals from committing crime again by punishing them. **General deterrence** is the prevention of people in general from engaging in crime by punishing specific individuals and making examples of them.

One of the problems with general deterrence as a rationale for punishment is that even though it makes intuitive sense, social science is unable to measure its effects. Only those people who have not been deterred come to the attention of social scientists and criminal justice personnel.

Rehabilitation   For much of the twentieth century, the primary rationale for punishing criminal offenders has been **rehabilitation,** which is the attempt to "correct" the personality and behavior of convicted offenders through educational, vocational, or therapeutic treatment. The goal has been to return them to society as law-abiding citizens. However, as mentioned earlier, the goal of rehabilitating offenders has been challenged on the grounds that we simply do not know how to correct or cure criminal offenders because the causes of crime are not fully understood. As was also mentioned before, beginning in the mid-1970s, the goal of rehabilitation was abandoned altogether in some states, or at least deemphasized in favor of the goals of retribution and incapacitation. In other states, attempts at rehabilitation continue in an institutional context that seems to favor retribution and incapacitation (as it probably always has). Some critics have

▲ Historically, many people have believed that public executions have a general deterrent effect. *Do you agree? Why or why not?*

suggested that punishment and rehabilitation are incompatible ways of preventing and controlling crime and that rehabilitation generally cannot be achieved in a prison setting. This criticism, however, has apparently not influenced judges, who continue to send criminal offenders to prison to rehabilitate them.

Restoration   Until recently, victims of crime and their survivors have generally been forgotten or neglected in criminal justice. They have not been important or respected participants in the adjudication process except, perhaps, as witnesses to their own or their loved ones' victimization. Beginning in the 1980s, however, because of increased scholarly attention to their plight and a fledgling victims' rights movement, attempts have been made to change the situation. Today, at least in some jurisdictions, a greater effort is being made to do something for victims and their survivors—to restore them, as much as possible, to their previous state and to make them "whole" again. Among the programs now being introduced on behalf of victims and their survivors are victim assistance and victim compensation programs.

The U.S. Supreme Court ruled in 1991 in *Payne v. Tennessee* that judges and juries may consider *victim-impact statements* in their sentencing decisions. **Victim-impact statements** are descriptions of the harm and suffering that a crime has caused victims and their survivors. Before the Court's 1991 decision, victim-impact statements were considered irrelevant and potentially inflammatory and were not allowed.

Another effort at restoration places equal emphasis on victims' rights and needs and the successful reintegration (and, in some cases, initial integration) of offenders into the community. Unlike retribution, which focuses almost entirely on offenders and their punishments, restorative justice seeks to restore the health of the community, repair the harm done, meet victims' needs, and require the offender to contribute to those repairs. Following Braithwaite's theory of reintegrative shaming, in restorative justice the criminal act is condemned, offenders are held accountable, participants are involved, and repentant offenders are encouraged to earn their way back into society.[6] Restitution and community service are two examples of restorative practices (they are used for other purposes as well). Restitution is a court requirement that a victims' convicted offender pay money or provide services to victims, survivors, or to the community that has been victimized. Unfortunately, a problem with restitution is that most offenders have neither the financial means nor the abilities to provide adequate restitution.

Organizational Considerations

A judge's sentence is also guided by organizational considerations. We have already discussed at some length the practice of plea bargaining and have shown that without it, the judicial process could not function. For practical reasons, judges almost always impose the sentence agreed upon during plea negotiations. If they did not, plea bargaining would not work. That is, if defendants could not be sure that judges would impose the agreed-upon sentence, there would be no reason for them to plead guilty. They might as well take their chances at trial.

CRIMINAL JUSTICE Online

Victim Assistance

The U.S. Department of Justice established the Office for Victims of Crime (OVC) in 1983. OVC provides federal funding for victim assistance and compensation programs throughout the country. It also develops policies and works with criminal justice professionals in order to support crime victims. Visit the OVC Web site by clicking the link at cj.glencoe.com. *Do you think that enough is being done to support crime victims?*

victim-impact statements Descriptions of the harm and suffering that a crime has caused victims and their survivors.

FYI

1984 Crime Control Act

The 1984 Federal Comprehensive Crime Control Act requires that when offenders convicted of federal violations are sentenced to probation, they must pay a fine, make restitution, perform community service, or do all three.

Sentencing, Appeals, and the Death Penalty   **CHAPTER 9**

Another organizational consideration is the capacity of the system. As we already have noted, many of the prisons in this country and some entire state prison systems are overcrowded and are under federal court order to reduce the problem. Judges in jurisdictions with overcrowded prisons are generally less inclined to sentence offenders to prison.

A third organizational consideration is the cost-benefit question. Every sentence involves some monetary and social cost. Judges must be sensitive to this issue and must balance the costs of the sentence they impose with the benefits that might be derived from it.

Presentence Investigation Reports

A purpose of **presentence investigation reports** (PSIs or PSIRs), used in the federal system and by the majority of states, is to help judges determine the appropriate sentence for particular defendants. They are also used in classifying probationers, parolees, and prisoners according to their treatment needs and security risk. Generally, a PSI is prepared by a probation officer, who conducts as thorough a background check as possible on a defendant. In some jurisdictions, probation officers recommend a sentence based on the information in the PSI. In other jurisdictions, they simply write the report and do not make a sentencing recommendation. Studies show that judges follow the sentencing recommendations in PSIs most of the time, although they are not required to do so.

In most jurisdictions, after the PSI has been submitted to the judge, a sentencing hearing is held at which the convicted defendant has the right to address the court before the sentence is imposed. This procedure is called **allocution**. During allocution, a defendant is identified as the person found guilty and has a right to deny or explain information contained in the PSI if his or her sentence is based on it. The defendant also has the opportunity to plead for a **pardon** (a "forgiveness" for the crime committed that stops further criminal processing). He or she may also attempt to have the sentencing process stopped or may explain why a sentence should not be pronounced. However, defendants are not entitled to argue during allocution about whether or not they are guilty. Among the claims that a convicted offender can make at allocution are the following:

1. That he or she is not the person who was found guilty at trial.
2. That a pardon has been granted for the crime in question.
3. That he or she has gone insane since the verdict was rendered. Rules of due process prohibit the sentencing of convicted offenders if they do not understand why they are being punished. Punishment must be deferred until they are no longer insane.
4. That she is pregnant. The sentence of a pregnant offender must be deferred or adjusted, especially in a capital case.

Personal Characteristics of Judges

Although extralegal factors are not supposed to influence a judge's sentencing decision, studies show that they invariably do. Judges, after all, are human beings with all of the human frailties and prejudices of other human beings. Among the personal characteristics of judges that have been found to affect their sentencing decisions are the following:

presentence investigation reports
Reports, often called PSIs or PSIRs, that are used in the federal system and the majority of states to help judges determine the appropriate sentence. They are also used in classifying probationers, parolees, and prisoners according to their treatment needs and security risk.

allocution
The procedure at a sentencing hearing in which the convicted defendant has the right to address the court before the sentence is imposed. During allocution, a defendant is identified as the person found guilty and has a right to deny or explain information contained in the PSI if his or her sentence is based on it.

pardon
A "forgiveness" for the crime committed that stops further criminal processing.

▲ A judge's sentencing is the result of a complex set of factors. *Which factors do you consider to be the most important and the least important? Why?*

1. Their socioeconomic backgrounds.
2. The law schools they attended.
3. Their prior experiences both in and out of the courtroom.
4. The number of offenders they defended earlier in their careers.
5. Their biases concerning various crimes.
6. Their emotional reactions and prejudices toward the defendants.
7. Their own personalities.
8. Their marital and sexual relations.

In summary, a judge's sentencing decision is the result of the complex interplay of several different factors. Those factors include statutory provisions, philosophical rationales, organizational considerations, presentence investigation reports, results of the allocution, and personal characteristics of the judge.

9.1 CRITICAL THINKING

1. What do you think are some of the most important issues to consider when sentencing a convicted criminal?

2. Do you think that victims should play more or less of a role in sentencing?

Court Reporter

My name is Debora Randolph, and I am an official court reporter with the Johnson Country, Kansas District Court. I have an associate of applied science degree in court reporting and also an associate's degree in specialized business.

I began thinking about a career in court reporting when I was in high school. At the time, Kansas City Business College was the only school that had a court reporting program but it was being phased out. I then enrolled in another program and received my specialized business degree. I worked as a secretary at first. Still having a desire to be a court reporter, I opened the phonebook hoping to find a school that offered such a program and came across Brown Mackie College. I enrolled in the evening program and attended school for two years while working a full-time job as an administrative assistant. I successfully completed the program and received an A.A. degree. I then took and passed the required state certification test and was hired by the state of Kansas. I subsequently received my national certification. I have also taught court reporting courses.

As an official court reporter for the state of Kansas, my job entails recording verbatim reports of judicial trials, conferences, and hearings. Notes are taken at a high rate of speed through the use of a stenotype machine. As an officer of the court, it is my responsibility to prepare a complete and accurate report of proceedings which may involve highly technical terminology used in a number of different fields. Although the proceedings may not be transcribed until some time later, I also provide "realtime" or instant-text translation feed to the attorneys and judges. Text is displayed on computer monitors for attorneys and judges to view during the proceedings. Additionally, I provide input to the judge and administrative assistant regarding docket management.

One of the things I like best about my job is I am constantly learning because of the varied cases I take. I also get to listen to some very interesting life experiences. Court reporting is an interesting, challenging, and rewarding career; however, because of the long hours involved, it can be overwhelming. I often work evenings and weekends producing transcripts. I would advise anyone who is thinking of court reporting as a career to be prepared to dedicate a considerable amount of time to the profession. Many aspiring court reporters do not make it past the first year of school. Training requires much practice time to learn to "write" up to 25 words per minute in addition to the other core requirements.

Which aspect of this job would you find the most rewarding?

9.2 Appeals

As described previously, defendants can appeal their convictions either on legal grounds (for example, defects in jury selection, improper admission of evidence at trial, mistaken interpretations of law) or on constitutional grounds (for instance, illegal search and seizure, improper questioning of the defendant by the police, identification of the defendant through a defective police lineup, incompetent assistance of counsel). However, they are not entitled to present new evidence or testimony on appeal if that evidence or testimony could have been presented at trial. If new evidence is discovered that was unknown or unknowable to the defense at trial, then an appeal can sometimes be made on the basis of that new evidence. However, in a recent death penalty case (*Herrera v. Collins*, 1993) the Supreme Court ruled that, absent constitutional grounds, new evidence of innocence is no reason for a federal court to order a new state trial. In any event, because the defendant has already been found guilty, the presumption of innocence no longer applies during the appellate process, and the burden of showing why the conviction should be overturned shifts to the defendant.

Generally, notice of intent to appeal must be filed within 30 to 90 days after conviction. Also within a specified period of time, an *affidavit of errors* specifying the alleged defects in the trial or pretrial proceedings must be submitted. If those two steps are followed, the appellate court must review the case. Nevertheless, very few appeals are successful. Nearly 80 percent of state trial court decisions are affirmed on appeal. (See Chapter 8 for more on the appellate courts.)

9.2 CRITICAL THINKING

Why do you think so few appeals are successful? Do you think the appeals process works effectively? Why or why not?

9.3 The Death Penalty

Before concluding this chapter, we will examine in some detail the death penalty in the United States, because, as the Supreme Court has acknowledged, "death is different."[7] Other sentencing options are discussed in later chapters of this book. As a punishment for the most heinous of crimes, the death penalty, or capital punishment, differs from all other criminal sanctions, not only in the nature of the penalty itself (the termination of life), but also in the legal procedures that lead to it. However, before describing the unique way in which capital punishment is administered in the United States, we will provide some background about the penalty.

A Brief History of the Death Penalty in the United States

When the first European settlers arrived in America, they brought with them the legal systems from their native countries, which included the penalty of death for a variety of offenses. For example, the English Penal Code at the time, which was adopted by the British colonies, listed more than 50 capital offenses, but actual practice varied from colony to colony. In the Massachusetts Bay Colony, 12 crimes carried the death penalty:

- Idolatry
- Witchcraft
- Blasphemy
- Rape
- Statutory rape
- Perjury in a trial involving a possible death sentence
- Rebellion
- Murder
- Assault in sudden anger
- Adultery
- Buggery (sodomy)
- Kidnapping

In the statute, each crime was accompanied by an appropriate biblical quotation justifying the capital punishment. Later the colony added arson, treason, and grand larceny to the list of capital offenses. In contrast, the Quakers adopted much milder laws. The Royal Charter for South Jersey (1646), for example, did not permit capital punishment for any crime, and in Pennsylvania, William Penn's Great Act of 1682 limited the death penalty to treason and murder. Most colonies, however, followed the much harsher British Code.

The earliest recorded lawful execution in America was in 1608 in the colony of Virginia. Captain George Kendall, a councillor for the colony, was executed for being a spy for Spain. Since Kendall, nearly 19,000 legal executions have been performed in the United States under civil authority. However, only about 2.5 percent of those people executed since 1608 have been women. Ninety percent of the women executed were executed under local, as opposed to state, authority, and the majority (87 percent) were executed before 1866. The first woman executed was Jane Champion in the Virginia colony in 1632. She was hanged for murdering and concealing the death of her child, who was fathered by a man other than her husband.

In addition, about two percent of those executed in the United States since 1608 have been juveniles, those whose offenses were committed prior to their 18th birthdays. The first juvenile executed in America was Thomas Graunger in Plymouth Colony in 1642, for the crime of bestiality. Since 1990, the United States is one of only five countries that has executed anyone under 18 years of age at the time of the crime; the others are Iran, Pakistan, Saudi Arabia, and Yemen. The United States has executed 17 juveniles since 1985 (as of October 1, 2000). About two percent of current death row inmates are juveniles.[8]

Enter the Supreme Court

Before 1968, the only issues the Supreme Court considered in relation to capital punishment concerned the means of administering the death penalty. The one exception was the case of *Powell v. Alabama* (1932), in which the Court held that failure to provide counsel in a capital case violates due process as required under the Fourteenth Amendment. In the other pre-1968 cases,

Women Executed

Of the 3,703 people on death rows in the United States, as of October 1, 2000, only about 1.5 percent were women. As of October 2000, only five women have been executed in the United States since 1962. The first was Velma Barfield, who was executed in North Carolina on October 2, 1984. The second through fifth were Karla Faye Tucker, who was executed in Texas on February 3, 1998; Judy Buenoano, who was executed in Florida on March 30, 1998; Bettie Lou Beets, who was executed in Texas on February 24, 2000; and Christina Marie Riggs, who was executed in Arkansas on May 2, 2000.

SOURCE: *Death Row, U.S.A.* (Fall 2000).

the Court upheld the constitutionality of the following methods of execution: shooting (*Wilkerson v. Utah,* 1878), electrocution (*In re Kemmler,* 1890), a second electrocution after the first attempt has failed to kill the offender (*Louisiana ex rel. Francis v. Resweber,* 1947), and hanging (*Andres v. United States,* 1948). Currently, there are five methods of execution in use: lethal injection, electrocution, lethal gas, hanging, and firing squad. Lethal injection is used by the most states. Figure 9–5 on page 324 lists the states that employ each method of execution.

Between 1968 and 1972, a series of lawsuits challenged various aspects of capital punishment as well as the constitutionality of the punishment itself. During this period, an informal moratorium on executions was observed, pending the outcome of the litigation, and no death row inmates were executed. Some of the suits were successful, and some of them were not. Finally, on June 29, 1972, the Supreme Court set aside death sentences for the first time in its history. In its decisions in *Furman v. Georgia, Jackson v. Georgia,* and *Branch v. Texas* (hereafter referred to as the *Furman* decision), the Court held that the capital punishment statutes in those three cases were unconstitutional because they gave the jury complete discretion to decide whether to impose the death penalty or a lesser punishment in capital cases. Although nine separate opinions were written—a very rare occurrence—the majority of five justices (Douglas, Brennan, Stewart, White, and Marshall) pointed out that the death penalty had been imposed arbitrarily, infrequently, and often selectively against people of color. According to the majority, those statutes constituted "cruel and unusual punishment" under the Eighth and Fourteenth Amendments. (The four dissenters were Chief Justice Burger and justices Blackmun, Powell, and Rehnquist.) It is important to emphasize that the Supreme Court did not rule that the death penalty itself was unconstitutional, only the way in which it was being administered.

The practical effect of the *Furman* decision was that the Supreme Court voided the death penalty laws of some 35 states, and more than 600 men and women had their death sentences vacated and commuted to a term of imprisonment. Although opponents of capital punishment were elated that the United States had finally joined all the other Western industrialized nations in abolishing capital punishment either in fact or in practice, the joy was short-lived. By the fall of 1974, 30 states had enacted new death penalty statutes that were designed to meet the Court's objections.

The new death penalty laws took two forms. Some states removed all discretion from the process by mandating capital punishment upon conviction for certain crimes (mandatory statutes). Other states provided specific guidelines that judges and juries were to use in deciding if death was the appropriate sentence in a particular case (guided-discretion statutes).

The constitutionality of the new death penalty statutes was quickly challenged, and on July 2, 1976, the Supreme Court announced its rulings in five

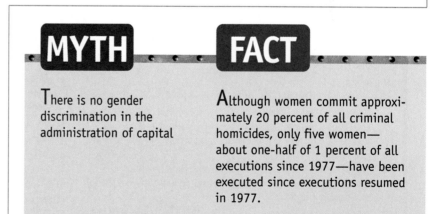

MYTH • • • • **FACT** • • • • •

There is no gender discrimination in the administration of capital

Although women commit approximately 20 percent of all criminal homicides, only five women—about one-half of 1 percent of all executions since 1977—have been executed since executions resumed in 1977.

FIGURE 9–5

Method of Execution, by Jurisdiction, August, 2000

Lethal Injection	Lethal Injection (continued)	Electrocution	Lethal Gas	Hanging	Firing Squad
Arizona [1, 2]	New Hampshire [8]	Alabama	Arizona [1, 2]	Delaware [1, 3]	Idaho [1, 9]
Arkansas [1, 4]	New Jersey	Arkansas [1, 4]	California [1, 5]	New Hampshire [8]	Oklahoma [6]
California [1, 5]	New Mexico	Florida [1, 12]	Maryland [7]	Washington [1]	Utah [1]
Colorado	New York	Georgia [1, 14]	Missouri [1]		
Connecticut	North Carolina	Kentucky [1, 11]	Wyoming [10]		
Delaware [1, 3]	Ohio [1]	Nebraska			
Florida [1, 12]	Oklahoma [6]	Ohio [1]			
Georgia [1, 14]	Oregon	Oklahoma [6]			
Idaho [1, 9]	Pennsylvania	South Carolina [1]			
Illinois	South Carolina [1]	Tennessee [13]			
Indiana	South Dakota	Virginia [1]			
Kansas	Tennessee [13]				
Kentucky [1, 11]	Texas				
Louisiana	Utah [1]				
Maryland [7]	Virginia [1]				
Mississippi	Washington [1]				
Missouri [1]	Wyoming [10]				
Montana	U.S. Government				
Nevada	U.S. Military				

SOURCE: The Death Penalty Information Center <www.deathpenaltyinfo.org>, August 28, 2000.

1. Authorizes two methods of execution.
2. Arizona authorizes lethal injection for persons sentenced after November 15, 1992; those sentenced before that date may select lethal injection or lethal gas.
3. Delaware authorizes lethal injection for those whose capital offense occurred after June 13, 1986; those who committed the offense before that date may select lethal injection or hanging.
4. Arkansas authorizes lethal injection for persons committing a capital offense after July 4, 1983; those who committed the offense before that date may select lethal injection or electrocution.
5. When lethal gas was challenged in *Fierro v. Gomez*, 77 F. 3d 301 (1996), the Ninth Circuit held this method of execution unconstitutional. Subsequently, the U.S. Supreme Court remanded the case for reconsideration in light of California changing its statute to provide that lethal injection be administered unless the inmate requests lethal gas. The Ninth Circuit, on remand, held that since Fierro had not chosen lethal gas, his claim was moot. However, the court held left open the reinstatement of the issue for an inmate actually facing the gas chamber.
6. Oklahoma authorizes electrocution if lethal injection is ever held to be unconstitutional and firing squad if both lethal injection and electrocution are held unconstitutional.

7. Maryland authorizes lethal injection for those whose capital offenses occurred on or after March 25, 1994; those who committed the offense before that date may select lethal injection or lethal gas.
8. New Hampshire authorizes hanging only if lethal injection cannot be given.
9. Idaho authorizes firing squad only if lethal injection is "impractical."
10. Wyoming authorizes lethal gas if lethal injection is ever held to be unconstitutional.
11. Kentucky authorizes lethal injection for those convicted after March 31, 1998; those who committed the offense before that date may select lethal injection or electrocution.
12. Florida lawmakers agreed to switch the state's primary method of execution from electrocution to lethal injection. The state will allow prisoners to choose between the two methods.
13. Tennessee authorizes lethal injection for those sentenced after Jan. 1, 1999 and those currently on death row will choose between the electric chair and lethal injection.
14. Georgia authorizes lethal injection for those sentenced after May 1, 2000. Those sentenced before May 1, 2000, will be executed by electrocution.

Hanging

Lethal Injection

Electrocution

Lethal Gas

KEEP OUTSIDE
OF RAILINGS

Firing Squad

▲ The five methods of execution currently used in the United States are lethal gas, electrocution, lethal injection, hanging, and firing squad. *Which method of execution do you think is preferable? Why?*

test cases. In *Woodson v. North Carolina* and *Roberts v. Louisiana,* the Court rejected "mandatory" statutes that automatically imposed death sentences for defined capital offenses. However, in *Gregg v. Georgia, Jurek v. Texas,* and *Proffitt v. Florida* (hereafter referred to together as the *Gregg* decision), the Court approved several different forms of guided-discretion statutes. Those statutes, the Court wrote, struck a reasonable balance between giving the jury some guidance and allowing it to consider the background and character of the defendant and the circumstances of the crime.

The most dramatic effect of the *Gregg* decision was the resumption of executions on January 17, 1977, when the state of Utah executed Gary Gilmore (at his own request) by firing squad. Since then, 667 people have been executed in 31 states (as of July 1, 2000).[10] More than half of the 667 executions have taken place in just three states—Texas (232), Virginia (79), and Florida (49). Figure 9–6 shows the states in which executions have taken place. Note that Texas alone accounts for more than one-third of all

FIGURE 9–6

State-by-State Count of Inmates Executed in 31 States Since Executions Resumed in 1977

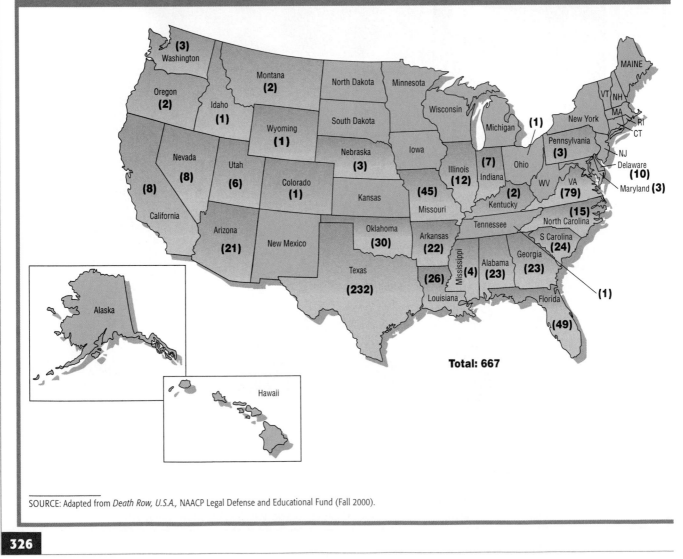

SOURCE: Adapted from *Death Row, U.S.A.,* NAACP Legal Defense and Educational Fund (Fall 2000).

PART 3   *The Courts*

FIGURE 9-7

Race or Ethnicity and Sex of Defendants Executed and Their Victims and Defendant-Victim Racial or Ethnic Combinations

Gender of Defendants Executed			Gender of Victims		
Total Number 667			Total Number 887		
Female	5	(0.75%)	Female	420	(47.35%)
Male	662	(99.25%)	Male	467	(52.65%)

Race of Defendants Executed			Race of Victims		
White	369	(55.32%)	White	727	(81.96%)
Black	239	(35.93%)	Black	111	(12.51%)
Latino	44	(6.60%)	Latino	29	(3.27%)
Native American	10	(1.50%)	Asian	20	(2.25%)
Asian	5	(0.75%)			

Defendant-Victim Racial or Ethnic Combinations		
White Defendant and		
White Victim	347	(52.02%)
Black Victim	11	(1.65%)
Asian Victim	3	(0.45%)
Latino Victim	3	(0.45%)
Black Defendant and		
White Victim	159	(23.84%)
Black Victim	62	(9.30%)
Latino Victim	7	(1.05%)
Asian Victim	6	(0.90%)
Latino Defendant and		
White Victim	25	(3.75%)
Latino Victim	15	(2.25%)
Black Victim	2	(0.30%)
Asian Victim	1	(0.15%)
Native American and White Victim	10	(1.50%)
Asian Defendant and		
Asian Victim	4	(0.60%)
White Victim	1	(0.15%)

SOURCE: *Death Row, U.S.A.,* NAACP Legal Defense and Educational Fund (Fall 2000).

post-*Furman* executions. Texas has executed almost three times as many offenders as any other state.

Figure 9–7 shows the race or ethnicity and gender of both the defendants executed and their victims, as well as defendant-victim racial or ethnic combinations. As can be seen in the figure, nearly all of the people executed since Gilmore's execution in 1977 have been male, while the gender of the victims is divided nearly evenly between males (53 percent) and females (47 percent). As for race, 55 percent of all people executed under post-*Furman* statutes have been white; about 36 percent have been black. Thus, the percentage of blacks who have been executed far exceeds their proportion of the general population (about 13 percent). Particularly interesting is that more than 80 percent of the victims of those executed have been white. What makes this finding interesting is that murders, including capital murders (all post-*Furman* executions have been for capital murders; see the following discussion), tend to be intraracial crimes. However, the death penalty is imposed primarily on the killers of white people, regardless of the race or ethnicity of the offender. The figures on defendant-victim racial or ethnic combinations (see Figure 9–7) further support this conclusion. Note that about 52 percent of executions have involved white killers of white victims, and about 24 percent of executions have involved black killers of white victims. On the other hand, only about 9 percent of executions have been of black killers of black victims, and there have been only 11 executions of white killers of black persons (less than 2 percent).

Currently (as of October 1, 2000), 40 jurisdictions have capital punishment statutes, although New Hampshire has no death sentences imposed. Thirteen jurisdictions do not have capital punishment statutes. Figure 9–8 shows the jurisdictions with and without capital punishment statutes.

MYTH

Capital punishment is no longer administered in a way that is racially discriminatory and legally impermissible.

FACT

Dozens of scientific studies clearly show that the death penalty continues to be administered in a legally impermissible and discriminatory fashion against blacks and the killers of whites.[9]

▲ The death penalty issue rouses intense passions on both sides of the debate. *Why do people feel so strongly about the death penalty?*

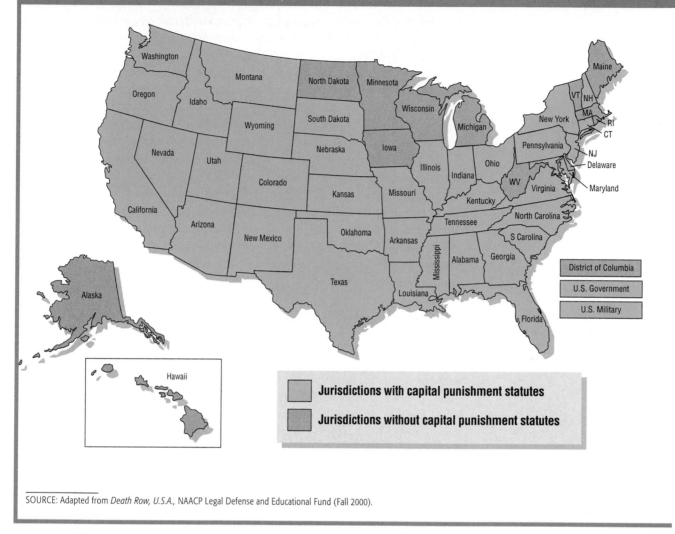

FIGURE 9-8

Jurisdictions With and Without Capital Punishment Statutes

Jurisdictions with capital punishment statutes

Jurisdictions without capital punishment statutes

District of Columbia

U.S. Government

U.S. Military

SOURCE: Adapted from *Death Row, U.S.A.,* NAACP Legal Defense and Educational Fund (Fall 2000).

In decisions since *Gregg,* the Supreme Court has limited the crimes for which death is considered appropriate and has further refined death penalty jurisprudence. In 1977, in the cases of *Coker v. Georgia* and *Eberheart v. Georgia,* the Court held that rape of an adult female (in *Coker*) and kidnapping (in *Eberheart*), where the victim was not killed, do not warrant death. Those two decisions effectively limited the death penalty to those offenders convicted of capital, or aggravated, murder.

In 1986, in *Ford v. Wainwright,* the Court barred states from executing inmates who have developed mental illness while on death row. In the 1989 case of *Penry v. Lynaugh,* however, the Court held that the Eighth Amendment does not prohibit the execution of a capital offender who is mentally retarded. In the 1988 case of *Thompson v. Oklahoma* and the 1989 cases of *Stanford v. Kentucky* and *Wilkins v. Missouri,* the Court effectively limited capital punishment to offenders who are 16 years of age or older at the time of their offenses. Another death penalty decision of the Supreme Court is the 1987 case of *McCleskey v. Kemp,* in which the Court held that state death penalty statutes are constitutional even when statistics indicate that they have been applied in racially biased ways. The Court ruled that racial discrimination must be shown in individual cases. The *McCleskey* decision was particularly disheartening to opponents of capital punishment because, for them, the case was the last best chance of having the Supreme Court declare the death penalty unconstitutional once and for all.

The 1994 federal crime bill (the Violent Crime Control and Law Enforcement Act) expanded the number of federal crimes punishable by death to about 50. (Estimates vary depending on whether statutes or offenses are counted, and how offenses are counted.) All but four of the federal crimes involve murder. The four exceptions are treason; espionage; drug trafficking in large quantities; and attempting, authorizing, or advising the killing of any public officer, juror, or witness in a case involving a continuing criminal enterprise—regardless of whether such a killing actually occurs. In addition, the bill reinstated the death penalty for federal crimes for which previous death penalty provisions could not pass constitutional muster. The new law brought the earlier statutes into compliance with guidelines established by the Supreme Court. The last execution by the U.S. government was on March 15, 1963, when Victor H. Feguer was hanged at Iowa State Penitentiary.

The Procedural Reforms Approved in *Gregg*

It is important to emphasize that the Supreme Court approved the new death penalty statutes in *Gregg* "on their face." That is, the Court assumed, without any evidence, that the new guided-discretion statutes would eliminate the arbitrariness and discrimination that the Court found objectionable in its *Furman* decision. The Court was particularly optimistic about the following procedural reforms: bifurcated trials, guidelines for judges and juries, and automatic appellate review.

bifurcated trial
A two-stage trial (unlike the one-stage trial in other felony cases) consisting of a guilt phase and a separate penalty phase.

Bifurcated Trials   A **bifurcated trial** is a two-stage trial—unlike the one-stage trial in other felony cases—consisting of a guilt phase and a separate penalty phase. If, in the guilt phase, the defendant is found guilty as charged, then at the penalty phase, the sentencing authority (judge or jury) must determine whether the sentence will be death or life in prison (there are no other choices except, in some states, life imprisonment without opportunity for parole). In most states, judges must follow the jury's sentencing recommendation. However, in Alabama, Delaware, Florida, and Indiana, the jury's recommendation is only advisory to the judge. In those states, the judge may impose death even if the jury recommends life, or may impose life even if the jury recommends death.

Some states require the selection of two separate juries in capital trials, one for the guilt phase and one for the penalty phase. During *voir dire* in capital cases, each side is generally allowed more peremptory challenges, necessitating a larger panel from which to select the jury. California, for example, allows 26 peremptory challenges in capital cases and only 10 in noncapital cases. During both phases of a bifurcated capital trial, evidence may be introduced and witnesses may be called to testify. In short, all of the procedures of due process apply to both phases of the bifurcated trial.

Guidelines for Judges and Juries What the Court found especially appealing about the guided-discretion statutes approved in *Gregg* is that judges and juries are provided with standards that presumably restrict, but do not eliminate, their sentencing discretion. Specifically, judges and juries, in most states, are provided with lists of aggravating and, at least in some states, mitigating factors. **Aggravating factors** are circumstances that make a crime worse than usual. **Mitigating factors** make a crime less severe than usual. The Court has since ruled (in *Lockett v. Ohio*, 1978; *Bell v. Ohio*, 1978; and *Hitchcock v. Dugger*, 1987) that judges and juries must consider any mitigating circumstance offered by the defense, whether it is listed in the statute or not. Figure 9–9 lists the aggravating and mitigating factors in Florida's current death penalty statute. The factors are typical of most states that provide them.

aggravating factors
In death sentencing, circumstances that make a crime worse than usual.

mitigating factors
In death sentencing, circumstances that make a crime less severe than usual.

FIGURE 9–9

Aggravating and Mitigating Factors in Florida's Death Penalty Statute

Aggravating Factors

1. The capital felony was committed by a person under sentence of imprisonment or placed on community control.
2. The defendant was previously convicted of another capital felony or of a felony involving the use or threat of violence to the person.
3. The defendant knowingly created a great risk of death to many persons.
4. The capital felony was committed while the defendant was engaged or was an accomplice, in the commission of, or an attempt to commit, or flight after committing or attempting to commit, any robbery, sexual battery, arson, burglary, kidnapping, or aircraft piracy or the unlawful throwing, placing, or discharging of a destructive device or bomb.
5. The capital felony was committed for the purpose of avoiding or preventing a lawful arrest or effecting an escape from custody.
6. The capital felony was committed for pecuniary gain.
7. The capital felony was committed to disrupt or hinder the lawful exercise of any governmental function or the enforcement of laws.
8. The capital felony was especially heinous, atrocious, or cruel.
9. The capital felony was a homicide and was committed in a cold, calculated, and premeditated manner without any pretense of moral or legal justification.
10. The victim of the capital felony was a law enforcement officer engaged in the performance of his official duties.
11. The victim of the capital felony was an elected or appointed public official engaged in the performance of his official duties if the motive for the capital felony was related, in whole or in part, to the victim's official capacity.

Mitigating Factors

1. The defendant has no significant history of prior criminal activity.
2. The capital felony was committed while the defendant was under the influence of extreme mental or emotional disturbance.
3. The victim was a participant in the defendant's conduct or consented to the act.
4. The defendant was an accomplice in the capital felony committed by another person, and his participation was relatively minor.
5. The defendant acted under extreme duress or under the substantial domination of another.
6. The capacity of the defendant to appreciate the criminality of his conduct or to conform his conduct to the requirements of law was substantially impaired.
7. The age of the defendant at the time of the crime.

SOURCE: Florida's Statutes Annotated, Chapter 921, Section 921.141.

Under Florida's death penalty statute, which is an "aggravating-versus-mitigating" type, at least one aggravating factor must be found before death may be considered as a penalty. If one or more aggravating factors are found, they are weighed against any mitigating factors. If the aggravating factors outweigh the mitigating factors, the sentence is death. However, if the mitigating factors outweigh the aggravating factors, the sentence is life imprisonment without opportunity for parole. As previously mentioned, in Florida the jury's recommendation is only advisory to the judge.

Another type of guided-discretion statute is Georgia's "aggravating-only" statute. In Georgia, if a jury finds at least one statutory aggravating factor, then it may, but need not, recommend death. The jury may also consider any mitigating factors, although mitigating factors are not listed in the statute, as they are in some states. The judge must follow the jury's recommendation.

A third type of guided-discretion statute is Texas's "structured-discretion" statute. In Texas, aggravating or mitigating factors are not listed in the statute. Instead, during the sentencing phase of the trial, the state and the defendant or the defendant's counsel may present evidence about matter that the court deems relevant to sentence, that is, any aggravating or mitigating factors. On conclusion of the presentation of the evidence, the court submits the following issues to the jury:

1. Whether the defendant would possibly commit criminal acts of violence that would constitute a continuing threat to society; and

2. (if raised by the evidence) whether the defendant actually caused the death of the deceased or did not actually cause the death of the deceased but intended to kill the deceased or another or anticipated that a human life would be taken.

During penalty deliberations, juries in Texas must consider all evidence admitted at the guilt and penalty phases. Then, they must consider the two aforementioned issues. To answer "yes" to the issues, all jurors must answer "yes"; to answer "no" to the issues, ten or more jurors must answer "no." If the two issues are answered in the affirmative, jurors are then asked if there is a sufficient mitigating factor or factors to warrant that a sentence of life imprisonment rather than a death sentence be imposed. To answer "no" to this issue, all jurors must answer "no"; to answer "yes," ten or more jurors must agree. If the jury returns an affirmative finding on the first two issues and a negative finding on the third issue, then the court must sentence the defendant to death. On the other hand, if the jury returns a negative finding on either of the first two issues or an affirmative finding on the third issue, then the court must sentence the defendant to life imprisonment.

Automatic Appellate Review The third procedural feature of most of the new death penalty statutes is automatic appellate review. Currently, 36 of the 38 states with death penalty statutes provide for automatic appellate review of all death sentences, regardless of the defendant's wishes. (Arkansas has no specific provisions for automatic review, and South Carolina allows the defendant to waive sentence review if the defendant is deemed competent by the court; also, the federal jurisdiction does not provide for automatic appellate review.) Most of the 36 states automatically review both the conviction and the sentence (Idaho, Indiana,

Oklahoma, and Tennessee review only the sentence).[11] Generally, the automatic review is conducted by the state's highest appellate court. If either the conviction or the sentence is overturned, then the case is sent back to the trial court for additional proceedings or for retrial. It is possible that the death sentence may be reimposed as a result of this process.

Some states are very specific in defining the review function of the appellate courts, while other states are not. Although the Supreme Court does not require it (*Pulley v. Harris,* 1984), some states have provided a proportionality review. In a **proportionality review,** the appellate court compares the sentence in the case it is reviewing with penalties imposed in similar cases in the state. The object of proportionality review is to reduce, as much as possible, disparity in death penalty sentencing.

In addition to the automatic appellate review, there is a dual system of collateral review for capital defendants. In other words, capital defendants may appeal their convictions and sentences through both the state and the federal appellate systems. Figure 9–10 shows the general appeals process in death penalty cases.

Some death row inmates whose appeals have been denied by the U.S. Supreme Court may still try to have the Supreme Court review their cases on constitutional grounds by filing a writ of *habeas corpus.* Recall that a writ of *habeas corpus* is a court order directing a law officer to produce a prisoner in court to determine if the prisoner is being legally detained or imprisoned. Critics maintain that abuse of the writ has contributed to the long delays in executions (currently averaging more than ten years after conviction) and to the high costs associated with capital punishment.

proportionality review

A review in which the appellate court compares the sentence in the case it is reviewing with penalties imposed in similar cases in the state. The object is to reduce, as much as possible, disparity in death penalty sentencing.

FIGURE 9–10

The Appellate Process in Capital Cases

Stage 1:

Step 1: Trial and Sentence in State Court
Step 2: Direct Appeal to the State Appeals Court
Step 3: U.S. Supreme Court for Writ of *Certiorari*

Stage 2:

Step 1: State Post Conviction
Step 2: State Court of Appeals
Step 3: U.S. Supreme Court for Writ of *Certiorari*

Stage 3:

Step 1: Petition for Writ of *Habeas Corpus* in Federal District Court
Step 2: Certificate of Probable Cause and Request for Stay of Execution
Step 3: U.S. Court of Appeals
Step 4: U.S. Supreme Court for Writ of *Certiorari*
Step 5: Request for a Stay of Execution

SOURCE: Raymond Paternoster, *Capital Punishment in America* (New York: Lexington, 1991), p. 203. Reprinted by permission.

Sentencing, Appeals, and the Death Penalty **CHAPTER 9**

Congress passed the Antiterrorism and Effective Death Penalty Act of 1996, in part to speed up the process and reduce costs. President Clinton signed it into law on April 24, 1996. The law requires that second or subsequent *habeas* petitions be dismissed when the claim had already been made in a previous petition. It also requires that new claims be dismissed, unless the Supreme Court hands down a new rule of constitutional law and makes it retroactive to cases on collateral review. Under the Act, the only other way the Supreme Court will hear a claim made for the first time is when the claim is based on new evidence not previously available. Even then, the new evidence must be of sufficient weight, by a clear and convincing standard of proof, to convince a judge or jury that the capital defendant was not guilty of the crime or crimes for which he or she was convicted.

The Act also made the federal appellate courts "gatekeepers" for second or subsequent *habeas corpus* petitions. Thus, to file a second or subsequent claim under the new law, a capital defendant must first file a motion in the appropriate appellate court announcing his or her intention. A panel of three judges must then hear the motion within 30 days. The judges must decide whether the petitioner has a legitimate claim under the new Act. If the claim is denied, the new law prohibits any review of the panel's decision, either by a rehearing or writ of *certiorari* to the Supreme Court. So far, the Supreme Court has upheld the constitutionality of the new law.

Some people argue that the appellate reviews are unnecessary delaying tactics (at least those beyond the automatic review). However, the outcomes of the reviews suggest otherwise. Nationally, between 1973 and 1998,

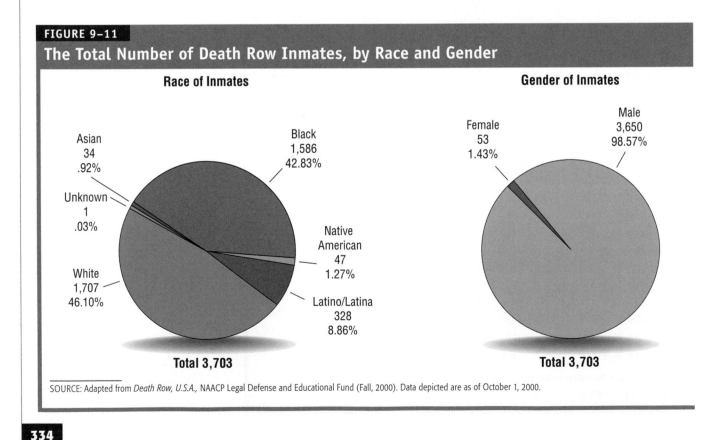

FIGURE 9–11

The Total Number of Death Row Inmates, by Race and Gender

Race of Inmates

Asian 34 .92%

Black 1,586 42.83%

Unknown 1 .03%

Native American 47 1.27%

White 1,707 46.10%

Latino/Latina 328 8.86%

Total 3,703

Gender of Inmates

Female 53 1.43%

Male 3,650 98.57%

Total 3,703

SOURCE: Adapted from *Death Row, U.S.A.*, NAACP Legal Defense and Educational Fund (Fall, 2000). Data depicted are as of October 1, 2000.

one-third of the initial convictions or sentences in capital cases were overturned on appeal,[12] and, contrary to popular belief, those reversals were generally not the result of so-called legal technicalities. They were the product of "such fundamental constitutional errors" as denial of the right to an impartial jury, problems of tainted evidence and coerced confessions, ineffective assistance of counsel, and prosecutors' references to defendants who refuse to testify.[13]

As noted previously, the number of persons currently on death rows in the United States is 3,682 (as of July 1, 2000). Figure 9–11 on page 334 shows the race, ethnic, and gender distributions of the death row population. Because there are so few executions each year (the largest number since 1977 was 98, in 1999),[14] the death row population in the United States continues to grow—there are about 200 to 300 new death sentences each year—but it grows much more slowly than one might expect. What keeps the death row population from growing at a much faster rate is that about half as many people have been removed from death row by having their convictions or sentences reversed as currently occupy it (1,710 as of April 1, 2000). In addition, since January 1, 1973, 54 death row inmates have committed suicide, 90 have received **commutations** (reductions in sentences, granted by a state's governor), and 165 have died of natural causes or have been killed.[15]

Prospects for the Future

These are interesting times when it comes to the death penalty in the United States. It appears that capital punishment is receiving more attention

commutations
Reductions in sentences, granted by a state's governor.

▲ The death row population in the United States has grown steadily in recent years. *What factors have kept it from growing even faster?*

Sentencing, Appeals, and the Death Penalty **CHAPTER 9**

than usual. Although less than half of the world's nations still have a death penalty, those that do have one seldom use it. Among western, industrialized nations, the United States stands alone as the only nation to employ capital punishment. However, even within the United States, as noted previously, 13 jurisdictions do not have a death penalty, and among the 40 jurisdictions that do have one, only a handful of them use it more than occasionally, and almost all of them are located geographically in the South.

Consider the distribution of the 667 executions conducted in the United States between January 17, 1977, and October 1, 2000:[16]

- The 667 executions have occurred in 31 of the 40 death penalty jurisdictions.
- Nine jurisdictions with death penalty statutes (including the U.S. government and the U.S. military) have not had a single execution.
- Thirteen jurisdictions, as noted, including the District of Columbia, do not have death penalty statutes.
- Seventeen of the 31 "executing" states (55 percent) have held fewer than 10 executions.
- Only 14 "executing" states (45 percent) have conducted ten or more executions.
- Nearly 70 percent of all executions have taken place in just six states—Texas, Virginia, Florida, Missouri, Oklahoma, and Louisiana.
- Fifty-four percent of all executions have taken place in just three states—Texas, Virginia, and Florida.
- Texas, alone, accounts for more than a third of all the executions.
- Of the states that have conducted ten or more executions, nine (64 percent) are southern states.
- More than 80 percent of all executions have occurred in the South.[17]

Thus, for all intents and purposes, the death penalty today is a criminal sanction that is used more than occasionally in only a few non-western countries and a few states in the American South. This is an important point because it raises the question of why those death penalty—or more precisely, executing—jurisdictions in the world need the death penalty, while all other jurisdictions in the world—the vast majority—do not.

There are several other reasons to believe that the death penalty in the United States is a waning institution. Four other factors, in particular, signal its demise. First, public support for the death penalty appears to be dropping. In four national public opinion polls conducted between May and July 2000, only 62 to 66 percent of adults or registered voters nationwide were in favor of the death penalty for a person convicted of murder.[18] This is the lowest level of support recorded in a national poll and likely the first time the level of support has fallen below 70 percent in more than 20 years. Moreover, for about a decade, national public opinion polls have shown that when given a choice between the death penalty and life imprisonment with absolutely no possibility of parole (LWOP), only about half of the public prefers the death penalty.[19]

Second, the American public is expressing greater concern about the way the death penalty is being administered. For example, an NBC News/*Wall*

Street Journal poll conducted in July 2000 found that 42 percent of registered voters nationwide thought that the death penalty is not applied fairly (42 percent believe it is applied fairly, 8 percent responded that it depends, and 8 percent are not sure).[20] Sixty-three percent of the respondents to that poll favor the suspension of the death penalty until questions about its fairness can be studied. A Harris poll conducted in July 2000 revealed that 94 percent of adults nationwide think that innocent people are sometimes convicted of murder. Perhaps even more telling, according to a CNN/*USA Today*/Gallup poll conducted in June 2000, 80 percent of adults nationwide think that in the past five years a person has been executed who was, in fact, innocent of the crime with which he or she was charged. A *Newsweek* poll conducted in June 2000 also found that more than 80 percent of adults nationwide think

MYTH	FACT
Most defendants facing the death penalty receive competent legal representation.	According to a *National Law Journal* study, criminal defendants in six southern states—Alabama, Florida, Georgia, Louisiana, Mississippi, and Texas (states that account for more than one-half of all post-*Furman* executions)—often wind up on death row after being represented by inexperienced, unskilled, or unprepared court-appointed lawyers. Many poor defendants sentenced to death had lawyers who had never handled a capital trial before, or lawyers who had been reprimanded or disciplined or were subsequently disbarred.[21]

that at least some innocent people have been wrongly executed since the death penalty was reinstated in the 1970s: 8 percent think that "many" innocent people have been wrongly executed; 33 percent think that only "some" innocent people have been wrongly executed; and 41 percent think that only a "very few" innocent people have been wrongly executed. That same poll discovered that 82 percent of adults nationwide think that states should make it easier for death row inmates to introduce new evidence that might prove their innocence, even if that might result in delays in the death penalty process. Ninety-five percent of adults nationwide think that states should permit DNA testing in all cases where it might prove a person's guilt or innocence (currently only Illinois and New York give inmates the right to have their DNA tested), and 88 percent of adults nationwide think that the federal government should require states to permit DNA testing under those circumstances. It appears that recent revelations about the quality of justice in capital murder trials, the overturning of several convictions as a result of DNA tests, and the resulting moratorium on executions in Illinois, have had an impact on public opinions about the death penalty.

A third factor is the positions taken by respected organizations within the United States, such as the American Bar Association (ABA) and organized religions. In 1997, the ABA adopted a resolution that requested death penalty jurisdictions to refrain from using the sanction until greater fairness and due process could be assured. In July 2000, the ABA's new president, Martha Barnett, a "reluctant supporter" of the death penalty, reiterated the call for a moratorium on executions. Besides inadequate counsel and a lack of due process, she cited racial bias, racial profiling, and the execution of the mentally retarded and juveniles as problems with the death penalty's

FIGURE 9-12

The Principal Executing Countries in the World Ranked by Number of Executions in 1998

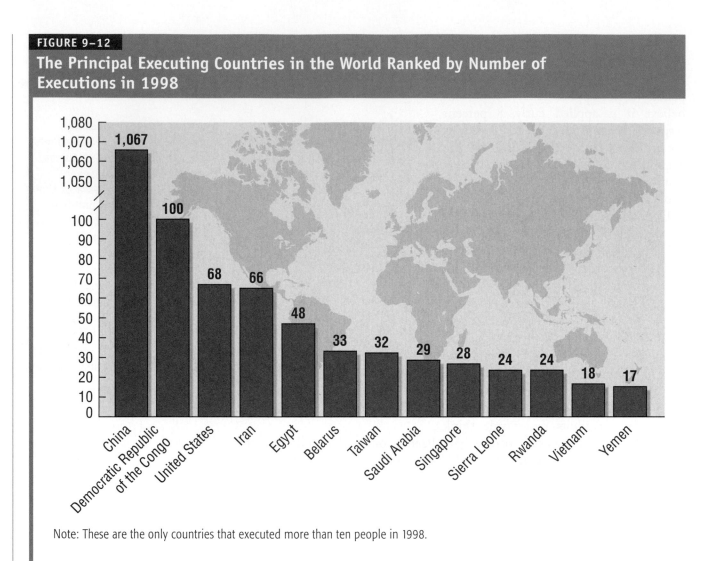

Note: These are the only countries that executed more than ten people in 1998.

SOURCE: Death Penalty Information Center.

administration.[22] The leaders of most organized religions in the United States—whether Catholic, Protestant, or Jewish—openly oppose capital punishment. The only religious organizations that support capital punishment are (1) the Southern Baptist Convention, (2) Jehovah's Witnesses, (3) Seventh Day Adventists, (4) the Church of Jesus Christ of Latter Day Saints (Mormons), and (5) certain conservative and orthodox Jewish groups.[23]

A fourth factor is world opinion. All of our major allies except Japan have abolished the death penalty. In Europe the death penalty is viewed as a violation of human rights.[24] Demonstrations protesting against the U.S. death penalty have recently been held in France, Spain, and Norway.[25] A condition for admittance into the European Union (EU) is the abolition of the death penalty. This criterion will force Turkey, for example, to abandon its death penalty system if it wants to join the EU, which it does. Admittance into the 40-nation Council of Europe also requires the renouncing of the death penalty. Georgia, a former republic of the Soviet Union, effectively abolished its death penalty in 1997 so that it could join the Council. Russia has promised to end its death penalty so that it, too, can secure membership in the Council. Figure 9–12 lists the principal executing countries of the world in 1998. The United Nations Commission on Human Rights has repeatedly condemned the death penalty in the United States, urging the U.S. government to stop all executions until it brings states into compliance with international standards and laws. Of particular importance, some foreign businesses may make economic decisions based on a state's use of the death penalty. In a 1998 letter to then Texas governor George W. Bush, a European Parliament official wrote, "Many companies, under pressure from shareholders and public opinion to apply ethical business practices, are beginning to consider the possibility of restricting the investment in the U.S. to states that do not apply the death penalty."

On the other hand, capital punishment in some states has proven stubbornly resilient. There are reasons to believe that in those U.S. states the death penalty will remain a legal sanction for the foreseeable future. One reason is that death penalty support among the American public, at least according to the major opinion polls, remains relatively strong. It is unlikely that the practice of capital punishment could be sustained if a majority of American citizens were to oppose it. In no year for which polls are available has a majority of Americans opposed the death penalty (the first national death penalty opinion poll was conducted in December 1936).[26]

Although life imprisonment without opportunity for parole (LWOP) seems to be a popular alternative to the death penalty in polls, a problem with the LWOP alternative is that the public is very skeptical about the ability of correctional authorities to keep capital murderers imprisoned for life. In a recent national survey, only 11 percent of registered voters believed that an offender sentenced to LWOP would never be released from prison.[27] Thus, although half of the public may say that it prefers LWOP to capital punishment, in practice, the public probably does not want to make the substitution because it fears that the alternative might not adequately protect it from the future actions of convicted capital offenders.

The abiding faith of death penalty proponents in the ability of legislatures and courts to fix any problems with the administration of capital punishment is another reason for its continued use in some places. However, the quarter-century record of "fine-tuning" the death penalty process remains ongoing. Legislatures and courts are having a difficult time "getting it right," despite spending inordinate amounts of their resources trying.

As for the positions against capital punishment taken by respected organizations in the United States, "true believers" in the death penalty could care less what others think, especially in the case of organizations such as the American Bar Association. This holds true for world opinion as well. In the case of organized religions, the situation is probably more complex. Although most people who consider themselves religious and are affiliated with religions whose leadership opposes capital punishment probably respect the views of their leaders, they obviously live their daily lives and hold beliefs about capital punishment (and other issues such as abortion) based on other values. This is clearly evident in public opinion polls that show that a large majority of Catholics and Protestants still favor the death penalty.[28]

Another sign of the death penalty's staying power in the United States is that no jurisdiction that adopted new death penalty statutes in the wake of *Furman* has abolished the penalty, including those jurisdictions that have

Justice Blackmun and the Death Penalty

For more than 20 years, Justice Harry A. Blackmun supported the administration of capital punishment in the United States. However, on February 22, 1994, in a dissent from the Court's refusal to hear the appeal of a Texas inmate scheduled to be executed the next day, Blackmun asserted that he had come to the conclusion that "the death penalty experiment has failed" and that it was time for the Court to abandon the "delusion" that capital punishment could be administered in a way that was consistent with the Constitution. He noted that "from this day forward, I no longer shall tinker with the machinery of death."

SOURCE: *Callins v. Collins,* 114 S. Ct. 1127 (1994).

The monetary costs of capital punishment are less than the monetary costs of life imprisonment without opportunity for parole.

The monetary costs of capital punishment (that is, the entire legal process) currently average between $2 million and $3.5 million per execution. The monetary costs of life imprisonment without opportunity for parole are unlikely to cost much more—and may cost much less—than $1 million per offender. It reportedly cost the state of Florida $10 million to execute serial killer Ted Bundy.[29]

never used it. If there were a serious threat to the retention of capital punishment—indeed, if it were abolished in some jurisdictions—then the effort to retain or reinstate it would likely begin in earnest. Currently, there is no need for such an effort.

Some death penalty opponents believe that a principal reason for the continuing support of capital punishment is that most people know very little about the subject and what they think they know is based almost entirely on myth. It is assumed that if people were educated about capital punishment, most of them would oppose it. Unfortunately, research suggests that educating the public about the death penalty may not have the effect abolitionists desire.[30] Although information about the death penalty can reduce support for the sanction—sometimes significantly—rarely is the support reduced to less than a majority.

What else, then, sustains the public's death penalty support? We believe that there are at least three more major factors:

1. The desire for vindictive revenge.
2. The incapacitative power of the penalty.
3. The symbolic value it has for politicians and law enforcement officials.

In a recent Gallup poll on the subject, 40 percent of all respondents who favored the death penalty selected "An eye for an eye/They took a life/Fits the crime" as a reason.[31] The reason selected second most often (by only 12 percent) was "Save taxpayers money/ Cost associated with prison." No other reasons were selected by more than ten percent of the death penalty proponents.

The choice of "An eye for an eye/They took a life/Fits the crime" indicates support of the penal purpose of retribution. Those who chose this reason want to repay the offender for what he or she has done. This response, moreover, at least the "eye for an eye" part, has a strong emotional component and thus has been called "vindictive revenge."[32] That the public may support the death penalty primarily for vindictive revenge raises two important questions. First, is the satisfaction of the desire for vindictive revenge a legitimate penal purpose? And second, does pandering to or legitimizing this desire for vindictive revenge contribute to the violence in our nation?

Another factor that sustains death penalty support is the unquestionable incapacitative power of the penalty: Once a capital offender has been executed, he or she can never kill again. Although this seems persuasive, it is not a reason often given by the public. Only four percent of Gallup-polled death penalty proponents chose it.

Nevertheless, research confirms that a small percentage of capital offenders released from prison have killed again. The execution of all convicted capital offenders would have prevented those killings. However, a problem with simply executing all convicted capital offenders is that, inevitably, innocent people are executed. The possibility of executing an innocent person does not seem to be a crucial problem for a majority of Supreme Court justices, given the Court's recent ruling in this area (see the FYI on *Herrera v. Collins,* 1993). It

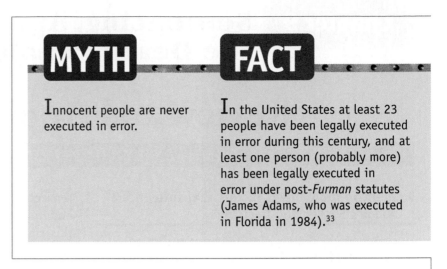

Innocent people are never executed in error.

In the United States at least 23 people have been legally executed in error during this century, and at least one person (probably more) has been legally executed in error under post-*Furman* statutes (James Adams, who was executed in Florida in 1984).[33]

might, however, be a problem for many Americans. In any event, to prevent capital offenders from killing again, doesn't it make sense simply to keep them imprisoned? At least then, if errors are made, they can be rectified to some degree.

A final factor that sustains death penalty support is the symbolic value it has for politicians and criminal justice officials. Politicians use support for the death penalty as a symbol of their toughness on crime. Opposition to capital punishment is invariably interpreted as symbolic of softness on crime. Criminal justice officials and much of the public often equate support for capital punishment with support for law enforcement in general. It is ironic that although capital punishment has virtually no effect on crime, the death penalty continues to be a favored political silver bullet—a simplistic solution to the crime problem used by aspiring politicians and law enforcement officials.

In short, the reasons provided for supporting capital punishment do not stand up well to critical scrutiny. But the American public has not been deterred from supporting it anyway. Together with the movement to replace indeterminate sentencing with determinate sentencing and to abolish parole, the death penalty is part of the "law and order" agenda popular in the United States since the mid-1970s. Whether this direction in criminal justice has run its course is anyone's guess. However, it appears that the effort to "get tough" with criminals has not produced the results desired by its advocates.

FYI

Herrera v. Collins

In *Herrera v. Collins* (1993) the Supreme Court held that in the absence of constitutional grounds, new evidence of innocence is no reason for the Court to order a new trial. According to the majority opinion: "Where a defendant has been afforded a fair trial and convicted of the offense for which he was charged, the constitutional presumption of innocence disappears. . . . Thus, claims of actual innocence based on newly discovered evidence [are not] grounds for . . . relief absent an independent constitutional violation occurring in the course of the underlying state criminal proceedings." For some, the decision is a reasonable response to the Court's need to limit its jurisdiction in *habeas corpus* cases.

9.3 CRITICAL THINKING

1. Do you think the death penalty helps to prevent crime in the United States? Why or why not?

2. Do you think the death penalty should continue to be legal in this country? Why or why not?

Review and Applications

1. Identify the General Factors that Influence a Judge's Sentencing Decisions

In sentencing, judges are limited by statutory provisions; guided by prevailing philosophical rationales, organizational considerations, and presentence investigation reports; and influenced by their own personal characteristics.

2. Describe how Judges Tailor Sentences to Fit the Crime and the Offender

Judges have several ways to tailor sentences to fit the crime and the offender. They can impose a combination sentence of imprisonment, probation, and a fine. They can suspend the imprisonment portion of a combination sentence, or they can suspend the entire sentence if the offender stays out of trouble, makes restitution to the victim, or seeks medical treatment. Judges can give offenders credit for time spent in jail while awaiting trial, deducting that time from any prison sentence. A judge may even impose a sentence of "time served" and release the offender. When an offender is convicted of two or more crimes, a judge can order the prison sentences to run concurrently or consecutively. Judges can also delay sentencing and retain the right to impose a sentence at a later date if conditions warrant it.

3. Distinguish Between Indeterminate and Determinate Sentences

An indeterminate sentence has a fixed minimum and maximum term of incarceration, rather than a set period. A determinate sentence, on the other hand, has a fixed period of incarceration and eliminates the decision-making responsibility of parole boards.

4. Explain the Three Basic Types of Determinate Sentences

There are three basic types of determinate sentences: flat-time, mandatory, and presumptive. With flat-time sentencing, judges may choose between probation and imprisonment but have little discretion in setting the length of a prison sentence. With mandatory sentencing, a specified number of years of imprisonment (usually within a range) is provided for particular crimes. Mandatory sentencing generally allows credit for good time but does not allow release on parole. Presumptive sentencing allows a judge to retain some sentencing discretion (subject to appellate review). It requires a judge to impose the normal sentence, specified by statute, on a "normal" offender who has committed a "normal" crime. However, if the crime or the offender is not normal—if there are mitigating or aggravating circumstances—then the judge is allowed to deviate from the presumptive sentence.

5. List Five Rationales or Justifications for Criminal Punishment

Five rationales or justifications for criminal punishment are retribution, incapacitation, deterrence, rehabilitation, and restoration.

6. Explain the Purposes of Presentence Investigation Reports

Presentence investigation reports (PSIs) help judges determine the appropriate sentences for particular defendants. PSIs are also used in the classification of probationers, parolees, and prisoners according to their treatment needs and their security risks.

7. List the Legal Bases for Appeal

Defendants can appeal their convictions either on legal grounds (such as defects in jury selection, improper admission of evidence at trial, mistaken interpretations of law) or on constitutional grounds (such as illegal search and seizure, improper questioning of the defendant by the police, identification of the defendant through a defective police lineup, and incompetent assistance of counsel).

8. Identify the Type of Crime for which Death May Be a Punishment

In the United States, death is the ultimate punishment. At the state level, death can be imposed only for the crime of aggravated murder and a few other seldom-committed offenses.

9. Summarize the Three Major Procedural Reforms the U.S. Supreme Court Approved for Death Penalty Cases in the *Gregg* Decision

The three major procedural reforms the Court approved in *Gregg* were bifurcated trials, guidelines for judges and juries to follow, and automatic appellate review.

KEY TERMS

restitution, p. 306
indeterminate sentence, p. 309
determinate sentence, p. 309
flat-time sentencing, p. 310
good time, p. 310
mandatory sentencing, p. 310
presumptive sentencing, p. 310
criminal sanctions or criminal
    punishment, p. 314
retribution, p. 315

revenge, p. 315
just desserts, p. 315
incapacitation, p. 315
special or specific deterrence,
    p. 316
general deterrence, p. 316
rehabilitation, p. 316
victim-impact statements, p. 317
presentence investigation reports,
    p. 318

allocution, p. 318
pardon, p. 318
bifurcated trial, p. 330
aggravating factors, p. 331
mitigating factors, p. 331
proportionality review, p. 333
commutations, p. 335

QUESTIONS FOR REVIEW

1. What are five general types of punishment currently being used in the United States?

2. What are some criticisms of determinate sentencing?

3. Which rationale for criminal punishment is the only one that specifically addresses what has happened in the past, and what are its two major forms?

4. What are three organizational considerations that may influence a judge's sentencing decision?

5. What is *allocution*?

6. What two steps must be taken before an appellate court will hear an appeal?

7. What was the landmark 1972 decision in which the Supreme Court set aside death sentences for the first (and only) time in its history?

8. What are the five methods of execution currently used in the United States?

EXPERIENTIAL ACTIVITIES

1. **Sentencing** Select a criminal case that is currently receiving publicity in your community. Conduct an informal survey, asking respondents what sentence they believe would be appropriate in the case. Ask them why they chose the sentence. Determine whether respondents tended to agree with each other or not. If they did not tend to agree, speculate on the reasons for the disagreement.

2. **Death Penalty Opinion** With family members or friends, discuss the death penalty. Ask them why they hold their particular positions (in favor, opposed, undecided). Also, ask them under what circumstances they would change their positions. Would any of the mitigating circumstances listed in the second Critical Thinking exercise that follows cause any of them to change their positions?

EXPERIENTIAL ACTIVITIES

INTERNET

3. Death Penalty Access the Death Penalty Information Center Web site through the link at cj.glencoe.com and the "Pro Death Penalty pages" from the links at cj.glencoe.com. Choose the same topic included in both sources, and review the information provided. Write a brief summary of the information you discovered and how it affected your view of capital punishment.

4. Mandatory Minimums Access the Web site of Families Against Mandatory Minimums through the link at cj.glencoe.com. Click on "Behind Bars" and select one or more of the federal or state MMS cases. Read the description of the case or cases and decide whether you agree or disagree with the sentence imposed. Provide reasons for your decision.

CRITICAL THINKING EXERCISES

The Three Strikes Law

1. In March 1995, a 27-year-old man who had stolen a slice of pizza from a group of children sitting outside a pizza parlor became the first person to be sentenced to 25 years to life in prison under California's "three strikes and you're out" law. Enacted March 7, 1995, the law was reinforced November 8, 1995 by a constitutional amendment supported by 72 percent of California voters. The "three strikes" law is triggered by two past felony convictions. In this case, the defendant was convicted of "petty theft with a prior felony conviction." He had already been convicted of robbery, attempted robbery, drug possession, and riding a stolen motorcycle.

   a. It will cost the taxpayers of California about $26,000 a year to incarcerate the man. Is it worth it? Is it a wise expenditure of tax dollars?

   b. Is the punishment proportional to the crime or crimes? Should it be?

   c. Do you think "petty theft with a prior conviction" is a legitimate trigger of a "three strikes" law?

   d. There is no question that the offender was a criminal. He had a reputation for being a bully. Nevertheless, are "three strikes and you're out" laws an ethically defensible way of dealing with such criminals? Why or why not?

Sentencing

2. You are a juror in a death penalty case. The defendant in the case has already been found guilty of capital murder during the guilt phase of the trial. During the penalty phase, you have to determine whether the defendant is to be sentenced to death or to life imprisonment without opportunity for parole (LWOP). The judge has instructed you (and the rest of the jury) to consider the aggravating and mitigating circumstances of the case. If the aggravating circumstances outweigh the mitigating circumstances, you are expected to vote for death. On the other hand, if the mitigating circumstances outweigh the aggravating circumstances, you are expected to vote for LWOP. The lone aggravating circumstance in the case is that the defendant committed the capital murder during the commission of a robbery. Though they are not aggravating circumstances, the defendant also has two prior convictions for robbery and one prior conviction for the sale of illegal drugs. Under which of the following mitigating circumstances would you vote for LWOP or death in this case? Explain the reasons for your decision.

   a. The defendant was 14 years old at the time the crime was committed.

   b. The defendant is a female with children.

c. The defendant is mentally retarded (that is, has an IQ of 60).

d. The defendant was seriously abused, both mentally and physically, as a child.

e. The defendant is legally insane.

ADDITIONAL READING

Acker, James R., Robert M. Bohm, and Charles S. Lanier (eds.). *America's Experiment with Capital Punishment: Reflections on the Past, Present, and Future of the Ultimate Penal Sanction.* Durham, NC: Carolina Academic Press, 1998.

Bedau, Hugo Adam (ed.). *The Death Penalty in America: Current Controversies.* New York: Oxford Univ. Press, 1997.

Bohm, Robert M., *Deathquest: An Introduction to the Theory and Practice of Capital Punishment in the United States.* Cincinnati, OH: Anderson, 1999.

Bowers, William J., with Glenn L. Pierce and John McDevitt. *Legal Homicide: Death as Punishment in America, 1864–1982.* Boston: Northeastern Univ. Press, 1984.

Haas, Kenneth C., and James A. Inciardi (eds.). *Challenging Capital Punishment: Legal and Social Science Approaches.* Newbury Park, CA: Sage, 1988.

Johnson, Robert. *Condemned to Die: Life Under Sentence of Death.* Prospect Heights, IL: Waveland, 1989.

Johnson, Robert. *Death Work: A Study of the Modern Execution Process,* 2d ed. Belmont, CA: Wadsworth, 1998.

Neubauer, David W. *America's Courts and the Criminal Justice System,* 5th ed. Belmont, CA: Wadsworth, 1996.

Paternoster, Raymond. *Capital Punishment in America.* New York: Lexington, 1991.

Van den Haag, Ernest, and John P. Conrad. *The Death Penalty: A Debate.* New York: Plenum, 1983.

Zimring, Franklin E., and Gordon Hawkins. *Capital Punishment and the American Agenda.* Cambridge:

ENDNOTES

1. In addition to the other sources cited, material on sentencing and appeals is from David W. Neubauer, *America's Courts and the Criminal Justice System,* 5th ed. (Belmont, CA: Wadsworth, 1996); Christopher Smith, *Courts, Politics, and the Judicial Process* (Chicago: Nelson-Hall, 1993); N. Gary Holten and Lawson L. Lamar, *The Criminal Courts: Structures, Personnel, and Processes* (New York: McGraw-Hill, 1991); Lawrence Baum, *American Courts,* 3d ed. (Boston: Houghton Mifflin, 1994); David Garland, *Punishment and Modern Society: A Study in Social Theory* (Chicago: Univ. of Chicago Press, 1990); Paul Wice, *Chaos in the Courthouse: The Inner Workings of the Urban Criminal Courts* (New York: Praeger, 1985); John Paul Ryan, Allan Ashman, Bruce D. Sales, and Sandra Shane-DuBow, *American Trial Judges* (New York: Free Press, 1980); Robert Satter, *Doing Justice: A Trial Judge at Work* (New York: Simon & Schuster, 1990);

Herbert Packer, *The Limits of the Criminal Sanction* (Stanford, CA: Stanford Univ. Press, 1968).

2. Timothy C. Hart and Brian A. Reeves, *Felony Defendants in Large Urban Counties,* 1996. U.S. Department of Justice, Bureau of Justice Statistics (Washington: GPO, 1999) p. 29, Table 29.

3. *American Correctional Association 2000 Directory: Juvenile and Adult Correctional Departments, Institutions, Agencies and Paroling Authorities* (Lanham, MD: American Correctional Association, 2000), p. 20

4. "Sentence Disparity in New York: The Response of Forty-One Judges," *New York Times,* March 30, 1979, p. B3.

5. See Robert M. Bohm, "Retribution and Capital Punishment: Toward a Better Understanding of Death Penalty Opinion," *Journal of Criminal Justice,* Vol. 20 (1992), pp. 227–35.

ENDNOTES

6. "Restorative Justice: An Interview With Visiting Fellow Thomas Quinn," *National Institute of Justice Journal,* No. 235 (March 1998), p. 10.

7. Unless indicated otherwise, material about the death penalty is from Robert M. Bohm, *Deathquest: An Introduction to the Theory and Practice of Capital Punishment in the United States* (Cincinnati, OH: Anderson, 1999); James R. Acker, Robert M. Bohm, and Charles S. Lanier (eds.), *America's Experiment with Capital Punishment: Reflections on the Past, Present, and Future of the Ultimate Penal Sanction* (Durham, NC: Carolina Academic Press, 1998); Hugo Alan Bedau, *The Death Penalty in America; Current Controversies* (New York: Oxford University Press, 1997), Hugo Adam Bedau (ed.), *The Death Penalty in America,* 3d ed. (London: Oxford Univ. Press, 1982); William J. Bowers, with Glenn L. Pierce and John McDevitt, *Legal Homicide: Death as Punishment in America, 1864–1982* (Boston: Northeastern Univ. Press, 1984); Raymond Paternoster, *Capital Punishment in America* (New York: Lexington, 1991); Robert M. Bohm, "Humanism and the Death Penalty, with Special Emphasis on the Post-Furman Experience," *Justice Quarterly,* Vol. 6 (1989), pp. 173–95; Victoria Schneider and John Ortiz Smykla, "A Summary Analysis of Executions in the United States, 1608–1987: The Espy File," in R. M. Bohm (ed.), *The Death Penalty in America: Current Research* (Cincinnati: Anderson, 1991), pp. 1–19.

8. *Death Row,* U.S.A (Summer 2000) <www.deathpenaltyinfo.org/DeathRowUSA1.html>.

9. For a summary of those studies, see United States General Accounting Office, *Death Penalty Sentencing: Research Indicates Pattern of Racial Disparities, Report to the Senate and House Committees on the Judiciary* (Washington: GPO, 1990). For the view that the evidence does not show racial discrimination, see William Wilbanks, *The Myth of a Racist Criminal Justice System* (Monterey, CA: Brooks/Cole, 1987).

10. Death Row, U.S.A., op. cit.

11. Bohm, op. cit., p. 30.

12. Tracy L. Snell, *Capital Punishment* 1998, U.S. Department of Justice, Bureau of Justice Statistics Bulletin (Washington: GPO, 1999), p. 15, appendix table 3.

13. Ibid., Paternoster, op. cit., pp. 208–9.

14. The Death Penalty Information Center, op. cit.

15. *Death Row,* U.S.A., (Spring 2000).

16. Unless otherwise indicated, these data are from *Death Row,* U.S.A. (Summer, 2000), a quarterly report by the Criminal Justice Project of the NAACP Legal Defense and Educational Fund.

17. Death Penalty Information Center <www.deathpenaltyinfo.org>, November 21, 2000.

18. <www.pollingreport.com/crime.htm#death>

19. See, for example, Alec Gallup and Frank Newport, "Death Penalty Support Remains Strong," *The Gallup Monthly Report* (June 1991); <www.pollingreport.com/crime.htm#death>.

20. <www.pollingreport.com/crime.htm#death>.

21. Marcia Coyle, Fred Strasser, and Marianne Lavelle, "Fatal Defense," *The National Law Journal,* Vol. 12 (June 11, 1990), pp. 29–44.

22. Death Penalty Information Center, op. cit.

23. Robert M. Bohm, *Deathquest,* op. cit., pp. 177 and 183.

24. "The Shadow Over America," *Newsweek,* May 29, 2000, p. 27.

25. Death Penalty Information Center, op. cit.

26. Bohm, *Deathquest,* op. cit.

27. Survey cited in Edmund F. McGarrell and Marla Sandys, "The Misperception of Public Opinion Toward Capital Punishment: Examining the Spuriousness Explanation of Death Penalty Support." *American Behavioral Scientist,* Vol. 39 (1996), pp. 500–13, p. 509.

28. See, for example, Gallup and Newport, op. cit.

29. Robert M. Bohm, "The Economic Costs of Capital Punishment: Past, Present, and Future," pp. 429–50 in James R. Acker, Robert M. Bohm, and Charles S. Lanier (eds.), *America's Experiment with Capital Punishment: Reflections on the Past, Present, and Future of the Ultimate Sanction* (Durham, NC: Carolina Academic Press, 1998).

30. Robert M. Bohm, Louise J. Clark, and Adrian F. Aveni, "Knowledge and Death Penalty Opinion: A Test of the Marshall Hypotheses," *Journal of Research in Crime and Delinquency,* Vol. 28 (1991), pp. 360–87; Robert M. Bohm and Ronald E. Vogel, "A Comparison of Factors Associated with Uninformed and Informed Death Penalty Opinions," *Journal of Criminal Justice,* Vol. 23 (1994), pp. 125–43; Robert M. Bohm, Ronald E. Vogel, and Albert A. Maisto, "Knowledge and Death Penalty Opinion: A Panel Study," *Journal of Criminal Justice,* Vol. 21 (1993), pp. 29–45.

31. The Gallup Organization <www.gallup.com/poll/surveys/2000/Topline000214/q42t47.asp>.

32. Bohm, "Retribution and Capital Punishment," op. cit.; see also Bohm and Vogel, "A Comparison of Factors Associated with Uninformed and Informed Death Penalty Opinions," op. cit.

33. Hugo Adam Bedau and Michael L. Radelet, "Miscarriages of Justice in Potentially Capital Cases," *Stanford Law Review,* Vol. 40 (1987), pp. 21–179; Michael L. Radelet, Hugo Adam Bedau, and Constance E. Putnam, *In Spite of Innocence: Erroneous Convictions in Capital Cases* (Boston: Northeastern Univ. Press, 1992).

PART 4

Corrections

CHAPTER 10
Institutional Corrections

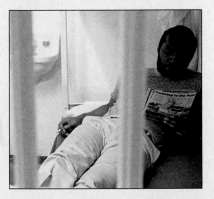

CHAPTER 11
Prison Life, Inmate Rights, Release, and Recidivism

CHAPTER 12
Community Corrections

Institutional Corrections

CHAPTER OBJECTIVES

After completing this chapter, you should be able to:

1. Summarize the purposes of confinement in Europe before it became a major way of punishing criminals.

2. Describe how offenders were punished before the large-scale use of confinement.

3. Explain why confinement began to be used as a major way of punishing offenders in Europe.

4. Describe the recent trends in the use of incarceration in the U.S.

5. List some of the characteristics of the incarcerated population in the U.S.

6. Describe how incarceration facilities are structured, organized, and administered by the government in the U.S.

7. Name some of the common types of correctional facilities in the U.S.

8. Identify some of the procedures that institutions employ to maintain security and order.

9. List the services and programs that are commonly available to inmates in prison.

10.1 Historical Overview of Institutional Corrections

Students often wonder why they must learn about the history of institutional corrections. One reason is that it is impossible to fully understand (and improve) the present state of affairs without knowledge of the past; the present developed out of the past. People who fail to remember the past are destined to repeat its mistakes. Another reason is that nothing helps us see how institutional corrections is linked to our larger society and culture better than the study of history. Try to keep those two points in mind when studying history.

European Background

In Europe, institutional confinement did not become a major punishment for criminals until the 1600s and 1700s. (In the United States, institutional confinement was not used extensively as a punishment until the 1800s.) As a practice, though, institutional confinement has existed since ancient times. Before the 1600s, however, it usually served functions other than punishment for criminal behavior. For example, confinement was used to:

1. Detain people before trial.
2. Hold prisoners awaiting other sanctions, such as death and corporal punishment.
3. Coerce payment of debts and fines.
4. Hold and punish slaves.
5. Achieve religious indoctrination and spiritual reformation (as during the Inquisition).
6. Quarantine disease (as during the bubonic plague).[1]

Forerunners of Modern Incarceration Unlike modern incarceration, which strives to change the offender's character and is carried out away from public view, popular early punishments for crime, which predated the large-scale use of imprisonment, were directed more at the offender's body and property; one basic goal was to inflict pain.[2] Furthermore, those punishments were commonly carried out in public to humiliate the offender and to deter onlookers from crime. Examples of such early punishments are fines, confiscation of property, and diverse methods of corporal and capital punishment. Some popular methods of corporal and capital punishment were beheading, stoning, hanging, crucifixion, boiling and burning, flogging, branding, or placement in the stocks or pillory.[3] As this brief list illustrates, the eventual shift to incarceration reduced the severity and violence of punishment.

MYTH

Throughout history, imprisonment has been the primary sentence for lawbreakers, and it still is today.

FACT

Viewed historically, imprisonment is a relatively recent sentence for lawbreaking. Even today in the United States, the number of people in prison is small compared with the number on probation or under other types of supervision in the community.

FYI

Mamertine Prison

Although it surely did not resemble today's prisons, one of the earliest known prisons was the Mamertine Prison, built around 64 B.C. under the sewers of Rome.

SOURCE: Robert Johnson, *Hard Time: Understanding and Reforming the Prison* (Monterey, CA: Brooks/Cole, 1987).

▲ Besides being painful, placement in the stocks or pillory was intended to humiliate and shame offenders. *Is a greater emphasis on the shame of punishment needed today? If so, how should it be accomplished?*

Two additional forerunners of modern incarceration were banishment and transportation. In essence, they were alternatives to the more severe corporal punishments or capital punishment. Originating in ancient times, **banishment** required offenders to leave the community and live elsewhere, commonly in the wilderness. The modern version of banishment is long-term incarceration (for example, life imprisonment without opportunity for parole). As population and urban growth displaced frontiers across Europe and as demands for cheap labor increased with the rise of Western capitalism, **transportation** of offenders from their home nation to one of that nation's colonies gradually replaced banishment. England, for instance, was transporting hundreds of convicts a year to North America by the early 1600s.[4] Transportation fell into disuse as European colonies gained independence.

The closest European forerunners of the modern U.S. prison were known as **workhouses** or *houses of correction*. Offenders were sent to them to learn discipline and regular work habits. The fruits of inmate labor were also expected to pay for facility upkeep and even to yield a profit. One of the first and most famous workhouses, the London Bridewell, opened in the 1550s, and workhouses spread through other parts of Europe thereafter. Such facilities were used extensively throughout the next three centuries, coexisting with such responses to crime as transportation, corporal punishment, and capital punishment. In fact, crowding in workhouses was a major impetus for the development of transportation as a punishment.

Reform Initiatives   As described in Chapter 3, the Enlightenment was a time of faith in science and reason as well as a period of humanistic reform. The Enlightenment thinkers and reformers of the 1700s and 1800s described the penal system of their day with such terms as *excessive, disorderly, inefficient, arbitrary, capricious, discriminatory* (against the poor), and *unjust*.

banishment
A punishment, originating in ancient times, that required offenders to leave the community and live elsewhere, commonly in the wilderness.

transportation
A punishment in which offenders were transported from their home nation to one of that nation's colonies to work.

workhouses
European forerunners of the modern U.S. prison, where offenders were sent to learn discipline and regular work habits.

Three reformers who were important to initiatives in corrections were Cesare Beccaria (1738–1794), John Howard (1726–1790), and Jeremy Bentham (1748–1832).

Graeme Newman and Pietro Marongiu contend that Beccaria's famous book, *On Crimes and Punishments* (1764), though often acclaimed for its originality, actually brought together the reformist principles espoused by other thinkers of the era, such as Montesquieu and Voltaire.[5] One of those principles concerned replacing the discretionary and arbitrary administration of justice with a system of detailed written laws describing the behaviors that constitute crime and the associated punishments. People need to know, Beccaria believed, exactly what punishments are prescribed for various offenses if the law is to deter criminal behavior. As part of his quest to deter crime, Beccaria declared that the punishment should fit the crime in two senses. First, the severity of punishment should parallel the severity of harm resulting from the crime. Second, the punishment should be severe enough to outweigh the pleasure obtainable from the crime. Furthermore, to deter crime, he believed, punishment needed to be certain and swift. Certainty implies that the likelihood of getting caught and punished is perceived as high. Swiftness implies that punishment will not be delayed after commission of the crime.

Beccaria did not ground his thinking firmly in empirical observations and did little to actively campaign for the reforms he advocated.[6] The work of John Howard, an English sheriff and social activist, presents an interesting contrast in that regard. Howard's 1777 book, *The State of the Prisons in England and Wales,* was based on his visits to penal institutions in various parts of Europe. Howard was appalled by the crowding, overall poor living conditions, and disorderly and abusive practices he observed in those facilities. He advocated that penal environments be made safe, humane, and orderly. Howard's opinion was that incarceration should do more than punish—that it should also instill discipline and reform inmates. Toward that end, he proposed an orderly institutional routine of religious teaching, hard work, and solitary confinement to promote introspection and penance.[7] Howard's work inspired the growing popularity of the term *penitentiary* to refer to penal confinement facilities.

In **penology,** the study of prison management and the treatment of offenders, Jeremy Bentham is perhaps best remembered for his idea that order and reform could be achieved in a prison through architectural design. His **panopticon** ("all-seeing" or "inspection-house") prison design consisted of a round building with tiers of cells lining the circumference and facing a central inspection tower so that prisoners could be watched by staff from the tower. Although no facilities completely true to Bentham's panopticon plan were ever

MYTH

The reason punishment fails to adequately deter crime in the United States is that it is not severe enough.

FACT

The United States has a higher rate of imprisonment and longer sentences than virtually any other nation. It is also one of the few advanced, industrialized nations to have retained the death penalty. It is hard indeed to support the argument that our punishment is not severe enough. Certainty and swiftness, however, are lacking, and that is the failure to which Beccaria would probably point.

penology
The study of prison management and the treatment of offenders.

panopticon
A prison design consisting of a round building with tiers of cells lining the inner circumference and facing a central inspection tower.

constructed, structures similar in design were erected at Illinois's Stateville Penitentiary (now Stateville Correctional Center), which opened in 1925.

In sum, the historical roots of the modern prison lie in Europe. It was in America, however, that the penitentiary concept was first put into wide practice.

Developments in the United States

In colonial America, penal practice was loose, decentralized, and unsystematic, combining private retaliation against wrongdoing with fines, banishment, harsh corporal punishments, and capital punishment. Local jails were scattered about the colonies, but they were used primarily for temporary holding rather than for punishment.[8] Some people, such as William Penn, promoted incarceration as a humane alternative to the physically brutal punishments that were common. However, that idea was largely ignored because there was no stable central governmental authority to coordinate and finance (through tax revenue) the large-scale confinement of offenders.

The Penitentiary Movement   In the aftermath of the American Revolution, it rapidly became apparent that the colonial system of justice would not suffice. Economic chaos and civil disorder followed the war. Combined with population growth and the transition from an agricultural society to an industrial one, they created the need for a strong, centralized government to achieve political and economic stability. The rise of the penitentiary occurred in that context.[9] Philosophically, it was guided by Enlightenment principles. In 1790, the Walnut Street Jail in Philadelphia was converted from a simple holding facility to a prison to which offenders could be sentenced for their crimes. It is commonly regarded as the nation's first state prison. In a system consistent with Howard's plan, its inmates labored in solitary cells and received large doses of religious teaching. Later in the 1790s, New York opened Newgate Prison. Other states quickly followed suit, and the penitentiary movement was born. By 1830, Pennsylvania and New York had constructed additional prisons to supplement their original ones.

Pennsylvania and New York pioneered the penitentiary movement by developing two competing systems of confinement.[10] The **Pennsylvania system,** sometimes called the *separate system,* required that inmates be kept in solitary cells so that they could study religious writings, reflect on their misdeeds, and perform handicraft work. In the New York system, or the **Auburn system** (named after Auburn Penitentiary and also referred to as the *congregate* or *silent system*), inmates worked and ate together in silence during the day and were returned to solitary cells for the evening. Ultimately, the Auburn system prevailed over the Pennsylvania system as the model followed by other states. It avoided the harmful psychological effects of total solitary confinement and allowed more inmates to be housed in less space because cells could be smaller. In addition, the Auburn system's congregate work principle was more congruent with the system of factory production emerging in wider society than was the outdated craft principle of the separate system. If prison labor was to be profitable, it seemed that the Auburn plan was the one to use.

It is interesting that although penitentiary construction flourished and the United States became the model nation in penology during the first half of the nineteenth century, there was serious discontent with the penitentiary

Pennsylvania system
An early system of U.S. penology in which inmates were kept in solitary cells so that they could study religious writings, reflect on their misdeeds, and perform handicraft work.

Auburn system
An early system of penology, originating at Auburn Penitentiary in New York, under which inmates worked and ate together in silence during the day and were placed in solitary cells for the evening.

▲ The Elmira Reformatory, which opened in 1876 in Elmira, New York, was the first institution for men that was based on reformatory principles. *What caused the change in penal philosophy?*

by the end of the Civil War. There were few signs penitentiaries were deterring crime, reforming offenders, or turning great profits from inmate labor. In fact, prisons were becoming increasingly expensive to run, and opposition was growing to selling prisoner-made goods on the open market. With faith in the penitentiary declining, the stage was set for a new movement—a movement that, rather than challenging the fundamental value of incarceration as a punishment, sought to improve the method of incarceration.

The Reformatory Movement The reformatory movement got its start at the 1870 meeting of the National Prison Association, in Cincinnati. The principles adopted there were championed by such leaders in the field as Enoch Wines (1806–1879) and Zebulon Brockway (1827–1920).[11] A new type of institution, the reformatory, was designed for younger, less hardened offenders, between 16 and 30 years of age. Based on a military model of regimentation, it emphasized academic and vocational training in addition to work. A classification system was introduced, in which inmates' progress toward reformation was rated. The sentences for determinate periods of time (for example, five years) were replaced with indeterminate terms, in which inmates served sentences within given ranges (for example, between two and eight years). Parole or early release could be granted for favorable progress in reformation.

It has been observed that indeterminate sentences and the possibility of parole facilitate greater control over inmates than with determinate sentences. Many inmates are interested, above all else, in gaining their freedom. The message conveyed by indeterminate sentences and the possibility of parole is this: "Conform to institutional expectations or do more time."

Institutions for Women Until the reformatory era, there was little effort to establish separate facilities for women. Women prisoners were usually confined in segregated areas of male prisons and generally received inferior treatment. The reformatory movement, reflecting its assumptions about differences between categories of inmates and its emphasis on classification, helped feminize punishment.[12] The first women's prison organized according to the reformatory model opened in Indiana in 1873. By the 1930s, several other women's reformatories were in operation, mainly in the Northeast and the Midwest. Most employed cottages or a campus and a family-style living plan, not the cell-block plan of men's prisons. Most concentrated on molding inmates to fulfill stereotypical domestic roles, such as cleaning and cooking, upon release.

10.1 CRITICAL THINKING

Do you think that any of the early forerunners to modern corrections (such as banishment, etc.) could be used today? Why or why not?

10.2 Developments in the Twentieth Century

John Irwin has provided a useful typology for summarizing imprisonment in the twentieth century.[13] According to Irwin, three types of institutions have been dominant. Each has dominated a different part of the century. The dominant type for about the first three decades was the "big house." In Irwin's words:

> The Big House was a walled prison with large cell blocks that contained stacks of three or more tiers of one- or two-man cells. On the average, it held 2,500 men. Sometimes a single cell block housed over 1,000 prisoners in six tiers of cells. Most of these prisons were built over many decades and had a mixture of old and new cell blocks. Some of the older cell blocks were quite primitive.[14]

It is important to realize that big houses were not new prisons, distinct from earlier penitentiaries and reformatories. They were the old penitentiaries and reformatories, expanded in size to accommodate larger inmate populations. Originally, big-house prisons exploited inmate labor through various links to the free market. Industrial prisons predominated in the North, while plantation prisons characterized much of the South. With the rise of organized labor and the coming of the Great Depression, free-market inmate labor systems fell into demise during the 1920s and 1930s. Big houses became warehouses oriented toward custody and repression of inmates.

What Irwin calls the "correctional institution" arose during the 1940s and became the dominant type of prison in the 1950s. Correctional institutions generally were smaller and more modern in appearance than big houses. However, correctional institutions did not replace big houses; they simply supplemented them, though correctional-institution principles spread to many big houses. Correctional institutions emerged as penologists turned to the field of medicine as a model for their work. During that phase of corrections, a so-called **medical model** came to be used, as crime was seen as symptomatic of personal illness in need of treatment. Under the medical model, shortly after being sentenced to prison, inmates were subjected to psychological assessment and diagnosis during classification processes. Assessment and diagnosis were followed by treatment designed to address the offender's supposed illness. The main kinds of treatment, according to Irwin, were academic and vocational education and therapeutic counseling. After institutional

▲ Big-house prisons, which consisted of large cell blocks containing stacks of cells, were the dominant prison design of the early twentieth century. *What are some problems with the big-house prison design?*

medical model
A theory of institutional corrections, popular during the 1940s and 1950s, in which crime was seen as symptomatic of personal illness in need of treatment.

Administrative Coordinator

My name is Pat Bryant and I am an administrative coordinator with the Central Visitation Center (CVC) for the South Carolina Department of Corrections (SCDC), Charleston, South Carolina. I have a bachelor of science degree in criminal justice from Benedict College, Columbia, South Carolina. I have held several positions with the South Carolina Department of Corrections during the course of my career to include administrative assistant, project developer, and business manager, to name a few. I have found these positions to be very rewarding.

The inmate visitation program is recognized by SCDC as an integral component of the rehabilitation process as it encourages inmates to have the opportunity to visit with family members and friends. The Central Visitation Center became operational in the fall of 1996 at which time I became the administrative coordinator.

A typical day as administrative coordinator for CVC involves communicating directly with family and friends of inmates in person, by telephone, or written correspondence and explaining to the prospective visitor the reason he/she may have been disapproved as a visitor, providing guidance and technical assistance as it relates to inmate visitation to the 31 correctional institutions within the SCDC and other law enforcement agencies as requested. One of the most significant aspects of this job is ensuring that all Requests for Visiting Privileges forms are reviewed and approved (if deemed appropriate) and an automated record is created for the prospective visitor. The CVC processes approximately 500–600 visitation applications per day. Some other aspects of this job include coordinating and conducting training for employees involved in the inmate visitation process and conducting semi-annual visits to each institution to ensure visitation procedures are being implemented according to policy.

While the job of administrative coordinator is certainly an interesting one, it can also be a challenge. The reward is knowing that you have assisted someone who may not have had a clear understanding of the visitation process and being a part of the solution.

Do you think communications skills are important in this position? Why?

treatment came parole, which amounted to follow-up treatment in the community. Importantly, the ways of achieving control over inmate behavior shifted from the custodial repression typical of the big house to more subtle methods of indirect coercion: inmates knew that failure to participate in treatment and exhibit "progress" in prison meant that parole would be delayed.

During the 1960s and 1970s, both the effectiveness and the fairness of coerced prison rehabilitation programming began to be challenged,[15] and the correctional institution's dominance began to wane. In Irwin's view, the third type of prison, the "contemporary violent prison," arose by default as the correctional institution faded. Gone were many of the treatment-program control mechanisms of the correctional institution. Further, many of the repressive measures used to control inmates in the big house became illegal after the rise of the inmates' rights movement during the 1960s (to be discussed later). In essence, what emerged in many prisons was a power vacuum that was filled with inmate gang violence and interracial hatred.

Recent Developments

As will be readily apparent in the next section of this chapter, the last two decades of the twentieth century are likely to be remembered for the largest incarceration boom to date and for desperate attempts to deal with prison crowding by developing alternatives to traditional incarceration.

One alternative to traditional confinement is the move toward **privatization,** the involvement of the private sector in the construction and operation of confinement facilities. The private sector has a long tradition in institutional corrections. For instance, such diverse services as food, legal aid, medical and psychiatric care, and education have long been provided through private vendors. There is a rich history of private labor contracting in the operation of prisons, and it is now witnessing something of a revival in certain jurisdictions. Also, the private sector has operated juvenile institutions for many years. But mounting prison populations, combined with space and budget limitations, have helped give privatization new twists. One of those twists entails having the private sector finance construction of institutions under what amounts to a lease-purchase agreement. The Potosi Correctional Center in Missouri was constructed under such a strategy. In another twist, the state contracts with private companies like U.S. Corrections Corporation to have them operate prisons. One of the earliest privately operated state prisons for adult felons, Kentucky's minimum-security Marion Adjustment Center, was opened in January 1986.

At the end of 1999, 14 private companies owned or managed 156 adult correctional institutions in 29 states, the District of Columbia, and Puerto Rico.[16] Nearly half of those institutions were located in Texas (with 42) and California (with 24). No other jurisdiction in the U.S. had more than nine private adult correctional institutions.[17] Together, those institutions have the capacity to hold approximately six percent of all local, state, and federal inmates.[18] Two companies—Corrections Corporation of America (with a 56 percent market share) and Wackenhut Corrections Corporation (with a 22 percent market share)—dominate the industry.[19]

Proponents of states' contracting to have the private sector finance construction and operate prisons often point to efficiency, flexibility, and cost effectiveness. Opponents frequently worry about liability issues, about creating a profit motive for incarcerating people, and about the incentive to trim inmate services and programs to maximize profits.

A second confinement alternative to traditional incarceration is **shock incarceration,** the placement of offenders in facilities patterned after military boot camps. Such facilities are ordinarily designed for young, nonviolent offenders without extensive criminal records. Instead of being given traditional prison sentences, those offenders are sentenced to shock incarceration facilities for relatively short periods (for instance, 90 days). There, they are subjected to a strict, military-style program of work, physical conditioning, and discipline. Boot camps vary considerably in their emphasis on treatment. After completing the program, inmates are released into the community on probation or parole. Shock incarceration is appealing to those who wish to

privatization
The involvement of the private sector in the construction and the operation of confinement facilities.

Prison Growth

Several states in the United States now have as many prisons in operation as some entire Western nations—or more. As of January 1, 1999, the states, the District of Columbia, and the federal government, combined, operated a total of 1,419 adult prisons.

SOURCE: Camille Graham Camp and George M. Camp, *The Corrections Yearbook 1999: Adult Corrections* (Middletown, CT: Criminal Justice Institute, 1999), p. 67.

shock incarceration
The placement of offenders in facilities patterned after military boot camps.

FYI

Wackenhut Corrections Corporation

In the first nine months of 1999, four inmates and a guard were killed in Wackenhut Corrections Corporation-run prisons in New Mexico.

SOURCE: "New Mexico transfers prisoners after uprising." *The Orlando Sentinel* (September 4, 1999), p. A–18.

convey a "tough on crime" message to the general public. However, as Doris Layton MacKenzie and James Shaw observe, the "studies examining the recidivism of boot camp releasees have been disappointing for those who expect the programs to affect offenders' activities after release."[20]

The popularity of boot camp programs has probably peaked. In 1997, the California state legislature ended the state's boot camp program after five years of operation. A California Department of Corrections evaluation found that the program reduced neither recidivism nor costs to the state.[21] Boot-camp prisons are considered an intermediate sanction, which will be discussed in Chapter 12 ("Community Corrections").

Cycles in History

The history of institutional corrections has evolved in cycles of accumulation. Developments viewed as innovative replacements for old practices almost always contain vestiges of the old practices, and the old practices seldom disappear when "new" ones are introduced. The new is implemented alongside the old and contains elements of the old. Penitentiaries were not torn down when reformatories were introduced, nor were big houses abolished when correctional institutions arose. Similarly, many jurisdictions have recently moved away from indeterminate sentences toward determinate ones. Those determinate sentences, although often seen as innovative, are hard to distinguish from the fixed sentences that preceded the move to indeterminate sentencing. Likewise, the modern trend toward boot camps revives the quasimilitary organization that was present at Elmira Reformatory. An interesting question is whether penological history represents progress or the coming back around of what went around before.

Chain gangs are another recent example of the "what goes around comes around" phenomenon. On May 3, 1995, Alabama became the first state to reintroduce the chain gang. Arizona became the second state to do so, on May 15, 1995. Arizona is also the first state to allow female prisoners to work on chain gangs. Both states put shackled prisoners to work along the roadside, cutting high weeds, picking up trash, and clearing muddy ditches. Prisoners were supervised by gun-toting guards. Alabama's experiment with chain gangs lasted less than four years. Among problems blamed for its demise were escape attempts, inmate fights, lack of productivity (people chained together move slowly), and the need for more guards inside prisons. As of this writing, Arizona was still using chain gangs on prison grounds. It suspended the use of chain gangs outside of prisons because of staffing shortages. In addition, unlike in Alabama where inmates were chained together, in Arizona, inmates are chained individually. In Florida in 1997, legislation was proposed to put chain gangs on state highways as a crime deterrent. The legislation failed because lawmakers felt the plan was too risky. Widespread use of chain gangs ended between the Depression and World War II, though it was not until the early 1960s that Georgia abolished the practice.

10.2 CRITICAL THINKING

Do you think that shock incarceration has any merit? Why or why not?

10.3 The Incarceration Boom

For most of the past 60 years, the incarceration rate was fairly steady. Only since 1973 has there been a continuing increase, with each year showing a new high.

Recent Trends

There were 329,821 inmates in state and federal prisons at the end of 1980 (305,458 state prison inmates and 24,363 federal prison inmates). By mid-decade, the total number of prison inmates had increased 52 percent, to 502,752 inmates, and by the end of the 1980s, there were a total of 712,967 inmates, an increase of 116 percent over 1980.[22] That represents an average increase of about nine percent per year.

A decade later, at year-end 1999, the adult prison population stood at a record high of 1,366,721 inmates (1,231,475 state prison inmates and 135,246 federal prison inmates), an increase of nearly 77 percent over the beginning of 1990 and an increase of 314 percent over 1980. (During the 20-year period, the state prison population increased 303 percent and the federal prison population increased 455 percent). In other words, between 1980 and 2000, the adult prison population (both state and federal) had more than quadrupled. However, the growth of the prison population slowed somewhat in the 1990s to an average of about 6.5 percent per year (from the approximately 9 percent per year during the 1980s). In 1999, the prison population grew 3.4 percent—the smallest yearly increase since 1988. Figure 10–1 on page 360 shows the jurisdictions with the largest and smallest numbers of prison inmates and the highest and lowest incarceration rates per 100,000 residents at year-end 1999. (We will discuss incarceration rates later in this section.)

It is important to emphasize that the approximately 1.4 million state and federal prison inmates do not include all persons incarcerated in the United States and its territories at year-end 1999. For example, not included in that number were the 63,635 state prison inmates being held in local jails, primarily because of prison crowding, the 605,943 local jail inmates (more about the jail population later), the 18,394 inmates held in territorial and commonwealth prisons, the 7,675 inmates held in facilities operated by or exclusively for the U.S. Immigration and Naturalization Service, the 2,279 inmates in military facilities, the 1,621 inmates in jails in Indian country, or the 105,790 inmates in juvenile facilities (discussed further in Chapter 13). Overall, the United States had more than two million people incarcerated at year-end 1999.[23]

We find similar, though somewhat less drastic, trends when we examine local jail populations. Between 1982 and 1990, the number of jail inmates increased nearly 89 percent, from 209,582 to 395,553. On June 30, 1999, the local jail population stood at a record high of 605,943 inmates, an increase of about 53 percent over the beginning of 1990 and 189 percent over 1982.[24] If the additional 82,030 persons being supervised outside a jail facility (in community service programs, weekender programs, by electronic monitoring, etc.) at midyear 1999 are added to the 605,943 confined inmates, the total number of people under the supervision of local jails increases to 687,973, an increase of nearly 3.5 percent over the previous year.[25] Figure 10–2 on page 361 lists the ten largest local jail jurisdictions in the United States, along with

Federal vs. State Prisons

Only about ten percent of all inmates at year-end 1999, were in federal prisons. The remaining 90 percent were in state and D.C. prisons.

SOURCE: Allen J. Beck, "Prisoners in 1999," U.S. Department of Justice, Bureau of Justice Statistics Bulletin (August 2000).

FIGURE 10–1

Jurisdictions With the Largest and Smallest Numbers of Prison Inmates and Rates per 100,000 Residents

Prison population	Number of inmates	Incarceration rates, 1999	Rate per 100,000 State residents[a]
10 largest:			
Texas	163,190	Louisiana	776
California	163,067	Texas	762
Federal	135,246	Oklahoma	662
New York	73,233	Mississippi	626
Florida	69,596	Alabama	549
Ohio	46,842	South Carolina	543
Michigan	46,617	Georgia	532
Illinois	44,660	Nevada	509
Georgia	42,091	Arizona	495
Pennsylvania	36,525	Delaware	493
10 smallest:			
North Dakota	943	Minnesota	125
Vermont	1,536	Maine	133
Wyoming	1,713	North Dakota	137
Maine	1,716	New Hampshire	187
New Hampshire	2,257	Rhode Island	193
South Dakota	2,506	West Virginia	196
Montana	2,954	Vermont	198
Rhode Island	3,003	Nebraska	217
West Virginia	3,532	Utah	245
Nebraska	3,688	Washington	251

[a]The number of prisoners with a sentence of more than one year per 100,000 residents in the state population. The Federal Bureau of Prisons and the District of Columbia are excluded.

SOURCE: Allen J. Beck, *Prisoners in 1999*, U.S. Department of Justice, Bureau of Justice Statistics Bulletin (Washington, DC: GPO, August 2000), p. 5, Table 7.

FIGURE 10-2

The Ten Largest Local Jail Jurisdictions With Their Average Daily Populations

Jurisdiction	Average Daily Population
Los Angeles County, CA	21,136
New York City, NY	17,524
Cook County, IL	9,297
Dade County, FL	7,836
Harris County, TX	7,781
Dallas County, TX	7,000
Maricopa County, AZ	6,910
Orleans Parish, LA	6,398
Philadelphia County, PA	5,753
San Diego County, CA	5,745

SOURCE: Adapted from Darrell K. Gilliard and Allen J. Beck, "Prison and Jail Inmates at Midyear 1998," U.S. Department of Justice, Bureau of Justice Statistics Bulletin (March 1999).

their average daily populations at midyear 1998 (the latest year for which data were available).

We must be cautious about looking exclusively at changes in the sheer number of people incarcerated, because such changes do not take into consideration changes in the size of the general population. We might wonder whether big increases in the number of people incarcerated simply reflect growth in the U.S. population. Researchers typically convert a raw figure to an **incarceration rate** to deal with that problem. The incarceration rate is calculated by dividing the number of people incarcerated by the population of the area and multiplying the result by 100,000:

$$\text{Incarceration rate} = \frac{\text{number incarcerated}}{\text{population}} \times 100,000$$

Figure 10–3 on page 362 is a display of the incarceration boom of recent years with shifts in the size of the general population taken into account. As shown in the figure, the U.S. adult prison incarceration rate was comparatively stable from the period before 1930 until the mid-1970s, at which time the dramatic upward climb began. Between 1980 and 2000, the prison incarceration rate rose approximately 242 percent, from 139 to 476 prisoners per 100,000 residents.[26] Likewise, between 1982 and 2000, the jail incarceration rate rose from 90 to 222 per 100,000 residents, or approximately 146 percent.[27]

Incarceration rates also differ significantly among nations. The data in Figure 10–4 on page 363 show the overall adult incarceration rates (both jail and prison populations) for 20 selected nations in 1995 (the latest year for which data were available). Note that the United States has one of the highest rates of incarceration in the world.

incarceration rate
A figure derived by dividing the number of people incarcerated by the population of the area and multiplying the result by 100,000; used to compare incarceration levels of units with different population sizes.

Incarceration Rates
Males are far more prone to crime and incarceration than females. At year-end 1999, the rate for men was 913 per 100,000, compared with 59 per 100,000 for women.

SOURCE: Allen J. Beck, "Prison and Jail Inmates at Midyear 1999," U.S. Department of Justice, Bureau of Justice Statistics Bulletin (April 2000), p. 5, Table 5.

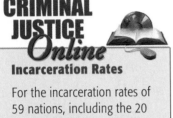
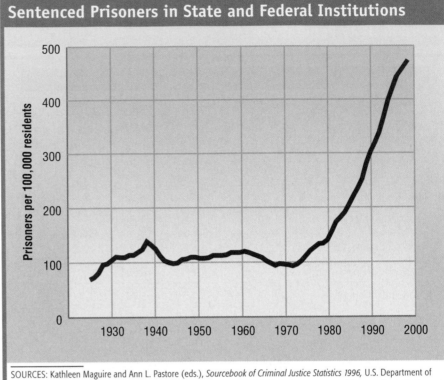

FIGURE 10–3

Sentenced Prisoners in State and Federal Institutions

SOURCES: Kathleen Maguire and Ann L. Pastore (eds.), *Sourcebook of Criminal Justice Statistics 1996*, U.S. Department of Justice, Bureau of Justice Statistics (Washington, DC: GPO, 1997), p. 517, Table 6.4 and p. 518, Table 6.21; Allen J. Beck, "Prisoners in 1999," U.S. Department of Justice, Bureau of Justice Statistics Bulletin (Washington, DC: GPO, August 2000).

Annual incarceration rates such as those depicted in Figure 10–4 and discussed earlier reflect the numbers of people admitted to institutions, the lengths of time those people serve, and (for purposes of international comparisons) the nations' levels of crime. Nations with higher levels of crime, with more people admitted to prison, and with prisoners serving longer terms can be expected to have higher annual rates of incarceration. Thus, James Lynch argues that the type of international comparisons depicted in Figure 10–4 may be misleading because the United States has a more serious crime problem than most other nations.[28] Lynch contends that if the analysis is controlled for nations' levels of crime, the differences between the United States and other nations in the use of imprisonment are smaller.

Cost Estimates   Total spending on state and federal prisons in fiscal year 1999 was budgeted at nearly $33 billion (33 percent more than in 1995), about $3.4 billion of it for capital improvements, about $1.4 billion for food, and nearly $3.2 billion for medical care. California budgeted the most of any state ($4.1 billion); North Dakota, the least ($21.6 million). The average daily cost of incarceration per inmate in 1998 was $56.26 ($20,534.90 per inmate per year). Alaska had the highest daily cost ($97.62, or $35,631.30 per year), and Louisiana had the lowest ($30.36, or $11,081.40 per year). The average daily cost per inmate for food was $3.70; the highest daily food cost was in Hawaii ($6.17), and the lowest in Mississippi ($1.50). The average daily cost per inmate for medical care was $6.81; the highest daily cost was $14.15 in Alaska, and the lowest was $1.28 in Oklahoma.[29]

For local jails for which data are available, the average amount budgeted in fiscal year 1998 was approximately $34 million per jail. (Only jail systems with capacities of 200 prisoners or more were surveyed.) The range was from a high of about $839 million in New York City to a low of about $1.5 million in Calhoun County, Alabama. The overall average 1998 cost per jail inmate was $54.39 per day (or $19,852.35 per year). Onondaga County, New York had the highest daily cost, $135.00 per inmate ($49,275.00 per year), and Calhoun County, Alabama, had the lowest daily cost, $10.00 per inmate ($3,650 per year).[30]

The Crowding Issue   Crowding has always been a problem in American prisons, but it has become especially troublesome over the past two decades. The increase in prison construction across the nation of late, while staggering, has failed to keep pace with the increase in prison populations, produced partly by the War on Drugs. Far more than half the states now have

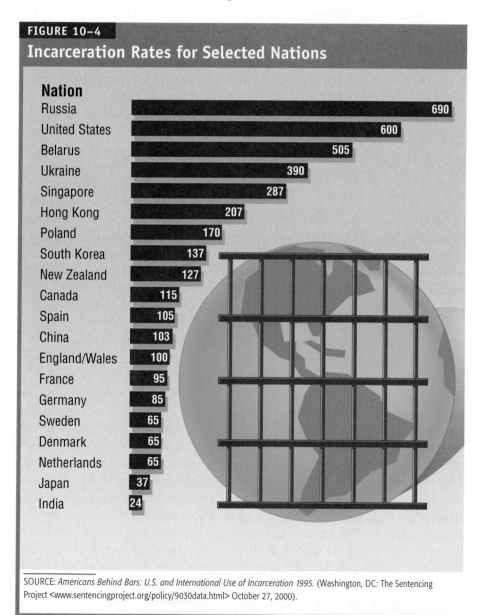

FIGURE 10-4

Incarceration Rates for Selected Nations

Nation

Nation	Rate
Russia	690
United States	600
Belarus	505
Ukraine	390
Singapore	287
Hong Kong	207
Poland	170
South Korea	137
New Zealand	127
Canada	115
Spain	105
China	103
England/Wales	100
France	95
Germany	85
Sweden	65
Denmark	65
Netherlands	65
Japan	37
India	24

SOURCE: *Americans Behind Bars: U.S. and International Use of Incarceration 1995.* (Washington, DC: The Sentencing Project <www.sentencingproject.org/policy/9030data.html> October 27, 2000).

at least one institution under court order to rectify crowded conditions, and many state prisoners are being held in local jails because of insufficient prison space. Furthermore, crowded prisons are often volatile prisons, and efforts to address problems related to crowding frequently end up diverting resources from inmate services and programs. How did we arrive at this state of affairs?

The most obvious explanation is that a massive outbreak of crime in the United States has fueled the growth of the prison population. But as author Nils Christie and a number of other observers have pointed out, that explanation is simply not supported by the data, which show relatively stable, and in some cases even declining, rates of crime for much of the period of the incarceration boom.[31] Likewise, there has not been an increase in the proportion of young adults, who constitute the most prison-prone age group, in the general population.

Franklin Zimring offers an interesting public opinion explanation.[32] Zimring claims that members of the public will think punishment for crime is too soft and will demand more imprisonment as long as they think crime is too high. The problem is that prisons generally do an unsatisfactory job of controlling crime, so the public continues to perceive crime as high, despite increases in the prison population. The inability of prisons to control crime fuels the public demand for still more punishment (such as more imprisonment). Zimring uses the analogy of a person who finds that the medicine he or she has been taking for a headache is not helping and decides to increase the dose of the same medication.

We can expand a bit on Zimring's perspective. Over the last 200 years, Americans have developed a tradition of strong reliance on the prison to control crime. It has never done very well. As Zimring observes, the typical response to high crime and high recidivism is to conclude that criminals are not being punished enough and to gradually increase the use of imprisonment. In pursuing that strategy, we get caught in a loop. We are continually forced to direct the greatest portions of our overall correctional budgets toward imprisonment. Relatively few resources are left to develop effective programs in community corrections and crime prevention programs that might reduce reliance on imprisonment. The lack of resources devoted to community corrections and crime prevention helps ensure that programs in those areas will fail to control crime. So there will always be an abundant supply of offenders to feed the prison population and escalate the cost of maintaining that population. The irony is clear and substantial. While crowding in correctional institutions suggests the need for effective alternatives in community corrections and crime prevention, that same crowding and the resources it consumes preclude such alternatives. Ineffectiveness in community corrections and crime prevention simply makes the crowding worse, thereby consuming even more resources.

Prison Inmate Characteristics

Who are the people in prison, and why are they there? First, we must distinguish between federal and state prisoners. At year-end 1999, 90 percent of all prisoners in the United States were state prisoners, while only 10 percent were federal prisoners.[34] Because most prisoners are state prisoners, we will focus on them. At the end of this section, however, we will indicate some important differences between state and federal prisoners. One last point before we begin: The characteristics of both state and federal prisoners are remarkably stable over time, that is, they do not change much from one year to the next.

From Figure 10–5 on page 366 it is evident that the largest proportion of state prisoners are male and black. In addition, a large proportion had not completed high school or did not have a GED, were under 35 years of age and never married, were employed full time prior to arrest, and had relatively low monthly incomes. Three things about these data bear mention. First, even though there is actually a greater percentage of females than males in the U.S. population, males make up nearly 94 percent of the state prison population (and almost 93 percent of the federal prison population); that is what is meant by saying that men are disproportionately represented in prison. Second, although 68 percent of the prisoners were employed in the month preceding their arrests, the monthly income figures reveal the low-paying jobs they held. More than half of all inmates had monthly incomes under $1,000 in the month prior to their current arrest. (However, only about ten percent of state inmates were homeless—living on the street or in a shelter—in the year prior to their incarceration.) Third, blacks are disproportionately represented in state prisons. While blacks make up approximately 13 percent of the general U.S. population, they account for nearly half of the state prison population. Further, the vast majority of blacks in prison are male, and black males constitute somewhere around half of all black persons in the United States. The overrepresentation of blacks in prison is a very heated issue in criminal justice today, and research has not established a consensus on the reasons for that overrepresentation. Currently, however, the weight of the evidence suggests that

Public Opinion

According to a public opinion poll, only a third of Americans support increasing taxes to build more prisons to reduce prison overcrowding.

SOURCE: Timothy J. Flanagan, "Reform or Punish: Americans' Views of the Correctional System," pp. 75–92 in Timothy J. Flanagan and Dennis R. Longmire (eds.), *Americans View Crime and Justice: A National Public Opinion Survey* (Thousand Oaks, CA: Sage, 1996), p. 90.

MYTH

Prisons have a revolving door, and inmates are now serving far shorter prison terms than in the past.

FACT

Since 1923, the average prison term served by inmates in the United States has remained constant at about two years. State prisoners are still serving sentences that average two years. Federal inmates, however, have been serving longer sentences since the passage of the Sentencing Reform Act of 1984 and the adoption of mandatory sentencing laws. The act introduced truth in sentencing in federal courts, which mandates that offenders serve a minimum of 85 percent of their sentences.[35]

FIGURE 10–5

Characteristics of State Prison Inmates

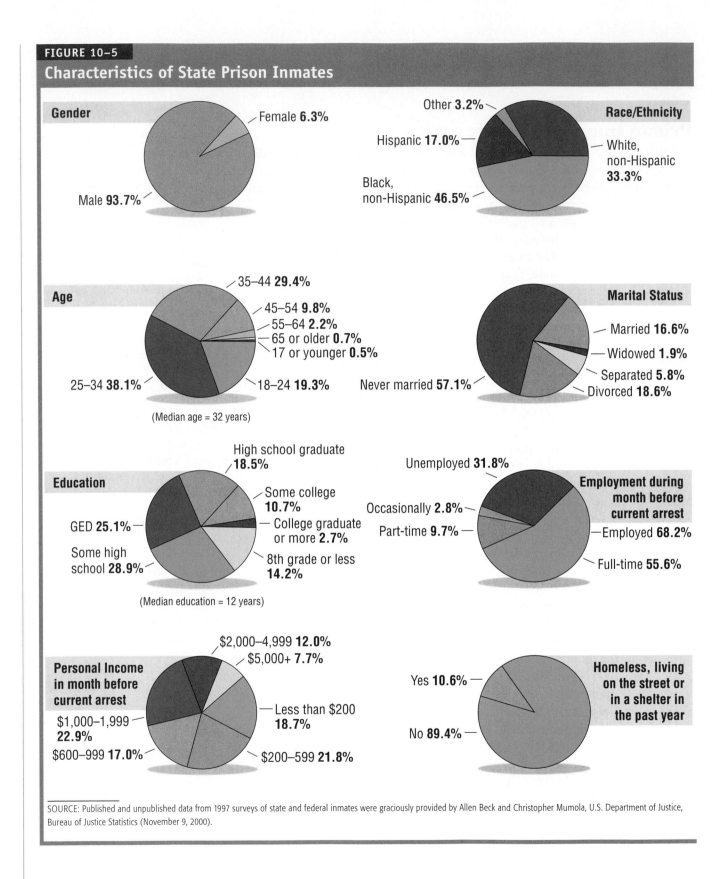

Gender

Female **6.3%**

Male **93.7%**

Race/Ethnicity

Other **3.2%**

Hispanic **17.0%**

Black, non-Hispanic **46.5%**

White, non-Hispanic **33.3%**

Age

35–44 **29.4%**

45–54 **9.8%**

55–64 **2.2%**

65 or older **0.7%**

17 or younger **0.5%**

25–34 **38.1%**

18–24 **19.3%**

(Median age = 32 years)

Marital Status

Never married **57.1%**

Married **16.6%**

Widowed **1.9%**

Separated **5.8%**

Divorced **18.6%**

Education

High school graduate **18.5%**

Some college **10.7%**

College graduate or more **2.7%**

GED **25.1%**

Some high school **28.9%**

8th grade or less **14.2%**

(Median education = 12 years)

Employment during month before current arrest

Unemployed **31.8%**

Occasionally **2.8%**

Part-time **9.7%**

Employed **68.2%**

Full-time **55.6%**

Personal Income in month before current arrest

$2,000–4,999 **12.0%**

$5,000+ **7.7%**

$1,000–1,999 **22.9%**

$600–999 **17.0%**

Less than $200 **18.7%**

$200–599 **21.8%**

Homeless, living on the street or in a shelter in the past year

Yes **10.6%**

No **89.4%**

SOURCE: Published and unpublished data from 1997 surveys of state and federal inmates were graciously provided by Allen Beck and Christopher Mumola, U.S. Department of Justice, Bureau of Justice Statistics (November 9, 2000).

FIGURE 10–6

Most Serious Offenses for Which State Inmates Were Serving Sentences in 1998

Offense	Percentage of Inmates
Violent Offenses	**47.7**
Murder/Nonnegligent manslaughter	11.8
Manslaughter	1.5
Rape	2.6
Other sexual assault	6.2
Robbery	13.9
Assault	9.6
Other violent offenses	2.0

Offense	Percentage of Inmates
Property Offenses	**21.3**
Burglary	10.3
Larceny	3.9
Motor vehicle theft	1.8
Fraud	2.6
Other property offenses	2.5

Offense	Percentage of Inmates
Drug Offenses	**20.7**
Public Order Offenses	**9.9**
Other/Unspecified Offenses	**0.2**

Note: Data are for inmates with a sentence of more than one year under the jurisdiction of state correctional authorities. The number of inmates by offense were estimated using 1997 Survey of Inmates in State Correctional Facilities and rounded to the nearest 100.

[a]Includes nonnegligent manslaughter.

[b]Includes weapons, drunk driving, court offenses, commercialized vice, morals and decency charges, liquor law violations, and other public-order offenses.

[c]Includes juvenile offenses and unspecified felonies.

SOURCE: Allen J. Beck, "Prisoners in 1999," U.S. Department of Justice, Bureau of Justice Statistics Bulletin (Washington, DC: GPO, August 2000), p. 10, Table 15.

offense seriousness and prior criminal record generally exert a stronger impact on decisions to imprison than do extralegal factors such as race.[36]

In 1998, nearly 48 percent of state prison inmates were serving sentences for violent offenses, about 21 percent were serving sentences for property offenses, approximately 21 percent were serving terms for drug offenses, and most of the remainder were doing time for public order offenses. A more detailed breakdown for the violent and property offense categories is shown in Figure 10–6.

The overall profile of inmate characteristics does not change drastically when we shift our attention to the federal prison population. However, there are some noteworthy differences. For example, in 1997, more than 57 percent of the federal prison population was white or Hispanic, and only about 38 percent was black. Federal inmates are, on average, somewhat older and possess higher education levels than state inmates. Also, more than 60 percent of federal inmates are serving time for drug offenses.[37]

Prison Resources

About two-thirds of all money spent on corrections is used to finance institutions. Roughly a quarter of all persons under correctional supervision are incarcerated. Therefore, about three-quarters of the correctional population must be accommodated with one-third of the resources.

10.3 CRITICAL THINKING

What do the characteristics of prison inmates say about American society as a whole?

U.S. Corrections

To learn more about a variety of issues that affect corrections in the United States, follow the links to the Corrections.com Web site at cj.glencoe.com. *What does this Web site tell you about the state of corrections in the U.S.?*

10.4 Incarceration Facilities

In the United States, the organizational and administrative structure of institutional corrections is diffuse and decentralized. Primary administrative responsibility for facilities lies with the executive branch of government, but the legislative and judicial branches are also involved. For example, the legislative branch appropriates resources and passes statutes that affect sentence length. The judicial branch sentences offenders to facilities and oversees the legality of institutional practices.

Organization and Administration by Government

Incarceration facilities exist at all three levels of government (federal, state, and local), and power and decision-making responsibility are widely distributed both among and within levels. Within broad guidelines, the federal level and the various state and local (county and city) jurisdictions have much autonomy to organize and carry out incarceration practices. As a general rule, the federal government operates its own prison system, each state operates its own prison system, and local jurisdictions operate their own jail systems. Decentralization and autonomy notwithstanding, there are interrelationships between levels. For example, federal requirements affect the operation of state prisons, and local jails are affected by both federal and state regulations.

Federal institutions are administered by the Federal Bureau of Prisons (BOP), which was established within the U.S. Justice Department in 1930 under the Hoover Administration. Before the BOP was created, there were seven federal prisons, each separately funded and each operated under policies and procedures established by its warden. The BOP's mission is "to protect society by confining offenders in the controlled environments of prison and community-based facilities that are safe, humane, and appropriately secure, and that provide work and other self-improvement opportunities to assist offenders in becoming law-abiding citizens."[38] The bureau's central office is in Washington, D.C., and there are six regional offices, in Philadelphia; Annapolis Junction, Maryland (near Baltimore); Atlanta; Dallas; Kansas City, Kansas; and Dublin, California (near San Francisco). The bureau also has three staff training centers and 29 community corrections offices. At the beginning of 1999, the BOP operated 98 institutions (see Figure 10–7 on page 369), with 21 more in various stages of construction. The bureau's facilities hold inmates convicted of violating the U.S. Penal Code. In 2001, the BOP assumes the added responsibility of incarcerating the District of Columbia's sentenced felons because of federal legislation passed in 1997.[39] The administrative organization of the bureau is shown in Figure 10–8 on page 370. The bureau has come to serve as a source of innovation and professionalization in the field of institutional corrections.

Although states vary in the way they organize institutional corrections, each state has a department of corrections or a similar administrative body to coordinate the various adult prisons in the state. Whether federal or state, correctional institutions are formal, bureaucratic organizations characterized by agency goals, rules and regulations, a staff chain of command, a staff division of labor, and similar features. Most adult prisons employ a

▲ Kathleen Hawk Sawyer, Director, Federal Bureau of Prisons. *What are the pros and cons of a woman heading the BOP?*

quasi-military model of administration and management. Figure 10–9 on page 371 displays the organizational chart for the California Department of Corrections.

Types of Facilities

Federal, state, and local institutions differ in their physical features, functions, and populations. We will consider some of the more common facility types.

Classification and Other Special Facilities
When offenders are sentenced to the custody of the department of corrections in most states, they are transported initially to a **classification facility** (sometimes referred to as an assessment, reception, or diagnostic center). Stays at classification facilities are ordinarily short (for example, 60 days). The process of classification entails assessing an offender's security risk and determining which program services (for instance, counseling and education) the offender

classification facility
A facility to which newly sentenced offenders are taken so that their security risks and needs can be assessed and they can be assigned to a permanent institution.

FIGURE 10–7

Locations of Institutions in Federal Bureau of Prisons

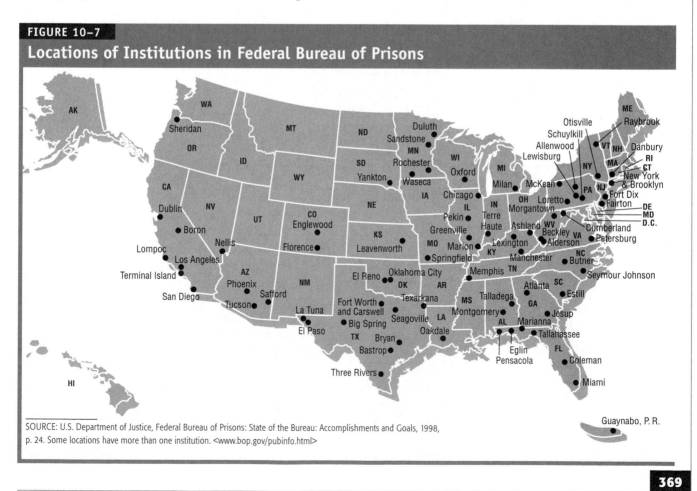

SOURCE: U.S. Department of Justice, Federal Bureau of Prisons: State of the Bureau: Accomplishments and Goals, 1998, p. 24. Some locations have more than one institution. <www.bop.gov/pubinfo.html>

Institutional Corrections **CHAPTER 10**

FIGURE 10–8

Organization of Federal Bureau of Prisons

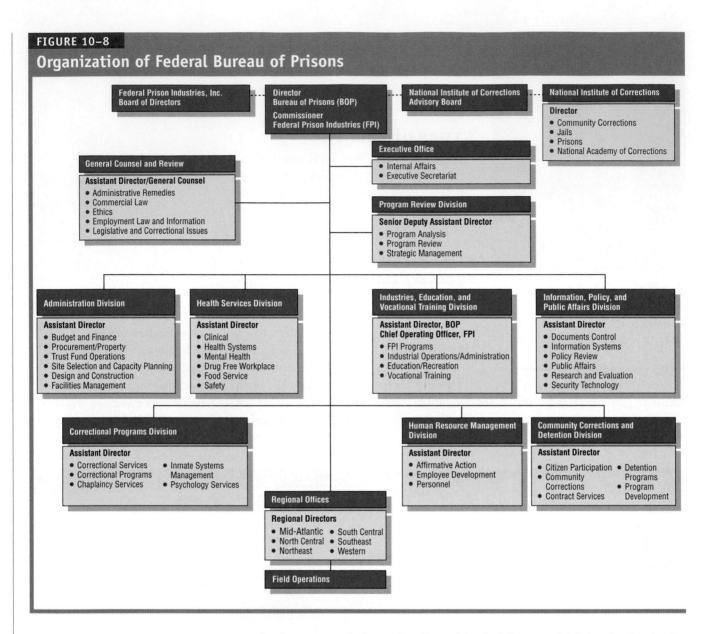

needs. Assessment information is used in deciding to which institution in the jurisdiction an offender will go to begin his or her term and which problems (such as alcohol dependency) the offender must address while imprisoned. A variety of other factors influence those decisions, including the nature of the offense; the offender's prior record (if any), propensity toward violence and escape, and vulnerability to victimization by other inmates; and the programs offered at the state's various institutions, as well as the levels of crowding at those institutions. The idea is to place inmates in facilities that can accommodate their risk-and-needs profiles.

Classification is not a one-time process; it occurs periodically throughout an inmate's sentence. Inmates are routinely monitored and reclassified to preserve institutional security and for purposes of transfer, programming, and release decisions.

Classification centers are not the only short-term-stay facilities. For example, the Federal Bureau of Prisons administers a number of medical institutions that receive inmates with health problems and provide them with

FIGURE 10–9

Organization of the California Department of Corrections

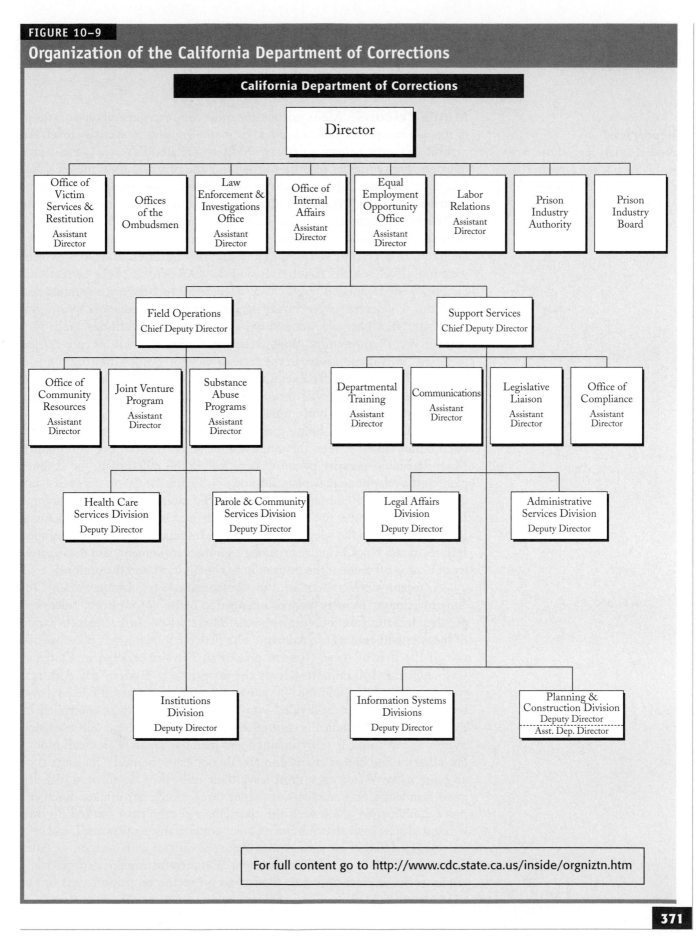

California Department of Corrections

Director

Office of Victim Services & Restitution — Assistant Director

Offices of the Ombudsmen

Law Enforcement & Investigations Office — Assistant Director

Office of Internal Affairs — Assistant Director

Equal Employment Opportunity Office — Assistant Director

Labor Relations — Assistant Director

Prison Industry Authority

Prison Industry Board

Field Operations — Chief Deputy Director

Support Services — Chief Deputy Director

Office of Community Resources — Assistant Director

Joint Venture Program — Assistant Director

Substance Abuse Programs — Assistant Director

Departmental Training — Assistant Director

Communications — Assistant Director

Legislative Liaison — Assistant Director

Office of Compliance — Assistant Director

Health Care Services Division — Deputy Director

Parole & Community Services Division — Deputy Director

Legal Affairs Division — Deputy Director

Administrative Services Division — Deputy Director

Institutions Division — Deputy Director

Information Systems Divisions — Deputy Director

Planning & Construction Division — Deputy Director / Asst. Dep. Director

For full content go to http://www.cdc.state.ca.us/inside/orgniztn.htm

371

health care services. If an inmate's condition improves, he or she is returned to the institution of origin or sent to another institution to complete the sentence. Other short-term facilities in various jurisdictions provide services for offenders with mental disorders.

Men's Prisons   Men's prisons, the most common general type of prison in the nation, are often distinguished from one another by **security level.** An institution's security level is determined by two related factors: (1) the degree of external or perimeter security surrounding the prison and (2) the measures taken to preserve internal security within the institution. The simplest security level categorization is maximum, medium, and minimum. Of the 1,419 adult correctional facilities in operation on January 1, 1999, 7.5 percent were maximum-security facilities, 24.7 percent were medium-security facilities, 18.2 percent were minimum-security facilities, and 20.8 percent were multilevel-security facilities. In addition, 4.8 percent of the correctional facilities were designated "high/close," a security level between maximum and medium, 6.6 percent were intake facilities, which include reception and diagnostic facilities and admissions and orientation facilities, and 17.5 percent were community (low) security facilities, such as pre-release facilities.[40] Jurisdictions vary in the security categorizations they use.

Maximum-security facilities are characterized by very tight external and internal security. A high wall or razor-wire fencing, with armed-guard towers, electronic detectors, or both, usually surrounds the prison. External armed patrol is also common. Some maximum-security institutions have a wide, open buffer zone between the outer wall or fence and the free community. Most maximum-security prison designs follow the radial plan, the Auburn plan, or the telephone pole plan, all shown in Figure 10–10 on pages 374 and 375. The Indiana Reformatory is based on the radial plan, the Kansas State Penitentiary illustrates the Auburn plan, and the Oregon State Correctional Institution displays the telephone pole design. Internal security consists of such features as cell-block living, restrictions on inmate movement, and the capability of closing off areas of the institution to contain riots and disruptions.

A recent development is the construction of "ultramaximum-" or "supermaximum-security" prisons intended to house notorious offenders and problem inmates from other institutions. These prisons utilize total isolation of inmates and constant lockdowns. The Federal Bureau of Prisons opened one of the first of these types of prisons in November 1994 in Florence, Colorado. The $60 million state-of-the-art prison (a modern-day Alcatraz) was custom-built to hold the 400 most predatory convicts in the federal system. The new prison is divided into nine units. Security is controlled by means of 1400 electronically controlled gates and shuttles and 168 television monitors. Each unit is self-contained and includes separate sick-call rooms, law libraries, and barber chairs. Inmates do not leave their cells for more than an hour a day. When they must leave their cells, they do so only with leg irons, handcuffs, and an escort of two or three guards per inmate. Each cell has a double-entry door, with the classic barred cage door backed up by a windowed steel door that minimizes voice contact among prisoners, and cells are staggered so that inmates cannot make eye contact with each other. After three years of this type of confinement, a successful inmate can gradually regain social contact by being allowed to go to the recreation yard or the cafeteria.[41] Currently, more than 30 states and the federal government are operating either one or more "supermax" units within existing maximum-security facilities or entire "supermax" facilities.[42] Pelican Bay Prison in northern California is another example of the ultramaximum- or super-maximum-security prison.

Compared with maximum-security prisons, medium-security institutions place fewer restrictions on inmate movement inside the facility. Cell blocks often coexist with dormitory- or barracks-type living quarters, and in some medium-security prisons, cells are relatively few. Typically, there is no wall for external security. Fences and towers exist but are less forbidding in appearance; razor wire may be replaced with less expensive barbed wire.

Compared with prisons at the other security levels, minimum-security prisons are smaller and more open. Inmates are frequently transferred to such prisons from more secure facilities after they have established records of good behavior or when they are nearing release. Dorm or barracks living quarters predominate, and often there are no fences. Some inmates may be permitted to leave the institution during the day to work (under *work release*) or study (under *study release*) in the community. Likewise, some inmates may be granted furloughs so that they can reestablish ties with family members, make living arrangements for their upcoming release, or establish employment contacts.

Custody level should be distinguished from *security level*. Whereas institutions are classified by security level, individual inmates are classified by custody level. An inmate's **custody level** indicates the degree of precaution that needs to be taken when working with that inmate. Confusion arises because custody levels are sometimes designated by the same terms used to designate institutional security levels (maximum, medium, and minimum). However, the two levels are independent of one another. For example, some inmates with medium or minimum custody levels may be housed in maximum-security prisons.

Women's Prisons and Co-correctional Facilities As pointed out earlier, women make up about six percent of the population of state prisons; they make up about seven percent of the population of federal institutions. In recent years, however, incarceration rates for females in the United States have grown faster than incarceration rates for males. For example, since 1990 the annual rate of growth of the female inmate population has averaged 8.3 percent, compared to a 6.4 percent average increase in the male inmate population. While the total number of male inmates has grown 75 percent since 1990, the number of female inmates has increased 106 percent. Nevertheless, at year-end 1999 there were 59 sentenced female inmates per 100,000 women in the United States, compared to 913 sentenced male inmates per 100,000 men.[43] One difference between male and female prisoners is that a somewhat greater proportion of women than men are serving sentences for property offenses (state = 27 percent female vs. 22 percent male; federal = 12 percent female vs. 6 percent male) and drug offenses (state = 34 percent female vs. 20 percent male; federal = 72 percent female vs. 62 percent male); a somewhat greater proportion of men are serving time for violent crimes (state = 49 percent male vs. 28 percent female; federal = 15 percent male vs. 7 percent female).[44] Other differences are that female inmates are more likely than male inmates to have dependent children and to be serving their first prison term.

custody level
The classification assigned to an inmate to indicate the degree of precaution that needs to be taken when working with that inmate.

Prison Misconduct

Ten federal prison guards at the supermaximum-security prison at Florence were indicted for 52 acts of abuse against at least 20 inmates from 1995 to 1997. The renegade group of guards, called "The Cowboys," was charged with kicking inmates, smashing their heads into walls, and mixing human waste into their food. In some cases, the guards injured themselves so they could claim the inmates had attacked them first. Some of the guards told prosecutors that they had a "green light" from prison authorities to "take care of business."

SOURCE: "Guards charged with abusing prisoners," *The Orlando Sentinel* (November 4, 2000), p. A10

FIGURE 10–10

Prison Architecture

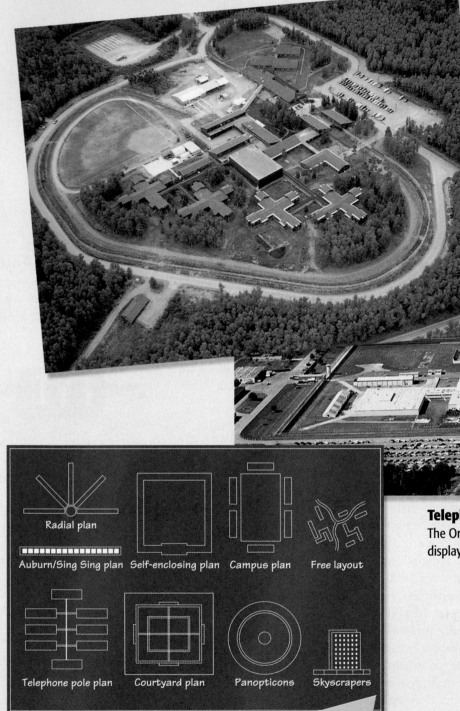

Free Layout Plan
Hiland Mountains Correctional Center in Eagle River, Alaska, which opened in 1982, displays the free layout design.

Radial plan

Auburn/Sing Sing plan Self-enclosing plan Campus plan Free layout

Telephone pole plan Courtyard plan Panopticons Skyscrapers

Telephone Pole Plan
The Oregon State Correctional Institution displays the telephone pole plan.

Skyscraper Plan
Piedmont Correctional Facility in North Carolina uses the skyscraper design.

Radial Plan
Pottsville Prison in Pennsylvania is setup on the radial plan.

Panopticon Plan
The Stateville Correctional Center in Illinois, which opened in 1925, is an example of the panopticon prison design.

In 2000, 87 percent of all state and federal adult prisons in the nation were for men only, 9 percent were for women only, and 4 percent were for both men and women.[45] Many states operate only one major prison for women. In general, prisons exclusively for women are smaller and house fewer inmates than institutions exclusively for men. Dorm and cottage plans are much more common than cell-block plans in institutions for women.

Co-correctional facilities, which house both male and female inmates, have been in operation (in contemporary form) since the 1970s. The goal of co-corrections is to normalize the prison environment by integrating the day-time activities of the sexes. In 2000, 36 co-correctional facilities were in operation in the United States (down from 97 in 1997).[46] Co-correctional prisons are usually small, and security is typically minimum. A recent comprehensive review of the effect of co-corrections on women prisoners paints a bleak picture: "[C]o-corrections offers women prisoners few, if any, economic, educational, vocational, and social advantages. Co-corrections benefits male prisoners and system maintenance."[47]

Jails and Lockups   A **lockup** is a very short-term (for instance, 24- to 48-hours) holding facility that is frequently located in or very near an urban police agency so that suspects can be held pending further inquiry into their cases by the police or the court. If there is cause, a suspect may be transferred from the lockup to the jail.

A **jail** is a facility that holds convicted offenders and unconvicted persons for relatively short periods. The modern term jail comes from the English term "gaol" (the pronunciation is identical), and English gaols have a history that dates to the 1100s. In contrast to prisons, most jails are administered at the county or city level of government. Excluding lockups, there are more jails (between 3,000 and 4,000) than any other kind of confinement facility in the United States. Although most jails in the United States are small (about half of them hold fewer than 50 people), some, such as those in Los Angeles and New York City, are very large (refer to Figure 10–2 on page 361).

The number of people being held in local jails has risen dramatically in recent years. The U.S. local jail population increased from 209,582 in 1982 to 605,943 at midyear 1999, an increase of about 189 percent (see Figure 10–11 on page 377). The jail incarceration rate was 96 inmates per 100,000 U.S. residents in 1983; by June 30, 1999, that number had climbed to 222 per 100,000, an increase of 131 percent.[48] Although just 1.6 percent of the jail population consisted of juveniles, that percentage amounts to 9,458 juveniles. The practice of holding juveniles in adult jails, where they are vulnerable to influence and victimization by adult criminals, is most common in rural areas, where there are no separate juvenile detention centers. That practice has been the target of much criticism and many policy initiatives for more than two decades. Nevertheless, the number of juveniles held in adult jails has been on the rise in recent years; the number increased by 120 percent between midyear 1993 and midyear 1999 (from 4,300 to 9,458).[49] Figure 10–12 on page 378, which displays selected characteristics of the jail population, also shows that the greatest proportions of jail inmates were male and black in 1999. Less than half of the jail population had been convicted of criminal activity. The remainder were unconvicted persons (usually awaiting trial or other case disposition).

co-correctional facilities
Usually small, minimum-security institutions that house both men and women with the goal of normalizing the prison environment by integrating the daytime activities of the sexes.

lockup
A very short-term holding facility that is frequently located in or very near an urban police agency so that suspects can be held pending further inquiry.

jail
A facility, usually operated at the local level, that holds convicted offenders and unconvicted persons for relatively short periods.

Most people think of the jail primarily as a short-term holding facility where unconvicted persons are detained pending further court processing, such as arraignment or trial. In practice, though, the jail serves a catchall function in criminal justice and corrections. For example, jails may hold convicted offenders who are serving short sentences (usually less than a year), convicted offenders awaiting transfer to prison, offenders who have violated their probation or parole, vagrants, drunks, homeless persons, the mentally ill, and others. The jail population is heterogeneous. Because the jail must be able to hold all types of people, including those who pose grave threats to security and the safety of others, the limited funds available through local taxes are directed primarily toward custody and security. Accommodations, services, and programs for inmates often suffer as a consequence.

In a classic study of jails,[50] author John Irwin found that, although members of the public tend to believe that jails are heavily populated with dangerous criminals, jails actually hold few such people. Jails are populated disproportionately with members of what Irwin calls the "rabble" class. The rabble class consists of people who are poor, undereducated, alienated from mainstream society, disreputable, and more likely than the general population to belong to an ethnic minority. Most of them have not committed serious offenses. In short, Irwin argues that the main function of the jail is to manage or control marginal members of our society and that as an unintended result of that process, the degradation those people experience in jail makes them even more marginal.

Jail Population

During 1998, the average daily population of the nine jails in Los Angeles County, California, the largest jail system in the nation, was 21,302 inmates.

SOURCE: Camille Graham Camp and George M. Camp, *The Corrections Yearbook 1999: Jails* (Middletown, CT: Criminal Justice Institute, 1999), p. 1.

FIGURE 10–11

Growth in Local Jail Population, 1982–Midyear 1999

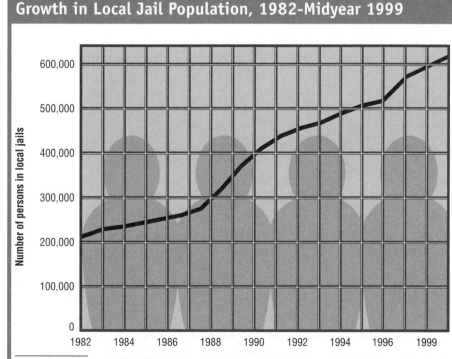

SOURCES: Adapted from Darrell K. Gilliard and Allen J. Beck, "Prison and Jail Inmates at Midyear 1997," U.S. Department of Justice, *Bureau of Justice Statistics Bulletin* (January 1998); Craig A. Perkins, James J. Stephan, and Allen J. Beck, "Jails and Jail Inmates 1993–1994," U.S. Department of Justice, *Bureau of Justice Statistics Bulletin* (April 1995); "Prison and Jail Inmates at Midyear 1999," U.S. Department of Justice, *Bureau of Justice Statistics Bulletin* (April 2000).

FIGURE 10–12
Selected Characteristics of Jail Inmates, Midyear 1999

Inmate Characteristic	Percent of Inmates (Total = 605,943)
Age	
Juvenile	1.6
Adult	98.4
Gender (adults only)	
Male	88.8
Female	11.2

Inmate Characteristic	Percent of Inmates (Total = 605,943)
Race/Hispanic Origin	
White, non-Hispanic	41.3
Black, non-Hispanic	41.5
Hispanic	15.5
Other	1.7
Legal Status (adults only)	
Convicted	45.9
Unconvicted	54.1

Incarceration Rate per 100,000 Residents in Each Group	
White, Non-Hispanic	127
Black, Non-Hispanic	730
Hispanic	288

SOURCE: Allen J. Beck, "Prison and Jail Inmates at Midyear 1999," U.S. Department of Justice, *Bureau of Justice Statistics Bulletin*, (April 2000).

However, a 1991 study of jail bookings challenges Irwin's conclusion that jails tend to house mostly "rabble." By analyzing the characteristics of persons booked into two jails (one urban, one rural), researchers found that nearly 47 percent had been charged with felonies, and more than 90 percent had been booked for a felony or a class A misdemeanor. Moreover, in one-day counts of those jails, the researchers discovered that 82.5 percent of those held had been either charged with or convicted of a felony offense. As the authors of the study observe, "These data do not appear to support Irwin's claims about detached and disreputable persons whose real problem is offensiveness, not serious criminality."[51]

Jails have traditionally represented, and continue to represent, one of the most problematic aspects of criminal justice. Many jails in the nation are old buildings plagued by overcrowding, a lack of services and programs for inmates, inadequate staffing, and unsanitary and hazardous living conditions. Some of the interrelated reasons for those problems are (1) the limited and unstable nature of local taxes to fund and staff jails, (2) a general lack of public support for jail reform, (3) rapid rates of inmate turnover, which make it difficult to coordinate programs, and (4) the sheer diversity of the risks and needs of the inmates. Also, in many areas, the chief jail administrator is the local sheriff, an elected or appointed political official. Because jails are usually under local administration, they are sometimes affected by the erratic and corrupt elements that often characterize local politics.

With increasing pressure from courts to reform jail conditions and management practices,[52] efforts at jail reform continue. A strategy pursued in a few jurisdictions has been to replace the traditional jail with a **new-generation jail.** A new-generation jail features architectural and programming innovations. The modular design typical of such jails consists of

new-generation jail
A replacement for traditional jails that features architectural and programming innovations.

individual cells organized into self-contained units. The jail is composed of two or more such units. Cells within each unit open into a common living area, where inmates from the unit can congregate for activities. Each congregate living area represents a staff post. Therefore, inmates have the opportunity to interact directly with other inmates and staff. (An arrangement that allows inmates to interact directly with staff is called *direct supervision*.)

In older jails, staff were separated from inmates by doors and bars, and inmates were separated from one another by cells. Preliminary analyses suggest that new-generation facilities may provide a less stressful environment for inmates and may enhance supervision.[53]

MYTH ••• FACT ••••••

Jails are heavily populated with dangerous criminals.

Most jail inmates have not committed violent offenses.

10.4 CRITICAL THINKING

1. What, if any, impact does a jail's architectural design have on inmates?

2. Do you agree that one of jails functions is to manage marginal members of society? Why or why not?

▲ The modular design of this new-generation jail allows inmates to interact directly with other inmates and staff. *What advantages do inmates gain from this interaction?*

10.5 Institutional Security, Services, and Programs

In many ways, an incarceration facility is like a miniature society within the larger society. Institutions have many of the same features as the wider society, such as security procedures for maintaining order and preserving the safety of inhabitants, as well as a variety of services and programs meant to provide for inmate needs and encourage inmates to better themselves.

Security and Inmate Discipline

An orderly and safe environment is the foundation for all else that happens in an institution. When the environment is not stable, everything else tends to become secondary. For that reason, security procedures strongly affect the daily activities of both staff and inmates.

In any prison, special security precautions are directed toward certain locations because of the importance of those locations to the institution's capacity for maintaining order. Examples of such locations include:

1. The front entry to the facility, through which all persons coming and going must pass.
2. The control room, which is usually located close to the front entry and is the heart of the institution's communication system.
3. The cell blocks or other quarters where the inmates live.
4. The dining area.
5. The area where the institution's confidential records and documents are maintained.
6. The indoor recreation areas and the outdoor recreation area or yard.
7. The sites where inmates work.

All institutions routinely employ a range of security procedures to maintain control over inmates. The classification of inmates by custody levels, mentioned earlier, is one such method. An inmate's custody level indicates the degree of precaution to be used when working with that inmate. In some facilities, certain inmates are given special custody designations that distinguish them from members of the general inmate population. Those inmates are not permitted to live among the general population of the facility. For example, inmates who are vulnerable to assault by other inmates may be designated for **protective custody,** meaning that they are to be kept segregated for their own safety. In contrast, inmates who represent a danger to other inmates or staff may be designated for **administrative segregation,** indicating that they must be kept in secure isolation so that they cannot harm others. Inmates who display signs of serious mental disorders may be segregated in a similar fashion.

As a basis for security procedures, institutions publish written rules that regulate the daily activities of inmates and staff alike. During the course of daily activities, staff routinely count inmates to detect escapes, and inmate whereabouts are constantly monitored within the facility. There are standard procedures for staff to follow when transporting certain inmates within the

protective custody
The segregation of inmates for their own safety.

administrative segregation
The keeping of inmates in secure isolation so that they cannot harm others.

facility or from the facility to an outside location, such as to another prison, to court, or to a hospital in the community. Much effort goes into controlling the property of the institution—for example, firearms, medicine, keys, tools, and basic commodities like clothes and food. In many prisons, searches of inmates' clothing and bodies and shakedowns of their cells are commonplace in an effort to control the flow of contraband, especially handmade knives and other weapons. There are special procedures and even special staff units for responding to riots, escapes, and other disturbances.

The mail and phone conversations of inmates may be monitored if there is sufficient security justification. Inmates may visit with relatives and friends only at designated times and may visit only those people the institution has approved. Although a small number of prisons permit **conjugal visits**— in which an inmate and his or her spouse or significant other visit in private to maintain their personal relationship—routine visits usually occur in large, open rooms with other inmates, their visitors, and staff present. Visits are supervised closely because of the potential for contraband to enter the prison.

It is important to emphasize that written rules and regulations are not the exclusive basis for institutional security. Written rules and regulations are part of an institution's formal bureaucratic structure, which was discussed earlier in this chapter. Within that formal structure, there develops an unwritten, informal structure of norms and relations that is vital to the operation of the facility. For example, most institutions have an elaborate **snitch system** in which staff learn from inmate informants about the presence of contraband, the potential for disruptions, and other threats to security. Informants often receive special concessions and protection in exchange for snitching on other inmates. Such arrangements can be very elaborate, as illustrated by the research of authors James Marquart and Ben Crouch. In their study of a Texas prison, Marquart and Crouch found that certain elite inmates, known as building tenders, actually functioned as extensions of the uniformed guard force to achieve control of the institution.[54] The use of inmates (building tenders or trustees) to discipline other inmates was formally outlawed in 1984.

Inmates who violate formal institutional regulations may be subjected to disciplinary measures. Staff members typically have broad discretion when they detect rule violations. They may simply overlook the infraction or may issue an informal warning. Alternatively, they may file a disciplinary report so that formal sanctions can be considered. The report usually leads to a disciplinary hearing, during which the charges and supporting evidence are presented to the institution's disciplinary committee or hearing officer. If the report is found to be valid, a number of sanctions are possible. For example, the inmate may have some of his or her privileges temporarily restricted (for instance, no commissary or store visits for 30 days), may be placed in solitary

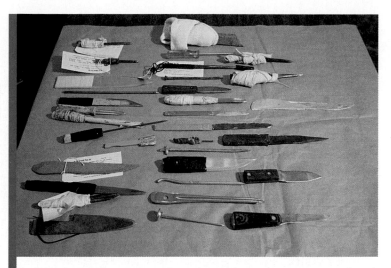

▲ Handmade weapons such as those shown here are contraband and make prisons and jails dangerous places. *Where do inmates get the materials for these weapons?*

conjugal visits
An arrangement whereby inmates are permitted to visit in private with their spouses or significant others to maintain their personal relationship.

snitch system
A system in which staff learn from inmate informants about the presence of contraband, the potential for disruptions, and other threats to security.

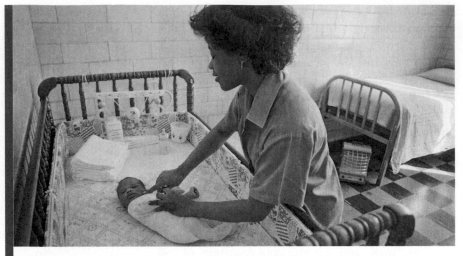

▲ Family visitation is extremely important to inmate morale. *What are other advantages and disadvantages of family visitation?*

confinement or "the hole" for a specified number of days, may forfeit some of the time that has been deducted from his or her sentence for good behavior, or may even be transferred to another facility. Because institutions have many rules governing the behavior of inmates, it should come as no surprise that rule infractions and disciplinary measures occur frequently.[55]

Services and Programs

Many of the human services and programs found in the free society are duplicated within institutions. At a minimum, inmates must be fed, clothed, and provided with such basic shelter requirements as warmth, electricity, and plumbing, and their health care needs must be addressed.

Food services are an important part of an institution's operation. Waste and inefficiency must be avoided to control expense, but inmate demand and dietary standards must be met.

Prisons and jails are buildings that, like all buildings, require maintenance and repair. A large portion of the maintenance and repair work is performed by inmates as part of their job assignments.

Courts have held that inmates are entitled to medical and dental services. Prisons normally have an infirmary where less serious ailments can be treated. More serious problems necessitate transfer to either a prison with more extensive medical services or a hospital in the local community.

Institutions make an array of services available to inmates for their leisure time. We have already mentioned mail, phone, and visitation services. In addition, institutions operate commissaries where inmates can purchase such items as food, tobacco, radios, reading materials, and arts and crafts supplies. A number of recreational facilities are also provided, such as weight-lifting equipment, softball fields, basketball courts, game tables, and television viewing areas. In addition, legal resources and religious services are available. They will be discussed in more detail in the next chapter. Although most prisons still offer a substantial number of services to prisoners, a movement to reduce services has arisen over the past decade. In a 1995 survey of U.S. state departments of corrections, 60 percent of the departments that responded had eliminated at least one inmate service in the previous year. Furthermore, 42 percent of the departments indicated that inmates had fewer privileges in 1995 than in 1985.[56]

Inmates With Special Needs   All institutions have special-needs populations. Although those populations generally consist of far fewer inmates than the general prison population, it is still necessary to provide services for them. For example, elderly inmates frequently need more medical attention than younger inmates. The number of elderly prison inmates is increasing. In 1990, 4.9 percent (or about 35,000) of state and federal prisoners were 50 or older. In 1999, 7 percent (or about 92,400) were 50 or older—an increase of 43 percent in the percentage of inmates 50 or older and an increase of 164 percent in the number of inmates 50 or older. In the federal prison system, each inmate 55 or older costs the government about $69,000 a year in maintenance costs, two or three times as much as is spent on inmates younger than 55. Most of the added expense is related to health costs. One health-related problem that has not been adequately addressed is the decreased mobility of older inmates—a problem that current prisons are rarely designed to accommodate.[57] Similarly, inmates with mental disorders may require segregated housing, frequent consultation with psychologists and psychiatrists, efforts to ensure that they take prescribed medication, and special safety precautions (for example, for a suicidal inmate, the use of paper sheets rather than cloth to prevent hanging).

Much controversy surrounds the presence of the human immunodeficiency virus (HIV) and acquired immune deficiency syndrome (AIDS) among institutional populations. As of year-end 1997, 2.1 percent of federal and state prison inmates were reported by prison officials to be HIV-positive (96 percent of HIV-positive inmates were in state prisons and 4 percent were in federal prisons). Of the HIV-positive inmates, 26 percent had confirmed cases of AIDS.[58] In 1997, 538 state prison inmates died of AIDS-related causes, down from 1,010 in 1995. In 1997, about one in five state prison inmate deaths was attributable to AIDS-related causes. Intravenous drug use is the key risk factor for AIDS among inmates. At the end of 1997, the rate of confirmed AIDS cases in state and federal prisons was 5-1/2 times the rate in the total U.S. population. At the end of 1997, 18 states and the federal government tested all inmates for HIV at some point during their sentences, a controversial practice known as *mass screening*. The remaining jurisdictions tested selected inmates. In addition to mass mandatory screening, other debated issues are whether HIV-positive inmates should be segregated and

MYTH   **FACT**

The high cost of incarceration is a product of amenities provided to inmates, such as cable television, law libraries, and weight-lifting equipment. Eliminating these "country club" add-ons will make prison costs more reasonable.

Actually, four out of every five dollars of prison operating costs are for employee salaries and facility maintenance. In addition, debt service to finance prison construction triples the original cost of construction. A maximum security prison in New York State, for example, costs about $100,000 per bed to build, but financing costs add another $200,000 per bed. Finally, costs have grown substantially as a result of the health care needs of an increasingly older and AIDS-afflicted inmate population.[59]

Aging Inmates
Correctional officials generally consider 50-year-old inmates geriatrics because their lives have probably been filled with violence, drug, alcohol and tobacco abuse, poor diets, and inadequate medical care.

SOURCE: "Virginia opens special prison for aging inmates," *The Dallas Morning News* (July 3, 1999) <www.dallasnews.com/national/0703nat4prison.html> (December 21, 2000).

the degree to which HIV-positive test results should be kept confidential by attending medical staff. At present, the trend seems to be away from blanket segregation and toward confidentiality.

Inmate Rehabilitation Programs Inmates hoping to better themselves during their incarceration normally have the opportunity to participate in a number of rehabilitation programs. The particular programs offered vary across jurisdictions and institutions. Examples are:

1. Self-improvement programs offered by religious and civic groups (Alcoholics Anonymous, the Jaycees, a Bible club).
2. Work programs.
3. Education and vocational training.
4. Counseling and therapy.

Work Programs Since the creation of the first houses of correction in Europe, there has been one constant: the belief that the imprisonment experience should improve inmates' work habits. Today, however, there is tremendous variation among institutions regarding work programs. In some institutions, all inmates who are physically able are required to work. In other institutions, the inmates who work are those who choose to do so. Likewise, there is great variation in the types of work inmates perform. Some inmates are employed to help the daily running of the institution and work in such areas as food services, maintenance and repair, laundry, health care, and clerical services. Other inmates work in factories at industrial tasks, such as wood or metal manufacturing. Still other inmates perform agricultural work.

As of January 1, 1999, the average daily wage earned by prison inmates working in agency-operated industries ranged from $2.17 to $8.94, up from $1.86 to $7.26 in 1997. The average workday was also up slightly to 7 hours per day from 6.9 hours. The average daily wage earned by prison inmates working in non-industry jobs ranged from $1.42 to $5.09, up from $.085 to $4.03 in 1997. The average workday was 6.3 hours, the same as in 1997. Some states, such as Georgia, do not pay inmates for their work. The state of Hawaii pays its inmates the most—$49.88 a day for work in agency-operated industries, while the state of Washington pays its inmates the most—$29.75 a day for work in non-industry jobs.[60]

Institutions also vary in the degree to which the private sector is involved in work programming. Although the early history of the prison in the United States was characterized by extensive ties between inmate labor and the free market, those ties diminished during the first half of the 1900s. That change was due to concern by organized labor about unemployment among free citizens, concern by businesses that did not employ convict

MYTH

The services and programs available to inmates make prisons seem like country clubs. Therefore, services and programs should be severely cut back or eliminated so that inmates receive punishment while incarcerated.

FACT

First, the services and programs available to inmates are sometimes of inferior quality when compared with those available in the free community. Second, programs and services perform a vital time management function. Institutions would be much more volatile and disorderly than they currently are without programs and services to fill time.

labor about their ability to compete on the open market, and concern by prison reformers about exploitation of inmates. Because of a series of laws restricting the private use of inmate labor, the *state-use system* became—and still is—the predominant way of arranging inmate work programs. Under that system, inmates are allowed to produce goods and services for the government. For example, in the main work program operated by the Federal Bureau of Prisons, known as UNICOR, inmates make a variety of products used by agencies of the federal government. Recently, however, legal restrictions on the private use of prison labor have been loosened, and the practice is witnessing somewhat of a resurgence in certain jurisdictions.

Education and Vocational Training   It has long been assumed that rehabilitation can be facilitated by improving inmates' academic skills and providing them with job skills. Many offenders enter prison with deficits in their education. It is not at all uncommon to encounter adult inmates who are reading, writing, and performing math operations at an elementary school level. Therefore, much prison education amounts to remedial schooling designed to prepare inmates to obtain their GEDs. College courses are made available in some prisons through correspondence or study release arrangements or by bringing college instructors to the prison to offer courses. However, low educational levels render college courses inappropriate for many inmates.

A recent study found that two-thirds of prison inmates have such poor reading and arithmetic skills that they are unable to write a brief letter explaining a billing error or to interpret a bar graph. Yet, over the past few years, while the prison population has expanded dramatically, more than half the states have cut back their educational and training budgets. The percentage of inmates enrolled in educational programs ranges from a high of 86 percent in Kentucky to a low of 7 percent in Nebraska. In most states, 25–50 percent of inmates take part in some form of education.[61]

Some prison vocational programs operate as part of job assignments (on-the-job training), and others are separate from job assignments. Either way, the goal is to provide inmates with job skills that will improve their marketability upon release. Most prison vocational training is geared toward traditional blue-collar employment, such as welding and auto mechanics. Vocational programs offered in women's prisons have often been criticized for concentrating excessively on stereotypical women's jobs, such as cosmetology.

Counseling and Therapy   A wide range of counseling techniques and therapy modalities are used in prisons across the nation. The description of specific techniques and modalities, however, is beyond the scope of this chapter.[62] Suffice it to say that the techniques and modalities used at a given institution ordinarily reflect the training and professional orientation of the treatment staff—caseworkers, religious counselors, social workers, psychologists, and psychiatrists.

A distinction is usually drawn between individual counseling, which involves one-on-one interaction between the counselor and the inmate, and group counseling, which involves the interaction of the counselor with a small group of inmates. Those categories of treatment may overlap, because an inmate receiving individual counseling may also be in group counseling,

Paying Prisoners

According to a public opinion poll, nearly 90 percent of Americans support "keeping prisoners busy constructing buildings, making products or performing services that the state would have to hire other people to do." Eighty percent of Americans favor paying "prisoners for their work, but [requiring] them to return two thirds of this amount to their victims or to the state for the cost of maintaining the prison."

SOURCE: Timothy J. Flanagan, "Reform or Punish: Americans' Views of the Correctional System," pp. 75–92 in Timothy J. Flanagan and Dennis R. Longmire (eds.), *Americans View Crime and Justice: A National Public Opinion Survey* (Thousand Oaks, CA: Sage, 1996), pp. 83–86, Table 6.2.

milieu therapy
A variant of group therapy that encompasses the total living environment so that the environment continually encourages positive behavioral change.

crisis intervention
A counselor's efforts to address some crisis in an inmate's life and to calm the inmate.

Educating Prisoners

A public opinion poll shows that more than 90 percent of Americans believe that before being released from prison, every inmate should be able to read and write and should have a skill or learn a trade so that he or she can get a job when released.

and many of the techniques and principles used in individual counseling are also applied to group settings. Still, the distinction has merit, because individual counseling is more appropriate for some inmates (for example, those with deep-seated problems who will require long-term help), and group counseling is more appropriate for other inmates (for example, those who are defensive, manipulative, and prone to denying their problems).

Group counseling is more popular than individual counseling in institutional settings, primarily because it is more economical and because there are large numbers of inmates who share similar backgrounds and problems. In fact, the members of a group are frequently selected on the basis of their common backgrounds and problem behavior patterns. For example, a group may consist of persons who have substance abuse problems or those who are sex offenders. Some institutions employ a variant of group therapy known as **milieu therapy** (also called a *therapeutic community*). Rather than having inmates attend periodic group sessions (one or two hourly sessions per week), milieu therapy encompasses the total living environment of inmates so that the environment continually encourages positive behavioral change. In effect, the entire inmate population becomes the group, and inmates have active roles in helping other inmates change.

Most counselors and therapists who work in prison spend a considerable portion of their time performing **crisis intervention.** Crisis intervention consists of a counselor's efforts to address some crisis that has erupted in an inmate's life (for example, suicidal thoughts, rejection by the spouse, a mental breakdown, or a conflict between inmates). Institutions are stressful living environments, so inmate crises are common. The counselor's task is to assist inmates in restoring a state of emotional calm and greater stability so that problems can be addressed rationally before inmates harm themselves or others.

Programs in Perspective We usually think of rehabilitation programs as serving one main objective: to help inmates better themselves. In practice, however, programs serve other, more subtle functions as well. Programs give inmates a way to occupy themselves; they help inmates manage time. They also help the institution achieve control over inmates. For example, inmates who are in counseling for displaying too much aggression toward other inmates may realize that unless they demonstrate "progress" in reducing their aggression, the counselor will not recommend them to the parole board for early release (in states where parole is available). Although such progress may be achieved quickly in prison, it may be short-lived upon release. Similarly, from the standpoint of inmates, the most desirable work assignments are those that give inmates access to valued resources (for instance, a kitchen job provides greater access to food). More desirable work assignments are routinely held out by the staff as privileges to be earned through good behavior.

Institutional programs are also plagued by a variety of problems that hinder their ability to effect rehabilitation. For example, prison work assignments frequently do not parallel work in the free world. In prison, workdays are often short and interrupted. In many cases, there is little concern for the quantity and quality of work. Furthermore, some of the jobs lack any real counterpart in the free world. The classic example is license plate manufacturing. In many prisons, educational programs suffer from a lack of funding.

Vocational training focuses primarily on traditional blue-collar jobs and thus prepares inmates to enter jobs for which there is already abundant competition. A dilemma is created by the argument that inmates should not receive highly technical or professional training (such as training in computer programming) because many members of the free, law-abiding community cannot afford such training. That argument is based on the **less-eligibility principle,** the position that prisoners should receive no service or program superior to the services and programs available to free citizens without charge. Moreover, prison education and vocational programs can do little to create jobs. If an inmate returns to a community with a poor economy and high unemployment, the education and training received in prison may do little more than raise the inmate's expectations to unrealistic levels.

For their part, counseling and therapy programs must operate against the harsh realities of the prison environment, where custody and security ordinarily take priority over rehabilitation. Despite those obstacles, some programs are able to bring about positive changes in offenders' attitudes and behavior. Author Ted Palmer has observed that although no single type of treatment can be identified as the most effective, one feature that seems to characterize programs that consistently reduce offender recidivism is the quality of the program's implementation. Thus, when the integrity of treatment efforts is allowed to take priority over institutional concerns for security and custody, offending can be reduced.[63] Also, as author Robert Johnson points out, many counseling programs place nearly exclusive emphasis on inmates' pasts and futures, with insufficient attention given to present coping patterns. Johnson recommends that programs begin teaching inmates to cope maturely and constructively with their present environment so that they will be better able to cope with life after release.[64]

less-eligibility principle
The position that prisoners should receive no service or program superior to the services and programs available to free citizens without charge.

10.5 CRITICAL THINKING

1. Do you think inmate rehabilitation programs can truly make a difference? Why or why not?

2. Do you think inmates should earn money for the work they do while in prison? Why or why not?

Review and Applications

1. Summarize the Purposes of Confinement in Europe Before it Became a Major Way of Punishing Criminals

Confinement became a major way of punishing criminals in Europe in the 1600s and 1700s. Before that, it was used to (1) detain people before trial, (2) hold prisoners awaiting other sanctions, such as death and corporal punishment, (3) coerce payment of debts and fines, (4) hold and punish slaves, (5) achieve religious indoctrination and spiritual reformation (as during the Inquisition), and (6) quarantine disease (as during the bubonic plague).

2. Describe How Offenders Were Punished Before the Large-Scale Use of Confinement

Before the large-scale use of confinement, punishments were directed more at the offender's body and property. One basic goal was to inflict pain. Those punishments were commonly carried out in public to humiliate the offender and to deter onlookers from crime. Examples of such punishments are fines, confiscation of property, and diverse methods of corporal and capital punishment.

3. Explain Why Confinement Began to be Used as a Major Way of Punishing Offenders in Europe

Enlightenment-era reforms led to an emphasis on deterring and reforming criminals through confinement. Confinement was also advocated as a humane alternative to older punishments. In addition, during the 1500s and 1600s, workhouses were established as places where offenders could be sent to learn discipline and productive work habits.

4. Describe the Recent Trends in the Use of Incarceration in the U.S.

There has been a dramatic increase since the mid-1970s in the number of people incarcerated in the United States, partly due to the War on Drugs. That increase has been accompanied by much concern over rising costs and institutional crowding. In response

to those problems, confinement alternatives to traditional incarceration have been developed. Two of those alternatives are contracts with the private sector for the construction or operation of some confinement facilities and the use of shock incarceration, or "boot camp" prisons, for young, nonviolent offenders without extensive prior criminal records.

5. List Some of the Characteristics of the Incarcerated Population in the U.S.

The incarcerated population in the United States is disproportionately male, black, young, single, undereducated, and poor. Nearly half of state prison inmates are serving time for violent offenses, whereas more than 60 percent of federal prison inmates are serving sentences for drug offenses. More than half of jail inmates are unconvicted, usually awaiting trial or other case disposition.

6. Describe How Incarceration Facilities are Structured, Organized, and Administered by the Government in the U.S.

Incarceration facilities in the United States are administered primarily by the executive branch of government. They exist at all three levels of government. Prisons are administered at the federal level and state levels, while jails tend to be locally administered. Despite this diversification, all the institutions have somewhat similar administrative structures, ranging from the warden or superintendent at the top to the correctional (line) officers at the bottom.

7. Name Some of the Common Types of Correctional Facilities in the U.S.

Common types of adult correctional facilities in the United States include (1) classification and special facilities, (2) "supermaximum-," maximum-, medium-, and minimum-security men's prisons, (3) women's and cocorrectional facilities, and (4) jails and lockups.

8. Identify Some of the Procedures That Institutions Employ to Maintain Security and Order

To maintain security and order, correctional institutions employ a number of procedures. Among them are the use of custody designations for inmates, inmate courts, property control, searches of inmates and their living quarters, and restrictions on inmate communication (mail, phone calls, and visits) with outsiders. Also, institutions commonly rely on inmate-informant, or snitch, systems to maintain security. Inmates found guilty of violating institutional rules may be subjected to a variety of disciplinary sanctions (such as loss of good time, restriction of privileges, and solitary confinement) to deter future rule infractions.

9. List the Services and Programs That Are Commonly Available to Inmates in Prison

Some of the services and programs available to prison inmates are subsistence services (food, clothing, and shelter), health care services, legal services, recreation, and religious services. There are also a number of programs designed to improve inmates' lives. They include low-paying work, education and vocational training, and group and individual counseling.

KEY TERMS

banishment, p. 351
transportation, p. 351
workhouses, p. 351
penology, p. 352
panopticon, p. 352
Pennsylvania system, p. 353
Auburn system, p. 353
medical model, p. 355
privatization, p. 357
shock incarceration, p. 357
incarceration rate, p. 361
classification facility, p. 369
security level, p. 372
custody level, p. 373
co-correctional facilities, p. 376
lockup, p. 376
jail, p. 376
new-generation jail, p. 378
protective custody, p. 380
administrative segregation, p. 380
conjugal visits, p. 381
snitch system, p. 381
milieu therapy, p. 386
crisis intervention, p. 386
less-eligibility principle, p. 387

Review and Applications

QUESTIONS FOR REVIEW

1. What did Cesare Beccaria, the Enlightenment thinker, mean when he said that a punishment should fit the crime?

2. What reforms in penal institutions did John Howard advocate in his book *The State of the Prisons in England and Wales* (1777)?

3. What is generally considered the first state prison in the United States, and of what did the daily routine of inmates in this prison consist?

4. How did the Pennsylvania system of confinement differ from the Auburn system of confinement, and which system became the model followed by other states?

5. What were the main features of the reformatory?

6. According to John Irwin, what three types of penal institutions have dominated different parts of the twentieth century?

7. What is an incarceration rate, and why is it used?

8. How does the incarceration rate of the United States compare with the incarceration rates of other countries?

9. How do the authors of this textbook explain the prison overcrowding crisis in the United States?

10. What are some major differences between the federal prison and state prison populations?

11. What is the official mission of the Federal Bureau of Prisons?

12. What are the purposes of inmate classification?

13. What are prison security and custody levels, and how do they differ?

14. What are the purposes of a jail?

15. Why do jails represent one of the most problematic aspects of criminal justice?

16. What are some objectives of inmate rehabilitation programs?

17. What is the less-eligibility principle, as applied to corrections?

EXPERIENTIAL ACTIVITIES

1. **Prison Tour** Many prisons and jails conduct tours for students in criminal justice courses. Arrange to visit one or more prisons and jails in your area. Compare and contrast what you see during your visit(s) with the material in this chapter. Also, if you tour both a prison and a jail, describe similarities and differences between the two institutions. Either present your findings orally in class or put them in writing for your instructor.

2. **Create a Prison** Design a prison conceptually and, perhaps, three-dimensionally. Decide what type of inmates the prison is to hold (men, women, or both; prisoners requiring maximum security, minimum security, etc.) and what the security level will be. Consider location, architectural design, bureaucratic structure, security and discipline procedures, and inmate services and programs.

INTERNET

3. **Federal Bureau of Prisons** Go to the Federal Bureau of Prisons Web site through the link at cj.glencoe.com. Access "Public Info" and then "Quick Facts and Statistics" from the topic list. Use the data provided to construct a current profile of inmates. Then access the "Weekly Population Report," and search for data about any federal prisons in your state. Write a brief report on what you find.

4. **Incarceration Worldwide** Examine international trends in rates of incarceration between 1985 and 1995 by accessing The Sentencing Project Web site through the link at cj.glencoe.com. Write a brief essay explaining what the changes in incarceration rates suggest about a country.

Prison Research

1. A Florida prison has recently been transformed into a combination hospital and prison where most inmates have HIV. They participate in tests of some of the newest HIV drugs being developed and have access to some of the nation's leading AIDS researchers. Only about 120 of the 3,000 or so state inmates who are known to be HIV positive are able to participate. Some inmates are due to be released in a few weeks or months; others are serving life sentences. On the street, the treatment would cost about $1,400 a month; participating inmates get it for free.

   The program is controversial. Although it has been praised as a model for the rest of the country's prisons to copy, it has also been criticized for conducting drug trials or medical studies on inmates. Because inmates are a captive audience, a major question is whether they can truly give informed consent to participate in the voluntary program. Before they are allowed to participate, inmates must sign a 5-page consent form that lists the possible benefits and side effects of the drugs. The state also has no relationship with the drug companies and accepts no money from them.

   Should the program continue and be spread to other prisons? Why or why not? In your answer, be sure and address these questions: Can inmates give informed consent? Does it matter? If inmates are allowed to participate, how should they be chosen from among all those who volunteer?

The Ex-Convict

2. To the average citizen, the ex-convict is an individual of questionable character. This image is reinforced by the fact that the only thing that is usually newsworthy about ex-convicts is bad news, such as when they are rearrested. Few citizens know a rehabilitated offender for obvious reasons. Yet, the rehabilitated ex-convict faces a variety of civil disabilities. Not the least among those is the difficulty of getting a "good" job. On virtually every job application, there is the question: "Have you ever been convicted of a felony or misdemeanor or denied bond in any state? In addition, prospective employers generally ask applicants to reveal their former substance abuse, which is a problem that most former offenders had. An affirmative answer to either question almost always eliminates a person's chance for employment.

   How can ex-offenders shed the ex-convict status? Should they be allowed to shed it? Why or why not?

ADDITIONAL READING

Carlie, Michael K. and Kevin I. Minor (eds.). *Prisons Around the World: Studies in International Penology.* Dubuque, IA: Wm. C. Brown, 1992.

Colvin, Mark. *The Penitentiary in Crisis: From Accommodation to Riot in New Mexico.* Albany, NY: State University of New York Press, 1992.

DiIulio, John J., Jr. *Governing Prisons: A Comparative Study of Correctional Management.* New York: Free Press, 1987.

Freedman, Estelle B. *Their Sisters' Keepers: Women's Prison Reform in America, 1830–1930.* Ann Arbor: University of Michigan Press, 1981.

Jacobs, James B. *New Perspectives on Prisons and Imprisonment.* Ithaca, NY: Cornell University Press, 1983.

Martin, Steve J. and Sheldon Ekland-Olson. *Texas Prisons: The Walls Came Tumbling Down.* Austin: Texas Monthly Press, 1987.

McKelvey, Blake. *American Prisons: A History of Good Intentions.* Montclair, NJ: Patterson Smith, 1977.

Mitford, Jessica. *Kind and Usual Punishment: The Prison Business.* New York: Vintage Books, 1974.

Morris, Norval and David J. Rothman (eds.). *Oxford History of the Prison.* Oxford: Oxford University Press, 1995.

Murton, Thomas O. *The Dilemma of Prison Reform.* New York: Holt, Rinehart and Winston, 1976.

Pisciotta, Alexander. *Benevolent Repression: Social Control and the American Reformatory-Prison Movement.* New York: New York University Press, 1994.

Rothman, David J. *The Discovery of the Asylum: Social Order and Disorder in the New Republic.* Boston: Little, Brown, 1971.

Sherman, Michael and Gordon Hawkins. *Imprisonment in America: Choosing the Future.* Chicago: University of Chicago Press, 1981.

Stone, W. G. *The Hate Factory: The Story of the New Mexico Penitentiary Riot.* Agoura, CA: Paisano Publications, 1982.

Thompson, Joel A. and G. Larry Mays (eds.). *American Jails: Public Policy Issues.* Chicago: Nelson-Hall, 1991.

ENDNOTES

1. See Robert Johnson, *Hard Time: Understanding and Reforming the Prison* (Monterey, CA: Brooks/Cole, 1987).
2. Michel Foucault, *Discipline and Punish: The Birth of the Prison* (New York: Pantheon, 1977).
3. See Graeme Newman, *The Punishment Response* (Albany, NY: Harrow and Heston, 1985).
4. Todd R. Clear and George F. Cole, *American Corrections*, 3d ed. (Belmont, CA: Wadsworth, 1994).
5. Graeme Newman and Pietro Marongiu, "Penological Reform and the Myth of Beccaria," *Criminology*, Vol. 28 (1990), pp. 325–46.
6. Ibid.
7. Clear and Cole, op. cit.
8. David J. Rothman, *The Discovery of the Asylum: Social Order and Disorder in the New Republic* (Boston: Little, Brown, 1971).
9. See Paul Takagi, "The Walnut Street Jail: A Penal Reform to Centralize the Powers of the State," *Federal Probation* (December 1975), pp. 18–26.
10. Rothman, op. cit.
11. Clear and Cole, op. cit.
12. Nicole Hahn Rafter, "Gender and Justice: The Equal Protection Issue," in L. Goodstein and D. L. MacKenzie (eds.), *The American Prison: Issues in Research and Policy* (New York: Plenum, 1989), pp. 89–109; and see Nicole Hahn

Rafter, *Partial Justice: Women in State Prisons, 1800–1935* (Boston: Northeastern University Press, 1985).
13. John Irwin, *Prisons in Turmoil* (Boston: Little, Brown, 1980).
14. Ibid., p. 3.
15. See Robert Martinson, "What Works? Questions and Answers About Prison Reform," The Public Interest, Vol. 42 (1974), pp. 22–54; see also The American Friends Service Committee, *Struggle for Justice: A Report on Crime and Justice in America* (New York: Hill & Wang, 1971).
16. From Charles W. Thomas, "Private Adult Correctional Facility Census: A 'Real-Time' Statistical Profile." <http://web.crim.ufl.edu/pcp/census/1999/Market.html> (December 19, 2000), Table 1 and Chart 3.
17. Ibid.
18. Ibid.
19. Ibid.
20. Doris Layton MacKenzie and James W. Shaw, "The Impact of Shock Incarceration on Technical Violations and New Criminal Activities," *Justice Quarterly*, Vol. 10 (1993), pp. 463–87; also see Doris Layton MacKenzie and Claire Souryal, *Multisite Evaluation of Shock Incarceration*, National Institute of Justice, November 1994.
21. "Poor Evaluation Brings End to California's Boot Camp," *Criminal Justice Newsletter*, Vol. 28, No. 15 (August 1, 1997), pp. 1–2.

22. United States Department of Justice, *Bureau of Justice Statistics Bulletin, Prisoners in 1992* (May 1993).

23. Beck, "Prisoners in 1999," op. cit.

24. Allen J. Beck, "Prison and Jail Inmates at Midyear 1999," U.S. Department of Justice, *Bureau of Justice Statistics Bulletin* (April 2000), p. 5, Table 5.

25. Ibid.

26. Beck, "Prisoners in 1999," op. cit. (for yearend 1999 figures).

27. Beck, "Prison and Jail Inmates at Midyear 1999," op. cit. (for midyear 1999 figures).

28. James P. Lynch, "A Cross National Comparison of the Length of Custodial Sentences for Serious Crimes," *Justice Quarterly,* Vol. 10 (1993), pp. 639–60.

29. Camp and Camp, op. cit., pp. 83–89.

30. Camille Graham Camp and George M. Camp, *The Corrections Yearbook 1999: Jails* (Middletown, CT: Criminal Justice Institute, 1999), pp. 39–42.

31. Nils Christie, *Crime Control as Industry: Toward Gulags Western Style?* (New York: Routledge, 1993).

32. Franklin E. Zimring, "The Great American Lockup," *Washington Post* National Weekly Edition (March 1991), pp. 4–10.

33. *Seeking Justice: Crime and Punishment in America,* Edna McConnell Clark Foundation (New York: 1997), p. 12.

34. Beck, "Prisoners in 1999," op. cit.

35. Ibid., p. 16; Beck, "Prisoners in 1999," op. cit.

36. See, for example, John Kramer and Darrell Steffensmeir, "Race and Imprisonment Decisions," *Sociological Quarterly,* Vol. 34 (1993), pp. 357–76; Ronald L. Akers, *Criminological Theories: Introduction and Evaluation,* Second Edition (Los Angeles: Roxbury, 1997). For different views, see Edmund F. McGarrell, "Institutional Theory and the Stability of a Conflict Model of the Incarceration Rate," *Justice Quarterly,* Vol. 10 (1993), pp. 7–28; Cassia Spohn and Jerry Cederblom, "Race and Disparities in Sentencing: A Test of the Liberation Hypothesis," Justice Quarterly, Vol. 8 (1991), pp. 305–27.

37. Published and unpublished data from 1997 surveys of state and federal inmates were graciously provided by Allen Beck and Christopher Mumola, U.S. Department of Justice, Bureau of Justice Statistics (November 9, 2000).

38. The Federal Bureau of Prisons, State of the Bureau: Accomplishments and Goals, 1998, p. 5 <www.bop.gov/pubinfo.html>

39. The Federal Bureau of Prisons, "The Bureau in Brief" www.bop.gov/pubinfo.html.

40. Camp and Camp, Adult Corrections, op. cit., p. 69.

41. Francis X. Clines, "A Futuristic Prison Awaits the Hard Core 400." *The New York Times,* national ed. (October 17, 1994), p. 1A.

42. Chase Riveland, "Supermax Prisons: Overview and General Considerations," U.S. Department of Justice, *National Institute of Corrections* (January 1999).

43. Beck, "Prisoners in 1999," op. cit., p. 5.

44. Published and unpublished data from 1997 surveys of state and federal inmates were graciously provided by Allen Beck and Christopher Mumola, U.S. Department of Justice, Bureau of Justice Statistics (November 9, 2000).

45. 2000 Directory: Juvenile and Adult Correctional Departments, Institutions, Agencies and Paroling Authorities, The American Correctional Association, 2000, p. 22.

46. Ibid.

47. John Ortiz Smykla and Jimmy J. Williams, "Co-Corrections in the United States, 1970–1990: Two Decades of Disadvantages for Women Prisoners," *Women and Criminal Justice,* Vol. 8 (1996), pp. 61–76.

48. Beck, "Prison and Jail Inmates at Midyear 1999," op. cit., p. 6.

49. Ibid.

50. John Irwin, *The Jail: Managing the Underclass in American Society* (Berkeley: University of California Press, 1985).

51. John A. Backstrand, Don C. Gibbons, and Joseph F. Jones, "Who Is in Jail: An Examination of the Rabble Hypothesis," *Crime and Delinquency,* Vol. 38 (1992), pp. 219–29.

52. See Dale K. Sechrest and William C. Collins, *Jail Management and Liability Issues* (Miami: Coral Gables Publishing, 1989).

53. Jeffrey D. Senese, "Evaluating Jail Reform: A Comparative Analysis of Popular/Direct and Linear Jail Inmate Infractions," *Journal of Criminal Justice,* Vol. 25 (1997), pp. 61–73; Linda L. Zupan, *Jails: Reform and the New Generation Philosophy* (Cincinnati: Anderson, 1991).

54. James W. Marquart and Ben M. Crouch, "Coopting the Kept: Using Inmates for Social Control in a Southern Prison," in M. K. Carlie and K. I. Minor (eds.), Prisons Around the World: Studies in International Penology (Dubuque, IA: Wm. C. Brown, 1992), pp. 124–38.

55. United States Department of Justice, Bureau of Justice Statistics Special Report, Prison Rule Violators (December 1989).

56. Amanda Wunder, "The Extinction of Inmate Privileges," *Corrections Compendium,* Vol. 20 (1995), pp. 5–24.

57. From Camp and Camp, Adult Corrections, op. cit., p. 25; "Longer Sentences Mean Older Prisoners and New Set of Problems," *The Orlando Sentinel* (September 1, 1996), p. A-15.

58. Information in this section about HIV and AIDS is from Laura Maruschak, *HIV in Prisons 1997,* U.S. Department of Justice, *Bureau of Justice Statistics Bulletin* (November 1999).

59. Seeking Justice, op. cit., p. 9.

60. Camp and Camp, Adult Corrections, op. cit., pp. 111–112; Camille Graham Camp and George M. Camp, *The Corrections Yearbook 1997* (South Salem, New York: Criminal Justice Institute), p. 88.

61. Tamar Lewin, "Locked in World of Illiteracy," *The Orlando Sentinel* (March 24, 1996), p. G-1; Flanagan, op. cit., pp. 83–84, Table 6.2.

62. For reference, see Anthony Walsh, *Understanding, Assessing, and Counseling the Criminal Justice Client* (Pacific Grove, CA: Brooks/Cole, 1988); also see Patricia van Voorhis, Michael Braswell, and David Lester, *Correctional Counseling and Rehabilitation,* 4th ed. (Cincinnati: Anderson, 2000).

63. Ted Palmer, *A Profile of Correctional Effectiveness and New Directions for Research* (Albany, NY: State University of New York Press, 1994).

64. Johnson, op. cit.

Chapter 11

Prison Life, Inmate Rights, Release, and Recidivism

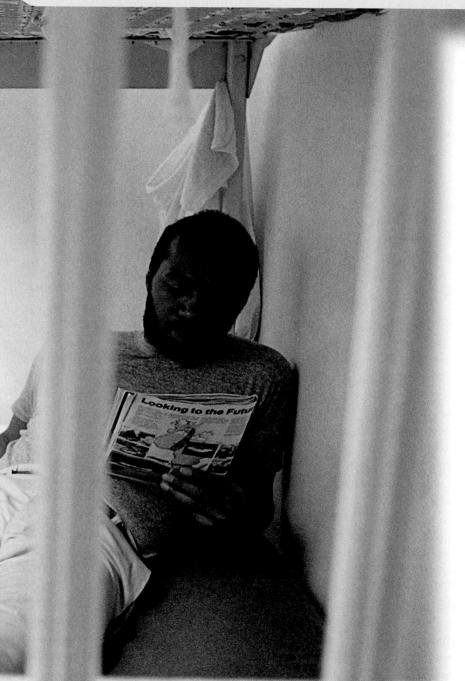

CHAPTER OBJECTIVES

After completing this chapter, you should be able to:

1. Distinguish between the deprivation and importation models of inmate society.

2. Explain how today's inmate society differs from those of the past.

3. Identify some of the special features of life in women's prisons.

4. Describe the profile of correctional officers and explain some of the issues that they face.

5. Identify prisoners' rights and relate how they were achieved.

6. List the two most common ways that inmates are released from prison and compare those two ways in frequency of use.

7. Summarize what recidivism research reveals about the success of the prison in achieving deterrence and rehabilitation.

11.1 Living in Prison

When people think of prisons, they usually imagine the big-house, maximum-security prison for men. Indeed, the majority of scholarly research on prison life has focused on this type of institution. In this chapter, we survey some of that research. However, we caution the reader to be careful about generalizing findings from studies of the big house to all institutions. As we have already seen, institutions are quite diverse.

Inmate Society

In his classic book *Asylums,* Erving Goffman described prisons as total institutions. Goffman defined a **total institution** as "a place of residence and work where a large number of like-situated individuals, cut off from the wider society for an appreciable period of time, together lead an enclosed, formally administered round of life."[1] As already pointed out and as further implied by Goffman's definition, a prison represents a miniature, self-contained society.

Although prisons are certainly influenced by the outside world,[2] they are also separated and closed off from that world. A society of prisoners, like any society, possesses distinctive cultural features (values, norms, and roles), and because prisoners do not serve their time completely isolated from other inmates, the features of the inmate society influence the way prisoners adjust to prison life.

Central to the inmate society of traditional men's prisons in the United States is the convict code. The **convict code** is a constellation of values, norms, and roles that regulate the way inmates interact with one another and with prison staff. For example, a principle of the convict code is that individual inmates should mind their own affairs and do their own time. Other principles are that inmates should not inform the staff about the illicit activities of other prisoners and that inmates' overall attitude and behavior should be indifferent to the staff and loyal to other convicts. "Conning" and manipulation skills are highly valued under the code, as is the ability to show strength, courage, and toughness.

Two major theories of the origins of the inmate society have been advanced: the deprivation model and the importation model. Advocates of the **deprivation model** (sometimes called the "indigenous origins model") contend that the inmate society arises in response to the prison environment and the painful conditions of confinement.[3] Specifically, imprisonment deprives inmates of such things as material possessions, social acceptance, heterosexual relations, personal security, and liberty. This environment of shared deprivation gives inmates a basis for solidarity. The inmate society and its convict code represent a functional, collective adaptation of inmates to this environment. When an inmate enters prison for the first time, the inmate is socialized into the customs and principles of the inmate society, a process author Donald Clemmer termed **prisonization**.[4] Clemmer believed that the longer inmates stayed in prison, the more "prisonized" they became and the more likely they were to return to crime after their release from prison.

An alternative to the deprivation model is the **importation model,** which holds that the inmate society is shaped by factors external to the prison environment—specifically, the preprison experiences and socialization patterns that inmates bring with them when they enter prison.[5] For example,

---

total institution

An institutional setting in which persons sharing some characteristics are cut off from the wider society and expected to live according to institutional rules and procedures.

convict code

A constellation of values, norms, and roles that regulate the way inmates interact with one another and with prison staff.

deprivation model

A theory that the inmate society arises as a response to the prison environment and the painful conditions of confinement.

prisonization

The process by which an inmate becomes socialized into the customs and principles of the inmate society.

importation model

A theory that the inmate society is shaped by the attributes inmates bring with them when they enter prison.

▲ Conflict builds when inmates form competing gangs along ethnic, racial, and geographic lines. *Why do inmates form gangs in prison?*

inmates who were thieves and persistently associated with other thieves before going to prison bring the norms and values of thieves into the prison. They will remain more loyal to those norms and values than to the staff while incarcerated. On the other hand, if an inmate primarily conformed to the law before entering prison, the inmate will probably exhibit greater loyalty to staff norms once in prison. In short, the deprivation model assumes that new inmates are socialized into the existing inmate society, which arises in response to the prison environment; the importation model suggests that the inmate society is the product of the socialization inmates experience before entering prison.

The deprivation and importation models were developed from studies of prisons of the pre-1960s era. Some scholars believe that the image of a fairly unified inmate society with an overarching convict code fails to characterize many of today's crowded and violent prisons. According to those scholars, several factors have rendered the inmate society fragmented, disorganized, and unstable:

1. Increasing racial heterogeneity
2. The racial polarization of modern prisoners
3. Court litigation
4. The rise and fall of rehabilitation
5. The increased politicalization of inmates

The order and stability provided by the old inmate subculture has been replaced by an atmosphere of conflict and tension, in which inmates align themselves into competing gangs (such as the Aryan Brotherhood, the Mexican Mafia, and the Black Guerrilla Family) and other inmate organizations (such as the Lifer's Club and the Muslims).[6]

Attica Prison Riot

The deadliest prison riot in the nation's history occurred at the Attica Correctional Facility in upstate New York in September 1971. The uprising began when inmates took over one of the prison yards, and held 49 guards hostage, demanding better living conditions within the facility. It ended four days later after state troopers, under orders from then-Governor Nelson Rockefeller, raided the prison, sparking violence that left 11 guards and 32 prisoners dead and more than 80 others wounded. On February 15, 2000, a U.S. District Court judge approved a settlement under which New York State, without admitting wrongdoing or liability, would pay $8 million to 1,280 inmates who were abused by law enforcement officials during the riot. The agreement concluded a long-stalled $2.8 billion class action lawsuit originally filed against prison and state officials in 1974.

SOURCE: "$8 Million Award Ends Attica Prison Suit," *Facts on File: World News Digest with Index*, No. 3097 (April 13, 2000), p. 248.

▲ Prison violence and disorder generally result spontaneously from particular circumstances. *What are some of those circumstances?*

Violence and Victimization   It is generally agreed that there is more physical violence by inmates in today's men's prisons than there was in earlier periods. In recent years, thousands of inmates and staff have been assaulted. In 1997, 75 inmates and, in 1998, 2 staff members, were killed by inmates in state prisons.[7] There is also consensus that staff violence against inmates is less common today. However, the number of inmates killed by staff in the last few years is unknown.

Commonly cited reasons for high rates of prison violence include improper management and classification practices by staff, high levels of crowding and competition over resources, the young age of most inmates in many prisons, and increases in racial tensions and prison gang activity. Although gang and racial conflicts surely play a role, it seems unlikely that the bulk of prison violence is extensively planned or gang-orchestrated. One reason is that many prisons across the United States lack well-developed gang structures and serious gang problems, but they are still plagued by violence. Furthermore, what we know about violent crime in general suggests that much prison violence is probably spontaneous, motivated by particular circumstances. Some common perpetrator motives for physical violence in prison are to (1) demonstrate power and dominance over others, (2) retaliate against a perceived wrong, such as the failure of another inmate to pay a gambling debt, and (3) prevent the perpetrator from being victimized (for example, raped) in the future.

A good deal of prison violence—but not all—has sexual overtones. It is important to realize that not all instances of sex in prison are violent, that not all instances are homosexual in nature, and that sexual encounters can involve both inmates and staff. Instances of prison sex can be further divided into three basic categories: (1) consensual sex for gratification, (2) prostitution, and (3) sexual assault. The third category obviously involves violence, and the first two sometimes have indirect links to violence. For example, a consensual sexual relationship between two inmates may have started out as a forced one. Likewise, an inmate who is vulnerable to sexual assault may perform sexual favors for an aggressive, well-respected prisoner in exchange for protection from other inmates. In the language of the prison, such vulnerable inmates are known as "punks." Prison sexual encounters can be intraracial or interracial; however, sexual assaults are more often interracial than intraracial.

Physical victimization is not the only or even the most frequent kind of victimization that takes place in prison. Lee Bowker identifies three other kinds: economic, psychological, and social.[8] As with physical victimization, these three kinds may be perpetrated by inmates against other inmates, by inmates against staff, or by staff against inmates. In addition, the four kinds of victimization are interrelated: combinations can occur, and one can lead to another.

All societies have an economy, and most have a black-market component. The inmate society is no exception. The **sub-rosa** (secret or underground) **economy** of an institution consists of the exchange of goods and services that, though often illicit, are in high demand among inmates. Examples of such goods and services include food, clothes, alcohol and other drugs, pornography, weapons, loan services, protection, sex, and gambling. Engaging in illicit economic exchanges is commonly referred to as "playing the rackets" or "hustling." Cigarettes often serve as the medium of exchange because currency is typically contraband. The money inmates earn from prison work is usually maintained in accounts from which they may deduct only specified amounts for specified purposes. Hence, packs and cartons of cigarettes assume the symbolic value of money in the sub-rosa economy. However, currency may also be used. Like any kind of contraband (drugs, for example), currency can enter the institution via mail, visits, or staff. The sub-rosa economy sets the stage for various types of economic victimization, including theft, robbery, fraud, extortion, loan-sharking, and price-fixing by gangs and cliques.

Psychological victimization consists of subtle manipulation tactics and mind games that occur frequently in prison. For example, a staff member may obtain sensitive confidential information from an inmate's file and proceed to "mess" with the inmate's mind by threatening to convey the information to other inmates. Likewise, an inmate may threaten to convey to superiors some instance of a staff member's corruption or failure to follow procedure. Examples of psychological victimization are numerous. Combined with the crowded and noisy living conditions, separation from

Smoking Ban

In 1997, the Florida legislature voted down a proposal to ban state prisoners from smoking, because of concerns that such a rule would make inmates unruly.

SOURCE: Lesley Clark, "Educators Were Smiling–Criminals Weren't," *The Orlando Sentinel* (May 4, 1997), p. A-22.

sub-rosa economy
The secret exchange of goods and services among inmates; the black market of the prison.

▲ Prostitution is part of prison culture at many institutions. *Why do some prisoners prostitute themselves?*

Prison Life, Inmate Rights, Release, and Recidivism **CHAPTER 11**

the outside world, and the threats to physical safety, psychological victimization contributes significantly to the stress of the prison environment. It is small wonder that many prisoners suffer from a host of psychological maladaptations, such as fear, paranoia, excess anxiety, depression, anger, and lack of trust in others.

Social victimization involves prejudice or discrimination against a person because of some social characteristic that person has. The social characteristic may be race, age, class background, religious preference, political position, or another factor. For example, racial segregation and discrimination against minorities was official policy in many prisons until the 1960s. Following the desegregation movement in the wider society, prisons, too, have become more racially integrated. Today, the segregation that remains is typically voluntary on the part of inmates. However, a recent study of a large state prison found white inmates receiving more desirable cell assignments.[9]

▲ Inmates develop a variety of coping mechanisms in prison. *If you were in prison, how would you cope?*

Inmate Coping and Adjustment

Living in prison is fundamentally different from living in the free community. In prison, for example, deprivation of personal freedom and material goods is much more pronounced. There is less privacy, there is more competition for scarce resources, and life is typified by greater insecurity, stress, and unpredictability. Moreover, prison life may encourage qualities counter to those required for functioning effectively in the free community. Author Ann Cordilia, expanding on the work of Erving Goffman, argues that prisons "desocialize" and alienate inmates by discouraging personal responsibility and independence, creating excessive dependency on authority, and diminishing personal control over life events.[10] One result is what Goffman called "self-mortification," a subduing or deadening of self-identity and self-determination.[11]

Therefore, a person coming from the free community into prison must learn to cope with and adjust to the institutional environment. Building on the ideas of author Hans Toch,[12] author Robert Johnson identifies two broad ways that inmates cope with imprisonment.[13] Some inmates enter what Johnson describes as the public domain of prison culture. Predatory, violent convicts, many of whom have lengthy prior records of incarceration (that is, are "state-raised youths") dominate this domain. Those convicts seek power and status in the prison world by dominating and victimizing others. Johnson claims that most inmates do not enter the public domain and live by its norms. Instead, most enter the prison's private culture. To understand this method of coping and adjustment, we must realize that each inmate brings a unique combination of personal needs into prison. That is, inmates vary in their needs for such things as privacy, environmental stimulation, safety, and emotional feedback. Entering the private culture of the prison means finding in the diverse environment of the institution a niche that will accommodate the inmate's unique combination of needs. For example, an inmate who has strong needs for privacy, safety, and intellectual stimulation may arrange to have a job in the prison library. The library becomes the inmate's niche. The private domain of prison culture consists of many diverse niches.

From another perspective, author John Irwin suggests that in coping and adjusting to prison, an inmate will develop a prison career or lifestyle.[14] Three such lifestyles are "doing time," "jailing," and "gleaning." Inmates who adopt the "doing time" lifestyle are primarily concerned with getting out of prison as soon as possible and avoiding hard time in the process. Avoiding hard time means maximizing comfort and minimizing discomfort in a way that does not threaten to extend the sentence or place the inmate in danger. The "jailing" lifestyle is often embraced by people with lengthy prior records of incarceration, who are more accustomed to life *in* an institution than life *outside* one. Those inmates are concerned with achieving positions of influence in the inmate society; prison is their world. "Gleaning" entails trying to take advantage of the resources available for personal betterment, such as obtaining marketable vocational skills. The idea is to prepare for life after release. Relatively few inmates adopt the gleaning lifestyle.

Life in Women's Prisons

Life in women's prisons is similar to life in men's prisons in some respects, but there are also important differences. For example, both female and male inmates must cope with the deprivations, stress, depersonalization, and authoritarian atmosphere of prison life. However, women's prisons are usually not characterized by the levels of violence, interpersonal conflict, and interracial tension found in men's institutions. Nor is the antistaff mentality of male prisoners as common among female inmates. Consequently, the environments of women's institutions are often less oppressive.

Those observations should not be taken to mean that female inmates generally do easier time than male inmates. Indeed, it has been suggested that women experience imprisonment more negatively than men.[15] A major reason for this is separation from friends and family.[16] Female inmates are more likely than male inmates to have children and to have been living with those children immediately before incarceration. In 1997, for example, 65 percent of female state prisoners had children under 18 years old, and about 64 percent of those women lived with their children before incarceration.[17]

Procedures for determining the custodial relationship between a female inmate and her child vary widely. In some cases, very young children of incarcerated women may live with their mothers in prison for a temporary period. In other cases, maternal custody might be terminated. The procedure depends on the jurisdiction and the particular circumstances. A common arrangement is for children to reside with their fathers, grandparents, or other relatives or friends during the period of incarceration. Visitation is often irregular or nonexistent, and the amount of visitation is dictated by institutional rules and the geographic distance between children and their mothers.[18]

Sonia Jacobs

For the first five years of her 17 years on death row, Sonia Jacobs was in isolation. From pacing all day, she moved on to meditating, writing letters, and painting with a brush made from her own hair. In 1981, the Florida Supreme Court commuted her sentence to life, releasing her into the general prison population, where she tutored fellow prisoners and taught meditation. After being granted a new trial, Jacobs—in an unusual legal formality—pleaded guilty without admitting guilt. She was released in 1992.

SOURCE: Jack Hayes and Jenny Allen, "Stolen Lives," *Life* (October 1994), p. 68.

▲ Female inmates are an increasing part of the nation's prison population. *Why?*

Pseudofamilies and Homosexuality   A distinguishing feature of the inmate society in many women's prisons is the presence of make-believe families, known as pseudofamilies. Studies have discovered that some female inmates adopt family roles, such as mother, daughter, sister, husband, and father to form kinship networks.[19] The number of inmates who adopt masculine roles, known as "butches," appears to be small in comparison with the number who take on feminine roles.[20] Furthermore, kinship ties may cut across racial lines, reflecting that race is not the divisive factor in women's prisons that it is in men's institutions. Pseudofamily structures are central to inmate society in women's prisons, providing social interaction and emotional support. Author Rose Giallombardo suggests that pseudofamilies provide imprisoned women with the family affiliation and bonding that they have been socialized to desire but have been deprived of by incarceration.[21]

Family activity and homosexual activity appear to be relatively independent of one another. A female prisoner who is involved in homosexuality may or may not be part of a family. Likewise, a female prisoner who is part of a make-believe family may or may not be involved in homosexuality. If she is, she may be having homosexual relations with someone who is part of the family or with someone who is not. The number of female prisoners who take part in family activities probably exceeds the number who participate in homosexuality. In addition, the majority of female inmates who participate in homosexuality are what authors David Ward and Gene Kassebaum call "turnouts," those who were heterosexual before incarceration and will return to heterosexuality upon release.[22] As in men's prisons, interracial homosexuality is quite common, but in contrast to men's prisons, the overwhelming majority of homosexual activity in women's institutions is consensual and is rooted in affection and attachment instead of dominance motives.

MYTH . . . FACT

Virtually all female prisoners are lesbians.

Although there are no totally reliable data on the proportion of female inmates who engage in homosexuality while incarcerated, a reasonable estimate (based on the literature) is approximately half. This proportion is comparable to the proportion of male prisoners who do so.

▲ Many women in prison are mothers or mothers-to-be, and the restrictions imprisonment imposes on them as they try to maintain relationships with their children affect their physical and emotional well-being. *How could the stress of a prison mother's parent/child relationship be reduced?*

Inmate Roles Author Esther Heffernan identified three roles that women commonly adopt when adjusting to prison. Heffernan's roles are very similar to roles identified by author Schrag in his work on male inmates.[23] The "square" role is adopted by women who were primarily noncriminals before coming to prison, and those women tend toward conventional behavior in prison. The square role discussed by Heffernan corresponds to the "square john" role identified by Schrag. Heffernan's "life" role is analogous to Schrag's "right guy" role. Inmates who assume the life role were habitual offenders before coming to prison, and they continue to adhere to antisocial and antiauthority norms in prison. The "cool" role, or what Schrag referred to as the "con politician," is occupied by sophisticated professional criminals. They try to do easy time by manipulating other inmates and the staff to their own advantage.

11.1 CRITICAL THINKING

1. In comparison to male prisons, why do you think that there is less violence, interpersonal conflict, and interracial tension in women's prisons?

2. Should very young children of incarcerated women be allowed to temporarily live with their mothers in prison? Why or why not?

11.2 Correctional Officers

In 1976, author Gordon Hawkins wrote, "It is in fact remarkable how little serious attention has been paid to prison officers in the quite extensive literature on prisons and imprisonment."[24] Although it has increased steadily since, research on prison staff remains sparse compared with research on inmates. Most studies of prison staff have concentrated on guards or correctional officers, and there is good reason for this. Correctional officers represent the majority of staff members in a prison, are responsible for the security of the institution, and have the most frequent and closest contact with inmates. Yet correctional officers should not be thought of as existing in isolation from the larger structure of the prison bureaucracy discussed in the last chapter.

As of January 1, 1999, there were 421,889 employees of adult correctional agencies in the United States, an increase of about 5.5 percent over the beginning of 1997.[25] Of those more than 400,000 employees, 250,740 (about 60 percent) were uniformed staff, an increase of 5.8 percent over 1997. Uniformed staff consists of all correctional security staff, including majors, captains, lieutenants, sergeants, and officers. Of the uniformed staff, 209,107 (83 percent of all uniformed staff and nearly half of all employees) were correctional officers. There were 39,535 new correctional officers hired in 1998 (19 percent of all correctional officers). Nearly 95 percent of both uniformed staff and correctional officers were employed by state agencies. About 80 percent of uniformed staff, including correctional officers, were male (though 31 percent of correctional officers hired in 1998 were female), and about 71 percent were white. The average ratio of correctional officers to inmates across the states in 1999 was one officer for every 5.9 inmates, and the average ratio in federal prisons was one correctional officer for every 8.7 inmates, both up less than one percentage point from prior years.

Correctional Officer Salaries

Starting salaries for entry-level state correctional officers ranged from a low of $15,324 in Louisiana to a high of $34,070 in New Jersey as of January 1, 1999. They averaged $21,855 (an increase of about 25 percent since 1990). The starting salary for entry-level federal correctional officers was $25,966. Salaries were subject to increases after completion of preservice training and a probationary period.

SOURCE: Camille Graham Camp and George M. Camp, *The Corrections Yearbook 1999: Adult Corrections* (Middletown, CT: Criminal Justice Institute), 1999, pp. 150–151.

▲ A correctional officer's custodial role is of primary importance. *Why?*

Inmate Assault

Although rates of inmate assaults on prison staff have been increasing, the likelihood of an individual staff member's being the victim of an inmate assault, especially a lethal assault, remains fairly low. The assault of staff by inmates is a serious problem and is always a threat in prison, but the risks should not be exaggerated.

Correctional officers face a number of conflicts in their work. Authors Richard Hawkins and Geoffrey Alpert observe that the job is characterized by both boredom and stimulus overload; officers assigned to the towers may experience the former, whereas officers assigned to work the cell blocks may experience the latter.[26] Much also has been written about the role ambiguity and role strain resulting from conflict between custody and treatment objectives. How does an officer supervise and discipline inmates and at the same time attempt to counsel and help them? Traditionally, the role of guards was clearer and less ambiguous; they were responsible for custody. With the advent of rehabilitation, guards became correctional officers, and the custodial role grew clouded with treatment considerations. In addition, a series of court decisions have given many officers the perception that they have lost

Correctional Sergeant

My name is Pietro DeSantis II and I am a Correctional Sergeant employed by the California Department of Corrections, assigned to the California Correctional Center (CCC) in Susanville, California. I have an Associate of Science Degree from Lassen Community College in Susanville. I began my career as a correctional officer with the department in November of 1986, and was promoted to sergeant in February of 1996. During my tenure with corrections I have also been Chapter President and Board member of the California Correctional Peace Officer Association and Commissioner and Curriculum Review Committee Chair of the Correctional Peace Officer Standards and Training (CPOST) Commission.

A normal workday starts as soon as you arrive on grounds and start talking to staff that are either beginning or ending their shift. Normal shifts at CCC are first watch (2200–0600 hours), second watch (0600–1400 hours), and third watch (1400–2200 hours). A normal day on all three watches starts with a security check of our safety equipment and security locks. First watch staff normally read the incoming and outgoing mail, count the inmate population three times, and ensure workers for the culinary service are awakened and report to work. Second watch staff normally feed breakfast and lunch to the inmates and supervise the inmate workers who clean the living quarters, inner perimeter yard areas, and the outside grounds. Third watch staff normally deliver the mail, count the inmates twice, feed them dinner, and house new arrivals from the transportation buses. As a sergeant, I could be assigned to supervise an office or unit with between zero and forty correctional officers.

Before entering into a career within corrections, I strongly suggest you do everything possible to become an effective communicator.

Why do you think it is important for a correctional officer to be an effective communicator?

power while inmates have gained it.[27] Officers generally have considerable discretion in discharging their duties within the constraints of rules, regulations, and policies. Yet, because they lack clear and specific guidelines on how to exercise their discretion, they feel vulnerable to second-guessing by their superiors and the courts.

A popular misconception has been that officers manage inmates with an iron fist and are therefore corrupted by the power they have over inmates. However, as Sykes realized, the limits on an officer's power may be the real source of corruption.[28] Although their formal role places them in a superior position over inmates, officers must still obtain a measure of voluntary compliance from inmates. In the modern prison, it is impossible to rely exclusively on force to gain compliance if bureaucratic inefficiency, mass inmate rebellion, and court litigation are to be avoided. Moreover, because of the nature of the prison environment, officers do not have many incentives they can use to solicit compliance, and they do not directly control many of the main rewards, such as release date. Still, officers' performance is often judged by how smoothly the officers interact with inmates and get inmates to go along with their wishes. Consequently, many officers seek inmate compliance through informal negotiation and exchange, and this practice can promote corruption. For example, an officer may gain compliance by becoming friendly with particular inmates, by granting inmates concessions in exchange for their cooperation, and by overlooking certain rule infractions in exchange for compliance with other rules. A study of a federal prison by author John Hewitt and his colleagues found that inmates reported committing, and officers reported observing, far more prison rule infractions than were documented in the institution's official disciplinary files.[29]

How do correctional officers respond to their roles and their work conditions? According to Hawkins and Alpert, some officers become alienated and cynical and withdraw from their work. Withdrawal can be figurative: an officer may minimize his or her commitment to the job and may establish a safe and comfortable niche in the prison, such as prolonged tower duty. Withdrawal can also be literal: turnover and absenteeism are high in many prison systems. Other officers become overly authoritarian and confrontational in a quest to control inmates by intimidation. Those officers put up a tough facade similar to that displayed by some inmates. Still other officers respond by becoming corrupt (for example, selling drugs to inmates in response to a low salary).[30] Finally, a number of officers respond by adopting a human-services orientation toward their work.[31] Those officers seek to make prison a constructive place for themselves and for inmates. They try to deliver goods and services to inmates in a regular and responsive manner, to advocate and make referrals on behalf of inmates when appropriate, and to assist inmates in coping with prison by providing protection and counseling.

Efforts are under way to transform prison work from a mere job into a profession, but a number of problems and issues surround those efforts. First, factors such as low pay, the nature and prestige of the work, and the remote location of many prisons make recruitment of new officers difficult in some jurisdictions. Some people take prison work simply because they believe that nothing better is currently available, with the intent of leaving as soon as a better job opens. Second, the general lack of competition for prison jobs in many jurisdictions makes it difficult to impose restrictive criteria for choosing among applicants. Most states require that applicants be of a certain age (18 or 21) and have completed high school or the GED. Some states have additional requirements, such as no prior felony convictions, related work experience, and the passing of certain tests. Third, in some jurisdictions, a backlash against affirmative action—which has increased female and minority representation among correctional officers—has resulted in tensions between the genders and races[32] and resentment by some white male officers. In jurisdictions where this backlash has occurred, efforts toward professionalization have been hampered. Fourth, once officers have been recruited and hired, they need to be trained, and the move toward professionalization has been

Turnover Rates

In 1998, the average turnover rate for correctional officers in state and federal prisons was 15.4 percent, up 19 percent from 1996. Arkansas had the highest turnover rate (36%), while New York had the lowest (2%). The turnover rate for correctional officers in the federal system was 6.4 percent, down about 5 percent from 1996.

SOURCE: Camille Graham Camp and George M. Camp, *The Corrections Yearbook 1999: Adult Corrections* (Middletown, CT: Criminal Justice Institute), 1999, pp. 152–153.

accompanied by increased attention to training. Officers are usually trained at the outset of their jobs and then receive annual training thereafter. At present, however, training standards are not uniform across or even within jurisdictions. Furthermore, when turnover rates are high, training costs are high, and training may start to be viewed as a waste of money and time. Fifth, professionalization has been accompanied by increased unionism among officers. As of 1994 (the latest year for which we found data), 86 percent of the officers in adult corrections departments in 43 jurisdictions had the right to organize, and nearly 70 percent of those officers were represented by unions or associations.[33] Although guard unions can help improve pay levels, job benefits, and work conditions, unions can also divide the superior and subordinate ranks. In addition, most guard unions have a very limited ability to engage in collective bargaining because strikes are commonly illegal. For example, in 1994, only 56 percent of officers in adult corrections departments had the right to engage in collective bargaining, and only about 12 percent had the right to strike.[34]

11.2 CRITICAL THINKING

1. What do you think could be done to further professionalize corrections work?

2. What are some ways you can think of to add selectivity to correctional worker recruitment?

Female Correctional Officers

In 1978, Linda Allen became the first female correctional officer to work at a high-security institution (the U.S. penitentiary at McNeil Island, Washington, now a Washington state correctional facility). Today it is commonplace for female correctional officers to work in federal and state high-security institutions.

SOURCE: Harry E. Allen and Clifford E. Simonsen, *Corrections in America: An Introduction, 8th Ed.* (Upper Saddle River, NJ: Prentice Hall, 1998), p. 539.

11.3 Inmate Rights and Prison Reform

Over the past four decades, the major means of reforming prisons has been court intervention. Until the middle of this century, the courts followed a **hands-off philosophy** toward prison matters. Under this hands-off philosophy, court officials were reluctant to hear prisoners' claims regarding their rights while they were incarcerated. Among other considerations, court officials questioned whether they had the necessary expertise in evaluating prison administration, and judges did not want to undermine the power of prison authorities. As a consequence of this inaction, prisoners, for all practical purposes, had no civil rights. (Remember that civil rights are those rights an individual possesses as a member of the state, especially those guaranteed against encroachment by the government.) This situation began to change as progress was made in civil rights in the wider society. Inmates were first granted rights of access to the courts, and the courts subsequently turned their attention to other rights.

hands-off philosophy
A philosophy under which courts are reluctant to hear prisoners' claims regarding their rights while incarcerated.

Access to the Courts and Legal Services

Ordinarily, prisoners want to get their cases into the federal courts because they perceive those courts as more receptive to their claims than state courts. In its 1941 landmark ruling in *Ex parte Hull*, the U.S. Supreme Court granted inmates the right of unrestricted access to the federal courts. Just three years later (in *Coffin v. Reichard*, 6th Cir., 1944), a federal circuit court held that prisoners may challenge in federal court not only the fact of their confinement but also the conditions under which they are confined. But the most important U.S. Supreme Court ruling in this area (*Cooper v. Pate*) did not occur until 1964, when Thomas Cooper, a Stateville inmate, first successfully used Section 1983 of the Federal Civil Rights Act of 1871 to challenge the conditions of confinement. Prior to the ruling in *Cooper*, inmates had relied primarily on *habeas corpus* petitions to obtain access to the federal courts. ***Habeas corpus*** is a court order requiring that a confined person be brought to court so that his or her claims can be heard. For various technical reasons, it has normally been easier for prisoners to win federal cases under Section 1983 than under *habeas corpus*. In effect, then, the *Cooper* decision launched the prisoners' rights movement by opening the door to a flood of Section 1983 claims from prisoners. Calling *Cooper v. Pate* "the Supreme Court's first modern prisoners' rights case," author James Jacobs writes:

▲ Inmates are entitled to adequate law library facilities. *Why do inmates have this right and should they?*

> But for the prisoners' movement it was not the breadth of the decision that mattered but the Supreme Court's determination that prisoners have constitutional rights; prison officials were not free to do with prisoners as they pleased. And the federal courts were permitted, indeed obligated, to provide a forum where prisoners could challenge and confront prison officials. Whatever the outcome of such confrontations, they spelled the end of the authoritarian regime in America penology.[35]

To get their cases to court, prisoners need access to legal materials, and many of them need legal assistance from persons skilled in law. The U.S. Supreme Court has recognized those facts. In *Johnson v. Avery* (1969), the Court held that inmates skilled in legal matters (so-called **jailhouse lawyers**) must be permitted to assist other inmates in preparing cases unless the government provides a reasonable alternative. Furthermore, in *Bounds v. Smith* (1977), the U.S. Supreme Court ruled that inmates are entitled to either an adequate law library or adequate legal assistance. So if a correctional institution does not wish to allow a jailhouse-lawyer system and does not wish to provide adequate library facilities for inmates, the implication is that the correctional institution should allow inmates to consult with licensed attorneys to obtain legal assistance.

Procedural Due Process in Prison

In the last chapter, we noted that inmates can face disciplinary action for breaking prison rules. The U.S. Supreme Court has moved to ensure that inmates receive minimal elements of due process during the disciplinary process. Probably the most important case in this area is *Wolff v. McDonnell* (1974). In *Wolff*, the Court held that although inmates facing a loss of good time for a rule infraction are not entitled to the same due-process protections

habeas corpus
A court order requiring that a confined person be brought to court so that his or her claims can be heard.

jailhouse lawyer
An inmate skilled in legal matters.

Civil Rights Violations

In 1996, prison inmates filed 68,235 petitions in federal district courts seeking release from prison or alleging civil rights violations. Those filings made up 25 percent of all civil filings in 1996. Except for death row inmates, who were represented by lawyers in 96 percent of the cases, inmates represented themselves in about 90 percent of cases. U.S. district courts ruled in favor of the inmates in fewer than two percent of the cases.

SOURCE: "Inmate Claims Burdening Courts, but Rate per Prisoner Is Down," *Criminal Justice Newsletter*, Vol. 28, No. 9 (October 1, 1997), p. 2.

as in a criminal trial, such inmates are entitled to (1) a disciplinary hearing by an impartial body, (2) 24 hours written notice of the charges, (3) a written statement of the evidence relied on and the reasons for the disciplinary action, and (4) an opportunity to call witnesses and present documentary evidence, provided that this does not jeopardize institutional security. The Court ruled that inmates are not entitled to confront and cross-examine people who testify against them or to have legal counsel.

First Amendment Rights

The First Amendment to the Constitution guarantees freedom of speech, press, assembly, petition, and religion. The U.S. Supreme Court has rendered numerous decisions affecting prisoners' rights to freedom of speech and expression and freedom of religion.

Free Speech   The significant case of *Procunier v. Martinez* (1974) dealt with censorship of prisoners' outgoing mail but is generally regarded as applicable to other aspects of correspondence and expression. In *Procunier,* the Supreme Court ruled that censorship is legal only if it furthers one or more of the following substantial government interests: security, order, and rehabilitation. Moreover, the degree of censorship can be no greater than that required to preserve the government interest in question.

Religious Freedom   With the demise of the hands-off policy, the first substantive right won by inmates was freedom of religion, which was awarded to Black Muslims in *Cooper v. Pate.* As a rule, inmates are free to practice either conventional or unconventional religions in prison, and prison officials are obligated to provide accommodations. However, restrictions may

▲ As a rule, inmates are free to practice their religion in prison. Religious symbols and practices that interfere with institutional security can be restricted. *Should religious practices be allowed in prisons? Why or why not?*

Commissioner of Corrections

My name is Robert L. Johnson and I am a commissioner of corrections. Shortly after Governor Ronnie Musgrove took office in January of 2000, I was invited by the state's new chief executive to come to Mississippi and become Commissioner of Corrections for the state's prison system.

Prior to accepting Governor Musgrove's invitation to head the prison system, I spent nearly 28 years in all phases of law enforcement. I held virtually every rank within the police profession. Throughout my career in the criminal justice system, my focus was centered on the law enforcement component.

As commissioner of corrections, my statutory responsibilities are to establish general policy of the department; to approve proposals for the location of new facilities, for major renovation activities, and for the creation of new programs, etc., and; to adopt administrative rules and regulations including, but not limited to, offender transfer

procedures, award of administrative earned time, personnel procedures, and employment practices.

The overall responsibilities of the commissioner are many and varied. Chief among those is to oversee the management of the state prison system which currently has over 19,000 inmates locked behind bars and nearly 19,000 offenders that are under some type of supervision in the community. Another important responsibility of commissioner is to make sure the agency remains in compliance with a court order arising from the *Gates v. Collier* class action suit.

My office also is responsible for assuring that the prison system is managed in the most cost efficient and economical manner possible.

The role of the commissioner is similar to other CEO positions in that you are confronted with often intractable problems. Generally these include tight budgets, limited resources, staff shortages and rising costs.

What personality characteristics do you think it would take to be the manager of a state prison?

be imposed, for example, where prison officials can demonstrate convincingly that religious practices compromise security or are unreasonably expensive. Granting special religious privileges can also be denied on the grounds that they will cause other groups to make similar demands. In general, the reasons given for restricting religious freedom must be compelling, and the restrictions imposed must be no more limiting than necessary.

Eighth Amendment Rights

As described in Chapter 4, the Eighth Amendment outlaws the imposition of cruel and unusual punishment. The courts have considered a number of issues under the umbrella of cruel and unusual punishment.

Medical Care   In 1976, the Supreme Court decided *Estelle v. Gamble*. The Court ruled that inmates, under the Eighth Amendment, have a right to adequate medical care, but that inmates claiming Eighth Amendment violations on medical grounds must demonstrate that prison officials have shown deliberate indifference to serious medical problems. Under these conservative and subjective criteria, medical services and circumstances usually have to be really bad—even extreme—for inmates to win cases. Furthermore, the deliberate-indifference standard formulated in *Estelle* now applies to Eighth Amendment challenges to any condition of confinement, medical or otherwise.[36]

Staff Brutality   Ironically, the Eighth Amendment has done little to protect inmates from staff brutality because brutality is normally construed as a tort rather than a constitutional issue.[37] (Recall that a tort is the breach of a duty to an individual that results in damage to him or her. It involves only duties owed to an individual as a matter of law.) However, whipping and related forms of corporal punishment have been prohibited under this amendment. Also, in *Hudson v. McMillian* (1992), the Supreme Court found that staff use of force against an inmate need not cause a significant physical injury to violate the Eighth Amendment.

Total Prison Conditions   Totality-of-conditions cases involve claims that some combination of prison practices and conditions (crowding, lack of services and programs, widespread brutality, and labor exploitation, for example) makes the prison, as a whole, unconstitutional under the Eighth Amendment. It is primarily in this area that the Eighth Amendment has been used. For example, in the famous case of *Holt v. Sarver* (1971), the entire Arkansas prison system was declared unconstitutional on grounds of totality of conditions and was ordered to implement a variety of changes.

▲ In 1981, the U.S. Supreme Court refused to hold that double-bunking in prison cells was cruel and unusual punishment. *Should double-bunking be allowed in prisons? Why or why not?*

Totality-of-conditions rulings were later handed down against prisons in Alabama (*Pugh v. Locke*, 1976) and Texas (*Ruiz v. Estelle*, 1982).

Prisons have long had the right to provide only the minimal conditions necessary for human survival. Such conditions include the necessary food, shelter, clothing, and medical care to sustain life. Whether institutional crowding violates the Eighth Amendment is typically determined in relation to total prison conditions. Instead of being treated as a separate issue, crowding is viewed as part of the totality of conditions. The Supreme Court has been reluctant to side with inmates in their challenges to crowding. In both *Bell v. Wolfish* (1979) and *Rhodes v. Chapman* (1981), the Court refused to prohibit the placing of two inmates in cells designed for one person ("double-bunking") as a response to crowding. Those rulings are frequently taken to mean that the more conservative Court is drawing the line on inmates' rights and is returning, at least partially, to a hands-off policy.

Fourteenth Amendment Rights

As described in Chapter 4, the Fourteenth Amendment guarantees U.S. citizens due process of law and equal protection under law. The due-process clause inspired the Supreme Court's decision in the previously discussed case of *Wolff v. McDonnell*, for example. Likewise, the equal-protection clause has led the Supreme Court to forbid racial discrimination (*Lee v. Washington*, 1968) and has led state courts to target gender discrimination (*Glover v. Johnson*, ED Mich., 1979). Compared with the rights of male inmates, however, the rights of female prisoners remain underdeveloped. The inmates' rights movement has been primarily a male phenomenon, and the rights of female prisoners deserve more attention from the courts in the future.

The Limits of Litigation

The progress toward prison reform resulting from the inmates' rights movement should not be underestimated. Nevertheless, one can question on a number of grounds the almost exclusive reliance, during the past four decades, on court intervention to reform the nation's prisons. Perhaps the most basic and compelling argument is that the monies being spent by prison systems to defend against inmate lawsuits and to comply with court orders (when inmate suits are successful) could have been spent better to reform the unacceptable practices that sparked the suits in the first place. Meanwhile, those prison systems are unable to address problems that help generate further inmate lawsuits precisely because they are defending against new suits and trying to comply with past court orders. The result is that even more money must be spent for legal defense and compliance with court orders. This cycle is difficult to break.

Court litigation is not just an expensive way to reform prisons; it is also a very slow and piecemeal way. A high percentage of lawsuits filed by inmates are judged frivolous and are therefore dismissed. If an inmate's suit is not judged frivolous, the inmate must still win the case in court, and many lose in the process. Even when inmates win a case, their success usually does not lead to wide-scale reforms. Successful, large-scale, class-action suits that have far-reaching impact on the prison system are relatively uncommon. Moreover, winning a case and then getting the desired changes implemented can take many years. Prison systems do not comply automatically with court decrees. Achieving compliance with court orders often requires sustained monitoring

Kansas v. Hendricks

By a 5–4 decision, in *Kansas v. Hendricks* (1997), the Supreme Court ruled that sexual predators judged to be dangerous may be confined indefinitely even after they finish serving their sentences. The decision allowed the state of Kansas to continue to hold an admitted pedophile, Leroy Hendricks, under the provisions of the state's Sexually Violent Predator Act. The Court's majority noted that such confinement, intended to protect society, does not violate the constitutional right to due process and is not double punishment for the same crime. Five other states—Arizona, California, Minnesota, Washington, and Wisconsin—have laws similar to the Kansas Sexually Violent Predator Act. Other states are likely to pass similar laws.

SOURCE: *Kansas v. Hendricks*, 117 S.Ct. 2072 (1997); "Court: Sex Predators Can Be Kept in Prison," *The Orlando Sentinel* (June 24, 1997), p. A-1.

413

by court-appointed officials as well as considerable negotiation and compromise by all parties involved to agree on a timetable and the specific nature of reforms. Finally, the transformation of traditional, ingrained practices in a prison system can render the prison environment chaotic and unstable, at least in the short run.

11.3 CRITICAL THINKING

1. What do you think are legitimate complaints from prisoners?

2. What constitutional rights do you think should be extended to prisoners? Or do you think prisoners already have too many rights? Why?

11.4 Release and Recidivism

Depending on the jurisdiction and the specific case, inmates may be released from prison in a number of ways. Examples include expiration of the maximum sentence allowed by law (known as "maxing out"); **commutation,** or reduction of the original sentence by executive authority; release at the discretion of a parole authority; and mandatory release. Of those ways, the two most common are release at the discretion of a parole authority and mandatory release.

The term **parole** has two basic meanings. It can refer to a way of being released from prison before the entire sentence has been served, or it can refer to a period of community supervision following early release. We are concerned here with the former meaning. In jurisdictions that permit parole release, inmates must establish eligibility for parole. Eligibility normally requires that inmates have served a given portion of their terms minus time served in jail prior to imprisonment and minus good time. **Good time** is time subtracted from the sentence for good behavior and other meritorious activity in prison. Once eligible, an inmate submits a parole plan stipulating such things as where he or she plans to live and work upon release. The parole authority, which may consist of a board, members of the board, or a representative of the board, then considers the inmate's plan. The parole authority also considers reports from institutional staff who have worked with the inmate. The decision to grant or deny parole is announced at a parole-grant hearing. Parole will be discussed more fully in the next chapter.

Mandatory release is release under the provisions of law, not at the discretion of a parole board. The inmate is released after serving his or her sentence or a legally required portion of the sentence, minus good-time credits. Mandatory release is similar to parole in that persons let out under either arrangement ordinarily receive a period of community supervision by a parole officer or the equivalent. Their freedom from prison is conditioned on following the rules of their community supervision (for example, obeying curfew, abstaining from drug use, and maintaining gainful employment) and on avoiding criminal activity.

commutation
Reduction of the original sentence given by executive authority, usually a state's governor.

parole
The conditional release of prisoners before they have served their full sentences.

good time
Time subtracted from an inmate's sentence for good behavior and other meritorious activities in prison.

mandatory release
A method of prison release under which an inmate is released after serving a legally required portion of his or her sentence, minus good-time credits.

In 1977, approximately 72 percent of inmates released from state prisons were released at the discretion of parole boards; only about 6 percent left prison under mandatory release that year. By contrast, in 1997, 28 percent were released by parole boards, compared with approximately 40 percent who received mandatory release.[38] This shifting pattern indicates the strong emphasis placed on determinate sentencing during the 1980s and the use of statistical guidelines to structure early-release decisions.

When inmates are released from correctional institutions, the hope is that as a result of deterrence or rehabilitation (discussed in Chapter 9), they will not return to criminal activity. Hence, we will conclude this chapter by considering **recidivism**—the return to illegal activity after release. Measuring recidivism and attributing the lack of recidivism to the influence of correctional programs are complicated by scientific methodological problems. Nevertheless, numerous studies conducted during the past couple of decades in several different jurisdictions reveal that recidivism rates, when recidivism is defined in a similar way, have remained remarkably stable. We will look at the results of several studies to show this troublesome stability in recidivism rates.

In a study of a representative sample of 1,205 individuals released from the Federal Bureau of Prisons in 1987, author Miles Harer found that within three years of release, 40.8 percent had been arrested again or had had their parole revoked. Similar studies using the same definition of recidivism had been made of federal prisoners released in 1970, 1978, 1980, and 1982. Each of those studies showed recidivism rates similar to those for the 1987 releasees. The average recidivism rate across the five studies was 43.76 percent. Some of Harer's other main findings are summarized in Figure 11–1 on page 416.[39]

recidivism
The return to illegal activity after release from incarceration.

▲ Most parole decisions are made by administrative boards whose members are appointed by state governors. An inmate's eligibility for release on parole depends on requirements set by law and on the sentence imposed by the court. *Should parole be abolished? Why or why not? If not, how could the decision-making process be improved?*

Early Release

Most offenders who receive lengthy prison terms (for example, 25 years) do not serve the entire term, and many do not even come close to doing so. The reason is the availability of parole, good time, and other mechanisms for reducing time served. Some opponents of those reductions in terms fail to understand that the mechanisms are essential to the operation of many current prison systems. Without them, many systems would be rendered dysfunctional by crowding. Additionally, without early release incentives for inmates, it would be extremely difficult to maintain order in prisons.

The largest follow-up study of its kind to date found that, of 108,580 inmates released from prisons in 11 states in 1983, an estimated 62.5 percent were rearrested for a felony or serious misdemeanor within three years of release. Approximately 22.7 percent of the released inmates were arrested for violent offenses. Nearly 47 percent were reconvicted, and 41.4 percent were returned to prison or jail.[40] With few exceptions, the findings of this study are similar to Harer's findings summarized in Figure 11–1. The results of the study indicated that the factor most strongly related to the likelihood of rearrest was prior arrest history; persons with more prior arrests were more likely to be arrested again. A similar study of nearly 4,000 young parolees who were released from prisons in 22 states in 1978 found that within six years of release, about 69 percent were rearrested, 53 percent were reconvicted, and 49 percent were reincarcerated.[41]

Finally, in a recent survey of state and federal recidivism rates, 39 states reported an average recidivism rate of 32.7 percent, based on postrelease tracking that averaged four years. In this survey, recidivism was defined as "the percentage of inmates being incarcerated for a new charge who have served a prior sentence." Utah had the highest recidivism rate (67 percent within three years after release). Montana had the lowest (11 percent within three years after release). The recidivism rate for the federal system was 40.8 percent within three years after release.[42]

FIGURE 11–1
Major Findings of Harer's Study of Recidivism Among Federal Inmates

Recidivism Rates Highest for:

First year of release

Blacks and Hispanics

Younger persons

Persons with less schooling

Those sent to prison for crimes against a person

Persons who were not employed full time or attending school before entering prison

Those with preprison histories of drug or alcohol dependency

Those having higher rates of misconduct in prison

Those who do not participate in educational programs while incarcerated

Recidivism Unrelated to:

Gender

Amount of time served in prison

SOURCE: Adapted from Miles D. Harer, *Recidivism Among Federal Prison Releasees in 1987: A Preliminary Report,* Federal Bureau of Prisons, Office of Research and Evaluation (December 9, 1993).

Obviously, those research findings are not good news for people who believe that imprisonment can achieve large-scale deterrence of crime and rehabilitation of criminals. More bad news for deterrence advocates comes from the research of author Ben Crouch, who found that newly incarcerated offenders frequently express a preference for prison over probation sentences. Crouch explains:

> A fundamental irony emerges in our justice system. That is, the lawbreakers whom middle-class citizens are most likely to fear and want most to be locked away . . . tend to be the very offenders who view prison terms of even two or three years as easier than probation and as preferable. To the extent that these views among offenders are widespread, the contemporary demand for extensive incarceration (but often for limited terms) may foster two unwanted outcomes: less deterrence and more prisoners.[43]

Similar research by author Kenneth Tunnell shows that most repeat property offenders are not threatened by the prospects of imprisonment.[44]

Unfavorable news for advocates of rehabilitation began trickling in even before the release, in 1974, of the famous Martinson report, which cast grave doubts on the ability of prisons to reform offenders.[45] In a later study, author Lynne Goodstein demonstrated that the inmates who adjusted most successfully to prison had the most difficulty adjusting to life in the free community upon release. About her research, Goodstein writes:

> These findings provide a picture of the correctional institution as a place which reinforces the wrong kinds of behaviors if its goal is the successful future adjustment of its inmates. In the process of rewarding acquiescent and compliant behavior, the prison may, in fact, be reinforcing institutional dependence.[46]

Of course, some people are deterred from crime by the threat of imprisonment, and the prison experience does benefit some inmates in the way rehabilitation advocates envision. We must be careful, however, not to hold unrealistic expectations about what imprisonment can accomplish in our society. Traditionally, we have placed undue confidence in the ability of imprisonment to control crime. But imprisonment is a reactive (versus proactive) response to the social problem of crime, and crime is interwoven with other social problems, such as poverty, inequality, and racism, in our wider society. We should not expect imprisonment to resolve or control those problems.

11.4 CRITICAL THINKING

1. Do you think anything could be done to lower recidivism rates amongst offenders? If so, what?

2. In your opinion, should prisoners be allowed to reduce their time in prison through parole or good time? Why or why not?

Review and Applications

SUMMARY BY CHAPTER OBJECTIVES

1. Distinguish Between the Deprivation and Importation Models of Inmate Society

The deprivation model of inmate society emphasizes the role of the prison environment in shaping the inmate society. The importation model of inmate society emphasizes attributes inmates bring with them when they enter prison.

2. Explain How Today's Inmate Society Differs From Those of the Past

Compared with prisons of the past, the inmate society in today's prisons is much more fragmented and conflict-ridden. Physical, psychological, economic, and social victimization are facts of life in many contemporary institutions. Inmates must learn to cope with this state of affairs. Some do so by becoming part of the prison's violent public culture. Others carve out niches and meet their needs in the prison's private culture.

3. Identify Some of the Special Features of Life in Women's Prisons

Life in women's prisons is somewhat different from life in men's prisons. In particular, women's prisons often have less stringent security measures, are less violent, and are characterized by pseudofamily structures that help the inmates cope.

4. Describe the Profile of Correctional Officers and Explain Some of the Issues that They Face

The growing number of correctional officers who staff prisons are predominantly white and male. Correctional officers face a number of problems in their work, including low pay, work-related conflicts, and a potential for corruption. They are also subject to role conflict because of their dual objectives of custody and treatment. Some officers respond to those problems more constructively than others. Efforts are ongoing to transform prison work into a profession, and issues surrounding those efforts include recruitment and selection, the backlash against affirmative action and other hiring practices, training, and unionism.

5. Identify Prisoners' Rights and Relate How They Were Achieved

The main way that prisoners have gained rights during the past four decades is through intervention by the courts. Until the 1960s, inmates had minimal rights. As the hands-off policy was lifted, prisoners gained a number of important rights: greater access to the courts, easier access to legal services in prison, and improved prison disciplinary procedures. They also gained certain rights under the First, Eighth, and Fourteenth Amendments.

6. List the Two Most Common Ways that Inmates Are Released from Prison and Compare Those Two Ways in Frequency of Use

Most inmates are released from prison at the discretion of a parole authority or under mandatory release laws. Mandatory release, a method of prison release under which an inmate is released after serving a legally required portion of his or her sentence minus good-time credits, has begun to rival parole release in frequency of use.

7. Summarize What Recidivism Research Reveals About the Success of the Prison in Achieving Deterrence and Rehabilitation

When inmates are released from prison, it is hoped that they will not return to crime. Studies show, however, that the rate of return to crime, or recidivism, is high. Studies also show that recidivism rates have remained fairly constant for a long time. Those studies call the deterrence and rehabilitation rationales into question. As a society, our expectations of what incarceration can accomplish are probably unrealistic.

KEY TERMS

total institution, p. 396
convict code, p. 396
deprivation model, p. 396
prisonization, p. 396
importation model, p. 396
sub-rosa economy, p. 399
hands-off philosophy, p. 408
habeas corpus, p. 409
jailhouse lawyer, p. 409
commutation, p. 414
parole, p. 414
good time, p. 414
mandatory release, p. 414
recidivism, p. 415

QUESTIONS FOR REVIEW

1. What did Erving Goffman mean when he wrote that prisons are *total institutions*?
2. What is the *convict code*, and why is it central to inmate society in traditional men's prisons?
3. What is *prisonization*?
4. What factors have rendered contemporary inmate society fragmented, disorganized, and unstable?
5. What are some of the reasons for high rates of prison violence?
6. What are four types of victimization that take place in prisons?
7. What are some of the general ways that inmates cope and adjust to the institutional environment, according to Johnson, Irwin, and Heffernan?
8. According to Hawkins and Alpert, what are four ways that correctional officers respond to their roles and their work conditions?
9. In *Wolff v. McDonnell* (1974), what rights were given to inmates facing disciplinary actions, and what rights were not extended?
10. How has court intervention limited prison reform?

EXPERIENTIAL ACTIVITIES

1. **Rehabilitation Programs** Contact a local prison or jail, and arrange to investigate one or more rehabilitation programs. Obtain pertinent written material, and observe the program in operation as much as possible. Assess how successful the program is in achieving its goals. Consider these specific issues:

   (1) What are the goals of the program?

   (2) Are the goals of the program clearly defined in some document?

   (3) Is the program administered in an effective way?

   (4) Is instruction adequate?

   (5) Is there adequate equipment (if applicable)?

   (6) Will the skills learned in the program be important to inmates upon release?

   (7) How likely are inmates to successfully complete the program?

   (8) Does the program have an evaluation component that would allow officials to determine the program's success or failure?

   (9) On what basis is the program's success or failure judged? After assessing the program, explain what changes, if any, you would recommend.

2. **Prison Films** Watch a video or movie about prison life. Good choices are *Murder in the First* with Kevin Bacon and Christian Slater, *The Shawshank Redemption* with Tim Robbins and Morgan Freeman, *Birdman of Alcatraz* with Burt Lancaster, *Brubaker* with Robert Redford, and *Cool Hand Luke* with Paul Newman. From what you have learned in this chapter, determine how realistic the portrayals are. Note common themes.

INTERNET

3. **Life in Prison** Visit the Web site of the North Carolina Department of Corrections, Division of Prisons, through the link at cj.glencoe.com. Access "24 Hours in Prison" and "Tour Central Prison" from the list of topics. Compare what you see to your own schedule and circumstances. Then choose any of the other topics that interest you and write a summary of what you learn.

4. **Virtual Prison Tour** Access the Florida Department of Corrections Web site by clicking the link at cj.glencoe.com and take the virtual prison tour through Florida prisons. In either an oral or written presentation describe your impressions of the prison. What surprised you? What, if anything, disturbed you? What changes, if any, should be made? As an option include North Carolina's Central Prison in your description—see Internet exercise 3.

Issues in Corrections

1. You are a correctional officer at a state prison. You face the following situations:

    a. You are ordered by a superior officer to help other officers remove an unruly inmate from a multiple-inmate holding area. The inmate is big and strong, and he resists the officers' best efforts to remove him peacefully. You and the other officers are ordered to remove him forcibly. Two of the officers immediately start punching the inmate into submission. What do you do?

    b. An inmate promises to pay you $10,000 in advance if you will deliver to him or her a small package (contents unknown). No correctional officer has ever been searched entering or leaving the facility. The inmate also tells you that his or her friends on the outside will kill your spouse and children if you do not do as he or she asks. What do you do?

    c. You learn that another correctional officer, with whom you work (and whom you like), has been smuggling contraband into the prison for inmates. What do you do? What if you know that the officer's family has been threatened?

    d. An inmate convinces you that he or she is innocent of the charges for which he or she was convicted and imprisoned. What do you do?

Religious Requests

2. As a corrections official, how would you respond to the following inmate religious requests? Be sure to justify your response.

    a. Inmates request religious literature of the "Hebrew Israelite" faith.

    b. Inmates ask to be allowed to practice the religion of an Islamic sect, the Temple of Islam. Your corrections department currently recognizes the Nation of Islam as a religion, and you believe the two are religiously identical.

    c. Native American inmates request the outdoor construction of a sweat lodge and a fire pit because the items are required for Native American worship.

    d. Native American inmates ask to be allowed to wear their hair long, as required by their religion.

    e. Inmates ask to be allowed to wear Orshiba beads under their clothes in conformity with the Santeria religion.

ADDITIONAL READING

Abbott, Jack Henry. *In the Belly of the Beast: Letters From Prison.* New York: Vintage Books, 1981.

Braly, Malcolm. *False Starts: A Memoir of San Quentin and Other Prisons.* New York: Penguin Books, 1976.

Early, Pete. *The Hot House: Life Inside Leavenworth Prison.* New York: Bantam Books, 1992.

Johnson, Robert and Hans Toch (eds.). *The Pains of Imprisonment.* Prospect Heights, IL: Waveland, 1988.

Lombardo, Lucien X. *Guards Imprisoned: Correctional Officers at Work,* 2d ed. Cincinnati: Anderson, 1989.

Pollock-Byrne, Joycelyn. *Women, Prison, and Crime.* Pacific Grove, CA: Brooks/Cole, 1990.

Rafter, Nicole Hahn. *Partial Justice: Women in State Prisons, 1800–1935.* Boston: Northeastern University Press, 1985.

ENDNOTES

1. Erving Goffman, *Asylums* (New York: Doubleday, 1961), p. xiii.

2. James B. Jacobs, *Stateville: The Penitentiary in Mass Society* (Chicago: University of Chicago Press, 1977).

3. See Donald Clemmer, *The Prison Community* (New York: Holt, Rinehart & Winston, 1940); Gresham M. Sykes, *The Society of Captives: A Study of a Maximum Security Prison* (Princeton, NJ: Princeton University Press, 1958).

4. Clemmer, op. cit.

5. John Irwin and Donald R. Cressey, "Thieves, Convicts, and the Inmate Culture," *Social Problems,* Vol. 10 (1962), pp. 142–55. Also see Clarence Schrag, "Some Foundations for a Theory of Corrections," in D. R. Cressey (ed.), *The Prison: Studies in Institutional Organization and Change* (New York: Holt, Rinehart & Winston, 1961), pp. 30–35.

6. See Richard Hawkins and Geoffrey P. Alpert, *American Prison Systems: Punishment and Justice* (Englewood Cliffs, NJ: Prentice Hall, 1989); John Irwin, *Prisons in Turmoil* (Boston: Little, Brown, 1980). Also see Leo Carroll, *Hacks, Blacks, and Cons: Race Relations in a Maximum Security Prison* (Lexington, MA: Heath, 1974); Geoffrey Hunt, Stephanie Riegel, Tomas Morales, and Dan Waldorf, "Changes in Prison Culture: Prison Gangs and the Case of the 'Pepsi Generation,'" *Social Problems,* Vol. 40 (1993), pp. 398–409; James B. Jacobs, *New Perspectives on Prisons and Imprisonment* (Ithaca, NY: Cornell University Press, 1983).

7. *Sourcebook of Criminal Justice Statistics Online* (January 2, 2001) p. 546, Table 6.81; Camille Graham Camp and George M. Camp, *The Corrections Yearbook 1999: Adult Corrections* (Middletown, CT: Criminal Justice Institute), p. 155.

8. Lee Bowker, *Prison Victimization* (New York: Elsevier, 1980).

9. Douglas C. McDonald and David Weisburd, "Segregation and Hidden Discrimination in Prisons: Reflections on a Small Study of Cell Assignments," in C. A. Hartjen and E. E. Rhine (eds.), *Correctional Theory and Practice* (Chicago: Nelson-Hall, 1992), pp. 146–61.

10. Ann Cordilia, *The Making of an Inmate: Prison as a Way of Life* (Cambridge, MA: Schenkman, 1983).

11. Goffman, op. cit., p. 14.

12. Hans Toch, *Living in Prison: The Ecology of Survival* (New York: Free Press, 1977).

13. Robert Johnson, *Hard Time: Understanding and Reforming the Prison* (Monterey, CA: Brooks/Cole, 1987).

14. Irwin, op. cit.

15. David Ward and Gene Kassebaum, "Homosexuality: A Model of Adaptation in a Prison for Women," *Social Problems,* Vol. 12 (1964), pp. 159–77.

16. Joycelyn Pollock-Byrne, *Women, Prison, and Crime* (Pacific Grove, CA: Brooks/Cole, 1990).

17. Christopher J. Mumola, "Incarcerated Parents and Their Children," U.S. Department of Justice, Bureau of Justice Statistics Special Report (Washington, D.C.: GPO: August 2000), p. 2, Table 1 and p. 3, Table 4.

18. Phyllis Jo Baunach, *Mothers in Prison* (New Brunswick, NJ: Transaction Books, 1985).

19. Rose Giallombardo, *Society of Women: A Study of a Women's Prison* (New York: Wiley, 1966); Esther Heffernan, *Making It in Prison: The Square, the Cool, and the Life* (New York: Wiley, 1972); Alice M. Propper, *Prison Homosexuality* (Lexington, MA: Heath, 1981).

20. Propper, op. cit.

21. Giallombardo, op. cit.

22. David Ward and Gene Kassebaum, *Women's Prison: Sex and Social Structure* (Chicago: Aldine, 1965).

23. Heffernan, op. cit.; Schrag, op. cit.

24. Gordon Hawkins, *The Prison: Policy and Practice* (Chicago: University of Chicago Press, 1976), p. 85.

25. Camille Graham Camp and George M. Camp, *The Corrections Yearbook 1999: Adult Corrections* (Middletown, CT: Criminal Justice Institute), 1999, pp. 130–161.

26. Hawkins and Alpert, op. cit.

27. Ibid.

28. Sykes, op. cit.

29. John D. Hewitt, Eric D. Poole, and Robert M. Regoli, "Self-Reported and Observed Rule-Breaking in Prison: A Look at Disciplinary Response," *Justice Quarterly,* Vol. 3 (1984), pp. 437–47.

30. Hawkins and Alpert, op. cit.

31. Lucien X. Lombardo, *Guards Imprisoned: Correctional Officers at Work,* 2d ed. (Cincinnati: Anderson, 1989). And see Johnson, op. cit.

32. Barbara A. Owen, "Race and Gender Relations Among Prison Workers," *Crime and Delinquency,* Vol. 31 (1985), pp. 147–59.

33. Vital Statistics 1994 (Laurel, MD: American Correctional Association, 1994), pp. 35–40.

34. Ibid.

35. Jacobs, op. cit., pp. 36–37.

36. *Wilson v. Seiter,* 111 S.Ct. 2321 (1991).

37. Hawkins and Alpert, op. cit.

38. U.S. Department of Justice, Bureau of Justice Statistics, Correctional Populations in the United States, 1997 (November 2000).

39. Miles D. Harer, *Recidivism Among Federal Prison Releasees in 1987: A Preliminary Report,* Federal Bureau of Prisons, Office of Research and Evaluation (December 9, 1993).

40. United States Department of Justice, Bureau of Justice Statistics Special Report, *Recidivism of Prisoners Released in 1983* (April 1989).

41. United States Department of Justice, Bureau of Justice Statistics Special Report, *Recidivism of Young Parolees* (May 1987).

42. Camp and Camp, op. cit., pp. 56–57.

43. Ben M. Crouch, "Is Incarceration Really Worse? Analysis of Offenders' Preferences for Prison over Probation," *Justice Quarterly,* Vol. 10 (1993), pp. 67–88.

44. Kenneth D. Tunnell, "Choosing Crime: Close Your Eyes and Take Your Chances," *Justice Quarterly,* Vol. 7 (1990), pp. 673–90.

45. Robert Martinson, "What Works? Questions and Answers About Prison Reform," *The Public Interest,* Vol. 42 (1974), pp. 22–54.

46. Lynne Goodstein, "Inmate Adjustment to Prison and the Transition to Community Life," in R. M. Carter, D. Glaser, and L. T. Wilkins (eds.), *Correctional Institutions,* 3d ed. (New York: Harper & Row, 1985), pp. 285–302.

Chapter 12
Community Corrections

CHAPTER OBJECTIVES

After completing this chapter, you should be able to:

1. Define community corrections and identify the goals and responsibilities of community corrections agencies and their staffs.

2. Define probation and summarize the research findings on recidivism rates.

3. Distinguish parole from probation.

4. Explain the functions of a parole board.

5. Describe how intermediate sanctions differ from traditional community corrections programs.

6. Explain two major concerns about intensive-supervision probation and parole (ISP).

7. Explain what day reporting centers and structured fines are.

8. Explain what home confinement and electronic monitoring are.

9. Identify the goal of halfway houses and compare them with other community corrections programs.

10. Summarize the purposes and outcomes of temporary-release programs.

12.1 Community Corrections: Definition and Scope

community corrections
The subfield of corrections in which offenders are supervised and provided services outside jail or prison.

Community corrections can be broadly defined as the subfield of corrections consisting of programs in which offenders are supervised and provided services outside jail or prison. For this reason, community corrections is sometimes referred to as noninstitutional corrections. Community corrections includes such programs as diversion, restitution, probation, parole, halfway houses, and various provisions for temporary release from prison or jail. Those programs are the subject of this chapter.

It is important to realize that community corrections is a generic term. Federal, state, and local jurisdictions differ widely in the way they organize and administer community corrections and in the specific procedures they use. Author David Duffee's delineation of three varieties of community corrections illustrates this diversity.[1] Community-run correctional programs are controlled by local governments, with minimal connection to state and federal authorities. In effect, local officials determine how such programs will be run within the broad guidelines of state and federal laws. In community-placed programs, as in community-run ones, offenders are handled by agencies within the local district, but agencies in community-placed programs are connected to central state or federal authorities, or both. Consequently, central authority affects program operation, and community-placed programs tend to be more isolated from local affairs than are community-run programs. Community-based correctional programs are a combination of the other two types. Connection to central authority for resources and other support services (a feature of community-placed programs) is combined with strong links between the program and the surrounding locality (a feature of community-placed programs).

MYTH Modern community correctional programs are invariably "soft on crime." They focus too much on rehabilitation, to the exclusion of punishment, deterrence, and incapacitation.

FACT Major prison crowding in the past 15 years or so has made it necessary to channel into the community, under supervision, many felons who formerly would have gone to (or stayed in) prison. The priorities and operations of community agencies have shifted to meet this challenge. Many community programs—especially the newer "intermediate sanctions," such as electronic monitoring—emphasize punishment, deterrence, and incapacitation as much as, if not more than, rehabilitation.

Goals and Staff Roles

As described in Chapter 9, the goals of sentencing, which also are the goals of corrections, include punishment, deterrence, incapacitation, and rehabilitation. Yet, as a subfield of corrections, community corrections has traditionally emphasized rehabilitation. Although community programs are concerned with supervising and controlling offenders and ensuring that they follow the rules of their sentences, there is frequently great emphasis on assisting offenders with personal problems and needs. Another emphasis is establishing stronger ties between the offender and the community, by helping the offender get and keep a job, for example. However, the traditional preoccupation of community corrections with rehabilitation has given way in recent years to concern with the other goals.

▲ One aspect of probation and parole is client counseling. *What kinds of counseling problems are probation or parole officers likely to encounter?*

Reform vs. Punishment

According to a public opinion poll, 90 percent of Americans support the development of local programs to keep more nonviolent and first-time offenders active and working in the community. Yet, only eight percent of Americans favor shortening sentences.

SOURCE: Timothy J. Flanagan, "Reform or Punish: Americans' Views of the Correctional System," pp. 75–92 in T. J. Flanagan and D. R. Longmire (eds.), Americans View Crime and Justice: A National Public Opinion Survey (Thousand Oaks, CA: Sage, 1996), p. 87.

The staff of community correctional programs have two potentially competing roles that reflect different goals. The first amounts to a law enforcement role: seeing that offenders comply with the orders of community sentences. This means that staff must supervise offenders, investigate possible rule infractions, and take action to address any serious or repeated rule violations.

The other role of staff is to help offenders identify and address their problems and needs. This role has three aspects. The first is the direct provision of services, such as counseling, to offenders. The second is commonly described as the "resource broker" role. In this role, staff identify particular problems and needs and refer offenders to various community agencies for help. An important advantage of community corrections is that correctional agencies can draw on the services of other agencies in the locality. For example, a probation officer may refer a client to a local mental health center for counseling. The third aspect of the helping role is advocacy. A community may not offer services that a significant number of offenders require, for example, opportunities for vocational training. It is the responsibility of staff to advocate greater availability for services that are lacking and to work with community leaders to develop those services.

Many people believe that community correctional staff *should* occupy the dual roles of enforcing the law and helping clients. Those people maintain that supervision and control are necessary to facilitate rehabilitation and that rehabilitation enhances supervision and control. Opponents of that position point to the potential for conflict between roles. They argue that such conflict creates undue stress for staff and makes it difficult to accomplish anything of value.

A recent study of the attitudes of community correctional staff toward their work found that staff attitudes have been shifting away from the helping role and toward the law enforcement role. The findings of this study indicate the declining emphasis on rehabilitation in community corrections and suggest that the potential for role conflict may lessen as well.[2]

CAREERS IN CRIMINAL JUSTICE

U.S. Probation Officer

My name is Steve E. Whisenant and I am an officer with the Federal Corrections and Supervision Division of the U.S. Courts, better known as the U.S. Pretrial and Probation Office. I supervise the Hickory and Statesville, North Carolina, offices, two of the five U.S. Pretrial and Probation Offices which serve the Western District of North Carolina.

My interest in criminal justice was initiated because law enforcement offered a challenging and exciting work environment. At age 20, I began employment with the Burke County, North Carolina, Sheriff's Office. While working as a deputy sheriff, I enrolled in a criminal justice program at Western Piedmont Community College in Morgantown, North Carolina. After receiving a police science associate degree, I transferred to an evening program to earn a Bachelor of Science degree in Social Science/Criminal Justice from Gardner-Webb University in Boiling Springs, North Carolina.

During my service with the sheriff's office as a patrol officer, detective, and captain of law enforcement operations, I met the U.S. probation officer who worked in Burke County. After nine rewarding years as a sheriff's deputy, the lure of a more stable work schedule and the absence of an election every four years made a position with the U.S. Probation Office appealing.

My career as a U.S. probation officer began in 1986. I worked in all three of our major units including (1) pretrial; (2) presentence writing; and (3) supervision. Each of these units offers unique and rewarding challenges. The pretrial unit completes background investigations, prepares written reports, and recommends release conditions for the magistrate's court. This unit also supervises defendants released under various bond conditions including electronic monitoring. Following a defendant's plea or verdict of guilty, the presentence unit conducts investigations and prepares detailed reports with sentencing recommendations for the district court. Their duties include contact with offenders, various law enforcement officers, U.S. attorneys, defense attorneys, and judges. The supervision unit supervises offenders who receive probation or who are released from imprisonment on parole or supervised release. They have contact with a number of persons including local law enforcement agencies, treatment providers, and offenders' employers, families, and acquaintances.

Some challenges faced by probation and pretrial staff include having little control over their workload numbers. Cases are generated by other federal agencies' arrests, releases from prison, and violations generated by the supervised offenders. Additionally, changes in the types of offenders and crimes committed, coupled with society's changing needs and expectations for supervising offenders require a successful organization to be flexible and innovative.

Our district's leadership solicits input from every employee in how to best accomplish the organization's mission. Opportunities to work on various committees and projects abound. Employees are encouraged to promote our organization's national vision statement to exemplify the highest standards in community corrections.

As a supervisor, I support a very competent and highly professional organization. My recommendation for anyone seeking a career within this organization is to excel in fields like criminal justice, psychology, sociology, or human relations.

What do you think are the most important abilities that one must have to be a successful probation officer?

The Importance of Community Corrections

A discussion of the definition and scope of community corrections would not be complete without stressing how other components of criminal justice depend on community programs. It is not feasible to send all convicted persons—or even all felons—to jail or prison; resources are simply too limited. Were it not for the availability of community programs, the courts and institutional corrections would be overwhelmed by the sheer number of cases.

To illustrate, examine Figure 12–1, which presents data on the number of adults under the supervision of state and federal corrections agencies at the end of 1980, compared with the end of 1999. Note that at the end of 1999,

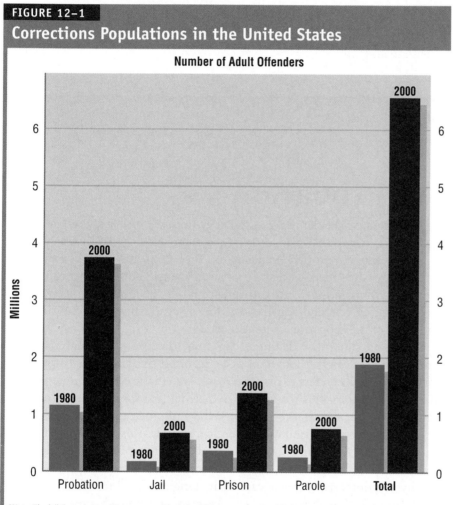

FIGURE 12–1

Corrections Populations in the United States

*Note: The jail figure is for midyear 1999 and includes jail inmates supervised in the community.

SOURCE: "U.S. Correctional Population Reaches 6.3 Million Men and Women Represents 3.1 Percent of the Adult U.S.Population," U.S. Department of Justice, Bureau of Justice Statistics Press Release (July 23, 2000) <www.ojp.usdoj.gov/bjs/pub/pdf/pp99pr.pdf>

Allen J. Beck, "Prisoners in 1999," U.S. Department of Justice, Bureau of Justice Statistics Bulletin (Washington, DC: GPO, August 2000).

Allen J. Beck, "Prison and Jail Inmates at Midyear 1999," U.S. Department of Justice, Bureau of Justice Statistics Bulletin (Washington, DC: GPO, April 2000).

Figures for 1980 are from Ann L. Pastore and Kathleen Maguire (eds.) Sourcebook of Criminal Justice Statistics 1999, U.S. Department of Justice, Bureau of Justice Statistics (Washington, DC: GPO, 2000), p. 484, Table 6.1.

Funding Corrections

Of all adults under some type of correctional supervision in the United States, approximately 30 percent are confined in prisons or jails. Approximately 70 percent are serving community sentences. Approximately 80 percent of all funds allocated to corrections in the United States are spent to build and run institutions, and about 20 percent are spent on community corrections. Thus, 80 percent of the funds are spent on 30 percent of the correctional population, and 20 percent of the funds are left to accommodate 70 percent of that population.

SOURCES: Thomas P. Bonczar and Lauren E. Glaze, Probation and Parole in the United States, 1998. U.S. Department of Justice, Bureau of Justice Statistics Bulletin (Washington, DC: GPO, August 1999), p. 2; Ann L. Pastore and Kathleen Maguire (eds.) Sourcebook of Criminal Justice Statistics 1999. U.S. Department of Justice, Bureau of Justice Statistics (Washington, DC: GPO, 2000), p. 11, Table 1.8.

probation
A sentence in which the offender, rather than being incarcerated, is retained in the community under the supervision of a probation agency and required to abide by certain rules and conditions to avoid incarceration.

diversion
Organized, systematic efforts to remove individuals from further processing in criminal justice by placing them in alternative programs; diversion may be pretrial or posttrial.

the number of offenders in jail and prison combined is considerably smaller than the number serving community sentences on probation and parole. Approximately 4.5 million adults were on probation or parole at the end of 1999, compared with about 2 million in jail or prison.

Figure 12–1 also shows that large increases in the prison and jail populations have been accompanied by large increases in the probation and parole populations. Between 1980 and 2000, the probation population increased by 238 percent, and the parole population by 223 percent. The comparable increases in the prison and jail populations were 328 percent and 277 percent, respectively.

12.1 CRITICAL THINKING

Which do you think is more beneficial to society: community corrections or prison? Why?

12.2 Probation

Probation can be defined as a sentence imposed by the courts on offenders who have either pleaded guilty or been found guilty. Instead of being incarcerated, an offender placed on probation is retained in the community under the supervision of a probation agency. The offender is provided with supervision and services. Continuation of probation (that is, avoidance of incarceration) depends on the offender's compliance with the rules and conditions of the probation sentence.

Probation should be distinguished from diversion, although, in broad terms, probation can be thought of as a type of posttrial diversion from incarceration. **Diversion** refers to organized and systematic efforts to remove people from the criminal justice process by placing them in programs that offer alternatives to the next, more restrictive stage of processing. Although diversion is commonly associated with juvenile justice, it is also used in adult criminal justice. Diversion can occur at any point from the initial police contact up to, and even in conjunction with, formal sentencing. For example, the police may divert a domestic violence case by making a referral to a family in crisis center instead of making an arrest. Instead of filing charges against an arrestee who is an alcoholic, a prosecutor may divert the case to a detoxification and counseling agency. Those are examples of *pretrial* diversion. *Posttrial* diversion—for example, probation—occurs when an offender who has pleaded guilty or been found guilty is placed in a program that is an alternative to a more restrictive sentence, such as incarceration.

There are five types of probation:

1. *Straight probation* occurs when an offender is sentenced only to probation, with no incarceration or other form of residential placement.

2. In *suspended-sentence probation,* the judge pronounces a jail or prison sentence but suspends the sentence on the condition that the offender performs well on probation.

3. With a *split sentence,* the judge divides a single sentence into a relatively short jail term followed by probation supervision (for example, a five-year probation sentence with the first six months to be served in jail).

4. *Shock probation* usually involves two sentences. The offender is initially sentenced to prison but is soon (perhaps after 120 days) recalled to court and placed on probation.

5. *Residential probation* involves placement of the probationer in a structured, but generally open, living environment, such as a halfway house. When residential probation is used, it is common for the probationer to spend the early part of the sentence in the residential facility and then, upon successful discharge, to complete the probation sentence living in the free community.

A probation agency has three fundamental objectives. The first is to assist the court in matters pertaining to sentencing. This is accomplished by conducting inquiries and furnishing the court with information about offenders' backgrounds and current situations. The second objective is to promote community protection by supervising and monitoring the activities of persons sentenced to probation. The third objective is to promote the betterment of offenders by ensuring that they receive appropriate rehabilitation services. Thus, probation agencies work closely with the courts to assist offenders and, when possible, help them avoid incarceration without compromising the safety and security of the community.

Historical Context

Probation developed out of various practices used under English common law. One such practice, known as benefit of clergy, allowed certain accused individuals to appeal to the court for leniency in sentencing by reading from the Bible. Another practice was judicial reprieve, whereby a convicted offender could ask the judge to suspend the sentence on the condition that the offender display good future behavior. Those and other practices were important forerunners of modern probation.

The more immediate origins of modern probation lie in the efforts of John Augustus (1785–1859), a Boston shoemaker, who is considered the "father" of probation. Starting in the early 1840s, Augustus volunteered to stand bail and assume custody for select, less serious offenders in exchange for the judge's deferring the sentence. Augustus was responsible for monitoring offenders' activities and later reporting to the judge on their performance in the community. If the judge was satisfied with community performance, charges were dropped; if not, sentencing proceeded.

Influenced by the efforts of Augustus, Massachusetts passed the first formal probation law in 1878. By 1920, a majority of the states allowed probation. However, it was not until 1957 that all states had probation statutes. The federal probation system was established in 1925.[3] In slightly more than 150 years, probation has grown from the efforts of a volunteer in Boston into the most frequently used sentence in criminal justice.

John Augustus

John Augustus, the prosperous Boston shoemaker who initiated the concept of probation, received no pay for his 18 years of court work. He used his own money and voluntary contributions from others to finance his efforts.

SOURCE: John Augustus, A Report of the Labors of John Augustus, For the Last Ten Years, In Aid of the Unfortunate (Boston: Wright and Hasty, 1852); reprinted as John Augustus, First Probation Officer (New York: National Probation Association, 1939).

Administration

As mentioned earlier in the chapter, probation is administered in many different ways across the nation. The federal government administers its own probation system under the Administrative Office of the Courts, and each state has responsibility for determining how to administer probation. In some states, such as Kentucky, probation is administered at the state level as part of a department of corrections or other state agency. In other states, such as California and Indiana, probation administration is a local function. Still other states combine state and local administration. Under *probation subsidy*, which became popular in the 1960s, states agree to financially support locally administered probation services in exchange for the localities' not sentencing all their offenders to the state prison system. The goal is to give localities a financial incentive to retain offenders in their communities when possible.

There are other variations in the way probation is administered. Depending on the jurisdiction, administrative responsibility may lie with the executive branch, the judicial branch, or both. Adult and juvenile probation services can be administered separately or jointly, as can misdemeanor and felony services. Finally, probation administration can be combined with parole administration, or the two may be separate.

Process and Procedures

A probation sentence can be viewed as a process with an identifiable beginning and end. The process consists of three basic stages:

1. Placement of an offender on probation by a judge

2. Supervision and service delivery for the probationer by probation officers

3. Termination of the probation

Before and during the process, probation agency staff employ a number of important procedures, which will be examined in the following subsections.

Placement on Probation   In deciding whether an offender should be sentenced to probation, a judge usually considers a host of factors, such as statutes outlining eligibility for probation, structured sentencing guidelines (in jurisdictions where they are used), recommendations from the prosecuting and defense attorneys, the offender's freedom or detention in jail before and during trial, the presentence investigation report prepared by the probation agency, and characteristics of the offender and offense. Judges ordinarily give great consideration to the seriousness of the current offense and the prior legal record of the offender. Cases involving more serious offenses or offenders with more extensive prior records are less likely to receive probation.

The Presentence Investigation   The **presentence investigation (PSI)** is conducted by the probation agency at the request of the judge, usually during the period between the finding or plea of guilt and sentencing. In performing a PSI, a probation officer conducts an inquiry into the offender's past and current social and psychological functioning as well as the offender's prior criminal record. The main task of the inquiry is to estimate the risk the offender presents to the community and to determine the offender's treatment needs. The probation officer obtains the necessary information by

presentence investigation (PSI)
An investigation conducted by a probation agency or other designated authority at the request of a court into the past behavior, family circumstances, and personality of an adult who has been convicted of a crime, to assist the court in determining the most appropriate sentence.

interviewing the offender and others who know the offender, such as an employer, family members, and victims. The officer also reviews relevant documents and reports. The information is assembled into a PSI report, which is submitted to the court.

A sample PSI checklist appears in Figure 12–2 on page 434. There are no universally accepted standards for PSI report format and content. However, reports typically contain the following basic elements:

1. A face sheet of identifying demographic data

2. A discussion of the instant or current offense as perceived by the police, the victim, and the offender

3. A summary of the offender's prior legal record

4. An overview of the offender's past and present social and psychological functioning

5. The probation officer's evaluation of the offender and the officer's recommendation for an appropriate sentence

The probation officer must convey the essential information in a concise and objective manner that supports the sentencing recommendation being offered.

Once prepared, the PSI report serves a variety of functions. It is useful in formulating supervision and treatment plans for persons who are given probation sentences. It also serves as the baseline for progress reports on probationers. When an offender is sent to prison, the report helps prison officials learn about and make decisions about the offender. However, the most well-known and immediate function of the PSI report is to assist judges in arriving at a proper sentence.

In most cases, there is a high degree of consistency between the sentencing recommendation in the PSI report and the actual sentence handed down

Presentence Investigation Reports

Probation personnel wrote more than a half million presentence investigation reports during 1999. Personnel in more than 80 percent of the agencies also supervised probationers. In 1999, probation staff in Texas wrote the most PSIs (103,157), while staff in South Carolina wrote the fewest (26).

SOURCE: Camille Graham Camp and George M. Camp, The Corrections Yearbook 1999: Adult Corrections (Middletown, CT: Criminal Justice Institute, 1999), p. 202.

▲ As part of a presentence investigation, a probation officer interviews an offender to obtain background information for the court. *What kinds of background information, if any, should influence the length and type of sentence? Why?*

FIGURE 12–2

Checklist for Completing a Presentence Investigation Report

Face sheet of identifying demographic information
    name, aliases, and address
    physical description
    social security number
    date and place of birth
    school history, occupation, marital status, family members

Instant offense
    offense and docket number
    name(s) of codefendants, if any
    prosecutor and defense attorney (names and addresses)
    means of conviction (trial, plea agreement, etc.)
    sentencing date

Presentence investigation
    defendant's version of events relating to offense
    victim impact, restitution needs
    jail time served in connection with offense
    previous record
    social history (family, friends, self-image)
    educational history
    marital history
    employment history
    economic situation
    religious association
    outside interests
    health (including drug and alcohol use)
    present attitudes of defendant
    plea agreement (if any)
    fiscal impact of sentencing option(s) to victim and state
    psychiatric insights
    statement of probation officer

Sentencing recommendation

Probation plan
    length of probationary period
    probationer reporting requirements
    job placement
    postemployment education training needs
    community service requirements
    other probation requirements

by the judge. As shown in the accompanying Myth/Fact box, however, this does not mean that judges are always strongly influenced by probation officers' sentencing recommendations. In some cases, probation officers recommend sentences that they believe are consistent with judicial expectations.

In addition to questions about the actual effect of PSI reports on sentencing decisions, another issue is whether courts should use PSIs conducted by private individuals and agencies rather than by probation agencies. Private PSIs became popular in the 1960s. Private individuals and agencies may conduct PSIs under contract with the defense or the court. Advocates of privately prepared PSIs argue that privatization reduces probation agency workloads and saves tax dollars (when such PSIs are commissioned by the defendant). Opponents argue that improper sentences may be recommended, that private PSIs can discriminate against the poor, and that the PSIs can reduce the credibility and funding of probation agencies.

The PSI report is usually the property of the court for which it is prepared. Once the report is submitted to the court, a copy is often provided to the defendant, defense counsel, and the prosecuting attorney. Both parties have the opportunity to review the report for accuracy and to bring any concerns to the court's attention. This process is known as "disclosure," and there has been controversy about it. Those who oppose the practice of disclosure maintain that people with important information may not make it available if the offender will see it and know who provided it. Those who support disclosure, on the other hand, argue that it is a matter of fairness that the offender be able to see the information on which the sentence is based, to ensure that it is accurate.

The Probation Order When an offender is sentenced to probation, the court files the appropriate documents indicating the length and conditions of the probation sentence (see Figure 12–3 on page 436).

Although the length of probation sentences varies between jurisdictions and between cases, it is common for adults placed on probation for misdemeanor offenses to receive one- to two-year terms. Those convicted of felonies and sentenced to probation generally receive longer terms (for example, five years). Some states allow sentences of lifetime probation. In some cases, the court has the authority to grant early discharge from probation for commendable performance, or to extend the term of probation.

Probation conditions are rules that specify what an offender is and is not to do during the course of a probation sentence. They are of crucial significance because the success or failure of the probationer is evaluated with respect to those rules. There are two types of conditions. *Standard* or *general conditions* apply to all persons placed on probation and pertain primarily to control and supervision of the offender. *Special conditions* are imposed at the discretion of the judge and probation officials and are designed to address the offender's particular situation. Special conditions frequently deal with treatment matters. For example, an offender may be ordered to participate in drug abuse counseling.

In recent years it has become increasingly common for jurisdictions to include restitution orders as part of probation, as either a standard condition or a special condition. (See standard condition 12 in Figure 12–3.)

MYTH . . . . **FACT** . . . .

An essential function of the PSI report is to individualize justice by helping judges structure their sentencing decisions around the offender's unique circumstances.

In an important study, author John Rosecrance found that experienced probation officers try to recommend sentences that are consistent with judicial expectations, given the seriousness of the offense and the offender's prior criminal record. Rosecrance found that officers selectively structure information in the report to support the recommendations they have already decided on. Information that is inconsistent with those recommendations is minimized in the report. Rosecrance's research implies that the PSI report merely gives the sentencing process a guise of individualized justice.[4]

probation conditions
Rules that specify what an offender is and is not to do during the course of a probation sentence.

FIGURE 12–3

Sample Probation Order

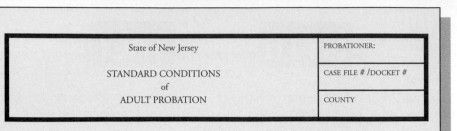

State of New Jersey

STANDARD CONDITIONS
of
ADULT PROBATION

PROBATIONER:

CASE FILE # /DOCKET #

COUNTY

The Court, believing that you are capable of living a useful and law-abiding life in the community, has sentenced you to probation for a period of _____ , beginning _____ _____ . While on probation, you will be under the supervision of a probation officer. You are required to comply with the conditions of probation listed below.

If there is probable cause to believ[e]
probation, the Court may commit you t[o]
probation, it may impose on you any se[ntence for which you could have origi]
nally convicted, up to and including the

1. You shall obey all federal, state, and [...]
   officer if you are arrested or issued a [...]

2. You shall report to your probation o[fficer ...]

3. You shall answer truthfully all inqui[ries ...]

4. You shall permit your officer to visit [...]

5. You shall submit at any time to a sea[rch of your]
   person, place of residence, vehicle, o[r ...]

6. You shall promptly report any chang[e ...]
   obtain permission from your probati[on ...]
   may not leave the state of New Jersey [...]
   tion officer.

7. You shall cooperate in any medical a[...]
   probation officer recommends.

8. You shall submit to drug or alcohol t[...]

9. You shall support your dependents a[...]

10. You shall seek and maintain gainful [...]
    your place of employment or find yo[ur ...]

11. You shall not have in your possessio[n ...]
    2C: 39 et seq. If you possess a firear[m ...]
    bation officer. In addition, if you pre[...]
    your local police department or to a[...]
    officer.

12. You shall make payments on any fine, penalty assessment, restitution or other financial obligation as provided by Court order. Failure to comply may result in further Court action, pursuant to *N.J.S.A.* 2C:46-2b; including attachment of your wages, filing of a civil judgment, and/or extension of your probation term.

| VCCB $_____ | DEDR $_____ | Fine $_____ |
| FLF $_____ | Restitution $_____ | Other $_____ |

Total Amount Ordered $_____. This will be paid at the rate of $_____ per _____ . If no payment schedule is established, the total is due forthwith. If the offense occurred on or after February 1, 1993, a transaction fee of up to $1.00 is to be paid on each occasion when a payment or installment payment is made (*N.J.S.A.* 2C:46-1d.).

Special Conditions

You must also comply with the following special conditions of probation imposed by the Court in accordance with *N.J.S.A.* 2C: 45-1 et seq.:

☐ ___ Hours of Community Service
☐ ___ Days in the County Jail
☐ Driver's License Suspended for _____
☐ Obtain a General Equivalency Diploma (GED)
☐ Complete Court Ordered Treatment Program
_____
Specify Program

☐ _____
☐ _____
☐ _____
☐ _____
☐ _____

I have received a copy of the rules and conditions of probation which have been read and explained to me. I understand the above rules and conditions of probation and that they apply to me, and I further understand that failure to comply on my part constitutes a violation of probation and will cause my return to Court. If I am arrested or detained in any other state or jurisdiction within the United States while I am on this term of probation, my signature below shall be deemed to be a waiver of extradition.

_____
PROBATIONER   DATE

_____
PROBATION OFFICER   DATE

ADDRESS: _____
_____
_____

Telephone: _____

DOB: ____/____/_____ SS#: _____

Driver's License #: _____

Restitution, you may recall, usually means that the offender provides either the victim or the community with money or work service.

In some areas, the court may later amend or modify conditions outlined in the initial probation order. The conditions can be made more or less restrictive, depending on the probationer's behavior. However, to be legal, it is necessary for all conditions, regardless of when they are imposed, to be clear, reasonable, permitted by the constitution, and related to the rehabilitation of the offender or the protection of society, or both.[5]

Supervision and Service Delivery Once offenders have been placed on probation, the probation agency must shift attention to supervision and service delivery. At this point, probationers must be assigned to probation officers. In making assignments, it is important to match officer and probationer characteristics. For example, a manipulative probationer who poses a risk to community security might be assigned to an officer with a law enforcement orientation. An offender who poses little risk but has pressing treatment needs might be assigned to an officer with more of a helping background.

Because not all persons placed on probation require the same amounts and types of supervision and services, an important task is to determine what is appropriate for each client. In recent years, this task has been facilitated by the development of risk-and-needs-assessment instruments such as the one shown in Figure 12–4 on page 438. The probation agency can more objectively determine the amount and type of supervision a probationer requires by examining the risk score. For instance, a probationer with a risk score in the maximum range might receive weekly contacts from the probation officer, whereas a probationer with a minimum-range risk score might receive monthly contacts. Likewise, the amount and kind of services are directed by the needs score. The point is to ensure that the highest levels of supervision are reserved for probationers who present the greatest risk to the community and that the highest levels of treatment services are reserved for those who present the greatest needs.

Once risk-and-needs assessment has been completed, the probation agency can formulate supervision and treatment plans for its clients. In effect, those plans further specify the conditions of probation and describe what is expected of probationers. Some of the requirements might include weekly contacts with the probation officer, random drug tests, weekly Alcoholics Anonymous meetings, or obtainment of a GED. Once supervision and treatment plans are set, the monitoring of probationers and the periodic filing of progress reports for the court can begin.

Termination of Probation Ultimately, the probation agency must make recommendations to the court about how probation is to be terminated. Clients who have generally fulfilled the conditions of their sentences and have served their terms are recommended for successful discharges. If a client has violated the conditions of probation, the probation agency may recommend **revocation,** which entails repealing the probation sentence and substituting a more restrictive sentence, such as a jail or prison term.

restitution
Money paid or services provided to victims, their survivors, or to the community by a convicted offender to make up for the injury inflicted.

Restitution

Although restitution is most commonly ordered as a condition of probation, it is used in other ways in community corrections. Restitution can be the sole sentence. It may also be a feature of diversion programming. For example, restitution is often part of victim-offender reconciliation programs, in which victims and offenders discuss the offense and arrive at an out-of-court settlement.

SOURCE: Belinda Rodgers McCarthy, Bernard J. McCarthy, Jr., and Matthew C. Leone, *Community-Based Corrections,* 4th ed. (Belmont, CA: Wadsworth, 2001), pp. 226–227.

revocation
The repeal of a probation sentence or parole, and substitution of a more restrictive sentence, because of violation of probation or parole conditions.

FIGURE 12–4

Sample Risk and Needs Assessment Instrument

DEPARTMENT OF CORRECTIONS
DIVISION OF PROBATION & PAROLE

Client No. _____   Client Name: _____   Officer No. _____

CLIENT RISK ASSESSMENT

Instructions: Enter numerical rating in box at right.

1. TOTAL NUMBER OF PRIOR FELONY CONVICTIONS:
   (include juvenile adjudications, if known)
   a. None .... Enter 0
   b. One .... Enter 2
   c. Two or more .... Enter 4

2. PRIOR NUMBER OF PROBATION/PAROLE SUPERVISION PERIODS:
   (include juvenile, if known)
   a. None .... Enter 0
   b. One or more .... Enter 4

3. PRIOR PROBATION/PAROLE REVOCATIONS:
   (adult only)
   a. None .... Enter 0
   b. One or more .... Enter 4

4. AGE AT FIRST KNOWN CONVICTION OR ADJUDICATION:
   (include juvenile, if known)
   a. 24 years or older .... Enter 0
   b. 20 through 23 years .... Enter 2
   c. 19 years or younger .... Enter 4

5. HISTORY OF ALCOHOL ABUSE:
   a. No history of abuse .... Enter 0
   b. Occasional or prior abuse .... Enter 2
   c. Frequent current abuse .... Enter 4

6. HISTORY OF OTHER SUBSTANCE ABUSE:
   (prior to incarceration for parolees)
   a. No history of abuse .... Enter 0
   b. Occasional or prior abuse .... Enter 1
   c. Frequent current abuse .... Enter 2

7. AMOUNT OF TIME EMPLOYED IN LAST 12 MONTHS:
   (prior to incarceration for parolees, based on 35 hr. week)
   a. 7 months or more .... Enter 0
   b. 4 months through 6 months .... Enter 1
   c. Less than 4 months .... Enter 2
   d. Not applicable .... Enter 0

8. AGENT IMPRESSION OF OFFENDER'S ATTITUDE:
   a. Motivated to change, receptive to assistance .... Enter 0
   b. Dependent or unwilling to accept responsibility .... Enter 3
   c. Rationalizes behavior, negative, not motivated to change .... Enter 5

9. RECORD OF CONVICTION FOR SELECTED OFFENSES:
   (include current offense, add categories and enter total)
   a. None of the following .... Enter 0
   b. Burglary, Theft, Auto Theft, Robbery .... Add 2
   c. Forgery, Deceptive Practices (Fraud, Bad Check, Drugs) .... Add 3

10. ASSAULTIVE OFFENSES:
    a. Crimes against persons which include use of weapon, physical force, threat of force, all sex crimes, and vehicular homicide
    ☐ Yes ☐ No

Total Score
(Range 0-34)

CLIENT NEED ASSESSMENT

Instructions: Enter numerical rating in box at right.

1. ACADEMIC/VOCATIONAL SKILLS:
   a. High school or above skill level .... Enter 0
   b. Has vocational training, additional not needed/desired .... Enter 1
   c. Has some skills; additional needed/desired .... Enter 3
   d. No skills, training needed .... Enter 5

2. EMPLOYMENT:
   a. Satisfactory employment for 1 year or longer .... Enter 0
   b. Employed, no difficulties reported, or homemaker, student, retired, or disabled and unable to work .... Enter 1
   c. Part-time, seasonal, unstable employment or needs additional employment; unemployed, but has a skill .... Enter 4
   d. Unemployed & virtually unemployable; needs training .... Enter 7

3. FINANCIAL STATUS:
   a. Longstanding pattern of self-sufficiency .... Enter 0
   b. No current difficulties .... Enter 1
   c. Situational or minor difficulties .... Enter 4
   d. Severe difficulties .... Enter 6

4. LIVING ARRANGEMENTS (Within last six months):
   a. Stable and supportive relationships with family or others in living group .... Enter 0
   b. Client lives alone or independently within another household .... Enter 1
   c. Client experiencing occasional, moderate interpersonal problems within living group .... Enter 4
   d. Client experiencing frequent and serious interpersonal problems within living group .... Enter 6

5. EMOTIONAL STABILITY:
   a. No symptoms of instability .... Enter 1
   b. Symptoms limit, but do not prohibit adequate functioning .... Enter 5
   c. Symptoms prohibit adequate functioning .... Enter 8

6. ALCOHOL USAGE (Current):
   a. No interference with functioning .... Enter 1
   b. Occasional abuse, some disruption of functioning, may need treatment .... Enter 4
   c. Frequent abuse, serious disruption, needs treatment .... Enter 7

7. OTHER SUBSTANCE USAGE (Current):
   a. No interference with functioning .... Enter 1
   b. Occasional substance abuse, some disruption of functioning, may need treatment .... Enter 4
   c. Frequent substance abuse, serious disruption, needs treatment .... Enter 6

8. REASONING/INTELLECTUAL ABILITY:
   a. Able to function independently .... Enter 1
   b. Some need for assistance, potential for adequate adjustment .... Enter 4
   c. Deficiencies suggest limited ability to function independently .... Enter 7

9. HEALTH:
   a. Sound physical health, seldom ill .... Enter 1
   b. Handicap or illness interferes with functioning on a recurring basis .... Enter 2
   c. Serious handicap or chronic illness, needs frequent medical care .... Enter 3

10. AGENT'S IMPRESSION OF CLIENT'S NEEDS:
    a. None .... Enter 0
    b. Low .... Enter 1
    c. Moderate .... Enter 4
    d. High .... Enter 6

Total Score
(Range 5-61)

SCORING AND OVERRIDE

Instruction: Check appropriate block
SCORE BASED SUPERVISION LEVEL ☐ Maximum ☐ Medium ☐ Minimum
Check if there is an override ☐ Override Explanation _____

FINAL CATEGORY OF SUPERVISION ☐ Maximum ☐ Medium ☐ Minimum

Date Supervision Level Assigned
MONTH   DAY   YEAR

APPROVED (Supervisor Signature and Date) _____   Agent

SOURCE: Anthony Walsh, *Understanding, Assessing, and Counseling the Criminal Justice Client* (Pacific Grove, CA: Brooks/Cole, 1988), p. 110. Reprinted by permission.

Revocation can be recommended for two general categories of violations. One category involves commission of new offenses. The second category, known as **technical violations,** involves failure to abide by the technical rules of the sentence. For example, a probationer might fail to report regularly to the probation officer or might leave the jurisdiction without the officer's consent. A recommendation of revocation is not automatic in the event of a violation, even if the violation is a new crime. Probation agents have considerable discretion on this matter. If the violation is a serious crime, a recommendation of revocation is very likely. On the other hand, a less serious offense or a technical violation may result in a warning, a tightening of probation conditions (perhaps the addition of a nightly curfew), or a brief jail term. Many probation agencies tend to let technical violations and petty offenses accumulate, with warnings and condition modifications along the way. However, repeated and excessive violations of this nature usually result in revocation recommendations.

If the probation agency asks the court to consider revocation of probation, the court must work within the guidelines of case law established by the U.S. Supreme Court. Two landmark cases are *Morrissey v. Brewer* and *Gagnon v. Scarpelli.* The Court's 1972 ruling in *Morrissey v. Brewer* dealt with parole revocation, but by virtue of the 1973 ruling in *Gagnon v. Scarpelli,* it also applies to probation revocation. *Morrissey* established that revocation is to be a two-stage process. In the first stage, there must be an informal, preliminary inquiry to establish probable cause that a violation has occurred. If probable cause is established, then in the second stage, there must be a formal court hearing to determine if the violation warrants revocation. Offenders have certain rights at both stages. They include the right to notice of the hearing

technical violations
Failure to abide by the technical rules or conditions of probation or parole (for example, not reporting regularly to the probation officer), as distinct from commission of a new criminal act.

Revocation

If probation is revoked, the judge can impose any sentence, including incarceration that was authorized for the offense for which the offender was originally placed on probation. Furthermore, the time already spent on probation, even though it may be several years, does not count as credit against the new sentence.

SOURCE: www.defgen.state.vt.us/lawbook/ch38.html

▲ Committing a new crime or violating the conditions of probation may lead to revocation of probation. *How serious should a new crime or violation of probation conditions be before probation is revoked?*

and charges, the right to be present at the hearing and to present evidence and witnesses, and the right to a detached and neutral hearing body.

The *Gagnon* decision extended the requirements of *Morrissey* to include probationers and also addressed the issue of right to counsel, which the *Morrissey* decision did not address. In *Gagnon,* the Court ruled that there is no absolute right to counsel at revocation proceedings. Whether the offender is provided with counsel is determined on a case-by-case basis, and if there is no compelling reason for providing counsel, counsel is unnecessary. However, the Court added that in probation revocation hearings, counsel should be provided when probationers present a timely claim that (1) they did not commit the violation, or (2) there are mitigating circumstances making revocation inappropriate. In other situations, attorneys are allowed at revocation hearings as long as defendants provide their own, at no cost to the state.

Issues in Probation

Probation is an evolving, changing field with many controversial issues. Several such issues have already been considered in this chapter. We now turn our attention to some additional issues.

Probation Fees   Increases in the probation population have been accompanied by increases in the financial costs of probation. Consequently, a trend has emerged toward having probationers pay fees (for example, $30 per month) to help offset the cost of their supervision and treatment. Probation fees—or supervision fees, as they are sometimes called—are distinct from fines, court costs, and restitution.

Advocates of probation fees argue that fees can help contain the increasingly high costs of probation. Advocates further contend that because the majority of probationers can afford reasonable monthly fees, it is only fair that those probationers be held responsible for supporting at least part of the services they receive. On the other hand, critics charge that fees are unfair for indigent offenders and that offenders should not have to pay for services they are mandated to receive. Critics also claim that the administrative costs associated with collecting fees can exceed the amount of money collected. Given the skyrocketing number of persons on probation and the high cost of supervision and treatment, it seems unlikely that the trend toward probation fees will decrease in the near future.

Legal Issues: Confidentiality and Privacy   Counseling is often an aspect of probation. It can be argued that to protect the counseling relationship, the information a probationer shares with a counselor should not be divulged to outside parties. However, it can also be argued that the counselor, who could be the offender's probation officer or a counselor to whom the probation officer has referred the offender, has a duty to divulge information about certain activities, particularly new crimes and technical violations, to appropriate authorities, such as police officers and judges. To what degree, then, should confidentiality govern the relationship between probation officer and probationer? In *Minnesota v. Murphy* (1984), the U.S. Supreme Court held that this relationship is not governed by the same degree of confidentiality as that between attorney and client or between physician and patient. Counselors taking probationer referrals can reveal information

Probation Fees

In 1929, Michigan became the first jurisdiction in the United States to impose probation supervision fees.

SOURCE: www.appa-net.org/

about a probationer's illegal activities to the probation officer, and the probation officer can notify the police.

Another issue is the conditions under which a probation officer may search a probationer's home for evidence. In its decision in *Griffin v. Wisconsin* (1987), the Supreme Court held that a search warrant based on probable cause is unnecessary for a probation officer to search a probationer's home; reasonable grounds is a sufficient basis for the search. This decision and the *Murphy* decision show that probationers are generally entitled to fewer due-process protections than free citizens who are not on probation. Whether this is just and fair is open to debate.

Caseload and Recidivism   With the probation population growing each year, it is not unusual for probation officers in larger urban jurisdictions to have as many as 200 offenders in their caseloads. Large caseloads, in turn, have been criticized for contributing to **recidivism** (the return of probationers to crime during or after probation). Clearly, it is difficult for probation officers with large caseloads to give each case individual attention and to provide proper supervision and services for all their clients.

Interestingly, however, research has generally failed to confirm that smaller caseloads, such as 25 cases per officer, are associated with decreased recidivism. In the words of author Jay S. Albanese and his colleagues, "It appears from many studies that the simple expedient of reducing caseloads will not of itself assure a reduction of recidivism."[6] In fact, it is reasonable to suppose that caseload reduction may sometimes be associated with an *increase* in recidivism detected by probation officers, because officers with smaller caseloads are able to scrutinize each probationer's activities more closely. There is some support for this supposition.[7] However, to the extent that (1) large caseloads promote recidivism because of the inability of probation officers to provide sufficient supervision and services and (2) smaller caseloads inflate recidivism numbers because of greater scrutiny of probationers' activities, probation agencies are in a no-win situation with respect to the issue of optimal caseload size.

How effective is probation in controlling recidivism? First, it should be noted that researchers attempting to address this question confront a variety of difficulties. One difficulty is deciding whether to define probationer recidivism in terms of technical violations, arrests for new crimes, new convictions, or revocations. The definition employed affects the amount of recidivism uncovered. Another important difficulty lies in accurately determining whether it is the probation experience or some additional factor that is responsible for the recidivism observed among a group of probationers. A simple finding that recidivism is low among a group of probationers does not necessarily mean that probation is containing recidivism. Other factors, such as improvements in the local economy or the selection of low-risk offenders for probation, may be responsible. To date, many studies of probation effectiveness have not been designed well enough to rule out the role of factors other than the probation experience. Difficulties like these must be kept in mind when reviewing studies on probation recidivism.

Research suggests that probation is less effective than many people would like in curtailing rearrests of felony offenders. In a well-known California study by author Joan Petersilia and her colleagues, approximately 1,700

recidivism
The return of probationers to crime during or after probation.

Probation Caseloads
In 1998, the average monthly regular-probation caseload in Rhode Island was 352 offenders.

SOURCE: Camille Graham Camp and George M. Camp, *The Corrections Yearbook 1999: Adult Corrections* (Middletown, CT: Criminal Justice Institute, 1999), p. 176.

Community Corrections   CHAPTER 12

felony offenders placed on probation were tracked for a period of 40 months. During this period, about two-thirds of the probationers were rearrested, more than half were reconvicted, and about one-third were sent to jail or prison.[8] In a similar but larger-scale study by the U.S. Justice Department, 79,000 felons sentenced to probation in 1986 by state courts in 17 states were followed for three years. By 1989, 43 percent of those felons had been arrested for new felonies; 8.5 percent were rearrested for violent offenses, 14.8 percent for property crimes, 14.1 percent for drug offenses, and the remainder for other crimes.[9]

In general, the recidivism figures associated with probation do not seem substantially higher or lower than those associated with incarceration. (See Chapter 11 for data on recidivism following incarceration.) Accordingly, it can be argued that when feasible, probation should be the preferred sentence because probation costs less than imprisonment. Of course, this logic holds true only if probation does not culminate in revocation followed by incarceration. If revocation and subsequent incarceration do occur, the combined costs of probation followed by incarceration may well exceed the cost of incarceration alone.

12.2 CRITICAL THINKING

1. What do you think makes an offender an ideal candidate for probation?

2. What are the benefits and drawbacks of probation vs. traditional jail time?

12.3 Parole

parole
A method of prison release whereby inmates are released at the discretion of a board or other authority before having completed their entire sentences; can also refer to the community supervision received upon release.

Recall that probation refers to the court-imposed sentence in which the offender, rather than being imprisoned, stays in the local community under the supervision of a probation officer. Two basic differences between probation and **parole** are that (1) parole is not a court-imposed sentence, and (2) parole is used with persons leaving prison. For purposes of definition, parole can be divided into two components. *Parole release* is one mechanism for releasing persons from prison. It involves releasing the inmate from prison, at the discretion of a parole board or similar paroling authority, before his or her sentence expires. *Parole supervision*, the aspect of parole that is often confused with probation, occurs after parole release. Essentially, parole supervision is a community-based continuation of the prison sentence. It involves supervision of the released offender in the community, often for a period roughly equal to the time remaining in the prison sentence.

Probation and parole supervision have similar features, which is why the two are sometimes confused. For example, both involve specific rules and conditions that offenders must follow to avoid revocation, and both entail providing offenders with supervision and services. In some instances, one officer may supervise both probationers and parolees. However, *probationer* and *parolee* are two distinct legal statuses. It is not uncommon for parole rules and conditions to be somewhat stricter and for officers to be less tolerant of

CAREERS IN CRIMINAL JUSTICE

Parole Agent

My name is Arthur J. Ramirez and I am a Parole Agent III (PA III) for the California State Department of Corrections (CDC) Parole and Community Services Division (P&CSD). Since 1983, I have also taught undergraduate and graduate criminal justice courses at California State University, Long Beach. I hold a bachelor of science degree in Criminal Justice, two master's degrees (Community Clinical Psychology and Criminal Justice), as well as a doctorate degree in Criminology. I chose to work with ex-felons in order to be in a unique position to improve the quality of life in our society.

As a PA III, I provide supervisory direction with respect to the philosophies, policies, and procedures of the CDC for the Long Beach I Parole Unit. I also complete a number of adjunct assignments for the department. A typical day includes reviewing my management formation system to ensure that the operations of the parole unit run smoothly. I hold case conferences with parole agents and/or review reports, written by them, related to the progress of parolees or parole violations committed by them. I review each case in order to determine the appropriate action. The actions may include: reviewing cases for discharge from parole; referring parolees to community programs that are in-line with their needs; approving funds to assist parolees; and reviewing activity reports to continue parolees on parole as a disposition after a parole violation. This allows the parolee to remain in the community and is often accompanied with a referral to a social program. I also make decisions to return parolees back into custody for parole violations. This includes reviewing the violation reports prior to submitting them to the Board of Prison Terms. Additionally, I review reports to initiate warrants for the arrest of parolees when they abscond from parole. Another typical day may also include traveling to Sacramento to attend a Commission on Correctional Peace Officer Standards and Training (CPOST) Curriculum Review Committee meeting. In this capacity, I review lesson plans submitted by youth and adult corrections agencies statewide and health care services to ensure that they are in-line with the professional training standards established and approved by CPOST.

It is very rewarding to see parolees making a positive adjustment in their reintegration back into society from imprisonment. It is also frustrating to see them being returned to prison for parole violations despite effective casework by a parole agent. Our society is currently faced with the challenge to provide the highest quality criminal justice services in order to respond to our criminal justice problems. I enjoy being a part of this process at the local and state levels. The field of criminal justice provides many career position opportunities for students. I fully believe that students today need to plan for their future careers systematically. Students interested in working in the field of criminal justice need to contact practicing professionals in the community in order to find out more about the position opportunities available in the field. I also recommend that students interested in working in parole should volunteer or enroll in an internship program with an agency that works with parolees or offenders. This will assist them in deciding whether a career in parole is for them.

Compare the information above with the career box on page 428 on probation officers. Which position would you be more attracted to? Why?

violations committed by parolees; revocation of parole may be sought quickly, even for a technical parole violation. In addition, parolees often face greater adjustment problems because of the stigma attached to their prison records and because of the time they have spent away from the free community.

Just as there are different types of probation (suspended-sentence probation, split-sentence probation, etc.), there are two general types of parole. In *straight parole,* offenders are released from prison directly into the community under the supervision of the parole agency. In *residential parole,* offenders serve part of the parole term in a community residential facility or halfway house. There are two variants of residential parole. In the first variant, offenders are released from prison into the residential facility, where they spend a temporary, transitional period before returning home. The idea is to make the release process a gradual one. In the second variant, a person who violates the conditions of parole is kept on parole and is placed in the residential facility for a period of structured living, rather than having parole revoked and being returned to prison.

There are four fundamental objectives of parole. Two of these are also objectives of probation and were discussed earlier in this chapter. As with probation, parole is meant to provide community safety and to promote offender betterment and reintegration into society. The other two objectives of parole are more subtle, often unstated, but no less important. They are to (1) relieve and contain prison crowding and (2) control the behavior of prison inmates.

Since its inception, parole has functioned as a "safety valve" for institutional corrections; crowding levels can be better contained if more inmates are granted early release. One of the clearest manifestations of this objective is the growing popularity of emergency release laws that permit executive authorities (usually governors) to accelerate parole eligibility for selected inmates when prison crowding reaches a particular level. Parole also gives prison officials some control over the behavior of inmates. The prospect of early release gives inmates an incentive to cooperate with prison officials and to avoid infractions of prison rules.

Historical Context

As with probation, parole emerged from earlier practices. One of those is the *tickets-of-leave* concept pioneered around the mid-1800s by Captain Alexander Machonochie off the coast of Australia and by Sir Walter Crofton in Ireland. Under this concept, inmates, after serving a portion of their sentences and exhibiting good performance in prison, could be granted tickets of leave, whereby they were released into the community under supervision. Release was made conditional on continuation of good behavior, so the practice was also known as conditional pardon.

▲ Some offenders are released on parole before the end of their sentences, on the condition that they remain law-abiding and follow the rules designed to control their movement and to help them adjust to society. *Should parole be abolished? Why or why not?*

The idea of releasing some prisoners early to community supervision and making release contingent on good conduct found its way to the United States. The idea was initially implemented, along with indeterminate sentencing, in the 1870s by Zebulon Brockway at Elmira Reformatory in New York. Brockway's system allowed prison officials to grant parole release to inmates they perceived as ready for release. Parole spread rapidly after its inception at Elmira. By the turn of the century, 20 states had provisions for parole, and by 1920, the majority of states had adopted such provisions.[10]

Administration

It is helpful to divide parole administration into two areas. The first area is the parole board, or a similar paroling authority, which makes parole release decisions. The second is the parole field service agency, which provides parole supervision in the community after release.

Parole administration, like probation administration, exhibits much variation across the nation. At the federal level, the paroling authority is the United States Parole Commission, and field services are administered by the Administrative Office of the Courts. Each state is responsible for administering its own parole system. Parole at the state level is generally an executive branch function, and each state has its own paroling authority. In most states, parole boards and field service agencies are administratively separate, although in some states, the board administers field services.[11] Whether probation and parole field services are jointly administered by the same government agency varies among the states. It has become quite common, however, for states to combine probation and parole administration. In Kentucky, for example, the same unit of the department of corrections administers both.

Another area of difference between states is whether the paroling authority or board is (1) administratively autonomous and independent of prison officials or (2) administratively consolidated with the department of corrections. Most parole boards are autonomous.[12]

In many ways the parole board is the centerpiece of parole administration; the board is very influential in establishing a jurisdiction's parole policies. A recent national survey of parole boards found that in most states, the governor, subject to legislative confirmation appoints parole board members. Appointment terms in most states are four to six years, and the vast majority of states use renewable appointments. The professional qualifications required for appointment differ across states. Interestingly, law in 23 jurisdictions requires no minimum professional qualifications. The number of parole board members also varies by state, with five and seven members being common. A minority of states employ part-time parole board members. Approximately two-thirds of the nations' board members are white, slightly over one-quarter are female, and 53 is the average age of board members.[13]

Process and Procedures

Besides helping establish the jurisdiction's parole policies, the parole board is generally responsible for managing parole release processes and making decisions to terminate parole supervision.

The Parole Board—Release and Termination Prior to appearing before the parole authority for a parole-grant hearing, a prisoner

Federal Parole

Anyone who has committed a federal crime after November 1, 1987, is no longer eligible for federal parole. (It has been abolished.) Such persons now must serve their entire sentences, less a maximum of 54 days a year good time, if granted. Those people sentenced or under supervision before November 1, 1987, are still eligible for federal parole supervision.

SOURCE: United States Parole Commission www.usdoj.gov/uspc/mission.html

must first become eligible for parole and complete a parole plan describing such things as where he or she plans to live and work after release. In addition, prison staff usually prepare a preparole report for the parole board. The report summarizes the characteristics of the inmate and his or her offense, reviews the inmate's adjustment to prison and his or her progress toward rehabilitation, and presents the inmate's parole plan. Reports sometimes contain a recommendation about whether the inmate should be paroled.

Depending on the jurisdiction and the particular case, the actual parole-grant hearing can be conducted by the full parole board, a partial board, or representatives of the board known as examiners or hearing officers. Roughly half of the states rely on hearing officers.[14] Other concerned parties, such as prison staff, prosecuting attorneys, and victims, may also be present. Parole hearings are typically quite short and routine. Parole authorities review relevant documents, such as the inmate's parole plan, the preparole report, and victim statements, and often interview the inmate. Authorities then vote on whether to grant or to deny parole release. In nearly 60 percent of the states, the inmate is notified of the outcome of voting at the hearing or immediately thereafter. In the remaining states, notification time frames range from one week to more than 30 days.[15] If parole is denied, the inmate is automatically eligible for a future hearing.

Increasingly, parole authorities are using structured instruments called **parole guidelines** to estimate the probability of recidivism and to direct their release decisions. Those guidelines are similar to the sentencing guidelines used by judges and the risk-and-needs-assessment instruments used in probation work. Currently, only about half the jurisdictions employ parole guidelines, and even in those jurisdictions, parole authorities often have the discretion to override guideline recommendations.[16] A sample parole guideline instrument, developed by the United States Parole Commission, is presented in Figure 12–5 on page 447.

Parole authorities consider a variety of factors in determining whether to grant or to deny an inmate parole. Furthermore, those factors tend to be assigned different levels of importance. A recent analysis of national data found that the four most important factors, in order, are:

1. Seriousness of the current offense
2. History of prior violent behavior
3. Prior felony convictions
4. Use of a firearm in committing the current offense

Other relevant factors include the number of prior incarcerations, prior adjustment on parole, prison disciplinary record, psychological reports, and victim input.[17]

Due process in parole release decisions was addressed by the U.S. Supreme Court in *Greenholtz v. Inmates of the Nebraska Penal and Correctional Complex* (1979). Noting that parole release is an act of grace, the Court held that release on parole is distinct from parole revocation. Thus, the Court declined to apply the provisions outlined in *Morrissey v. Brewer*, discussed earlier in this chapter, to parole release. Consequently, what constitutes acceptable due process in release decision making is largely case-specific. Jurisdictions vary considerably in their due process provisions for parole

FIGURE 12–5

Parole Guideline Instrument

Item A.   PRIOR CONVICTIONS/ADJUDICATIONS
(ADULT OR JUVENILE) . . . .❑
    None . . . .= 3
    One . . . .= 2
    Two or three . . . .= 1
    Four or more . . . .= 0

Item B.   PRIOR COMMITMENT(S) OF MORE THAN
THIRTY DAYS (ADULT OR JUVENILE) . . . .❑
    None . . . .= 3
    One . . . .= 2
    Three or more . . . .= 0

Item C.   AGE AT CURRENT OFFENSE/PRIOR
COMMITMENTS . . . .❑
    Age at commencement of the current offense:
        26 years of age or more . . . .= 2*
        20–25 years of age . . . .= 1*
        19 years of age or less . . . .= 0
    *EXCEPTION: If five or more prior commitments of
    more than thirty days (adult or juvenile), place an "x"
    here___ and score this item . . . .= 0

Item D.   RECENT COMMITMENT-FREE PERIOD
(THREE YEARS) . . . .❑
    No prior commitment of more than thirty days (adult
    or juvenile) or released to the community from last
    such commitment at least three years prior to the
    commencement of the current offense . . . .= 1
    Otherwise . . . .= 0

Item E.   PROBATION/PAROLE/CONFINEMENT/ESCAPE
STATUS VIOLATOR THIS TIME . . . .❑
    Neither on probation, parole, confinement, or
    escape status at the time of the current offense, nor
    committed as a probation, parole, confinement, or
    escape status violator this time . . . .= 1
    Otherwise . . . .= 0

Item F.   HEROIN/OPIATE DEPENDENCE . . . .❑
    No history of heroin/opiate dependency . . .= 1
    Otherwise . . . .= 0

TOTAL SCORE . . . .❑

SOURCE: Paul F. Cromwell and George C. Hellinger, *Community-Based Corrections*, 3d ed. (St. Paul, MN: West, 1994), p. 232

hearings. Roughly two-thirds of the jurisdictions allow inmates to be represented by attorneys.[18]

Once inmates receive parole release, they begin the period of parole supervision, discussed later, which continues until it is terminated. In addition to its responsibility for release decisions, the parole board is responsible for parole termination decisions. In most jurisdictions, the board can discharge individuals from parole supervision; this is commonly done upon the recommendation of the parole supervision agency. Alternatively, if no board action is taken, the individual is discharged from parole upon expiration of the legal sentence.

Parole revocation is also the responsibility of the parole board and can occur in response to new crimes or technical violations. Parole revocation is quite similar to probation revocation and is governed by the same case law (*Morrissey v. Brewer* and *Gagnon v. Scarpelli*). As is true in the field of probation, parole officers enjoy considerable discretion when deciding whether to recommend revocation for violations. If revocation is sought, the two-stage hearing process required under *Morrissey* becomes applicable. Although parole authorities consider various factors in determining whether to revoke parole, a recent study suggests that the two most important factors are the seriousness of the violation and the recommendation of the supervising parole officer.[19]

Field Services—Supervision and Service Delivery

Traditionally, most parole supervision or field service agencies were administered by parole boards. This situation has changed dramatically since the 1960s. Currently, field service agencies are administratively separate from the parole board in 42 jurisdictions.[20] In most of those 42 jurisdictions, parole supervision is administered by the department of corrections. Nevertheless, the basic task of field service agencies has remained constant through the years—to provide control and assistance for persons reentering the community from prison.

Virtually everything that was stated earlier in this chapter about probation supervision and service delivery applies to parole supervision and service delivery. The subtle differences between the two are overshadowed by the many similarities. However, one difference warrants mention. Specialization is more common in parole than in probation supervision. Under specialization, offenders who pose a similar threat to public safety or those who share similar treatment needs are grouped together and assigned to the same officers. Specialization by parole officers is used in slightly more than half the jurisdictions. The two most common areas for specialization are with sex offenders and substance-abusing offenders.[21]

Author Richard McCleary conducted what is considered a classic sociological study of a parole supervision agency.[22] In his book *Dangerous Men*, McCleary observes that parole officers are very concerned with avoiding "trouble" from parolees. Trouble is defined broadly as anything that runs

MYTH ···· **FACT** ····

If parole is revoked, return to prison is automatic.

Though reincarceration is common, other options are usually possible, such as placement in a halfway house or reinstatement of parole. Much discretion is involved.

counter to the status quo of the parole agency. Trouble can threaten the agency's public image, thus bringing the agency pressure—and possibly increased structure—from political officials. The likelihood of trouble is reduced to the extent that officers can anticipate what clients might do in response to threats of various punishments and rewards from officers. "Dangerous men" are parolees who do not respond predictably to officers' threats and promises. Dangerous men are not necessarily prone to violent behavior; they are merely unpredictable. Because unpredictability implies possible trouble, officers try to identify dangerous men as soon as possible in the supervision process. The dangerous-man label is used sparingly because it means greater supervision and more documentation and paperwork for officers. However, the label can protect the supervising officer and the agency from subsequent criticism because, early on, it conveys that problems

▲ Parole officers frequently meet their clients at the clients' workplaces. *What problems, if any, might be created by this practice?*

may be expected from a particular parolee. Concerned parties in the parole bureaucracy are alerted to what might happen, and the potential for "surprises" is reduced. Once parolees have acquired the dangerous-man label, the agency is quick to seek reasons to revoke their paroles. McCleary's research underscores the crucial significance of agency bureaucratic dynamics in shaping supervision practices.

Parole Issues

Since the 1970s, discretionary parole release has been among the most controversial issues in criminal justice. Proponents of parole release argue, for example, that early release provisions are essential for controlling prisoners' behavior and for containing institutional crowding. However, several criticisms have been directed at parole release. Some critics claim that parole undermines both retribution and deterrence because offenders are permitted to leave prison early, sometimes many years before finishing their maximum sentences. Similarly, critics argue that because prisons generally fail to reform offenders and it is impossible for parole boards to accurately predict which offenders will commit new crimes, parole does not sufficiently guarantee public safety. Other critics believe that parole is unfair to offenders. Those opponents charge that parole leads to significant disparities in time served in prison for offenders who should be serving equal amounts of time. For example, two offenders in the same jurisdiction with very similar prior legal backgrounds may be convicted of committing armed robbery under very similar circumstances. One offender may serve five years in prison and receive parole, whereas the other may serve twice as long before release. Another contention of critics is that linking the degree of participation in prison treatment programs to the possibility of early parole amounts to subtly coercing inmates into programs that are often of questionable effectiveness.

Those and other criticisms helped persuade a number of jurisdictions to curtail discretionary parole release. Instead, they moved from indeterminate sentencing to determinate sentencing, decreased reliance on parole release and increased reliance on mandatory release, and devised both sentencing

Public Opinion

According to a recent public opinion poll, nearly two-thirds of all Americans support allowing prisoners to earn early release through good behavior and participation in educational and work programs. However, only 21 percent of Americans are willing to give parole boards more authority to release offenders early, and 75 percent of Americans do not want to parole prisoners who have been paroled before for a serious crime.

SOURCE: Timothy J. Flanagan, "Reform or Punish: Americans' Views of the Correctional System," pp. 75–92 in T. J. Flanagan and D. R. Longmire (eds.), *Americans View Crime and Justice: A National Public Opinion Survey* (Thousand Oaks, CA: Sage, 1996), p. 87.

and parole guidelines. There were even forceful calls and some initiatives undertaken to completely abolish parole release, although the movement to abolish parole seems to have peaked.[23] Currently, 14 states (Arizona, 1994; Delaware, 1990; Florida, 1983; Illinois, 1978; Indiana, 1977; Kansas, 1993; Maine, 1975; Minnesota, 1980; Mississippi, 1995; North Carolina, 1994; Ohio, 1996; Oregon, 1989; Washington, 1984; and Wisconsin, 1999) and the federal government have abolished early release by discretion of a parole board for all offenders (year abolished in parentheses). However, parole boards still have discretion over inmates who were sentenced for crimes committed prior to the effective date of the law that eliminated parole board release. A few other states have abolished parole release for certain violent or felony offenders (Alaska, New York, Tennessee, and Virginia) or for certain crimes against a person (Louisiana). California allows discretionary release by a parole board only for offenders with indeterminate life sentences. It is important to note that while discretionary release from prison by a parole board has been eliminated by some states, post-release supervision still exists and is generally referred to as community or supervised release. Parole boards, in various forms, have the responsibility to set conditions of release for offenders under community or supervised release, the authority to return an offender to prison for violating the conditions of supervised release, and the power to grant parole for medical reasons.[24]

Besides the issue of whether parole release should exist, there are a number of other pressing concerns surrounding parole. They include legal issues, strained parole resources, and parolee adjustment and recidivism.

Legal Issues   There are two general categories of legal issues that relate to parole: (1) parolees' civil rights and (2) the liabilities of parole officials.

Individuals forfeit a variety of civil rights when they are convicted of a felony. Some of those include the right to hold public office and certain other jobs, the right to jury service, and the right to obtain some types of licenses and insurance. Although the specific rights forfeited vary by jurisdiction, in many instances parolees must seek court action to restore their rights following release from incarceration. Only ten jurisdictions grant their parole boards authority to restore ex-offenders' rights.[25]

People who support denying released inmates certain rights argue that the practice is necessary to preserve public safety and maintain high moral standards in society. Opponents argue that it is unfair to continue penalizing individuals who have "paid their debts." They point out that denial of civil liberties contributes to poor adjustment on parole. Given the current posture of the nation toward felons and ex-felons, it seems unlikely, at least in the foreseeable future, that the majority of persons coming out of prison will have their rights fully restored.

Can parole board officials and field service agents be held legally liable if a parolee's actions cause harm to a victim or victims? The answer is a qualified yes. Even though the vast majority of paroling authorities enjoy some type of immunity from liability (through constitution, statute, or case law), such immunity has been eroding in recent years.

According to author John Watkins, Jr., three central elements must be proven to establish liability on the part of parole and probation officials.

1. The existence of a legal duty owed the public.
2. Evidence of a breach of the required standard of duty.
3. An injury or damage to a person or group proximately caused by the breach of duty.

Watkins further observes that as a general rule, tort liability applies to injuries, or damages, caused by the negligent or improper performance of ministerial functions, but not to injuries caused by unsatisfactory performance of discretionary functions. A *discretionary* function is one "that may involve a series of possible choices from a wide array of alternatives, none of which may be absolutely called for in a particular situation." A *ministerial* function is "one regarding which nothing is left to discretion—a simple and definite duty imposed by law, and arising under conditions admitted or proved to exist."[26] An example of a breach of a ministerial function would be if a parole board were to completely disregard parole guidelines that the board is legally bound to consider before releasing inmates. Thus, if parole and probation officials wish to minimize the likelihood of being held liable, those officials should determine what is legally required of them in their jurisdiction and make good faith efforts to abide by those requirements.

Strained Parole Resources Parole supervision agencies across the nation are currently attempting to manage record numbers of parolees. On December 31, 1999, for example, 712,700 adults were under active parole supervision. This represents an increase of about 34 percent over the total number of parolees on December 31, 1990.[27] Moreover, an increasingly large proportion of parolees have been released from prison early because of pressures to relieve institutional crowding, rather than because those persons have been judged good candidates for parole. Such parolees often require above-average levels of supervision and services. Because most jurisdictions are facing pressure to expand prison space, it is not surprising that parole resources, such as budgets and staffing, have failed to keep pace with those developments.

The long-term implications of this predicament are often unappreciated. Parolee recidivism is normally quite high, partly because of the strained resources of parole agencies. The typical public and political response to high parolee recidivism is to demand a "get-tough" stance that culminates in the return of large numbers of parolees to prison. This exacerbates both prison crowding and the tendency to rely on parole release to relieve crowding. The result is further strain on parole resources and, consequently, further recidivism.

Parolee Adjustment and Recidivism A key to successful community adjustment for inmates leaving prison is **reintegration,** which means rebuilding former prosocial ties to the community and establishing new ties. An important part of reintegration is finding a satisfactory job and obtaining adequate subsistence funds through legal means.

The stigma of a prison record can result in grim employment prospects, especially without the assistance of the parole agency. Yet, research suggests that obtaining employment improves adjustment to community life. In a study of the effects of postrelease employment on the emotional well-being of a sample of ex-felons in Texas and Georgia, it was found that employment enhanced emotional well-being by providing wages and improving perceptions of self-worth. The research discovered that sustained unemployment caused

FYI

Parole Officer Caseloads

The average parole officer caseload for 23 jurisdictions with separate probation and parole agencies during 1998 was 67. The range was from a low of 40 in Nebraska to a high of 100 in New York. The average caseload in the 22 jurisdictions with combined probation and parole agencies was 94. The range was from 51 in Ohio to 154 in Arkansas. In jurisdictions with separate probation and parole agencies, probation caseloads are nearly always larger than parole caseloads—frequently much larger.

SOURCE: Camille Graham Camp and George M. Camp, *The Corrections Yearbook 1999: Adult Corrections* (Middletown, CT: Criminal Justice Institute, 1999), p. 176.

reintegration
The process of rebuilding former ties to the community and establishing new ties after release from prison.

emotional distress. This distress reduced the motivation of releasees to search for jobs. In the words of the study's author, "Unemployment fed on itself by creating psychological stress which in turn reduced effectiveness in finding work."[28] Related evidence suggests that providing newly released ex-inmates with temporary unemployment benefits can decrease the recidivism rate, although it is important that such benefits not create a work disincentive.[29]

In 1987, the U.S. Justice Department released its findings from a six-year follow-up study of nearly 4,000 individuals between the ages of 17 and 22 who were paroled from prisons in 22 states in 1978.[30] Over the six-year period, approximately 69 percent were rearrested, 53 percent were reconvicted, and 49 percent were returned to prison. As Figure 12–6 suggests, the probability of recidivism was highest in the early phases of follow-up. Within one year of release, 32 percent of the parolees had been rearrested, and 47 percent had been rearrested within two years. Roughly three-fourths of the persons who were paroled after serving time for property offenses were rearrested, compared with approximately two-thirds of those who were paroled after serving time for violent crimes. Time spent in prison was not consistently related to the likelihood of recidivism. Although the 1987 study is dated, current trends are similar.[31]

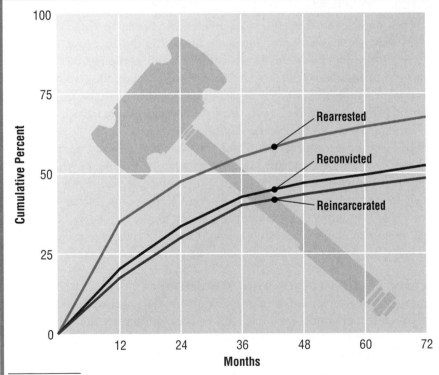

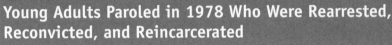

FIGURE 12–6

Young Adults Paroled in 1978 Who Were Rearrested, Reconvicted, and Reincarcerated

SOURCE: U.S. Department of Justice, Bureau of Justice Statistics Special Report, *Recidivism of Young Parolees* (May 1987).

Parole Violations

A 54 percent increase in the number of offenders returned to prison for parole violations underlies the growth in the state prison population between 1990 and 1998. In 1998, 206,751 of the offenders entering state prison had violated the conditions of their parole, up from 133,870 in 1990. Based on reports from inmates in state prisons in 1997 (the latest data), 60 percent of the inmates had their paroles revoked for being arrested or convicted of new crimes; 19 percent for absconding or failing to report to a parole officer; 14 percent from a drug-related violation and 14 percent for other reasons (such as gun possession). Percentages add to more than 100 because inmates may have had more than one reason.

SOURCE: Allen J. Beck, "Prisoners in 1999," U.S. Department of Justice, Bureau of Justice Statistics Bulletin (August 2000), p. 11.

12.3 CRITICAL THINKING

1. How much weight do victim impact statements get in the decision to grant parole?

2. Given what you have read, do you think there are ways to improve the parole process? If so, what can be done?

12.4 Intermediate Sanctions

Recent dramatic increases in prison, parole, and probation populations have fundamentally altered the field of community corrections. Community corrections has been forced to accommodate (1) growing numbers of the types of offenders the field has traditionally accommodated, plus (2) offenders who would have been sent to—or remained in—prison had sufficient space been available. At the same time, the field has witnessed a general decline in philosophical support for rehabilitation, coupled with a growing emphasis on punishing and controlling offenders. Since the 1980s, the intermediate-sanction trend has grown within this context.

In restrictiveness and punitiveness, **intermediate sanctions** lie somewhere between traditional probation and traditional imprisonment or, alternatively, between imprisonment and traditional parole supervision (see Figure 12–7 on page 454). Intermediate sanctions are designed to widen the range of incarceration alternatives and to calibrate that range according to the differential risks and needs of offenders.

As a rule, the newer intermediate sanctions are oriented less toward rehabilitation and more toward retribution, deterrence, and incapacitation than older community correctional programs. However, the distinction between intermediate sanctions and older, more traditional programs has become somewhat blurred because some traditional programs, such as restitution and halfway houses, have been incorporated into the intermediate-sanction category. The specific intermediate sanctions to be discussed in this section include intensive-supervision probation and parole, day reporting centers, structured fines (or day fines), home confinement and electronic monitoring, and halfway houses.

intermediate sanctions
Sanctions that, in restrictiveness and punitiveness, lie between traditional probation and traditional imprisonment or, alternatively, between imprisonment and traditional parole.

Intensive-Supervision Probation and Parole (ISP)

Intensive-supervision probation and parole (ISP) provides stricter conditions, closer supervision, and more treatment services than traditional probation and parole. Offenders are often selected for ISP on the basis of their scores on risk-and-needs-assessment instruments. Alternatively, they may be placed on ISP after violating regular probation or parole. Most ISP programs are for nonviolent felons.

The ISP programs in existence across the nation are diverse, and some programs come much closer than others to providing supervision and services that are genuinely intensive. In theory, ISP programs have the following features:

1. Specially trained intensive-supervision officers with small caseloads (for example, 25 cases per officer).

2. Inescapable supervision, such as multiple weekly contacts between officers and clients and frequent testing for drug use.

3. Mandatory curfews.

4. Mandatory employment or restitution requirements, or both.

5. Mandatory or voluntary participation in treatment.

6. Supervision fees to be paid by clients.

intensive-supervision probation and parole (ISP)
An alternative to incarceration that provides stricter conditions, closer supervision, and more treatment services than traditional probation and parole.

FIGURE 12–7

Relationship of Intermediate Sanctions to Traditional Sanctions

No Sanction	Traditional Probation	Intermediate Sanctions	Traditional Imprisonment	Intermediate Sanctions	Traditional Parole Supervision

net-widening

A phenomenon that occurs when the offenders placed in a novel program are not the offenders for whom the program was designed. The consequence is that those in the program receive more severe sanctions than they would have received had the new program remained unavailable.

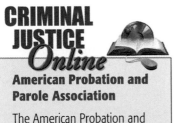

American Probation and Parole Association

The American Probation and Parole Association explores issues relevant to the field of community corrections. You can visit their Web site through the link at cj.glencoe.com. *Would a career in probation or parole be of interest to you? Why or why not?*

ISP usually lasts six months to two years. Typically, offenders must pass through a series of phases that become progressively less restrictive during the period of intensive supervision.

The majority of states have implemented ISP programs for adult probationers and parolees.[32] However, out of all persons placed on probation or parole, relatively few are placed under intensive supervision because of resource limitations and the small caseloads required by ISP. Although it is commonly argued that ISP costs less money than incarceration, provided it is not followed by incarceration due to revocation, ISP generally costs more than traditional probation or parole. For this reason, it is used rather sparingly.

Although a number of concerns have been raised about ISP, two of the most important are (1) the potential for net-widening and (2) the lack of demonstrated reduction of recidivism.

Net-widening takes various forms and can plague virtually any type of community correctional program. Net-widening occurs when the offenders placed in a novel program like ISP are not the offenders for whom the program was intended. The consequence is that those in the program receive more severe sanctions than they would have received had the new program remained unavailable. Suppose, for example, that a jurisdiction facing a prison crowding crisis establishes a new intensive probation program so that a substantial number of nonviolent offenders can be sentenced to ISP rather than prison. That is, the ISP target group consists of nonviolent felons who would have gone to prison had ISP not become available. If only persons who would formerly have gone to prison are placed on ISP, net-widening has not taken place. However, if persons who would formerly have been placed on regular probation are now placed on ISP, net-widening has occurred. To the degree that such net-widening is the result, ISP becomes a costly addition to ordinary probation, instead of serving its intended function of providing a cost-efficient alternative to imprisonment.

Again, it is important to realize that almost all community correctional programs, especially those specifically designed to divert offenders from more severe sanctions, are vulnerable to net-widening. Net-widening can be avoided or minimized by establishing and following standard criteria for assigning offenders to programs. If the goal of an intensive probation program is to divert offenders from prison, then only prison-bound offenders should be placed in the program. Offenders who would have been placed on regular probation had the intensive program been unavailable should continue to be placed on regular probation. When modern ISP programs were introduced in the early 1980s, there was much optimism that a cost-efficient means of diverting offenders from prison and controlling their recidivism had been found. Writing about the Georgia ISP program, authors Billie Erwin and Lawrence Bennett stated that "the recidivism rates are considerably better . . . than for groups under regular probation and for those released from prison. [ISP] offenders commit fewer and less serious crimes."[33] Erwin and Bennett also estimated that Georgia saved $6,775 for each case diverted from prison into ISP.

Unfortunately, the initial optimism surrounding ISP has not been sustained according to subsequent, well-designed research by Joan Petersilia and her colleagues. In one study, authors Petersilia and Turner compared offenders who had been randomly assigned to either intensive or regular probation in three California counties. Efforts were made to ensure that only high-risk, serious offenders were included in the study, and offenders were followed for six months after program placement. Across counties, an average of 30 percent of the ISP cases had technical violations, and about 20 percent had new arrests. In two counties, ISP clients were significantly more likely than regular probationers to incur technical violations, but neither more nor less likely to incur new arrests. In the other county, ISP cases and regular probationers did not differ significantly in technical violations or new arrests. Petersilia and Turner observe that in the first two counties, the increased supervision of ISP may simply have increased awareness of clients' technical violations. That is, regular probationers may have committed just as many technical violations, but more of the violations may have escaped detection because of less supervision. More important, Petersilia and Turner point out that if ISP simply increases awareness of technical violations and if the official response to such violations is swift revocation of ISP followed by incarceration, two things may occur. First, because offenders are no longer at risk of recidivism in the community once they are incarcerated, the artificial impression may be created that ISP is associated with low arrest rates. Second, ISP will fuel the prison crowding problem it is intended to relieve.[34]

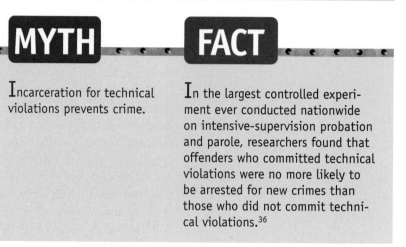

MYTH

Incarceration for technical violations prevents crime.

FACT

In the largest controlled experiment ever conducted nationwide on intensive-supervision probation and parole, researchers found that offenders who committed technical violations were no more likely to be arrested for new crimes than those who did not commit technical violations.[36]

In another study, Petersilia and Turner evaluated a national ISP demonstration project in 14 jurisdictions across nine states.[35] The 14 programs were implemented between 1986 and 1991 and involved approximately 2,000 offenders. In each program, offenders were assigned randomly to either ISP or an alternative sanction, such as regular probation, prison, or regular parole. They were then followed for one year. The average results across jurisdictions are summarized in Figure 12–8 on page 456. ISP was associated with a substantially higher percentage of technical violations than the alternative sanctions. Again it appears that ISP may have increased detection of technical violations and thereby inflated incarceration rates. The data suggest that if ISP is to relieve prison crowding in any meaningful way, officials will have to become more reluctant to revoke ISP and impose incarceration for technical violations.

Day Reporting Centers

day reporting centers
Facilities that are designed for offenders who would otherwise be in prison or jail and that require offenders to report regularly to confer with staff about supervision and treatment matters.

Day reporting centers, a relatively new facet of the intermediate-sanction movement, emerged in Great Britain in the 1970s and were pioneered in the United States in Massachusetts in 1986. The centers can be administered publicly or privately and are designed primarily for offenders who would otherwise be in jail or prison. This includes offenders such as those on ISP and those awaiting trial who did not receive release on recognizance or bail. Offenders are permitted to live at home but must report to the center regularly to confer with center staff about supervision and treatment matters. Program components commonly focus on work, education, counseling, and community service.[37] The program objectives devised for offenders by the Metropolitan Day Reporting Center in Boston are illustrated in Figure 12–9 on page 457.

Structured Fines, or Day Fines

structured fines, or **day fines**
Fines that are based on defendants' ability to pay.

Another relatively new intermediate sanction, at least in the United States, is structured fines, or day fines.[38] **Structured fines,** or **day fines,** differ fundamentally from the fines (called *tariff fines*) more typically imposed by American criminal courts. Whereas tariff fines require a single fixed amount of money, or an amount of money within a narrow range, to be paid by all defendants convicted of a particular crime, *without regard to their financial circumstances,* structured fines are based on defendants' ability to pay. The basic premise of structured fines is that "punishment by a fine should be proportionate to the seriousness of the offense and should have roughly similar impact (in terms of economic sting) on persons with differing financial resources who are convicted of the same offense."

The creation of a structured fine is a two-part process. In the first part, the number of fine units for a crime is determined from a scale that ranks crimes according to their seriousness. In the second part, the dollar amount of the fine is determined by multiplying the number of fine units by a proportion of the defendant's net daily income (hence the term *day fine*), adjusted to account for dependents and special circumstances.

Structured fines were first introduced in the 1920s in Sweden and soon thereafter were adopted by other Scandinavian countries. West Germany began employing them in the early 1970s. Those Western European nations have made day fines the sanction of choice in a large proportion of criminal

Structured Fines

Regarding the use of structured fines, or day fines, in the United States, authors Norval Morris and Michael Tonry make this interesting observation: "It is paradoxical that a society that relies so heavily on the financial incentive in its social philosophy and economic practice should be so reluctant to use the financial disincentive as a punishment of crime."

SOURCE: Norval Morris and Michael Tonry (eds.), *Between Prisons and Probation: Intermediate Punishments in a Rational Sentencing System* (New York: Oxford University Press, 1990), p. 111.

FIGURE 12–8

Offender Recidivism Averages in Petersilia and Turner's Study of ISP in 14 Jurisdictions

Sanction	Percentage Arrested	Percentage with Technical Violations	Percentage Returned to Prison
ISP	37	65	24
Alternative	33	38	15

SOURCE: Joan Petersilia and Susan Turner, *Evaluating Intensive Supervision Probation/Parole: Results of a Nationwide Experiment,* U.S. Department of Justice, National Institute of Justice Research in Brief (Washington, DC: GPO, 1993).

I , _____, agree to participate in the activities and to adhere to the schedule of this contract. I understand that this contract may be modified during my participation in the Day Reporting Center and I agree to those modifications as determined by my participation.

Objectives   *Time frame*

Reporting: I will report in to the Center at the times designated by my case manager and as noted on my daily itinerary.

I will call in to the Center at the times designated by my case manager and as noted on my daily itinerary.

Supervision: I will be available for phone calls or house checks by Day Reporting Center staff at the locations listed on my daily itinerary.

Employment: Employer: _____
Address: _____

Contact Person: _____
Telephone: _____
Hours: _____
Salary: _____
_____
_____

Financial: I agree to submit my pay stub to the Center for verification of my employment. I further agree to work with my case manager on budgeting my money; including the payment of any court ordered fines or other restitution. Details:_____
_____
_____

Substance Abuse Treatment: I agree to participate in the following program to address my substance abuse problems: _____

Urinalysis: I agree to submit to urinalysis testing upon the request of Day Reporting Center staff. _____

Curfew: I understand that I am to be at my residence from the hours of _____ P.M. to _____ A.M., and that I may be contacted by Day Reporting Center staff during that time. _____

Other Objectives: _____
_____
_____
_____
_____
_____
_____
_____
_____
_____
_____
_____

_____   _____
Client   Date

I agree to assist _____ to achieve the listed objectives of this contract in my capacity as case manager.

_____   _____
Case Manager   Date

cases, including many involving serious offenses. For example, in Germany, day fines are used as the only sanction for three-fourths of all offenders convicted of property crimes and for two-thirds of all offenders convicted of assaults.

The first structured-fine program in the United States began in 1988 in Richmond County (Staten Island), New York, as a demonstration project. Other structured-fine demonstration projects have been established in Maricopa County (Phoenix), Arizona; Bridgeport, Connecticut; Polk County (Des Moines), Iowa; and in four counties in Oregon (Marion, Malheur, Josephine, and Coos). An evaluation of the Richmond County project, sponsored by the National Institute of Justice, showed very promising results.

Among the presumed advantages of structured-fine or day-fine programs are:

1. Offender accountability—"The offender is, quite literally, made to pay his or her debt to society"

2. Deterrence—"Structured fines provide an economic disincentive for criminal behavior"

3. Fairness—Structured fines are fairer than tariff fines because tariff fines frequently are too low to be meaningful to wealthier offenders and too high for poorer offenders to pay

4. Effective and efficient use of limited system resources— "Structured fines are relatively inexpensive to administer compared with most other types of intermediate sanctions"

5. Revenue—"Structured fines can be more effective than tariff fines in generating revenue"

6. Credibility for the court—Because offenders pay in full in a very large proportion of cases, the sanction has credibility with the offender and the community

Among the problems with structured fines are:

1. Collection problems—"If judges are not convinced that such fines will be paid in a high proportion of cases, or if offenders assume that the fines need not be paid, the usefulness of the structured fine as a criminal sanction is seriously eroded"

2. The effect of other monetary penalties—In most U.S. jurisdictions, defendants convicted of crimes have a variety of monetary penalties to pay, for example, penalty assessment fees, crime victim compensation fees, indigent defense fees, and probation fees. Those monetary sanctions create a high cost to a defendant, even before a fine is imposed. A fine added to those costs may exceed the ability of poorer defendants to pay.

Home Confinement and Electronic Monitoring

home confinement
A program that requires offenders to remain in their homes except for approved periods of absence; commonly used in combination with electronic monitoring.

In **home confinement** programs (also known as home incarceration, home detention, and house arrest), offenders are required by the court to remain in their homes except for preapproved periods of absence. For example, offenders may be permitted to leave home to go to work, school, or church or to run errands. Home confinement is usually considered more punitive than ISP but is often used in conjunction with ISP. For example, home confinement may be required during the initial phase of intensive probation or may be ordered if an offender violates probation or parole. Home confinement can also serve as an alternative to pretrial detention in jail.

electronic monitoring
An arrangement that allows an offender's whereabouts to be gauged through the use of computer technology.

House arrest has traditionally been employed in the military and has a long history of limited use in criminal justice. However, home confinement programs did not gain wide popularity until **electronic monitoring** equipment became readily available during the 1980s. Electronic monitoring allows an offender's whereabouts to be gauged through the use of computer technology. Before the use of electronic monitoring, it was time-consuming and expensive for officials to ensure that offenders were complying with home confinement orders. Electronic monitoring rendered home confinement more practical and cost-effective because officials did not have to rely on personal phone calls and home visits to assess compliance with home detention orders. Today, it is very common for home confinement programs to have electronic monitoring components.

Electronic monitoring devices are used to verify, either through phone lines or radio signals, that offenders are at their designated locations at particular times. The two most popular electronic monitoring devices are the continuously signaling and programmed contact systems. In the continuously signaling system, an offender wears a small transmitter, usually on the ankle, that sends encoded signals to a nearby receiver at regular intervals. In essence, the receiver communicates with the monitoring agency's computer, which contains the offender's schedule, so staff can determine whether the offender is in the designated location at the required time. Under the programmed contact arrangement, the agency's computer generates either random or scheduled phone calls to the designated location, and the offender must respond to the calls. The type of response required from the offender depends on the specific device. For example, some devices require the offender to insert a wristlet into a verifier box hooked on the phone. Others require the offender to speak for purposes of voice verification.

Home confinement and electronic monitoring have not yet been evaluated extensively. However, a national survey found that electronic monitoring has expanded rapidly since its inception. Furthermore, there appears to be a trend toward using electronic monitoring with offenders who have committed more serious crimes.

As might be expected, home confinement and electronic monitoring are controversial practices. This is particularly true of monitoring. Supporters argue that home confinement and monitoring are cost-effective alternatives to incarceration in jail or prison that allow offenders to receive more supervision and punishment than they would receive on traditional probation or parole. Another argument is that offenders are spared the potentially harmful effects of institutionalization, one of the most important of which is the breaking of family ties.

Critics counter with a variety of claims. One important criticism is that home confinement and monitoring encroach on the constitutional rights to privacy, protection against self-incrimination, and protection against unreasonable search and seizure. Critics maintain that not only the offender's rights are threatened, but also the rights of persons who share the offender's residence. However, it seems unlikely that the use of those sanctions will be severely restricted on constitutional grounds in the foreseeable future. As del Carmen and Vaughn observe, "A review of decided cases in probation and parole indicates that while the use of electronic devices raises constitutional issues, its constitutionality will most likely be upheld by the courts, primarily based on the concept of diminished rights [for offenders]."[39]

Some people worry that home confinement and electronic monitoring may discriminate against economically disadvantaged persons, who are less likely to have homes and telephone systems for the installation of monitoring devices. Others are concerned that offenders and manufacturers of monitoring equipment have become locked in a perpetual and costly battle to outwit one another. Manufacturers continually work to devise monitors that will resist offender tampering. Meanwhile, offenders seek ways to manipulate the

Electronic Monitoring

Electronic monitoring has rapidly become one of the most widespread and controversial innovations in community corrections since the idea was first introduced, in the 1960s. The first statewide home confinement program without electronic monitoring was implemented in Florida in the early 1980s. St. Louis was one of the cities to pioneer such programming in the early 1970s. Among the first jurisdictions to implement an electronic monitoring program was Palm Beach County, Florida, in 1984.

SOURCE: J. R. Lilly and R. A. Ball (1987) "A Brief History of House Arrest and Electronic Monitoring." *Northern Kentucky Law Review* 13(3): 343–74.

latest monitoring innovations on the market. This situation, of course, is potentially lucrative for equipment vendors, but it is potentially costly for taxpayers and for offenders who must pay monitoring fees. A broader criticism is that a profit incentive is being created to subject more and more persons to government surveillance.

Finally, some people object to monitoring on the grounds that it is impersonal, thus removing the human and helping elements from community corrections. Those critics suggest that by reducing the need for skill and professionalism on the part of probation and parole officers, monitoring may undermine rehabilitation. As author John Conrad writes:

> Probation and parole were once intended to help men and women in the worst kind of trouble to find ways to lead law abiding lives. No more. Official services to offenders in the community have been transformed into a cat-and-mouse game in which surveillance, not service, has become the primary, if not the exclusive requisite . . . . Electronic surveillance is a recent and welcomed contribution of high technology to the community control of convicted offenders. We settle for temporary control in place of a serious program for changes in attitude, behavior and style of life.[40]

Halfway Houses

Halfway houses (sometimes referred to as community correctional centers) are community-based residential facilities that are an alternative to confinement in jail or prison. Although those facilities are an alternative to more secure and restrictive placements, they provide a much more controlled environment than is possible with traditional probation and parole, or even with ISP and home confinement. As the term *halfway* implies, the offender is midway between jail or prison and the free community.

The goal of halfway houses is to provide offenders with a temporary (for instance, six-month) period of highly structured and supportive living so that they will be better prepared to function independently in the community upon discharge. To this end, most programs place a heavy emphasis on addressing offenders' educational and employment deficits. For example, persons who have not completed high school are encouraged to obtain the GED, individuals who have few marketable job skills are encouraged to complete vocational training, and those who lack employment are assisted in finding and keeping jobs.

Halfway houses have existed in the United States since the mid-1800s and, prior to the 1960s, were used primarily for persons coming out of prison and making the transition back into the community. During the 1960s, the number and functions of halfway house programs in the nation expanded. In addition to providing services for parolees and prereleasees (prisoners nearing their release dates), houses began to service probationers, pretrial detainees, and persons on furlough from prison. More recently, in the 1980s, halfway houses became an integral part of the intermediate-sanction movement. They are now sometimes used in conjunction with other intermediate sanctions. For example, as part of a probation sentence, an offender may complete a stay in a halfway house before being discharged to ISP, or a person who has violated a home confinement order may be placed in a halfway house program to give authorities added control.

halfway houses
Community-based residential facilities that are less secure and restrictive than prison or jail but provide a more controlled environment than other community correctional programs.

Costs of Electronic Monitoring

In 1998, the average costs per day for electronic monitoring of probationers and parolees were $6.59 and $13.82, respectively. This compares with average daily costs of $9.62 and $8.34 for intensive probation and parole supervision, $1.90 and $4.18 for regular probation and parole supervision, and $56.26 for prison incarceration.

SOURCE: Camille Graham Camp and George M. Camp, *The Corrections Yearbook 1999: Adult Corrections* (Middletown, CT: Criminal Justice Institute, 1999), pp. 89 and 188.

Halfway houses are quite diverse. Not all houses are for offenders; some facilities serve other populations, such as those with mental disorders or drug addictions. Programs for offenders may serve a specific category of offenders, such as all probationers or all parolees, or some combination of offender groups. In addition, a halfway house's population may be all male, all female, or both male and female. Some houses rely heavily on referrals to other local agencies to ensure that offenders' treatment needs are met, whereas others provide extensive in-house treatment. Programs can be administered publicly or privately, but private administration is more common. Public programs may be administered at the federal, state, or local level of government.

Procedures Halfway house programming involves five basic procedures:

1. Referral
2. Administrative screening
3. Intake and orientation
4. Program participation
5. Termination of the stay

Referral of clients to a halfway house may be done by a correctional institution (as in the case of prereleasees), a court, or a probation or parole agency. The fundamental issue referral sources must confront is whether the offender will benefit from halfway house placement without compromising community safety. Thus, such factors as the offender's propensity for violence and degree of employment and educational deficits are generally given great weight in determining whether to make a referral.

When a referral is made, the next step is *administrative screening*, in which halfway house administrators examine the case and decide whether to accept the offender into the program. Some house administrators have more authority to reject referrals than others. Administrators of private houses often have more discretion to decline referrals than do administrators of public programs. An important point to note is that referral sources and house administrators are sometimes motivated by differing objectives. For instance, correctional institution staff may be motivated by the desire to reduce crowding in their facilities, whereas house administrators may wish to maximize the rate of successful discharge from their programs.

If administrative screening results in a decision to accept the referral, the focus shifts to *intake and orientation*. This entails assessing the new resident's risks and needs as well as orienting him or her to the rules, expectations, and routines of the program. An important aspect of intake and orientation is determining exactly what the resident should accomplish during the stay to improve his or her life and reduce the likelihood of recidivism. That determination is usually written as a treatment plan with specific goals and objectives.

With respect to *program participation*, many halfway houses have a series of levels, or phases, through which residents must pass to receive a successful discharge. Typically, each level is associated with progressively more demanding goals and responsibilities for the resident to meet and also with more privileges and freedoms. For example, a requirement for an offender to move from the entry level to the second level may be the successful completion of a

Intensive Probation and Parole

In 1998, the average caseloads for regular probation and parole supervision were 124 and 67, respectively. By contrast, the 1998 average caseloads for intensive probation and parole supervision were 25 each. The 1998 average costs per day for regular probation and parole supervision were $1.90 and $4.18, respectively, while the 1998 average costs per day for intensive probation and parole supervision were $9.62 and $8.34, respectively. It is important to note, however, that caseloads and amounts spent on the two types of probation and parole supervision varied greatly across the nation. The average daily cost per prison inmate in 1998 was $56.26.

SOURCE: Camille Graham Camp and George M. Camp, *The Corrections Yearbook 1999: Adult Corrections* (Middletown, CT: Criminal Justice Institute, 1999), pp. 176–177, 187–188 and 89.

FIGURE 12–10
Intermediate Sanctions

Intermediate sanctions lie between traditional probation and traditional imprisonment or, alternatively, between imprisonment and traditional parole.

Community Service

Community service sanctions require offenders to perform a specified number of hours for the community. Traditionally, the offender paid restitution directly to the victim. Community service is restitution to the community.

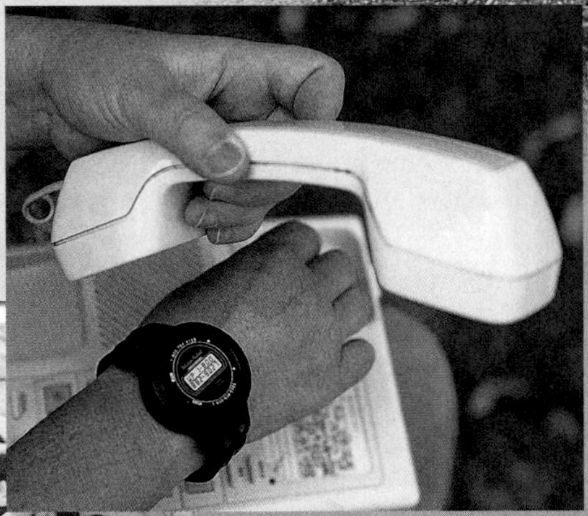

Home Confinement

Home confinement requires offenders to remain in their homes except for preapproved periods of absence. Most programs use electronic monitoring equipment to verify that offenders are at their designated locations at particular times.

Halfway Houses

Halfway houses may be operated by private for-profit or not-for-profit contractors or by public agencies. Some provide room, board, and help with employment. Others provide remedial education, individual or group counseling, and other types of life skills training.

ISP and Parole

Intensive-Supervision Probation (ISP) and parole programs impose strict requirements for reporting to a probation or parole officer with a limited caseload. Often, mandatory curfews, employment, and restitution are part of the program.

Day Reporting Centers

Day reporting centers , which may be publicly or privately operated, are corrections centers where offenders must report regularly to comply with a sentence. Most day center programs include employment, counseling, education, and community service components.

job skills class. Upon promotion to level two, the offender may receive one weekend furlough per month to spend with family and friends. Promotion to level three may carry additional furlough time and require that the offender obtain a job and complete a class on job retention skills.

As noted previously, halfway houses usually provide a variety of treatment services, such as employment counseling and training, life skills training, substance abuse intervention, and remedial education. Those services are provided either directly by house staff or indirectly through referrals to community agencies. To allow control and supervision, houses have a number of rules that govern both the in-house behavior of residents and residents' activities away from the facility. Those rules cover such matters as interaction between residents, care of facility property, curfews, and the use of alcohol. Progress through program levels requires completion of the goals and responsibilities associated with a particular level, participation in relevant treatment components, and compliance with house rules. Failure to achieve goals, to complete treatment components, or to abide by rules can result in the resident's staying at a given level or being demoted to a lower level.

A resident's behavior must be monitored and periodically reviewed throughout the term of program participation because, ultimately, the house administration must decide the resident's *termination*, or discharge, status. Residents who have satisfactorily completed all of the required levels are discharged into the community, frequently under probation or parole supervision. If a resident fails to make satisfactory progress through levels in a reasonable time, compiles an excessive number of less serious rule violations, or commits a serious rule infraction (such as another felony), the resident can also be discharged from the facility. An unsuccessful discharge can be granted at any point in a resident's stay and is frequently followed by incarceration.

Issues   Several issues surround the use of halfway houses. Two of the most critical issues are (1) the relations between a halfway house and the local community of which it is a part and (2) recidivism among persons who have been discharged from the house.

For a halfway house to be established in a community and to operate effectively, cooperative relations between the staff of the house and members of the community are essential. Halfway house staff often depend on the surrounding community for such things as resident health care, counseling services, educational programming, and job placements. Furthermore, unfavorable reactions from community members toward residents will simply reinforce the sense of marginalization and alienation that many offenders already experience. To the extent that community members feel threatened by residents or have poor relations with staff, the halfway house program is in jeopardy.

Virtually all halfway houses must confront the issue of community resistance, and some must confront outright hostility from community members. There are at least two keys to doing this effectively. First, halfway house officials must actively cultivate support and assistance from community members by engaging in open, honest communication with them from the earliest possible stage of the halfway house's existence. Many fears that community members have of residents are founded on inaccurate, media-fueled stereotypes and can be reduced with realistic, factual information. Second, it is very helpful if community members can see that the halfway house is contributing

Community Concern

Neighbors of a halfway house in Orlando, Florida, were upset about the placement of John Crutchley, the "vampire rapist." Crutchley was moved to the halfway house after serving 10 years of a 25-year sentence for the 1986 abduction and rape of a 19-year-old hitchhiker, whose blood he drank after he took her to his home and attacked her. Under special arrangements, Crutchley was to be under constant surveillance and supervision while at the halfway house and would be escorted and monitored when he left the house for a job interview or to make permanent living arrangements. Although the average stay at the halfway house is about four months, a judge gave approval for Crutchley to stay up to 364 days if necessary. Both community residents and law enforcement officials said they will do everything possible to encourage Crutchley to move out of the county.

SOURCE: Sherri M. Owens, "Neighbors Are Worried by Arrival of Rapist Who Drank Victim's Blood," *The Orlando Sentinel* (August 9, 1996), p. A–1.

something of value to the community, rather than simply consuming resources. For example, house residents can be involved in well-publicized and highly visible community service projects that save tax dollars. Also, in houses where a high proportion of residents are employed, community residents should be frequently reminded that residents are contributing to the tax base instead of consuming public revenue as jail or prison inmates. If community members can be convinced that the halfway house has a positive, contributing side, they are likely to be more accepting of the house.

Just as there are ways to facilitate cooperative community relations, there also are ways to create unfavorable relations. One way to almost ensure poor relations is for the halfway house to be sprung on the community without any notice of the desire of officials to establish the house and without community input in the early planning process. Another common mistake is for halfway house officials to be content with a low-profile image once the house is established. Believing that adequate community relations will exist as long as offenders are controlled and unfavorable media exposure is avoided, officials may try to minimize exposure of house operations to the public. The typical result is an atmosphere of secrecy, suspicion, and distrust. When the inevitable negative incident occurs, such as a crime by a resident against a community member, public outcry against the house is likely.

MYTH **FACT**

When an offender halfway house is established in a neighborhood, crime rates increase and property values fall.

Research on this subject has confirmed neither of those assumptions. Crime rates and property values tend to remain the same.

How many persons placed in halfway houses successfully complete their stays, and how high is recidivism among former residents after discharge? Those questions were addressed in a recent study of 156 probationers admitted to a halfway house in Michigan.[41] The study found that nearly 60 percent of all probationers received unsuccessful discharges. However, other studies have discovered successful discharge figures as high as 60 percent.[42] The Michigan study tracked former halfway house residents for seven years after their discharges. The researchers found that approximately 67 percent of the former residents were arrested at least once during the seven-year period for some type of criminal activity; about 60 percent were arrested at least once for felonies. However, persons who had successfully completed the halfway house program were significantly less likely to incur new arrests than the persons who had not done so. For instance, 44 percent of the persons who had received successful discharges were arrested for new felonies, compared with 68.8 percent of those who had received unsuccessful discharges.

In another study, the recidivism of offenders who had been placed in halfway house programs was compared with the recidivism of those placed on regular probation supervision. Using a three-year follow-up period, the researchers found that 29.5 percent of the former halfway house residents and 30.7 percent of the regular probationers experienced new criminal convictions. Slightly more than 40 percent of the halfway house residents had failed to complete their programs successfully.[43]

Research clearly suggests that a large number of offenders placed in halfway houses do not successfully complete their programs. However, those who do receive successful discharges seem less likely to commit new crimes than those who do not. Yet, there is little reason to believe that halfway houses are associated with less recidivism than other types of community corrections programs.

12.4 CRITICAL THINKING

1. Do you think people should have the right to reject the placement of a halfway house in their neighborhood?

2. What could be done to bring about good relations between a community and the halfway house located within the community?

12.5 Temporary-Release Programs

temporary-release programs
Programs that allow jail or prison inmates to leave the facility for short periods to participate in approved community activities.

Temporary-release programs allow inmates in jail or prison to leave the facility for short periods to participate in approved community activities. Those programs are designed to permit inmates to establish or maintain community ties, thereby gradually preparing them for reentry into society. The programs also give institutional authorities a means of testing the readiness of inmates for release as well as a means of controlling institutional behavior. Not surprisingly, opportunities for temporary release create a major incentive for inmates to engage in the conduct desired by officials.

Three common temporary-release programs are work release, study release, and furloughs. The persons involved in such programs may be prison or jail inmates, or halfway house residents. As should be apparent from the previous section of this chapter, temporary release is an integral aspect of halfway houses. In prisons and jails, temporary release is reserved for inmates who have demonstrated that they are appropriate candidates to participate in community-based activities.

Organized temporary-release programs are not new in American corrections. Although the programs date to the early 1900s, they did not gain widespread popularity until the 1960s, when the emphasis on community corrections began to grow. Today, almost all states offer temporary release.[44]

In work-release programs, inmates leave the facility for certain hours each day to work for employers in the free community. Work-release inmates are paid prevailing wages, but they are usually required to submit their paychecks to corrections officials to deduct for such things as dependent support and restitution orders before placing the balance in inmates' accounts. Inmates may withdraw some money while in the facility but are usually required to save a certain amount for their ultimate release from incarceration. A limitation of such programs is that most inmates must settle for low-skilled and low-paying jobs. This limitation exists because:

1. A large proportion of inmates lack the educational and vocational backgrounds needed to secure higher-paying employment.

2. There is more competition for higher-paying jobs.

3. Many employers are reluctant to hire work-release inmates, especially for jobs that pay well and require skill and responsibility.

Study-release inmates can leave prison for high school equivalency classes, vocational training, or college coursework. A limitation of study release is that, unlike work release, it does not generate financial resources. If inmates cannot pay for their own educational programs or obtain financial aid, study release must be funded by the jurisdiction. Even in the unlikely event that a jurisdiction has resources to fund study release, there may still be reluctance to do so because of the argument that inmates are getting free education at taxpayers' expense.

In furlough programs, inmates are granted leaves of absence for brief periods (for example, 48 hours) to accomplish specific things. Inmates may be granted furloughs to spend time with family members, to attend funerals, or to search for employment and housing before release.

One commonly voiced fear about temporary-release programs is that inmates will flee or commit serious crimes while away from the facility. In fact, research shows that most inmates neither flee nor commit serious offenses. The most frequent problems are late returns and the use of alcohol and illegal drugs.

Temporary-release programs became a significant issue in the U.S. presidential election campaign of 1988. Massachusetts Governor Michael Dukakis, the Democratic presidential nominee, was heavily criticized by Vice President George Bush, the Republican nominee, for allowing temporary release of inmates with records of violence. Willie Horton, a black man who had been serving a first-degree murder sentence at a Massachusetts institution, committed violent crimes against a white couple during his tenth furlough from the institution. Bush made much of the "liberal" prison release policies of Massachusetts in an attempt to discredit Dukakis.

Around the same time, an evaluation of temporary release in Massachusetts was being conducted. The evaluation was published in 1991.[45] The researchers studied persons released from Massachusetts facilities between 1973 and 1983. Offenders were tracked for one year after release, and recidivism was defined as return to prison. The recidivism of persons who participated in furloughs, prerelease-center (halfway house) programs, and both furloughs and prerelease centers was compared with the recidivism of persons who participated in neither. Using statistical controls for differences in offenders' backgrounds, researchers concluded that "prerelease programs following prison furloughs, and prison furloughs alone, appear to reduce dramatically the risks to public safety after release." This study implies that eliminating or significantly curtailing temporary-release programs is likely to result in a long-term decline in community safety and an increase in recidivism.

12.5 CRITICAL THINKING

1. Do you think offenders should be allowed to take college courses, at taxpayers' expense, through study-release programs?

2. Do you think temporary-release programs help rehabilitate offenders? Why or why not?

Review and Applications

SUMMARY BY CHAPTER OBJECTIVES

1. Define Community Corrections and Identify the Goals and Responsibilities of Community Corrections Agencies and their Staffs

Although community corrections programs are very diverse across the nation, the common feature of those programs is that they provide supervision and treatment services for offenders outside jails and prisons. The dual emphasis on supervision and treatment creates a potential role conflict for community corrections staff. There is some indication, however, that the traditional focus on treatment has been declining relative to the growing emphasis on supervision.

2. Define Probation and Summarize the Research Findings on Recidivism Rates

The most commonly used type of community sentence is probation. Offenders placed on probation are supervised and provided with various services in the community instead of being incarcerated. In return, they are required to abide by the rules of the probation sentence. Overall, studies indicate that probation is about as effective as incarceration in controlling recidivism. Available data indicate that recidivism is quite high among felons sentenced to probation. Furthermore, research has not found a strong association between probation officers' caseloads and the likelihood of probationer recidivism. If anything, reduced caseloads seem to increase the probability that instances of recidivism will be detected.

3. Distinguish Parole from Probation

Unlike probation, parole is not a court-imposed sentence. Parole is a mechanism of releasing persons from prison and a means of supervising them after release, instead of an alternative to an incarceration sentence. Parole supervision is often confused with probation because the two share many similarities.

Four major objectives of parole agencies are to:
(1) preserve community safety by supervising the behavior of parolees
(2) promote the betterment of parolees by responding to their treatment needs
(3) control prison crowding
(4) control the behavior of prison inmates by providing early release opportunities in exchange for good prison conduct.

4. Explain the Functions of a Parole Board

In general, a parole board directs a jurisdiction's parole policies and manages the parole release and termination processes. Parole board members (or their representatives) conduct parole-grant hearings to determine which inmates should receive early release from prison. Boards also determine whether to revoke the parole of persons who have violated parole conditions. In most states, field service agencies are administratively independent of parole boards. A field service agency provides community supervision and treatment services for persons who have been granted parole release by the board and makes recommendations to the board concerning termination of parole.

5. Describe How Intermediate Sanctions Differ from Traditional Community Corrections Programs

Compared with traditional programs in community corrections, intermediate sanctions are oriented less toward rehabilitation and more toward retribution, deterrence, and incapacitation. They are more punitive and more restrictive. The recent popularity of intermediate sanctions is attributable largely to the record high levels of prison crowding that plague many jurisdictions and a corresponding need to devise acceptable alternatives to imprisonment.

6. Explain Two Major Concerns About Intensive-Supervision Probation and Parole (ISP)

Two major concerns about ISP are
(1) the potential for net-widening
(2) the lack of demonstrated reduction of recidivism.
Net-widening occurs when offenders placed in a novel program such as ISP are not the offenders for whom the program was intended. The consequence is that those in the program receive more severe sanctions than they would have received had the new program been unavailable. Studies show that ISP is associated with a substantially higher percentage of technical violations than alternative sanctions such as regular probation, prison, or regular parole.

7. Explain What Day Reporting Centers and Structured Fines Are

Day reporting centers allow offenders to live at home but require them to report to the center regularly to confer with center staff about supervision and treatment matters. Program components commonly focus on work, education, counseling, and community service. Structured fines, or day fines, differ fundamentally from the fines (called *tariff fines*) more typically imposed by American criminal courts. Whereas tariff fines require a single fixed amount of money, or an amount within a narrow range, to be paid by all defendants convicted of a particular crime, without regard to their financial circumstances, structured fines, or day fines, are based on defendants' ability to pay. The basic premise of structured fines is that punishment by a fine should be proportionate to the seriousness of the offense and should have a roughly similar economic impact on persons with differing financial resources who are convicted of the same offense.

8. Explain What Home Confinement and Electronic Monitoring Are

In home confinement programs (also known as home incarceration, home detention, and house arrest), offenders are required by the court to remain in their homes except for preapproved periods of absence. Electronic monitoring, which is generally coupled with home confinement, allows an offender's whereabouts to be gauged through the use of computer technology.

9. Identify the Goal of Halfway Houses and Compare Them With Other Community Corrections Programs

The goal of halfway houses is to provide offenders with a temporary (for instance, six-month) period of highly structured and supportive living so that they will be better prepared to function independently in the community upon discharge. To this end, most programs place a heavy emphasis on addressing offenders' educational and employment deficits. Research clearly suggests that a large number of offenders placed in halfway houses do not successfully complete their programs. However, those who do receive successful discharges seem less likely to commit new crimes than those who do not. Yet, there is little reason to believe that halfway houses are associated with less recidivism than other community corrections programs.

10. Summarize the Purposes and Outcomes of Temporary-Release Programs

By allowing incarcerated persons to temporarily leave their facilities to participate in approved activities in the community, temporary-release programs are intended to foster ties between inmates and their communities, thus gradually preparing inmates for return to society. These programs also give officials a way to judge the readiness of inmates for release, and since most inmates want to participate in temporary release, the programs give inmates an incentive to maintain good institutional behavior. Although fear and other forms of resistance from community members often plague the programs, there is evidence that participation in temporary release is associated with a decreased likelihood of recidivism upon release from incarceration. Some common types of temporary release include work release, study release, and furlough.

KEY TERMS

community corrections, p. 426
probation, p. 430
diversion, p. 430
presentence investigation (PSI), p. 432
probation conditions, p. 435
restitution, p. 437
revocation, p. 437
technical violations, p. 439
recidivism, p. 441
parole, p. 442
parole guidelines, p. 446

reintegration, p. 451
intermediate sanctions, p. 453
intensive-supervision probation and parole (ISP), p. 453
net-widening, p. 454
day reporting centers, p. 456
structured fines, or day fines, p. 456
home confinement, p. 458
electronic monitoring, p. 458
halfway houses, p. 460
temporary-release programs, p. 466

QUESTIONS FOR REVIEW

1. What are David Duffee's three varieties of community corrections, and how do they differ?

2. What are three aspects of the helping role of community corrections staff?

3. Why is community corrections important?

4. What are five types of probation?

5. What are three fundamental objectives of probation agencies?

6. What is a probation subsidy, and what is its goal?

7. What is the main task of the PSI?

8. What are two types of probation conditions, and how do they differ?

9. For what general types of violations can probation be revoked?

10. What two landmark Supreme Court cases define the procedural guidelines for revoking probation or parole?

11. What are two general types of parole, and what is their function?

12. According to a recent study, what are the four most important factors parole authorities consider before granting release on parole?

13. What are some criticisms of parole release?

14. What are two ways that halfway house officials might effectively confront community resistance?

1. **Tour a Probation Agency** Take a guided tour of the probation or parole agency in your community.
(1) Ask the guide to explain the various activities of the agency. Also ask to speak with various officers about their work.
(2) Request sample copies of agency documents, such as risk-and-needs-assessment instruments.
(3) Write a short essay describing what the agency documents reveal about the work of the agency.

2. **Evaluate Halfway House Rules** Obtain a copy of the rules of behavior for a halfway house.
(1) Evaluate the rules, and decide whether you think they are too strict, not strict enough, or on target.
(2) Rewrite any rules that you think need changing.

INTERNET

3. **Local Community Corrections** Visit the Sedgwick County, Kansas, Department of Corrections, Community Corrections Web site or the North Carolina Department of Correction, Division of Community Corrections Web site by clicking the links at cj.glencoe.com. Choose from the topics provided, and write a brief summary of the information you find and how it is related to community corrections.

4. **U.S. Parole Commission** Visit the Web site of the United States Parole Commission through the link at cj.glencoe.com and click on "Our History" to read a contextual history of the federal parole system. Then click on "Answering Your Questions" for the answers to many commonly asked questions about federal parole. Write a short essay explaining why you support or oppose the 1987 abolition of federal parole.

Probation/Parole Officer

1. You are a probation or parole officer. Your caseload averages 100 clients.

   a. A client tells you that her boss is treating her unfairly at work because of her criminal record and probation or parole status. Your client is afraid of being fired and having her probation or parole revoked. What do you do?

   b. You discover that a client is using marijuana. You like the client, and other than the marijuana use, he has been doing well on probation or parole. What do you do?

   c. You have a problem client who is using drugs (marijuana and cocaine), hanging out with a "bad" group of people, and probably (though you have no hard evidence) committing petty thefts to support her drug habit. You have warned the client to stop this behavior, but she has ignored your warnings. Furthermore, the client has threatened to harm you and your family should you revoke her probation or parole. What do you do?

   d. You have a client who, as a condition of his probation or parole, is required to earn his GED. Although the client has been attending classes regularly and seems to be trying very hard, his teacher informs you that the client just does not have the intellectual capacity to earn the GED. What do you do?

Halfway House

2. As an employee of your state department of corrections, you have been asked to establish a halfway house for parolees, all of whom are former substance abuse offenders, in the nice, middle-class community where you live. Assuming that you take the job, how would you address the following questions?

    a. Would you communicate to the community your intention of establishing the halfway house? Why or why not?

    b. How would you address community resistance to the halfway house should it arise?

    c. Would you ask community residents to aid you in your efforts? Why or why not?

    d. Besides community resistance, what other problems might arise in your effort to establish the halfway house? How would you handle them?

    e. Would you be willing to remain a resident of the community after the halfway house is established (especially if you have a family with small children)? Why or why not?

ADDITIONAL READING

Allen, Harry E., Chris W. Eskridge, Edward J. Latessa, and Gennaro F. Vito. *Probation and Parole in America.* New York: Free Press, 1985.

Ball, Richard A., C. Ronald Huff, and J. Robert Lilly. *House Arrest and Correctional Policy: Doing Time at Home.* Beverly Hills, CA: Sage, 1988.

Byrne, James M. (ed.). *Smart Sentencing: The Emergence of Intermediate Sanctions.* Beverly Hills, CA: Sage, 1992.

Champion, Dean. *Probation, Parole and Community Corrections.* Upper Saddle River, NJ: Prentice Hall, 1996.

Clear, Todd R., Val B. Clear, and William D. Burrell. *Offender Assessment: The Presentence Investigation Report.* Cincinnati: Anderson, 1989.

Clear, Todd R. and Vincent O'Leary. *Controlling the Offender in the Community.* Lexington, MA: Lexington Books, 1983.

Cromwell, Paul F. and George G. Killinger. *Community-Based Corrections: Probation, Parole, and Intermediate Sanctions,* 3d ed. Minneapolis/St. Paul: West, 1994.

Dillingham, Steven D., Reid H. Montgomery, Jr., and Richard W. Tabor. *Probation and Parole in Practice,* 2d ed. Cincinnati: Anderson, 1990.

Duffee, David E. and Edmund F. McGarrell (eds.). *Community Corrections: A Community Field Approach.* Cincinnati: Anderson, 1990

Ellsworth, Thomas (ed.). *Contemporary Community Corrections.* Prospect Heights, IL: Waveland Press, 1992.

Galaway, Burt and Joe Hudson (eds.). *Criminal Justice, Restitution, and Reconciliation.* Monsey, NY: Criminal Justice Press, 1990.

Keller, Oliver J. Jr. and Benedict S. Alpert. *Halfway Houses.* Lexington, MA: Lexington Books, 1970.

Klein, Andrew R. *Alternative Sentencing: A Practitioner's Guide.* Cincinnati: Anderson, 1988.

McCarthy, Belinda R. (ed.) *Intermediate Punishments: Intensive Supervision, Home Confinement and Electronic Surveillance.* Monsey, NY: Criminal Justice Press, 1987.

McCarthy, Belinda Rodgers, Bernard J. McCarthy, Jr., and Matthew C. Leone. *Community-Based Corrections,* 4th ed. Belmont, CA: Wadsworth, 2001.

McCleary, Richard. *Dangerous Men: The Sociology of Parole.* Beverly Hills, CA: Sage, 1978.

McShane, Marilyn D. and Wesley Krause. *Community Corrections.* New York: Macmillan, 1993.

Morris, Norval and Michael Tonry. *Between Prison and Probation: Intermediate Punishments in a Rational Sentencing System.* New York: Oxford University Press, 1990.

Petersilia, Joan, Susan Turner, James Kahan, and Joyce Peterson. *Granting Felons Probation: Public Risks and Alternatives.* Santa Monica, CA: Rand, 1985.

Rothman, David J. *Conscience and Convenience: The Asylum and Its Alternatives in Progressive America.* Boston: Little, Brown, 1980.

Smykla, John Ortiz, and William L. Selke (eds.) *Intermediate Sanctions: Sentencing in the 1990s.* Cincinnati: Anderson, 1994.

Travis, Lawrence F., III (ed.) *Probation, Parole, and Community Corrections: A Reader.* Prospect Heights, IL: Waveland Press, 1985.

Walsh, Anthony. *Understanding, Assessing, and Counseling the Criminal Justice Client.* Pacific Grove, CA: Brooks/Cole, 1988.

Zvekic, Ugljesa (ed.) *Alternatives to Imprisonment in Comparative Perspective.* Chicago: Nelson-Hall, 1994.

ENDNOTES

1. David E. Duffee, "Community Corrections: Its Presumed Characteristics and an Argument for a New Approach," in D. E. Duffee and E. F. McGarrell (eds.), *Community Corrections: A Community Field Approach* (Cincinnati: Anderson, 1990), pp. 1–41.

2. Patricia M. Harris, Todd R. Clear, and S. Christopher Baird, "Have Community Supervision Officers Changed Their Attitudes Toward Their Work?" *Justice Quarterly,* Vol. 6 (1989), pp. 233–46. And see Robert T. Sigler, "Role Conflict for Adult Probation and Parole Officers: Fact or Myth," *Journal of Criminal Justice,* Vol. 16 (1988), pp. 121–29.

3. David J. Rothman, *Conscience and Convenience: The Asylum and Its Alternatives in Progressive America.* Boston: Little, Brown, 1980, p. 44; www.ohnd.uscourts.gov/U_S_Probation/U_S_Probation_Employment/u_s_probation_employment.html

4. John Rosecrance, "Maintaining the Myth of Individualized Justice: Probation Presentence Reports," *Justice Quarterly,* Vol. 5 (1988), pp. 235–56.

5. Rolando V. del Carmen, "Legal Issues and Liabilities in Community Corrections," in T. Ellsworth (ed.), *Contemporary Community Corrections* (Prospect Heights, IL: Waveland Press, 1992), pp. 383–407.

6. Jay S. Albanese, Bernadette A. Fiore, Jerie H. Powell, and Janet R. Storti, *Is Probation Working? A Guide for Managers and Methodologists* (New York: University Press of America, 1981), p. 65.

7. Ibid.

8. Joan Petersilia, Susan Turner, James Kahan, and Joyce Peterson, Granting Felons *Probation: Public Risks and Alternatives* (Santa Monica, CA: Rand, 1985).

9. United States Department of Justice, Bureau of Justice Statistics Special Report, *Recidivism of Felons on Probation, 1986–89* (Washington, DC: GPO, February 1992).

10. Rothman, op. cit.

11. John C. Runda, Edward E. Rhine, and Robert E. Wetter, *The Practice of Parole Boards* (Lexington, KY: Host Communications Printing, 1994).

12. Ibid.

13. Ibid.

14. Ibid.

15. Ibid.

16. Ibid.

17. Ibid.

18. Ibid.

19. Ibid.

20. Ibid.

21. Ibid.

22. Richard McCleary, *Dangerous Men: The Sociology of Parole* (Beverly Hills, CA: Sage, 1978).

23. Peggy B. Burke, *Abolishing Parole: Why the Emperor Has No Clothes* (Lexington, KY: American Probation and Parole Association, 1995); Peggy B. Burke, "Issues in Parole Release Decision Making," in C. A. Hartjen and E. E. Rhine (eds.), *Correctional Theory and Practice* (Chicago: Nelson-Hall, 1992), pp. 213–32.

24. Paula M. Ditton and Doris James Wilson, "Truth in Sentencing in State Prisons," U.S. Department of Justice, Bureau of Justice Special Report (Washington, DC: GPO, January 1999), p. 3.

25. Burke, *Abolishing Parole,* op. cit.

26. John C. Watkins, Jr., "Probation and Parole Malpractice in a Noninstitutional Setting: A Contemporary Analysis," *Federal Probation,* Vol. 53 (1989), pp. 29–34 (quotations from p. 30). Also see Rolando V. del Carmen, op. cit.

27. Calculated from "U.S. Correctional Population Reaches 6.3 Million Men and Women Represents 3.1 Percent of the Adult U.S. Population," U.S. Department of Justice, Bureau of Justice Statistics Press Release (July 23, 2000), Table 1. <www.ojp.usdoj.gov/bjs/pub/pdf/pp99pr.pdf>

28. Jeffrey K. Liker, "Wage and Status Effects of Employment on Affective Well-Being Among Ex-Felons," *American Sociological Review,* Vol. 47 (1982), pp. 264–83 (quotation from p. 282).

29. Richard A. Berk and David Rauma, "Capitalizing on Nonrandom Assignment to Treatments: A Regression-Discontinuity Evaluation of a Crime-Control Program,"

ENDNOTES

Journal of the American Statistical Association, Vol. 78 (1983), pp. 21–27. And see Peter H. Rossi, Richard A. Berk, and K. J. Lenihan, *Money, Work, and Crime: Experimental Evidence* (New York: Academic Press, 1980).

30. U.S. Department of Justice, Bureau of Justice Statistics Special Report, Recidivism of Young Parolees (Washington, DC: GPO, May 1987).

31. "U.S. Correctional Population Reaches 6.3 Million Men and Women Represents 3.1 Percent of the Adult U.S. Population," U.S. Department of Justice, Bureau of Justice Statistics Press Release (July 23, 2000) www.ojp.usdoj.gov/bjs/pub/pdf/ pp99pr.pdf

32. Runda et al., op. cit. Also see United States G.A.O., *Intermediate Sanctions: Their Impacts on Prison Crowding, Costs, and Recidivism Are Still Unclear* (Washington, DC: General Accounting Office, 1990).

33. Billie S. Erwin and Lawrence A. Bennett, *New Dimensions in Probation: Georgia's Experience With Intensive Probation Supervision,* United States Department of Justice, National Institute of Justice, Research in Brief (Washington, DC: GPO, 1987), p. 4.

34. Joan Petersilia and Susan Turner, "Comparing Intensive and Regular Supervision for High-Risk Probationers: Early Results From an Experiment in California," *Crime and Delinquency,* Vol. 36 (1990), pp. 87–111.

35. Joan Petersilia and Susan Turner, *Evaluating Intensive Supervision Probation/Parole: Results of a Nationwide Experiment,* United States Department of Justice, National Institute of Justice, Research in Brief (Washington, DC: GPO, 1993). For further detail see Joan Petersilia and Susan Turner, "Intensive Probation and Parole," in M. Tonry and A. J. Reiss (eds.), *Crime and Justice: A Review of Research,* Vol. 17 (Chicago: University of Chicago Press, 1993), pp. 281–335.

36. Ibid.

37. Dale G. Parent, *Day Reporting Centers for Criminal Offenders: A Descriptive Analysis of Existing Programs,* United States Department of Justice, National Institute of Justice, Issues and Practices (Washington, DC: GPO 1990).

38. Material in this section is from How to Use Structured Fines (Day Fines) as an Intermediate Sanction, U.S. Department of Justice, Bureau of Justice Assistance (November 1996).

39. Rolando V. del Carmen and Joseph B. Vaughn, "Legal Issues in the Use of Electronic Surveillance in Probation," in T. Ellsworth (ed.), *Contemporary Community Corrections* (Prospect Heights, IL: Waveland Press, 1992), p. 426.

40. John P. Conrad, "Concluding Comments: VORP and the Correctional Future," in B. Galaway and J. Hudson (eds.), *Criminal Justice, Restitution, and Reconciliation* (Monsey, NY: Criminal Justice Press, 1990), p. 229.

41. David J. Hartmann, Paul C. Friday, and Kevin I. Minor, "Residential Probation: A Seven-Year Follow-Up Study of Halfway House Discharges," *Journal of Criminal Justice,* Vol. 22 (1994), pp. 503–15.

42. Patrick G. Donnelly and Brian E. Forschner, "Client Success or Failure in a Halfway House," *Federal Probation,* Vol. 48 (1984), pp. 38–44. Also see R. E. Seiter, H. Bowman Carlson, J. Grandfield, and N. Bernam, Halfway Houses: National Evaluation Program: Phase I, Summary Report, U.S. Department of Justice (Washington, DC: GPO, 1977).

43. Edward J. Latessa and Lawrence F. Travis, "Halfway House or Probation: A Comparison of Alternative Dispositions," *Journal of Crime and Justice,* Vol. 14 (1991), pp. 53–75.

44. Belinda Rodgers McCarthy, Bernard J. McCarthy, Jr., and Matthew C. Leone, *Community-Based Corrections,* 4th ed. (Belmont, CA: Wadsworth, 2001). Unless otherwise noted, the material in the remainder of this section draws on pp. 148-156 of this source.

45. Daniel P. LeClair and Susan Guarino-Ghezzi, "Does Incapacitation Guarantee Public Safety? Lessons From the Massachusetts Furlough and Prerelease Programs," *Justice Quarterly,* Vol. 8 (1991), pp. 9–36 (quotation from p. 26).

PART 5

Juvenile Justice

CHAPTER 13
Juvenile Justice

Juvenile Justice

CHAPTER OBJECTIVES

After completing this chapter, you should be able to:

1. Describe some of the early institutions used to respond to wayward and criminal youths.

2. Explain the effects of some landmark U.S. Supreme Court cases on the juvenile justice system.

3. Identify and describe factors that influence the ways that police process juvenile cases.

4. Summarize the rationale for the use of diversion in juvenile justice.

5. Describe the adjudication hearing in juvenile justice.

6. Describe the disposition hearing and the types of dispositions available to the juvenile court.

7. Identify the types and describe the effectiveness of community-based correctional programs for juveniles.

8. Summarize recent trends in juvenile incarceration.

9. Identify the types and describe the effectiveness of institutional programs for juveniles.

13.1 Historical Development of Juvenile Justice

juvenile delinquency
A special category of offense created for youths who, in most U.S. jurisdictions, are persons between the ages of 7 and 18.

From a historical perspective, juvenile delinquency and a separate justice process for juveniles are recent concepts. So, too, are the ideas of childhood and adolescence. **Juvenile delinquency,** as you may recall from Chapter 2, is a special category of offense created for youths—that is, in most U.S. jurisdictions, persons between the ages of 7 and 18. Through most of recorded history, the young have not enjoyed the statuses of childhood and adolescence as special times during which the young need nurturing and guidance for their healthy development.

Before the sixteenth century, the young were viewed either as property or as miniature adults who, by the age of five or six, were expected to assume the responsibilities of adults. They were also subject to the same criminal sanctions as adults. However, in the sixteenth and seventeenth centuries, a different view of the young emerged that recognized childhood as a distinct period of life, and children as corruptible but worth correcting.[1] Youths began to be viewed, not as miniature adults or as property, but rather as persons who required molding and guidance to become moral and productive members of the community. American colonists brought with them those new ideas about childhood as well as European mechanisms for responding to violators of social and legal rules.

During the colonial period, the family was the basic unit of economic production and the primary mechanism through which social control was exerted. Survival depended on the family's ability to produce what it needed, rather than relying on the production of others. Consequently, a primary responsibility of the family was overseeing the moral training and discipline of the young. During this period, two age-old mechanisms were employed to teach children who were difficult to handle or needed supervision a trade to allow them an opportunity to earn a livelihood. One of those mechanisms was the **apprenticeship system,** which served as a primary means for teaching skilled trades to the children of the middle and upper classes. The other tradition was the binding-out system, which was reserved for poor children. Under the **binding-out system,** children were bound over to masters for care. However, under this system, masters were not required to teach the youths a trade. As a result, boys were often given farming tasks, while girls were assigned to domestic duties.[2]

apprenticeship system
The method by which middle- and upper-class children were taught skilled trades by a master.

binding-out system
Practice in which children were "bound over" to masters for care. However, under the binding-out system, masters were not required to teach youths a trade.

Religion, particularly in New England, was another powerful force that shaped social life in the colonies. Regular church attendance was expected, and religious beliefs dominated ideas about appropriate behavior. Present-day concerns about the separation of church and state were nonexistent. What was believed to be immoral was also unlawful and subject to punishment by the authorities. Punishments such as fines, whipping, branding, and the use of stocks and the pillory served as reminders to both young and old that violations of community norms would not go unpunished.[3]

By the early 1800s, the social organization of colonial life began to change as a result of economic and social developments. The family-based production unit that had characterized colonial social life was giving way to a factory-based system in the growing towns. As parents—particularly

▲ Until the early 1900s, children were subject to same punishments as adults. *Should children be punished in the same way as adults? Why or why not?*

fathers—and children began to leave the home for work in a factory, fundamental changes occurred in the relationships between family members and in the role of the family in controlling the behavior of children. Further, as industry developed and as towns grew, communities became more diverse and experienced problems on a scale unheard of during earlier periods.

The Development of Institutions for Youths

At the time of the American Revolution, Philadelphia had fewer than 20,000 residents, and other large towns, such as New York, Boston, Newport, and Charleston, had fewer than 15,000 inhabitants each. However, by 1820, the population of New York City was about 120,000 and was growing rapidly as a result of immigration. Immigration, in turn, was changing the composition of communities, which had been more homogeneous during colonial times.

The Houses of Refuge   Accompanying those changes in the social and economic life of the growing cities were a host of social problems, such as poverty, vagrancy, drunkenness, and crime, including crimes committed by children. In response to those conditions, the first correctional institutions specifically for youths developed. Those institutions were called **houses of refuge.** The first was established in New York City in 1825, and houses of refuge soon spread to other cities such as Boston and Philadelphia.[4]

A primary goal of the houses of refuge was to prevent pauperism and to respond to youths who were ignored by the courts. Houses of refuge were meant to be institutions where children could be reformed and turned into hard-working members of the community. To accomplish this mission, youths were placed in houses of refuge for indeterminate periods or until their 18th or 21st birthdays. Placement, moreover, did not require a court hearing. A child could be committed to a house of refuge by a constable, by a parent, or on the order of a city alderman.[5]

Juvenile Crime Wave
Each generation of Americans seems to believe that the country is experiencing a "juvenile crime wave."

SOURCE: Thomas J. Bernard, *The Cycle of Juvenile Justice* (New York: Oxford University Press, 1992).

houses of refuge
The first specialized correctional institutions for youths in the United States.

While there, children engaged in a daily regimen of hard work, military drills, and enforced silence, as well as religious and academic training. It was also common practice for outside contractors to operate shops within the houses of refuge. In those shops, children produced goods such as shoes or furniture, and in return, the houses of refuge were paid 10 to 15 cents per youth each day. This arrangement allowed houses of refuge to pay a substantial percentage of their daily operating expenses.[6] When the youthful inmates failed to meet production quotas, they were often punished. After "reformation," boys were frequently indentured to masters on farms or to tradesmen, and girls were placed in domestic service.[7]

Placing Out   Soon after the establishment of houses of refuge, reformers began to recognize the inability of those institutions to accommodate the large numbers of children needing placement and to either reform or control youths. One early response to those problems was the development of placing out. **Placing out,** which involved the placing of children on farms in the West and Midwest, was believed to have several advantages over the houses of refuge. First, placing out was seen as a way of removing children from the supposedly corrupting influences of their parents, who frequently were immigrants, and especially of the cities, which reformers viewed as breeding grounds for idleness and crime. Second, many reformers recognized that the conditions in the houses of refuge were counterproductive to the goal of reform. Third, rural areas were assumed to be an ideal environment for instilling in children the values the reformers cherished—values that stressed discipline, hard work, and piety.

Agents hired by charitable organizations would take children west by train and place them with farm families. Although some children were placed in caring homes and were treated as members of the family, others were not so lucky. Many of the children who were placed out were required to work hard for their keep, were abused, were not accepted as members of the family, and never saw their own families again.

Probation   Another effort to deal with troubled children was initiated by a Boston shoemaker, John Augustus. As described in Chapter 12, Augustus spent considerable time observing the court and became convinced that many minor offenders could be salvaged. As a result of his concern and his willingness to work with offenders, Augustus was permitted to provide bail for his first probation client in 1841.

Augustus's first client was a drunkard who showed remarkable improvement during the period in which he was supervised. The court was impressed with Augustus's work and permitted him to stand bail for other minor offenders, including children.

After Augustus died, the Boston Children's Aid Society and other volunteers carried on his work. Then, in 1869, the state of Massachusetts formalized the existing volunteer probation system by authorizing visiting probation agents, who were to work with both adult and child offenders who showed promise. Under this arrangement, youths were allowed to return home to their parents, provided they obeyed the law.[8] In 1878, an additional law was passed in Boston that provided for paid probation officers.[9] Subsequently, several other states authorized the appointment of probation

placing out
The practice of placing children on farms in the Midwest and West to remove them from the supposedly corrupting influences of their parents and the cities.

▲ Juveniles incarcerated at the turn of the century were put into job training programs that would help them when they were released. Typically, male offenders learned industrial trades; female offenders learned ironing, laundry work, and cooking. *Should these practices be revived? Why or why not?*

officers. However, it was not until after the turn of the century and the development of the first juvenile court that probation gained widespread acceptance.[10]

Reform Schools, Industrial Schools, and Training Schools
By the late 1800s, the failure of houses of refuge was well known. Dislocations produced by the Civil War placed tremendous strain on houses of refuge and the placing out system. Perhaps most disappointing, the number of problem youths was growing. In response, state and city governments took over the administration of institutions for juvenile delinquents. Another response was the establishment of **reform, industrial,** or **training schools,** correctional facilities that focused on custody.[11] Those institutions were of two types: cottage reformatories and institutional reformatories.

Cottage reformatories were usually located in rural areas to avoid the negative influences of the urban environment. They were intended to closely parallel family life. Each cottage contained 20–40 youths, who were supervised by cottage parents charged with the task of overseeing residents' training and education.[12]

In addition to cottage reformatories, larger, more institutional reformatories were developed in many states. Like the cottage reformatories, the institutional reformatories were usually located in rural areas in an effort to remove youths from the negative influences of city life. However, the institutions were frequently large and overcrowded.

Another development, in the late 1800s, was the establishment of separate institutions for females. Previously, girls had been committed to the same institutions as boys, although there was strict gender segregation in those institutions. Moreover, girls were often committed by parents or relatives for moral, as opposed to criminal, offenses. Those moral offenses consisted of such actions as "vagrancy, beggary, stubbornness, deceitfulness, idle and vicious behavior, wanton and lewd conduct, and running away."[13] The expressed goal of those institutions was to prepare girls to be good

reform, industrial, or **training schools**
Correctional facilities for youths, first developed in the late 1800s, that focused on custody. Today, those institutions are often called training schools and although they may place more emphasis on treatment, they still rely on custody and control.

cottage reformatories
Correctional facilities for youths, first developed in the late 1800s, that were intended to closely parallel family life and remove children from the negative influences of the urban environment. Children in those facilities lived with surrogate parents, who were responsible for the youths' training and education.

housewives and mothers. Yet, the institutions, like those for boys, were little different from the prisons of that era.

The reform, industrial, and training schools placed more emphasis on formal education than did the houses of refuge, but in many other respects there was little difference. Indeed, those institutions confronted many of the same problems as the houses of refuge had. Moreover, the conditions in the reformatories were certainly no better than those in the houses of refuge, and in many cases they were worse.

The Development of the Juvenile Court

By the end of the 1800s, a variety of institutions and mechanisms had been developed in response to problem children. Still, the problems presented by children who were believed to be in need of correctional treatment—problems such as homelessness, neglect, abuse, waywardness, and criminal behavior—proved difficult to solve. Consequently, during the late 1800s a new group of reformers, the *child savers,* began to advocate a new institution to deal with youth problems. This new institution was the juvenile court.

The Social Context of the Juvenile Court   The period from 1880 to 1920, a period historians refer to as the Progressive Era, was a time of major change in the United States. Although industrialization and urbanization were well under way, and previous waves of immigrants had added to the population of the country, the pace of industrialization, urbanization, and immigration quickened.

In an effort to respond to the problem of youth crime and waywardness, reformers again sought to save children from the crime-inducing conditions of the cities. Supported by important philanthropic and civic organizations, the child savers worked to improve jail and reformatory conditions. However, the primary outcome of the child-saving movement was the extension of governmental control over children's lives. The child savers argued for stricter supervision of children, and they improved legal mechanisms designed to regulate children's activities.[14] In short, the child savers felt that children needed to be protected and that the best institutions for protecting them were government agencies such as the police and the courts, as well as local charitable organizations.

The Legal Context of the Juvenile Court   By the late 1800s, legal mechanisms for treating children differently and separately from adults had existed for some time. For example, jurisdictions had set the minimum age at which a child could be considered legally responsible for criminal behavior. Minimum ages for placement in adult penitentiaries were also enacted during the first half of the 1800s.[15] Moreover, special institutions for dealing with youths had been in existence since 1825, when the first house of refuge was established in New York City. Yet, cases involving juveniles were still heard in criminal courts. Many of the child savers believed that criminal courts failed to respond adequately to many of the transgressions of the young.

The legal philosophy justifying state intervention in the lives of children, the doctrine of ***parens patriae*** (the state as parent), was given judicial

The Progressive Era

The city of Chicago provides a good example of the changes experienced during the Progressive Era. Between 1890 and 1910, Chicago's population grew from one million to two million. Between 1880 and 1890, the number of factories nearly tripled. By 1889, nearly 70 percent of the inhabitants of the city were immigrants.

SOURCE: Harold Finestone, *Victims of Change* (Westport, CT: Greenwood Press, 1976).

parens patriae
The legal philosophy justifying state intervention in the lives of children when their parents are unable or unwilling to protect them.

endorsement in the case *Ex parte Crouse* (1838). Mary Ann Crouse had been committed to the Philadelphia House of Refuge by her mother against her father's wishes. Mary Ann's father contested his daughter's placement, arguing that she was being punished even though she had committed no criminal offense. However, the Pennsylvania Supreme Court ruled that Mary Ann's placement was legal because (1) the purpose of the Philadelphia House of Refuge was to reform youths, not to punish them, (2) formal due-process protections provided to adults in criminal trials were unnecessary because Mary Ann was not being punished, and (3) when parents were unwilling or unable to protect their children, the state had a legal obligation to do so.[16]

However, the right of the state to intervene in the lives of children did not go unchallenged. In *People v. Turner* (1870), for example, the Illinois Supreme Court ruled that Daniel O'Connell, who was committed to the Chicago House of Refuge against both his parents' wishes, was being punished and not helped by his placement. The court also decided that because placement in the house of refuge actually was punishment, due-process protections were necessary.[17] The ruling, together with increasing concern over the willingness or ability of the criminal courts to protect or control youths, led reformers in Chicago to consider other mechanisms by which their aims might be achieved. The mechanism they created was the first juvenile court, which was established in Chicago in 1899 by passage of the Juvenile Court Act in Illinois.[18] Some scholars argue that the Juvenile Court Act was a means for the child savers, intent on salvaging poor children—especially poor immigrant children—to get around the *Turner* decision's requirement of due-process protections for youths.

The Operation of Early Juvenile Courts   The Juvenile Court Act of 1899 gave the Chicago juvenile court broad jurisdiction over persons under the age of 16 who were delinquent, dependent, or neglected. In addition, the act required:

1. The court to be overseen by a special judge.
2. Hearings to be held in a separate courtroom.
3. Separate records to be kept of juvenile hearings.[19]

It also made probation a major component of the juvenile court's response to offenders and emphasized the use of informal procedures at each stage of the juvenile court process. Indeed, this informality has been a hallmark of the juvenile court since its beginning, a key feature distinguishing it from criminal court proceedings. The major reason for this informality is that the juvenile court has traditionally focused not on the act, but on the *whole child*.

In practice, the informality of the juvenile court allowed complaints against children to be made by almost anyone in the community. It also allowed juvenile court hearings to be held in offices, instead of in traditional courtrooms, and to be closed to the public, unlike criminal trials, which were open to the public. In the typical juvenile court hearing, the only persons present were the judge, the parents, the child, and the probation officer, who met and discussed the case. Also, few (if any) records were kept of hearings, proof of guilt was not necessary for the court to intervene in children's lives, and little or no concern for due process existed. Finally, judges exercised wide

Daniel O'Connell

Like Mary Ann Crouse, who was committed by her mother against her father's wishes, Daniel O'Connell was institutionalized even though he had committed no criminal offense. He was placed in the house of refuge because he was perceived to be in danger of becoming a pauper or a criminal. However, Daniel's case differed from Mary Ann's because both his parents objected to his placement and, even more important, because the court ruled that Daniel's placement was harmful, not helpful.

▲ The use of informal procedures is characteristic of the juvenile court system. *Are the juvenile court's informal procedures desirable? Why or why not?*

discretion in how they dealt with children, ranging from a warning to placement in an institution.[20]

The idea of a juvenile court spread rapidly after the passage of the Juvenile Court Act. Within a decade, ten states had established special courts for children, and by 1925 all but two states had juvenile courts.[21] Moreover, those juvenile courts followed closely the model developed in Chicago of an informal court intended to "serve the best interests of children."

Despite the growing popularity of the new courts, they did not go completely unchallenged. In the case *Commonwealth v. Fisher* (1905), for example, the Pennsylvania Supreme Court again examined the juvenile court's mission, the right to intervene, and the due-process protections owed to children. In this case, Frank Fisher, a 14-year-old male, was indicted for larceny and committed to the house of refuge until his 21st birthday. Frank's father objected to his placement, claiming that Frank's seven-year sentence for a minor offense was more severe than he would have received in criminal court.[22]

In its ruling, the Pennsylvania Supreme Court upheld the idea of the juvenile court, and in many respects repeated the arguments it had made in the *Crouse* decision. The court found that the state may intervene in families when parents are unable or unwilling to prevent their children from engaging in crime, and that Frank was being helped by his placement in the house of refuge. It further ruled that due-process protections were unnecessary when the state acted under its *parens patriae* powers.[23]

The *Fisher* case set the legal tone for the juvenile court from its beginnings until the mid-1960s, when new legal challenges began to be mounted. Those legal challenges attempted primarily to expand juveniles' due-process protections. Critics of the juvenile courts recognized that despite their expressed goal of "serving the best interests of children," the established institutions of juvenile justice often did the opposite.

The Legal Reform Years: The Juvenile Court after *Gault*

The 1960s and 1970s provided the social context for a more critical assessment of American institutions, including juvenile justice. Beginning in the mid-1960s and continuing though the mid-1970s, a number of cases decided by the U.S. Supreme Court altered the operation of the juvenile court. The most important of those cases was *In re Gault*, which expanded the number of due-process protections afforded juveniles within the juvenile court. However, a number of other cases also helped define juveniles' rights within juvenile justice and contributed to the legal structure found in juvenile courts today. The first of those cases was *Kent v. United States* (1966).

In re

The Latin phrase *in re* in the description of court cases (for example, *In re Gault*) means, literally, "in the matter of" or "concerning." It is used when a case does not involve adversarial parties.

Morris Kent was a 16-year-old juvenile on probation who was transferred to criminal court to stand trial on charges of robbery and rape. Although the juvenile court judge received several motions from Kent's attorney opposing the transfer, he made no ruling on them. Further, after indicating that a "full investigation" had been completed, the juvenile court judge transferred Kent to criminal court for trial.[24] Thus, an important decision had been made, the decision to try Kent as an adult, even though no hearing had been held. Kent's attorney had no opportunity to see or to question material that had been used to make the decision to transfer jurisdiction, and no reasons for the court's decision were given.

The *Kent* case is important for several reasons. It was the first major ruling by the U.S. Supreme Court that closely examined the operation of the juvenile courts. It also made clear the need for due-process protections for juveniles who were being transferred to criminal court for trial. The Court noted that even though a hearing to consider transfer to criminal court is far less formal than a trial, juveniles are still entitled to some due-process protections. Specifically, the Court ruled that before a juvenile court could transfer a case to criminal court, there must be a hearing to consider the transfer, the defendant must have the assistance of defense counsel if requested, defense counsel must have access to social records kept by the juvenile court, and the reasons for the juvenile court's decision to transfer must be stated.[25]

Having given notice that it would review the operations of the juvenile court, the Supreme Court, within a year of the *Kent* decision, heard another landmark case. This case, *In re Gault* (1967), went far beyond the ruling in *Kent* in its examination of juvenile court practices. The *Gault* case is important because it extended a variety of due-process protections to juveniles. In addition, the facts of the case clearly demonstrate the potential for abuse in the informal practices of the traditional juvenile court.

Gerald Gault was 15 years old when he, along with a friend, was taken into custody by the Gila County, Arizona, sheriff's department for allegedly making an obscene phone call to a neighbor, Ms. Cook. At the time of his arrest, Gerald was on six-months probation as a result of his presence when another friend had stolen a wallet from a woman's purse. Without notifying his mother, a deputy took Gerald into custody on the oral complaint of Ms. Cook and transported him to the local detention unit.

When Ms. Gault heard Gerald was in custody, she went to the detention facility. The superintendent of the facility told her that a juvenile court hearing would be held the next day. On the following day, Gerald, his mother, and the deputy who had taken Gerald into custody appeared before the juvenile court judge in chambers. The deputy had filed a petition alleging that Gerald was delinquent. Ms. Cook, the complainant, was not present. Without being informed that he did not have to testify, Gerald was questioned by the judge about the telephone call and was sent back to detention. No record was made of this hearing, no one was sworn, and no specific charge was made, other than an allegation that Gerald was delinquent. At the end of the hearing, the judge said he would "think about it." Gerald was released a few days later, although no reasons were given for his detention or release.

Juvenile Courts

Each state has at least one court with juvenile jurisdiction, but only in a few states is it called juvenile court. Other names include district, superior, circuit, county, family, or probate court. Regardless of the name, courts with juvenile jurisdiction are generally referred to as juvenile courts.

SOURCE: Howard N. Snyder and Melissa Sickmund, *Juvenile Offenders and Victims: 1999 National Report.* U.S. Department of Justice, National Center for Juvenile Justice, Office of Juvenile Justice and Delinquency Prevention (Washington, DC: GPO, September 1999) p. 99.

adjudication
The juvenile court equivalent of a trial in criminal court, or the process of rendering a judicial decision regarding the truth of the facts alleged in a petition.

On the day of Gerald's release, Ms. Gault received a letter indicating that another hearing would be held a few days later about Gerald's delinquency. The hearing was held and, again, the complainant was not present. Again, there was no transcript or recording of the proceedings, and what was said was later disputed by the parties. Neither Gerald nor his parent was advised of a right to remain silent, a right to be represented by counsel, or any other constitutional rights. At the conclusion of the hearing, Gerald was found delinquent and was committed to the state industrial school until he was 21 years old, unless released earlier by the court. This meant that Gerald received a sentence of up to six years for an offense that if committed by an adult, would have been punished by a maximum sentence of two months in jail and a $50 fine.

When the case finally reached the Supreme Court, the Court held that a youth has procedural rights in delinquency hearings where there is the possibility of confinement in a state institution. Specifically, the Court ruled that juveniles have a right against self-incrimination, a right to adequate notice of charges against them, a right to confront and to cross-examine their accusers, and a right to assistance of counsel. In addition, the Court's ruling implied that juveniles also have the rights to sworn testimony and appeal.

The landmark *Gault* decision was not the last Supreme Court decision to influence juvenile court procedures. The Supreme Court further expanded protections for juveniles three years after *Gault*. In a 1970 case, *In re Winship*, the Court ruled that delinquency charges must be proven beyond a reasonable doubt where there was a possibility that a youth could be confined in a locked facility. Until the *Winship* ruling, the standard of proof typically employed at the adjudication stage of the juvenile justice process was a preponderance of the evidence, the level of proof employed in civil proceedings. **Adjudication** is the juvenile court equivalent of a trial in criminal court, or the process of rendering a judicial decision regarding the truth of the facts alleged in a petition. Under the preponderance-of-the-evidence standard of proof, juveniles could be adjudicated delinquent (found guilty) if the weight of the evidence was slightly against them, a much lower standard of proof than the standard required in criminal courts.

It is important to note that both the *Gault* and *Winship* decisions not only increased procedural formality in juvenile court cases, but also shifted the traditional focus from the "whole child" to the child's act. Once this shift occurred, it was only a short step to offense-based sentencing and the more punitive orientation that is characteristic of the juvenile justice system today.

The Supreme Court's extension of due-process protections to juveniles slowed in the year following the *Winship* decision. In a 1971 ruling, *McKeiver v. Pennsylvania*, the Court held that juveniles were not entitled to a trial by jury. The Court cited several reasons for the decision:

1. The Court did not want to turn the juvenile court into a fully adversarial process.
2. The Court determined that bench trials could produce accurate determinations.
3. The Court felt that it was too early to completely abandon the philosophy of the juvenile court and its treatment mission.

To grant juveniles all of the protections accorded adults, the Court surmised, would make the juvenile court indistinguishable from the criminal court.

The continued informality of the juvenile court may explain why very few youths contest charges against them and why a surprising number of youths who are not adjudicated delinquent (found guilty) are placed on probation. Indeed, most youths who appear before the juvenile court admit to the charges against them.[26] Moreover, data collected by the National Center for Juvenile Justice indicate that in 1997, 23 percent of youths who were not adjudicated delinquent in juvenile courts were still placed on some form of probation (see also Figure 13–3 on page 497).[27]

Today, juveniles have been granted many, but not all, of the due-process protections given adults in criminal trials. However, the daily operation of juvenile courts calls into question the extent to which court-mandated changes in juvenile justice procedures have influenced the traditional informality of the juvenile court. Juvenile court procedures are still characterized by an informality that most people would find unacceptable if it were applied to adults in criminal court.

CRIMINAL JUSTICE Online

Juvenile Justice by State

Go to cj.glencoe.com to access the Web site for the National Center for Juvenile Justice to find descriptive information and analyses of the various juvenile justice systems in the United States. Compare your state's juvenile justice system to that of another state. *How are the two states similar? Different?*

▲ In the 1967 landmark case of *In re Gault,* Supreme Court Justice Abe Fortas wrote that, "Due process of law is the primary and indispensable foundation of individual freedom." *Do you agree with Justice Fortas? Why or why not?*

13.1 CRITICAL THINKING

1. Should youths in juvenile court proceedings be granted the same due-process protections as adults in criminal trials? Why or why not?

2. Historically, what do you think was the most significant change in the treatment of juvenile offenders? How did the change occur?

13.2 The Processing of Juvenile Offenders

Juvenile delinquency in the United States is widespread, and people respond to it both formally and informally. Informal responses consist of actions taken by members of the public that do not rely on official agencies of juvenile justice. Formal responses, on the other hand, rely on official agencies of juvenile justice such as the police and juvenile court. Figure 13–1 on page 490 depicts the stages in the formal juvenile justice process. Before providing a detailed examination of the formal juvenile justice process, however, the informal juvenile justice process is briefly discussed.

The Informal Juvenile Justice Process

An examination of the juvenile justice process usually begins with the police, and the police do play a critical role in juvenile justice. However, any discussion of the juvenile justice process should really begin with the public, because police involvement with juveniles is typically the result of citizen complaints.

The informal actions taken by citizens to respond to delinquency constitute an **informal juvenile justice** process that operates outside the official agencies of juvenile justice. Many illegal behaviors by juveniles are handled informally by neighbors, business owners, teachers, and others who are not part of the formal juvenile justice apparatus. The informal processing of juveniles is important because it is one of the mechanisms that operates to control youths' behavior. The more citizens rely on informal control and the more effective it is, the less necessary the formal processing of juveniles becomes.

Although many delinquent actions are handled informally, in other instances members of the public decide to call the police or the juvenile court and to request action from the formal agencies of juvenile justice. Thus, most youths become involved in the formal juvenile justice process when the

informal juvenile justice
The actions taken by citizens to respond to juvenile offenders without involving the official agencies of juvenile justice.

Illegal Behavior

Although few juveniles commit serious violent crimes, self-report studies show that most juveniles have engaged in some type of illegal behavior. For example, a 1998 national survey of high school seniors revealed that more than 74 percent of them had consumed alcohol illegally during the last 12 months, and 52 percent of them had consumed alcohol illegally within the previous 30 days.

SOURCE: Kathleen Maguire and Ann L. Pastore (eds.), *Sourcebook of Criminal Justice Statistics 1998.* U.S. Department of Justice, Bureau of Justice Statistics (Washington, DC: GPO, 1999), p. 233, Table 3.72 and p. 234, Table 3.73.

▲ Teachers are an important part of the informal juvenile justice process. *What can teachers do to keep students from becoming delinquent?*

people who make up the informal process decide, in their discretion, to involve the police or the juvenile court. This means that some combination of the public and the police plays a major role in determining who the clientele of juvenile justice will be.

The Formal Juvenile Justice Process

The police represent the primary gatekeepers to the formal juvenile justice process. For example, in 1997, 85 percent of delinquency cases referred to the juvenile courts came from police agencies.[28] This percentage has remained about the same for more than a decade. In the case of status offenses, however, the percentage of cases referred from police agencies varies greatly by offense. In 1997, for example, 94 percent of status liquor law violation cases were referred by police agencies to the juvenile courts, while only 40 percent of cases of running away, 11 percent of ungovernability (being beyond the control of parents or guardians) cases, and 8 percent of truancy cases were referred from police agencies.[29] **Status offenses,** as you may recall, are acts that are not crimes when committed by adults but are illegal for minors.

status offenses
Acts that are not crimes when committed by adults but are illegal for minors (for example, truancy or running away from home).

The Police Response to Juveniles Like citizens, the police exercise discretion in handling juvenile cases. Typical responses that police officers may employ are to:

1. Warn and release
2. Refer to parents
3. Refer to a diversionary program operated by the police or another community agency
4. Refer to court

In some communities, an officer may have a variety of options, while in other communities available options are more limited.

Describing the typical police response to juveniles in trouble is difficult because there is considerable variation in the ways individual officers approach juvenile offenders. A number of factors influence the ways police officers handle juvenile suspects. Among those factors are:

1. The seriousness of the offense
2. The police organization
3. The community
4. The wishes of the complainant
5. The demeanor of the youth
6. The gender of the offender
7. The race and social class of the offender

MYTH ••• FACT ••••••

The commission of serious, violent crime by juveniles is widespread.

In 1998, there were 370 arrests for every 100,000 juveniles 10 to 17 years of age for murder and nonnegligent manslaughter, forcible rape, robbery, and aggravated assault. If each of those arrests involved a different juvenile (which is very unlikely), then fewer than one-half of one percent of all persons aged 10 to 17 in the United States were arrested for one of those four crimes in 1998.[30]

489

FIGURE 13–1

The Formal Juvenile Justice Process

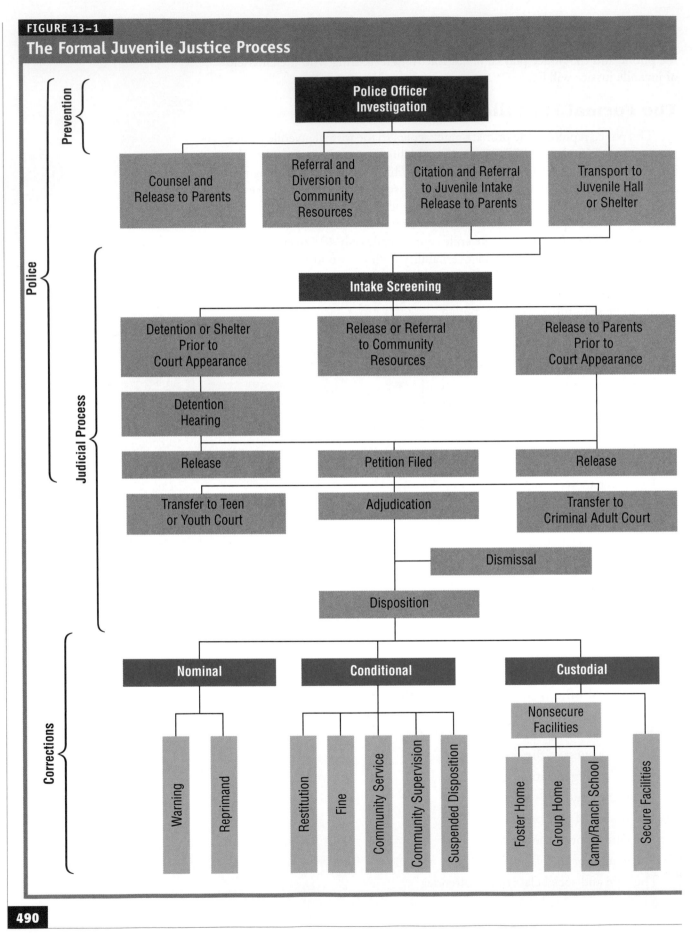

Offense Seriousness   The most important factor in the decision to arrest is the seriousness of the offense. Regardless of the subject's demeanor or other factors, as the seriousness of the offense increases, so does the likelihood of arrest. Most police-juvenile encounters involving felony offenses result in an arrest. However, most police-juvenile encounters involve minor offenses. When offenses are minor, a number of other factors have been found to influence police decision making.

The Police Organization   As described in Chapter 6, police departments develop their own particular styles of operation. Those styles, in turn, help structure the way officers respond to juvenile offenders. For example, in one study that categorized police departments by the extent to which they employed a legalistic style of policing, characterized by a high degree of professionalism and bureaucratic structure, it was discovered that officers in most legalistic departments were more likely to arrest juvenile suspects than were officers in less legalistic departments.[31] Thus, the ways that police department personnel respond to juvenile offenders is to some extent a product of the organizational characteristics and policies developed by their individual departments. However, police departments do not operate in a political and social vacuum. They are also influenced by the communities in which they operate.

The Community   Communities influence policing in a variety of ways. Through their interactions with residents of a community, police develop assumptions about the communities they police, the people who live in those communities, and the ability and willingness of community residents to respond to crime and delinquency. Research suggests that police operate differently in lower-class communities than in wealthier communities. Police expect lower-class communities to have higher levels of crime and delinquency because more arrests are made in those communities and because they know that lower-class communities have fewer resources with which to respond informally to the array of problems experienced there. Consequently, when police have contact with juveniles in lower-class communities, formal responses become more likely because informal responses are believed to be ineffective in most cases. Indeed, research that has examined the effect of neighborhood socioeconomic status has found that as the socioeconomic status of the neighborhood increases, the likelihood that a police-juvenile encounter will end in arrest declines.[32]

The Wishes of the Complainant   As noted earlier, many police-juvenile interactions occur because of a citizen complaint to the police. What police do in those situations often depends on whether the complainant is present, what the complainant would like the police to do, and, sometimes, who the complainant is.

The Demeanor of the Youth   As one might expect, how youths behave toward the police can influence whether an arrest is made. Interestingly, youths who are either unusually antagonistic or unusually polite are more likely to be arrested. In contrast, youths who are moderately respectful to the police are less likely to be arrested—as long as the offense is not serious.[33]

Juveniles and Curfew

Juvenile arrests for curfew and loitering violations increased 178 percent between 1989 and 1998. In 1998, 27 percent of curfew arrests involved juveniles under the age of 15 and 30 percent involved females.

SOURCE: Howard N. Snyder, *Juvenile Arrests 1998* (Washington, DC: OJJDP, December 1999).

▲ A juvenile's demeanor can influence arrest decisions. *How would you advise a juvenile to act if he or she is stopped by a police officer?*

The Gender of the Offender   Gender also appears to influence the decision to arrest, particularly when status offenses are involved. A number of studies have found that female status offenders are more likely to be formally processed than male status offenders.[34]

When it comes to criminal offenses, however, research results are mixed. Some of the research shows that girls are less likely than boys to be arrested for criminal offenses, even when prior record and seriousness of offense are taken into account.[35] Other research suggests that any gender bias that existed in the past has diminished or disappeared.[36]

The Race and Social Class of the Offender   There is strong evidence that a juvenile's race and social class influence police decision making. The evidence is clear that minority and poor youths are represented disproportionately in arrest statistics. For example, according to 1999 UCR data, white youths accounted for 72 percent of all arrests of persons under 18 years of age. They accounted for 69 percent of arrests for index property offenses and about 57 percent of arrests for index violent offenses. In contrast, African-American youths accounted for about 25 percent of all arrests of persons under 18 years of age, 27 percent of index property-crime arrests, and approximately 41 percent of index violent-crime arrests. Other racial groups accounted for the remainder of arrests of persons under 18 years of age.[37] Thus, although white youths account for the majority of juvenile arrests, African-American youths are arrested in disproportionate numbers, since they comprise only 15.5 percent of the U.S. population under 18 years of age.[38]

The UCR does not report arrests by social class. However, self-report data reveal that the prevalence of delinquency (that is, the proportion of the youth population involved in delinquency) does not differ significantly between social classes when all types of offenses are considered. In other words, the proportions of middle-class and lower-class youths who engage in delinquency are similar. However, when different types of offenses are examined, significant social class differences appear. Middle-class youths have higher rates of involvement in such offenses as stealing from their families, cheating on tests, cutting classes, disorderly conduct, and drunkenness. Lower-class youths, on the other hand, have higher rates of involvement in more serious offenses, such as felony assault and robbery.[39]

Police Processing of Juvenile Offenders   When a police officer encounters a juvenile who has committed an illegal act, the officer must decide what to do. One option is to make an arrest. (In some jurisdictions, this is referred to as "taking into custody.") For practical purposes, an arrest takes place whenever a youth is not free to walk away.

As a general rule, the basis for arresting a juvenile is the same as for arresting an adult. An officer needs to have probable cause. There are, however, several differences between arrests of adults and juveniles. First, the police can arrest juveniles for a wider range of behaviors. For example, juveniles, but not adults, can be arrested for status offenses. (Technically, juveniles are not "arrested" for status offenses, because such offenses are not crimes. Also, because status offenses are not crimes, the apprehension of juveniles for status offenses does not require probable cause.) Second, at least in some jurisdictions, juveniles are given the *Miranda* warnings in the presence of a parent, guardian, or attorney. This is not necessary, however, because the Supreme Court, in *Fare v. Michael C.* (1979), ruled that parents or attorneys do not have to be present for juveniles to waive their rights. Third, in many jurisdictions, juveniles are more likely than adults who have committed similar offenses to be detained pending adjudication. In *Schall v. Martin* (1984), the Supreme Court ruled that preventive detention of juveniles is acceptable.

Concern about the detention of juveniles generally focuses on the use of preventive detention. Some critics argue that it amounts to punishment before a youth has been found guilty of an offense. The conditions juveniles are sometimes exposed to in detention units and adult jails raise additional concerns.

The exact procedures that the police must follow when taking a juvenile into custody vary from state to state and are specified in state juvenile codes. However, those codes typically require officers to notify a juvenile's parents that the juvenile is in custody. Police often ask parents to come to the police station. Sometimes, an officer transports a youth home prior to any questioning. When an officer feels that detention of a juvenile is appropriate, the juvenile is transported to a juvenile detention facility. If such facilities are not available, the youth may be taken to an adult jail in some jurisdictions. In cases where a juvenile is released to his or her parents, the juvenile and the parents are informed that they will be contacted by the court at a later date about the case. After a juvenile is released, an officer completes the complaint, collecting any additional information needed, and then forwards it to the next stage of the juvenile justice process for further action. When a juvenile is detained in a juvenile detention facility or an adult jail, the processing of the complaint is expedited because juvenile codes require a detention hearing (and therefore, a specific complaint) to determine the appropriateness of detention.

Juvenile Arrests

The National Center for Juvenile Justice estimates that almost one-third of all juveniles will have arrest records by the time they reach 18 years of age.

SOURCE: Gary F. Jensen and Dean Rojek, *Delinquency and Youth Crime*, 2d ed. (Prospect Heights, IL: Waveland Press, 1992), p. 5.

Juveniles and Jail

On a typical day in 1999, 9,458 juveniles were confined in adult jails in the United States—a 311 percent increase from 1990. In states that allow the jailing of juveniles, statutes usually prevent youths from being placed in cells with adults. This means that jail administrators must provide separate rooms and supervision for juveniles within their facilities. For juveniles, separation often means isolation, which is in turn related to an increased risk of self-destructive behavior. A national study found that the suicide rate for juveniles in adult jails was almost five times the suicide rate for juveniles in the general population, and nearly eight times the suicide rate of juveniles in juvenile detention facilities.

SOURCE: Allen J. Beck, "Prison and Jail Inmates at Midyear, 1999," US Department of Justice, Bureau of Justice Statistics Bulletin (Washington, DC: GPO, April 2000), p. 6, Table 6. Community Research Center, *An Assessment of the National Incidence of Juvenile Suicide in Adult Jails, Lockups, and Juvenile Detention Centers.* (Champaign, IL: Community Research Center, 1980).

radical nonintervention
A practice based on the idea that youths should be left alone if at all possible, instead of being formally processed.

Trends in Police Processing of Juveniles   In 1998, approximately 70 percent of all juveniles taken into police custody were referred to juvenile court, about 22 percent were handled within the police department and released, and nearly 7 percent were referred to adult or criminal courts.[40] However, an examination of such data over time reveals a trend toward increased formal processing of cases (referral to court) by police agencies. For example, in 1972, approximately 51 percent of youths taken into custody by the police were referred to the juvenile court, 45 percent were handled within the police department and released, and only about 1 percent were referred to criminal courts. Figure 13–2 on page 495 shows that there has been a trend toward:

1. Referring more youths to juvenile court.
2. Handling fewer cases within police departments.
3. Referring more cases to criminal courts.

Diversion   The goal of juvenile diversion programs is to respond to youths in ways that avoid formal juvenile justice processing. Diversion can occur at any stage of the juvenile justice process, but it is most often employed before adjudication.

Diversion programs are based on the understanding that formal responses to youths who violate the law, such as arrest and adjudication, do not always protect the best interests of the youths or the community. Consequently, efforts to divert youths *from* the juvenile justice process by warning and releasing them, as well as efforts to divert youths *to* specific diversionary programs, such as counseling, have long been a part of juvenile justice practice. This is especially true for status offenders. Since the enactment of the Juvenile Justice and Delinquency Act of 1974, which stipulated that status offenders not be placed in secure detention facilities or secure correctional facilities, the number of status offenders diverted from formal juvenile justice processing has increased dramatically.

Today, diversion strategies are of two basic types. Some diversion strategies are based on the idea of radical nonintervention. Other strategies are designed to involve youths, and possibly parents, in a diversionary program. **Radical nonintervention** is based on the idea that youths should be left alone if at all possible, instead of being formally processed. The police practice of warning and releasing some juvenile offenders is an example of radical nonintervention. The practice of referring juveniles to community agencies for services such as individual or family counseling is an example of a strategy that involves youths in a diversionary program.

Contemporary diversion programs are operated by both juvenile justice and community agencies. Interventions employed in those programs include providing basic casework services to youths; providing individual, family, and group counseling; requiring restitution; and imposing community service.

Detention   Sometimes a youth is held in a secure detention facility during processing. There are three primary reasons for this practice: (1) to protect the community from the juvenile, (2) to ensure that the juvenile appears at a subsequent stage of processing, and (3) to secure the juvenile's own safety. In 1997, juveniles were held in detention facilities at some point between

FIGURE 13-2

Percentage Distribution of Juveniles Taken Into Police Custody, by Method of Disposition

	Referred to Juvenile Court Jurisdiction	Handled Within Department and Released	Referred to Criminal or Adult Court	Referred to Other Police Agency	Referred to Welfare Agency
1972	50.8%	45.0%	1.3%	1.6%	1.3%
1973	49.5	45.2	1.5	2.3	1.4
1974	47.0	44.4	3.7	2.4	2.5
1975	52.7	41.6	2.3	1.9	1.4
1976	53.4	39.0	4.4	1.7	1.6
1977	53.2	38.1	3.9	1.8	3.0
1978	55.9	36.6	3.8	1.8	1.9
1979	57.3	34.6	4.8	1.7	1.6
1980	58.1	33.8	4.8	1.7	1.6
1981	58.0	33.8	5.1	1.6	1.5
1982	58.9	32.5	5.4	1.5	1.6
1983	57.5	32.8	4.8	1.7	3.1
1984	60.0	31.5	5.2	1.3	2.0
1985	61.8	30.7	4.4	1.2	1.9
1986	61.7	29.9	5.5	1.1	1.8
1987	62.0	30.3	5.2	1.0	1.4
1988	63.1	29.1	4.7	1.1	1.9
1989	63.9	28.7	4.5	1.2	1.7
1990	64.5	28.3	4.5	1.1	1.6
1991	64.2	28.1	5.0	1.0	1.7
1992	62.5	30.1	4.7	1.1	1.7
1993	67.3	25.6	4.8	0.9	1.5
1994	63.2	29.5	4.7	1.0	1.7
1995	65.7	28.4	3.3	0.9	1.7
1996	68.6	23.3	6.2	0.9	0.9
1997	66.9	24.6	6.6	0.8	1.1
1998	69.2	22.2	6.8	0.9	1.0

Note: Because of rounding, percentages may not add to 100.

SOURCE: Sourcebook of Criminal Justice Statistics Online. www.albany.edu/sourcebook/1995/pdf/t426.pdf Table 4.26.

intake screening
The process by which decisions are made about the continued processing of juvenile cases. Decisions might include dismissing the case, referring the youth to a diversion program, or filing a petition.

petition
A legal form of the police complaint that specifies the charges to be heard at the adjudication.

transfer, waiver, or certification
The act or process by which juveniles who meet specific age, offense, and (in some jurisdictions) prior-record criteria are transferred to criminal court for trial.

referral to court and case disposition in 19 percent of all delinquency cases disposed. The percentage of juveniles detained during processing has not changed very much since 1988.[41] Federal rules require that a juvenile who is detained in an adult jail or lockup be held for no more than six hours and in a separate area out of sight or sound of adult inmates.[42]

Intake Screening   When the decision to arrest a youth is made, or a social agency such as a school alleges that an offense has occurred, the next step in the juvenile justice process is **intake screening.** The purpose of intake screening is to make decisions about the continued processing of cases. Those decisions and others made during juvenile court processing of delinquency cases in 1997 are shown in Figure 13–3 on page 497. The location of the intake screening and the educational background and training of the person who conducts it vary from jurisdiction to jurisdiction. Traditionally, intake screening has been performed by probation officers. However, in recent years there has been a move toward involving the prosecuting attorney in the intake process. In fact, in some jurisdictions, such as Colorado and Washington, intake screening is now the responsibility of the prosecuting attorney's office.[43] In other states, such as Michigan, intake screening is done by an intake officer (probation officer) who works for the juvenile court, although the prosecuting attorney's office reviews most complaints for legal sufficiency.

Possible intake decisions might include dismissing the case or having youths and parents in for a conference or an informal hearing to collect additional information for making the intake decision. Other decisions include referral of the youth to a diversion program (for example, informal probation or counseling at a community agency), filing a **petition** (a legal form of the police complaint that specifies the charges to be heard at the adjudication), and waiver or transfer of the case to criminal court.

As in police decision making, a number of factors have been found to influence intake screening decisions. For example, youths who have committed serious offenses, those with prior records, and those who are uncooperative are more likely to have petitions filed. In addition, lower-class minority males, at least in some jurisdictions, are more likely than other groups to receive more formal responses at intake. Finally, there is considerable evidence that female status offenders are likely to be treated more harshly at intake than are their male counterparts, at least in some jurisdictions.[44]

Transfer, Waiver, or Certification to Criminal Court
Since the early days of the juvenile court, state legislatures have given juvenile court judges statutory authority to transfer certain juvenile offenders to criminal court. In some jurisdictions, transfer is called waiver or certification. **Transfer, waiver,** or **certification** may occur in cases where youths meet certain age, offense, and (in some jurisdictions) prior-record criteria. For example, in North Carolina, waiver may occur if a youth has reached 13 years of age and has committed a felony. In Michigan, a juvenile must be 14 years of age and must have committed one of a number of felonies specified by law. In many states, before a youth is transferred to an adult criminal court, a separate transfer or waiver hearing must be conducted to determine the waiver's appropriateness.

FIGURE 13-3

Juvenile Court Processing of Delinquency Cases, 1997, National Estimates

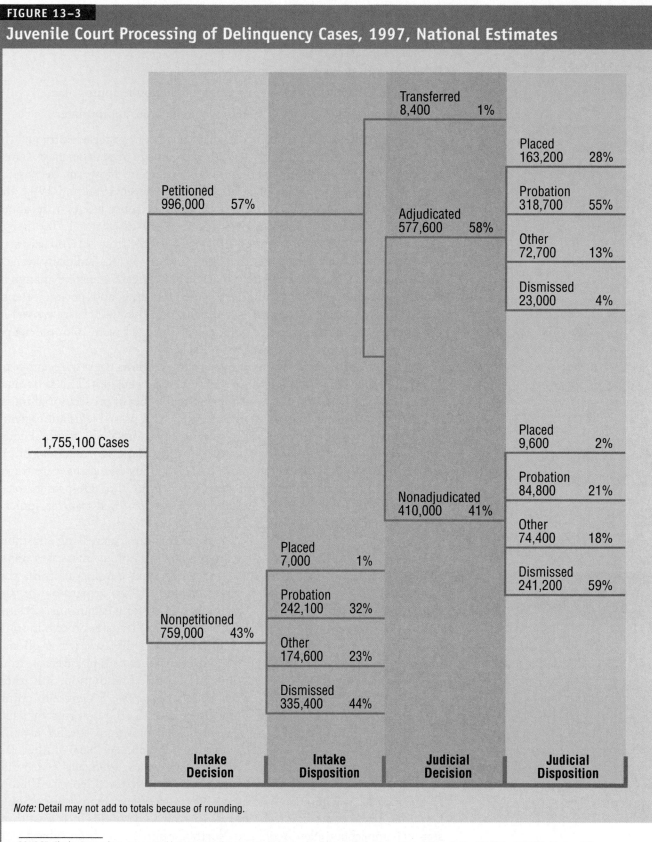

1,755,100 Cases

Petitioned
996,000   57%

Transferred
8,400   1%

Adjudicated
577,600   58%

Placed
163,200   28%

Probation
318,700   55%

Other
72,700   13%

Dismissed
23,000   4%

Nonadjudicated
410,000   41%

Placed
9,600   2%

Probation
84,800   21%

Other
74,400   18%

Dismissed
241,200   59%

Nonpetitioned
759,000   43%

Placed
7,000   1%

Probation
242,100   32%

Other
174,600   23%

Dismissed
335,400   44%

Intake Decision   **Intake Disposition**   **Judicial Decision**   **Judicial Disposition**

Note: Detail may not add to totals because of rounding.

SOURCE: Charles Puzzanchera, Anne L. Stahl, Terrence A. Finnegan, Howard N. Snyder, Rowen S. Poole, Nancy Tierney, *Juvenile Court Statistics 1997* (Washington, DC: U.S. Department of Justice, Office of Juvenile Justice and Delinquency Prevention, May, 2000), p. 9., Figure 2.

The judicial waiver process varies from state to state, but at the typical waiver hearing, probable cause must be shown. In addition, in many states the prosecutor must show that:

1. The youth presents a threat to the community.
2. Existing juvenile treatment programs would not be appropriate.
3. Programs within the adult system would be more appropriate.

Historically, judicial transfer authority has been exercised infrequently. For example, between 1988 and 1997, the percentage of petition cases transferred to criminal court remained around one percent. However, because of changes in the total number of petition cases between 1988 and 1997, the number of delinquency cases waived by juvenile court judges rose about 75 percent between 1988 and 1994 (from 6,700 cases to 11,700 cases), then dropped 28 percent between 1994 and 1997 (from 11,700 cases to 8,400 cases). The net result was that the number of cases judicially waived was 25 percent higher in 1997 than in 1988. The greatest relative change in waived cases between 1988 and 1997 was for drug and person offense cases (78 percent and 74 percent, respectively). In the 8,400 cases waived in 1997, 95 percent of the juveniles were male, 87 percent were 16 or older, and 50 percent were white (46 percent were black).[45]

The number of juvenile cases transferred to criminal court in recent years is actually much larger than the aforementioned data suggest. This is because there are no national statistics available on the number of prosecutorial transfers. Prosecutorial transfers occur in states that have passed legislation giving prosecutors discretion to file certain juvenile cases directly in criminal court when a youth meets certain age, offense, and (in some jurisdictions) prior-record criteria. In Florida alone, more than 7,000 juvenile cases were transferred to criminal court in fiscal year 1995–1996 through prosecutorial transfer. Today, because of the availability of prosecutorial transfer, judicial waiver is almost never used in Florida.[46]

Besides the increasing number (though not rate) of juvenile cases transferred, additional developments in this area include (1) an expansion of the number of transfer mechanisms, (2) simplification of the transfer process in some states, including the *exclusion* of offenders charged with certain offenses from juvenile court jurisdiction, or their *mandatory* or *automatic waiver* to criminal court, and (3) the lowering by some states of the maximum age for juvenile court jurisdiction. As part of that last development, since 1995, all 17-year olds in at least ten states (Georgia, Illinois, Louisiana, Massachusetts, Michigan, Missouri, New Hampshire, South Carolina, Texas, and Wisconsin) and all 16- and 17-year olds in at least three states (Connecticut, New York, and North Carolina) have been subject only to criminal court jurisdiction. Additionally, in many states, juveniles who have been convicted as adults must be prosecuted in criminal court for any

MYTH

Greater use of transfer or expansion of transfer criteria will reduce crime because of the adult sanctions that will be applied.

FACT

Youths transferred to criminal court are more likely to commit further crimes than others retained in the juvenile justice system. There is no evidence that transfer has any deterrent effect.[47]

subsequent offenses (the "Once an adult, always an adult" provision). Those developments reflect a shift in many jurisdictions toward a more punitive orientation toward juvenile offenders.[48]

The Adjudication Hearing   When a petition is filed at intake and the case is not transferred to criminal court, the next step is adjudication. As noted previously, adjudication is the juvenile court equivalent of a trial in criminal court. In some states, such as Michigan, adjudication is now called a trial. It is at adjudication, moreover, that a juvenile begins to develop an official court record.

Before adjudication can take place, several preliminary actions are necessary. A petition must be filed, a hearing date must be set, and the necessary parties (such as the youth, the parents, and witnesses) must be given notice of the hearing. Notice is typically given through a summons or subpoena. A summons, which is an order to appear in court, is issued to the youth; copies are also given to the parents or guardians. The summons specifies the charges and the date, time, and location of the hearing, and it may list the youth's rights, such as a right to an attorney. Subpoenas are issued to witnesses, instructing them to appear on a certain day, time, and place to provide testimony or records.

When charges specified in the petition are contested by a juvenile and the juvenile is represented by an attorney, another critical event often takes place before adjudication—a plea bargain. Plea bargaining, including its problems, was discussed in detail in Chapter 8. Although the extent of plea bargaining in juvenile justice is unknown, it is believed to be a common practice in many juvenile courts.

There are two types of adjudications: contested ones (in which juveniles dispute the charges) and uncontested ones. Contested adjudications are similar to trials in criminal courts, which were described in Chapter 8. They typically employ the same rules of evidence and procedure. Most contested adjudications are bench adjudications, in which the hearing officer—a judge, referee, court master, or commissioner—makes a finding of fact based on the evidence presented. A **hearing officer** is a lawyer, empowered by the juvenile court to hear juvenile cases. In some jurisdictions, contested adjudications are jury trials. However, as noted earlier in this chapter, juveniles do not have a constitutional right to a jury trial, and even in states that give juveniles the right to a jury trial, jury trials are rare.

Like their criminal court counterparts, the vast majority of juvenile court adjudications are uncontested. Uncontested adjudications are generally brief and consist of a reading of the charges, advice of rights, and possibly brief testimony by the youth or other parties, such as a probation officer. After this, the youth, or frequently the youth's attorney, admits the charges. In some states, an uncontested adjudication is called an arraignment.

The majority of cases that are not adjudicated are dismissed. Surprisingly, however, many juveniles whose cases are neither adjudicated nor dismissed are still placed on informal probation or treated in some other way. For example, of the estimated 410,000 delinquency cases filed but not adjudicated in 1997, 59 percent were dismissed. In 21 percent, the juvenile was placed on informal probation, and the remaining 20 percent were disposed of in other ways (see Figure 13–3 on page 497). However, the majority of cases

Plea Bargaining

In a recent nationwide study of plea bargaining in juvenile courts, it was found that "much of the country has either not addressed at all or has not fully developed standards regarding the guilty plea process in juvenile court." It was also discovered that there was considerable variability in the ways that plea bargaining was carried out in various courts. For example, urban courts were more likely to institute formal procedures to regulate plea bargaining than were suburban or rural courts.

SOURCE: Joseph B. Sanborn, Jr. "Pleading Guilty in Juvenile Court," *Justice Quarterly,* Vol. 9 (1992), pp. 127–50.

hearing officer
A lawyer empowered by the juvenile court to hear juvenile cases.

▲ Uncontested adjudications are generally brief. At the end, the youth or the youth's attorney admits the charges. *Why do you suppose most adjudications are uncontested?*

Juvenile Court Cases

The number of juvenile court cases increased 48 percent between 1988 and 1997, to more than 1.7 million cases. The increase for homicides between 1988 and 1997 was 31 percent (2,000 cases in 1997); for forcible rape, 48 percent (6,500 cases in 1997); for aggravated assault, 66 percent (67,900 cases in 1997); and for robbery, 55 percent (33,400 cases in 1997).

SOURCE: Puzzanchera et al., *Juvenile Court Statistics 1997,* (Washington, DC: GPO, May 2000), p. 5, table 1, US Department of Justice

in which petitions are filed are adjudicated. In 1997, for example, 58 percent of the delinquency cases in juvenile courts were adjudicated (see Figure 13–3). Although 58 percent may not seem like a large percentage, keep in mind that many cases not adjudicated still receive some court supervision, such as informal probation.

Recently, a relatively small number of juvenile offenders (65,000 nationwide in 1998) have been adjudicated in teen courts or youth courts instead of juvenile courts or adult courts.[49] Teen courts or youth courts are a new way of dealing with relatively young and usually first-time offenders charged with offenses such as theft, misdemeanor assault, disorderly conduct, and possession of alcohol. In 1998, there were between 400 and 500 teen court programs in the United States, up from about 50 in 1991.

Teen courts are based on one of four models:

1. Adult judge—An adult serves as judge and rules on legal matters and courtroom procedure. Youths serve as attorneys, jurors, clerks, bailiffs, etc.

2. Youth judge—Similar to the adult judge model, but a youth serves as judge.

3. Tribunal—Youth attorneys present the case to a panel of three youth judges, who decide the appropriate disposition for the defendant. A jury is not used.

4. Peer jury—This model does not use youth attorneys; the case is presented to a youth jury by a youth or adult. The youth jury then questions the defendant directly.

Nearly half of all teen courts use the adult judge model.

Most teen courts do not determine guilt or innocence. Rather they serve as diversion alternatives and youths must admit to the charges against them to qualify for teen court. The most common disposition used in teen court cases is community service. Other frequently used dispositions included

Juvenile Probation Officer

My name is Kelly Webster. I am a deputy probation officer (P.O.) with Los Angeles County Probation Department. I work at Camp Scott, a boot camp housing females ages 12–19. Camp Scott is the only female boot camp in L.A. County. Minors sentenced to camp are wards of the court and spend from four months to a year incarcerated. They are sentenced to camp for any crime leading up to attempted murder, so their sentences vary.

To become a P.O., a four-year degree is required, in any subject. I have a B.A. in social welfare from the University of California, Berkeley. However, I never intended on becoming a social worker. My interest has always been in the criminal justice system. I became a P.O. by looking into county job openings upon completing my undergraduate degree. The Probation Department had an opening as a detention services officer in juvenile hall. I worked there for a year before promoting to a P.O.

The only difference in the two jobs is the degree required, because of the court report writing.

I work a 56-hour shift, meaning that I work two days and then I have four and a half days off; I sleep at work for two nights. My routine consists of supervising approximately 115 minors at all times. Because camp is structured like the military, I wear fatigues, as do the minors. Minors must ask permission to speak, salute me when walking by, and march around the facility calling cadences.

During the week, the minors are in school. On the weekends, they are cleaning, receiving visits on Sunday, or writing letters in the dormitory. They do physical training every day and twice on the weekend.

When I am not with the whole group, I have time assigned to counsel my own caseload. I am responsible for about five minors at a time. I write court reports when the minor is scheduled for release, informing the judge of the minor's behavior in camp. I recommend release or more time, depending on how they have progressed. Camp's philosophy is family reunification, so I have as much contact with the minor's family as possible.

What I like most about being a juvenile P.O. is the ability to affect some minors. What I like least about the job is that some of these "hardened" children cannot be helped. It is difficult to hear about what some of these children have endured.

Which aspects of this job would you find most difficult? Why?

---

victim apology letters, apology essays, teen court jury duty, drug/alcohol classes, and monetary restitution.

Disposition   **Disposition** is the juvenile court equivalent of sentencing in criminal court. At the disposition hearing, the court makes its final determination of what to do with the juvenile officially labeled delinquent. Some of the options available to juvenile courts are probation, placement in a diversion program, restitution, community service, detention, placement in foster care, placement in a long-term or short-term residential treatment program, placement with a relative, and placement with the state for commitment to a state

disposition
The juvenile court equivalent of sentencing in criminal court. At the disposition hearing, the court makes its final determination of what to do with the juvenile officially labeled delinquent.

facility. In addition, the court may order some combination of those dispositions, such as placement on probation, restitution, and a short stay in detention. However, disposition possibilities are limited by the available options in a particular jurisdiction. In a few jurisdictions, they are also limited by statutory sentencing guidelines. In practice, the disposition options available to most juvenile courts are quite narrow, consisting of probation or incarceration. When incarceration is used, an indeterminate period of commitment or incarceration is the norm.[50]

As part of the disposition, the court also enters various orders regarding the youth's behavior. Those orders consist of rules the youth must follow. Also, the court may enter orders regarding parents, relatives, or other people who live in the home. For example, the court may order parents to attend counseling or a substance abuse treatment program, a boyfriend to move out of the house, or parents to clean up their house and pay for court costs or services provided, such as counseling caseworker services. If parents fail to follow those orders, at least in some jurisdictions, they may be held in contempt of court and placed in jail.

In making the disposition, the hearing officer usually relies heavily on a presentence investigation report (sometimes called a predisposition report), which is completed by a probation officer or an investigator before the disposition. Presentence investigation reports for criminal courts were described in detail in Chapter 9.

The most frequently used disposition in juvenile courts is probation, followed by placement. In 1997, for example, approximately 55 percent of the youths adjudicated delinquent were placed on probation; 28 percent received some type of commitment. Relatively few delinquency cases received other dispositions or were released after adjudication (see Figure 13–3 on page 497).

Because of recent heightened concerns about violent juvenile offenders, many states have legislatively redefined the juvenile court's mission by deemphasizing the goal of rehabilitation and stressing the need for public safety, punishment, and accountability in the juvenile justice system. Along with this change in purpose has been a fundamental philosophical change in the focus of juvenile justice, from offender-based dispositions to offense-based dispositions, which emphasize punishment or incapacitation instead of rehabilitation. These changes are reflected in new disposition or sentencing practices, including (1) the use of *blended sentences,* which combine both juvenile and adult sanctions, (2) the use of mandatory minimum sentences for specific types of offenders or offense categories, and (3) the extension of juvenile court dispositions beyond the offender's age of majority, that is, lengthening the time an offender is held accountable in juvenile court.[51]

13.2 CRITICAL THINKING

Which do you think is a better way to handle juvenile crime—the informal or formal process? Why?

13.3 Correctional Programs for Juveniles

As noted, when youths are adjudicated, a number of disposition options are available to juvenile courts, although the options typically used in any one jurisdiction are fairly narrow. Three general types of dispositions are:

1. Dismissal of the case, which is used in a small percentage of cases.
2. The use of a community-based program.
3. The use of an institutional program.

Because both community-based and institutional correctional programs for adults were the subjects of previous chapters of this book, only the features of those programs that are unique to juveniles will be discussed in the following sections.

Community-Based Correctional Programs for Juveniles

Among the community-based correctional programs for juvenile offenders are diversion, pretrial release, probation, foster care, group home placement, and parole. Some of those programs are designed to provide services to youths in their own homes, while others provide services to youths who have been removed from their homes, at least for short periods of time. Moreover, although all community-based programs are intended to control offenders and provide sanctions for their behavior, they are also designed to accomplish a variety of additional objectives. Those objectives include allowing youths to maintain existing ties with the community, helping them restore ties and develop new and positive ones with the community (reintegration), avoiding the negative consequences of institutional placement, providing a more cost-effective response to offenders, and reducing the likelihood of recidivism. Some of the community-based correctional programs for juveniles are examined in the following sections.

Probation   Probation is the most frequently used correctional response for youths who are adjudicated delinquent in juvenile courts. Although the actual practice of juvenile probation varies from one jurisdiction to the next, probation officers usually perform four important roles in the juvenile justice process:

1. They perform intake screening.
2. They conduct presentence investigations.
3. They supervise offenders.
4. They provide assistance to youths placed on probation.

In some jurisdictions, all of those roles are performed by the same individual. In other jurisdictions, each probation officer specializes in only one of the roles.

A recent trend in juvenile probation is the development of intensive-supervision (probation) programs, which in some jurisdictions involves home

FYI

Nathanial Abraham

On January 13, 2000, 13-year-old Nathaniel Abraham, the youngest American ever convicted of murder as an adult, was sentenced by a family court judge in Pontiac, Michigan, to a seven-year term at a maximum-security juvenile facility. The sentence allows Abraham to be released when he turns 21. In sentencing Abraham, who at age 11 shot and killed a stranger, the judge criticized the growing tendency of the U.S. judicial system to treat children as adults. He believed that the boy had a chance of being rehabilitated.

SOURCE: *Facts on File: World News Digest with Index,* Vol. 60, No. 3094, March 23, 2000, p. 196; "Young killer gets another chance," *The Orlando Sentinel* (January 14, 2000), p. A-3.

confinement. Intensive-supervision programs are intended to ensure regular contact between probationers and probation officers. They are also intended to serve as an intermediate response that is more restrictive than standard probation but less restrictive than incarceration. However, like standard probation programs, the frequency of contact between probation officers and probationers varies considerably.[52]

Although there is wide variation in the meaning of intensive supervision, there is some indication that programs that provide frequent supervision of offenders, as well as services, are as effective as incarceration at reducing recidivism.[53] The same research also suggests that intensive-supervision programs are more cost-effective than incarceration, provided they actually divert a sizable number of youths from institutions.

A recent trend in intensive supervision of juveniles is the use of home confinement, which began to be used with juvenile offenders in the 1970s[54] and has grown in popularity since that time. Today, home confinement programs use two mechanisms to monitor youths: frequent probation officer contacts and electronic monitoring. Electronic monitoring requires an offender to wear a tamper-resistant electronic device that automatically notifies the probation department if the juvenile leaves home or another designated location.

The use of home confinement employing electronic monitoring of juvenile offenders began in the 1980s and has grown substantially.[55] However, because electronic monitoring technology is diverse, rapidly developing, and relatively new, little evidence of its effectiveness exists. Still, there are good reasons that some jurisdictions find electronic monitoring attractive:

1. It eases the problem of detention overcrowding.

2. It allows youths to participate in counseling, education, and vocational programs without endangering public safety.

3. It allows youths to live with supervision in a more natural environment than an institution.

4. It allows court workers to better assess the ability of youths to live in the community under standard probation after they leave the program.[56]

Besides probation, juvenile courts in some jurisdictions employ several other types of community-based interventions with juvenile offenders, such as restitution or community service programs, wilderness probation programs, and day treatment programs. In practice, probation is often combined with one of those other community-based interventions.

Restitution　　Restitution programs, as you may recall, require offenders to compensate victims for damages to property or for physical injuries. The primary goal of restitution programs is to hold youths accountable for their actions. In practice, there are three types of restitution:

1. *Monetary restitution,* a cash payment to the victim for harm done.

2. *Victim-service restitution,* in which the youth provides some service to the victim.

3. *Community-service restitution,* in which the youth provides assistance to a community organization.

CRIMINAL JUSTICE *Online*

OJJDP

Visit the Office of Juvenile Justice and Delinquency Prevention Web site to review the various programs offered by the organization. *Which programs do you think would help deter juvenile crime?*

Despite the growing popularity of juvenile restitution programs, as well as some programs' effective reduction of recidivism, there are potential problems with some of those programs. Problems include poorly managed, informal programs with low compliance rates; high recidivism rates in some programs; and hearing officers' ordering restitution that it is unrealistic to expect juveniles to complete. There is also a potential for net-widening, and restitution requirements can be subject to discretionary abuse; some jurisdictions, however, have established restitution guidelines to remedy this problem. Thus, rather than achieving the goals of accountability, offender treatment, and victim compensation, restitution programs may fail to protect community safety. Moreover, they are likely to produce negative perceptions of juvenile justice by both offenders and victims.

Wilderness Probation (Outdoor Adventure) Programs

Wilderness probation or outdoor adventure programs for juvenile offenders are based, in part, on ideas derived from programs such as Outward Bound. (Outward Bound is a company that sells outdoor experiences such as mountain climbing, backpacking, and mountain biking.) A basic assumption of those programs is that learning is best accomplished by acting in an environment where there are consequences for one's actions. Consequently, the programs involve youths in a physically and sometimes emotionally challenging outdoor experience intended to help them develop confidence in themselves, learn to accept responsibility for themselves and others, and develop a relationship of trust with program staff. This is done by engaging youths in a variety of activities, such as camping, backpacking, rock climbing, canoeing, sailing, negotiating rope courses, and a solo experience (spending one or more nights alone in the wilderness).[57]

Evaluations of several wilderness probation programs have shown that they can produce positive effects, such as increases in self-esteem and a decrease in criminal activity both during and after the program.[58] However,

Wilderness Probation

You can learn more about wilderness probation programs by accessing The Hope for Youth Web site from the link at cj.glencoe.com. *What do you think are some of the benefits and drawbacks of wilderness probation?*

▲ Some juvenile treatment programs strive to provide physically and emotionally challenging experiences to help youthful offenders gain confidence and learn responsibility for their actions. *What are the benefits and drawbacks of these kinds of programs?*

research also indicates that the positive effects of the programs may diminish over time or may be no greater than the effects produced by probation programs that provide regular and meaningful contacts between probation officers and probationers.[59]

Day Treatment Programs   Day treatment programs for juvenile offenders operate in a number of jurisdictions around the United States. The programs often target serious offenders who would otherwise be candidates for institutionalization. They provide treatment or services to youths during the day and allow them to return home at night. Because they are viewed as alternatives to incarceration, they are believed to be cost-effective. Because they provide highly structured programs for youths during the day, it is assumed that they protect community safety as well. The range of services or treatments can be quite varied and may include academic remediation, individual and group counseling, job skills training, job placement, and social-skills training. Although some evidence suggests that day treatment programs are as effective as, or more effective than, institutional placement, some programs may be no more effective at reducing recidivism than standard probation.[60]

Foster Homes   Foster homes are out-of-home placements intended to resemble, as much as possible, a family setting. Foster parents are licensed to provide care for one or more youths (usually one to three) and are paid a daily rate for the costs of care. Foster placement is often used by a court when a youth's home life has been particularly chaotic or harmful. In such a case, foster care is used to temporarily separate the youth from the parents or guardian in an effort to resolve the problems that resulted in the youth's removal. Foster homes are also used to remove youths from particular neighborhoods and for some nonviolent offenders instead of more restrictive placements, such as institutionalization. When used in those ways, they are considered "halfway-in programs." In other instances, foster homes are used as transitions to home and are considered "halfway-out programs."

Although foster homes are widely used by juvenile courts in some jurisdictions, there are few sound evaluations of their effectiveness. The limited research that exists indicates that foster care is generally not effective and may even be counterproductive.

Group Homes   Similar to foster homes, group homes are open, nonsecure community-based facilities used in both "halfway-in programs" and "halfway-out programs." However, they are somewhat larger and frequently less family-like than foster homes. The purpose of many group homes is to avoid requiring youths to accept "substitute parents," because many youths are in the process of developing emotional independence from parental figures. Nevertheless, group homes are generally less impersonal than institutions and are less expensive than institutional placements. In addition, their location allows residents to take advantage of community services. Youths who live in group homes usually go to school in the home or in the community or work in the community. Treatment typically consists of group or individual counseling provided by group-home staff or outside counselors.

Group Homes

Although group homes are used extensively in juvenile justice, relatively little sound recent research has examined their effectiveness. One well-known, but older, study of a group home program, the Silverlake Experiment, found that youths placed in the program for approximately six months were no more likely to commit further crimes than similar youths who were randomly assigned to an institutional placement. In other words, placement in the program was neither more nor less effective than institutionalization at reducing recidivism.

Aftercare Programs   Aftercare involves the provision of services to assist youths in successfully making the transition from juvenile institutions to life back in the community. The services are the same as those provided by other types of community-based programs and may include foster care, shelter or group-home placement, home placement, or efforts to help youths live on their own. Parole, too, is one form of aftercare.

Unfortunately, the quality of many aftercare programs is questionable, and in some cases, youths fail to receive any services after institutional release. As in probation, parole supervision, in practice, may involve very little contact between parole officers and parolees. Moreover, large caseloads carried by aftercare workers may prevent the provision of meaningful services.

Institutional Programs for Juveniles

A variety of correctional institutions house juveniles within the United States, including detention centers, adult jails, shelter facilities (some of them more community based), reception and diagnostic centers, ranches, forestry camps, farms, and training schools. These institutions hold a variety of youths, including those who are status offenders as well as those who have committed violent offenses against others. They are administered by either state or local governments or by private agencies.

Juvenile Correctional Institutions   What distinguishes institutional programs from their community-based counterparts is that institutional programs typically restrict youths' access to the community more than community-based programs do. Indeed, institutional programs are the most restrictive placements available to juvenile courts. However, juvenile institutions vary in the extent to which they focus on custody and control.

For example, some juvenile institutions employ a variety of security hardware: perimeter fencing or walls, barbed or razor wire, and surveillance and detection devices, such as motion detectors, sound monitors, and security cameras. Those juvenile institutions, classified as secure facilities, closely monitor residents' movement within the facility and restrict residents' access to the community. Most public and private detention centers, reception and diagnostic centers, and state training schools are secure facilities. In contrast, other juvenile institutions rely much less on security devices. Those facilities have no perimeter fencing, and some do not lock entrances or exits at night. Classified as open institutions, they rely more heavily on staff than on physical security. Most private facilities, as well as most public shelters, ranches, forestry camps, and farms, are open institutions.[61]

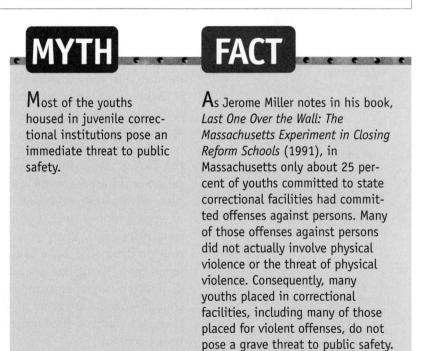

MYTH

Most of the youths housed in juvenile correctional institutions pose an immediate threat to public safety.

FACT

As Jerome Miller notes in his book, *Last One Over the Wall: The Massachusetts Experiment in Closing Reform Schools* (1991), in Massachusetts only about 25 percent of youths committed to state correctional facilities had committed offenses against persons. Many of those offenses against persons did not actually involve physical violence or the threat of physical violence. Consequently, many youths placed in correctional facilities, including many of those placed for violent offenses, do not pose a grave threat to public safety.

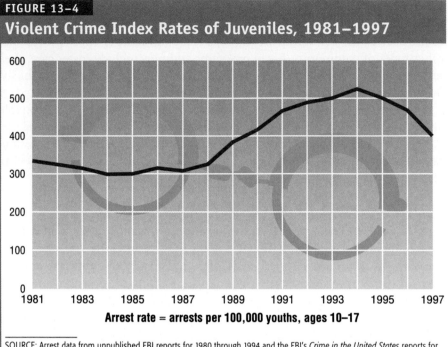

FIGURE 13-4

Violent Crime Index Rates of Juveniles, 1981–1997

Arrest rate = arrests per 100,000 youths, ages 10–17

SOURCE: Arrest data from unpublished FBI reports for 1980 through 1994 and the FBI's *Crime in the United States* reports for 1995, 1996, and 1997 and population data from the Bureau of the Census for 1980 through 1989 from *Current Population Reports*, P25–1095, and for 1990 through 1997 from *Estimates of the population of States by age, sex, race, and Hispanic origin: 1990–1997* [machine-readable data files].

Public versus Private Facilities

There is considerable variation between the average time youths spend in public facilities and the average time they spend in private facilities. There is also variation by status. For example, in 1997, the average stays in public facilities were 192 days for committed youths, 37 days for detained youths, and 25 days for voluntarily committed youths. The average stays in private facilities, in contrast, were 174 days for committed youths, 70 days for detained youths, and 195 days for voluntarily committed youths.

SOURCE: Howard N. Snyder and Melissa Sickmund, *Juvenile Offenders and Victims: 1999 National Report.* U.S. Department of Justice, National Center for Juvenile Justice, Office of Juvenile Justice and Delinquency Prevention (Washington, DC: GPO, September 1999), p. 202.

In addition to differences in the use of security hardware, juvenile correctional institutions also differ in a number of other ways. Some of the institutions are privately operated institutions, although the majority are public institutions. The majority of both private and public institutions are small, housing 40 or fewer residents, although some large, state-operated institutions have a legal capacity of 800 or more. Some institutions are coed; others are single-gender institutions.

Institutions also differ in the average length of time that residents stay in the facility. Typically, youths stay longer in private facilities than in public facilities. However, some private and public facilities are for short-term placements, while others are for long-term placements. Institutions such as detention centers and diagnostic and reception centers are typically for short-term placements. Detention centers usually house youths awaiting adjudication or those who have been adjudicated and are awaiting disposition. In some cases, youths are placed in those institutions for a period of time as a disposition. Other institutions, such as ranches, forestry camps, farms, and training schools, are generally for long-term placements. Youths are placed in them as a result of disposition or possibly assessment at a reception and diagnostic center.

Juvenile institutions also differ in types of programming and quality of care. Almost all juvenile correctional institutions offer basic educational and counseling programs for their residents. Moreover, more than half of all institutions offer family counseling, employment counseling, peer group meetings, a point system, or behavioral contracts. However, there is considerable variability in the extent to which institutions offer more specialized educational or counseling programs for clients and the extent to which residents participate in the programs. For example, fewer than half of all institutions offer vocational training, GED courses, tutoring, suicide prevention, or programs for special offender types, such as violent offenders, sex offenders, or drug offenders.[62]

An examination of the history of juvenile institutions reveals that children have often been subjected to abuse and inhumane treatment in juvenile correctional institutions. Certainly, the overall quality of institutional life in correctional facilities today is vastly improved over that experienced by most youths placed in houses of refuge and early reform and training schools. Many juvenile institutions are administered by competent, caring, and professional administrators, who oversee skilled and caring staff in delivering a variety of high-quality services to their residents. Yet, many of the problems that have historically plagued juvenile correctional institutions are still evident. In the most comprehensive study ever undertaken of the conditions of confinement in American juvenile correctional facilities, researchers found a number of widespread problems. Conducted between 1990 and 1992, this study found overcrowding that resulted in the following substantial deficiencies: a lack of adequate living space, security practices that resulted in escapes or injuries to residents, inadequate health care for residents, and inadequate mechanisms for controlling suicidal behavior. In addition, the study discovered that such "deficiencies were distributed widely across facilities."[63]

Despite the long history of juvenile correctional institutions, there is surprisingly little information on the effectiveness of this response to juvenile offenders. Moreover, what is known is not encouraging. Although there is some indication that effective institutional programs for juveniles exist,[64] the bulk of the evidence indicates that many juvenile institutions have little effect on recidivism. For example, a review of the re-arrest rates of youths released in states that rely heavily on institutions found that the percentage of youths re-arrested ranged from 51 percent to more than 70 percent.[65] The results may not be surprising, considering the quality of life in many juvenile institutions.

Boot Camps

In response to the significant increase in juvenile arrests and repeat offenses from the mid-1980s to the mid-1990s, a few states and many localities have established juvenile boot camps, modeled after adult boot camps. Evaluations of three juvenile boot camp pilot projects found that program completion rates were high, academic skills improved, and many participants found jobs during aftercare. However, none of the projects reduced recidivism. For one of them, recidivism among participants was greater than among juvenile offenders confined in traditional juvenile correctional facilities.

SOURCE: Eric Peterson, "Juvenile Boot Camps: Lessons Learned," U.S. Department of Justice, Office of Juvenile Justice and Delinquency Prevention, Fact Sheet #36 (Washington, DC: GPO, June 1996).

▲ Historically, large juvenile institutions have proven ineffective at preventing youths from offending again. *What do you think could be done to make these institutions more effective?*

FYI

Correctional Facility Conditions

A recent survey of 984 detention centers, training schools, ranches, farms, and camps holding 65,000 juveniles found that only 20 to 26 percent had adequate bed space, health care, security, or suicide control. The survey discovered that more than 11,000 juveniles committed 18,000 acts of attempted suicide, suicidal gestures, or self-mutilation, and that institutions frequently failed to provide appropriate housing for suicidal juveniles. Nearly half the facilities exceeded their design capacity, and only 24 percent of detained youths were in places that met all living-space standards.

SOURCE: Dale J. Parent, Valerie Leiter, Stephen Kennedy, Lisa Livens, Daniel Wentworth, and Sarah Wilcox, *Conditions of Confinement: Juvenile Detention and Corrections Facilities Research Summary* (Washington, DC: OJJDP, 1994) p. 5.

Recent Trends in Juvenile Incarceration

Among recent trends in juvenile incarceration are (1) its increased use (at least until recently), (2) the use of both public and private facilities, (3) the disproportionately large percentage of males and racial or ethnic minorities that are incarcerated, and (4) the increasing number of juveniles being incarcerated in local adult jails and state prisons. Incarceration has become an increasingly popular response to delinquency, though that trend may be moderating somewhat. For example, as of October 29, 1997 (the latest date for which data were available), nearly 106,000 juvenile offenders were held in residential placement facilities, down slightly from the approximately 109,000 held in 1995.[66] The juvenile incarceration rate (the number of juveniles incarcerated in relation to the size of the juvenile population) decreased, from about 382 (per 100,000 youths aged 10–17) in 1995 to approximately 368 in 1997. The District of Columbia had the highest juvenile incarceration rate in 1997 (662 per every 100,000 juveniles in the population), while Vermont had the lowest (70).

Ninety-three percent of juveniles placed in residential facilities in 1997 committed delinquency offenses; only seven percent committed status offenses. The delinquency offenses included violent person offenses (25 percent of all offenses for which juveniles were incarcerated), other person offenses (8 percent), property offenses (30 percent), drug offenses (9 percent), and public order offenses (21 percent). Furthermore, whether a juvenile was placed in a public or private facility depended primarily on whether a delinquency or status offense was committed. Of the juveniles who were placed for delinquency offenses, 75 percent were placed in public facilities and 25 percent were placed in private facilities. Conversely, of the juveniles placed for status offenses, 26 percent were placed in public facilities and 74 percent were placed in private facilities. However, states varied greatly in the extent to which they used public or private residential facilities. At one extreme, Mississippi placed 99 percent of its juvenile offenders in public facilities; at the other extreme, Massachusetts placed 64 percent of its juvenile offenders in private facilities.

A disproportionately large percentage of males and racial or ethnic minorities are incarcerated in juvenile facilities. Although juvenile males comprised half of the U.S. juvenile population aged 10-17 in 1997, 86 percent of all juveniles incarcerated in 1997 were males. However, females were much more likely than males to be incarcerated for status offenses (23 percent of females versus 4 percent of males). Nearly half of all females incarcerated for status offenses (45 percent) were placed in private as opposed to public facilities.

As for racial and ethnic minorities, in 1997, minorities (that is, nonwhites) comprised 34 percent of the American population aged 10–17. Yet, minorities accounted for more than 60 percent of all juveniles in custody in 1997. About two-thirds (67 percent) of all juveniles in public facilities and more than half (55 percent) of all juveniles in private facilities in 1997 were members of minority groups. Figure 13–5 on page 514 illustrates the racial and ethnic composition of public and private juvenile incarceration facilities in 1997. Whites are underrepresented in both public and private facilities, blacks are overrepresented in both, Hispanics are overrepresented in public facilities and are underrepresented in private facilities, Asians and Pacific Islanders are underrepresented in both, and Native Americans are overrepresented in private facilities and represented proportionally in public facilities. The Juvenile Justice and Delinquency Prevention Act of 1974, as amended, requires states to determine whether minorities are disproportionately represented in confinement. If overrepresentation is found, the state must reduce it.

MYTH A new type of violent juvenile offender, one for whom violence is a way of life—a "superpredator"—emerged in the late 1980s and early 1990s.

FACT Although evidence shows that in the early 1990s, juvenile arrest rates for violent crimes broke out of their historic range and increased to a level greater than in previous generations, the evidence also shows that by 1995 arrest rates for juvenile violence had returned to a level comparable to that of a generation ago. Ironically, because of the myth of the "superpredator," nearly every state legislature made it easier to handle juveniles as adult offenders.[68]

Juveniles have also been increasingly held in local adult jails and state prisons. Those juveniles are not included in the aforementioned total of approximately 106,000 juveniles who were incarcerated. In 1997, local adult jails held 9,100 juveniles, an increase of 35 percent from 1994. Seven thousand of the juveniles were being held as adults, and 2,100 were being held as juveniles. Another 5,600 juveniles were being held in adult prisons in 1997. Three-quarters of those juveniles were 17 years old.

In conclusion, as juvenile justice in the United States enters the twenty-first century, several important problems remain unresolved. Many of the problems are the same ones that have plagued juvenile justice since the first specialized institutions for children were established in the early 1800s. The problems include:

1. Providing adequate due-process protections to youths at all stages of the juvenile justice process.

2. Continuing to build on knowledge of effective correctional interventions and developing a range of effective and humane correctional responses, from diversion to institutional aftercare programs.

3. Eliminating the abusive treatment of youths placed in correctional programs.

4. Working out the appropriate balance between community-based and institutional correctional programs.

5. Conducting rigorous evaluations of juvenile justice agencies and programs.

6. Recognizing the limits of correctional responses in solving the juvenile crime problem.

7. Working out an appropriate balance between preventing and correcting delinquency.

FYI

New Prison for Females

In 2000, Florida opened its first maximum security prison devoted to women ages 13 to 21. The prison, surrounded by razor wire and concrete walls, houses about 50 females who have committed crimes such as murder, armed robbery, drug dealing, and prostitution, as well as some women who have suffered physical and sexual abuse. The goal is to rehabilitate girls. The girls must attend school and therapy sessions during their 18-month to three-year stays. Previously, one year was the longest sentence that could be imposed on a girl committed to a juvenile justice program.

SOURCE: "Girls get a prison of their own," *The Orlando Sentinel* (March 21, 2000) p. D-3.

FIGURE 13–5

Racial and Ethnic Composition of Inmate Population of Public and Private Juvenile Incarceration Facilities, 1997

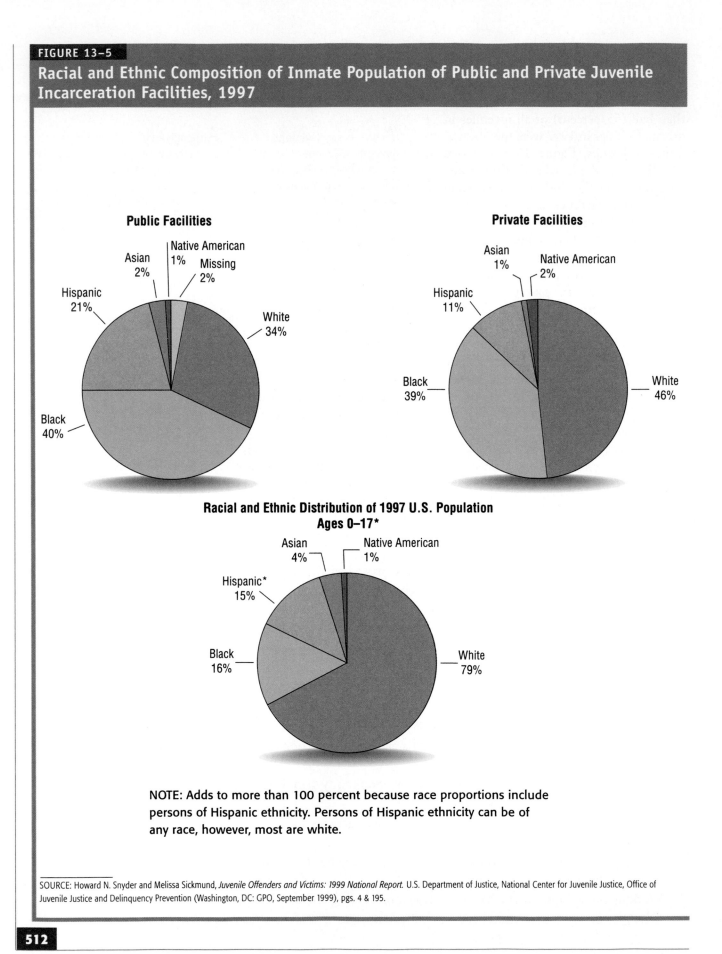

Public Facilities

Native American
1% Missing
2%

Asian
2%

Hispanic
21%

White
34%

Black
40%

Private Facilities

Asian
1% Native American
2%

Hispanic
11%

Black
39%

White
46%

Racial and Ethnic Distribution of 1997 U.S. Population Ages 0–17*

Asian
4% Native American
1%

Hispanic*
15%

Black
16%

White
79%

NOTE: Adds to more than 100 percent because race proportions include persons of Hispanic ethnicity. Persons of Hispanic ethnicity can be of any race, however, most are white.

SOURCE: Howard N. Snyder and Melissa Sickmund, *Juvenile Offenders and Victims: 1999 National Report.* U.S. Department of Justice, National Center for Juvenile Justice, Office of Juvenile Justice and Delinquency Prevention (Washington, DC: GPO, September 1999), pgs. 4 & 195.

BARJ Coordinator

My name is Donald J. Haldemann. I am the balanced and restorative justice (BARJ) coordinator for the Delaware County Juvenile Court in Southeastern Pennsylvania. I also supervise our Victim Services Unit with a staff of six. I have a bachelor's in history, a master's in administration of justice, and a juris doctor from Widener Law School in Delaware.

I worked with 1,300 juveniles as a juvenile probation officer for 21 years before embarking on the quest for restorative justice. In 1995, Pennsylvania's Juvenile Act was amended to include the concept of restorative justice. Slowly, with grant money from the Pennsylvania Commission on Crime and Delinquency, individual counties hired restorative justice specialists and I jumped at the opportunity to join this elite fraternity. So what is restorative justice and how can you join the movement?

A crime is considered to be an offense against the "State" under the traditional model but restorative justice views crime as a harm against individual victims and the community. Offenders need to accept responsibility for the harm they have caused and participate in victim and community restoration.

On a daily basis my job consists largely of educating my staff, criminal justice professionals, social agencies, schools, and communities on restorative justice and how it can be a win/win proposition for all stakeholders in the process.

I can't possibly list all the positives about my job. I get to promote a philosophy of justice which is based on practices used in cultures all over the world for hundreds of years. What I find most difficult about my job is the reluctance of many criminal justice "players" to welcome a new way of looking at crime, opting instead to hang on to a process which has served no one's best interest. Offenders have not been helped to accept responsibility, victims have been ignored, and communities have been trained to believe that crime is a government problem and not their concern.

If you are thinking about becoming a restorative justice coordinator, I recommend you take a restorative justice training like the one sponsored by Florida Atlantic University in partnership with the National Institute of Corrections. The more exposure you have to restorative justice philosophy and practitioners, the better.

Do you share this BARJ coordinator's enthusiasm for this philosophy of justice? Why or why not?

13.3 CRITICAL THINKING

1. Which of the community-based correctional programs described in the chapter (e.g., restitution, wilderness probation, and day treatment) do you think would be most effective at rehabilitating youths? Why?

2. What do you think are the pros and cons of institutional programs for juveniles?

Review and Applications

1. Describe Some of the Early Institutions Used to Respond to Wayward and Criminal Youths

Among the early institutions used to respond to wayward and criminal youths were houses of refuge, placing out, reform schools, industrial schools, and training schools.

2. Explain the Effects of Some Landmark U.S. Supreme Court Cases on the Juvenile Justice System

Landmark Supreme Court cases on juvenile justice include *Ex parte Crouse, People v. Turner, Commonwealth v. Fisher, Kent v. United States, In re Gault, In re Winship,* and *McKeiver v. Pennsylvania.* Some of the effects of those cases on juvenile justice are the right to adequate notice of charges, protection against compelled self-incrimination, the right to confront and to cross-examine accusers, and the right to the assistance of counsel.

3. Identify and Describe Factors that Influence the Ways that Police Process Juvenile Cases

Among the factors that influence the ways that police process juvenile cases are (1) the seriousness of the offense, (2) the community, (3) the wishes of the complainant, (4) the demeanor of the youth, (5) the gender of the offender, (6) the race and social class of the offender, and (7) the police organization.

4. Summarize the Rationale for the Use of Diversion in Juvenile Justice

Diversion programs in juvenile justice are based on the understanding that formal responses to youths who violate the law, such as arrest and adjudication, do not always protect the best interests of children or the community. Indeed, some formal responses may be harmful to many youths and may increase the likelihood of future delinquent behavior. This is because formal processing may cause youths to develop negative or delinquent self-images, may stigmatize youths in the eyes of significant others, or may subject youths to inhumane treatment.

5. Describe the Adjudication Hearing in Juvenile Justice

There are two types of adjudication: contested ones (in which juveniles dispute the charges) and uncontested ones. Contested adjudications are similar to trials in criminal courts. Most contested adjudications are bench adjudications, in which the hearing officer makes a finding of fact based on the evidence presented. In some jurisdictions, contested adjudications are jury trials. At an uncontested adjudication hearing, the youth, or frequently the youth's attorney, admits to the charges. The vast majority of juvenile court adjudications are uncontested.

6. Describe the Disposition Hearing and the Types of Dispositions Available to the Juvenile Court

The disposition is the juvenile court equivalent of sentencing in criminal court. At the disposition hearing, the court makes its final determination of what to do with the youth who is officially labeled delinquent. At the disposition, the court also enters various orders regarding the youth's behavior. Those orders consist of various rules the youth must follow. Also, the court may enter orders regarding parents, relatives, or other people who live in the home.

7. Identify the Types and Describe the Effectiveness of Community-Based Correctional Programs for Juveniles

Community-based correctional programs include diversion, pretrial release, probation, foster care, group home placements, and parole. Evaluations of some programs indicate that they are effective at reducing recidivism or that they are as effective as institutional placement. In contrast, evaluations of other community-based programs indicate that they have little effect on subsequent offenses.

8. Summarize Recent Trends in Juvenile Incarceration

Among recent trends in juvenile incarceration are (1) its increased use (at least until recently), (2) the use of both public and private facilities, (3) the disproportionately large percentage of males and racial or ethnic minorities that are incarcerated, and (4) the increasing number of juveniles being incarcerated in local adult jails and state prisons.

9. Identify the Types and Describe the Effectiveness of Institutional Programs for Juveniles

In the United States, a variety of correctional institutions house juveniles, including detention centers, adult jails, shelter facilities, reception and diagnostic centers, ranches, forestry camps, farms, and training schools. There is some evidence that small, secure treatment facilities for violent or chronic offenders are effective at reducing recidivism. However, many institutions, particularly large state institutions, have often been found to have little positive effect on youths' subsequent delinquent behaviors. In fact, they may increase the likelihood that youths will commit further offenses.

KEY TERMS

juvenile delinquency, p. 478
apprenticeship system, p. 478
binding-out system, p. 478
houses of refuge, p. 479
placing out, p. 480
reform, industrial, or training schools, p. 481
cottage reformatories, p. 481
parens patriae, p. 482
adjudication, p. 486

informal juvenile justice, p. 488
status offenses, p. 489
radical nonintervention, p. 494
intake screening, p. 496
petition, p. 496
transfer, waiver, or certification, p. 496
hearing officer, p. 499
disposition, p. 501

QUESTIONS FOR REVIEW

1. What changes occurred in the sixteenth and seventeenth centuries in the ways the young were viewed?

2. What were the purposes of houses of refuge?

3. What is *parens patriae*, and what was the legal context in which it arose?

4. What was the social and historical context in which the juvenile court was created?

5. Historically, what has been the fundamental difference between the procedures used in juvenile courts and those employed in criminal courts?

6. What is the informal juvenile justice process, and why is it important?

7. What are four typical responses that police officers employ when handling juvenile cases?

8. What are three recent trends in police processing of juveniles?

9. What are five possible intake decisions that might be made in the juvenile justice process?

10. What are five recent trends in the practice of transferring juvenile cases to criminal court, and what do they suggest about the current orientation of juvenile justice?

11. In practice, what two dispositions are typically available to juvenile court judges in most jurisdictions, and which one is most frequently used?

12. What are three new dispositional or sentencing practices employed by juvenile court judges?

13. What are six objectives of community-based correctional programs for juveniles?

14. In the most comprehensive study ever undertaken of the conditions of confinement in juvenile correctional facilities in the United States, what four problems were found to be most widespread?

15. What are some important problems that remain unresolved as juvenile justice in the United States enters the twenty-first century?

EXPERIENTIAL ACTIVITIES

1. **Debate Juvenile Justice** With fellow students, family members, or friends, debate whether the juvenile justice system ought to be abolished and juvenile offenders treated as adults.

2. **Compare Correctional Facilities** Visit different juvenile correctional facilities in your community, both community-based facilities and institutional facilities. Compare what you observe at these facilities based on the following criteria:

   a. How do terms for similar offenses compare at each facility?

   b. How are juveniles treated?

   c. Are there educational or rehabilitation opportunities?

   d. How does the way of life compare?

INTERNET

3. **Juvenile Information Center** Go to cj.glencoe.com for links to access the Justice Information Center Web site. Click on Juvenile Justice and then on Delinquency Prevention under Documents. Choose one of the documents (for example, "What Works: Promising Interventions in Juvenile Justice"). Read the document and then write a brief summary of it.

4. **Research Parenting Issues** Go to cj.glencoe.com to access the *Parenting Resources for the 21st Century* online guide. Select one or more of the seven major subject headings (except Resources) and then choose one or more of the specific topics to read. Write a report on the delinquency implications of the various parenting issues. (It may be helpful to review theories of delinquency in Chapter 3.)

The Case of Paul

1. Paul, a 15-year-old, sexually assaulted, robbed, and killed Billy, an 11-year-old. Billy was missing for two days. Paul hid Billy's body for those two days in his family's garage before dumping it in a wooded area near the house. Neighbors describe Paul as quiet and introverted. His parents state that he grew increasingly violent after they kept him from a 43-year-old man named Smith who Paul had met in a chat room. Smith was subsequently charged with sexually assaulting Paul. The two apparently had sex in motels five times during the previous four months.

    a. Should Paul be handled by the justice system (either juvenile or adult) or be diverted, perhaps to a mental health facility? Why?

    b. Should he be charged with first-degree murder (as well as the other crimes)? Why or why not?

    c. Should he be transferred to criminal court and tried as an adult?

    d. If tried as an adult, should he enter a plea of not guilty by reason of insanity? A plea of guilty but insane? Why or why not?

    e. If Paul is convicted of any of the charges, what sentence should be imposed? Why?

The Case of James

2. Seventeen-year-old James lives in a nice lower-middle-class neighborhood in central Florida. A few years ago, James began running with a bad crowd. His parents tried a variety of punishments, to no avail. James was eventually arrested for burglary, theft, and other crimes. A juvenile court judge placed him on probation and ordered him to receive counseling. James violated probation, stopped going to counseling sessions, and began committing crimes again. After a subsequent arrest, James was ordered into a residential rehabilitation program for several months. After finishing the program, he was placed in a special school, from which he soon ran away. He was next placed in another residential program, one designed for youths "needing more structure." He ran away. After he was caught, a juvenile court judge returned him to the residential program for about six months.

    James's father states that the rehabilitation programs are a waste of time and money, because they are disorganized and ineffectual. He fears James will kill or be killed, and he wants James to be locked up until the age of 19. However, space is limited in the most secure juvenile institutions. In Florida, youths must commit an average of 12 crimes before they are placed in such institutions.

    a. Should James be handled by the justice system (either juvenile or adult) or be diverted? Why?

    b. If he is diverted, what type of program would benefit him most? Why?

    c. If James is retained in the juvenile justice system, what disposition would be most appropriate and beneficial for him?

ADDITIONAL READING

Bartollas, Clemens and Stuart J. Miller, *Juvenile Justice in America*, 3rd ed. Upper Saddle River, NJ: Prentice Hall, 2000.

Bernard, Thomas J. *The Cycle of Juvenile Justice.* New York: Oxford University Press, 1992.

Feld, Barry C. "Criminalizing the American Juvenile Court." In Michael Tonry (ed.). *Crime and Justice: A Review of Research*, Vol. 17. Chicago: University of Chicago Press, 1993, pp. 197–280.

Jacobs, Mark D. *Screwing the System and Making It Work: Juvenile Justice in the No-Fault Society.* Chicago: University of Chicago Press, 1990.

Krisberg, Barry and James F. Austin. *Reinventing Juvenile Justice*, 2d ed. Newbury Park, CA: Sage, 1993.

Miller, Jerome G. *Last One Over the Wall: The Massachusetts Experiment in Closing Reform Schools.* Columbus, OH: The Ohio State University Press, 1991.

Platt, Anthony M. *The Child Savers: The Invention of Delinquency.* Chicago: University of Chicago Press, 1969.

Rothman, David J. *The Discovery of the Asylum: Social Order and Disorder in the New Republic.* Boston: Little, Brown, 1971.

Schwartz, Ira M. *(In)Justice for Juveniles: Rethinking the Best Interests of the Child.* Lexington, MA: Lexington Books, 1989.

Whitehead, John T. and Steven P. Lab. *Juvenile Justice: An Introduction*, 3rd ed. Cincinnati: Anderson, 1998.

ENDNOTES

1. Philippe Aries, *Centuries of Childhood: A Social History of Family Life*, translated by Robert Baldick (New York: Random House, 1962).
2. Barry Krisberg and James F. Austin, *Reinventing Juvenile Justice* (Newbury Park, CA: Sage, 1993), p. 9.
3. Harry Elmer Barnes, *The Story of Punishment*, 2d ed. (Montclair, NJ: Patterson Smith, 1972).
4. David J. Rothman, *The Discovery of the Asylum* (Boston: Little, Brown, 1971).
5. Thomas J. Bernard, *The Cycle of Juvenile Justice* (New York: Oxford University Press, 1992), p. 63; Rothman, op. cit., p. 207.
6. Robert M. Mennel, *Thorns and Thistles* (Hanover, NH: University Press of New England, 1973); Steven L. Schlossman, *Love and the American Delinquent* (Chicago: University of Chicago Press, 1977).
7. Alexander Pisciotta, "Treatment on Trial: The Rhetoric and Reality of the New York House of Refuge, 1857–1935," *The American Journal of Legal History*, Vol. 29 (1985), pp. 151–81; Rothman, op. cit., p. 231.
8. Clemens Bartollas and Stuart J. Miller, *Juvenile Justice in America* (Englewood Cliffs, NJ: Regents/Prentice Hall, 1994), p. 136.
9. LaMar T. Empey and Mark C. Stafford, *American Delinquency: Its Meaning and Construction*, 3d ed. (Belmont, CA: Wadsworth, 1991), p. 368.
10. Belinda R. McCarthy and Bernard J. McCarthy, Community-Based Corrections, 2d ed. (Pacific Grove, CA: Brooks/Cole, 1991), p. 98.
11. Krisberg and Austin, op. cit., pp. 23–4; Hastings Hart, *Preventive Treatment of Neglected Children* (New York: Russell Sage, 1910), p. 70.

12. Bartollas and Miller, op. cit., p. 209; John T. Whitehead and Steven P. Lab, *Juvenile Justice: An Introduction* (Cincinnati: Anderson, 1990), p. 47.
13. Cited in Meda Chesney-Lind and Randall G. Shelden, *Girls, Delinquency, and Juvenile Justice* (Pacific Grove, CA: Brooks/Cole, 1992), p. 111.
14. Anthony M. Platt, *The Child Savers: The Invention of Delinquency* (Chicago: University of Chicago Press, 1969), p. 99.
15. Ibid., pp. 101–2.
16. Bernard, op. cit., pp. 68–9.
17. Ibid., pp. 70–1.
18. Platt, op. cit., pp. 134–36; Bernard, op. cit., p. 73.
19. Empey and Stafford, op. cit, pp. 58–9.
20. Bartollas and Miller, op. cit., p. 92; Empey and Stafford, op. cit., p. 59.
21. Krisberg and Austin, op. cit., p. 30.
22. Bernard, op. cit., p. 96.
23. Ibid., pp. 96–7.
24. Walter Wadlington, Charles H. Whitebread, and Samuel M. Davis, *Cases and Materials on Children in the Legal System* (Mineola, NY: Foundation Press, 1983), p. 202; Bernard, op. cit., p. 110.
25. M. A. Bortner, *Delinquency and Justice: An Age of Crisis* (New York: McGraw-Hill, 1988), p. 60.
26. Bernard, op. cit., p. 141.
27. Charles Puzzanchera, Anne L. Stahl, Terrence A. Finnegan, Howard N. Snyder, Rowen S. Poole, and Nancy Tierney, *Juvenile Court Statistics 1997* (Washington, DC: U.S. Department of Justice, Office of Juvenile Justice and Delinquency Prevention, May 2000), p. 9, Figure 2.
28. Puzzanchera et al., op. cit., p. 7, Table 4.
29. Ibid., p. 38, Table 53.

30. Howard N. Snyder, *Juvenile Arrests 1998*, Juvenile Justice Bulletin (Washington: U.S. Department of Justice, Office of Justice and Delinquency Prevention, December 1999), p. 6.

31. Douglas A. Smith, "The Organizational Context of Legal Control," *Criminology*, Vol. 22 (1984), pp. 19–38.

32. Robert J. Sampson, "Effects of Socioeconomic Context on Official Reaction to Juvenile Delinquency," *American Sociological Review*, Vol. 51 (1986), pp. 876–85; also see A. Cicourel, *The Social Organization of Juvenile Justice* (New York: Wiley, 1968).

33. Donald Black and Albert J. Reiss, "Police Control of Juveniles," *American Sociological Review*, Vol. 35 (1970), pp. 63–77; Richard J. Lundman, Richard E. Sykes, and John P. Clark, "Police Control of Juveniles: A Replication," in Ralph Weisheit and Robert G. Culbertson (eds.), *Juvenile Delinquency: A Justice Perspective* (Prospect Heights, IL: Waveland Press, 1978), pp. 107–15; Irving Piliavin and Scott Briar, "Police Encounters With Juveniles," *American Journal of Sociology*, Vol. 70 (1964), pp. 206–14.

34. Marvin D. Krohn, James P. Curry, and Shirley Nelson-Kilger, "Is Chivalry Dead? An Analysis of Changes in Police Dispositions of Males and Females," *Criminology*, Vol. 21 (1983), pp. 417–37; Katherine Teilmann and Pierre H. Landry, "Gender Bias in Juvenile Justice," *Journal of Research in Crime and Delinquency*, Vol. 18 (1981), pp. 47–80; see also William G. Staples, "Law and Social Control in Juvenile Justice Dispositions," *Journal of Research in Crime and Delinquency*, Vol. 24 (1987), pp. 7–22; Meda Chesney-Lind, "Judicial Paternalism and the Female Status Offender: Training Women to Know Their Place," *Crime and Delinquency*, Vol. 23 (1977), pp. 121–30.

35. Robert J. Sampson, "Sex Differences in Self-Reported Delinquency and Official Records: A Multiple-Group Structural Modeling Approach," *Journal of Quantitative Criminology*, Vol. 1 (1985), pp. 345–67; Dale Dannefer and Russell K. Schutt, "Race and Juvenile Justice Processing in Court and Police Agencies," *American Journal of Sociology*, Vol. 87 (1982), pp. 1113–32.

36. Merry Morash, "Establishment of a Juvenile Police Record: The Influence of Individual and Peer Group Characteristics," *Criminology*, Vol. 22 (1984), pp. 97–111; Krohn et al., op. cit.; D. Elliott and H. L. Voss, *Delinquency and Dropout* (Lexington, MA: Lexington Brooks, 1974).

37. Federal Bureau of Investigation, *Crime in the United States 1999*, U.S. Department of Justice (Washington: GPO, 2000), p. 231, Table 43.

38. *Statistical Abstract of the United States* (1999), p. 22, Table No. 22.

39. Delbert S. Elliott and David Huizinga, "Social Class and Delinquent Behavior in a National Youth Panel," *Criminology*, Vol. 21 (1983), pp. 149–77.

40. *Sourcebook of Criminal Justice Statistics Online*, Table 4.26.

41. Puzzanchera et al., op. cit., p. 7, Table 5.

42. Howard N. Snyder and MeLissa Sickmund, *Juvenile Offenders and Victims: 1999 National Report*. U.S. Department of Justice, National Center for Juvenile Justice, Office of Juvenile Justice and Delinquency Prevention (Washington: GPO, September 1999), p. 97.

43. Ted Rubin, "The Emerging Prosecutor Dominance of the Juvenile Court Intake Process," *Crime and Delinquency*, Vol. 26 (1980), pp. 299–318.

44. For a review of this literature, see Chesney-Lind and Shelden, op. cit., pp. 137–39.

45. Puzzanchera et al., op. cit., pp. 12-13, Tables 11 and 12; Charles M. Puzzanchera, "Delinquency Cases Waived to Criminal Court, 1988-1997," U.S. Department of Justice, Office of Juvenile Justice and Delinquency Prevention, Fact Sheet #02 (Washington: GPO, February 2000).

46. Florida Department of Juvenile Justice, Bureau of Data and Research, *Florida's Profile of Delinquency and Youths Referred: FY 1991–92 Through FY 1995–96* (Tallahassee: Florida Department of Juvenile Justice, November 1996).

47. Donna M. Bishop, Charles E. Frazier, Lonn Lanza-Daduce, and Lawrence Winner, "The Transfer of Juveniles to Criminal Court: Does It Make a Difference?" *Crime and Delinquency*, Vol. 42 (1996), pp. 171–91; Jeffrey Fagan, "Separating the Men From the Boys: The Comparative Advantage of Juvenile Versus Criminal Court Sanctions on Recidivism Among Adolescent Felony Offenders," in James C. Howell, Barry Krisberg, J. David Hawkins, and John Wilson, eds., *A Sourcebook: Serious, Violent, and Chronic Juvenile Offenders* (Thousand Oaks, CA: Sage, 1995), pp. 213–37; Eric Jensen and Linda Metsger, "A Test of the Deterrent Effect of Legislative Waiver on Violent Juvenile Crime," *Crime and Delinquency*, Vol. 40 (1994), pp. 96–104.

48. Unless indicated otherwise, material in this section is from the following sources: Barry C. Feld, "Criminalizing the American Juvenile Court," in Michael Tonry (ed.), *Crime and Justice: A Review of Research*, Vol. 17 (Chicago: University of Chicago Press, 1993), pp. 197–280; Joseph B. Sanborn, Jr., "Policies Regarding the Prosecution of Juvenile Murderers: Which System and Who Should Decide," Law & Policy, Vol. 18 (1996), pp. 151–78; Joseph B. Sanborn, Jr., "Certification to Criminal Court: The Important Policy Questions of How, When, and Why," *Crime and Delinquency*, Vol. 40 (1994), pp. 262–81; Howard N. Snyder, *Juvenile Arrests 1995*, U.S. Department of Justice, Office of Juvenile Justice and Delinquency Prevention, Juvenile Justice Bulletin (Washington: GPO, February 1997), p. 12; Barry C. Feld, "The Juvenile Court Meets the Principle of the Offense: Legislative Changes in Juvenile Waiver Statutes," *Journal of Criminal Law and Criminology*, Vol. 78 (1987), pp. 471–533; Barry Krisberg, Ira M. Schwartz, Paul Litsky, and James Austin, "The Watershed of Juvenile Justice Reform," *Crime and Delinquency*, Vol. 32 (1986), pp. 5–38; Donna Hamparian, Linda Estep, Susan M. Muntean, Ramon R. Prestino, Robert G. Swisher, Paul L. Wallace, and Joseph L. White, *Youth in Adult Court: Between Two Worlds* (Washington: OJJDP, 1982); and personal communications from Donna M. Bishop and Joseph B. Sanborn, Jr.

49. Information about teen courts or youth courts is from Jeffrey Butts, Dean Hoffman, and Janeen Buck, "Teen Courts in the United States: A Profile of Current Programs," U.S. Department of Justice, Office of Juvenile Justice and Delinquency Prevention, OJJDP Factsheet #118 (Washington: GPO, October 1999).

50. Martin L. Forst, Bruce A. Fisher, and Robert B. Coates, "Indeterminate and Determinate Sentencing of Juvenile Delinquents: A National Survey of Approaches to Commitment and Release Decision-Making," *Juvenile and Family Court Journal* (Summer 1985), pp. 1–12.

51. Patricia Torbert, Richard Gable, Hunter Hurst IV, Imogene Montgomery, Linda Szymanski, and Douglas Thomas, *State Responses to Serious and Violent Juvenile Crime*, U.S. Department of Justice, Office of Juvenile Justice and Delinquency Prevention (Washington: GPO, July 1996), Chap. 3.

52. Troy L. Armstrong, "National Survey of Juvenile Intensive Supervision" (Parts I and II), *Criminal Justice Abstracts*, Vol. 20 (1988), pp. 342–48 (Part I) and 497–523 (Part II).

53. Richard G. Wiebush, "Juvenile Intensive Supervision: The Impact on Felony Offenders Diverted From Institutional Placement," *Crime and Delinquency,* Vol. 39 (1993), pp. 68–89; William H. Barton and Jeffrey A. Butts, "Viable Options: Intensive Supervision Programs for Juvenile Delinquents," *Crime and Delinquency,* Vol. 36 (1990), pp. 238–56.

54. Richard A. Ball, Ronald Huff, and Robert Lilly, *House Arrest and Correctional Policy: Doing Time at Home* (Newbury Park, CA: Sage, 1988).

55. See Marc Renzema and David T. Skelton, "Use of Electronic Monitoring in the United States: 1989 Update," National Institute of Justice, Research in Brief (Washington: National Institute of Justice, 1990); Daniel Ford and Annesley K. Schmidt, "Electronically Monitored Home Confinement," National Institute of Justice, Research in Action (Washington: National Institute of Justice, 1985).

56. Joseph B. Vaughn, "A Survey of Juvenile Electronic Monitoring and Home Confinement Programs," *Juvenile and Family Court Journal,* Vol. 40 (1989), pp. 1–36.

57. Kevin I. Minor and Preston Elrod, "The Effects of a Probation Intervention on Juvenile Offenders' Self-Concepts, Loci of Control, and Perceptions of Juvenile Justice," *Youth and Society,* Vol. 25 (1994), pp. 490–511; Gerald L. Golins, Utilizing Adventure Education to Rehabilitate Juvenile Delinquents (Las Cruces, NM: Educational Resources Information Center, Clearinghouse on Rural Education and Small Schools, 1980).

58. See, for example, R. Callahan, "Wilderness Probation: A Decade Later," *Juvenile and Family Court Journal,* Vol. 36 (1985), pp. 31–51; John Winterdyk and Ronald Roesch, "A Wilderness Experiential Program as an Alternative for Probationers: An Evaluation," *Canadian Journal of Criminology,* Vol. 24 (1982), pp. 39–49.

59. H. Preston Elrod and Kevin I. Minor, "Second Wave Evaluation of a Multi-Faceted Intervention for Juvenile Court Probationers," *International Journal of Offender Therapy and Comparative Criminology,* Vol. 36 (1992), pp. 247–62; John Winterdyk and Curt Griffiths, "Wilderness Experience Programs: Reforming Delinquents or Beating Around the Bush?" *Juvenile and Family Court Journal,* Vol. 35 (1984), pp. 35–44; Winterdyk and Roesch, op. cit.

60. Ted Palmer, *The Re-Emergence of Correctional Intervention* (Newbury Park, CA: Sage, 1992); Office of Juvenile Justice and Delinquency Prevention, Project New Pride: Replication (Washington: OJJDP, 1979); LaMar T. Empey and Maynard L. Erickson, *The Provo Experiment: Evaluating Community Control of Delinquency* (Lexington, MA: Lexington Books, 1972).

61. Terrence P. Thornberry, Stewart E. Tolnay, Timothy J. Flanagan, and Patty Glynn, *Office of Juvenile Justice and Delinquency Prevention Report on Children in Custody 1987: A Comparison of Public and Private Juvenile Custody Facilities* (Washington: OJJDP, 1991).

62. Thornberry et al. (1991), op. cit.

63. Dale G. Parent, Valerie Leiter, Stephen Kennedy, Lisa Livens, Daniel Wentworth, and Sarah Wilcox, *Conditions of Confinement: Juvenile Detention and Corrections Facilities Research Summary* (Washington: OJJDP, 1994), p. 5.

64. See, for example, Barry Krisberg, "Juvenile Justice: Improving the Quality of Care," *National Council on Crime and Delinquency* (San Francisco: NCCD, 1992); Carol J. Garrett, "Effects of Residential Treatment on Adjudicated Delinquents," *Journal of Research in Crime and Delinquency,* Vol. 22 (1985), pp. 287–308.

65. Barry Krisberg, Robert DeComo, and Norma C. Herrera, *National Juvenile Custody Trends 1978–1989* (Washington: OJJDP, 1992), p. 2; Also see Steven Lab and John T. Whitehead, "A Meta-Analysis of Juvenile Correctional Treatment," *Journal of Research in Crime and Delinquency,* Vol. 26 (1989), pp. 276–95.

66. Unless indicated otherwise, data in this section are from Snyder and Sickmund, op. cit., chap. 7.

67. Howard N. Snyder and Melissa Sickmund, Juvenile Offenders and Victims: 1999 National Report. U.S. Department of Justice, Office of Juvenile Justice and Delinquency Prevention (Washington: GPO, September 1999), p. 62.

68. "Challenging the Myths," U.S. Department of Justice, Office of Juvenile Justice, and Delinquency Prevention, *1999 National Report Series: Juvenile Justice Bulletin* (Washington: GPO, February 2000).

PART 6

The Future of Criminal Justice in America

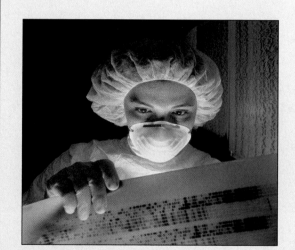

CHAPTER 14
Understanding and Predicting the Future of Criminal Justice

CHAPTER OUTLINE

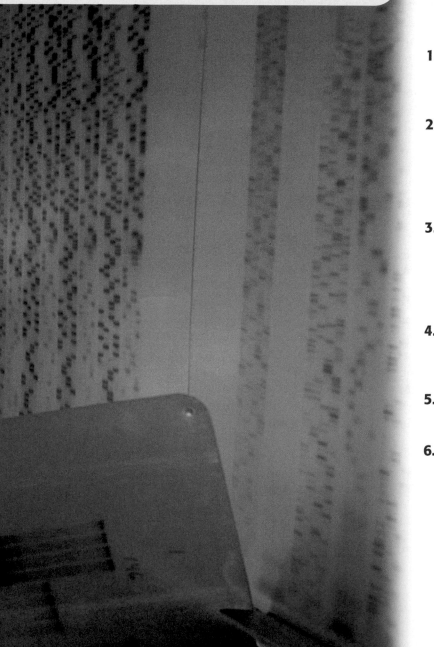

Understanding and Predicting the Future of Criminal Justice

CHAPTER OBJECTIVES

After completing this chapter, you should be able to:

1. Point out major differences between Packer's crime control and due process models.

2. Describe the possible future of law enforcement if the crime control model dominates, and the possible future if the due process model dominates.

3. Describe the possible future of the administration of justice if the crime control model dominates, and the possible future if the due process model dominates.

4. Identify perhaps the most divisive issue that will confront correctional policy makers in the future.

5. Describe the possible future of corrections.

6. List some of the cost-reduction strategies likely to be advocated in corrections in the future.

14.1 A Framework for Understanding the Future of Criminal Justice

In the preceding chapters of this book, you have learned about the nature of crime and its consequences in the United States, theories of crime and delinquency causation, criminal law and its application, and the historical development of criminal and juvenile justice. You have also examined in detail the current operation of criminal and juvenile justice and have analyzed problems associated with each. In this last chapter, you will explore the directions that American criminal and juvenile justice might take in the future and consider some predictions. Excluded from this chapter are predictions about future trends in crime and delinquency, because that subject is too far afield. However, crime and delinquency, in whatever new forms they take, are likely to remain pervasive social problems in the United States for the foreseeable future.

The principal guide that informs predictions of the future directions of criminal and juvenile justice is Herbert Packer's model of the U.S. criminal justice process.[1] For us, Packer's model has had considerable explanatory power for more than 30 years, and it seems that its explanatory power will remain strong in the future. However, in making predictions, this text will not limit itself to Packer's vision of possible futures for criminal and juvenile justice, but will instead peer into its own crystal ball—and those of others—to venture some predictions in areas where Packer's model is silent.

In his influential 1968 book entitled *The Limits of the Criminal Sanction*, legal scholar Herbert Packer describes the criminal justice process in the United States as the outcome of competition between two value systems. Those two value systems, which represent two ends of a value continuum, are the basis for two models of the operation of criminal justice—the crime control model and the due process model. Figure 14–1 depicts this continuum. From a political standpoint, the **crime control model** reflects traditional conservative values, while the **due process model** embodies traditional liberal values.[2] Consequently, when politically conservative values are dominant in

crime control model
One of Packer's two models of the criminal justice process. Politically, it reflects traditional conservative values. In this model, the control of criminal behavior is the most important function of criminal justice.

due process model
One of Packer's two models of the criminal justice process. Politically, it embodies traditional liberal values. In this model, the principal goal of criminal justice is at least as much to protect the innocent as it is to convict the guilty.

FIGURE 14–1
Two Models of the Criminal Justice Process

Due Process Model	Crime Control Model
Traditional liberal values	Traditional conservative values

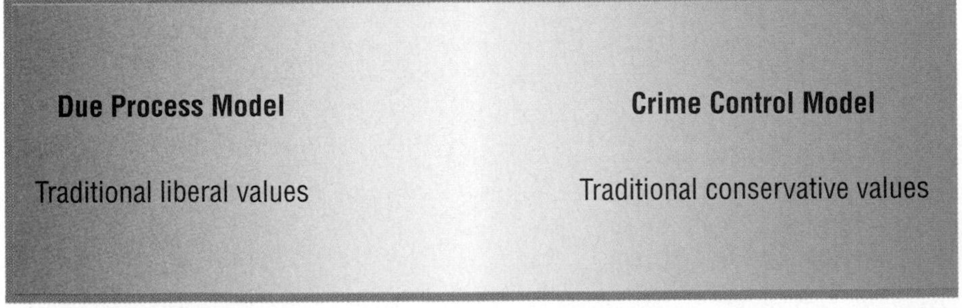

society, as they are currently, the principles and policies of the crime control model seem to dominate the operation of criminal justice. During more politically liberal periods, such as the 1960s and 1970s, the principles and policies of the due process model seem to dominate criminal justice activity.

The models are ideal types, neither of which corresponds exactly to the actual day-to-day practice of criminal justice. Rather, they both provide a convenient way to understand and discuss both the current and the future operation of criminal justice in the United States. In practice, the criminal justice process represents a series of conflicts and compromises between the value systems of the two models. In the following sections, Packer's two models are described in detail.

The Crime Control Model

In the crime control model, the control of criminal behavior is by far the most important function of criminal justice. Although the means by which crime is controlled are important in this view (illegal means are not advocated), they are less important than the ultimate goal of control. Consequently, the primary focus of this model is on efficiency in the operation of the criminal justice process. Advocates of the crime control model want to make the process more efficient—to move cases through the process as quickly as possible and to bring them to a close. Packer characterizes the crime control model as "assembly-line justice." To achieve "quick closure" in the processing of cases, a premium is placed on speed and finality. Speed requires that cases be handled informally and uniformly; finality depends on minimizing occasions for challenge, that is, appeals.

To appreciate the assembly-line metaphor used by Packer and to understand how treating cases uniformly speeds up the process and makes it more efficient, consider the way that McDonald's sells billions of hamburgers. When you order a Big Mac from McDonald's, you know exactly what you are going to get. All Big Macs are the same, because they are made uniformly. Moreover, you can get a Big Mac in a matter of seconds most of the time. However, what happens when you order something different, or something not already prepared, such as a hamburger with ketchup only? Your order is taken, and you are asked to stand to the side because your special order will take a few minutes. Your special order has slowed down the assembly line and reduced efficiency. This happens in criminal justice, too! If defendants ask for something special, such as a trial, the assembly line is slowed and efficiency is reduced.

As described in Chapter 8 ("The Administration of Justice"), even when criminal justice is operating at its best, it is a slow process. The time from arrest to final case disposition can typically be measured in weeks or months. If defendants opt for a jury trial, as is their right in most felony cases, the cases are handled formally and are treated as unique; no two cases are the same in their circumstances or in the way they are handled. If defendants are not satisfied with the outcome of their trials, then they have the right to appeal. Appeals may delay by years the final resolution of cases.

To increase efficiency—meaning speed and finality—crime control advocates prefer plea bargaining. As described in Chapter 8, plea bargaining is an informal process that is used instead of trial. Plea bargains can be offered and accepted in a relatively short time. Also, cases are handled uniformly because the mechanics of a plea bargain are basically the same; only the substance of the deals differs. Additionally, with successful plea bargains, there is no opportunity for challenge; there are no appeals. Thus, plea bargaining is the perfect mechanism for achieving the primary focus of the crime control model—efficiency.

The key to the operation of the crime control model is "a presumption of guilt." In other words, advocates of this model assume that if the police have expended the time and effort to arrest a suspect and the prosecutor has formally charged the suspect with a crime, then the suspect must be guilty. Why else would police arrest and prosecutors charge? Although the answers to that question are many (see the discussions in Chapters 7 and 8 of the extralegal factors that influence police and prosecutorial behavior), the fact remains that a presumption of guilt is accurate most of the time. That is, most people who are arrested and charged with a crime or crimes are, in fact, guilty. A problem—but not a significant one for crime control advocates—is that a presumption of guilt is not accurate all of the time; miscarriages of justice do occur (see the discussion in Chapter 4, "The Rule of Law"). An equally important problem is that a presumption of guilt goes against one of the oldest and most cherished principles of American criminal justice—that a person is considered innocent until proven guilty.

Reduced to its barest essentials and operating at its highest level of efficiency, the crime control model consists of an administrative fact-finding process with two possible outcomes: a suspect's exoneration or the suspect's guilty plea.

The Due Process Model

Advocates of the due process model, by contrast, reject the informal fact-finding process as definitive of factual guilt. They insist, instead, on formal, adjudicative fact-finding processes in which cases against suspects are heard publicly by impartial trial courts. In the due process model, moreover, the factual guilt of suspects is not determined until the suspects have had a full opportunity to discredit the charges against them. For those reasons, Packer characterizes the due process model as "obstacle-course justice."

What motivates this careful and deliberate approach to the administration of justice is the realization that human beings sometimes make mistakes. The police sometimes arrest the wrong person, and prosecutors sometimes charge the wrong person. Thus, contrary to the crime control model, the demand for finality is low in the due process model, and the goal is at least as much to protect the innocent as it is to convict the guilty. Indeed, for due process model advocates, it is better to let a guilty person go free than it is to wrongly convict and punish an innocent person.

The due process model is based on the doctrine of legal guilt and the presumption

▲ Legal guilt results when factual guilt is determined at a fair trial. *Should a defendant be freed if he or she is found not legally guilty at trial, even though he or she is factually guilty? Why or why not?*

of innocence. According to the **doctrine of legal guilt,** people are not to be held guilty of crimes merely on a showing, based on reliable evidence, that in all probability they did in fact do what they are accused of doing. In other words, it is not enough that people are factually guilty in the due process model; they must also be legally guilty. Legal guilt results only when factual guilt is determined in a procedurally regular fashion, as in a criminal trial, and when the procedural rules, or due-process rights, designed to protect suspects and defendants and to safeguard the integrity of the process are employed. Many of the conditions of legal guilt—that is, procedural, or due-process, rights—were described in Chapter 4. They include:

- Freedom from unreasonable searches and seizures
- Protection against double jeopardy
- Protection against compelled self-incrimination
- A speedy and public trial
- An impartial jury of the state and district where the crime occurred
- Notice of the nature and cause of the accusation
- The right to confront opposing witnesses
- Compulsory process for obtaining favorable witnesses
- The right to counsel
- The prohibition of cruel and unusual punishment

In short, in the due process model, factual guilt is not enough. For people to be found guilty of crimes, they must be found *both* factually and legally guilty.

This obstacle course model of justice is championed by due process advocates because they are skeptical about the ideal of equality on which American criminal justice is supposedly based. They recognize that there can be no equal justice where the kind of trial a person gets, or whether he or she gets a trial at all, depends substantially on how much money that person has. It is assumed that in an adversarial system of justice (as described in Chapter 8 and employed in the United States), an effective defense is largely a function of the resources that can be mustered on behalf of the accused. It is also assumed that there are gross inequalities in the financial means of criminal defendants. Most criminal defendants are indigent, and because of their indigence, they are frequently denied an effective defense. Although procedural safeguards, or conditions of legal guilt, cannot by themselves correct the inequity in resources, they do provide indigent defendants, at least theoretically, with a better chance for justice than they would receive without them.

Fundamentally, the due process model defends the ideal of personal freedom and its protection. The model rests on the assumption that preventing tyranny by the government and its agents is the most important function of the criminal justice process.

Crime Control versus Due Process

As noted earlier, which of the models dominates criminal justice policy in the United States at any particular time depends on the political climate. Currently, the United States is in the midst of a prolonged period—beginning in the mid-1970s—in which traditional politically conservative values

doctrine of legal guilt
The principle that people are not to be held guilty of crimes merely on a showing, based on reliable evidence, that in all probability they did in fact do what they are accused of doing. Legal guilt results only when factual guilt is determined in a procedurally regular fashion, as in a criminal trial, and when the procedural rules designed to protect suspects and defendants and to safeguard the integrity of the process are employed.

have dominated the practice of criminal and juvenile justice. Thus, it should come as no surprise that the crime control model of criminal justice more closely resembles the actual practice of criminal and juvenile justice in the United States today. At the time Packer wrote and published his book, however, politically liberal values and, thus, the principles and policies of the due process model dominated the operation of criminal and juvenile justice.

In any event, neither model is likely to completely control criminal justice. Even though the current operation of criminal and juvenile justice reflects the dominance of the crime control model, elements of the due process model remain evident. How long this trend will continue is anybody's guess. Many suspect that the American people will eventually get tired of seeing their tax dollars spent on programs and a process that is not providing them with the safety from criminal behavior that they so desperately desire. However, if Packer's model of criminal justice is correct, a shift in criminal justice practice will come only after a shift in the values held by American political leaders and, of course, American citizens.

Using Packer's model as a guide, and barring any radical or fundamental changes, some predictions about the future of criminal and juvenile justice are made in the following three sections: law enforcement, the administration of justice, and corrections. Future directions in juvenile justice are considered in the section on the administration of justice.

14.1 CRITICAL THINKING

1. What do you think are some of the fundamental problems with the crime control model? What are the benefits of this model?

2. What do you think are some of the fundamental problems with the due process model? What are the benefits of this model?

14.2 The Future of Law Enforcement

If the future of law enforcement increasingly reflects the principles and policies of the crime control model, then you might expect fewer limitations on how the police attempt to combat crime. For example, the practice of detaining and arresting suspects for investigation without probable cause is likely to increase, as is the length of time a suspect may be held before being charged. The Supreme Court may augment those practices by granting good-faith exceptions to the Fifth Amendment protection against compelled self-incrimination. If the crime control model is fully embraced, it is possible that the Court's decision in *Miranda v. Arizona* could be overturned and that coerced confessions would be admissible at trial.

The investigative abilities of the police should be improved and made easier by the expansion of community policing. Although the current meaning of community policing remains vague (see Chapter 6), it will ultimately be defined by the way it is actually employed. If it is employed according to crime control principles, American citizens can expect greater intrusion into their lives. Privacy will be sacrificed for efficiency in crime control.

Greater intrusion into people's lives will be facilitated by advances in electronic surveillance. For example, advances in **bionics** (the replacing of human body parts with mechanical parts) may someday produce bionic eyes powerful enough for law enforcement officers to see for miles or through walls, and bionic ears sensitive enough to enable law enforcement officers, from a considerable distance, to clearly hear conversations held behind closed doors.[3] Already, computer-controlled supersensitive listening and video devices are able to accomplish the same things.[4] To the extent that the crime control model is followed, there may be fewer or, perhaps, no limitations on the future uses of electronic surveillance. According to this scenario, George Orwell's vision of a society monitored totally by Big Brother (the state and its agents) may become a reality in the United States, as it did to varying degrees in the totalitarian nations of Eastern Europe, Communist China, and the former Soviet Union. In other words, to facilitate efficient crime control, according to the logic of the crime control model, it is conceivable that every move you make, every word you say and, possibly, every thought you think will be recorded for future incrimination, if the need arises.

Moreover, advanced electronic surveillance devices and other new technologies in law enforcement (to be discussed in more detail later in this chapter) should be available sooner than might normally be expected, because of the end of the Cold War. Billions of tax dollars that would have been spent on military hardware during the Cold War will probably be shifted to defense conversion programs. A primary beneficiary of the new programs will undoubtedly be domestic law enforcement.

On the other hand, if Americans see a shift to the principles and policies of the due process model, they should expect existing limitations on how the police combat crime to remain intact or even be expanded. Certainly, the practice of detaining and arresting suspects for investigation without probable cause will end or, at least, be decreased substantially. The present 48-hour limitation—with certain exceptions—on the length of time a suspect may be held before being charged will be standard operating procedure. Good-faith exceptions to protections against compelled self-incrimination will not be allowed, and current good-faith exceptions to the exclusionary rule may be eliminated. Adherence to the *Miranda* requirements will become even more routine among police officers than it is currently. Perhaps suspects will no longer be allowed to waive their rights.

Regardless of which of Packer's two models dominates in the future, community policing is likely to become standard practice throughout the country, as police officers become known as *public service officers*.[5] Community policing will at least make citizens feel much safer in their homes and communities (and, perhaps, reduce the likelihood of victimization by predatory criminal behavior) than did previous forms of policing. However, if community policing adheres to principles of the due process model, it will not in any way violate the privacy of citizens unless there is probable cause (strictly defined) to do so. Instead, for citizens and communities that seek help, community policing will help reduce the incidence of criminal victimization and, by doing so, improve the conditions of life—while respecting the privacy of citizens who do not want help.

As described more fully in Chapter 6, a recent development in criminal investigation is DNA profiling. Although this new technology is still controversial, it will probably become a routine law enforcement tool in the

bionics
The replacing of human body parts with mechanical parts.

CRIMINAL JUSTICE *Online*

Bionics

Visit *Scientific American's* Web site by accessing the link at cj.glencoe.com to learn more about scientific research in bionics. *Do you think the use of bionics could have a significant impact on law enforcement in the future? Why?*

Carnivore

The FBI has implemented a new surveillance system, called *Carnivore*. The system, when placed at an Internet service provider such as America Online, will allow law enforcement agents to intercept and analyze huge amounts of incoming and outgoing E-mail in connection with the target of a criminal investigation.

SOURCE: "Right groups fight e-mail tap." *The Orlando Sentinel* (July 13, 2000), p. A-3.

near future. Perhaps the most thorny issue with this new technology is how the DNA database will be collected and used. If the principles of the due process model prevail in the future, then the DNA database will probably comprise DNA samples taken only from booked suspects (and criminal justice personnel upon hiring), as is the current practice with fingerprints. Such a policy is unlikely to be very controversial or to attract much public resistance. On the other hand, if policy reflects the principles of the crime control model, then the DNA database may comprise DNA samples taken shortly after birth from all infants born in the United States. This latter strategy would clearly make the DNA database more complete and, therefore, a more efficient tool in the effort to solve crimes. It would also be much more controversial and would probably be resisted by a large segment of the population as a violation of privacy rights.

To the extent that the due process model shapes future law enforcement practice, electronic surveillance will not be allowed under any circumstances or will at least be strictly limited to a few types of crimes (for example, crimes that threaten national security, such as treason and espionage).

Advances in law enforcement technology are inevitable, but technology employed according to due process principles will be used to protect citizens and law enforcement personnel. For example, robots will be employed with greater frequency to perform a variety of law enforcement duties. Robots have been used by law enforcement personnel since the mid-1970s for handling bombs, and they are currently being used in other law enforcement situations, usually in SWAT or other dangerous circumstances.[6] In the future, they may be used routinely in hostage situations and in the arrest of dangerous suspects.

DNA

You can learn more about DNA profiling by visiting the National Institute of Justice's National Commission on the Future of DNA Evidence Web site by accessing the link at cj.glencoe.com. *Do you think that DNA profiling will play an important role in the future of law enforcement? Why?*

▲ Some law enforcement agencies use robots to handle bombs and other dangerous assignments. *Should all law enforcement agencies have access to robots? If so, how should they be financed and distributed?*

Some other ideas currently on drawing boards are:

- A pocket-sized, voice-activated voice-stress analyzer that police officers could use to determine whether suspects or witnesses experienced stress during questioning, indicating possible dishonest answers (used like current polygraph machines).

- An ultrasmall, two-way cellular phone (like a Dick Tracy wrist communicator), possibly implanted in officers' larynxes, that would allow police officers to be in constant contact with headquarters, fellow officers, or anyone around the world.

- A universal translator (that is, an ultrasmall computer) that could instantly translate speech from one language to another, allowing police officers to question suspects, witnesses, or crime victims without the language barrier they frequently confront today.[7]

- An ultra-wideband device that will allow police officers to detect motions through surfaces such as walls (for example, to determine whether there are people inside a room before they knock down a door).[8]

- A "smart" gun that would electronically disable itself if taken away from a police officer during a struggle.

- A microwave device to shut off a car's ignition, stopping fleeing suspects without the risk of a high-speed chase.

- A supersticky foam that could be sprayed on armed suspects, neutralizing them by temporarily gluing their arms to their bodies.

- Spikes embedded in retractable panels beneath roads that could be raised by remote control to blow out a getaway car's tires.[9]

- Jet packs that officers could wear on their backs so that they could patrol by air.[10]

- A hand-held scanner that will allow remote body-cavity searches.[11]

- Nanosized computer chips that can be placed in the neural networks (such as the human brain) of police officers to give them access to billions of gigabytes of instantly accessible data (such as criminal records of suspects).[12]

The future of law enforcement in the United States is likely to be very different from law enforcement today. New styles of policing, such as community policing, will be embraced and new technologies employed. The form that the change ultimately takes, however, will depend substantially on whether there is a dramatic shift toward the principles and policies of the crime control model or toward the principles and policies of its due process counterpart. In the next section, possible future developments in the administration of justice are considered.

Robot Security

The Los Angeles Art Museum currently uses a cybermotion robot sentry to patrol at night. The robot checks for intruders, leaky pipes, or fire. If it finds a door open that should be closed, it calls security and takes a video picture of the scene.

SOURCE: Gene Stephens, "Drugs and Crime in the Twenty-First Century," *The Futurist* (May-June, 1992), pp. 19–22.

14.2 CRITICAL THINKING

1. What impact do you think DNA profiling will have on the future of law enforcement?

2. Can you think of any other technological advances not listed above that could significantly impact law enforcement in the future?

14.3 The Future of the Administration of Justice

If, in the future, the administration of justice in the United States is more in line with the crime control model, then the right to legal counsel (both court-appointed and privately retained) at critical pre- and posttrial stages may be scaled back significantly. Advocates of the crime control model consider legal representation at any stage, other than perhaps at trial, a luxury and an unnecessary impediment to the efficient operation of the process. Advocates of the crime control model argue that prior to trial (for example, during interrogation), providing counsel to a suspect only hampers the ability of police to investigate a case. After trial, during the appellate process, the availability of legal counsel further reduces the speed with which a case can be brought to closure. Crime control model supporters maintain that in both situations, a crafty lawyer may be able to win the freedom of a factually guilty client by means of a legal technicality.

If the principles and policies of the due process model dominate the future of the administration of justice, however, then it is likely that the current right to counsel at a variety of critical stages in the process will be retained and, perhaps, even extended somewhat (for example, to appeals beyond the first one). Advocates of the due process model believe that legal counsel is crucial throughout the process and must be made available immediately after arrest. Otherwise, the likelihood that innocent people will be subject to harassment, or worse, by agents of the state (police officers and prosecutors) is increased to an intolerable level.

Preliminary Hearing   Along with a greatly reduced role for legal counsel in the administration of justice, crime control model enthusiasts advocate the abolition of the preliminary hearing. They argue that it is a waste of time and money to conduct a preliminary testing of the evidence and the charges imposed, because prosecutors have no reason to pursue cases that are unlikely to lead to conviction. Recall from the discussion in Chapter 8 that prosecutors' reputations and chances of achieving higher political office depend at least partially on the proportion of convictions they are able to obtain. Besides, for several reasons, including the sheer volume of cases that must be handled in the lower courts, the evidence against a suspect is rarely tested at the preliminary hearing anyway. Today, the preliminary hearing is used mostly for making decisions about bail.

Due process model advocates, however, believe that the preliminary hearing is a critical stage in the administration of justice. Although they concede that this hearing is not currently being used as it is supposed to be, they argue that it needs reform instead of abandonment. As described previously, due process model advocates are skeptical about the motivations of prosecutors in criminal cases. History has certainly recorded numerous incidences of prosecutorial misbehavior. Because most criminal cases are resolved through plea bargaining rather than criminal trial, the preliminary hearing may be the only opportunity for a judicial officer to scrutinize the prosecutor's work. Elimination of the preliminary hearing (as it is supposed to operate in theory) would substantially reduce the effectiveness of the entire adversary process of justice.

Grand Jury   Instead of elimination of the preliminary hearing, due process model enthusiasts are more inclined to argue for elimination of the grand jury. As described in Chapter 8, the grand jury is another vehicle by which the evidence and charges brought by a prosecutor against a suspect are examined by an impartial body. However, in practice, the grand jury is even more of a sham than the preliminary hearing, having become nothing more than a tool or a rubber stamp for the prosecutor. Invariably, a grand jury will indict or not indict a suspect if that is what the prosecutor wants. Moreover, abuses of the process are more likely to occur in grand jury proceedings, which are conducted in private—away from the watchful eyes of defense attorneys and the public—than in preliminary hearings, which allow the presence of defense attorneys and are open to the public.

If the crime control model dominates the administration of justice in the future, it is likely that the use of pretrial detention will be expanded. Advocates of the crime control model maintain that expanded use of pretrial detention will encourage more factually guilty offenders to plead guilty—they would have nothing to gain by not doing so—and will better protect society from the crimes those people are likely to commit if not confined. As for the protection of society, perhaps in the future the pretrial detention of potentially dangerous suspects will be unnecessary because of technical advances in electronic monitoring. For example, the use of electronically monitored house arrest, in which suspects are connected to monitors by electrodes (perhaps surgically implanted in their bodies) that shock them intermittently when they are outside designated areas, may be sufficient to ensure that suspects do not pose a threat to society while awaiting trial.[13] If this type of monitoring is employed, it is likely that suspects would be given a choice between it and jail. Most suspects would probably choose electronic monitoring.

Due process model supporters argue that pretrial detention should be used sparingly if at all. They believe that people accused of crimes should be entitled to remain free until they are found guilty, unless they are unlikely to appear when required or they pose a significant threat to society. Regarding those two exceptions to pretrial release, due process model advocates believe that nonappearance problems can be handled adequately through the existing bail system. They do admit, however, that the present bail system discriminates against the poor. That discrimination is another problem that must be rectified. As for the pretrial detention of defendants who presumably pose a significant threat to society, due process model advocates doubt that prosecutors and judges can predict accurately which defendants actually pose a significant threat and which do not. The result is that many defendants who do not need to be jailed prior to trial will be jailed—or electronically monitored—because of inevitable false predictions. Due process model enthusiasts also suggest that both exceptions to pretrial release—nonappearance and potential threat to society—could be handled by methods other than pretrial detention—for example, by a prompt trial, as required by the Sixth Amendment.

As mentioned earlier in this chapter, a key to the crime control model's efficiency in the administration of justice is heavy reliance on plea bargaining. Thus, if the crime control model dominates the administration of justice in

FIGURE 14–2

Technology and Criminal Justice

Emission Tomography
Criminologists are using emission tomography to peer into the brains of violent offenders and try to determine whether those brains are fundamentally different.

DNA Mapping
Forensic scientists can map DNA patterns in samples of skin, blood, semen, or other body tissues or fluids. The DNA patterns can then be stored, analyzed, and compared.

Imaging Systems
With document-imaging systems, attorneys do not have to go to the courthouse to see a document and can file lawsuits and other legal documents electronically.

the future, Americans should expect even fewer criminal trials than today. If there is instead a dramatic shift to the principles and policies of the due process model, plea bargaining will probably be discouraged, and the number of criminal cases that go to trial will increase substantially. For due process model supporters, a principal problem with plea bargaining is that after a guilty plea has been accepted, the possibility of any further judicial examination of earlier stages of the process is eliminated. In other words, with the acceptance of a guilty plea, there is no longer any chance that police or

Infrared Surveillance
Infrared devices allow through-the-wall surveillance of a room in a building.

Telephone Sensors
Special telephone units with alcohol sensors in the mouthpiece are being used by probation and parole departments to monitor offenders sentenced to home detention.

Hard-Drive Investigation
Criminal investigators use computer-evidence recovery techniques to uncover evidence from computers that have been used in criminal activities.

prosecutorial errors before trial will be detected. Plea bargaining will probably not be eliminated entirely, however, even in a legal atmosphere dominated by due process model principles and policies, because eliminating it would be impractical. The time and expense involved in subjecting every criminal case to a trial would be prohibitive.

As discussed in Chapter 9 ("Sentencing, Appeals, and the Death Penalty"), more jurisdictions are eliminating or significantly reducing judicial discretion in sentencing by enacting mandatory sentencing statutes and using sentencing guidelines. This policy seems to reflect crime control model principles, although a due process model argument could be made that the restriction of judicial discretion in sentencing will reduce unwarranted judicial disparity in sentencing. In any event, if the trend continues, it is likely that in the area of sentencing, judges in the future will function simply as automatons, empowered only to apply the specific sentence dictated by law.

If the crime control model dominates the future of the administration of justice, it is likely that appeals—following the few trials that occur—will be strongly discouraged and limited. Crime control model advocates consider appeals a remote and marginal part of the process. They do recognize that the appellate process can correct errors in procedure or in the determination of factual guilt, and they endorse that role. They believe, however, that such errors occur only occasionally. For crime control model supporters, the appellate process can impede the efficient operation of the administration of justice.

If the due process model dominates the administration of justice in the future, there will probably be no limitations on the right to appeal. Due process model advocates, in contrast to their crime control model counterparts, believe that the right to appeal is a significant and indispensable part of the process, one where earlier errors and infringements of rights can be corrected. Perhaps even more important, due process model enthusiasts maintain that the prospect, if not the actual act, of appellate review can deter the commission of similar errors and other forms of misbehavior in subsequent cases. Due process model proponents argue that without the real prospect of appellate review, there would be no effective deterrent of police, prosecutorial, or judicial misbehavior or error.

Because the population of the United States in the future will have greater cultural and racial diversity, criminal courts may be forced to adapt their routines and personnel to those changing demographics. Among the changes that may be required in the future are:

1. A greater sensitivity of court personnel to cultural diversity issues.
2. An increased ability of court personnel to communicate effectively with non-English-speaking people (this will require the employment of interpreters and multilingual staff, as well as the provision of other language services, to ensure that due-process rights are protected).
3. A more culturally and racially diverse workforce that better reflects the demographic characteristics of the population it serves.[14]

As the number of people aged 65 and over increases, the operation of criminal courts will probably have to change in other ways as well. In the first place, the types of cases routinely heard in criminal courts are likely to change somewhat and to reflect more and more the problems confronted by the elderly. For example, crimes committed by and against the elderly will probably increase, as will consideration of such issues as the right to die and the appropriate use of new medical technologies.[15] An older population will also put new demands on the way criminal courts conduct business. At the very least, courts will have to better accommodate people with physical disabilities, such as hearing and visual impairments. For example, to serve hearing-impaired clients, a text telephone (telecommunications device for the deaf, or TDD) or an interpreter will probably become a standard fixture

Bilingual Courts

On January 19, 2000, the New Mexico Supreme Court ruled that people cannot be disqualified from serving as jurors simply because they do not speak English. The decision will require the use of translators in New Mexico courtrooms.

SOURCE: "Court: Jurors don't have to speak English to serve," *The Orlando Sentinel* (January 20, 2000), p. A-10.

▲ Courts are already adapting to the future by employing signers for hearing-impaired persons. *In what other ways will courts of the future have to change?*

in courtrooms of the future. Likewise, court personnel might be trained to establish eye contact when addressing people with hearing impairments, to provide verbal prompts to people with visual impairments, and to sit down when talking to people who are confined to wheelchairs.[16]

If the crime control model dominates the future, criminal courts will probably have to handle an increasing number of juvenile offenders, too, as the practice of transferring juvenile offenders to criminal court for trial increases (see the discussion in Chapter 13). Moreover, to the extent that crime control model principles guide the practice, Americans should expect younger and younger juvenile offenders to be transferred. If this trend becomes the norm, it is conceivable that sometime in the future the juvenile court, and possibly the entire juvenile justice system, could be eliminated entirely, in which case juvenile offenders would be treated similarly to adult criminal offenders.

Ironically, even if due process model principles guide the future, juvenile justice might be eliminated anyway. Juvenile courts are currently providing juvenile offenders with a greater number of procedural rights and are adopting more adversarial procedures (reflecting due process model principles). They are also increasingly replacing paternalistic, treatment-oriented correctional strategies with more punitive ones. As a result of those changes, there may be no practical need for a separate juvenile justice process in the future. In other words, if juvenile offenders are going to be treated exactly the same as adult criminal offenders, why have a separate juvenile justice process?

Regardless of which model of criminal justice dominates the future, it is likely that most conflicts—with the possible exception of the more serious ones—that today are dealt with through the adversary process of justice will be handled differently through alternative dispute resolution programs. In other words, criminal courts will become the arenas of last resort for most conflicts, used only when all other methods of resolving disputes have been exhausted. The two alternative methods of dispute resolution that will probably be used most widely in the future are mediation and arbitration.

The Aging Population

According to U.S. Bureau of Census forecasts, the percentage of the U.S. population 65 or older, which was 8.1 percent in 1950 and 12.7 percent in 1998, will reach 16.5 percent in 2020 and 20.4 percent by the middle of the twenty-first century.

mediation
A dispute resolution process that brings disputants together with a third party (a mediator) who is trained in the art of helping people resolve disputes to everyone's satisfaction. The agreed-upon resolution is then formalized into a binding consent agreement.

arbitration
A dispute resolution process that brings disputants together with a third party (an arbitrator) who has the skills to listen objectively to evidence presented by both sides regarding a conflict, to ask probing and relevant questions of each side, and to arrive at an equitable solution to the dispute.

restorative justice
A process whereby an offender is required to contribute to restoring the health of the community, repairing the harm done, and meeting victims' needs.

reintegrative shaming
A strategy in which disappointment is expressed for the offender's actions, the offender is shamed and punished, and, more importantly, following the expression of disappointment and shame is a concerted effort on the part of the community to forgive the offender and reintegrate him or her back into society.

Gene Stephens, a criminologist who specializes in the future of crime and criminal justice, proposes a model, based on current neighborhood justice centers, that integrates mediation and arbitration into a process he calls "participatory justice."[17] **Mediation** brings disputants together with a third party (a mediator) who is trained in the art of helping people resolve disputes. The job of the mediator is to help the disputants talk out their problems, to offer suggestions about possible resolutions, and, if possible, to achieve consensus about how the dispute can be resolved to everyone's satisfaction. The agreed-upon resolution is then formalized into a binding consent agreement. **Arbitration,** on the other hand, brings disputants together with a third party (an arbitrator) who has the skills to listen dispassionately to evidence presented by both sides of a conflict. The arbitrator asks probing and relevant questions of each side and arrives at an equitable solution to the dispute. The process is concluded when the arbitrator imposes a resolution of the dispute, which is binding on all parties.

For Stephens, the goal of both methods is to resolve any conflicts through a consent agreement completed by all parties involved in the dispute. Mediation is the primary method of resolution. Arbitration is a backup procedure used only when mediation fails or is inappropriate (for example, in contract murder cases). In Stephens's model, appeals from mediation would be unnecessary because of the consent agreement, while appeals from arbitration would be limited to a single appeal to a three-member board of arbitrators. A variety of resolutions, whether by consent agreement or imposed arbitration, would be available. They include monetary restitution, community service, therapy, and even incarceration. Violations of consent agreements would be handled through arbitration, and violations of imposed arbitration resolutions would be dealt with through increasingly coercive measures—probably ending with incarceration. Stephens maintains that participatory justice would be cheaper, faster, and more equitable than the current adversary process of justice.[18]

Participatory justice is a form of restorative justice, an alternative to the punitive justice currently used in the United States and many other countries. The primary goals of **restorative justice** are to restore the health of the community, meet victims' needs, repair the harm done, and require the offender to contribute to those repairs. Another form of restorative justice that may be adopted in the United States in the future is Australian criminologist John Braithwaite's "reintegrative shaming."[19] **Reintegrative shaming** is a strategy in which disappointment is expressed for the offender's actions, the offender is shamed and punished, but, what is more important, following the expression of disappointment and shame is a concerted effort on the part of the community to forgive the offender and reintegrate him or her back into society. Braithwaite contends that the practice of reintegrative shaming is one of the primary reasons for Japan's relatively low crime rate.

Clearly, the future of the administration of justice in the United States should be quite different from what it is today. The exact differences will depend on which model's principles and policies dominate. Areas in which differences and changes are likely to be most pronounced include the availability of legal counsel at various stages in the process; retention or abolition of the preliminary hearing, the grand jury, and juvenile justice; and the extent of pretrial detention, plea bargaining, alternative dispute resolution procedures, judicial sentencing flexibility, and the appellate process. Courts of the future will also have to adapt to the needs of an increasingly older and more racially and culturally diverse population.

Before considering the future of corrections in the United States, it is important to emphasize that advances in technology are likely to influence the administration of justice in the future, just as they will affect the future of law enforcement. The possible substitution of electronically monitored house arrest for pretrial detention has already been examined. Additionally, in many jurisdictions in the United States today it is no longer necessary for defendants to physically appear in court for the initial appearance, preliminary hearing, arraignment, or even trial. Interactive television can be used to administer justice to defendants without incurring the risks involved in physically transporting them to a courtroom. This development has allowed jails to be built in more remote areas of municipalities, affording greater protection to the citizens of a community and reducing the costs of constructing jails because they need not be built in expensive urban locations. Courts are also allowing witnesses to provide videotaped depositions when they are physically unable to be present in court and allowing children to testify via interactive television in some child sex abuse cases.[20] Those practices are likely to continue and be expanded.

Perhaps, someday, determination of guilt or innocence, as well as the truthfulness of testimony, will become a routine matter of simply employing mind-reading technology. For example, the transfer to the public domain, via computer or some other device, of ribonucleic acid (RNA) structures that form memories will make deception and privacy of thoughts nearly impossible.[21] Sometime in the future, it may even be possible to retrieve memories of the events of a crime from the stored RNA memory chains (or "memory banks") of deceased victims and witnesses.[22] Imagine the constitutional questions raised by such technological abilities.

Mediation

A Department of Justice evaluation of the Neighborhood Justice Center in Atlanta, Georgia, found that, in 88 percent of the mediation cases handled, both sides were satisfied with the process.

SOURCE: Gene Stephens, "Crime and Punishment: Forces Shaping the Future," *The Futurist* (January-February 1987), p. 22.

▲ The use of interactive television in the administration of justice is likely to be expanded in the future. *Besides those mentioned, what are some of the other benefits of having interactive television in the courtroom?*

Among other technological advances that people should expect in the administration of justice in the future (some are available today) are the following:

1. More efficient processing and recording of information by computer (thus eliminating the need for paper files).

2. Instantaneous long-distance communication between integrated court systems.

3. Use of artificial intelligence to assist in legal research and various decision-making duties, such as sentencing.

4. Use of computer-generated graphics to reconstruct crime incidents.

5. Use of computers to create a virtual reality in which court participants can experience an interactive three-dimensional re-creation of a crime scene.

6. Use of a computer that can extract the events of a crime from the conscious and unconscious memory of a witness.

7. Kiosk jurisprudence, that is, court information stations located throughout the community, where 24 hours a day, citizens can conduct court business such as filing complaints or paying fines, or receive court information such as the court's daily calendar, the estimated time of an arraignment, and the outcomes of cases that have already been heard.[23]

14.3 CRITICAL THINKING

1. Can you think of any other technological advances that could impact the administration of justice in the future?

2. Review the FYI on Bilingual Courts presented on page 536. Do you think that people who don't speak English should be allowed to serve as jurors? Why or why not?

14.4 The Future of Corrections

The crime control and due process models used in the previous sections do not lend themselves as well to a consideration of the future of corrections. The primary reason is that in the area of corrections, crime control is, and probably will remain, the paramount goal. This does not mean that due process concerns are unimportant, however. Whatever new strategies are employed in corrections in the future will have to conform to constitutional restrictions. Specifically, the Eighth Amendment protection against cruel and unusual punishment—however that phrase is interpreted in the future—will have to be respected and will no doubt set the outer limits of what corrections in the future might be.

Perhaps the most divisive issue that will confront correctional policy makers in the future is whether increasingly scarce resources should be devoted more to punishment (to achieve the goals of retribution and incapacitation) or to rehabilitation (to achieve the goals of specific deterrence and successful reintegration). If the current trend continues, the answer is easy: scarce correctional dollars will be devoted primarily to punishment. In fact, it has recently been argued that a "new penology" has already emerged—a penology that has abandoned rehabilitation in favor of efficiently managing large numbers of prisoners.[24] Success for this new penology is not measured by reductions in recidivism (a standard measure of correctional success used in the past), but rather by how efficiently correctional systems manage prisoners within budgetary constraints.[25]

Most people knowledgeable about corrections in the United States paint a rather bleak picture of its future. They believe that the number of citizens under correctional custody—in jail, in prison, on probation, or on parole—will continue to increase. Increasing numbers of offenders under correctional supervision, in turn, are likely to consume increasingly larger proportions of city, county, state, and federal budgets.

To make matters worse, scholars knowledgeable about corrections predict that alternatives to incarceration will not prevent the need to fund hundreds of costly new jails and prisons in the immediate future. In the first place, they contend, recent history demonstrates that increases in the use of alternatives to incarceration do not necessarily lead to decreases in the use of incarceration. Instead, increases in the use of alternatives coincide with increases in the use of incarceration, through net-widening, for example. This phenomenon occurred in the 1980s, when the use of community-based supervision nearly tripled and the use of incarceration almost doubled.[26]

A second reason that alternatives to incarceration will probably not reduce the need for more jails and prisons is that only a small percentage of future prisoners are likely to be good candidates for alternative programs. According to one authority, more than 95 percent of current prisoners are either violent offenders or repeat offenders with two or more felony convictions. Only five percent of prisoners can be considered low-risk offenders and thus good candidates for alternatives to incarceration.[27] This ratio of high-risk prisoners to low-risk prisoners is not likely to change dramatically in the future.

Prisons of the Future
Prisoners in the future may be incarcerated in self-supporting undersea or space prisons, as the old practice of transporting prisoners is revived.

SOURCE: Gene Stephens, "Prisons," in G. T. Kurian and G. T. T. Molitor (eds.), *Encyclopedia of the Future* (New York: Simon & Schuster, Macmillan), 1996, p. 751.

▲ The federal super maximum-security prison in Florence, Colorado, was one of the first of the "new penology" institutions that has abandoned rehabilitation in favor of efficiently managing a large population of violent offenders. *What are some of the problems of abandoning rehabilitation as a goal of punishment?*

Privatization

At year-end 1999, about 14 private companies owned or managed nearly 156 correctional institutions in 29 states, the District of Columbia, and Puerto Rico. Two companies, Corrections Corporation of America (with a 56 percent market share) and Wackenhut Corrections Corporation (with a 25 percent market share), dominated the industry.

SOURCE: From Charles W. Thomas, "Private Adult Correctional Facility Census: A 'Real-Time' Statistical Profile." <http://web.crim.ufl.edu/PCP/census/1999/market.html> (December 19, 2000). Table 1 and Chart 3.

cryonics
A process of human hibernation that involves freezing the body.

Future expenditures of tax dollars on corrections by governments at all levels will be made grudgingly, after much wrangling and debate. Every attempt will be made to carry out corrections functions as inexpensively as possible. Because the vast majority of correctional clientele will be members of the underclass, as is the case today, there will be little public resistance to low-cost management strategies. Indeed, corrections in the future is likely to take on "a kind of waste management function."[28]

Among the cost-reduction strategies likely to be advocated in the future are various alternatives to incarceration. For example, most persons convicted of minor offenses may be required to perform community service such as litter control and maintenance and construction of government buildings and grounds.[29] However, as described earlier, the cost savings of alternatives to incarceration tend to be illusory. In any case, most offenders who otherwise would be sent to prison will be considered poor candidates for the available alternatives.

Another cost-reduction strategy likely to receive increasing support in the future is the privatization of corrections. As described in Chapter 10 ("Institutional Corrections"), the private sector has been involved in corrections in various ways for a long time. Recently, private companies have entered the business of operating entire jails and prisons, and this practice, no doubt, will increase dramatically in the future.

However, a problem with the operation of jails and prisons by private companies—and a reason that cost savings from this strategy may prove minimal at best—is that private companies are in business to make a profit. If the companies are publicly owned, there is tremendous pressure on management to maximize shareholder value. As a result, it can be expected that private or public correctional companies will do all in their power to protect and enhance their interests by lobbying government officials for more favorable terms of operation and by using marketing to produce a greater demand for their products (that is, more offenders jailed or imprisoned).[30]

A third cost reduction strategy—potentially the most effective one—is the use of new technology. For example, the use of cameras to watch prisoners and robots to service them, as well as the use of sensing devices on an institution's perimeter, would reduce the need for most correctional officers. The use of ultrasound may be the solution to costly prison riots. "Piping high-pitched sound over improved intercom systems would momentarily render everyone in the affected area unconscious and allow staff to enter, disarm, and regain custody."[31] If the death penalty continues to be employed in the United States, ultrasound may provide a more humane and cost-effective method of execution. In the near future, ultrasound could be provided at levels that would literally dematerialize the offender (eliminating the costs of disposing of the body).[32] Another possibility is instant death by laser ray.[33] The costs of building or enlarging more jails and prisons because of overcrowding would be reduced significantly in the future through the use of **cryonics** (freezing) and other forms of human hibernation.[34] Many prisoners could be "stored" in a small amount of space with the use of such technologies. In fact, they could literally be stacked on top of each other in coffinlike containers.

You have already learned about the use of electronically monitored house arrest for pretrial detainees (using electrodes connected to a monitor, perhaps surgically implanted, that would intermittently shock clients while they were outside a designated area). The same technology could be used for

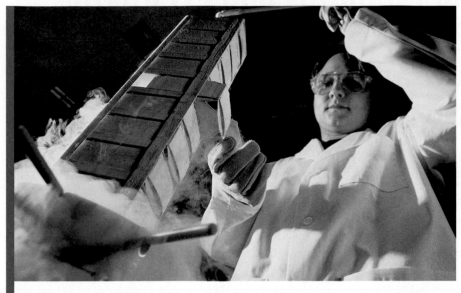

▲ Prison overcrowding could someday lead to the use of cryonics and other forms of human hibernation. *What problems might arise if cryonics were used to deal with prison overcrowding?*

probationers and parolees, reducing the number of probation and parole officers needed. In addition, a subliminal-message player might be implanted in probationers, parolees, and prisoners that would provide 24-hour anticrime messages, such as "Obey the law" or "Do what is required of you," or synthesized body chemicals could be implanted that would keep offenders under constant control.[35] The costs related to future violations could be reduced dramatically through such methods.

However, it is important to keep in mind that several possible factors might significantly reduce or negate the tremendous cost savings anticipated from new correctional technologies. For example, the success of the strategy may create incentives for net-widening, which will reduce or eliminate any anticipated cost savings.[36] In addition, technology has its own costs: Experts must be employed, staff must be trained, equipment must be serviced, and systems must be upgraded as new technologies are introduced.[37]

You may have noticed that this discussion did not cover an important subject: crime and delinquency prevention—the effort to prevent criminal and delinquent acts from being committed in the first place. Although crime and delinquency prevention will probably be a priority in the future, it will be mostly the responsibility of government agencies and philanthropic organizations outside the criminal justice process (for example, social, health, and welfare agencies). Because the focus of this book is criminal justice in the United States, speculate future crime and delinquency prevention strategies will not be addressed.

14.4 CRITICAL THINKING

1. When it comes to corrections, to what do you think more money should be devoted: punishment or rehabilitation? Why?

2. Of the possible future technology advances presented above, which do you think could have the most significant impact on corrections in the future? Why?

Review and Applications

SUMMARY BY CHAPTER OBJECTIVES

1. Point Out Major Differences Between Packer's Crime Control and Due Process Models

From a political standpoint, the crime control model of criminal justice reflects traditional conservative values, while the due process model embodies traditional liberal values. In the crime control model, the control of criminal behavior is by far the most important function of criminal justice. Consequently, the primary focus of this model is on efficiency in the operation of the criminal justice process. The goal of the due process model, on the other hand, is at least as much to protect the innocent as it is to convict the guilty. Fundamentally, the due process model defends the ideal of personal freedom and its protection, and rests on the assumption that the prevention of tyranny on the part of government and its agents is the most important function of the criminal justice process.

2. Describe the Possible Future of Law Enforcement if the Crime Control Model Dominates, and the Possible Future if the Due Process Model Dominates

If law enforcement in the future increasingly reflects the principles and policies of the crime control model, then Americans might expect fewer limitations on how the police attempt to combat crime. However, if there is a shift to the principles and policies of the due process model, Americans should expect existing limitations on how the police combat crime to remain intact or even to be expanded.

3. Describe the Possible Future of the Administration of Justice if the Crime Control Model Dominates, and the Possible Future if the Due Process Model Dominates

If the crime control model dominates the administration of justice in the future, then the right to legal counsel at critical pre- and posttrial stages may be scaled back significantly, the preliminary hearing may be abolished, and the use of pretrial detention may be expanded; there may be fewer criminal trials and more plea bargaining, and appeals may be strongly discouraged and limited. If the due process model dominates, then the current right to counsel at a variety of critical stages in the process is likely to be maintained or, perhaps, extended somewhat (for example, to appeals beyond the first one); the grand jury may be eliminated; plea bargaining probably will be discouraged, and the number of criminal cases that go to trial is therefore likely to increase substantially; and there will probably be no limitations on the right to appeal.

4. Identify Perhaps the Most Divisive Issue that will Confront Correctional Policy Makers in the Future

Perhaps the most divisive issue that will confront correctional policy makers in the future is whether increasingly scarce resources will be devoted more to punishment (to achieve the goals of retribution and incapacitation) or to rehabilitation (to achieve the goals of specific deterrence and successful reintegration).

5. Describe the Possible Future of Corrections

Most people knowledgeable about corrections in the United States paint a rather bleak picture of its future: an increasing number of offenders under correctional supervision, consuming larger and larger proportions of state and federal budgets. Future expenditures of tax dollars on corrections by governments at all levels will be made grudgingly, after much wrangling and debate. Every attempt will be made to carry out corrections functions as inexpensively as possible.

6. List Some of the Cost-Reduction Strategies Likely to Be Advocated in Corrections in the Future

Among the cost reduction strategies likely to be advocated in corrections in the future are various alternatives to incarceration. However, cost savings from those alternatives may be illusory. Another cost reduction strategy likely to receive increasing support in the future is the privatization of corrections. A third cost reduction strategy, and potentially the most effective one, is the use of new technology.

KEY TERMS

crime control model, p. 524
due process model, p. 524
doctrine of legal guilt, p. 527
bionics, p. 529
mediation, p. 538

arbitration, p. 538
restorative justice, p. 538
reintegrative shaming, p. 538
cryonics, p. 542

QUESTIONS FOR REVIEW

1. Why does Packer use the metaphors of *assembly-line justice* and *obstacle-course justice* to characterize his crime control and due process models of criminal justice?

2. What are the bases (that is, the presumptions or doctrines) of Packer's crime control and due process models of criminal justice?

3. How might community policing based on the crime control model of criminal justice differ from community policing based on the due process model?

4. How might bionics affect law enforcement in the future?

5. What is perhaps the thorniest issue regarding the use of DNA technology as a law enforcement tool?

6. What is a principal problem with plea bargaining for due process model supporters?

7. How might the changing demographics of the U.S. population affect the operation of criminal courts?

8. What is the principal difference between mediation and arbitration?

9. What are restorative justice and reintegrative shaming, and how do they differ from punitive justice?

10. What is the *new penology,* and how is its measurement of success different from the measurement of correctional success in the past?

11. What is cryonics, and how might it be used in corrections in the future?

EXPERIENTIAL ACTIVITIES

1. **Compare Models of Criminal Justice** After briefly describing Packer's crime control and due process models to fellow students, family members, or friends, discuss with them whether the crime control model or the due process model ought to dominate criminal justice in the future.

2. **Criminal Justice in the Movies** There are numerous science fiction movies or videos that depict criminal justice in the future. Examples are *Blue Thunder, Escape From New York, Demolition Man, Blade Runner,* and the *RoboCop* series. Watch one or more of those movies or videos, and consider how plausible they seem in light of what you have read in this chapter. Have any of the innovations of these futuristic justice systems become a part of the current American justice system? Are any of these innovations discussed in this chapter?

INTERNET

3. **Explore New Technologies** Go to the Justice Technology Information Network by accessing the link at cj.glencoe.com. Click on Law Enforcement, Corrections, or Forensics. Survey the new technologies available or those on the drawing board. Write a three-page scenario of how law enforcement, corrections, or forensics will change if the new technology is implemented.

4. **Evaluate Programs** Access "Creating a New Criminal Justice System for the 21st Century: Findings and Results From State and Local Program Evaluations" through cj.glencoe.com. Read some of the program evaluations. Write a short essay on why the programs may or may not be important in the twenty-first century.

5. **Research the Police Futurists** Access the Web site of Police Futurists International through cj.glencoe.com. Click on "Issue Papers." Read one of these papers. Write an essay on why you agree or disagree with the ideas presented in it.

CRITICAL THINKING EXERCISES

Corrections in the Future

1. It is the year 2028, and you have been asked to serve on a citizens' committee charged with providing input about the creation of a new supermaximum-security federal prison. The prison will be built either several hundred feet beneath the ocean's surface off the east coast of the United States or on the moon. The rationale for these locations is to better isolate prisoners from the law-abiding population and to take advantage of prison labor for the high-risk jobs of either marine farming or the mining of new and useful materials in space. The technology and the resources to build the prison, though expensive, are available.

   a. Which location would be preferable? Why?

   b. Should public tax dollars be used to fund the project, or should a private corporation be allowed to build and operate the facility at its own expense and keep any profits from the farming or mining business?

   c. What special problems might arise because of the location of the prison?

Law Enforcement in the Future

2. It is the year 2028 in Washington, D.C., and public service officers, formerly called police officers, are flying routine patrol with the aid of their new jet packs. While flying over a condo near the city's center, two of the officers, using their bionic eyes and ears, detect what appear to be a half dozen men plotting to bomb the White House. Surveying the condo from their sky perch, the officers see, stored in a bedroom closet, enough of a new, illegal, and largely undetectable hydrogen-based explosive to do the job. The officers, using the ultrasmall two-way communication devices implanted in their larynxes, communicate to headquarters what they have seen. They await further orders.

   a. Do the officers have probable cause to obtain a search warrant from a magistrate or to make an arrest? If you were a proponent of Packer's crime control model, what would your answer be? If you were a proponent of Packer's due process model, what would your answer be?

   b. How might the legal issues of the right to privacy, the admissibility of evidence, the exclusionary rule, and the plain-view doctrine affect the use of this new technology by law enforcement officers?

   c. What restraints, if any, should be imposed on the use of this new technology by law enforcement officers? If you were a proponent of Packer's crime control model, what would your answer be? If you were a proponent of Packer's due process model, what would your answer be?

ADDITIONAL READING

Dilulio, John J. Jr., *No Escape: The Future of American Corrections.* New York: Basic Books, 1991.

Klofas, John and Stan Stojkovic (eds.). *Crime and Justice in the Year 2010.* Belmont, CA: Wadsworth, 1995.

Maguire, Brendan and Polly Radosh (eds.). *The Past, Present, and Future of American Criminal Justice.* New York: General Hall, 1995.

Packer, Herbert. *The Limits of the Criminal Sanction.* Palo Alto, CA: Stanford University Press, 1968.

ENDNOTES

1. Herbert Packer, *The Limits of the Criminal Sanction* (Stanford, CA: Stanford University Press, 1968).

2. See, for example, Walter B. Miller, "Ideology and Criminal Justice Policy: Some Current Issues," *Journal of Criminal Law and Criminology,* Vol. 64 (1973), pp. 141–62.

3. Gene Stephens, "High-Tech Crime: The Threat to Civil Liberties," *The Futurist* (July–August 1990), pp. 20–25.

4. Gene Stephens, "Law Enforcement," in G. T. Kurian and G. T. T. Molitor (eds.), *Encyclopedia of the Future* (New York: Simon & Schuster, Macmillan, 1996), p. 538; Jeff Kunerth, "You have no right to privacy you seek." *The Orlando Sentinel* (August 8, 1999), p. A-1.

5. Jack Cheevers, "Beyond '*RoboCop*': Concern for Officer Safety Fuels Innovation," *The Charlotte Observer* (August 26, 1994), p. 14A.

6. Gene Stephens, "Drugs and Crime in the Twenty-First Century," *The Futurist* (May–June 1992), pp. 19–22.

7. Stephens (1996), op. cit., p. 539; "Police test voice translator box." *The Orlando Sentinel* (December 5, 1999), p. A-17.

8. "New ultra-wideband could make walls see-through," *The Orlando Sentinel* (June 15, 2000), p. A-3.

9. Cheevers, op. cit.

10. Stephens (1996), op. cit., p. 539.

11. Terry D. Anderson, Kenneth D. Gisborne, Marilyn Hamilton, Pat Holiday, John C. LeDoux, Gene Stephens, and John Welter, *Every Officer Is A Leader: Transforming Leadership in Police, Justice, and Public Safety.* Boca Raton, FL: St. Lucie Press (2000), p. 368.

12. Ibid.

13. Stephens (1990), op. cit.

14. Anita Neuberger Blowers, "The Future of American Courts," in B. Maguire and P. Radosh (eds.), *The Past, Present, and Future of American Criminal Justice* (New York: General Hall, 1995).

15. Ibid.

16. Ibid.

17. Gene Stephens, "Crime and Punishment: Forces Shaping the Future," *The Futurist* (January–February 1987), pp. 18–26.

18. Ibid.

19. John Braithwaite, *Crime, Shame and Reintegration* (Cambridge: Cambridge University Press, 1989).

20. Blowers, op. cit.

21. Stephens (1990), op. cit.

22. Ibid.

23. Blowers, op. cit.

24. Malcolm M. Feeley and Jonathan Simon, "The New Penology: Notes on the Emerging Strategy of Corrections and Its Implications," Criminology, Vol. 30 (1992), pp. 449–74.

25. Ibid.

26. John J. Dilulio, Jr., *No Escape: The Future of American Corrections* (New York: Basic Books, 1991), p. 4.

27. Ibid.

28. Feeley and Simon, op. cit., p. 470.

29. Stephens, "Prisons," op. cit.

30. See Francis T. Cullen and John P. Wright, "The Future of Corrections," in B. Maguire and P. Radosh (eds.), *The Past, Present, and Future of American Criminal Justice* (New York: General Hall, 1995).

31. Stephens (1990), op. cit.

32. Ibid.

33. Stephens, "Prisons," op. cit., p. 751.

34. Stephens (1990), op. cit.

35. Ibid.

36. Cullen and Wright, op. cit.

37. Ibid.

Glossary

Adjudication The juvenile court equivalent of a trial in criminal court or the process of rendering a judicial decision regarding the truth of the facts alleged in a petition. (13)

Administrative segregation The keeping of inmates in secure isolation so that they cannot harm others. (10)

Aggravated factors In death sentencing, circumstances that make a crime worse. (9)

Aggressive patrol The practice of having an entire patrol section make numerous traffic stops and field interrogations. (6)

Allocution The procedure at a sentencing hearing in which the convicted defendant has the right to address the court before the sentence is imposed. During allocution, a defendant is identified as the person found guilty and has a right to deny or explain information contained in the PSI if his or her sentence is based on it. (9)

Anomie For Durkheim, the dissociation of the individual form the collective conscience. For Merton, the contradiction between the cultural goal of achieving wealth and the social structure's inability to provide legitimate institutional means for achieving the goal. For Cohen, it is caused by the inability of juveniles to achieve status among peers by socially acceptable means. (3)

Appellate jurisdiction The power of a court to review a case for errors of law. (8)

Arbitration A dispute resolution process that brings disputants together with a third party (an arbitrator) who has the skills to listen objectively to evidence presented by both sides regarding a conflict, to ask probing and relevant questions of each side, and to arrive at an equitable solution to the dispute. (14)

Arraignment A pretrial stage to hear the formal information or indictment and to allow the defendant to enter a plea. (8)

Arrest The seizure of a person or the taking of a person into custody, either actual physical custody, as when a suspect is handcuffed by a police officer, or constructive custody, as when a person peacefully submits to a police officer's control. (4)

Arrest warrant A written order directing law enforcement officers to arrest a person. (1)

Arrest warrant A written order directing law enforcement officers to arrest a person. The charge or charges against a suspect are specified on the warrant. (8)

Atavist A person who reverts to a savage type. (3)

Auburn system An early system of penology, originating at Auburn Penitentiary in New York, under which inmates worked and ate together in silence during the day and were placed in solitary cells for the evening. (10)

Bail bond/bail Usually a monetary guarantee deposited with the court that is supposed to ensure that the suspect or defendant will appear at a later stage in the criminal justice process. (8)

Banishment A punishment, originating in ancient times, that required offenders to leave the community and live elsewhere, commonly in the wilderness. (10)

Bench trial A trial before a judge without a jury. (8)

Bench warrant or _capias_ A document that authorizes a suspect's or defendant's arrest for not appearing in court as required. (8)

Beyond a reasonable doubt The standard of proof necessary to find a defendant guilty in a criminal trial. (4)

Bifurcated trial A two-stage trial (unlike the one-stage trial in other felony cases) consisting of a guilt phase and a separate penalty phase. (9)

Biological inferiority According to biological theories, a criminal's innate physiological makeup produces certain physical or genetic characteristics that distinguish criminals from non-criminals. (3)

Glossary

Bionics The replacing of human body parts with mechanical parts. (14)

Booking The administrative recording of an arrest. Typically, the suspect's name, the charge, and perhaps the suspect's fingerprints or photograph are entered into the police blotter. (1)

Chicago School A group of sociologists at the University of Chicago who assumed in their research that delinquent behavior was a product of social disorganization. (3)

Civil law One of two types of law practiced in the United States (other is criminal law); a means of resolving conflicts between individuals. It includes personal injury claims (torts), the law of contracts and property; and subjects such as administrative law and the regulation of public utilities. (4)

Classical theory A product of the Enlightenment, based on the assumption that people exercise free will and are thus completely responsible for their actions. In classical theory, human behavior, including criminal behavior, is motivated by a hedonistic rationality in which individual theory weigh the potential pleasure of an action against the possible pain associated with it. (3)

Classification facility A facility to which newly sentenced offenders are taken so that their security risks and needs can be assessed and they can be assigned to a permanent institution. (10)

Clear and convincing evidence The standard of proof required in some civil cases and, in federal courts, the standard of proof necessary for a defendant to make a successful claim of insanity. (4)

Co-correctional facilities Usually small, minimum-security institutions that house both men and women with the goal of normalizing the prison environment by integrating the daytime activities of the sexes. (10)

Collective conscience The general sense of morality of the times. (3)

Community corrections The subfield of corrections in which offenders are supervised and provided services outside jail or prison. (12)

Community policing A contemporary approach to policing that actively involves the community in a working partnership to control and reduce crime. (5)

Commutation Reduction of the original sentence given by executive authority, usually a state's governor. (8)

Complaint A charging document specifying that an offense has been committed by a person or persons named or described. It is usually used for misdemeanors and ordinance violations. (8)

Conditional release A form of release that requires a suspect/defendant to maintain contact with a pretrial release program or undergo regular drug monitoring or treatment. (8)

Confession An admission by a person accused of a crime that he or she committed the offense charged. (4)

Conflict theory A theory that assumes society is based primarily on conflict between competing interest groups and that criminal law and the criminal justice system are used to control subordinate groups. Crime is caused by relative powerlessness. (3)

Conjugal visits An arrangement whereby inmates are permitted to visit in private with their spouses or significant others to maintain their personal relationship. (10)

Constable-Watch system A system of protection in early England in which citizens, under the direction of a constable, or chief peacekeeper, were required to guard the city and to pursue criminals. (5)

Contraband An illegal substance or object. (4)

Contract security Protective services that a private security firm provides to people, agencies, and companies that do not employ their own security personnel or that need extra protection. Contract security employees are not peace officers. (5)

Convict code A constellation of values, norms, and roles that regulate the way inmates interact with one another and with prison staff. (8)

Glossary

Cottage reformatories Correctional facilities for youths, first developed in the late 1800s, that were intended to closely parallel family life and remove children from negative influences of the urban environment. Children in those facilities lived with surrogate parents, who were responsible for the youths' training and education. (13)

Crime control model One of Packer's two models of the criminal justice process. Politically, it reflects traditional conservative values. In this model, the control of criminal behavior is the most important function of criminal justice. (14)

Criminal anthropology The study of "criminal" human beings. (3)

Criminal law One of two general types of law practiced in the United States (the other is civil law); "a formal means of social control [that uses] rules…interpreted [and enforced] by the courts…to set limits to the conduct of the citizens, to guide the officials, and to define…unacceptable behavior." (4)

Criminal sanctions or criminal punishment Penalties that are imposed for violating criminal law. (9)

Criminalization process The way people and actions are defined as criminal. (3)

Criminological theory The explanation of criminal behavior, as well as the behavior of police, attorneys, prosecutors, judges, correctional personnel, victims, and other actions in the criminal justice system. (3)

Crisis intervention A counselor's efforts to address some crisis in an inmate's life and to calm the inmate. (10)

Cryonics A process of human hibernation that involves freezing the body. (14)

Custody level The classification assigned to an inmate to indicate the degree of precaution that needs to be taken when working with that inmate. (10)

Cybercrime The use of computer technology to commit crime. (6)

D

Day reporting centers Facilities that are designed for offenders who would otherwise be in prison or jail. Offenders are required to report regularly to confer with staff about supervision and treatment matters. (12)

Defendant A person against whom a legal action is brought, a warrant is issued, or an indictment is found. (1)

Deprivation model A theory that the inmate society arises as a response to the prison environment and the painful conditions of confinement. (8)

Determinate sentence A sentence with a fixed period of incarceration, which eliminates the decision-making responsibility of parole boards. (9)

Differential association Sutherland's theory that persons who become criminal do so because of contacts with criminal patterns and isolation from anticriminal patterns. (3)

Directed patrol Patrolling under guidance or orders on how to use patrol time. (6)

Disposition An order of the court specifying what is to be done with a juvenile who has been adjudicated delinquent. A disposition hearing is similar to a sentencing hearing in criminal court. (13)

Diversion Organized, systematic efforts to remove individuals from further processing in criminal justice by placing them in alternative programs; diversions may by be pretrial or post-trial. (12)

Doctrine of fundamental fairness The rule that makes confessions inadmissible in criminal trials if they were obtained by means of either psychological manipulation or "third-degree" methods. (4)

Glossary

Doctrine of legal guilt The principle that people are not to be held guilty of crime merely on a showing, based on reliable evidence, that in all probability they did in fact commit the crime they are accused of committing. Legal guilt results only when factual guilt is determined in a procedurally regular fashion, as in a criminal trial, and when the procedural rules designed to protect suspects and defendants and to safeguard the integrity of the process are employed. (14)

Double jeopardy The trying of a defendant a second time for the same offense when jeopardy attached in the first trial and a mistrial was not declared. (4)

Dual court system The court system in the United States, consisting of one system of state and local courts and another system of federal courts. (8)

Due process model One of Packer's two models of the criminal justice process. Politically, it embodies traditional liberal values. In this model, the principal goal of criminal justice is at least as much to protect the innocent as it is to convict the guilty. (14)

Due process The rights of people suspected of or charged with crimes. The procedures followed by courts to ensure that a defendant's constitutional rights are not violated. (8)

Electronic monitoring An arrangement that allows an offender's whereabouts to be gauged through the use of computer technology. (12)

Exclusionary rule The rule that illegally seized evidence must be excluded from trials in federal courts. (4)

Extinction A process in which behavior that previously was positively reinforced is no longer reinforced. (3)

Felony A relatively serious offense punishable by death or by confinement in prison for more than one year. (1)

Feminist theory A perspective on criminality that focuses on women's experiences and seeks to abolish men's control over women's labor and sexuality. (3)

Field interrogation A temporary detention in which officers stop and question pedestrians and motorists they find in suspicious circumstances. (6)

Flat-time sentencing Sentencing in which judges may choose between probation and imprisonment but have little discretion in setting the length of a prison sentence. (9)

Frisking Conducting a search for weapons by lightly patting the outside of a suspect's clothing, feeling for hard objects that might be weapons. (4)

G

General deterrence The attempt to prevent people in general from engaging in crime by punishing specific individuals and making examples of them. (8)

General jurisdiction The power of a court to hear any type of case. (8)

GIS crime mapping A technique that involves the charting of crime patterns within a geographic area. (6)

Good time The number of days deducted from a sentence by prison authorities for good behavior or for other reasons. (9)

Grand jury Generally a group of 12 to 23 citizens who meet in closed sessions to investigate charges coming from preliminary hearings or to engage in other responsibilities. A primary purpose of the grand jury is to determine whether there is probable cause to believe that the accused committed the crime or crimes. (8)

Glossary

Grand jury indictment A written accusation by a grand jury charging that one or more persons have committed a crime. (8)

H

Habeas corpus A court order requiring that a confined person be brought to court so that his or her claims can be heard. (8)

Halfway house Community-based residential facilities that are less secure and restrictive than prison or jail but provide a more controlled environment than other community correctional programs. (12)

Hands-off philosophy A philosophy under which courts are reluctant to hear prisoners' claims regarding their rights while incarcerated. (8)

Hearing officer A lawyer empowered by the juvenile court to hear juvenile cases. (13)

Highway patrol model A model of state law enforcement services in which officers focus on highway traffic safety, enforcement of the state's traffic laws, and the investigation of accidents on the state's roads, highways, and property. (5)

Home confinement A program that requires offenders to remain in their homes except for approved periods of absence; commonly used in combination with electronic monitoring. (12)

Houses of refuge The first specialized correctional institutions for youths in the United States. (13)

Hung jury The result when jurors cannot agree on a verdict. The judge declares a mistrial. The prosecutor must decide whether to retry the case. (8)

I

Imitation or modeling A means by which a person can learn new responses by observing others without performing any overt act or receiving direct reinforcement or reward. (3)

Importation model A theory that the inmate society is shaped by the attributes inmates bring with them when they enter prison. (8)

Incapacitation The removal or restriction of the freedom of those found to have violated criminal laws. (9)

Incarceration rate A figure derived by dividing the number of people incarcerated by the population of the area and multiplying the result by 100,000; used to compare incarceration levels of units with different population sizes. (10)

Indeterminate sentence A sentence with a fixed minimum and maximum term of incarceration, rather than a set period. (9)

Indictment A document that outlines the charge or charges against a defendant. (8)

Informal juvenile justice The actions taken by citizens to respond to juvenile offenders without involving the official agencies of juvenile justice. (13)

Information A document that outlines the formal charge or charges, the law or laws that have been violated, and the evidence to support the charge or charges. (8)

Initial appearance A pretrial stage in which a defendant is brought before a lower court to be given notice of the charge(s) and advised of her or his constitutional rights. (1)

Institution of social control An organization that persuades people, through subtle and not-so-subtle means, to abide by the dominant values of society. (1)

Intake screening The process by which decisions are made about the continued processing of juvenile cases. Decisions might include dismissing the case, referring the youth to a diversion program, or filing a petition. (13)

Intensive Supervision Probation and Parole (ISP) An alternative to incarceration that provides stricter conditions, closer supervision, and more treatment services than traditional probation and parole. (12)

Glossary

Intermediate sanctions Sanctions that, in restrictiveness and punitiveness, lie between traditional probation and traditional imprisonment or, alternatively, between imprisonment and traditional parole. (12)

J

Jail A facility, usually operated at the local level, that holds convicted offenders and unconvicted persons for relatively short periods. (10)

Jailhouse lawyer An inmate skilled in legal matters. (8)

Jurisdiction The right or authority of a justice agency to act in regard to a particular subject matter, territory, or person. (5)

Just desserts The punishment rationale based on the idea that offenders should be punished automatically, simply because they have committed a crime — they "deserve" it — and the idea that the punishment should fit the crime. (9)

L

Labeling theory A theory that emphasizes the criminalization process as the cause of some crime. (3)

Learning theory A theory that explains criminal behavior and its prevention with the concepts of positive reinforcement, negative reinforcement, extinction, punishment, and modeling or imitation. (3)

Left realists A group of social scientists who argue that critical criminologists need to redirect their attention to the fear and the very real victimization experienced by working-class people. (3)

Less-eligibility principle The position that prisoners should receive no service or program superior to the services and programs available to free citizen without charge. (10)

Limbic system A structure surrounding the brain stem that, in part, controls the life functions of heartbeats, breathing, and sleep. (3)

Lockup A very short-term holding facility that is frequently located in or very near an urban police agency so that suspects can be held pending further inquiry. (10)

M

Mandatory release A method of prison release under which an inmate is released after servicing a legally required portion of his or her sentence, minus good-time credits. (8)

Mandatory sentencing Sentencing in which a specified number of years of imprisonment (usually within a range) is provided for particular crimes. (9)

Mediation A dispute resolution process that brings disputants together with a third party (a mediator) who is trained in the art of helping people resolve disputes to everyone's satisfaction. The agreed-upon resolution is then formalized into a binding consent agreement. (14)

Medical model A theory of institutional corrections, popular during the 1940s and 1950s, in which crime was seen as symptomatic of personal illness in need of treatment. (10)

Mere suspicion The standard of proof with the least certainty; a "gut feeling." With mere suspicion, a law enforcement officer cannot legally even stop a suspect. (4)

Milieu therapy A variant of group therapy that encompasses the total living environment so that the environment continually encourages positive behavioral change. (10)

Misdemeanor A less serious crime generally punishable by a fine or by incarceration in jail for not more than one year. (1)

Mitigating factors In death sentencing, circumstances that make a crime less severe than usual. (9)

Myths Beliefs based on emotion rather than analysis. (1)

Glossary

N

Negative reinforcement The removal or reduction of a stimulus whose removal or reduction increases or maintains a response. (3)

Neoclassical theory A modification of classical theory in which it was conceded that certain factors, such as insanity, might inhibit the exercise of free will. (3)

Net-widening A phenomenon that occurs when the offenders placed in a novel program are not the offenders for whom the program was designed. The consequence is that those in the program receive more severe sanctions than they would have received had the new program remained unavailable. (12)

New-generation jail A replacement for traditional jails that features architectural and programming innovations. (10)

Nolle prosequi (nol pros) The notation placed on the official record of a case when prosecutors elect not to prosecute. (8)

Nolo contendre Latin for "no contest." When defendants plead *nolo*, they do not admit guilt but are willing to accept punishment. (8)

O

Operational styles The different overall approaches to the police job. (6)

Ordinance violation Usually the violation of a law of a city or town. (1)

Original jurisdiction The authority of a court to hear a case when it is first brought to court. (8)

P

Panopticon A prison design consisting of a round building with tiers of cells lining their inner circumference and facing a central inspection tower. (10)

Pardon A "forgiveness" for the crime committed that stops further criminal processing. (9)

Parens patriae The legal philosophy justifying state intervention in the lives of children when their parents are unable or unwilling to protect them. (13)

Parole A method of prison release whereby inmates are released at the discretion of a board or other authority before having completed their entire sentences; can also refer to the community supervision received upon release. (12)

Parole guidelines Structured instruments used to estimate the probability of parole recidivism and to direct the release decisions of parole boards. (12)

Patriarchy Men's control over women's labor and sexuality. (3)

Peacemaking criminology An approach that suggest the solutions to all social problems, including crime, are the transformation of human beings, mutual dependence, reduction of class structures, the creation of communities of caring people, and universal social justice. (3)

Peel's principles of policing A dozen standards proposed by Robert Peel, the author of the legislation resulting in the formation of the London Metropolitan Police Department. The standards are still applicable to today's law enforcement. (5)

Penal code The criminal law of a political jurisdiction. (4)

Penal sanction An ideal characteristic of criminal law; the principle that violators will be punished or at least threatened with punishment by the state. (4)

Pennsylvania system An early system of U.S. penology in which inmates were kept in solitary cells so that they could study religious writings, reflect on their misdeeds, and perform handicraft work. (10)

Glossary

Penology The study of prison management and the treatment of offenders. (10)

Personal jurisdiction A court's authority over the parties to a lawsuit. (8)

Petition A legal form of the police complaint that specifies the charges to be heard at the adjudication. (13)

Placing The practice of placing children on farms in the Midwest and West to remove them from the supposedly corrupting influences of their parents and the cities. (13)

Plea bargaining or plea negotiating The practice whereby the prosecutor, the defense attorney, the defendant, and — in many jurisdictions — the judge agree on a specific sentence to be imposed if the accused pleads guilty to an agreed-upon charge or charges instead of going to trial. (8)

Politicality An ideal characteristic of criminal law, referring to its legitimate source. Only violations of rules made by the state, the political jurisdiction that enacted the laws, are crimes. (4)

Positive reinforcement The presentation of a stimulus that increases or maintains a response. (3)

Posses Groups of able-bodied citizens of a community, called into service by a sheriff or constable to chase and apprehend offenders. (5)

Postmodernism An area of critical thought which, among other things, attempts to understand the creation of knowledge, and how knowledge and language create hierarchy and domination. (3)

Power differentials The ability of some groups to dominate other groups in a society. (3)

Precedent A decision that forms a potential basis for deciding the outcomes of similar cases in the future; a by-product of decisions made by trial and appellate court judges, who produce case law whenever they render a decision in a particular case. (4)

Preliminary hearing a pretrial stage used in about one-half of all states and only in felony cases. Its purpose is for a judge to determine whether there is probable cause to support the charge or charges imposed by the prosecutor. (8)

Preponderance of evidence Evidence that outweighs the opposing evidence, or sufficient evidence to overcome doubt or speculation. (4)

Pre-Sentence Investigative Reports (PSIs or PSIRs) Reports that are used in the federal system and the majority of states to help judges determine the appropriate sentence. They are also used in classifying probationers, parolees, and prisoners according to their treatment needs and security risks. (9)

Pre-Sentence Investigation (PSI) An investigation conducted by a probation agency or other designated authority at the request of a court into the past behavior, family circumstances, and personality of an adult who has been convicted of a crime, to assist the court in determining the most appropriate sentence. (12)

Presumptive sentencing Sentencing that allows a judge to retain some sentencing discretion, subject to appellate review. The legislature determines a sentence range for each crime. The judge is expected to impose the typical sentence, specified by statute, unless mitigating or aggravating circumstances justify a sentence below or above the range set by the legislature. (9)

Preventative patrol Patrolling the streets with little direction. Between responses to radio calls, officers are "systematically unsystematic" and observant in an attempt to both prevent and ferret out crime. Also know as random patrol. (6)

Preventive detention Holding suspects or defendants in jail without giving them an opportunity to post bail, because of the threat they pose to society. (8)

Prisonization The process by which as inmate becomes socialized into the customs and principles of the inmate society. (8)

Privatization The involvement of the private sector in the construction and the operation of confinement facilities. (10)

Probable cause The amount of proof necessary for a reasonably intelligent person to suspect that a crime has been committed or that items connected with criminal activity can be found in a particular place. It is the standard of proof needed to conduct a search or to make an arrest. (4)

Probation A sentence in which the offender, rather than being incarcerated, is retained in the community under the supervision of a probation agency and required to abide by certain rules and conditions to avoid incarceration. (12)

Probation conditions Rules that specify what an offender is and is not to do during the course of a probation sentence. (12)

Procedural law The body of law that governs the ways substantive laws are administered; sometimes called *adjective* or *remedial* law. (4)

Proportionality review A review in which the appellate court compares the sentence in the case it is reviewing with penalties imposed in similar cases in the state. The object is to reduce, as much as possible, disparity in death penalty sentencing. (9)

Proprietary security In-house protective services that a security staff, which is not classified as sworn peace officers, provide for the entity that employs them. (5)

Protective custody The segregation of inmates for their own safety. (10)

Psychopaths, sociopaths, or antisocial personalities Persons characterized by no sense of guilt, no subjective conscience, and no sense of right and wrong. They have difficulty in forming relationships with other people; they cannot empathize with other people. (3)

Punishment The imposition of a penalty for criminal wrongdoing. (8)

R

Radical nonintervention A practice based on the idea that youths should be left alone if at all possible, instead of being formally processed. (13)

Radical theories Theories of crime causation that are generally based on a Marxist theory of class struggle. (3)

Reasonable doubt A standard of proof that is more than a gut feeling. It includes the ability to articulate reasons for the suspicion. With reasonable suspicion, a law enforcement officer is legally permitted to stop and frisk a suspect. (4)

Recidivism The return to illegal activity after release from incarceration. (8)

Reform, industrial, or training schools Correctional facilities for youths, first developed in the late 1800s, that focused on custody. Today, these institutions are often called training school and although they may place more emphasis on treatment, they still rely on custody and control. (13)

Regularity An ideal characteristic of criminal law: the applicability of the law to all persons, regardless of social status. (4)

Rehabilitation The attempt to "correct" the personality and behavior of convicted offenders through educational, vocational, or therapeutic treatment and to return them to society as law-abiding citizens. (8, 9)

Reintegration The process of rebuilding former ties to the community and establishing new ties after release from prison. (12)

Reintegrative shaming A strategy in which disappointment is expressed for the offender's actions, the offender is shamed and punished, and, more importantly, following the expression of disappointment and shame is a concerted effort on the part of the community to forgive the offender and reintegrate him or her back into society. (14)

Relative powerlessness In conflict theory, the inability to dominate other groups in society. (3)

Release on own recognizance (ROR) A release secured by a suspect's written promise to appear in court. (8)

Restitution Money paid or services provided by a convicted offender to victims, their survivors, or the community to make up for the injury inflicted. (9)

Restorative justice A process whereby an offender is required to contribute to restoring the health of the community, repairing the harm done, and meeting victims' needs.

Glossary

Retribution A dominant justification for punishment. (9)

Revenge The punishment rationale expressed by the biblical phrase, "An eye for an eye, and a tooth for a tooth." People who seek revenge want to pay back offenders by making them suffer for what they have done. (9)

Revocation The repeal of a probation sentence or parole, and substitution of a more restrictive sentence, because of violation of probation or parole conditions. (12)

Role The right and responsibilities associated with a particular position in society. (6)

Role conflict The psychological stress and frustration that results from trying to perform two or more incompatible responsibilities. (6)

Role expectation The behavior and actions that people expect from a person in a particular role. (6)

Rules of discovery Rules that mandate that a prosecutor provide defense counsel with any exculpatory evidence (evidence favorable to the accused that has a effect on the guilt or punishment) in the prosecutor's possession. (8)

S

Searches Exploration or inspections, by law enforcement officers, of homes, premises, vehicles, or persons, for the purpose of discovering evidence of crimes or persons who are accused of crimes. (4)

Security level A designation applied to a facility to describe the measures taken, both inside and outside, to preserve security and custody. (10)

Seizures The taking of persons or property into custody in response to violations of the criminal law. (4)

Self-incrimination Being a witness against oneself. If forced, it is a violation of the Fifth Amendment. (4)

Shire reeve In medieval England, the chief law enforcement officer in a territorial area called a shire; later called the sheriff. (5)

Shock incarceration The placement of offenders in facilities patterned after military boot camps. (10)

Slave patrols The earliest form of policing in the South. They were a product of the slave codes. (5)

Snitch system A system in which staff learn from inmate informants about the presence of contraband, the potential for disruptions, and other threats to security. (10)

Social contract An imaginary agreement to sacrifice the minimum amount of liberty necessary to prevent anarchy and chaos. (3)

Social contract theory A view in which people are expected to commit crime and delinquency unless they are prevented from doing so. (3)

Social disorganization The condition in which the usual controls over delinquents are largely absent, delinquent behavior is often approved of by parents and neighbors, there are many opportunities for delinquent behavior, and there is little encouragement, training, or opportunity for legitimate employment. (3)

Special jurisdiction The power of a court to hear only certain kinds of cases. (8)

Special or specific deterrence The prevention of individuals from committing crime again by punishing them. (3)

Specificity An ideal characteristic of criminal law, referring to its scope. Although civil law may be general in scope, criminal law should provide strict definitions of specific acts. (4)

Stare decisis The principle of using precedents to guide future decisions in court cases; Latin for "to stand by decided cases." (4)

State police model A model of state law enforcement services in which the agency and its officers have the same law enforcement powers as local police but can exercise them anywhere within the state. (5)

Status offenses Acts that are not crimes when committed by adults but are illegal for children (for examples, truancy or running away from home). (13)

Structured fines or day fines Fines that are based on defendants' ability to pay. (12)

Subject matter jurisdiction The power of a court to hear a particular type of case. (8)

Subpoena A written order issued by a court that requires a person to appear at a certain time and place to give testimony. It can also require that documents and objects be made available for examination by the court. (4)

Sub-rosa economy The secret exchange of goods and services that, though often illicit, are in high demand among inmates; the black market of the prison. (8)

Substantive law The body of law that defines criminal offenses and their penalties. (4)

Summary trial An immediate trial without a jury. (1)

System A smoothly operating set of arrangements and institutions directed toward the achievement of common goals. (1)

Technical violations Failure to abide by the technical rules or conditions of probation or parole (for example, not reporting regularly to the probation officer), as distinct from commission of a new criminal act. (12)

Temporary-release programs Programs that allow jail or prison inmates to leave the facility for short periods to participate in approved community activities. (12)

Theory An assumption (or set of assumptions) that attempts to explain why or how things are related to each other. (3)

Tithing system A private self-help protection system in early medieval England, in which a group of ten families, or a tithing, agreed to follow the law, keep the peace in their areas, and bring law violators to justices. (5)

Tort A violation of the civil law. (4)

Total institution An institutional setting in which persons sharing some characteristics are cut off from the wider society and expected to live according to institutional rules and procedures. (8)

Traffic accident investigation crews In some agencies, the special units assigned to all traffic accident investigations. (6)

Transfer, waiver or certification The act or process by which juveniles who meet specific age, offense, and (in some jurisdictions) prior-record criteria are transferred to criminal court for trial. (13)

Transportation A punishment in which offenders were transported from their home nation to one of that nation's colonies to work. (10)

Trial *de novo* A trial in which an entire case is reheard by a trial court of general jurisdiction because there is an appeal and there is no written transcript of the earlier proceeding. (8)

Uniformity An ideal characteristic of criminal law; the enforcement of the laws against anyone who violates them, regardless of social status. (4)

Unsecured bond An arrangement in which bail is set but no money is paid to the court. (8)

Utility The principle that a policy should provide "the greatest happiness shared by the greatest number." (3)

Venire The pool from which jurors are selected. (8)

Venue The place of the trial. It must be geographically appropriate. (4)

Victim-impact statement Descriptions of the harm and suffering that a crime has caused victims and their survivors. (9)

Glossary

Voir dire The process in which potential jurors who might be biased or unable to render a fair verdict are screened out. (8)

W

Warrant A written order from a court directing law enforcement officers to conduct a search or to arrest a person. (4)

Workhouses European forerunners of the modern U.S. prison, where offenders were sent to learn discipline and regular work habits. (10)

Writ of *certiorari* A written order, from the U.S. Supreme Court to a lower court whose decision is being appealed, to send the records of the case forward for review. (8)

Writ of *habeas corpus* An order from a court to an officer of the law to produce a prisoner in court to determine if the prisoner is being legally detained or imprisoned. (8)

Case Index

Subject Index

Subject Index

Subject Index

Subject Index

Subject Index

Subject Index

Subject Index

Subject Index

Subject Index

K

Subject Index

Subject Index

Subject Index

Subject Index

Subject Index

Subject Index

Subject Index

Subject Index

Subject Index

Tutorial Simulations